"Moments Are the Elements of Profit"

"Moments Are the Elements of Profit"

Overtime and the Deregulation of Working Hours Under the Fair Labor Standards Act

Marc Linder

Fănpìhuà Press
Iowa City
2000

Printed in the United States of America

Suggested Library of Congress Cataloging
Linder, Marc, 1946—
"Moments are the elements of profit":
Overtime and the deregulation of working hours
under the Fair Labor Standards Act/by Marc Linder
xvii, 524; 23 cm.
Includes bibliographical references and index
ISBN 0-9673899-3-3
1. Hours of labor--law and legislation--United States--history.
2. United States. Fair Labor Standards Act of 1938.
KF3525L56
344.0125722—dc21 Library of Congress Control Number 00-092178

You cannot get more out of a man than is in him, and if you take too much one day, there will be so much less to obtain on succeeding days. As stated by Professor Clark of Columbia University: "If you want a man to work for you one day and only one day, and secure the greatest possible amount of work he is capable of performing you must make him work for twenty-four hours. If you would have him work a week it will be necessary to reduce the time to twenty hours; if you want him to work for a month a still further reduction to eighteen hours a day. For the year, fifteen hours a day will do; for several years, ten hours; but if you wish to get the most out of a man for a working lifetime, you will have to reduce his hours of labor to eight each day."

John Mitchell, *Organized Labor: Its Problems and Ideals and the Present and Future of American Wage Earners* 123-24 (1903)

Except perhaps for the Social Security Act, it [the Fair Labor Standards Act] is the most far-reaching, far-sighted program for the benefit of workers ever adopted here or in any other country. ... Do not let any calamity-howling executive with an income of $1,000 a day, who has been turning his employees over to the Government relief rolls in order to preserve his company's undistributed reserves, tell you—using his stockholders' money to pay the postage for his personal opinions—that a wage of $11 a week is going to have a disastrous effect on all American industry.

President Franklin D. Roosevelt, Fireside Chat, June 24, 1938, in *Public Papers and Addresses of Franklin D. Roosevelt: 1938 The Continuing Struggle for Liberalism* 391, 392 (1941)

The FLSA, in actuality, made no difference to most American workers, some of whom were brutally exploited.

Jonathan Grossman, "Fair Labor Standards Act of 1938: Maximum Struggle for a Minimum Wage," 101 (6) *Monthly Lab. Rev.* 22-30 at 29 (June 1978) (U.S. Dept. of Labor official historian)

Contents

Tables

Preface

It is wrong for the Government to deny our citizens the privilege of working as long as they wish so long as the choice is theirs and so long as the opportunity presents itself.[1]

[M]y grandfather at the turn of century fought for the 40 hour [week]. His slogan used to be, "8 hours for work, 8 hours for rest and 8 hours for what we will." I am not sure what the slogan is for a 72 hour week or a 96 hour overtime over a three week period.[2]

The enormous increases in the productivity and intensity of labor that have brought about a post-industrial, hi-tech, information society have done little to abate capitalism's drive to impose a longer workday and workweek than millions of workers want to work. Although rising productivity makes shorter working hours possible and heightened fatigue associated with greater intensity of labor should make them necessary,[3] employers and economists still regard longer hours as a means of boosting the rate of growth and accumulation.[4] Nor has the rhetoric of the new virtual economy rid capitalists of their venerable habit, as Victorian factory inspectors put it, of "petty pilferings of minutes"[5] of unpaid labor, which, when practiced systematically, enhance profitability considerably.

The end of the nineteenth and beginning of the twentieth century witnessed large-scale campaigns by organized labor for the eight-hour day. A century later the legislative initiative on hours regulation in the United States has passed back to capital. The so-called maximum hours provision of the Fair Labor Standards Act (FLSA),[6] which in reality is merely a "maximum nonovertime hours" provision,[7] has never prohibited employers from working their adult employees

---

[1]*Overtime Penalty Pay Act of 1964: Hearings Before the Select Subcommittee on Labor of the House Committee on Education and Labor*, 88th Cong., 2d Sess. Pt. 2 at 768 (1964) (statement of Rep. John B. Anderson).

[2][Maine] *Legislative Record*, H-2022 (Rep. Samson, Mar. 30, 1998). The word "week" has been substituted in brackets for "day," which was manifestly a typo or a misspeaking.

[3]Edward Denison, *Why Growth Rates Differ: Postwar Experience in Nine Western Countries* 59 (1969 [1967]).

[4]Edward Denison, *The Sources of Economic Growth in the United States and the Alternatives Before Us* 35-66 (1962).

[5]*Reports of the Inspectors of Factories for the Half Year Ending 31st October, 1856*, at 48 (C. 2153, 3 Parl. Pap. 1857 Sess. 2).

[6]The title of the overtime provision is "Maximum Hours." Fair Labor Standards Act of 1938, ch. 676, § 7, 52 Stat. 1060, 1063 (current version at 29 U.S.C. § 207 (1994)). As a court noted with regard to a related statutory term (used in § 218): "'Maximum workweek' does not in fact limit the number of hours an employee may work. ... It must refer to that number of excess hours worked for which an overtime rate must be paid." State v. Comfort Cab, Inc., 286 A.2d 742, 748 (N.J. Super. 1972).

[7]29 C.F.R. § 778.101 (1999).

for as long as firms find necessary: "Not only may an employee be worked twenty-four hours per day; but one hundred and twenty-four hours of overtime per week would not violate the law so long as the employee was paid for all such overtime at the required rate."[8]

As the FLSA's time and a half for overtime provision has increasingly lost its deterrent force and brought about the de facto deregulation of working hours, the labor movement has sought to make a virtue of the market-knows-best Zeitgeist by claiming that the "purpose of the FLSA's overtime provision is not to create an entitlement of employees, who work long hours for premium pay for overtime work. Rather, its purpose is to generate a national system in which employers are discouraged from requiring overtime work. The overtime provisions of the Act are intended to be a free market mechanism to enforce a national 'hours of work' rule."[9] However, this effort to salvage some elements of hours regulation ignores the contradiction inherent in basing mandatory labor standards on anarchic free labor markets, which tend to reach equilibrium at the lowest common denominator of needy workers and greedy employers.

The labor movement's self-contradictory position also overlooks the close affinity between "free-market" overtime laws and nineteenth-century declaratory or hortatory legal day's work statutes. New Hampshire enacted the first in 1847, entitled, "An Act regulating the hours of labor in manufactories." It provided: "In all contracts for or relating to labor, ten hours of actual labor shall be taken to be a day's work, unless otherwise agreed by the parties; and no person shall be required to or holden to perform more than ten hours of labor in any one day, except in pursuance of an express contract requiring a greater time."[10] Such statutes, which indiscriminately classified involuntary overwork as consensual, reflected a conviction, not alien to that underlying the FLSA, that state intervention on behalf of workers "should not curtail individual liberty to contract, but could be effective without so doing."[11]

Nevertheless, the mere fact that the FLSA modestly charges employers for

---

[8]Missel v. Overnight Motor Transp. Co., 126 F.2d 98, 104 (4th Cir. 1942).

[9]Michael Leibig, "The Attack on the Forty-Hour Week," in *Hearings on the Fair Labor Standards Act: Hearings Before the Subcommittee on Workforce Protections of the House Committee on Economic and Educational Opportunities*, 104th Cong., 1st Sess. 211, 213 (1996). Leibig is a long-time union-side labor lawyer.

[10]1847 N.H. Laws, ch. 488, § 1 at 465-66. The Illinois legislature has never repealed its meaningless eight-hour law: "On and after the first day of May, 1867, eight hours of labor between the rising and the setting of the sun, in all mechanical trades, arts ane employments, and other cases of labor and service by the day, except farm employments, shall constitute and be and legal day's work, where there is no special contract or agreement to the contrary." 820 ILCS 145/1 (1999).

[11]Elizabeth Brandeis, "Labor Legislation," in 3 John Commons et al., *History of Labor in the United States, 1896-1932*, at 397-697 at 541 (1935).

the privilege of violating the aspirational norm of a 40-hour week triggered employers' efforts in the 1990s, after the Republicans had gained a majority in both Houses of Congress, to repeal the act's "rigid and inflexible" hours provisions.[12] Associations of big and small businesses, represented by the Labor Policy Association and the Flexible Employment, Compensation, and Scheduling Coalition, have prepared an "assault" on labor's "most sacred icon—the 40-hour week."[13] Employers are poised to persuade Congress to create 80-hour two-week or even 160-hour four-week pay periods, during which they would be free to work their employees any number of hours during an individual week without being required to pay time and a half for hours beyond 40 per week.[14] (Perversely, the U.S. Supreme Court has anticipatorily approved this policy inversion by adducing employers' privilege under the act to "tell the employee to take off an afternoon, a day, or even an entire week" as flowing from the FLSA's purpose of protecting workers from "'the evil of overwork.'")[15] In contrast, the labor movement, even if successful in warding off such thrusts under a Democratic president, is in no position to secure enactment of statutory protection against employers' power-based imposition of mandatory overtime, let alone to persuade Congress that a shorter workweek is possible and desirable.

In spite of the considerable attention paid to employers' recent campaign to roll back hours regulation, participants and observers have overlooked capital's vigorous opposition to such state intervention literally since the day the FLSA went into effect in 1938. The balance of social and ideological forces has become so skewed that without having to fear public ridicule in the press, senators can characterize bills that empower firms to eliminate the 40-hour week as "put[ting] work schedule decisionmaking back in the hands of employees."[16] Management, in turn, buttresses the claim that it "has retained its inherent right...to require that employees shall respond to its call for overtime"[17] on the grounds that anarchy is the unthinkable alternative: rolling electrical blackouts are "of course, possible,

---

[12]141 *Cong. Rec.* S 11787, 11788 (1995) (Sen. Ashcroft) (Lexis).

[13]Saul Friedman, "Time Short for 40-Hour Week? Partisan Clash over OT Rules," *Newsday*, Sept. 4, 1995, at A21 (Lexis).

[14]E.g., Work and Family Integration Act, S. 1129, § 2, 104th Cong., 1st Sess. (1995) (160 hours); H.R. 2723, § 2, 104th Cong., 1st Sess. (1995) (160 hours); Family Friendly Workplace Act, S. 4, § 3(b), 105th Cong., 1st Sess. (1997) (80 hours) (filibustered by Democrats); Family Friendly Workplace Act, S. 1241, § 3, 106th Cong., 1st Sess. (1999) (80 hours, permitting up to 50-hour workweek without overtime liability, sponsored by 38 Republicans).

[15]Christensen v. Harris County, 68 U.S.L.W. 4343, 4345 (U.S. May 1, 2000).

[16]141 *Cong. Rec.* S 11787, 11788 (Aug. 7, 1995) (Sen. John Ashcroft, R. Mo.).

[17]Van Dorn Co., 48 Lab. Arb. (BNA) 925, 928 (1967).

if there is a law that says that overtime can't be mandatory."[18] Even in 1960, in the midst of the postwar Keynesian boom and cooperation between strong unions and management, a monumental Brookings Institution study of collective bargaining found nothing paradoxical in asserting that some plants had become "vulnerable to employee control of leisure" and asking: "Who is to control the use of their leisure time?"[19]

Although, as even Friedrich Engels conceded, the working hours of a modern factory are incompatible with individual workers' autonomy,[20] the compulsion to keep invested capital continuously in motion, as Sidney and Beatrice Webb agreed, makes it "a special aggravation of this subordination, that, under the circumstances of the modern capitalist industry, the employer's decision will perpetually be biassed in favor of lengthening the working day." Yet this "autocratic judgment of their employer,"[21] which may typically reflect firms' inexorable prioritizing of the demands of competition and profitability over workers' needs, is not the only conceivable countermodel; democratic co-determination of the length of the workday is also thinkable. However, as long as the dominant ideology ordains, as *The New York Times* editors put it in 1912, that "[t]he interest of the public is rather in the output than in the length of the working day,"[22] the compulsions of production will prevail over human needs.

In a pseudo-antipaternalistic turn, factory autocrats sought to invert this logic

---

[18] 1 [California] Senate Committee on Industrial Relations, *Interim Hearings on AB 1295—Mandatory Overtime* 177 (Nov. 8, 1977) (statement of Wayland Bonbright, ind. rels. mgr., Pac. Gas & Elec. Co.). Bonbright's invocation of alleged mass refusals to work overtime in the British electrical power industry at the time of the hearings was misleading since overtime was a minor aspect of the labor action. More importantly, no British law empowered workers to refuse to work overtime, and union officials opposed the actions. The point here is that if workers feel strongly enough about their working conditions to strike and thus impose considerable inconvenience on the rest of the working class and society, they may do so with or without legal sanction. "Power Cuts Unofficial But Effective," *Economist*, Nov. 5, 1977, at 110 (Lexis); "Pay Policy Under Public-Sector Siege," *Economist*, Nov. 12, 1977, at 85 (Lexis).

[19] Sumner Slichter, James Healy, and E. Livernash, *The Impact of Collective Bargaining on Management* 238 (1960).

[20] Friedrich Engels, "Dell'Autorità," in I:24 Karl Marx [and] Friedrich Engels, *MEGA (Gesamtausgabe)* 82, 85 (1984 [1873]). Only disingenuousness can account for the following response by the Master Builders Society of London on August 26, 1858, to a request by carpenters for a reduction in hours from ten to nine with no change in pay: "inasmuch as there is no compulsion by which workmen are obliged to labour for a given number of hours, it really amounts to an alteration in the rate of wages." G. Shaw Lefevre and Thomas Bennet, "Account of the Strike and Lock-Out in the Building Trades of London, in 1859-60," in *Trades' Societies and Strikes: Report of the Committee on Trades' Societies, Appointed by the National Association for the Promotion of Social Science* 53-76 at 55 (1860).

[21] Sidney Webb and Beatrice Webb, *Industrial Democracy* 327, 334 (new ed., 1920 [1897]).

[22] "The Eight-Hour Day," *N.Y. Times*, July 2, 1912, at 10, col. 3.

by projecting the collective normalization of the working day as an expropriation of the worker. In rhetoric that still resonates with free-marketeers, Alfred I. Du Pont, vice-president of E. I. Du Pont Company, testified to Congress in 1904 against federal regulation of government contractors: "To peremptorily establish the eight-hour limitation, denying the right to labor more than eight hours a day...must clearly militate against the laborer in the exercise of his labor, which is his property and the privilege of contracting or marketing his property rights."[23] That the Du Ponts were fantasizing about workers who could exercise their labor 24 hours a day emerged two decades later from a prediction by Irénée du Pont, president of the company:

> "[T]here are a number of great things which chemistry can and will do....
>
> "[A] study of the ductless glands will likely lead to the identification of some "reagent" which...will maintain the vigor of youth far beyond three-score-years-and-ten. This does not refer only to sexual vigor, but to the power—more important to maintain—which enables a young man to work longer hours and withstand fatigue which can not be withstood by men who have reached their mental prime of life.
>
> "I think it likely that material will be found which, taken into the human system, will accomplish the results of eight hours' sleep. This will change the active existence of a man from sixteen hours a day to twenty-four hours a day...."[24]

As is always the case with state-imposed labor standards, overcoming the imperatives of capital's self-valorization must confront resistance based on employers' more prosaic principal argument—that national labor laws exert a harmful impact in a world in which global competition is no longer a menacing tendency dimly visible on the horizon, but a force to be reckoned with daily in ways big and small. In the words of the chairman of the House Economic Opportunities Committee: "As each American firm encounters the challenges of the modern global economy, it faces a seriously outdated and inflexible federal scheme of regulating employee compensation and scheduling."[25] The defense is venerable. As far back as the 1840s, British employers defended overtime work as "necessary to compete with the lightly-taxed foreigner...."[26] In the late nineteenth century, when the federal government was said to be still merely "a

---

[23]*Eight Hours for Laborers on Government Work: Report by the Hon. Victor H. Metcalf, Secretary Department of Commerce and Labor, on H. R. 4064* (Eight-Hour Bill) 33-34 (H. Doc. No. 413, 58th Cong., 3d Sess. 1905).

[24]"Chemistry's Tremendous Tomorrow," 79(5) *Literary Digest* 23-24 (Nov. 3, 1923).

[25]William Goodling, "National Press Club Remarks" (Jan. 10, 1995) (Lexis) (formerly House Labor Committee).

[26]J. Binns, *Prize Essay on Systematic Overtime Working and Its Consequences, Moral, Physical, Mental, and Social* 7 (1846).

state of courts and parties,"[27] expanding monopolies deployed the same capital-logic. Testifying before Congress against a bill to establish an absolute eight-hour day for laborers, workmen, and mechanics on public works or work performed for the United States government, the representative of the Bethlehem and Carnegie steel companies observed:

> it is evident that the interests of many of the largest manufacturing concerns would be injured by the passage of this act. In the world's competition for foreign trade the cheapest product secures the market. Any effort by Congress to indirectly reduce the hours of labor...must militate against the manufacturing interests of this country, compelling them ultimately to do work and produce results at a disadvantage in competition with manufacturers in other parts of the world beyond the paternal control of the Congress of the United States.[28]

To the owner of a shipbuilding company with six million dollars invested in plant, it made a "vast difference" whether a worker and hence that plant worked eight hours or nine.[29] The passage of a century has done little to alter this capital-logic as developments in the 1990s at an "immense, windowless" AT&T/Lucent Technologies microelectronics factory in Orlando, Florida, revealed:

> [M]ore and more American factory workers are being assigned the short-week, extended-hour schedules.
>
> Management experts call them compressed workweeks. At factories like Lucent's, the eight-hour-a-day, five-day workweek has all but vanished and given way to schedules that management deems efficient, even if they ignore the calendar's seven-day cycles and community patterns of work, sleep and play....
>
> Abbreviated workweeks...have been a growing trend in manufacturing. Nearly all automobile tire companies and most big semiconductor companies have shifted to the new schedules. The big General Motors plant...that turns out Saturn automobiles has adopted one, too. ...
>
> Efforts are being made in Congress to speed the shift to abbreviated workweeks. Many companies want Congress to change overtime provisions of the Fair Labor Standards Act...that require employers to pay time and a half for any work beyond 40 hours a week, with one proposal seeking a monthly ceiling instead.
>
> "The week is getting redistributed toward work," said Jerome M. Rosow, president

---

[27]Stephen Skowronek, *Building a New American State: The Expansion of National Administrative Capacities, 1877-1920* (1984 [1982]).

[28]*Hours of Labor for Workmen, Mechanics, Etc., Employed Upon Public Work of the United States*, Sen. Doc. No. 318, 55th Cong., 2d Sess. 5 (1898) (testimony of Joseph McCammon).

[29]*Hours of Labor for Workmen, Mechanics, Etc., Employed Upon Public Work of the United States* at 74 (testimony of Charles Cramp, pres., William Cramp & Sons Ship and Engine Building Co.).

of the Work in America Institute.... Part of the price, he said, is the traditional weekend: "Leisure is getting squeezed out."

The impetus, experts say, is a redoubled emphasis on efficient production, the same pressure that has been driving the tides of corporate downsizing. It is another tactic to wrest additional profits and lower-cost production from factories.

[M]anagement decided that to hold its own in competition...worldwide, it could not let its machinery sleep when people do. "The equipment has to keep running," said the plant manager, Robert B. Koch.

Before, the company had been running on a less-compressed week with four 10-hour days. But that meant that for several hours a day the machinery stood idle. "The company eyeballed that quiet time," said Thomas S. Christian, president of Local 2000 of the International Brotherhood of Electrical Workers, who helped negotiate the schedule with 12-hour shifts. ...

An extreme form of workweek compression is the product of something...experts call best cost scheduling. Under that concept people work 12-hour shifts for three days and take three days off. They also work for 30 days and then switch to nights for 30 days. ...

Four years ago the A. E. Staley Manufacturing Company...imposed the schedule on its workforce. The union local...voted 96 percent against it, precipitating a 30-month lockout before the workers acquiesced....

To give management greater flexib[ility] in setting workers' hours, Senator John Ashcroft...has proposed legislation that would replace the 40-hour week with a 160-hour month. ...

Unions...see the bill as an effort to restore the sweatshop hours of the turn of the century. ... "[C]learly this is an effort to let employers get overtime without paying for it."[30]

Labor's rhetoric, however, did modulate during the twentieth century. It is difficult to imagine a labor leader in the early twenty-first century echoing the sentiments of Samuel Gompers, the president of the American Federation of Labor and chief public disputant of the manufacturing interests in 1898, that the eight-hour day gave workers the opportunity for "more rest, so that they may have the means by which they can think for themselves, rather than having our captains of industry doing all the thinking for them."[31] By the late twentieth century, when millions of workers had come to rely on overtime pay to make ends meet, it had even become rare for union officials to be blunt enough to complain, as they did in the 1960s, that "employers use overtime as a substitute for decent hourly rates."[32] And the opposition that an Alaska state senator

---

[30]Peter Kilborn, "Factories that Never Close Are Scrapping 5-Day Week," *N.Y. Times*, June 4, 1996, at A1, col. 5 (Lexis).

[31]*Hours of Labor for Workmen, Mechanics, Etc., Employed Upon Public Work of the United States* at 41.

[32]*Amendments to the Fair Labor Standards Act: Hearings Before the Subcommittee on Labor of the Senate Committee on Labor and Public Welfare*, Pt. 1, 89th Cong., 1st Sess.

mounted in 1919 against the presence of a time and a half overtime provision in an eight-hour bill on the grounds that it offered a premium for the violation of the proposed law would doubtless stamp him as an enemy of labor today.[33]

143 (1965) (statement of William Du Chessi, vice pres., Textile Workers Union).

[33]"8 Hour Law May Not Pass Senate," *Weekly Nome Industrial Worker*, Apr. 26, 1919, at 1, col. 4 (Sen. John Ronan). To be sure, since Ronan was a member of a mine owners association who had supported the ten-hour day and helped break strikes by recruiting strikebreakers, it seems unlikely that he was speaking as an avid advocate of the absolute eight-hour day. Evangeline Atwood, *Frontier Politics: Alaska's James Wickersham* 171 (1979).

Acknowledgments

Although this book is the most extensive analysis ever published of the history of hours regulation under the FLSA, its four essays do not deal with all aspects of a law that is profoundly flawed by an enormous number of exclusions and exemptions.[1] Chapter 1, by far the longest, is new and offers a detailed historical sweep of the origins and development of the overtime provision and its fecklessness as a safeguard against firms' imposition of mandatory overtime. Chapters 2, 3, and 4 are revisions of earlier works. Chapter 2, which deals with the exclusion of so-called executive employees from the overtime provision, is a thorough revision, expansion, and update of "Closing the Gap Between Reich and Poor: Which Side Is the Department of Labor On?" 21 *N.Y.U. Review of Law and Social Change* 1-32 (1993) (©Marc Linder). Chapter 3, which explains how and why much of the time workers are required to travel, change clothes, and engage in other activities for employers' benefit, came to be noncompensable, is a revision incorporating new material and an update of "Class Struggle at the Door: The Origins of the Portal-to-Portal Act of 1947," 39 *Buffalo Law Review* 53-180 (1991) (©Buffalo Law Review, with whose permission the original article is used here). Chapter 4, which reveals how construction and other employees in small firms came to be excluded from the overtime law, updates and makes minor revisions to "The Small-Business Exemption Under the Fair Labor Standards Act: The 'Original' Accumulation of Capital and the Inversion of Industrial Policy," 6 *Journal of Law and Policy* 403-535 (1998) (©Marc Linder).

Several archivists and scholars were extremely helpful in unearthing materials about the remarkable Alaska eight-hour law of 1917, the first-ever account of which appears in Chapter 1. With resourcefulness and tenacity Judy Skagerberg at the Alaska State Archives in Juneau located a huge volume of crucially important documents. Sylvie Savage at the Alaska and Polar Regions Archives, Rasmuson Library, University of Alaska Fairbanks, provided correspondence from the papers of Governor Riggs and Judge Bunnell. Diane Kodiak at the National Archives and Records Administration in Anchorage furnished the record in the test case that held the law unconstitutional. John Stewart, the chief archivist at the Alaska State Archives, Joe Sullivan of Brown University, and Prof. Mary Mangusso of the University of Alaska at Fairbanks History Department all pointed the way to sources.

---

[1]Omitted, for example, is an account of the exclusion of farmworkers from the overtime provision of the FLSA, which was analyzed in Marc Linder, "Farm Workers and the Fair Labor Standards Act: Racial Discrimination in the New Deal," 65 *Texas L. Rev.* 1335-93 (1987), and updated in Marc Linder, *Migrant Workers and Minimum Wages: Regulating the Exploitation of Agricultural Labor in the United States* 125-75 (1992).

1

Overtime over Time: The Long and Unfinished Road from the Realm of Necessity to the Realm of Freedom

The saying goes that "the loyal union man, out for a good time, not only expects a good time, but a time and a half."[1]

The concept of "overtime" implies a normal or basic workday or workweek, but the loss in English of the synonymy between it and "overwork"[2] (or, in the even more pathos-generating older term, "overtoil"),[3] still preserved in other languages,[4] clothes abnormally long working time with such a self-explanatory

[1]Jerome Rosow, "Overtime Pay Policies for Executive, Administrative, and Professional Employees," 30 (2) *Personnel* 105-12 at 112 (Sept. 1953).

[2]The first modern use of "Over-time" and "Over-work" cited in the *Oxford English Dictionary* is Peter Simmonds, *The Dictionary of Trade Products, Commercial, Manufacturing, and Technical Terms* (1858), which (though by no means the first use) defines the two terms (in one entry) as "extra labour done beyond the regular fixed hours of business." *Id.* at 269; 7 *Oxford English Dictionary* 331, 338 (1961 [1933]). The New Zealand Factories Act, 1894, which for the first time permitted overtime, at premium rates, for women and children, used an unusual hybrid term: "The Inspector shall keep a list of the names of all those women or young persons for whom permission to work overtime has been granted, and shall note against the name of each the hours of overtime worked by him or her, so that the full amount of overwork-time be not in any case exceeded." The Factories Act, 1894, § 55, N.Z. Stat., No. 31, at 144-45. Prof. David McCabe, a historian of labor relations, testified at an important FLSA-overtime trial in 1946 that the first use of the word "overtime" in the United States that he could recall was a resolution of the iron moulders at their 1876 convention; "overwork" was the preferred term until the 1880s. Testimony of David McCabe, Transcript of Record at 419, in Bay Ridge Operating Co. v. Aaron, 334 U.S. 446 (1947). New York State's legal day's work statute of 1897 did not "prevent an agreement for overwork at an increased compensation...." 1897 N.Y. Laws, ch. 415, § 3 at 461, 463. According to a computer database search, only one court has used the word "overwork" in a FLSA case since World War II except for quoting from a 1942 U.S. Supreme Court case, which in turn was quoting from President Roosevelt's message. Overnight Motor Transportation Co. v. Missel, 316 U.S. 572, 578 (1942). And even that one court used "overwork" merely in citing the plaintiffs' complaint and did not adopt the term. Assocation of Court Reporters of Superior Court v. Superior Court for the District of Columbia, 424 F. Supp. 90, 91 (D.D.C. 1976).

[3]The *OED* quotes a source from 1872: "These died of overtoil in the Lowell carpet factories." 7 *Oxford English Dictionary* at 331. British unions in the nineteenth century commonly made the connection between overtoil and oversupply. Sidney Webb and Beatrice Webb, *The History of Trade Unionism* 288 (new ed. 1902 [1894]).

[4]E.g. Danish. See Lov om Forbud mod Overarbejde (Act: Prohibition of Overtime), in ILO, *Legislative Series*, 1937—Den. 3.

patina that it is workers' resistance to, rather than employers' demand for, overtime work that seems to require justification. In the words of one economist: "The existence of 'overtime unemployment'—that is, of offers to work at premium rates that are not taken up—is evidence of disequilibrium of some kind."[5] But generally economists perceive the best of all possible equilibria: "Premium rates of time and one-half or double time are more than adequate to offset any natural disinclination to work overtime...."[6]

In contrast, the fundamental purpose behind the struggle for the normal workday of eight hours or workweek of 40 hours lay in withdrawing all time beyond that norm from the economic play of forces and economic calculations—whether by employers or workers—and committing it exclusively to workers' nonproduction-oriented personal development. No matter what the length of the workday, as the AFL Executive Council declared in 1919, "sufficient remuneration should be received by the workers to make it possible to live comfortably without working overtime...."[7] Normalization of the workday also means knowing in the morning whether capital will demand overwork later that day.[8] In this important sense, universalist, collective, and egalitarian elements prevailed with regard to the distribution of work within the working class as a whole and avoidance of the creation of subclasses of overworked and unemployed workers.[9]

The institutionalization of overwork has long blinded market-knows-besters to its nonconsenual aspects, although the enveloping rhetoric has grown more sophisticated. In 1859, when one of the demands of London building tradesmen striking for a reduction in their working day from ten to nine hours was abolition of "systematic overtime,"[10] the *Times* reported that "the great object of the masters is to crush once and for ever those trade societies which, in their view, interfere so arbitrarily and so vexatiously in trade arrangements between the employer and his men. ... For example, the masons...will not allow...overtime."[11]

---

[5]Frederic Meyers, "The Economics of Overtime," in *Hours of Work* 95-110 at 95 (Clyde Denkert et al. eds. 1965).

[6]Albert Rees, *The Economics of Trade Unions* 147 (1962).

[7]*Report of the Proceedings of the Thirty-Ninth Annual Convention of the American Federation of Labor* 454 (1919).

[8]Dale Buss, "Overtime Debate: Economics v. Exhaustion," *Automotive News*, Sept. 13, 1999, at 30U (Westlaw).

[9]Christoph Deutschmann, "Arbeitszeit und Arbeitsmarkt: Historische und institutionelle Aspekte," in *Arbeitszeitpolitik: Formen und Folgen einer Neuverteilung der Arbeitszeit* 33-45 at 42 (C. Offe, K. Hinrichs, H. Wiesenthal eds.; 2d ed. 1983 [1981]).

[10]George Potter, letter to editor, (London) *Times*, July 30, 1859, at 5, col. 2 (secretary of United Building Trades).

[11]"The Nine Hours Movement," (London) *Times*, Aug. 5, 1859, at 3, col. 3.

Workers resisted systematic overtime because it "reduced the normal day to a nullity."[12]

A century later, the discourse had been purged of any trace of conflict. Operating with a presumption that work schedules constitute an "optimum for the majority of workers," blackboard economics posits that "overtime pay will always induce the typical worker to offer his services beyond the standard schedule...." Indeed, economists are puzzled by those who prefer more leisure, chalking it up to "inertia, or lack of other opportunities...."[13]

Such economists also ignore the costs to workers of overwork. If a collectively bargained or statutorily imposed overtime rule is required to bring about a substitution of unemployed workers at straight-time wages for already employed workers at premium rates, they infer an increase in unit labor costs "since presumptively employers would have substituted additional workers for additional hours of existing workers even without such a rule if such a course would have been efficient."[14] Overlooked is the cost of the shortened working lives of workers, which overtime premiums cannot internalize.

1. What is a Normal Workday? From Surplus Value to Family Values

This is a family values law. It gives somebody out there that doesn't dare to say, I don't want to work because I will lose my job, a chance to do so.[15]

Labor Unions over a century ago fought for the 40-hour workweek. What we are seeing today is workers working 60-hour weeks. There should be a healthy balance: eight hours of work, eight hours of sleep and eight hours with the family.[16]

Historically the concept of overtime ("over-hours" in nineteenth-century Britain)[17] did not arise until coercive collective action, either through labor unions or the state, had created a normal or standard working day. And even then,

---

[12]Webb and Webb, *History of Trade Unionism* at 333. Legal restriction of systematic overtime was one of the British unions' primary legislative goals in the early twentieth century. E. H. Phelps Brown, *The Growth of British Industrial Relations: A Study from the Standpoint of 1906-14*, at 303-304 (1974 [1959]).

[13]Richard Perlman, "Observations on Overtime and Moonlighting," 33 (2) *Southern Econ. J.* 237-44 at 237, 238 (Oct. 1966).

[14]Meyers, "The Economics of Overtime" at 106.

[15][Maine] *Legislative Record*, H-2021 (Rep. Hatch, Mar. 30, 1998).

[16]House of Representatives, Commonwealth of Pennsylvania, [Hearing on] House Bills 1940 and 1941 Before House Labor Relations Committee 8 (Jan. 18, 2000) (testimony of Teresa Ruhl, regional COPE director, Penn. AFL-CIO).

[17]Factories Inquiry Commission, *First Report of the Central Board* 12 (1833).

workers paid by the hour or the piece did not initially benefit from the normalization if employers continued to work them at the regular rate; only workers receiving a fixed daily wage for a day's work consisting of a variable number of hours could gain—provided that the employer did not lower the day wage.[18]

The advantages of overtime work to employers paying workers on a daily or weekly basis can be illustrated today in terms of salaried employees who are required to work unlimited hours for a fixed salary.[19] The impact of an atomized labor market, unregulated by the state, on the length of the working day is also exemplified by the situation of 10,000 low-paid female department store employees in New York City around the time of World War I:

> "Most of us think that the girls' work...is over at 6 o'clock, but this is not true. It is the custom to keep the girls until 7, 8, 9, 10 and later to sort stock, to put things in order, to change departments. In most of the stores they receive nothing for this overtime, but in some of them they are given 35 cents for supper money. One store pays 17 cents an hour for overtime."[20]

The change that labor standards legislation could bring about was documented in New Zealand at the end of the nineteenth century, when adult men were excluded from the Factories Act. As the Department of Labour there observed: "If a woman works overtime she had not only to be paid for it, but a minimum wage for it is fixed, and the employer is liable to suffer for a breach of the law if such wage is not paid. The man, on the contrary, may be worked not only outrageously long hours at his ordinary day's work, but kept on at overtime, without pay, till either his strength or his patience is exhausted."[21]

Karl Marx provided an economic analysis of this regime in the 1860s. Assuming that the average workweek consisted of six 12-hour days and that 10 of those 12 hours were devoted to creating the value that reproduced the worker, leaving the capitalist with two hours of surplus value, Marx set a hypothetical case in which the workday was extended by one hour or six hours weekly. Since

---

[18]Webb and Webb, *History of Trade Unionism* at 333 n.3; Robert Leiter, "The Principle of Overtime," 2 *Lab. Law J.* 24-30 at 24 (June 1951). As late as 1920 the Webbs wrote that some unorganized workers in Britain "are still required to work longer hours to cope with a press of orders without getting any additional pay for the extra labor." Sidney Webb and Beatrice Webb, *Industrial Democracy* 329 n.1 (1920 [1897]).

[19]See below chapter 2.

[20]"Demands Better Pay for Girl Employees," *Brooklyn Daily Eagle*, Jan. 12, 1914, at 7, col. 8 (quoting speech, "What Is the Matter with Our Department Stores?," by Mrs. Frank H. Kathryn, chairman of the committee for the organization of department store workers of the Woman's Trades Union).

[21]New Zealand, *Report of the Department of Labour* iv (Sess. II.—1897).

these six hours were all devoted to creating surplus value, the capitalist was getting a very good deal: otherwise he would have to pay wages to an additional worker for three days or three additional workers for one day to extract six hours of surplus value.[22] That European workers as late as 1880 did not always receive premium wages for overwork is clear from a questionnaire that Marx devised: "Are extra wages—and which—paid in case of overtime?"[23]

Marx also furnished a general framework for understanding struggles over the length of the workday or workweek. On the surface, this struggle centers on the conflict between the buyer and the seller of a commodity which generates special problems because, unlike the situation with a general run-of-the-mill commodity, the body and mind of the human seller of labor power cannot be separated from its daily use by the buyer. Since the law of exchange of commodities, however, does not recognize any special rules for this particular exchange, the capitalist buyer tries to extract the greatest possible profit from the use of the worker's labor power for the day's or week's worth he has bought. The question then becomes: how long is a workday or workweek? Since the human seller lives beyond the day, he must make sure that he sells his only commodity for a price high enough to enable him to reappear at work the next day with his labor power in a condition of strength and health that meets the standards set by his competitors. But the worker as a rational labor market participant must also exercise sufficient foresight to husband his only economic asset for a lifetime—or at least the standard working life of his type of labor. If the daily value of his commodity equals its lifetime value divided by 30 years or approximately 10,000 workdays, then he must make sure that overlong workdays and workweeks do not force him to expend so much additional energy that he uses up 1/5,000 or 1/3,333 of his lifetime supply for only 1/10,000 of its lifetime value.[24] For this reason socialist unions regarded eight-hour laws as "life lengthening" acts.[25]

The worker therefore regards such overwork as crossing the line from the capitalist's rightful use to plundering of his labor power and, as such, a breach of their contract and of the law of the exchange of commodities. His demand for a workday or workweek of normal length—defined by its compatibility with a

---

[22]Karl Marx, "Zur Kritik der politischen Ökonomie (Manuskript 1861-1863)," in II:1 Karl Marx [and] Friedrich Engels, *Gesamtausgabe (MEGA)* 162-63 (1976).

[23]Karl Marx, "Questionnaire for Workers," in 25 Karl Marx [and] Friedrich Engels, *Gesamtausgabe (MEGA)* 199, 204 (1985 [1880]). In 1836, members of the machinists union in London, who had worked a 10 and a half hour day and often an additional two hours at the ordinary rate, successfully struck for time and a quarter and time and a half for overtime hours. James Jefferys, *The Story of the Engineers, 1800-1945*, at 21 (n.d. [1945]).

[24]1 Karl Marx, *Das Kapital*, in 23 Karl Marx [and] Friedrich Engels, *Werke* 247-48 (1962 [1867]).

[25]"Illegally Overworked," *Alaska Labor News*, Mar. 31, 1917, at 4, col. 1 (editorial).

healthy 30-year worklife—is as rightful as the capitalist's demand that the worker work as long as possible each day and week. Because the capitalist is not a slaveholder, he has no (capital-) invested interest in the length of the worklife of his individual employees: "A quick succession of unhealthy and short-lived generations will keep the labour market as well supplied as a series of vigorous and long-lived generations."[26] Thus as long as the employer can find equivalent replacements in the labor market when he needs them, this private contractual dispute cannot be resolved between individual buyer and seller. The resulting "antinomy" of right against right[27] must, Marx argued, be decided by "the respective powers of the combatants." But since "in its merely economic action capital is the stronger side," a class-wide settlement of the hours issue was possible only through "general political action," which meant "legislative interference" under pressure from the working class.[28] Consequently, the normalization of the workday and workweek appears historically as a struggle between the "aggregate capitalist, i.e., the class of capitalists, and the aggregate worker, or the working class."[29]

In contrast, neoclassical economics has tried to reduce this society-defining struggle between two rights into mere market failure: "the marginal social cost of longer workweeks exceeded the marginal private cost to employers. In the absence of government intervention these divergencies persisted because low family incomes did not permit many women and children the luxury of turning down jobs with low wages and long hours...." The overtime penalty can then be "thought of as a tax to make employers bear the full marginal social cost of their hours decisions." [30]

The sea change in the conflict over a shorter workweek is captured by the current union refrain that "'[t]he question is...[s]hould workers be forced to work or should they be given the choice to spend time with their families?'"[31] This individualistic "family values" public relations approach stands in sharp contrast to the nineteenth- and early twentieth-century collectivist context, when labor "predicated its demand for leisure as a means to the creation of a better social order. To produce intelligent citizens, essential to the existence of a democracy, everybody should have sufficient leisure to permit attendance at night schools,

---

[26]Karl Marx, *Value, Price and Profit* 57 (Eleanor Marx Aveling ed. 1935 [1865]).

[27]1 Marx, *Das Kapital* at 249.

[28]Marx, *Value, Price and Profit* at 58-59.

[29]1 Marx, *Das Kapital* at 249.

[30]Ronald Ehrenberg and Paul Schuman, "The Overtime Pay Provisions of the Fair Labor Standards Act," in *The Economics of Legal Minimum Wages* 264-95 at 265, 287 (Simon Rottenberg ed. 1981).

[31]"Mandatory Overtime Seen as Key Bargaining Issue," 161 *Lab. Rel. Rep.* 435 (Aug. 2, 1999) (quoting Rick Bank, director, AFL-CIO Center for Collective Bargaining).

time for reading, discussion, and attendance at political meetings."[32] Around the time of the Civil War, the eight-hours movement was in part driven by the demand that a bright line be drawn between the time during which workers were wage-slaves to capital and the time during which they were free.[33] The thousand-page brief that Louis Brandeis, Felix Frankfurter, and Josephine Goldmark produced in support of the 1913 Oregon ten-hour law when its constitutionality was attacked before the U.S. Supreme Court collected massive evidence on the detrimental impact of long hours on workers' health, safety, morals, and citizenship.[34]

Press accounts of long workweeks have been common for years, even decades, though they appear in cycles. Often they have one-sidedly focused on factory workers who volunteer to work "unbelievable amounts of overtime"—upwards of 80 hours a week—over months and even years in order to achieve six-figure annual incomes to finance consumption patterns otherwise unattainable for the manual working class. Such presentations do mention the disruptive impact such total absorption by work can exert on workers' family lives and also allude to the greater exposure to injuries associated with the attendant fatigue, but they insist on the consensual nature of the choices.[35] Even the United Automobile Workers (UAW), arguably the country's strongest union and collective bargaining partner of the automobile manufacturers, which have adamantly insisted on the practice for decades, is said not to "press too hard because its members tend to enjoy the extra income from those overtime hours more than they're distressed by having to work them." The president of one Ford UAW local in Michigan estimated in 1999 that "'probably 70 percent of my people would be pretty upset if the UAW helped get restrictions on overtime.'"[36] Such attitudes underscore how profound the sea change has been since the AFL representative told Congress in 1948 that the FLSA "was established to reduce unemployment and put everybody on a 40-hour week. ... [T]he intent of the act is not to give the worker more money for overtime but to reduce unemployment."[37]

---

[32]Marion Cahill, *Shorter Hours: A Study of the Movement Since the Civil War* 14 (1932).

[33]David Montgomery, *Beyond Equality: Labor and the Radical Republicans, 1862-1872*, at 237-39 (1967).

[34]Felix Frankfurter, *The Case for the Shorter Work Day* (n.d. [ca. 1915]).

[35]Aaron Lucchetti, "Overdrive: An Auto Worker Earns More Than $100,000, But at a Personal Cost," *Wall St. J.*, Aug. 1, 1996, at A1 (Westlaw). For related examples among truck drivers, including one who works 3,400 hours a year for only $40,000, see Peter Kilborn, "In a Nonstop Economy, Truckers Keep Rolling," *N.Y. Times*, Nov. 24, 1999, at A14, col. 1 (nat. ed.).

[36]Dale Buss, "Overtime Debate: Economics v. Exhaustion."

[37]*Fair Labor Standards Act Amendments: Hearings Before a Subcommittee of the Senate Committee on Labor and Public Welfare*, 80th Cong., 2d Sess., Pt. 1 at 129-30

Nevertheless, by the end of the 1990s, employers' unrelenting appropriation of their employees' time began "wearing down" assembly line workers, making "many fatigued workers finally...ready to value a normal workweek more than the considerable financial incentives...." Average weekly overtime in manufacturing in the mid- and late 1990s reached their highest levels since the Bureau of Labor Statistics (BLS) began collecting such data in 1956. Prior to 1993, the highest average weekly level of overtime in manufacturing had been 4.1 hours at the height of the Vietnam War boom in early 1966; from January 1993 on, the figure virtually never fell below 4 hours, reaching annual averages between 4.4 and 4.8 hours from 1995 through 1998, and exceeding five hours in some months.[38] As corporate strategies polarized the labor force into "overtimers" and "temps"—already Marx had observed that such terms reduced workers to nothing but "personified labor time"[39]—reporters could point to the self-identified "greedy" "'overtime hogs'" and those who "are grabbing all the hours they can...merely to stay afloat in a time of stagnating wages."[40]

At times the press also turns its attention to overtime imposed by employers on unwilling workers, who are fired for refusing to work. Such accounts raise the question as to how much has changed with regard to control over the length of the workweek exerted by the compulsions of spontaneous labor markets and employers' autocracies since the middle of the nineteenth century, when British factory inspectors reported on (and Marx immortalized) adult male cotton spinners who preferred to work 10-hour days for less wages, but were compelled to work as many as five hours of overtime daily lest they be forced to change places with the unemployed.[41] The *Wall Street Journal*, for example, in the wake of the Reagan depression of the early 1980s, quoted a worker bemoaning the

---

(1948) (testimony of Walter Mason).

[38]2 BLS, *Employment, Hours, and Earnings: United States, 1909-94*, at 1195-96 (Bull. 2445, 1994); BLS, *Employment, Hours, and Earnings: United States, 1988-96*, at 432-33 (Bull. 2481, 1996); 42 (1) *Employment and Earnings*, tab. B-15 at 102 (Jan. 1995); 46 (1) *Employment and Earnings*, tab. 50 at 230 (Jan. 1999). The BLS defines overtime hours as those worked by production workers "for which overtime premiums were paid because the hours were in excess of the number of hours of either the straight-time workday or the workweek" during the survey pay period. 46 (1) *Employment and Earnings* 252 (Jan. 1999). This methodology overstates overtime since some workers receiving premium pay for working more than eight hours daily do not work 40 hours weekly. A BLS survey from May 1985 revealed that 1.6 million or 15 percent of the 10.5 million workers receiving overtime pay worked 40 hours or fewer. Darrell Carr, "Overtime Work: An Expanded View," 109 (11) *Monthly Lab. Rev.*, Nov. 1986, at 36-39.

[39]1 Marx, *Das Kapital* at 257-58 (referring to the terms "full times" and "half times" used in Victorian Britain for factory workers).

[40]Sandra Livingston, "Overdosing on Overtime: Workers See Companies Increase Their Hours Instead of Work Force," Cleveland *Plain Dealer*, Oct.2, 1994, at 1A (Lexis).

[41]1 Marx, *Das Kapital* at 301.

irony that at the end of the twentieth century "'we're working the same hours our grandfathers worked.'" The reporters were even alive to the need to educate the paper's typical readers that not all overtime is created equal:

> Americans with steady, white-collar jobs, many of whom also work 50 to 60 hours a week, often without extra pay, may find it hard to identify with factory workers bitter about working overtime following a recession when many were laid off. But office work tends to be more interesting than running a stamping press. And office workers are free to sit down, take a few minutes for coffee and, if necessary, slip out to the dentist.[42]

Until the 1990s, governmental concern with and union opposition to overtime work were largely rooted in fears of exacerbating already high levels of unemployment. More recently, the trigger has been its coercive character and corrosive impact on workers' lives. The declining volume of unemployment in the mid- and late 1990s brought on a resurgence of and opposition to overtime. While firefighters allege in a lawsuit that extended forced overtime violates the constitutional prohibition against involuntary servitude,[43] workers scheduled for only four hours of work daily complain that they are not even permitted to call home or take a break when the boss informs them at the end of their workday: "'You can't leave, it's busy, I got to hold you over...three hours...." This version of compulsory overtime is especially insidious because it enables employers "to hold the people over at no extra cost...."[44]

In the 1990s, resistance, especially in the automobile industry, periodically took the form of strikes. In 1994, for example, General Motors workers in Flint, Michigan, who had been working six days a week as long as 11 and a half hours a day for two years, struck, demanding that the company hire additional workers. The psychological and physical toll that such unrelenting work had taken caused the modal middle-aged workers to realize that even $60,000 annual incomes could not make them "bounce back" from injuries or fatigue as they could when they were younger; they simply needed more non-worktime.[45] An agreement was reached in this instance, but the UAW continues to regard GM's overtime levels as "'relentless'" as the company insists on reducing its unionized workforce

---

[42]Gregory Stricharchuk and Ralph Winter, "Worked Up: As the Recovery Gains, Compulsory Overtime Becomes a Rising Issue," *Wall St. J.*, Jan. 20, 1984 (Westlaw).

[43]Rachel Gottlieb, "Fire Union Calls Forced Overtime Form of Slavery," *Hartford Courant*, Sept. 13, 1999, at B6 (Westlaw).

[44]1 Senate Committee on Industrial Relations, *Interim Hearing on AB 1295—Mandatory Overtime* 289-90 (Nov. 8, 1977) (statement of Frank Bradburn, Retail Clerks Union, Local 770).

[45]Doron Levin, "G.M. Impasse: Work Strain vs. Rising Car Sales," *N.Y. Times*, Sept. 29, 1994, at B10, col. 1 (Lexis).

through attrition.[46]

Ironically, even the compellers at times recognize the irrationality of compulsory overtime from their own perspective in confrontation with workers acting as rational owners of the commodity labor power seeking to preserve its long-term value against opportunistic depredations by employers[47]: "Prolonged overtime often cuts productivity...because workers pace themselves to be able to stand the extra hours."[48] One company that relentlessly imposes overtime on its employees, US West, seemed to portray itself as its own hapless victim when it asserted that it was "just as interested in reducing mandatory overtime because it wants its employees to be rested and refreshed when they begin work." The US West case is especially important because it reveals that although forced overtime has become a "'big flashpoint'" for unions, even strong unions such as the Communication Workers of America (CWA) have been relatively powerless to resist employers' demands. In 1998, when the union made overtime a key issue because members "'were missing Little League games and sometimes even church services,'" the best the CWA could achieve after a two-week strike by 35,000 workers was capping mandatory overtime at 16 hours weekly in 1999 and 8 hours in 2000, and a guarantee of at least one five-day week per month in 1999 and two in 2001.[49] When the same issue confronted members of the International Brotherhood of Electrical Workers employed by GTE, one local union business manager said "he would settle only reluctantly for limiting the amount of required overtime to 16 hours a week. 'This bothers all unions.... Our forefathers in the labor movement died to get the 8-hour work day.'"[50]

Resistance to demands for overtime has been undermined by administrative and judicial rulings, dating back to the inception of the National Labor Relations Act (NLRA), vindicating employers' claims that, just as "[f]ailure to work overtime hours is the same as failure to work regular straight-time hours,"[51] employers' autocratic rule applies to both. The National Labor Relations Board disqualifies such a refusenik as seeking to "dictate the terms of his employment" and thus engaging in "unprotected insubordination" leaving him "legitimately

---

[46]"UAW-GM Talks Reflect Difficult Relationship," 156 *Lab. Rel. Rep.* 373, 374, 375 (Nov. 17, 1997). After a three-day strike GM agreed to hire some additional workers. Doron Levin, "G.M. and Auto Workers Reach an Accord," *N.Y. Times*, Oct. 1, 1994, at 7, col. 1 (Lexis).

[47]1 Marx, *Das Kapital* at 568-70.

[48]Stricharchuk and Winter, "Worked Up."

[49]"Mandatory Overtime Seen as Key Bargaining Issue" at 436.

[50]Eve Tahmincioglu, "Strain from Overtime Piles Up for Workers," *St. Petersburg Times*, Aug. 28, 1999, at 1E (Westlaw) (quoting Danny Johnson, Local 824 in Florida).

[51]Van Dorn Co., 48 Lab. Arb. (BNA) 925, 926 (1967).

subject to discipline."[52]

Consequently, workers who concertedly refuse to work overtime while continuing to work the normal working day forfeit their rights under the NLRA; their employers may lawfully consider them strikers and permanently replace them. The legal basis for this outcome is judges' rejection of guerrilla warfare as protected activity—the notion that "an employee can be on a strike and at work simultaneously. We think he must be on the job subject to the authority and control of the employer, or off the job as a striker, in support of some grievance." The monopoly hold that this binary world has on the judicial mind stems, in turn, from a deeper bias concerning capitalist control of the workplace as the natural order of things and codetermination as anarchy or tyranny: "We are aware of no law or logic that gives the employee the right to work upon terms prescribed solely by him. ... It is not a situation in which employees ceased work in protest against conditions imposed by the employer, but one in which the employees sought and intended to work upon their own notion of the terms which should prevail. If they had a right to fix the hours of their employment, it would follow that a similar right existed by which they could prescribe all conditions...affecting their employment."[53]

One point virtually everyone agrees on is that: "Employers can force their employees to work overtime—no matter how much they object." Employees, according to the U.S. Department of Labor (DOL), "must work as many extra hours as their employers demand or face losing their jobs. ... '(Labor laws) don't give employees any protection if they refuse to work overtime,' Richard Backer, assistant district director for the U.S. Department of Labor, said...."[54] The more aseptic version in the DOL regulations explains: "Since there is no absolute limitation...on the number of hours that an employee may work in any workweek, he may work as many hours a week as he and his employer see fit" so long as the

---

[52]Mead Corp.-Publishing Paper Div.-Escanaba, 275 NLRB 323, 324 (1985). See also Poppin Fresh Pies, Inc., 256 NLRB 233, 234 (1981), in which a Spanish-speaking married couple at a pie factory were fired for refusing to work overtime because the employer had not paid them properly for previous overtime: "'me no work no more overtime for this company, this company no pay overtime, and me and Hortencia is going la casa'" (Member Jenkins, concurring in part and dissenting in part).

[53]C.G. Conn, Ltd. v. NLRB, 108 F.2d 390, 397 (7th Cir. 1939). See also NLRB v. Mt. Clemens Pottery Co., 147 F.2d 262 (6th Cir. 1945). First Nat. Bk. Omaha v. NLRB, 413 F.2d 921 (8th Cir. 1969), upheld the same principle, but enforced the Board's order of reinstatement both because the employer had committed the form error of not replacing the women who walked off the job in the middle of their involuntary overtime before they had returned to work the next morning and the weight of the evidence did not support the employer's claim that "the girls intended to walk off the job again if their overtime demands were not met...." *Id.* at 924.

[54]Marcelene Edwards, "Employers Have Right to Demand Overtime," *Idaho Statesman*, Aug. 22, 1998, at 1d (Lexis).

required overtime compensation is paid.[55] Under state labor laws, too, "adult employees can be required to work overtime as long as they're paid time and a half for more than a 40-hour week...." A Washington state labor official offered this explanation of employer behavior: "'If I have two employees, I have to pay two Labor and Industries coverage, two medical-care payments, two Social Security.... If I can take one employee and work the heck out of him, then my overall costs are going to be down.'"[56]

To be sure, workers under union collective bargaining agreements may grieve particularly egregiously motivated dismissals. For example, a telephone repairman with 24 years of seniority won his arbitration 18 months after he had been discharged for refusing to work overtime on the grounds that as a divorced parent with sole custody he had to pick up his two children after school; the employer had found the "excuse" unreasonable on the grounds that he could have made other arrangements.[57] However, for the overwhelming majority of workers in the United States, who lack union representation, no such protection from autocratic employers is available.

But even in the unionized sector, in 1980 only 19.3 percent of major collective bargaining agreements conferred on 21.6 of all workers covered by such contracts the right to refuse overtime.[58] In the mid-1970s, fewer than 5 percent of a sample of collective bargaining agreements entitled workers to refuse overtime without limitations, while another 19 percent permitted them to do so under certain conditions such as a reasonable excuse or the availability of a replacement worker.[59] And "[i]n the absence of an express contractual stipulation or a binding prior understanding, arbitrators universally rule that management has the right to require employees to work reasonable amounts of overtime."[60]

---

[55]29 C.F.R. § 778.102 (1999).

[56]Tamra Fitzpatrick, "Compulsory Overtime Creates Much Heartache," Seattle *Times,* May 2, 1999, at K1 (Lexis).

[57]Kevin Galvin, "Some Workers Protest Rise in Forced Overtime," Chattanooga *Free Press*, Nov. 22, 1998, at A4 (Lexis).

[58]Calculated according to BLS, *Characteristics of Major Collective Bargaining Agreements, January 1, 1980*, tab. 4.1 at 61 (Bull. 2095, 1981). Major agreements were defined as covering 1,000 or more workers. According to a 1970 survey, only 18 percent of workers reported that they could not refuse to work overtime without being penalized. University of Michigan Survey Research Center, *Survey of Working Conditions: Final Report on Univariate and Bivariate Tables*, tab. 7.14 at 231 (1971).

[59]BLS, *Hours, Overtime and Weekend Work* 20-22 (BLS Bull. 1425-15, 1974).

[60]Roger Abrams and Dennis Nolan, "Time at a Premium: The Arbitration of Overtime and Premium Pay Disputes," 45 *Ohio St. L. J.* 837, 845 (1984). See also Marvin Hill, Jr. and Anthony Sinicropi, *Management Rights: A Legal and Arbitral Analysis* 513 (1986) ("Management's right to require that an employee work overtime has been consistently recognized by arbitrators"). For proof that arbitrators have not universally vindicated employers' power to compel overtime work, see Connecticut River Mills, Inc. 6 Lab. Arb.

A case involving a strong union that failed to negotiate any express limitation on overtime illustrates both the power that even unionized firms may retain and the modicum of freedom that counter-organization secures unionists. In 1947 the Ford Motor Company announced at one of its plants that, beginning six days later, workers would work nine hours daily until further notice. Near the end of the very first day of the new schedule, "Supervision instructed the employees to continue working until the production schedule for that day was completed." Two workers who refused to remain at work beyond the already lengthened workday were initially discharged but then reinstated with a three-day lay-off penalty. After asserting that the amount of overtime requested would not have endangered the workers' health, the high-profile arbitrator, Harry Shulman, rejected the UAW's argument that work beyond the standard 40-hour week was optional with the workers: it flew in the face of an express contractual provision—only recently added—according to which Ford "'retains the sole right...to determine the starting and quitting time and the number of hours to be worked.'"[61] Despite this clear basis, Shulman also found that a worker's refusal to work overtime may be justified under certain circumstances:

> Except when specifically so hired, employees are not on continuous call 24 hours a day. While they must recognize that they may be called upon to work overtime, they may properly plan their lives on the basis of their customary work schedules. Under the parties' present Agreement, when an employee is asked to work overtime, he may not refuse merely because he does not like to work more than eight hours, does not need the extra money, or for no reason at all. But if the overtime work would unduly interfere with plans he made, then his refusal may be justified. If he is given advance notice sufficient to enable him to alter his plans, he must do so. But if the direction is given to him without such notice, then it would be arbitrary to require him to forego [sic] plans which he made in justifiable reliance upon his normal work schedule—unless, indeed, his commitments are of such trivial importance as not to deserve consideration.[62]

Despite the fact that management had handed down its order shortly before quitting time, Shulman ruled that one of the workers was unjustified in refusing to work without offering any reason; nevertheless, the arbitrator's award reduced his suspension without pay to one day. Shulman then rescinded Ford's punishment of the other worker altogether because overtime work would have

(BNA) 1017, 1019 (1947), in which the arbitrator held that under a contract providing that an 8-hour day, 40-hour week "shall be in effect without revision," work beyond these hours was "solely within the discretion of the employee" even where workers had been working 6-day, 48-hour weeks for some time; employers who required scheduling flexibility would have to include express language in their contracts.

[61]Ford Motor Co., 11 Lab. Arb. (BNA) at 1159.

[62]Ford Motor Co., 11 Lab. Arb. (BNA) at 1160.

caused him to lose his ride home with another worker and to take public transportation, which would have taken a substantially longer amount of time, which was also disproportionate to the amount of overtime. The arbitrator added that if Ford had given the worker notice a day or two earlier, the case would have been different.[63]

This arbitral mercy, based on the common law of the unionized shop, continues to characterize arbitrations, which subject managerial prerogatives in this area to a reasonableness criterion: employers' power to order overtime may be overridden where the extended work period is unreasonably long, inconsistent with workers' health, safety, and endurance, or is imposed under unreasonable circumstances.[64] This sphere of autocracy tempered by reasonableness may be contrasted with the fate of workers in the union-free sector. When a key punch operator was told on a Thursday that mandatory overtime was scheduled for Saturday, she reminded her supervisor that she would not be able to work because she had planned a birthday party for her husband. Working for a nonunion firm, Deborah Butler could not challenge her discharge; instead, her legal dispute focused merely on whether she was entitled to unemployment compensation. Under Colorado law, as in many other states, resolution of that question pivoted on whether organizing her spouse's birthday party constituted good cause for refusing mandatory overtime; that standard was defined by reference to "compelling personal reasons affecting either the worker or his immediate family."[65] The court glossed those reasons by adopting phraseology from other courts: "'quitting must be for such a cause as would, in a similar situation, reasonably motivate the average able-bodied and qualified worker to give up his or her employment with its certain wage rewards in order to enter the ranks of the unemployed.' ... While claimant understandably desired to give the birthday party for her husband, we do not think a reasonable person would refuse to work overtime and thereby sacrifice employment for this reason."[66]

Employers' entitlement to exact overtime is so deeply anchored in the

---

[63]Ford Motor Co., 11 Lab. Arb. (BNA) at 1160-61. In contrast, in a nonunion case involving a minimum wage worker who sought unemployment benefits after quitting a job which for three months had required four hours of commuting daily on public transportation following the demise of his truck which he could not afford to repair, the court ruled that such commutes in the Los Angeles area were too common to make the claimant's travel time unreasonable. Zorrero v. Unemployment Ins. App. Bd., 47 Cal.App.3d 434 (1975).

[64]Donald Peterson, "Arbitration of Employee Refusal to Work Overtime," *Dispute Resolution J.*, Jan. 1997, at 21-27.

[65]Action Key Punch Service, Inc. v. Industrial Comm'n of Colorado, 709 P.2d 970, 971 (Col. Ct. App. 1985) (quoting Col. Rev. Stat. § 8-73-108(4)(k) (1984 Cum. Supp.)).

[66]Action Key Punch Service, Inc. at 972 (quoting Evenson v. Unemployment Ins. App. Bd., 62 Cal.App.3d 1005, 1016 (1976)). This language apparently derives from 81 *Corpus Juris Secundum* § 226 at 449-50 (1977).

judicial mind that even a worker who had been injured on the job and whose physician suggested that he not work more than eight hours a day was denied relief under the Americans with Disabilities Act (ADA) after his employer had rejected his request that it accommodate his disability by not assigning him overtime. A federal appeals court held that the Florida Power & Light Company's "aggressive same-day" policy of meeting consumer demand by connecting and disconnecting electric meters within 24 hours made the performance of mandatory overtime an essential function of the job by creating fluctuating production requirements so that the worker, who could not work overtime, failed to meet the ADA's threshold requirement and therefore suffered no unlawful discrimination when he was fired.[67] Thus an employer's prestatutory power to force workers to work overtime instead of hiring additional workers trumps this protective statute: the company can bootstrap itself into the privilege of firing workers injured on the job who can no longer work 216 overtime hours per year simply by understaffing the workplace in terms of the long-term health of its employees.[68]

2. The Self-Contradictions of Overtime Premiums

There was a man who sold spears and shields. Holding up a shield to the people, he cried: "My shields! They are extraordinarily solid—no matter how good the spear, nothing can pierce them." Then he picked up a spear and shouted: "My spears! They are very sharp—no matter how hard and solid the shield, there is nothing they cannot pierce."

Those standing on the side listened and snickered. One of them asked him: "So according to what you said, your spears are the sharpest and your shields are the strongest. What happens if your spear is used to pierce your shield?" Disconcerted, the man could not give an answer.[69]

In the workingman's world there is something called an "overtime hog." The name, a union epithet, refers to the worker who is forever trying to put in overtime. Among the biggest of all headaches shop stewards have is the question of who is going to put in overtime and get its premium pay. These days, it seems, there is not enough overtime to go around. The average in manufacturing industries reaches two to three hours a week or about half an hour a day per worker. So it raises all the dangers of favoritism.

---

[67]Davis v. Florida Power & Light Co., 205 F.3d 1301 (11th Cir. 2000).

[68]To be sure, the ADA regulations state that a "job function may be considered essential...because of the limited number of employees available among whom the performance of that job function can be distributed." 42 CFR § 1630.2(n)(2)(ii) (1999). But the definition is circular if "can" merely means that the employer has for reasons of profitability decided not to hire additional workers.

[69]The Book of Han Fei Zi (3rd century B.C.).

That someone can favor a friend by seeing that he gets overtime work may sound at first like a teacher's keeping the good boys after school to write on the blackboard one hundred times, "I have been a good boy."[70]

If an hours law is aimed at creating macrosocial norms such as shielding life spheres from the demands of production, preserving workers' health, or spreading employment, it must withhold from individual workers the decision whether to overwork or not. In particular, an overtime premium law like the FLSA is addressed to the employer, who, as Shulman recognized, "must determine whether the overtime work is worth the greater cost to him. ... No deterrence is accomplished by leaving the choice with the employee for whom the premium must act as an encouragement rather than as a deterrence."[71] In the early twentieth century, unionists saw the need to educate the "'over-time hogs,' who have no concern in the organization other than the amount of money in their pay envelopes."[72] Thus union officials who concede that "where people want to voluntarily work overtime, that's their determination to make,"[73] have already abandoned the compulsory-collectivist principle that they would never consider yielding with regard to minimum wages.

Since not even the AFL-CIO believes in the existence of significant congressional support for the double or triple overtime penalty that would be needed to restore its deterrent value, its function may have degenerated into a mere entitlement to a modest premium for overwork. Many current defenders of the overtime premium, accordingly, advocate its retention on the grounds of its efficacy in preserving living standards especially for low-paid workers. Such friends of labor are unaware that the argument was long ago a favorite among labor's enemies, who used it to attack unions' advocacy of eight-hour laws without overtime. For example, in 1912, when Congress, after two decades of union urging, enacted such a statute to cover government contracts, *The New York Times* taunted labor: "Overtime is forbidden, although extra pay at higher rates is a boon to the wage-earner. ... Eight hours' work and eight hours' pay are not attractive under the present narrow margins of wages above the cost of living. For some there is no such margin, and any such reduction of pay would be...a

---

[70]Sebastian de Grazia, *Of Time, Work, and Leisure* 131 (1964 [1962]).

[71]Ford Motor Co., 11 Lab. Arb. (BNA) at 1159-60.

[72]*Report of the Proceedings of the Thirty-Ninth Annual Convention of the American Federation of Labor* 453 (1919) (executive council quoting delegate Tracy, Cal. State Fed. of Labor).

[73]1 [California] Senate Committee on Industrial Relations, *Interim Hearing on AB 1295—Mandatory Overtime* at 18 (William Robertson, exec. sec'y-treas., L.A. Cty. Fed. Lab.).

calamity for them...."[74]

This question was prominently raised in 1997 in connection with unsuccessful congressional efforts to enact the so-called Family Friendly Workplace Act amending the FLSA to empower employers to offer compensatory time off in lieu of premium pay.[75] The minority Senate Democrats protested the proposal because

> the very workers who currently rely most heavily on overtime pay are the employees most vulnerable to coercion and retaliation by their employer.
>
> Thus, to understand the real world impact of this bill, we must look at the workers who are currently depending on overtime pay to make ends meet. Overwhelmingly, they are working for low wages. [O]ne-fourth of workers earning overtime earn under $12,000 per year. 44 percent of workers who depend on overtime earn $16,000 per year or less, and 61 percent earn $20,000 per year or less. ... These are classic low-wage jobs, where workers need every dollar of pay they can earn. Furthermore, overtime pay makes up a significant percentage of many hourly workers' take-home pay. When they work overtime, manufacturing workers find that an average of nearly 15 percent of their take-home pay is attributable to the extra hours. ... If this bill becomes law, many of them will lose overtime pay that they depend on to pay the rent, buy food, and provide clothing for their children. ...
>
> Millions of those who rely on overtime earn only the minimum wage.[76]

Wage and Hour Administrators use similarly self-contradictory reasoning. In attacking big business's drive to undermine the 40-hour week and the payment of penalty overtime wages, Maria Echaveste charged: "'The issue is not about flexibility.... It's about money. And the net result of change will not be flexibility but the loss of money out of the pockets of workers who need the overtime.'"[77] Echaveste correctly unmasked employers' efforts to camouflage their attack on the FLSA as motivated by the desire to lower wage costs, but her ledger-book logic equating money saved and money lost stands the historical struggle over shorter hours on its head. And her successor, T. Michael Kerr, apparently saw no contradiction in explaining the "purpose and importance of overtime pay" to Congress in these terms:

> Protecting the integrity of the regular rate is key to ensuring workers overtime rights. An important purpose of the overtime premium pay requirement is to limit the burden of excessive work hours for employees and their families, and to ensure workers are fairly

---

[74]"The Eight-Hour Day," *N.Y. Times*, July 2, 1912, at 10, col. 3 (editorial).

[75]S. 4, 105th Cong., 1st Sess. (1997).

[76]S. Rep. No. 11: *Family Friendly Workplace Act*, 105th Cong., 1st Sess. 38-39 (1997).

[77]Friedman, "Time Short for 40-Hour Weeks?" (quoting Maria Echaveste).

compensated when they are required to work long hours. For many workers, overtime pay is an important part of their income that helps them make ends meet. ... Average weekly overtime hours have been at or near record levels for much of the 1990s. [O]vertime hours and overtime pay have become increasingly important to many workers...as the amount of overtime work has trended upward.[78]

Employers, too, have used the same argument to attack legislative efforts to put an end to mandatory overtime. As the Ford Motor Company informed the California Senate Committee on Industrial Relations a quarter-century ago: "in the automotive industry, a substantial number of employes [sic] look upon overtime pay as being an integral part of their paycheck or earning capacity. Indeed, our experience at Ford is that substantially all of our overtime grievances are submitted by employes who believe that they have been improperly denied overtime as opposed to protesting the fact that if it is scheduled, they were required to work."[79]

Even a resolutely pro-labor economist who has untiringly defended the FLSA against employer attacks, loses sight of logic in asserting: "When an employer insists on long hours per week, the costs spill over onto family and parenting time, student time, leisure, and volunteer time. In a sense, the overtime premium makes employers bear more of the social spillover costs imposed by their own hours decisions."[80] It is unclear what "sense" Lonnie Golden can mean since no matter how much money the premium redistributes from the employer to the overtime worker, it cannot restore to the worker the lost time that he will never be able to spend in these nonproduction activities.

Regardless of whether reliance on overtime premiums is a rational means of raising the annual incomes of low-wage workers, it is irreconcilable with using the statutory overtime penalty to discourage overtime work and promoting work sharing. In the context of an unprincipled Democratic opposition to Republican efforts to dismantle the New Deal, promoting the overlong workweeks that the labor movement struggled for decades to abolish does not even provoke demands for an explanation as to why the traditional goals of shorter hours and work sharing should be sacrificed for marginal increases in weekly wages that tendentially depress hourly wage rates.

Evidence of the perverse result of relying on overtime to bolster low-waged

---

[78]Treatment of Stock Options Under the Fair Labor Standards Act: Hearing Before the House Committee on Education and the Workforce (Mar. 2, 2000) (statement of T. Michael Kerr) (Lexis).

[79]Senate Committee on Industrial Relations, *Interim Hearing on AB 1295—Mandatory Overtime: Appendices* at 225, 227 (Halton Axtell, industrial relations mgr., Ford Motor Co. San Jose assembly plant).

[80]Lonnie Golden, "Family Friend or Foe? Working Time, Flexibility, and the Fair Labor Standards Act," at 7 (Economic Policy Institute Briefing Paper, 1997).

workers' incomes is provided by numerous BLS surveys showing that a below-average proportion of labor union members work overtime, but an above-average proportion are paid premium overtime when they do work long weeks. In May 1978, for example, 23.2 percent of blue-collar unionists worked 41 hours a week or more compared with 31.4 percent of nonunionists, while 83.3 percent of unionists but only 62.4 percent of nonunionists received premium pay. Among construction wage and salary workers, 13.2 percent of unionists and 27.5 percent of nonunionists worked overtime, while 73.6 percent of unionists and only 50.1 percent of nonunionists were paid overtime premiums. In manufacturing, the corresponding figures were 23.4 and 30.3 percent, and 88.7 and 56.3 percent, respectively.[81] On average, employees of establishments imposing overtime do not receive compensatory higher straight-time wages, but union workers do.[82]

Female piece-rate bookbinders in London in 1877 were neither the first nor last workers to learn the Sisyphean lesson that "if overtime were continued for a few weeks together their earnings would soon fall to about the same amount as when they worked the regular hours."[83] Although workers "reap no permanent advantage" from long hours, premium pay, as nineteenth-century trade unionists gradually learned, instead of discouraging overtime work, "stimulated the men in various trades to desire it."[84]

The fundamental defect in unions' and Democrats' rhetoric—and it is mere rhetoric devoid of any principle or theory—to combat efforts by employers and Republicans to undermine the 40-hour week lies in the wholesale adoption of their enemies' individualist-consensual framework. Two centuries of union campaigns have demonstrated that regulation of the length of the workday or workweek cannot be based on worker or employer voluntarism; on the contrary, the very existence of normal working hours presupposes collective-compulsory principles embedded in collective bargaining agreements or statutes.

As Sidney and Beatrice Webb explained a century ago, the failure to proceed along such lines results in an inexorable drift toward longer hours if not lower wage rates. The history of British union agreements regarding overtime work in the nineteenth century, which bears startling resemblances to the late-twentieth-

---

[81]BLS, *Long Hours and Premium Pay, May 1978*, supp. tab. C at A-8 (Spec. Lab. Force Rep. 226, 1979). For similar data for 1977, see BLS, *Long Hours and Premium Pay, May 1977*, supp. tab. E at A-6 (Spec. Lab. Force Rep. 214, 1978). See also Stephen Trejo, "Overtime Pay, Overtime Hours, and Labor Unions," 11 (2) *J. Lab. Econ.* 253-78 (1993).

[82]Ronald Ehrenberg and Paul Schumann, "Compensating Wage Differentials for Mandatory Overtime"? 22 *Econ. Inquiry* 460-78 (Oct. 1984).

[83]*Reports of the Inspectors of Factories for the Half-Year Ending 31st October 1877*, at 14 (C.-2001, 1878).

[84]George Howell, *Trade Unionism: New and Old* 79, 78 (1891).

century experience in the United States, revealed that when the employer had been deprived of the unilateral power to extend the working day as he wished, he insisted, "in conceding a customary fixed working day," that workers accommodate him with respect to emergencies and sudden rush orders by working beyond the usual hours. Unable to refute this claim, union leaders turned the concession into "a source of extra wages" for their members by negotiating for higher time and a quarter or time and a half rates.

This arrangement appeared a reasonable compromise, advantageous to both parties. The employers gained the elasticity they declared to be necessary to the profitable carrying on of their business.... The workmen...were recompensed by a higher rate of payment for the disturbance of their customary arrangement of life, and the extra strain of continuing work in a tired state. The concession involved a deviation from the Normal Day, but the exaction of extra rates would...restrict overtime to real emergencies. ...

Further experience of these extra rates for overtime work has convinced nearly all Trade Unionists that they afford the smallest degree of protection to the Normal Day, whilst they are productive of evil consequences to both parties. In spite of the extra rates, employers have...adopted the practice of systematically working their men for one or two hours a day overtime, for months at a stretch, and, in some cases, even all the year round. ... The result is that the long hours become customary, and subject to alteration at the will of the employer. Nor has the individual workman any genuine choice. ...

Whilst the practice of systematic overtime deprives the workman of any control over his hours of labor, the Trade Unionists are beginning to realise that it insidiously affects also the rate of wages. If there is any truth in the economists' assumption that it is the customary standard of life of each class of workers which, in the long run, subtly determines their average weekly earnings, systematic overtime, if paid for as an extra, must...tend to lower the rate per hour. That frequent opportunities are afforded for working overtime is...often given by employers as an excuse for paying a low rate of weekly wages. Where payment is made by the piece, it is usually impossible...to distinguish between "time" and "overtime," and in such cases a promise of systematic overtime, enabling the men to make up their total earnings to the old standard, is a common inducement to them to submit to a reduction of their piecework rates. But the timeworker is...as much at the mercy of the employer as the pieceworker. The promise of "time and a quarter" for the extra hours is a powerful temptation to the stronger men to acquiesce in a reduction of the Standard Rate of payment for the normal working day.

Moreover, when bad times come, and the demand for a particular kind of labor falls off, there is an almost irreversible tendency for the amount of overtime to increase. The employers see in it a chance of reducing the cost of production by spreading the heavy items of rent, interest on machinery, and office charges over more hours of work. The workmen are tempted to make up, by extra labor, their drooping weekly earnings. Exactly at the moment when the community needs...ten per cent less work from its...building operatives, a large number of these are pressed and tempted to give ten per cent more work—to the end that nearly twenty per cent of the trade can find no employment whatever! ... Even the employers are now beginning to object to the arrangement. They feel that it is unbusinesslike to pay higher rates for tired work.[85]

Significantly, the Webbs told a similar cautionary tale about statutory hours regulation. When Parliament extended the ten-hours regime from textile and allied industries to other factories and workshops, it failed to retain the scheme of rigidly fixed uniform hours: "Endeavours were made, by sanctioning overtime under certain conditions,...to meet the varying circumstances of different industries." The result, they reported, was that the "overtime regulations hailed as one of the sensible advantages of the Act of 1878, have gone far to neutralise any regulation of hours at all." In the end, overtime seldom remained the exception that the law contemplated.[86]

The same analysis was accepted by trade unionists in the United States. Writing in 1903, John Mitchell, the president of the United Mine Workers, stressed it was "absolutely essential to regulate the question of overtime" in order to limit working hours:

> The ideal of an agreement upon the working day should be to limit its length to a reasonable number of hours, while at the same permitting the employer in cases of emergency to keep his men at work for a longer period. It has been shown in practice, however, that where overtime is paid for at the same rate as ordinary time, so-called emergencies multiply, overtime is resorted to systematically, and the normal working day is broken down. The men who have thus secured an eight-hour day find that they are regularly working eight hours per day plus, say, two hours overtime, and after a few years, they may receive for their ten hours no more, if not actually less, than formerly for their eight hours of work. To remedy this evil and to avert this peril, trade unionists have in many cases been obliged to charge for overtime at a considerably higher rate, such as time and a quarter, time and a half, or double time. This is fair to the wage earner, since the last hour of work is harder for him than any other, whereas to the employer, who pays most for this last hour, it is the least valuable, since the workman is tired. Theoretically, therefore, the employer will work overtime only in especially good seasons or in emergencies. In actual practice, however, overtime, even when paid for at a higher rate, tends often to become systematic and to lengthen the working day without permanently increasing wages. Consequently, unions have frequently been compelled to prohibit overtime entirely, to limit the maximum amount of overtime per week or month, or to make other provisions that overtime, while serving the employer's purpose, may not be used to break down the standard working day.[87]

---

[85]Sidney Webb and Beatrice Webb, *Industrial Democracy* 344-47 (new ed. 1920 [1897]).

[86]Webb and Webb, *Industrial Democracy* at 349-50; Factory and Workshop Act, 1878, 41 Vict. ch. 16, §§ 53-57, at 137, 157-59.

[87]John Mitchell, *Organized Labor: Its Problems, Purposes, and Ideals and the Present and Future of American Wage Earners* 127-28 (1903).

Clarity about the self-defeating character of premium overtime compensation was a commonplace among unionists in the early twentieth century also in the statutory context. Between 1892 and 1912, when Congress debated an eight-hour law for employees of contractors on government works, union leaders repeatedly urged legislators not to yield to employers' requests to include an overtime provision. Employers alleged that "the chance to work overtime" was a "privilege," which a foreman handed out to workers he "wants to be good to...."[88] The president of a shipyard representing the National Metal Trades Association and the National Association of Manufacturers (NAM), whose more than 4,000 members employed 1.7 million workers, testified to the Senate Labor Committee that overtime was a "Godsend to tens of thousands of young men who are working." Purporting to speak on behalf of these firms' employees, Wallace Downey declared:

> The overtime that is paid to those men upon Friday or Saturday night is in itself so much money that it would seem fabulous were I to mention it. You gentlemen do not hear anything about it, but the wives at home and the children hear about it. The overtime money is a very important part of the man's earnings. His whole year's living is laid out on the basis of his average wages and average time made, and the overtime money he makes is something for his wife to get something extra for herself and her children with.[89]

The president of the AFL, Samuel Gompers, was most vociferous in warning that such payments were dysfunctional for workers. "As a matter of fact," he told the House Labor Committee in 1902:

> it is not extra pay; that is, only temporarily is it extra pay, for as the hours of labor are increased generally wages fall to the wages earned in the shorter workday.
>
> In other words, I say that for a ten-hour day, and when overtime is practiced, there is an increase of pay to those who have this overtime. When the overtime becomes general, the wages earned in the lengthened day's work is not more, but generally less, than the wages earned in the shorter workday. This is the universal economic law, from which there is absolutely no deviation.[90]

Gompers had also expressed the labor movement's adamant opposition to

---

[88] *Eight-Hour Law: Hearings Before the Senate Committee on Education and Labor*, 62d Cong. 265 (1912) (testimony of R. Bickford, general counsel, Newport News Shipbuilding and Dry Dock Co.).

[89] *Eight-Hour Law: Hearings Before the Senate Committee on Education and Labor*, 62d Cong. 306 (1912) (testimony of Wallace Downey, pres. Downey Ship Yard and Marine Co.).

[90] *Eight Hours for Laborers on Government Work: Hearings Before the House Committee on Labor*, 57th Cong., 1st Sess. 92 (1902).

overtime two years earlier to the U.S. Industrial Commission. Outlining the same reequilibration process, he added that "after a while it happens that overtime—overwork—becomes the rule and is no longer overwork."[91]

A decade later, the president of a machinists union local explained to the Senate Labor Committee that the union negotiated premium overtime provisions in its collective bargaining agreements with private firms "to prevent the manufacturers from using overtime, and not for the sake of getting extra money, because we know very well that if we work overtime continuously, that becomes a new basis for our day's work, and eventually we will have to work a longer time, and that the straight time will become the regular time, for the same old pay."[92]

3. Overtime Regulation Before the FLSA

> Every one at all conversant with labour questions knows that overtime is extremely common, and that the men themselves are the greatest supporters of the system. And yet the men, in their meetings and by their formal declarations, are constantly protesting against the practice. Nor is it difficult to reconcile these two facts. The men, acting in a body and thinking of their common interests, protest against overtime, because they know that it restricts the area of employment and lowers the rate of wages. But when each individual man comes to deal with his own case, these considerations are replaced by others of a very different character. To the individual workman, a request to work overtime presents itself mainly...as an offer of more money.... From his point of view he would be a fool to reject the offer. Moreover, if he reflects on the matter...from a wider point of view, he will probably argue that his refusal will do no particular good to his comrades. One man who stands out against overtime will not abolish the practice. The system is there, and he may as well take advantage of it. If he doesn't, somebody else will. There is...nothing illogical...in the contradiction between the speech and action of the average trade unionist in the matter of overtime. He does the best he can for himself and family by working overtime, and he does the best he can for his society and his class by protesting against the practice.[93]

Applying financial disincentives to employers in the form of overtime penalties was not the only method available to Congress to limit the workweek

---

[91]7 *Report of the Industrial Commission on the Relations and Conditions of Capital and Labor Employed in Manufactures and General Business* 614 (56th Cong., 2d Sess. H. Doc. No. 495, 1901).

[92]*Eight-Hour Law: Hearings Before the Senate Committee on Education and Labor*, 62d Cong. 373 (1912) (testimony of N. Alifas, pres., District No. 44, Government Employees' International Association of Machinists).

[93]Sidney Webb and Harold Cox, *The Eight Hours Day* 154-5 (1891).

when it was considering the FLSA in 1937-38. To be sure, in 1916 Congress enacted the Adamson law establishing eight hours as the basic workday for workers operating railways and requiring additional compensation for overtime,[94] but 20 years later Congress could simply have prohibited employing any worker for more than a specified number of hours per day or week.

One such counter-model available to Congress was Senator Hugo Black's 30-hour bill, which would have denied access to the channels of interstate commerce to any products produced in establishments that employed anyone more than five days per week or six hours per day,[95] and which the Senate passed by a large majority in 1933. The New Deal, according to one interpretation, rejected this approach that year when the forces advocating increased production and employment prevailed over the continuing campaign for shorter hours; the overtime provision of the FLSA, on this view, was later intended by President Roosevelt as a diluted accommodation of the demand by the AFL for work sharing and a 30-hour work week.[96] The 30-hour bill that Representative Connery introduced in the House in 1937 made the proposal more flexible by authorizing the Secretary of Labor to exempt employers from the law with respect to certain employees if the employer could prove that special conditions required them to be employed more than five days or six hours.[97]

---

[94]Act of Sept. 5, 1916, ch. 436, §§ 1, 3, 39 Stat. 721, 722.

[95]This approach was reminiscent of the program of the Boston Eight-Hour League, which in 1872 proposed amending the patent law so that a patent would be forfeited if the firm that produced the patented product worked any of its employees more than eight hours. Marion Cahill, *Shorter Hours: A Study of the Movement Since the Civil War* 39 (1932).

[96]Benjamin Hunnicutt, *Work Without End: Abandoning Shorter Hours for the Right to Work* ch. 5-7 (1988). The most important legislative history may be consulted in: *Thirty-Hour Work Week: Hearings Before a Subcommittee of the Senate Committee on the Judiciary*, 72d Cong., 2d Sess (1933); H. Rep. No. 124: *Thirty-Hour Week Bill*, 73d Cong., 1st Sess. (1933); *Thirty-Hour Week Bill: Hearings Before the House Committee on Labor*, 73d Cong., 1st Sess. (1933); *Thirty-Hour Week Bill: Hearings Before the House Committee on Labor*, 73d Cong., 2d Sess. (1934). See also Grant Farr, *The Origins of Recent Labor Policy* 59-76 (Univ. Colo. Studies, Ser. in Econ. No. 3, 1959); Stanley Vittoz, *New Deal Labor Policy and the American Industrial Economy* 73-96 (1987). On employers' positive attitude toward work sharing during the Depression, see National Industrial Conference Board, *Shorter Work Periods in Industry* 35-43 (1932); on the view of the Communist Party of the U.S.A. that work sharing appealed to employers as a device for wage cutting, see Labor Research Association, *The History of the Shorter Workday* 34-36 (1942).

[97]H.R. 1606, § 1, 75th Cong., 1st Sess. (Jan. 5, 1937). Black's bill that had passed the Senate 53-30 in 1933 included an amendment to the same effect. This approach resembled that of a World War I-era bill that prohibited shipment in interstate commerce of any commodity produced in any lumber mill, logging camp, or woodworking establishment on which "any labor employed has been permitted to work more than eight hours in any day," but authorized the secretary of labor to permit labor to be employed more than eight hours in emergencies as determined by him. H.R. 11599, 65th Cong., 2d Sess. (1918).

In addition to such rigid or flexible maximum 30-hour bills, Congress could also have looked to an array of federal and state statutes that for decades had limited the daily hours of labor on government work to eight with no provision for overtime work, subject only to exceptions for emergencies. For example, in 1892 Congress enacted such a law on behalf of laborers and mechanics employed by the United States or any contractor or subcontractor on public works of the United States, making violation of the law a misdemeanor.[98] Twenty years later, Congress enacted a similar law for the benefit of employees of federal government contractors, imposing a contract penalty for violations of five dollars per day per worker.[99]

Not surprisingly, such regimes were anathema to employers, who saw them as an opening wedge to "enforcing in private employment a universal eight-hour day, and a rigid eight-hour day at that, not one in which double pay for overtime was to be allowed, but one in which...no...laborer...would be permitted to sell more than eight hours of his own skill and labor...no matter what his necessities might be...."[100] During the many congressional hearings on such proposals during the 1890s and early 1900s, employers' representatives made it clear that the bills' denunciation and prohibition of overtime "of course creates an absolute revolution in every industrial establishment in this country where Government work is performed."[101] Yet the Senate Education and Labor Committee, in reporting out the bill that was enacted in 1912, not only mocked the objection that it was "revolutionary," but declared that whatever "inconvenience" the eight-hour day might cause employers was "of minor importance compared to the general benefit...for laborers. We believe it means better work, better citizens, and in the end better for society."[102]

To be sure, during World War I, Congress authorized the president with respect to national emergencies to suspend the two eight-hour laws for work

---

[98]Act of Aug. 1, 1892, ch. 353, 27 Stat. 340.

[99]Act of June 19, 1912, ch. 174, 37 Stat. 137. See generally, H. Rep. No. 165: *The Eight-Hour Law*, 62d Cong., 1st Sess. (1911); Cahill, *Shorter Hours* at 261-67. For earlier statutes, see Matthew Kelly, "Early Federal Regulation of Hours in the United States," 3 (3) *Indus. & Lab. Rel. Rev.* 362-74 (Apr. 1950). In addition, in 1936 South Carolina enacted a statute that absolutely prohibited employers from employing employees more than 40 hours per week in textile mills, but it did not go into effect because it was conditioned on the enactment of similar legislation in North Carolina and Georgia. 1936 S.C. Acts No. 832 at 1568.

[100]*Eight-Hour Day: Hearings Before the Senate Committee on Education and Labor*, 62d Cong., Pt. 4, at 131-32 (1912) (testimony of James Emery, NAM).

[101]*H.R. 11651—Eight Hours for Laborers on Government Work: Hearings Before the House Committee on Labor* 60 (59th Cong., 1906) (testimony of Lewis Payson, former Republican Representative from Illinois, representing employers).

[102]S. Rep. No. 601: *Hours of Daily Service of Laborers and Mechanics upon Government Contracts*, 62d Cong., 2d Sess. 7, 3 (1912).

performed for the U.S. Navy or under War Department contracts for constructing military buildings or public works for purposes of national defense, and to authorize payment of time and a half for work beyond eight hours.[103] Once President Wilson's executive orders inaugurated this wartime overtime regime,[104] employers complained not about the universal eight-hour day—which had ceased to be a threat—but about the market-induced compulsion to pay premium overtime to workers engaged in civilian work in a factory that was also engaged in government work. The federal government itself took this objection seriously since the application of the overtime regulation to the many dual-purpose firms "would have the effect of disturbing the conditions in their factories, upsetting the well-developed organization of some of the most important factories of the country...." Because the federal government could not attain its goal of standardizing war-related wage scales without also standardizing overtime wages, it faced a dilemma, which it never resolved: "On the one hand it is desirable to eliminate a great cause of labor trouble, put an end to a sense of injustice in the workers resulting from what must to them appear to be an arbitrary discrimination.... On the other hand, it is very important in this crisis not to interfere with the normal and effective flow of the production of the supplies needed by the Army."[105]

Some state laws limiting the hours of female workers in effect when Congress was debating the FLSA imposed absolute caps on the workday and/or workweek, while others permitted overtime work.[106] (Thirty years later, in the wake of the enactment of federal antidiscrimination legislation and the failure of state legislatures to re-enact gender-neutral hours law, the United States lost "even the limited protection against hours deemed long enough to be hazardous to the health of women....")[107] The statute for the District of Columbia, which Congress enacted in 1914, was of the first type, rigidly limiting female workers' daily hours to eight.[108] To prevent overtime from undermining the laws' purpose, some states provided for time and a quarter, time and a half, and/or double time,

---

[103]Act of Mar. 4, 1917, ch. 180, 39 Stat. 1168, 1192. See also U.S. DOL, WHD, *Annual Report for the Fiscal Year Ended June 30, 1940*, at 31-32 (1941).

[104]Exec. Order No. 2559-A, Mar. 24, 1917; Exec. Order No. 2605, Apr. 28, 1917.

[105]"Federal Eight-Hour Law and Executive Orders Pertaining Thereto," 7 *Monthly Lab. Rev.* 193-96 at 195-96 (1918) (memorandum to War Labor Policies Board from committee appointed to investigate applicability of eight-hour laws).

[106]For an international survey at the turn of the century, see 16 *Report of the Industrial Commission* 22-48 (57th Cong., 1st Sess., H. Doc. No. 185, 1901).

[107]Denison, *Why Growth Rates Differ* at 69 n.33. On the rise and demise of gendered hours laws, see Marc Linder and Ingrid Nygaard, *Void Where Prohibited: Rest Breaks and the Right to Urinate on Company Time* 67-127 (1998).

[108]Act of Feb 28, 1914, ch. 28, § 1, 38 Stat. 291.

while others authorized daily overtime so long as the weekly total did not exceed the maximum; other states confined overtime to a certain number of days, while still others required employers to prove to a state agency that irreparable injury would result without overtime. California, for example, prescribed a maximum eight-hour day, six-day, 54-hour week in the fruit and vegetable canning industry, but permitted longer hours in emergencies if one and one-quarter the minimum rate was paid for all daily hours up to 12 and double-time for hours beyond 12. Indeed, the California Industrial Welfare Commission, in justifying the switch from a limit of 10 hours per day and time and a quarter overtime and a limit of 72 hours per week to nine hours per day and time and a quarter overtime up to 12 hours and double time thereafter, argued that

> it has taken a long step in more drastically penalizing overtime than by the legal limitation of seventy-two hours per week. Double time rate, except as an emergency measure, is practically prohibitive. With juries of men in country districts whose fruit may perish if not canned, conviction for violation of the limitation of hours law is most difficult to achieve, some canners even saying they were willing to pay a $50 or $100 fine if necessary to save their fruit.[109]

The Texas 9-hour day/54-hour week law permitted longer hours in extraordinary emergencies, but only with the employee's consent and at double-time rates. A Kansas six-day, 54-hour week regulation permitted one 10-hour working day per week provided the weekly limit was not exceeded. Under Wyoming's eight and one-half hour law, overtime was authorized only in emergencies and if time and one-half was paid for daily overtime. Finally, the weekly hours laws for textile workers in Georgia, Mississippi, and South Carolina imposed various limitations on overtime. In South Carolina, 60 hours of overtime were permitted annually to make up for time lost by accidents or other unavoidable causes, but this time had to be made up within three months. The Mississippi statute permitted indefinite overtime for emergencies or public necessity.[110]

Historical experience in Britain and the United States had shown that unless such terms as "emergencies" were precisely defined, "advantage may easily be

---

[109]Industrial Welfare Commission, State of California, *Report on the Regulation of Wages, Hours and Working Conditions of Women and Minors in the Fruit and Vegetable Canning Industry of California* 7 (Bull. No. 1, May, 1917). In the Australian state of Victoria, nineteenth-century factory acts for women and children provided for time and one half plus tea money. 2 William Pember Reeves, *State Experiments in Australia and New Zealand* 45 (1903).

[110]For an overview of the overtime provisions state by state, see U.S. Women's Bureau, *Labor Laws for Women in the States and Territories,* charts II-VI at 17-31 (Bull. No. 98, 1932).

taken of the exception to permit unnecessary overtime.[111] British hours statutes for women and children in textile factories, the country's most important in the nineteenth century, absolutely prohibited overtime, while later laws governing various other industries permitted overtime during seasonal rush orders or unforeseen events.[112] Advocates of strict enforcement criticized such permissiveness, and unionists argued that such partial exemptions were self-fulfilling prophecies: sudden spurts in orders were the result of customers' very knowledge of this overtime provision.[113] In New Zealand, too, after the Factories Act was amended in 1894 to permit some overwork by women and boys under 16 years of age in exchange for a premium, legislative expectations were disappointed: "When trade was brisk the employers paid the extra money rather than delay to execute orders."[114]

Perhaps the best-known statute imposing an absolute limit on hours—apart from New York's 1897 60-hour bakeries statute struck down by the U.S. Supreme Court's infamous *Lochner* decision in 1905 as exceeding the police power[115]—had been enacted in Utah in 1896 and provided: "The period of employment of workingmen in all underground mines or workings shall be eight hours per day, except in cases of emergency where life or property is in imminent danger." Identical language prohibited work beyond eight hours in "smelters and all other institutions for the reduction or refining of ores or metals," and violations of either provisions were declared misdemeanors.[116] The statute's renown arose from a employer's challenge to its constitutionality on the grounds that it deprived him of his property without due process of law and interfered with employers' and employees' freedom to contract. The U.S. Supreme Court upheld its constitutionality as a reasonable exercise of the police power to protect

---

[111]John Common and John Andrews, *Principles of Labor Legislation* 121 (4th ed. 1936 [1916]).

[112]Factory and Workshop Act, 1878, 41 Vict. ch. 16, §§ 53-57, at 137, 157-59.

[113]Webb and Cox, *The Eight Hours Day* at 157-63; B. Hutchins and A. Harrison, *A History of Factory Legislation* 181 (2d ed. 1911); Leiter, "The Principle of Overtime" at 25.

[114]2 Reeves, *State Experiments in Australia and New Zealand* at 42.

[115]Lochner v. New York, 198 U.S. 45 (1905). The New York labor law provided: "No employé shall be required or permitted to work in a...bakery...more than sixty hours in any one week, or more than ten hours in any one day...." 1897 N.Y. Laws ch. 425, art. 8, § 110.

[116]1896 Utah Laws ch. 72. The "emergency where life or property is in imminent danger" exception, adopted by other states, was interpreted narrowly. In Arizona, for example, the attorney general ruled that the loss of revenue arising from the halting of production would not in itself justify working more than eight hours; moreover, the emergency would have to be so unforeseen, unexpected, and threatening as to "place a reasonable and prudent man to the instant defense of either life or property." Ariz. Op. Atty. Gen. No. 73--17.

the health of workers exposed to especially dangerous work environments, but it also went much further:

> The legislature has also recognized the fact...that the proprietors of these establishments and their operatives do not stand upon an equality, and that their interests are, to a certain extent, conflicting. The former naturally desire to obtain as much labor as possible from their employes, while the latter are often induced by the fear of discharge to conform to regulations which their judgment, fairly exercised, would pronounce to be detrimental to their health or strength. In other words, the proprietors lay down the rules and the laborers are practically constrained to obey them. In such cases self-interest is often an unsafe guide, and the legislature may properly interpose its authority.
>
> [A]lthough the prosecution in this case was against the employer of labor..., his defence is not so much that his right to contract has been infringed upon, but that the act works a peculiar hardship to his employes, whose right to labor as long as they please is alleged to be thereby violated. The argument would certainly come with better grace and greater cogency from the latter class. But the fact that both parties are of full age and competent to contract does not necessarily deprive the State of the power to interfere where the parties do not stand upon an equality, or where the public health demands that one party to the contract shall be protected against himself.[117]

Employers did indeed make such superficially anti-paternalistic arguments on behalf of their workers. At the same time that mine and metals employers were unsuccessfully attacking the Utah statute, their counterparts in Colorado succeeded in thwarting the will of the vast majority of the electorate, which had voted in favor of an eight-hours law. One of the arguments that the chairman of the board of the powerful Colorado Fuel and Iron Company used to oppose it was the alleged injustice it did to miners who would have been deprived of the opportunity to work overtime so that they could earn enough money to educate their sons and elevate them to higher social positions.[118] A representative of the Bethlehem and United States Steel companies, attributing the meteoric rise of some managers to the college educations that they had been able to finance with overtime earnings, went so far as to assert before Congress in 1902 that the ban on overtime work in a proposed eight-hours law for workers on government works was actually designed

> to prevent such careers.... It is to compel men to remain on the same dead level, to prevent men from having the opportunity to rise above their fellow-men. That is the purpose, the direct purpose...of the bill. It is to say to one man of somewhat superior natural ability, "You shall not go faster than your brother who has not the mental capacity

[117]Holden v. Hardy, 169 U.S. 366, 397 (1898).

[118]*A Report on Labor Disturbances in the State of Colorado, from 1880 to 1904*, 58th Cong., 3d Sess., S. Rep. No. 122, at 62 (1905) (quoting John Osgood).

that you have. ... If you have more muscle, you must not be permitted to exert it.[119]

In 1912, a perennial congressional employer-witness against overtimeless eight-hour bills for federal government works alleged: "On one occasion I declared that I could go before the people of my district and defeat...the Member from that district, if he supported a bill of this character, and that I would make the contest with him over the question whether or not he was in favor of striking down the rights of the American workingman to work overtime for overtime pay, which is the very purpose of this bill."[120]

The overtime approach also differed fundamentally from the aspirations expressed in older labor discourse. At its 1887 annual convention, for example, the AFL had advised strongly against overtime work, which interfered with the eight-hour movement, while many workers were unemployed: "It is an instigator of the basest selfishness, a radical violation of union principles...."[121] In the late nineteenth century, unions began prohibiting their members from working overtime while other members were unemployed, as well as demanding that employers distribute overtime to the unemployed.[122] Others, like the National Cotton Mule Spinners, did not shy away from "censur[ing] all those who are guilty of working overtime without a protest."[123] The U.S. Industrial Commission reported in 1901 that only a few unions "felt themselves strong enough to forbid overtime absolutely" to their members by means of fines and other sanctions.[124]

Behind these demands lay the insight that overtime work enables employers to increase the supply of labor without increasing the supply of laborers so that this artificial oversupply, by increasing the number of unemployed, depresses the wage level of the employed.[125] By 1919, when premium overtime rates had appeared in the contracts of virtually all AFL international unions, the AFL

---

[119] *Eight Hours for Laborers on Government Work: Hearings Before the House Committee on Labor*, 57th Cong., 1st Sess. 93 (1902) (testimony of Joseph McCammon).

[120] *Eight-Hour Law: Hearings Before the Senate Committee on Education and Labor*, 62d Cong. 12 (1912) (statement of Daniel Davenport, American Antiboycott Assoc.).

[121] 1 American Federation of Labor, *History, Encyclopedia, Reference Book* 309 (1919) (citing the Report of the Proceedings of the AFL from 1887 at 43, although there is no such page in that report and this passage also appears nowhere else in that publication).

[122] *30th Annual Report of the Massachusetts Bureau of Statistics of Labor: March 1900*, at 79 (1900) (Lowell Spinners Union).

[123] *30th Annual Report of the Massachusetts Bureau of Statistics of Labor: March 1900*, at 141 (referring to Lowell).

[124] *Reports of the Industrial Commission on Labor Organizations, Labor Disputes, and Arbitration, and on Railway Labor* XVII-XVIII (57th Cong., 1st Sess., H. Doc. No. 186, 1901).

[125] Karl Marx, *Zur Kritik der politischen Ökonomie (Manuskript 1861-1863)*, in II:3.6 Karl Marx [and] Friedrich Engels, *Gesamtausgabe (MEGA)* 1910 (1982).

convention declared that overtime work should be discouraged and penalized by demands for double time.[126] A decade later, the convention, which found it contrary to union principles that some workers engaged in avoidable overtime while others were unemployed, recommended the abolition of overtime wherever possible and its use only for reasons beyond the control of management and workers.[127]

Looking back at the history of overtime in 1947, labor historian and economist Philip Taft testified at trial in one of the most important FLSA overtime cases that the desire for additional compensation had never been a general principle: "the one predominant feeling—it is a feeling because it is not a worked out intellectual concept—of labor throughout its history, is the fear of unemployment, even in good times; as you examine the conventions of the different unions..., you find this constantly repeated over and over again, that we do not want overtime. We want to reduce the hours of labor to spread the work."[128] Indeed, at the time Taft was testifying some collective bargaining agreements still instantiated this venerable demand: "Except in cases of emergency, there shall be no regularly scheduled overtime in a classification as long as any employee on the company's pay roll in that classification who is qualified to perform the work, remains laid off without being given the opportunity of returning to work."[129] The trial judge even adopted Taft's position as a finding of fact: "The purpose of the demand of organized labor in American industry for penalty compensation for overtime was...prompted by the laborers' desire for a shorter work day, and was not generally intended as a method of increasing earnings."[130]

For decades unions, with varying degrees of success, had included overtime penalties in collective bargaining agreements to discourage employers from working employees overlong hours where they could not be prohibited outright.[131]

---

[126]*Report of the Proceedings of the Thirty-Ninth Annual Convention of the American Federation of Labor* 450-51, 454 (1919).

[127]*Report of the Proceedings of the Forty-Ninth Annual Convention of the American Federation of Labor* 378 (1929).

[128]Testimony of Prof. Philip Taft, Transcript of Record at 346-47, Bay Ridge Operating Co. v. Aaron, 334 U.S. 446 (1947). Taft stressed that economists did not accept the underlying view that the amount of labor is limited. *Id.* at 329.

[129]BLS, *Collective Bargaining Provisions: Hours of Work, Overtime Pay, Shift Operations* 66 (Bull. No. 908-18, 1950).

[130]Findings of Fact 28 (c), Transcript of Record at 605, Bay Ridge Operating Co.

[131]E.g., *Report of the Eight-Hour Commission* 481-82 (1918) (on railway unions). For a collection of overtime provisions in collective bargaining agreements from various trades, see Supplemental Memorandum for Defendant in Error 4-6, Bunting v. Oregon, 243 U.S. 436 (1917). According to Merle Vincent, "Time and Money," 30 (11) *Survey Graphic* 621-23, 654-55, at 621-22 (Nov. 1941), time and a half overtime had prevailed in the electrical, cement, paper and pulp, furniture, printing, and machine trades prior to

Fewer contracts imposed absolute bans or requirements that each instance of overtime be authorized by the union.[132] In congressional hearings on bills to prohibit overtime (except for emergencies) and mandate the eight-hour day on government works, union leaders were interrogated by employers' spokesmen as to why they sought by legislation what they themselves did not include in their own private-sector contracts. Unionists repeatedly testified that their contracts permitted overtime only in "extraordinary emergencies," which in some instances only the union shop steward was authorized to declare. Under such circumstances, overtime was "almost wiped out" because "[t]here is nobody who cares to pay time and half time." One union official testified in 1904 that his union's entire 800 members did not work a total of even 10 hours' overtime annually.[133] Samuel Gompers added that the bill provided for overtime for the government "in cases of emergency, of war, flood, and so forth; while with the employer we can make no such provisions, because the employer has no war."[134]

In the early twentieth century unions protested against overtime work out of collective-compulsory principle. Gompers repeatedly declared to congressional committees considering a ban on overtime work on government works that "we want no overtime. We want no man to have even the opportunity of overtime...unless there be an extraordinary emergency...."[135] When a Congressman asked him whether unions were opposed to workers' "having the privilege of working overtime for extra pay," Gompers rejected the premise; instead, he urged enactment of "a law to prevent the employers of labor either directly or indirectly making conditions such as to compel the workmen to work more than eight hours a day by any species of inducement that shall have the general tendency to

---

enactment of the FLSA.

[132]Testimony of Prof. Philip Taft, Transcript of Record at 329-30, Bay Ridge Operating Co. A few minutes later, however Taft testified that "there is no union contract that I know—there may be some—that explicitly prohibits work beyond a certain time, because there may be a job that is in the middle, you may spoil materials, you may require the filling of an order. ... I know of no single contract where it is absolutely prohibited, and that certainly would be a very foolish clause...." *Id.* at 357, 384. In fact, a BLS study of overtime provisions in collective bargaining agreements in force at precisely the time of Taft's testimony offered examples of absolute bans. BLS, *Collective Bargaining Provisions: Hours of Work; Overtime Pay; Shift Operations* 64 (Bull. No. 908-18, 1950).

[133]*Eight Hours for Laborers on Government Work: Hearings Before the House Committee on Labor*, 58th Cong. 418 (1904) (testimony of Herman Schulteis, Knights of Labor, and Milford Spohn, chairman, legis, comm., Central Labor Union, Washington, D.C.).

[134]*Hours of Labor for Workmen, Mechanics, etc., Employed upon Public Works of the United States: Hearings Before the House Committee on Labor*, 56th Cong. 1st Sess. 413 (1900).

[135]*Eight Hours for Laborers on Government Work: Hearings Before the House Committee on Labor*, 58th Cong. 458 (1904).

increase the hours of labor."[136]

The building trades unions had, going back to the middle of the nineteenth century, bargained for time and a half or double time to regulate overtime as part of the overriding purpose of equalizing their members' work opportunities.[137] Unions sometimes reinforced this approach by giving overtime work only to their unemployed members or by prohibiting members from working overtime for any firm other than their regular-hours employer. Employers' skepticism toward the claim that construction unions were merely trying to protect the standard workweek was based on the counterclaim that building deadlines made overtime an ongoing necessity.[138] Indeed, employers insisted not only that employees in general and construction workers in particular "covet" overtime,[139] but that unions insisted on premium overtime rates not to discourage overtime work, but "[f]or the simple reason that they can get it."[140]

However, the whole point of penalty overtime rates was turned on its head in the nineteenth century as employers came to accept shorter standard workweeks in return for overtime. For example, among construction workers in Britain in the second half of the nineteenth century: "Overtime was converted from a disincentive on the employer to an incentive for the men."[141] Consequently, "where there were no restrictions on overtime work the determination of the hours of work was in effect returned to the individual bargain where each individual's leisure was purchasable at some premium rate of pay. Thus the overtime rate became one of the means through which the employer could undermine the union attempts to restrict supply. Ironically the unions had originally pressed for its introduction as part of their effort to restrict supply." Instead of deterring employers from overworking employees, premium rates became "a means of inducing employees to spend longer hours at work."[142] For example, the machinists union, which was adamantly opposed to systematic overtime in the mid-nineteenth century, by 1874 saw no remedy for it, and by the

---

[136]*Eight Hours for Labor on Government Work: Hearings Before the House Committee on Labor*, 57th Cong., 1st Sess. 91 (1902) (colloquy with Rep. William Warnock).

[137]For the example of London masons in 1853, see M. Bienefeld, *Working Hours in British Industry: An Economic History* 85 (1972).

[138]William Haber, *Industrial Relations in the Building Trades* 228-30 (1930).

[139]*H.R. 15651: Eight Hours for Laborers on Government Work: Hearings Before Subcommittee No. 1, House Committee on Labor* 31 (60th Cong., 1908) (testimony of Joseph Richardson, D.C. Bldg. Trades Employers Assoc.).

[140]*H.R. 15651: Eight Hours for Laborers on Government Work* at 148 (testimony of W. Post, vice president of Post and McCord, largest steel erector in the United States).

[141]Richard Price, *Masters, Unions and Men: Work Control in Building and the Rise of Labour 1830-1914*, at 146 (1980).

[142]Bienefeld, *Working Hours in British Industry* at 209.

beginning of the twentieth century had deleted the term from its vocabulary as it was constrained to accept collective bargaining agreements that not only permitted up to 40 overtime hours per month, but included "urgency and emergency" clauses that could be interpreted broadly enough "to make overtime practically unlimited."[143]

Historically, this insight that overtime premiums would make workers complicit in the undermining of their class's own standards even inspired state court judges to deny the overtime compensation claims of workers who had complied with employers' requests to work more than the maximum number of hours in states with statutes that absolutely prohibited and criminalized employment beyond a certain number of hours. In the best-known such case, decided under the aforementioned Utah statute, the state supreme court upheld the trial judge's ruling:

> "Had the employe the right to waive this protection, both for himself and the state, it can readily be seen that it rests entirely with him to abrogate the operation of the law, and to cause it to become a dead letter. He may make the period of employment eight, ten, twelve or any greater number of hours, at his option, with the result that the conditions of relating to the period of employment in mines and mills would now exist as before enactment of this law—a matter purely of contract between the parties."[144]

Even under statutes not interpreted to hold workers criminally co-liable for their violation, courts denied compensation on the grounds that granting recovery would permit them to gain from thwarting the enforcement of a benevolent public policy.[145]

As the FLSA was wending its way through Congress in 1937, the Bureau of National Affairs (BNA) published a study of workweek and overtime provisions in representative collective bargaining agreements of important industries and firms. The near ubiquity in the contracts of the 40-hour normal workweek prompted the BNA to conclude that "the 40-hour week may almost be regarded as a national standard already on the way to general acceptance." A 50-percent overtime premium was also "[t]he usual custom," although many unions had also secured time and a half for hours beyond eight per day as well as double time for holidays and Sundays.[146] Such union achievements, however, were not customary among unorganized workers before the New Deal, and not until industrial

---

[143]Jefferys, *Story of the Engineers* at 36, 90, 148, 158 (quotes).

[144]Short v. Bullion-Beck & Champion Mining Co., 57 P. 720, 721 (Utah 1899).

[145]Lewis v. Ferrari, 34 Cal.App.2d Supp. 767 (App. Dept. San Diego Cty., 1939); Martinez v. Johnson, 119 P.2d 880 (Nev. 1941).

[146]"Work Week and Overtime Pay in Contracts," 1 *Labor Relations Reports* 97 (Sept. 27, 1937).

organizing vastly expanded in 1936-37 did the practice of overtime rates spread with it.[147] As late as the 1920s, for example, thousands of automobile workers worked forced overtime without premium wages.[148] And members of the United Mine Workers in the crucial Appalachian area did not secure premium overtime pay until 1937, tonnage and piecerate workers not gaining time and a half rates until 1943.[149]

4. The Legislative History and Purposes of the FLSA Overtime Provision

According to Mr. Justice Murphy, the purpose of the overtime provisions was twofold: "to spread employment by placing financial pressure on the employer through the overtime pay requirement...and...to compensate employees for the burden of a workweek in excess of the hours fixed in the Act." ... The learned Justice's statement fails to dispel a lingering doubt as to whether Congress in 1938 actually regarded workweeks over forty hours as burdensome.[150]

Enactment of the FLSA overtime provision was accompanied by a sea change in public evaluation of hours regulation. In the 1920s, a standard international text on state regulation of working time noted that rules merely governing premiums for overtime were not of a fundamental character.[151] As late as 1935, Elizabeth Brandeis, one of the country's leading experts on and advocates of labor standards legislation, frankly characterized state hours laws similar to what would soon be enacted under the FLSA as "of the unenforceable type permitting overtime for extra pro rata pay."[152] Yet, three years later President Roosevelt

---

[147]Testimony of Prof. David McCabe, Transcript of Record at 420-21, Bay Ridge Operating Co.

[148]BLS, *Wages and Hours of Labor in the Motor Vehicle Industry: 1925*, at 23-24 (Bull. No. 438, 1927); BLS, *Handbook of Labor Statistics 1924-1926*, at 772 (Bull. No. 439, 1927); Robert Dunn, *Labor and Automobiles* 94-95 (1929).

[149]"Wage Chronology No. 4: Bituminous-Coal Mines, 1933-48," 68 (3) *Monthly Lab. Rev.* 303-307 at 305 (Mar. 1949).

[150]E. Merrick Dodd, "The Supreme Court and Fair Labor Standards, 1941-1945," 59 *Harv. L. Rev.* 321, 321 n.2 (1945).

[151]Emil Lederer and Jakob Marschak, "Arbeiterschutz," in 9:2 *Grundriss der Sozialökonomik: Das soziale System des Kapitalismus: Die autonome und staatliche soziale Binnenpolitik im Kapitalismus* 259-319 at 287-88 (1927).

[152]Elizabeth Brandeis, "Labor Legislation," in 3 John Commons et al., *History of Labor in the United States, 1896-1932*, at 397-697 at 551 (1935). Even a critical leftist seemed unaware of the contradiction between confirming that an 1868 statute limiting the workday on government contracts to eight hours was ineffective because it permitted agreements to work overtime and asserting that the FLSA did not interfere with overtime

tried to persuade the millions of listeners to his fireside chat on the eve of the FLSA's enactment that the new law "sets...a ceiling over hours of labor."[153] To be sure, this public relations effort may have been facilitated by the act itself, whose overtime provision is conveniently mislabeled, "Maximum Hours."[154]

Despite such misleading cues, Frances Perkins, the Secretary of Labor during the entire Roosevelt administration and one of the most ardent advocates of the FLSA, unambiguously vindicated employers' power to make their employees work unlimited hours under the new law:

> It has been said that one reason for the collapse of the French Republic was the adoption of the 40-hour week. The French 40-hour-week law was a rigid statute which prohibited all overtime beyond 40 hours, not only for the individual worker but also for the entire industrial establishment. ... The American hour laws, however, were very carefully framed to avoid this rigidity, and any employer in the land can legally and automatically ask his employees to work as many hours beyond 40 as he cares to without asking permission of the Government so long as he pays the overtime rate of time and one-half.[155]

Perkins was wrong about France,[156] but she stated the record correctly for the United States, and her Wage and Hour Administrator[157] and the U.S. Supreme

---

work. Irving Richter, "Four Years of the Fair Labor Standards Act of 1938: Some Problems of Enforcement," 51 (2) *J. Political Economy* 95-111, at 96, 98 (Apr. 1943).

[153]*Public Papers and Addresses of Franklin D. Roosevelt: 1938: The Continuing Struggle for Liberalism* 391, 392 (1941[June 24, 1938]).

[154]Fair Labor Standards Act of 1938, ch. 676, § 7, 52 Stat. 1060, 1063.

[155]*Twenty-Eighth Annual Report of the Secretary of Labor for the Fiscal Year Ended June 30 1940*, at 5 (1940). Perkins made this statement in a speech to the Seventh National Conference on Labor Legislation; "Calls Short Hours Best in Emergency," *N.Y. Times*, Dec. 10, 1940, at 18, col. 3.

[156]As Perkins herself knew or should have known, at the same time she made this statement her own Wage and Hour Administrator was publishing a detailed account of the French hours law concluding that the "frequently repeated statement that the French 40-hour law contributed to the defeat of France by bringing about curtailment of production, is subject to correction in the light of history. The act was fully in effect but a short time, liberal provision was made for the exemption of defense industries, and even general relaxations were permitted many months before the outbreak of war...." U.S. DOL, WHD, *Annual Report for the Fiscal Year Ended June 30, 1940*, at 63 (1941). A decree of Nov. 12, 1938, not only made a worker's refusal to work overtime in the interest of national defense a breach of contract, subjecting him to forfeiture of unemployment benefits for six months, but criminalized any attempts to induce others not to work overtime. *Id.* at 57.

[157]"It is clear that there is no absolute limitation upon the number of hours that an employee may work. If he is paid time and a half for overtime, he may work as many hours a week as he and his employer see fit." WHD, Interpretative Bull. No. 4 (Dec. 20, 1939 [Oct. 21, 1938]), reprinted in BNA, *Wage and Hour Manual* at 95 (1940 ed.).

Court agreed.[158]

In the face of the FLSA's manifestly permissive regulation of hours, both the Right and the Left have perpetuated myths about workers' statutory entitlement to the 40-hour week. Disconnected from reality is a Republican congressman's recent assertion that the "rights" to the minimum wage and 40-hour workweek created by the FLSA "have become as ingrained as constitutional guarantees."[159] Similarly fanciful is the leftist pathos that the FLSA "made the eight-hour day and forty-hour week the law of the land...."[160] Much closer to the mark was the characterization by Donald Nelson, chairman of the War Production Board, in opposition to efforts by employers to suspend the overtime law during World War II: "It governs wages rather than the hours in which a man may work."[161] More accurate, too is a later scholar's judgment that the FLSA "did not really establish the forty-hour week norm so much as it buttressed management's insistence that there be no further reductions in weekly work time standards"[162] even if employers did not support the FLSA's creation of that norm.[163]

Some of the confusion that has fogged over understanding of the purposes of the overtime penalty/premium can be lifted by scrutinizing the FLSA's legislative history. The immediate precedents for the overtime provision under the FLSA were the President's Reemployment Agreement (PRA or blanket code), with which Roosevelt asked employers to comply in July 1933 pending adoption of codes for their industries, and various industry codes promulgated under the National Industrial Recovery Act (NIRA) in 1933 and 1934.[164] The PRA

---

[158]Overnight Motor Transp. Co. v. Missel, 316 U.S. 572 (1942).

[159]142 *Cong. Rec.* E 1789 (Sept. 27, 1996) (Rep. Thomas Petri, R. Wis.). Similarly, Rep. Wood (D. Mo.) was wrong in asserting at the 1937 FLSA hearings that "this bill would take away from the employee the right to work for as low wages as he pleased and for as many hours as he pleased." *Fair Labor Standards Act of 1937: Joint Hearings Before the Senate Committee on Education and Labor and the House Committee on Labor*, 75th Cong., 1st Sess. 139 (1937). He was right about the minimum wage, but not about long hours.

[160]David Roediger and Philip Foner, *Our Own Time: A History of American Labor and the Working Day* 257 (1989).

[161]*Hearings on H. R. 6790, to Permit the Performance of Essential Labor on Naval Contracts Without Regard to Laws and Contracts Limiting Hours of Employment, to Limit the Profits of Naval Contracts, and for Other Purposes Before the House Committee on Naval Affairs*, 77th Cong., 2d Sess. 2576 (1942).

[162]Ronald Edsforth, "Why Automation Didn't Shorten the Work Week: The Politics of Work Time in the Automobile Industry," in *Autowork* 155-79 at 162 (Robert Asher & Ronald Edsforth eds., 1995).

[163]David Roediger, "The Limits of Corporate Reform: Fordism, Taylorism, and the Working Week in the United States, 1914-1929," in *Worktime and Industrialization: An International History* 135-54 at 148 (Gary Cross ed. 1988).

[164]The PRA and the codes were precursors to the FLSA overtime provision also with respect to the exclusion of executive employees; see below chapter 2.

provided that employers would not, for example, work any factory worker more than 35 hours per week, but conferred the right on them to work a maximum workweek of 40 hours during a period of six weeks; however, this provision did not apply to "very special cases where restrictions on hours of highly skilled workers on continuous processes would unavoidably reduce production but, in any such special case, at least time and a third shall be paid for hours worked in excess of the maximum."[165]

Under the codes:

> The need for establishing rates of pay for overtime work arose from the very general occurrence of provisions permitting an extension of the regular working time either by allowing hours to be averaged over specific periods or by fixing definite additions to the usual schedule in periods of concentrated demand. Such extensions were sometimes regarded as part of the usual scheduled hours but more often they were considered overtime for which extra compensation had to be paid. [T]he principle of extra pay for such employment was recognized in 86 percent of the approved codes.
>
> Time and a half was the rate at which overtime was most generally compensated, with time and a third ranking next in frequency. ...
>
> Of the small number of codes that did not provide for overtime pay, a few either prohibited such employment or made no allowance for employment beyond the scheduled maximum.[166]

President Roosevelt himself commended the use of overtime premiums under the codes. In a statement on the extension of the automobile manufacturing code in 1935, he highlighted as one of the code's most important advances the establishment of the "principle" of payment of time and a half for overtime in excess of 48 hours, which "will benefit the employees through additional compensation for any necessary overtime work and deter the employment of workers in any unnecessary overtime."[167] (The automobile code did not

---

[165]BLS, *Handbook of Labor Statistics: 1936 Edition* 500 (Bull. No. 616, 1936).

[166]BLS, *Handbook of Labor Statistics: 1936 Edition* at 523. Without any evidence, the Office of National Recovery Administration, Div. of Review, *Work Materials* No. 35: *The Content of NIRA Administrative Legislation*, Part B: *Labor Provisions in the Codes* 81 (written by Ruth Reticker) (Spec. Studies Sect., Feb. 1936) claimed: "Historically, overtime rates were provided in union agreements for work beyond certain specified hours known as the basic day or basic week. This was primarily a wage device, intended to increase pay rather than to limit hours. In the NRA codes the purpose of the overtime provision seems to have been to provide some elasticity for employers who were reducing basic hours to the NRA standards, an elasticity protected against abuse by the requirement of penalty rates for overtime hours."

[167]"Statement by the President on the Extension of the Automobile Code," in 4 *Public Papers and Addresses of Franklin D. Roosevelt: The Court Disapproves: 1935*, at 70, 71 (1938 [Jan. 31, 1935]). Roosevelt characterized the "payment of overtime where permitted in exceptional circumstances, such as extraordinary seasonal demand" as having

originally provide for premium overtime and even the amended version was to little effect since the weekly hours could be averaged over the entire model year.)[168]

A labor standards bill that Secretary of Labor Perkins had her department's solicitor, Charles Gregory, draft in 1935 also provided for administrative discretion in setting the overtime premium.[169] And less than a year before Congress began debating the FLSA it enacted the Walsh-Healey Government Contracts Act, which prohibited the employment of any person in excess of eight hours per day or 40 hours per week under any contract with the United States for the manufacture or furnishing of any materials in an amount exceeding $10,000, but authorized the Secretary of Labor to permit longer hours for which time and a half was mandatory.[170]

Unlike many of the aforementioned statutes that prohibited work beyond a certain number of hours, from its very earliest drafts the FLSA merely required employers to pay workers a 50 percent premium for overtime hours. Despite the enormous changes that the bill underwent over more than a year, this provision was a constant. In the confidential draft that President Roosevelt's legislative brain-trusters, Thomas Corcoran and Benjamin Cohen, prepared on April 30, 1937—as the bill's congressional opponents never ceased repeating, the bill was filled with "Cohenisms and Corcoranisms"[171]—a section headed, "Exemptions from fair labor standards," provided that "the maintenance...of an oppressive or substandard work week shall not be deemed to constitute a substandard labor condition if the employees so employed receive additional compensation for such overtime employment at the rate of one and one-half times the regular hourly rate at which such employees are employed."[172] The administration's FLSA bill that was introduced in the Senate and House on May 24, 1937, contained identical language.[173] Indeed, President Roosevelt himself, in his message to Congress

---

been established as one of the policies implementing the principles underlying the NRA. "The President Hails the First N.R.A. Code," in 2 *Public Papers and Addresses of Franklin D. Roosevelt: The Year of Crisis: 1933*, at 275, 277 (note) (1938 [July 9, 1933]).

[168]Edsforth, "Why Automation Didn't Shorter the Work Week" at 157-58.

[169]Frances Perkins, *The Roosevelt I Knew* 254 (1946).

[170]Act of June 30, 1936, ch. 881, §§ 1(c), 6, 49 Stat. 2036, 2037, 2038-39. The act was later amended to provide for an exception pursuant to § 7(b) of the FLSA pertaining to union collective bargaining agreements. Act of May 13, 1942, ch. 306, 56 Stat. 277.

[171]82 *Cong. Rec.* 1487 (1937) (Rep. James Mott, R. Ore.).

[172]Confidential Revised Draft: Fair Labor Standards Act of 1937, § 5(b) (Apr. 30, 1937) (National Archives, Labor Dept. Records, Labor Standards—1937 File, Fair Labor Standards Bill). See also Confidential Revised Draft: Fair Labor Standards Act of 1937, § 6(b) (May 20, 1937) (National Archives, Labor Dept. Records, Labor Standards—1937 File, Fair Labor Standards Bill).

[173]S. 2475, § 6(b), 75th Cong., 2d Sess. (May 24, 1937).

accompanying the bill, optimistically stated that "permitting longer hours on the payment of time and a half for overtime, it should not be difficult to define a general maximum working week." [174]

All later versions of the House and Senate FLSA bills during 1937 and 1938 included either language identical with that of the original bill or some variant of this time and one-half for overtime provision.[175] An unsuccessful House floor amendment filed on behalf of the AFL would simply have made it unlawful to employ anyone for more than eight hours a day or 40 hours a week and permitted "emergency work" in excess of such hours for which employers were required to pay time and one half.[176] And a Senate floor amendment would have imposed absolute limits on the length of the workweek. Introduced by Senator Francis Maloney (D. Conn.), it would have required the proposed Labor Standards Board to take a census of unemployment; if it counted more than 8 million unemployed, it would have been required to set the working week at 30 hours; at the other end of the spectrum, if fewer than 2 million people were unemployed, the working week had to be established at 40 hours. Without debate the amendment was defeated 45 to 37, with the strongest FLSA supporters generally opposing it.[177]

The earliest FLSA draft bills also enforced compliance by means of the same financial disincentive. Any employee employed for more hours per week than the maximum work week required by a labor standard order "shall be entitled to receive as reparation from his employer additional compensation for the time that he was employed in excess of such maximum work week at the rate of one and one-half times the agreed wage at which he was employed or the minimum wage, if any, for such time established by this act or by an applicable labor standard order, whichever is higher, less the amount actually paid to him for such time by the employer."[178]

Contemporaries were not confused about the distinction between a 40-hour week law and an overtime law. In sharp contrast to the permissive hours regulation scheme that Congress was preparing, a majority of the population favored caps on working hours. Public opinion polls revealed that in July 1937, 60 percent of those surveyed thought that "the federal government ought to set a limit on the number of hours employees should work in each business...." Some

---

[174]S. Rep. No. 884: Fair Labor Standards Act, 75th Cong., 1st Sess. 1, 3 (1937).

[175]E.g., S. 2475, § 6(a), 75th Cong., 2d Sess. (House bill, Dec. 17, 1937); S. 2475, § 5, 75th Cong., 3d Sess. (House bill, Apr. 21, 1938).

[176]82 *Cong. Rec.* 1591 (Dec. 15, 1937). The amendment, which was offered by Rep. Griswold (D. Ind.), was defeated 162-131. *Id.* at 1604.

[177] 81 *Cong. Rec.* 7952-54 (July 31, 1937).

[178]Confidential Revised Draft: Fair Labor Standards Act of 1937, § 20(a) (Apr. 30, 1937). The administration bill introduced on May 24, 1937, contained identical language. S. 2475, § 21(a).

insight into the class-based conflict over hours is furnished by the fact that in May 1937, just a week before the FLSA bill was introduced in Congress, when 58 percent of respondents favored such limits, 68 percent of Democrats agreed as opposed to only 34 percent of Republicans. Indeed, just a few months earlier, 65 percent of respondents expressed themselves in favor of the thirty-hour week. According to a survey conducted in May 1942, 84 percent of respondents knew that a 40-hour week in a plant meant merely that the employees had to be paid overtime—not that they could not work there more than 40 hours.[179]

Although the distinction between a ban and a financial disincentive was well known, it was widely assumed that the overtime deterrent would be effective. *The New York Times*, which was militantly skeptical of the FLSA, editorialized: "The House wage-hour bill, it is true, does not absolutely prohibit a working week in excess of forty hours, but provides that hours in excess of that must be paid for at the rate of one and one-half times the regular rate. For many marginal firms and others this will be equivalent to prohibition, particularly in view of the increases in regular hourly rates by the bill."[180] (During World War II, when the work-spreading argument had lost its vitality and Secretary Perkins defended the overtime premium instead on the grounds that it did not really restrict hours, the *Times* pointed out that this claim ignored the law's purpose of making overtime "prohibitively costly....")[181]

In 1939 a scholar confirmed that few doubted that "both the expected and the probable effect of the hours provision...will be to restrict working hours to the maximum permitted at straight time."[182] A contemporaneous study of the automobile industry confirmed that the "overtime differential makes extra work so costly as to be impractical except under very unusual conditions." With respect to the FLSA and to even stricter provisions in collective bargaining agreements, management "would like to be able to operate 45 or 48 hours a week during 20 weeks each year without paying overtime rates. This would enable them to rely more completely on their best employees, and there would be less need for the temporary hiring of less efficient men. ... Such a change is now impossible owing both to union attitudes and to the Wage-Hour Act."[183]

---

[179]*Public Opinion: 1935-1946*, at 290 (quote), 292 (Hadley Cantril ed., 1951).

[180]"The Question of Hours," *N.Y. Times*, May 22, 1938, sect. IV, at 8, col. 1, 2 (editorial). The paper repeated this claim in "Working Hours," *N.Y. Times*, May 26, 1938, at 24, col. 3.

[181]"Fighting the War on a 40-Hour Week," *N.Y. Times*, Feb. 16, 1942, reprinted in 88 *Cong. Rec.* 1328 (1942). See also below section 7.

[182]Orme Phelps, *The Legislative Background of the Fair Labor Standards Act: A Study of the Growth of National Sentiment in Favor of Governmental Regulation of Wages, Hours, and Child Labor* 41 (1939).

[183]William McPherson, *Labor Relations in the Automobile Industry* 71, 72 (1940).

Identifying Congress's precise intent in enacting the overtime penalty is not simple. The Supreme Court's interpretation from the early 1940s, which has been repeated ad nauseam ever since, that spreading employment was the principal goal[184]—occasionally the Court added that the overtime penalty was also designed to compensate workers "for the burden of a workweek beyond the hours fixed in the Act"[185]—is, to be sure, neither implausible nor bereft of a basis in the legislative history.[186] Nevertheless, it cannot be anchored in the most authoritative texts such as the House and Senate reports or the FLSA bills.[187] That the goal was in the air is obvious from a *New York Times* editorial the day after the administration bills were filed. While the editors did not object to the maximum hour provisions if the law's aim was "simply to protect labor from oppressively long hours," the bill aroused their suspicions because it "evidently aims at quite different purposes. This is to keep hours short for the purposes of 'spreading the work' and 'creating employment.'" The *Times* cared about the difference because it deemed the latter conception fallacious: "The nation cannot be made richer by working less. Hours legally frozen below the number necessary to insure health and efficiency and reasonable leisure simply reduce our national production of wealth...and reduce the demand for labor by at least as much as they reduce the working week."[188]

Nor can it be denied that work-spreading had been a venerable goal of government hours legislation. Indeed, its impeccable conservative pedigree was on display as far back as 1890, when future president William McKinley, then

---

[184]E.g., Southland Gasoline Co. v. Bayley, 319 U.S. 44 , 48 (1943) (citing Overnight Motor Transportation Co. v. Missel for the proposition that FLSA "sought a reduction in hours to spread employment as well as to maintain health"). Montgomery, *Beyond Equality* at 237, noted that the early post-Civil War eight-hours movement, unlike that in the early twentieth century, did not focus on work-spreading or reduction of injuries. Yet by the mid-1880s the Illinois Bureau of Labor Statistics reported that in the previous 20 years "the plane of the shorter-day demand" had shifted from the beneficial physical, mental, and moral results for workers to the need to deal with unemployment caused by overproduction resulting from maintenance of long hours despite proliferation of labor-saving machinery. *Fourth Biennial Report of the Bureau of Labor Statistics of Illinois: 1886*, at 474 (1886).

[185]Overnight Motor Transp. Co. v. Missel, 316 U.S. 572, 578 (1942). See also Walling v. Helmerich & Payne, Inc., 323 U.S. 37, 40 (1944) (citing *Overnight* and *Southland* for the proposition that purpose of the FLSA overtime provision was to spread employment and compensate workers for the burden of long hours).

[186]As Denison, *The Sources of Economic Growth in the United States* at 39, noted: "It is at least doubtful that standard weekly hours would have been set where they were if the reduction had not been expected to result in more employment rather than entirely in less work being done."

[187]For an argument that spreading work by means of an overtime premium designed to reduce the workweek would lower productivity, raise prices, and decrease employment, see Fred Best, *Work Sharing: Issues, Policy Options and Prospects* 120-36 (1981).

[188]"Federal Wage-and-Hour Control," *N.Y. Times*, May 25, 1937, at 26, col. 2.

Republican leader of the House of Representatives, spoke in favor of an absolute eight-hours bill governing laborers and mechanics employed by the Federal government or by contractors on public works:

It has been said that it is a bill to limit the opportunity of the workingman to gain a livelihood. This is not so; it will have the opposite effect. [W]hen we constitute eight hours a day's work, instead of ten hours, every four days give an additional day's work to some workingman who may not have any employment at all. [Applause.] It is one more day's work, one more day's wages, one more opportunity for work and wages, an increased demand for labor. ... The tendency of the times the world over is for shorter hours for labor, shorter hours in the interest of health, shorter hours in the interest of humanity, shorter hours in the interest of the home and the family....[189]

A few members of Congress also spoke out clearly along these lines during the FLSA floor debates. Senator (and future Vice President) Alben Barkley may have been the strongest advocate of this position:

If we have arrived at a time in this country when we must choose between two horns of a dilemma, one of which is that all our people may work three-fourths of the time and the other that three-fourths of them may work all the time and one-fourth of them never work, then I choose the former. I believe it will be socially, economically, and industrially more wholesome and safe for all the available labor in America to be able to work three-fourths of the time than for three-fourths of it to work all the time and one-fourth never to work.

The bill makes a modest beginning by undertaking to establish among the laborers who are not organized, who have no voice around the conference table, who have no mechanics through which to make a choice of representatives in collective bargaining, an opportunity and possibility of spreading employment among all those able and willing to perform it in order that those who are willing and able to perform it may obtain work.[190]

A seemingly persuasive piece of legislative history supporting the work-spreading interpretation arose during the House floor debates in December 1937. Representative Alfred Bulwinkle (D. N.C.) offered an amendment that would have prohibited the employment of any employee between midnight and 6 o'clock in the morning in any manufacturing industry that did not require continuous production unless the employee was paid time and a half. Bulwinkle explained that the amendment's purpose was to eliminate the graveyard shift in several industries, chiefly textiles, because "largely but not altogether chiselers, carry this night work on, which is detrimental to the health of the employees

---

[189] 21 *Cong. Rec.* 9300-9301 (1890).

[190] 81 *Cong. Rec.* 7941 (July 31, 1937).

and...to industry...."[191] The provision was in fact taken from a textile bill—hearings on which had been going on when the FLSA was introduced in May and which was shelved to make way for the FLSA[192]—in which it was designed to "take the profit out of the graveyard shift...and yet permit its use whenever a special seasonal profit would justify the payment of time and a half."[193]

Night work had proliferated in cotton manufacturing in the twentieth century from two sources: "when business was good each mill hastened to get as much of the market as possible when the getting was good, and when business was bad the spreading of the overhead costs over a greater volume of production meant that in the depressed market of slim margins the double-shift mill had a slight edge over the single-shift mill." Even after the World War I textile boom had subsided, southern mills retained the night shift, despite workers' aversion, higher wage rates, and lower productivity, because continuous operation reduced unit costs. The resulting overproduction led to losses, but the logic of competition prevented individual firms from eliminating night work and individual states from banning it unless their competitors did likewise.[194]

The importance, if not the quantification, of these microeconomic factors was present to mind when the House Labor Committee held hearings, just 12 days before the FLSA bill was introduced, on a so-called little National Recovery Act bill to regulate the textile industry. The subcommittee chairman, Representative Kent Keller (D. Ill.), who was opposed to graveyard shifts on economic and social grounds, was reluctant to enact an outright ban because "it may limit a manufacturer who has necessarily to deal with a temporary condition, such as a shift in styles. If we should allow that practice in a case like that, a manufacturer could afford to work that shift and labor would also be benefited. The operator certainly would not use the graveyard shift unless it paid to do so."[195] Keller then asked the chief economist of the BLS, F.A. Hinrichs, whether imposing time and a half for all hours worked between 11 p.m. and 7 a.m. would discourage night work while permitting it where profitable:

MR. HINRICHS. I am quite sure that the payment of penalty overtime rates rather than

---

[191] 82 *Cong. Rec.* 1695 (Dec. 16, 1937).

[192] "Basic 40-Hour Work Week, 40 Cts. Hour Minimum Pay, Planned in Federal Bill," *N.Y. Times*, May 22, 1937, at 1, col. 1.

[193] 82 *Cong. Rec.* at 1696 (Rep. Keller). On the textile industry as the New Deal "guinea pig," see Stanley Vittoz, *New Deal Labor Policy and the American Industrial Economy* 14, 24, 28-32 (1987).

[194] Herbert Lahne, *The Cotton Mill Worker* 143-44 (1944).

[195] *To Regulate the Textile Industry: Hearings Before the Subcommittee of the House Committee on Labor,* 75th Cong., 1st Sess., pt. 3 at 178 (1937).

the fixing of flat maxima gives a larger degree of flexibility. There ought to be a sufficient penalty so that the practice would be indulged in only under the most favorable market circumstances. I should say that normally the payment of 50 percent more than the going rate for labor would effectively bar the use of such overtime. One could not produce for stock under those conditions.

MR. KELLER. Do you think that would be an effective means of doing away with the abuses of the graveyard shifts?

MR. HINRICHS. The only reason I hesitate to answer in the affirmative absolutely is that I do not know the exact amount by which the overhead of a mill will be reduced by three rather than two shifts. I do not know the balance between the cut in overhead and the increase in 50 percent in labor costs; but a 50-percent increase in labor costs, if not offset, would be a complete barrier.[196]

Representative Keller may never have received the underlying data he requested to determine whether the 50-percent premium sufficed to make night work unprofitable in textiles, but an analogous calibration underlay the overtime penalty under the FLSA. There its purpose was not to overcome the fixed scale economies of 100-percent capacity utilization, but to overcome the economies of fixed or quasi-fixed benefits paid to workers regardless of how many hours they worked. In both cases, however, achieving the legislative objective depended on calculating the correct empirical data, adapting the appropriate premium, and keeping it up to date as the underlying variables changed over time. Just as Congress assumed that the number of workers employed by firms that were already paying time and a half and on which the FLSA would have no impact was relatively small, it must also have assumed that the penalty rate might have to be adjusted upwards from time to time to keep the hiring of additional workers profitable when they had to be paid financially significant benefits that increased little or not at all when employees already on the payroll worked overtime.

One congressman immediately opposed the Bulwinkle amendment because it abandoned "the theory behind" the FLSA: by seeking to curtail production, it would merely promote capital intensification on the other two shifts employing the same number of workers.[197] This objection prompted the chair of the House Labor Committee, Representative Mary Norton (D. N.J.), to reply that evidence available to the committee contradicted that claim: "In fact, it has been proven to us that if we could do this it would do more to spread employment than any other thing concerned in the bill. That is the purpose of the bill—to try to spread employment." Several representatives were understandably puzzled by how preventing overproduction by eliminating one-fourth of the aggregate working time available to the entire covered working class (as opposed to shortening some

---

[196]*To Regulate the Textile Industry* at 178.

[197]82 *Cong. Rec.* at 1696 (Rep. Smith, Conn.).

workers' working days) could possibly be consistent with work sharing; nevertheless, the amendment was agreed to, although the House bill itself was not passed.[198]

The dubious work-sharing capacity of the anti-graveyard shift proposal was underscored later in the debate when Michigan Representative Shafer successfully prevailed on the House to exempt the food processing industry from the provision in order not to disadvantage the Kellogg plant in Battle Creek, which had converted its three eight-hour shifts to four six-hour shifts during the Depression to combat unemployment. Shafer feared that the Bulwinkle amendment would make Kellogg "close down one of these shifts, thereby causing a number of men to lose their jobs." When another congressman, who was skeptical of the Bulwinkle amendment itself, asked whether the same argument did not apply to any manufacturing process using a night shift but lacking a great excess of machinery on which the discharged workers could work during the day, Shafer agreed, but his amendment was nevertheless agreed to.[199]

Employers' later efforts to persuade the courts that the FLSA overtime premium applied only to the minimum wage were also not totally bereft of a purchase in the legislative history. Perhaps the most powerful evidence supporting their view was found in the report issued by the Senate in July 1937 recommending passage of an amended FLSA bill:

> The right of individual or collective employees to bargain with their employers concerning wages and hours is recognized and encouraged by this bill. It is not intended that this law shall invade the right of employer and employee to fix their own contracts of employment, wherever there can be any real, genuine bargaining between them. It is only those low-wage and long-working-hour industrial workers, who are the helpless victims of their own bargaining weakness, that this bill seeks to assist to obtain a minimum wage.[200]

This explanation clearly eschewed any policy of creating an across-the-board norm for the length of the workweek or of work sharing. Its only motivation was combating impoverishment among sweated workers. The House report a month later added the goal of expanded purchasing power, but also emphasized that the bill "only attempts in a modest way to raise the wages of the most poorly paid workers and to reduce the hours of those most overworked."[201]

Even the single most important textual warrant in the legislative history

---

[198]82 *Cong. Rec.* at 1696-97.

[199]82 *Cong. Rec.* at 1775. See generally, Benjamin Hunnicutt, *Kellogg's Six-Hour Day* (1996).

[200]S. Rep. No. 884: *Fair Labor Standards Act*, 75th Cong., 1st Sess. 3-4 (1937).

[201]H. Rep. No. 1452: *Fair Labor Standards Act*, 75th Cong., 1st Sess. 9 (1937).

offers only tenuous support for the U.S. Supreme Court's assertion in 1942 that the statutory overtime premium was designed to apply "financial pressure...to spread employment to avoid the extra wage.... In a period of widespread unemployment and small profits, the economy inherent in avoiding extra pay was expected to have an appreciable effect in the distribution of available work."[202] Though the Court cited no source to document its assertion, the Fourth Circuit, on whose opinion it relied heavily, pointed to President Roosevelt's message to Congress in connection with the introduction of the FLSA bill on May 24, 1937, for its claim that: "It seems plain from the legislative history of the Act that...one of the fundamental purposes of the Act was to induce worksharing and relieve unemployment by reducing hours of work."[203] Yet Roosevelt had merely said: "We know that overwork and underpay do not increase the national income when a large portion of our workers remain unemployed. Reasonable and flexible use of the long-established right of government to set and change working hours can, I hope, decrease unemployment in those groups in which unemployment today principally exists."[204] Yet this presidential hope raises more questions than it answers. In particular it fails to explain why workers who are not underpaid should receive a state mandated overtime premium and what the purpose of the mandatory premium vis-à-vis groups not suffering from unemployment or at times when unemployment in general was low.

The work-spreading argument is further undermined by the fact that employers were privileged to ignore the disincentive effect of the overtime premium to employ workers beyond 40 hours by reducing their hourly wages so that they could continue to work the same number of overtime hours for the same total weekly wages. Although the DOL initially took the position that this tactic violated the FLSA, it acquiesced in it after several courts upheld its legality provided that the lower wage still exceeded the statutory minimum. This result hinged, in turn, on judicial rulings that the language in the FLSA stating that "[n]o provision of this Act shall justify any employer in reducing a wage paid by him which is in excess of the applicable minimum wage under this Act"[205] was merely precatory and unenforcible. Declaring this provision legally meaningless was facilitated by comparison with the original FLSA bill, which had authorized a proposed Labor Standards Board to issue labor standard orders that it deemed "necessary or appropriate to prevent the established minimum wage becoming the maximum wage and to prevent the discharge or reduction in wages of employees receiving more than the established minimum wage"; the Board would also have

---

[202]Overnight Motor Transp. Co. v. Missel, 316 U.S. 572, 578 (1942).

[203]Missel v. Overnight Motor Transp. Co., 126 F.2d 98, 103 (4th Cir. 1942).

[204]S. Rep. No. 884 at 3.

[205]FLSA, § 18.

been empowered to "prevent the circumvention or evasion" of its orders.[206] Significantly, even this provision, which had teeth but was deleted before enactment, revealed the FLSA's intended limitations when it went on to confine the Board's power to establish minimum wage standards to those that "will affect only those employees in need of legislative protection without interfering with the voluntary establishment of appropriate differentials and higher standards for other employees in the occupations to which such orders relate."[207]

Just a few days before Senator Black's labor committee redrafted the bill as a whole in mid-1937, *Business Week* portrayed employers as too preoccupied with their rebellious workers to focus on the potentially disastrous statute: "Little imagination is necessary to translate the effect of this provision and others on labor costs, manufacturing costs, and price levels, but most industrialists do not appear to be concerned, either because they are too busy or because they are afraid to turn their back on their employees and come to Washington when labor trouble looms so large at home."[208]

President Roosevelt himself could have served as a prime witness for those arguing for a minimalist interpretation of the FLSA. In a fireside chat to the nation on October 12, 1937, explaining why he was calling an extraordinary session of Congress for the next month, Roosevelt, after mentioning "the millions of men and women and children who still work at insufficient wages and overlong hours," stated: "I am a firm believer in fully adequate pay for all labor. But right now I am most greatly concerned in increasing the pay of the lowest-paid labor...." More specifically he added: "A few more dollars a week in wages, a better distribution of jobs with a shorter working day will almost overnight make millions of our lowest-paid workers actual buyers of billions of dollars of industrial and farm products."[209] Then on November 15, 1937, the opening day of the extraordinary session, in his message to Congress Roosevelt focused his labor agenda on the proposition that the "exploitation of child labor and the undercutting of wages and the stretching of the hours of the poorest-paid workers in periods of business recession have a serious effect on purchasing power." He therefore characterized as the "two immediate purposes" of the proposed legislation "banish[ing] child labor and protect[ing] workers unable to protect themselves from excessively low wages and excessively long hours."[210]

---

[206]S. 2475, § 12(6) and (7) (May 24, 1937).

[207]S. 2475, § 12(6) (May 24, 1937).

[208]"Wage-Hour Fate—and Politics," *Bus. Wk.*, July 3, 1937, at 24.

[209]"A 'Fireside Chat' Discussing Legislation to Be Recommended to the Extraordinary Session of the Congress," in *Public Papers and Addresses of Franklin D. Roosevelt: 1937 Volume: The Constitution Prevails* 429-38 at 435 (1941).

[210]"Message from the President," in 82 *Cong. Rec.* 9, 11 (1937).

Roosevelt's State of the Union address to Congress on January 3, 1938, shifted the emphasis somewhat toward long hours generally. He noted that the minimum wage and maximum hours provisions promulgated under industry codes pursuant to the NIRA had proved their social and economic worth, and insisted that "the people of this country, by an overwhelming vote, are in favor of having the Congress—this Congress—put a floor below which industrial wages shall not fall, and a ceiling beyond which the hours of industrial labor shall not rise." Concealing the fact that no FLSA bill imposed such a ceiling on hours, he then returned to the perspective of impoverishment by referring to those who opposed wage and hour legislation on the grounds that it would impede the flow of capital to and foster its exodus from localities that survived "only because of existing low wages and long hours." Roosevelt rejected such growth strategies: "In the long run the profits from child labor, low pay, and overwork inure not to the locality or region where they exist but to the absentee owners who have sent their capital into these exploited communities to gather larger profits for themselves." He argued that new firms would be more likely to bring "permanent wealth" to communities that insisted on "good pay and reasonable hours" because the workers would be more efficient and happier. Finally, resuming the minimalist theme, the president sought to reassure Congress that the FLSA did not aim for "drastic change": "We are seeking, of course, only legislation to end starvation wages and intolerable hours; more desirable wages are and should continue to be the product of collective bargaining."[211]

These conflicting, confused, and understated policy reasons underlying the overtime provision may be contrasted with those apparently buttressing what until the FLSA had been the country's most famous overtime statute—Oregon's 1913 law covering men and women in factories.[212] It prohibited employing anyone in a factory more than ten hours a day (except when engaged in emergency work), but permitted up to three hours a day of overtime if it was compensated at time and one-half the regular wage.[213] Its preamble articulated a public policy that working any person more than ten hours a day in a factory "is injurious to the physical health and well-being of such person, and tends to prevent him from acquiring that degree of intelligence that is necessary to make him a useful and desirable citizen of the state."[214]

Accordingly, the Oregon Supreme Court, in passing on the law's

---

[211]83 *Cong. Rec.* 8, 9 (1938).

[212]Its fame was a result of the fact that the U.S. Supreme Court upheld its constitutionality despite its limitation on the hours of adult men. Bunting v. Oregon, 243 U.S. 425 (1917).

[213]1913 Or. Laws ch. 102, § 2.

[214]1913 Or. Laws ch. 102, § 3.

constitutionality, elaborated on the legislative policies in a manner wholly unlike later judicial interpretation of the FLSA. It divined that "the legislative mind" viewed long hours as increasing the risk of injuries in factories with high-powered machinery, but it also observed that "a man who day in and day out labors more than 10 hours must not only deteriorate physically, but mentally. The safety of a country depends upon the intelligence of its citizens, and if our institutions are to be preserved the state must see to it that the citizen shall have some leisure which he may employ in fitting himself for those duties which are the highest attributes of good citizenship."[215]

The problem with this pathos-radiating rhetoric is that it failed to deal with the obvious fact that employers were privileged to work their employees 13 hours—and thus expose them to greater risks of injury and make them unfit for good citizenship—provided that they paid time and a half for the last three hours. As the leading turn-of-the-century treatise on the police power observed, "where the time for all street railroad employees is fixed at ten hours per day, with the right to work overtime for special compensation, the justification on the ground of public safety evidently fails. If safety or health really forbid excessive work, special compensation does not remove the objection, and the fact that it is allowed indicates that the restriction rests on economic grounds."[216]

More puzzling was the success with which Felix Frankfurter, who represented the state of Oregon, persuaded the U.S. Supreme Court in *Bunting v. Oregon* to uphold the statute as regulating health and hours rather than wages. Frankfurter's argument that it was "an hours law and not at all a wage law" was implicitly based on his contention that there was so little overtime work in Oregon industry that the law made little difference. The overtime provision "merely...allow[ed] for a limited and reasonable flexibility in time of unusual business pressure," but "even now, when employers do not have to pay time and a half, over 93 per cent find it unprofitable to employ men beyond ten hours as a normal standard." His assertion that the statute was reasonable in "safeguarding abuse of the exception by the punitive provision"[217] reveals that an overtime law would cease being reasonable if its punitive provision no longer deterred employers. The U.S. Supreme Court accorded only "a certain verbal plausibility" to the employer's contention that the law was intended to permit 13 hours' work

---

[215]State v. Bunting, 139 P. 731, 735 (Or. 1914).

[216]Ernst Freund, *The Police Power: Public Policy and Constitutional Grounds* 301 (1904).

[217]Supplemental Memorandum for Defendant in Error at 1-2, Bunting v. Oregon, 243 U.S. 436 (1917). Frankfurter incorrectly reported his own data, which in fact showed that in 1909 93.7 percent of industrial workers in Oregon were employed less than 10 hours a day. Supplemental Brief for Defendant in Error upon Re-Argument at 63, Bunting v. Oregon, 243 U.S. 436 (1917).

for 14 and a half hours' pay; that the legislature chose to "achieve its purpose through the interest of those affected" rather than by a "rigid prohibition" was not fatal.[218]

Oddly, although labor standards advocates characterized the Oregon statute as "of a very ineffective type" for permitting three hours of overtime at time and a half, the FLSA was not attacked for permitting 16 hours a day of premium overtime.[219]

5. Employers' Struggle Against Statutorily Imposed Premium Overtime Wages for Non-Minimum Wage Workers: 1938-1942

> Another difference of opinion which might be clarified by court action hinges on the question of hours. This controversy, if it is a controversy, seems rather strange in view of the statute's moderate hour provision. The Act does not even satisfy the perennial demand of labor—the 8-hour day. The Act does not tell the employer what hours in any day he may work his men. It simply says...he shall not work his employees more than 44 hours without paying them time and a half for overtime. In fact, the overtime provision is where the rub comes in. There has been much talk about ways and means of an employer working his men more than 44 hours without paying them any more than they were paid prior to the effective date of the Act.[220]

The Wage and Hour Division (WHD) engaged in extensive public education during the run-up to the act's date of effectiveness. Two national radio networks gave the Wage and Hour Administrator, Elmer Andrews,[221] fifteen minutes the night before and a third broadcast a program the next day.[222] Yet even before the FLSA went into effect at 12:01 a.m., Monday, October 24, 1938, the WHD had received "[e]vidence of employer resistance" from several states.[223] Already a week earlier an employer had telegraphed the WHD seeking the general counsel's blessing for his "'painless compliance'" scheme to lower "the hourly wage of every worker in his place, from president to office boy, to 25 cents an hour for the

---

[218]Bunting v. Oregon, 243 U.S. at 436-37.

[219]Brandeis, "Labor Legislation" at 681.

[220]Elmer Andrews, "FLSA Problems for Congress or the Courts," 1 *Wage and Hour Reporter* 419 (1938) (address at Brookings Institution, Dec. 20, 1938).

[221]Elmer Andrews (1890-1964), had, before Roosevelt appointed him the first Wage and Hour Administrator, been the New York State industrial commissioner. 4 *Who Was Who in America* (1961-1968) at 31 (1968).

[222]Elmer Andrews, "The Tribulations of a Wage-Hour Administrator," 4 (1) *Public Opinion Q.* 25-34 at 27 (Mar. 1940).

[223]"Wage-Hour Law: Variety of Interpretations As Strict Enforcement Is Promised," 1 *Wage and Hour Reporter* 233 (Oct. 24, 1938)

first 44 hours and 37½ cents overtime" and to guarantee the difference between that amount and the weekly compensation prior to October 24.[224]

Such reports prompted Andrews to declare preemptively: "'Millions of Americans look forward to Monday...as the beginning of a new advance in the nation's offensive against exploitation and hardship. These millions welcome the opportunity to help inoculate our economic system against the virus of sweatshops. Unfortunately, however, there is a small and scattered minority who apparently are unwilling or incapable of contributing to the common good. These delinquents, whose number and importance are magnified by their isolation, resort to subterfuge in an effort to camouflage their selfishness and blame the Fair Labor Standards Act for their own anti-social conduct."[225] The intensity and longevity of this important conflict contradicts the later scholarly claim that "[f]or several months, Andrews enjoyed his honeymoon."[226]

Roosevelt himself may have been disappointed that the bill "had been so watered down in its long journey through Congress that it could have little impact on the national economy,"[227] but employers, who had failed to voice such apprehensions at the hearings in 1937, feared a "very violent" "shock." For example, the economist of the Chase National Bank, Benjamin Anderson, Jr., conceded that at 48 or 50 hours, overtime was a "serious burden" warranting labor unions' "good rule" of time and a half to protect workers' health. But a mandatory 50 percent premium for hours above 40 "creat[ed] an inelasticity" which could plunge the next business upturn into a "needlessly violent and premature crisis." Anderson found the FLSA altogether "unfortunate," but especially could not "contemplate with equanimity" a 50-percent overtime penalty after a mere 40 hours for all industry within two years.[228]

The chief dispute on the eve of October 24 was the payment of overtime to salaried employees.[229] The BNA's authoritative *Wage and Hour Reporter* argued that "[t]he root of the controversy" stemmed from a statement that Administrator Andrews had made before the Southern States Industrial Council in Birmingham on September 29. It is implausible that Andrews' statement provided anything

---

[224]"FLSA and 'Painless' Compliance," 1 *Wage and Hour Reporter* 375 (Nov. 21, 1938).

[225]"Wage-Hour Law: Variety of Interpretations As Strict Enforcement Is Promised," 1 *Wage and Hour Reporter* 233, 234 (Oct. 24, 1938).

[226]George Paulsen, *A Living Wage for the Forgotten Man: The Quest for Fair Labor Standards 1933-1941*, at 137 (1996).

[227]James MacGregor Burns, *Roosevelt: The Lion and the Fox* 343-44 (1956).

[228]"Banker's View of Wage-Hour Act," 1 BNA, *Wage and Hour Reference Manual* 13-14 (1939) (address to the Chamber of Commerce of Kansas City, Dec. 14, 1938).

[229]On employers' coordinated efforts from 1938 to 1940 to amend the FLSA to broaden the exclusion of white-collar workers, see below chapter 2.

but a pretext for employers' resistance that would have emerged anyway, especially since the WHD's official Interpretative Bulletin No. 4 ("Maximum Hours and Overtime Compensation"), published on October 21, contradicted Andrews' statement,[230] which he himself later disowned ("certain impromptu remarks I made...in reply to random questions asked me at the end of the speech").[231] Indisputably, however, Andrews had put his foot in his mouth in the following colloquy:

> Q.—Many clerical and non-supervisory employees are on a monthly or weekly wage basis. Is it necessary for such wages to be recalculated to an hourly basis and time and one-half paid for hours over forty-four?
>
> MR. ANDREWS—... Clerical forces, we all feel, are included in the Act. But I cannot see where there is going to be any practical difficulty there because your clerical force in any plant of any consequence certainly is earning on a basis of more than 25 cents an hour, weekly wages divided by the hours they work. If they are well above 25 cents an hour, it seems to me that there would not be much question about time and a half for overtime, because you could figure in that weekly wage that time and a half over the 44 hours had been given consideration as remuneration for their full week's work."[232]

That Andrews's slip was not inadvertent was clear from his answer to a similar question in Birmingham that was not trotted out in the later debate. In response to a question concerning overtime liability for office employees of steamship companies who were paid more than the statutory minimum wage, Andrews replied: "They still get enough wages, I am sure, that if you want to break it up into so much per hour, so much for time and a half, it would still work out."[233] Nevertheless, those who wanted to make much ado of these ignorant off-the-cuff remarks ignored the disclaimer that the BNA had appended to their publication already three weeks after the Birmingham meeting: "it should be kept in mind that the Administrator's answers are not final on any point and that he reserves the right to 'change his mind'...." They also conveniently overlooked Andrews's own self-deprecating admission at Birmingham about a similar gaffe that he had committed soon after his appointment as deputy labor commissioner in New York State.[234]

---

[230]"Interpretative Bulletin No. 4," in 1 *Wage and Hour Reporter* 236-38 (Oct. 24, 1938).

[231]"Salaried Employees: Overtime," in 1 BNA, *Wage and Hour Reference Manual* 59, 61 (1939).

[232]"Some Employers' Questions Answered," 3 *Labor Relations Reporter* 194, 195 (Oct. 17, 1938).

[233]"Some Employers' Questions Answered" at 196.

[234]"Some Employers' Questions Answered" at 194.

Employers' focus on the FLSA's overtime premium in the period immediately after enactment was driven by the fact that more than four times as many workers were affected by it than by the minimum wage provision. In 1938, 1,384,000 workers were covered and working more than 44 hours; by 1939, 1,751,000 workers were predicted to be covered and working more than 42 hours, and by 1940, 2,184,000 workers. In contrast, in 1938 only 300,000 workers were earning less than the minimum wage of 25 cents, while the Wage and Hour Administrator predicted that by 1939 550,000 would be earning less than the minimum wage of 30 cents. The manufacturing industries with the greatest overtime liability were food, lumber, and textiles.[235]

During the congressional hearings on the FLSA, it had been the very rare employer who, when asked by Senator Hugo Black whether "there should be any permission to work longer than 40 [hours] on payment of overtime," replied, as did Donald Comer, president of Avondale Mills and former president of the American Cotton Manufacturers Association: "No. Get another man."[236] Employers launched a many-sided campaign against the overtime provision of the FLSA as soon as the law went into effect.[237] During its very first week, enforcement officials were occupied with employers' efforts to achieve costless compliance with the overtime rule. An Ohio steel foundry, for example, planned to cut the hourly wage from 70 to 40 cents, on which time and a half would be paid, and then add back a 30-cent an hour bonus.[238] A trade association suggested to its members that they could achieve costless compliance by reducing the hourly wage of an employee who worked 48 hours from 50 cents to 46 cents. However, if the worker insisted on his old 50-cent wage, employers should offer him only 40 hours, leaving him with a total weekly wage of $20: "'Naturally employees are going to be quite willing to take the slight hourly rate cut and a full weekly pay envelope rather than contribute $4 for the privilege of having an extra day off with nothing to do but spend his money.'"[239]

Remarkably, unions had long been aware that such evasions were predictable.

---

[235]"Analysis of FLSA Coverage," 2 *Wage and Hour Reporter* 96, 97 (Feb. 13, 1939).

[236]*Fair Labor Standards Act of 1937: Joint Hearings* at 451.

[237]Carroll Daughterty, who had been the chief economist of the BLS and WHD, incorrectly stated in his labor economics textbook: "Under the business conditions of 1938 and 1939 most employers seemed to have no great difficulty in adjusting their operations to the Act's requirements. But the rise in business activity caused by the government's expenditures for national defense in 1940 led some employers to begin agitating for modification of the Act's hours provisions." 1 Carroll Daugherty, *Labor Problems in American Industry* 191 (1944 [1941]).

[238]"Vanguard of Wage-Hour Field Force; Some Novel Methods of Compliance," 1 *Wage and Hour Reporter* 281 (Oct. 31, 1938).

[239]"Complaint Form; First Violations Reported," 1 *Wage and Hour Reporter* 291, 292 (Nov. 7, 1938).

As far back as 1912, when Congress was in the final throes of a two-decade debate on an eight-hour law for employees of federal government contractors that did not provide for overtime work, N. P. Alifas, the president of a government machinists union local testified against employers' request for overtime on the grounds that it would be misused:

> [I]f a manufacturer secured a contract...he could very easily evade the law like this: For instance, here is John Smith who gets $3.60 for a nine-hour day. That is 40 cents an hour. The employer might say: "Mr. Smith, we have secured this contract from the Government on condition that we work the men an eight-hour day, and with the provision that the men are to be allowed to work overtime." He may also say: "I secured this contract on a very low bid. You know there is a great deal of competition among employers, and, Mr. Smith, you have been in the habit of working nine hours for me for $3.60; surely you will be willing to help me overcome the technicality of this law, and instead of 40 cents an hour accept 38 cents an hour for the eight hours, and accept time and a half for the extra hour, or 57 cents, which will make just $3.61 instead of $3.60 as heretofore.[240]

Significantly, Alifas then added what no one would criticize about the FLSA a quarter-century later: the existence of such a permissive overtime provision "would be dangerous, as it would utterly nullify the real intention of the law. It is just such contractors as the one cited here that make a rigid law necessary...."[241]

One of the more primitive evasions was reported on the front page of *The New York Times* just a few weeks after the FLSA went into effect: some employers stamped or printed a waiver of overtime payments on pay checks on the assumption that workers' acceptance of the check would act as a waiver of their FLSA rights.[242] The two chief thrusts to employers' resistance, however, were economic and legal. The former focused on readjusting wages and hours to avoid the bite of the overtime premium. The object of litigation was to secure rulings that the overtime premium was applicable only to the minimum wage in opposition to the WHD's interpretation that section 7 of the FLSA clearly makes the employee's "regular rate" and not the minimum wage the base for the overtime premium.[243]

---

[240]*Eight-Hour Law: Hearings Before the Senate Committee on Education and Labor*, 62d Cong. 372 (1912) (statement of N. Alifas, pres., District No. 44, Government Employees' International Association of Machinists).

[241]*Eight-Hour Law: Hearings Before the Senate Committee on Education and Labor*, 62d Cong. at 372 (1912).

[242]"Workers Cannot Waive Wages Act Hours; Andrews Warns Employers Not to Try Idea," *N.Y. Times*, Nov. 21, 1938, at 1, col. 2.

[243]Fair Labor Standards Act of 1938, ch. 676, § 7, 52 Stat. 1060, 1063; WHD, Interpretative Bull. No. 4, in 1 BNA, *Wage and Hour Reference Manual* 197 (1939 [Oct. 21, 1938]).

The WHD's first line of defense against this attack was reliance on section 18 of the FLSA: "No provision of this Act shall justify any employer in reducing a wage paid by him which is in excess of the applicable minimum wage under this Act, or justify any employer in increasing hours of employment maintained by him which are shorter than the maximum hours applicable under this Act."[244] At his Birmingham question and answer session on September 29, Andrews had also put his foot in his mouth on this issue. When asked whether an employer paying higher wages than his competitor could reduce wages "to meet the competitive situation where he observes the minimum," the Wage and Hour Administrator replied:

> I have heard of that in some of the communications industries, that that is being contemplated. Of course, the Act contains a pious wish that that should not be done. I think it is not going to make for any happier industrial relationship...between employer and employee. I think it is economically unsound and pretty generally unfair, but that is all I can say about it.[245]

Andrews's infamous "pious wish" may have been as accurate a label as could be placed on section 18, but the WHD was not deterred from dressing it up in the agency's initial (and ambiguous) interpretation. In Interpretative Bulletin No. 4 of October 21, the WHD asked and answered hypothetical questions about the regular rate against the background of section 18. If an employer, who before the FLSA went into effect had employed his workers for 48 hours at a flat hourly rate well in excess of the 25-cent minimum wage, reduced its employees' wage rate to an amount still above the minimum wage so that their total weekly wages including time and a half for overtime remained the same, the WHD was not yet prepared to "give any definite interpretation" of the applicability of section 18. It merely pointed out that "it is not safe to assume that a section of an Act of Congress is meaningless," and speculated that if the same employer tried to use the section to "justify" the wage reduction in negotiations with its employees, a court "might" be warranted in holding that the reduction "is not really a reduction in legal contemplation," and that therefore the regular rate remained the pre-FLSA higher rate.[246]

In mid-November 1938, the WHD's assistant general counsel informed the Fifth National Conference on Labor Legislation: "if the effect of what the employer does is to reduce the hourly wage being received at the time the act

---

[244]Fair Labor Standards Act of 1938, § 18, 52 Stat. at 1069.

[245]"Some Employers' Questions Answered," 3 *Labor Relations Reporter* 194 (Oct. 17, 1938).

[246]WHD, Interpretative Bull. No. 4, in 1 BNA, *Wage and Hour Reference Manual* 197, 198 (1939).

went into effect, he is violating the spirit of the act. We cannot assume that Congress put that in there for nothing, and I think that the employer who engages in such a practice is running a big risk of having to pay twice the amount which he was paying at the time to his employees...."[247]

The possible interpretations of section 18 had not passed unnoticed in the press when it suddenly appeared in the bill as it emerged from the House-Senate conference committee. The *Times* was immediately and remained for years exercised over this "potential joker." It conceded in June 1938 that it had probably been inserted "with the best of intentions"—namely, to assuage fears that the statutory minimum wage would tend to become the maximum and maximum hours the minimum. However, the editors speculated that the "ambiguous sentence...may prove to be a very mischievous joker. There will be those who will try to interpret it to mean that all existing wages above the minimums now fixed and all existing hours below the maximums now existing must be frozen at their present levels—or that all existing wages can only move in one direction—upward. Such an interpretation...would paralyze the American economy."[248] Two months later, repeating much of its earlier editorial verbatim, the *Times* saw its premonitions coming true as the national director of the Congress of Industrial Organizations (CIO) asserted that two large employers intended to use the FLSA as a cover for reducing wages in tandem with reducing weekly hours from 48 to 40. To be sure, the paper found a silver lining in the CIO's lament that the lack of an enforcement provision in section 18 gave employers a "'technical loophole.'"[249]

The NAM immediately launched an aggressive campaign to undermine the effectiveness of the overtime provision with respect to employees whose hourly wage exceeded the new statutory minimum. It also contended that there was "a serious legal question" whether salaried employees were covered by the overtime provision at all. Through its general counsel, John Gall, the NAM called attention to Andrews' admission that section 18 "was nothing more than a 'pious hope' on the part of Congress.'" Gall also pointed out that even if an employer wished to respect the spirit of a provision that lacked any sanction, section 18 did not refer to wage rates, but merely "a wage"; consequently, so long as the total weekly pay was not reduced, employers could comply with the alleged spirit of the law despite reducing wage rates. Moreover, Gall argued that the FLSA permitted employers to pay salaried employees for more than 44 hours weekly

---

[247]*Proceedings of the Fifth National Conference on Labor Legislation: Washington, D.C., November 14, 15, 16, 1938*, at 32 (DOL, Div. Lab. Standards, Bull. No. 25, 1939) (statement of Rufus Poole).

[248]"A Potential Joker," *N.Y. Times*, June 16, 1938, at 22, col. 2.

[249]"Interpreting the Wage Act," *N.Y. Times*, Aug. 16,, 1938, at 18, col. 2.

at their existing weekly compensation provided that the base hourly rate did not fall below 25 cents and the overtime rate was at least 37.5 cents. The NAM argued that "if the employer could not modify the basic rate so as to work salaried employes for the same weekly hours as before, at the same total compensation, the employer was 'forever prevented from lowering a present wage rate even if it resulted in no lowering of total compensation.'" Gall asserted that if the NAM's view did not prevail, "'unscrupulous'" employers would have an incentive to fire their existing employees and hire new ones at the lower, minimum rates of 25 and 37.5 cents.[250]

The Wage and Hour Administrator, perceiving this interpretation as a direct threat to the new law's effectiveness, struggled to draw out Congress's intent from the overtime provision:

> "Congress refrained from taking the more drastic step of prescribing an absolute maximum work week, but made it unlawful for an employer to work an employe for longer than forty-four hours a week unless such employe receives compensation...in excess of the hours above specified at a rate not less than one and a half times the regular rate at which he is employed....
>
> "Congress thus made it economically disadvantageous to an employer to maintain a work week in excess of forty-four hours. The expectation evidently was that this provision would tend to bring down the customary work week to forty-four hours. The question now is whether this expectation can be defeated by various devices, with the probable result the coming Congress will renew consideration of more far-reaching proposals."[251]

In the weeks following the FLSA's effective date (Oct. 24, 1938), high ranking WHD officials attended numerous employers' meetings to discourage them from running afoul of section 18. The agency's general counsel, Calvert Magruder, warned the annual meeting of the Manufacturers' Association of Connecticut against "the effort to make a huge joke of the overtime provisions...."[252] Speaking to the Executives Association of Greater New York on November 16, Paul Sifton, the deputy Wage and Hour administrator (and former leftist playwright), also advised against reducing the hourly base rates of

---

[250]"Salaried Employees: Overtime," 1 *Wage and Hour Reporter* 355, 356 (Nov. 14, 1938).

[251]"Disputes Hirers on Overtime Law," *N.Y. Times*, Nov. 6, 1938, at 2, col. 1. Even the liberal economist and later Senator Paul Douglas agreed with the NAM that it would be "very dubious public policy" to enforce section 18 because its effect would be to "freeze existing wage scales at their present levels and prevent any future reductions, whether caused by a depression, a fall in prices...." Paul Douglas and Joseph Hackman, "The Fair Labor Standards Act of 1938: II," 54 *Pol. Sci. Q.* 29, 35 (1939).

[252]Calvert Magruder, "What Did Congress Intend? Mr. Magruder's View," 1 *Wage and Hour Reporter* 357, 358 (Nov. 14, 1938) (address delivered Nov. 10).

employees working more than 44 hours: "The work week is not merely to be shortened for the lowest-paid workers, but for all industry, and if devices for circumventing the overtime provisions are permitted, then the act's intent falls down."[253]

In an appearance at the same time before the Structural Clay Products Industry, George McNulty, the WHD's associate general counsel, included among the "'obvious subterfuges'" reducing employees' hourly rate to 25 cents but guaranteeing them their old total pay, reducing base wages only during peak periods so that employees would receive the same total wages as during normal weeks, and declaring that henceforth workweeks would be 56 hours in order to calculate a lower hourly rate. McNulty also categorized as a subterfuge the then proliferating ruse of lowering the hourly rate from well above 25 cents to an amount still above 25 cents, but calibrated exactly so that, despite complying with the new time and a half rule, employers could continue to employ workers for 48 hours weekly without having to pay any more than before the act went into effect. He warned employers that even in the unlikely case that the bookkeeping schemes they were devising for "juggling purported regular hourly rates" were later found to be legal, "'is it wise to assume that Congress will sit supinely by?' If a huge joke is made of Section 7 (which sets the maximum hours), Mr. McNulty said he doubted that 'Congress will join in the laughter. Passage of the Black-Connery Thirty-Hour Bill was once seriously considered and may be again.... If flexibility is incompatible with enforcement, then Congress may well vote for enforcement without flexibility.'"[254]

A few days later, the *Times* reported on its front page, the Wage and Hour Administrator said flatly that any employers reducing wages to 25 cents an hour "as a result of the act were acting in a 'most illegal manner.'" However, despite his assurance that the intent of the act was to prevent wages from being reduced to the minimum wage, Andrews revealed some legal uncertainty when he added that he was considering suggesting a clarifying amendment to Congress "'to be sure that the penalty applies to all sections where penalties should apply....'" Yet even in the absence of such congressional action, Andrews was eager to litigate such reductions: "'In our opinion it is illegal.... You can say it just as often as

---

[253]"Industry Warned on Wage 'Juggling,'" *N.Y. Times*, Nov. 18, 1938, at 40, col. 1. Sifton, who together with his wife had written the play *1931*, later became a lobbyist for liberal causes. "Paul F. Sifton, 74, Ex-Lobbyist, Reuther Aide and Writer, Dead," *N.Y. Times*, Apr. 7, 1972, at 39, col. 1.

[254]"Industry Warned on Wage 'Juggling,'" *N.Y. Times*, Nov. 18, 1938, at 40, col. 1. WHD assistant general counsel Rufus Poole stated that employers asked the division for its opinion about lowering wages to maintain a constant total weekly wage after premium overtime more often than any other question. BNA, *Wage and Hour Manual* 112-13 (1940 ed.).

you want to. It would tickle me to death. So many people say it can be done.'"[255]

Contrary to a popular misconception, employer resistance was not confined to the South. In 1940, for example, a large employer association in New York was indicted for having conspired to effect an industry-wide violation of the FLSA.[256] The stratagems used by employers, large and small, to avoid the financial bite of the overtime law is nicely captured by some of the high-profile litigation. One such case arose two days before the FLSA went into effect when a superintendent of the General Mills plant at Larrowe, Ohio, near Toledo, met, on instructions from the company main office, with the watchmen, who had been working 56 hours weekly at 60 cents per hour for total weekly wages of $33.60, and advised them that "under the statute the company could put on other men to do the work as watchmen for 60 cents an hour instead of paying overtime of 90 cents to the present employees for a large part of the work."[257] He explained that they could either work 40 hours at the same hourly wage or, if they wished to continue working a 56-hour week, at a reduced hourly wage of 52.5 cents for the first 40 hours and time and a half for the remaining 16 hours, leaving their total wages unchanged. Since the 40-hour option would have left them with only 71 percent of their then weekly wage—but would have required the employment of at least two other watchmen—the workers "were willing to work 56 hours 'if it was legal' for the company to make such an arrangement." In their FLSA suit against General Mills, Samuel Williams and his coworkers demanded the statutory time and a half overtime based on their real regular rate, which had been 60 cents an hour, during more than two years. In mid-1941 Judge Frank Picard (who would shortly achieve national fame as the trial judge in the Mt. Clemens Pottery portal-to-portal case)[258]formulated the point of the litigation this way: "There is no denying that this was an attempt, by contract, to circumvent the purpose of the Fair Labor Standards Act by reducing wages, maintaining the same number of hours and giving the workman the same pay he was receiving before the act went into effect. No one disputes this, and the question simply is: Did the defendant company have the right to enter into a contract with its men previous to the effective date of the Fair Labor Standards Act as long as the minimum rate paid was not below the rate set by the act?"[259]

---

[255]"Wage Cuts to 25¢ Minimum Held 'Illegal'; Andrews Seeks 'Good Cases' to Prosecute," *N.Y. Times*, Nov. 23, 1938, at 1, col. 6.

[256]Richter, "Four Years of the Fair Labor Standards Act" at 99.

[257]General Mills v. Williams, 132 F.2d 367, 368 (6th Cir. 1942).

[258]See below chapter 3.

[259]Williams v. General Mills, Inc., 39 F. Supp. 849, 850 (N.D. Ohio, 1941). The plaintiffs were members of an AFL union, but the union, preoccupied with the plant's larger departments, apparently did not intervene. *Id.* Judge Picard was a federal district judge in Michigan, but heard this case in the Western Division of the Northern District of

From the FLSA's finding of "labor conditions detrimental to the maintenance of the minimum standard of living necessary for health, efficiency, and general well-being of workers," and its declared policy of eliminating those conditions "without substantially curtailing employment or earning power,"[260] Picard concluded that Congress condemned long hours not so much as being unhealthful but as generating unemployment: "Congress...anticipated that many industrial leaders would not be adverse to giving more employment as long as it didn't cost anything and to meet any possible circumvention the policy of the Act itself enunciated the doctrine that the eventual change to a 40-hour week should be made generally without affecting the 'earning power' of the workers of the United States." Picard saw this congressional intent buttressed by section 18, which "notifies the employer that nothing in the act 'justifies' him in reducing a wage paid by him which is in excess of the applicable minimum wage...."[261]

Focusing on what he regarded as the economic realities, Picard found nothing ambiguous in section 18:

> It clearly shows that Congress, composed of men the majority of whom had reason to believe from past experience that there would always be a few employers who would not enter into the spirit of the intention of such legislation, had in mind that minority and desired to place a barrier against the very thing that happened here. If all industrial leaders had reduced the wage rate in anticipation of this act, they would probably have found their men willing to work overtime to get the same wages. Congress knew that. They sought to prevent the act's frustration because the evil was not so much in the length of time men worked but, with nine, ten or twelve million unemployed..., the problem was to cut into that unemployment without financially hurting industry or its employees. It was hoped to cut at least four or five millions from the unemployment ranks. This it appears was the big objective of the...Fair Labor Standards Act.[262]

In response to General Mills's defense that Congress attached no remedy to violations of section 18, Judge Picard stated merely that congressional intent had to be derived from the act as a whole; in that sense he concluded that employers and employees were not privileged to contract for a nominal regular rate

---

Ohio. The following year, citing his decision in this case, he handed down a similar ruling in Anuchick v. Transamerican Freight Lines, Inc., 46 F. Supp. 861, 866 (E.D. Mich. 1942). Plaintiffs' lawyer, Edward Lamb, was also a high-profile portal-pay litigator, whom the chairman of the House Un-American Activities Committee accused of being a communist. See below chapter 3.

[260]FLSA, § 2, 52 Stat. at 1060.

[261]Williams v. General Mills, 39 F. Supp. at 851. Picard offered no evidence for his claim: "Except in certain fields of industrial endeavor, very few who have studied the problem contend that 48 hours or more of labor per week are detrimental to health." *Id.*

[262]Williams v. General Mills, 39 F. Supp. at 851-52.

regardless of the real rate in order to nullify the overtime provision. Finally, Picard, reaching far beyond the statute, refused to enforce a contract that was against public policy because it was based on coercion of the employees by the employer and simultaneously "almost amounted to a conspiracy between the men and the company against an act of Congress—the men conspired to keep others out of work and the company to refrain from paying higher wages." Despite the workers' quasi-conspiracy to hog rather than share work, Picard awarded them their overtime pay and damages.[263]

Picard's vindication of section 18 in *General Mills v. Williams* was, however, short-lived: in December 1942 the Sixth Circuit Court of Appeals reversed the lower court decision on the basis of the Supreme Court's June 1942 decision in *Walling v. A. H. Belo*, which had ruled that the FLSA in general and section 18 in particular did not prevent employers from contracting to employ their employees at the same wage so long as the new rate exceeds the statutory minimum.[264]

A number of similar complaints reached the courts in the early 1940s, producing divergent outcomes. In one of the earliest, *Gurtov v. Volk*, decided less than four months after the FLSA went into effect by the Small Claims Part of the Municipal Court of New York City in Brooklyn, plaintiff-shipping clerk had been earning $12 for 50 hours of work or 24 cents an hour. In contemplation of the FLSA, the employer raised his wages on July 15, 1938 to $15 weekly, which remained his wage until he left defendant's employ in December. The court ruled against the worker's claim for time and one-half on the grounds that it was unreasonable to regard the overtime provision as a "penalty against employers who, in apparent good faith, have paid wages in excess of the amount prescribed by the act. Such employers appear to be exempt from the operation of the statute."[265] The defect in this decision was the incorrect assumption that overtime is due only on the minimum wage and the failure to compute the regular rate on which overtime was due, which here at the very least would have been 30 cents ($15/50 hours), thus producing overtime wages of 90 cents per week (15 cents x 6 hours). As a federal judge observed two years later, the employers "insist if, what defendants were paid can be so allocated as to cover the statutory minimum for the statutory maximum hours and, in addition, one and one half for all

---

[263]Williams v. General Mills, 39 F. Supp. at 852.

[264]General Mills, Inc. v. Williams, 132 F.2d at 369-70; Walling v. A.H. Belo Corp., 316 U.S. 624 (1942). Almost half a century after this battle was lost, John Owen, *Reduced Working Hours: Cure for Unemployment or Economic Burden?* 47 (1989), still mistakenly believed that "the FLSA specifically prohibits reducing hourly wages below the rate paid before the law went into effect. It is likely that a new reduction in the standard workweek would be accompanied by a similar prohibition."

[265]Gurtov v. Volk, 11 NYS2d 604, 605 (Munic. Ct. NYC 1939).

overtime, that such a salary meets the requirements of the law. ... The proposition seems very plausible, but, unless such was an arrangement agreed to by the parties...it is not compliance, because perchance it might figure out that way. ... It is not enough that the salaries...may be allocated or spread so as to cover the minimum and one and a half for overtime. It may even exceed the 30¢ minimum and the 45¢ for overtime and yet be a violation of the law."[266]

In another early federal court case, from May 1940, an oil refinery worker who had been receiving a fixed monthly salary of $150 told his employers a week after the FLSA went into effect that he wanted the benefit of shorter hours conferred by the new law; his foreman informed him that shorter hours would bring lower pay in their wake, but no changes ever took place. The federal court in Abilene, Texas, found for the defendant-employer on the grounds that the pay exceeded the minimum wage and overtime (on the minimum wage) for the number of hours worked.[267]

A complaint based directly on section 18 was filed in Maryland federal court by a hosiery knitter whose piece rate had amounted to the comparatively high weekly wage of $40 before the FLSA went into effect. At that time the Easton Hosiery Mills lowered his piece rate by five cents in order to finance the wage increase that the employer had to implement to comply with the FLSA vis-à-vis the low-wage helpers. The court dismissed the complaint because section 18 provided no relief, Congress did not intend to freeze wages above the minimum, and, even if it did so intend, it lacked the power to do so. The court noted that the original FLSA bill had authorized administrative action to prevent precisely what Easton Hosiery Mills had done, but the House had deleted the provision, and a proposed amendment to achieve the same end was not adopted. The court conceded that the legislative proponents intended section 18 to serve as a mandate and not a mere policy statement, but they had failed to embody that intent in any statutory language.[268]

Another high-profile judicial decision arose out of a complaint filed by the WHD against a Minnesota manufacturing firm that on the eve of the FLSA had employed 18 workers working 50 to 56 hours a week at hourly rates varying between 45 and 80 cents. In the interim between enactment of the FLSA and October 25, 1938, the employer told the employees that with low profits it would have to adjust wages to comply with the new law. To avoid premium overtime rates, it would have to reduce hours to 44, but since it wished to maintain the

---

[266]St. John v. Brown, 38 F. Supp. 385, 388-89 (N.D. Tex. 1941).

[267]Reeves v. Howard County Refining Co., 33 F. Supp. 90 (N.D. Tex. 1940).

[268]Remer v. Czaja, 36 F. Supp. 629 (D. Md. 1941). The court's reasoning compelled it to reject the WHD's interpretation of the regular rate as meaning the wage in effect when the Act went into effect and requiring ignoring reductions in violation of section 18 in computing overtime wages. Interpretative Bull. No. 4.

workers' weekly wages, it planned to lower hourly wages by 10 cents; it would pay time and a half on the lower rate, and if the total still failed to reach their present wages, it would make up the difference with a weekly bonus or gratuity. In response to the workers' hostile reaction, the employer stated that it would drop the plan and reduce their hours to 44. Because the workers objected to a loss of wages and were willing to continue the long work weeks, they were unwilling to agree to the alternative proposal; although they feared that the bonus scheme was illegal, they ultimately accepted it. The court in *Fleming v. Carleton Screw Products Company* agreed with the WHD's argument that the new wage rates were fictitious, the pre-FLSA rates being the real regular rates; to accept the employer's defense that it was free to agree with its employees to hold them harmless while protecting itself against higher overtime costs would have nullified the FLSA's purpose of making long hours more expensive and thus creating more employment by cutting those hours.[269] On appeal, the Eighth Circuit expressly rejected the employer's claim that the FLSA does not apply to employers paying in excess of the minimum wages and one and one-half times that minimum for overtime hours.[270] The Sixth Circuit came to a similar conclusion in a suit against the Continental Baking Company.[271]

Despite employers' campaign of civil disobedience, Major A. L. Fletcher, the Assistant Administrator in Charge of Cooperation and Enforcement, expressed the belief in early December 1938 that the FLSA might yet be "properly administered by capital, labor" and the WHD.[272] And in spite of this organized resistance to the overtime law, the Wage and Hour Administrator assured the NAM that only a "delinquent minority" who "contaminated the whole business community" had prevented businessmen from eliminating the "evils of sweatshops, of unfair competition and of low purchasing power" and had made necessary "some sort of compulsion,...the power of organized society applied through legislation...."[273] Yet Andrews himself found the controversy that the NAM and employers had provoked odd since the FLSA's hour provision is permissive and does not even prescribe the eight-hour day.[274] (In fact, the president of the AFL had alluded to the need for overtime pay after eight hours

---

[269]Fleming v. Carleton Screw Products Co., 37 F. Supp. 754 (D. Minn. 1941).

[270]Carleton Screw Products Co. v. Fleming, 126 F.2d 537 (8th Cir. 1942).

[271]Bumpus v. Continental Baking Co., 124 F.2d 549 (6th Cir. 1941).

[272]"Enforcement of Wage-Hour Law," 1 *Wage and Hour Reporter* 394, 395 (Dec. 5, 1938) (address delivered at Duke University, Dec. 3, 1938).

[273]"Mr. Andrews' Address to N.A.M.," 1 *Wage and Hour Reporter* 413 (Dec. 19, 1938) (address of Dec. 9, 1938).

[274]Andrews, "FLSA Problems for Congress or the Courts" at 419.

as an aside at the 1937 FLSA hearings,[275] and at the end of 1938 the Textile Workers Organizing Committee proposed amending the FLSA to provide penalty overtime pay after eight hours daily and four hours on Saturdays, but it was not enacted then or since.)[276]

By mid-1939, when deputy administrator Sifton addressed the Iowa Bankers Association, the WHD, while still insisting that lowering the wage rate to cancel the effect of the overtime premium ran contrary to congressional expectations of employment spreading and increased purchasing power, seemed almost to be reduced to pleading with employers, on moral rather than legal or economic grounds, not to litigate the force of section 18. In a puzzling non sequitur, Sifton asked employers, in view of the uncertainty of predicting judicial outcomes: "If you win, will it be worth it?"[277]

Other employers organizations were not content with legislating or litigating the details of federal wage-hour regulation. At the end of April 1939 the Chamber of Commerce of the United States demanded congressional repeal of "curbs on business" including the FLSA.[278] By early 1940, claiming that "[f]ew legislative enactments have produced greater confusion or have been more bitterly criticized," the Committee on Manufacture of the Chamber of Commerce also called for outright repeal. Dissatisfied with the mere "palliatives" that the scores of proposed amendments might have constituted, the committee recommended relegating to the states all regulation of wages, hours, and working conditions to prevent the "oppression" of "special classes of workers...." Significantly, the overtime provisions, especially their application to office and salaried workers, were at "the heart of the Committee's objections" to the FLSA. With respect to employees who were accorded "privileges" such as paid vacations and sick leave, the Chamber asserted a generally held view that mandatory overtime pay was "inequitable to the employer and...tend[ed] to restrict the opportunities of the worker to improve his status."[279]

In light of employers' single-minded attack on the scope of the overtime provision, it seems odd that the Wage and Hour Administrator reassured the NAM

---

[275]*Fair Labor Standards Act of 1937: Joint Hearings* at 231 (testimony of William Green).

[276]"Possible Changes in Wage-Hour Law," 1 *Wage and Hour Reporter* 419 (Dec. 26, 1938). The California Eight-Hour-Day Restoration and Workplace Flexibility Act of 1999 imposes time-and-a-half compensation for hours beyond eight daily and double-time compensation for hours beyond 12. Cal. Labor Code § 510(a) (Deering 1999).

[277]Paul Sifton, "Two-Week Pay Period and Overtime," BNA, *Wage and Hour Manual* 108, 109-10 (1940 ed.) (address of June 7, 1939).

[278]"Chamber Demands Congress Repeal Curbs on Business," *N.Y. Times*, May 1, 1939, at 1, col. 5.

[279]"Case for Repeal of Wage-Hour Law," 3 *Wage and Hour Reporter* 47, 49, 50 (Feb. 5, 1940).

in late 1940 that protest about the 40-hour week stemmed from journalists and academics, "not from manufacturers. Perhaps this is the reason: In 1909 average weekly hours worked in factories were 53; in 1929, 46 hours; in 1939, 38 hours. The 40-hour week had arrived in manufacturing industries long before the law made it mandatory."[280] Yet despite the fact that in 1939 fewer than one-eighth of covered workers were working more than 44 hours and thus benefiting from the overtime provision—in contrast to only 3 percent of covered workers whose wages were lifted by the 25-cent minimum wage[281]—a wide cross-section of employers had resolved to undo the new law.

Although the WHD had insisted that reducing wage rates in order to offset the overtime penalty was "contrary to the purpose of the Act," by the time of World War II it was constrained to concede that because "no penalty is provided in the Act for action contrary to its purpose in this respect," the division "does not...proceed against an employer who reduces a rate of pay to avoid the effect of the overtime penalty."[282]

6. The Supreme Court Spreads Confusion Instead of Employment

Perhaps Congress should have gone further and prohibited any employee from working over 42 hours in any event. This, however, it did not see fit to do. ... True, the detriment to well-being of workers exists as much in a case where overtime is worked and paid for as where it is worked without being paid for. Had it desired to do so, Congress might have absolutely forbidden the employment of any worker beyond a certain number of hours.... Presumably, however, it felt it more desirable to attempt to achieve the same result by merely imposing a penalty for the overtime....[283]

The only reason that the administration did not recommend an arbitrary statutory prohibition against working over 40 hours, which is what they were seeking, was because there were certain cases, particularly in the seasonal industries, where it was desirable for short periods to work over 40 hours, and they didn't want to absolutely bar that, so they put in a penalty, and the purpose of the time and a half...was to create a competitive situation where one man could not abuse working overtime when all the rest of them were playing fair, because his costs would go up so high that in a competitive market he could

---

[280]Philip Fleming, Address before the NAM, New York City, Dec. 12, 1940, in 86 *Cong. Rec.* at 6963.

[281]Elmer Andrews, "Making the Wage-Hour Law Work," 29 (2) *Am. Lab. Leg. Rev.* 53-61 at 55 (June 1939).

[282]BNA, *Wage and Hour Manual* 233 (1944-1945 ed.).

[283]Letter from Philip Fleming (Wage and Hour Administrator) to J. Capper (May 18, 1940), in 86 *Cong. Rec.* A3787, A3789.

not survive.[284]

At the time of the congressional debates over the FLSA in 1937-38, large employers in general, and especially those that had entered into collective bargaining agreements, had not anticipated that compliance with the law would be burdensome; after all, most of them were already paying time and one-half for overtime and more than the minimum wage.[285] For example, General Motors adopted time and a half for hours over eight per day and forty per week in November 1936, while Chrysler followed suit in 1937.[286] At the FLSA hearings that year the Commissioner of Labor Statistics told Congress that the industries, such as automobiles, steel, and agricultural implements, with the greatest employment were working more than 40 hours and were "for the most part paying overtime rates."[287]

Employers' position toward statutorily imposed overtime penalties, as the preceding section revealed, soon changed. Counsel for the NAM expressed large capital's exasperation with the WHD's early enforcement priorities when he urged it to focus on sweatshops rather than on regular-rate cases "where the wages and employment conditions are far superior to anything remotely intended to be covered by the wage-hour law."[288] When large firms finally realized that relatively highly paid organized workers were also protected by the FLSA, they began to lobby Congress to cut back on the Supreme Court's expansive interpretations of the regular rate for overtime purposes. Yet while echoing the views of Supreme Court dissenters in a number of the FLSA cases to the effect that Congress never

---

[284]*Hearings on H. R. 6790, to Permit the Performance of Essential Labor on Naval Contracts Without Regard to Laws and Contracts Limiting Hours of Employment, to Limit the Profits of Naval Contracts, and for Other Purposes Before the House Committee on Naval Affairs*, 77th Cong., 2d Sess. 2771 (1942) (testimony of Rep. Melvin Maas (Rep. Minn).

[285]*See* DOL, *Fair Labor Standards in Wartime: Annual Report, Wage and Hour Division, Public Contracts Division, For the Fiscal Year Ended June 30, 1942*, at 5 (1943).

[286]*Overtime Penalty Pay Act of 1964: Hearings Held Jointly Before the General Subcommittee on Labor and Select Subcommittee on Labor of the House Committee on Education and Labor*, 88th Cong., 2d Sess. , Pt. 1 at 250 (1964) (statements of Louis Seaton, vice president for personnel, GM and William O'Brien, vice president for personnel, Chrysler Corp.)

[287]*Fair Labor Standards Act of 1937: Joint Hearings* at 343 (testimony of Isador Lubin).

[288]*Regulating the Recovery of Portal-to-Portal Pay, and For Other Purposes: Hearings Before Subcomm. No. 2 of the House Comm. on the Judiciary*, 80th Cong., 1st Sess. 448 (1947) (statement of Raymond Smethurst). Smethurst co-edited a casebook on the FLSA; Raymond Smethurst and Reuben Haslam, *Cases on the Fair Labor Standards Act of 1938 (Federal Wage and Hour Law)* (1949). Haslam was also counsel for the NAM.

intended the Act to impinge on the outcomes of legitimate collective bargaining,[289] the NAM, unlike the Chamber of Commerce of the United States, apparently did not seek outright repeal of the FLSA.[290]

Capital's litigation strategy against statutory overtime premiums culminated in two U.S. Supreme Court cases decided the same day in June 1942.[291] The most straightforward legal gambit was the ultimately unsuccessful claim that "the regular rate" on which overtime had to be paid was merely the minimum wage.[292] In *Missel v. Motor Overnight Transportation Co.,* Administrator Andrew's loose lips in his 1938 Birmingham talk came back to haunt workers as the press declared that the federal district court had adopted the "Birmingham Doctrine" when it ruled in 1941 that a salaried employee being paid considerably more than the minimum wage for indefinite hours was entitled only to time and one-half calculated on the statutory minimum wage. William Missel, a rate clerk and dispatcher for a trucking company between 1937 and 1940, had been paid a weekly salary of $25.50 and later $27.50 for a workweek varying between 40 and 75 hours. The trial court rejected Missel's claim that his regular rate was to be calculated by dividing his salary by the maximum number of non-overtime hours in effect at the time. The trial judge's reasoning was shaped by his unsubstantiated interpretation of the FLSA's "underlying purpose" as merely to raise minimum wages gradually: "the overtime provisions...were not inserted...to discourage or limit overtime work, but merely as an essential part of a plan to raise sub-standard wages by providing definite pay for overtime work...."[293]

The amicus brief of the American Trucking Associations had apparently persuaded the judge that the plaintiff-worker's position was a parade of horribles: "'According to plaintiff's contention, it would make no difference whether he was paid $27.50 or $1,000 a week, he would always be underpaid and the employer would always owe him money for every minute over straight-time hours that he might be required to be on duty.'"[294]

---

[289]In various cases, Justices Roberts, Jackson, Stone, Frankfurter, and Burton stressed this point repeatedly without success. See below chapter 3.

[290]In the course of testifying before Congress on the issue of portal pay in 1945, the NAM advocated furthergoing changes in the FLSA unrelated to that problem. *Limiting the Time for Bringing Certain Actions under the Laws of the United States: Hearing Before Subcomm. No. 4 of the House Comm. on the Judiciary*, 79th Cong., 1st Sess. 21-23 (1945) (testimony of Raymond Smethurst, counsel, NAM); *Portal to Portal Wages: Hearings Before a Subcomm. of the Senate Comm. on the Judiciary*, 80th Cong., 1st Sess. 106-107 (1947) (testimony of Raymond Smethurst, counsel NAM).

[291]See generally, E. Merrick Dodd, "The Supreme Court and Fair Labor Standards, 1941-1945," 59 *Harv. L. Rev.* 321 (1946).

[292]E.g., Sunshine Mining Co. v. Carver, 41 F. Supp. 60, 66-67 (D. Idaho, 1941).

[293]Missel v. Overnight Motor Transp. Co., 40 F. Supp. 174, 178-79 (D. Md. 1941).

[294]"Minimum Wage As Overtime Base," 4 *Wage and Hour Reporter* 205, 206 (Apr.

The widespread support in the press for employers' implausible claim that "the regular rate" on which the time and one-half premium had to be paid was merely the minimum wage rate seems especially odd in light of the fact that Representative Hartley, one of the most extreme northern opponents of the FLSA, had expressly declared during the House floor debates that the FLSA would not affect only the lower wage scales "inasmuch as requirement for payment of time and a half for overtime is based upon the regular rate of pay whether that be 40 cents an hour or $1 an hour."[295] Yet the NAM, through its general counsel, began almost immediately after the enactment of the FLSA propagating the position that employers were required to pay the 50 percent premium only on the minimum wage.[296]

As the principal test cases were pending in the Supreme Court in 1941, *Modern Industry*, a management magazine, observed that the Court "may soon decide whether the Fair Labor Standards Act is primarily a minimum wage law or a maximum hours law. ... The outcome is of interest to an estimated 1.5 million white-collar workers getting more than the statutory minimum. If the decision stands, the Wage and Hour Division contends, it will largely eliminate the law's benefits for them and will make it chiefly a minimum wage law."[297]

The Fourth Circuit—which asserted that the magazine was referring to *Missel* despite the article's express reference to *Walling v. A. H. Belo Corp.*, which was decided against the Wage and Hour Administrator without the predicted dire consequences[298]—cited this article as evidence of the importance of the question and the need for granting the Administrator amicus status.[299] The strongest policy argument that the appellate court devised in reversing the trial judge and refuting employers' claim that the "regular rate" meant the minimum wage was based on the underlying congressional intent to discourage excessively long hours: "Such a construction would wholly defeat this policy, for if an employee was getting a fairly high wage, one and one-half times the minimum would in such a case be less than the actual wage the employee was receiving.... This would encourage rather than discourage overtime, and the plain purpose of Congress...would be defeated."[300]

Despite this astute policy logic, the court's reasoning made no sense when it

---

28, 1941).

[295]83 *Cong. Rec.* 9258 (1938).

[296]"Salaried Employees: Overtime," in 1 *Wage and Hour Reference Manual* 59 (1939) (BNA).

[297]"New Test for Wage-Hour Act," *Modern Industry*, Oct. 15, 1941, at 42.

[298]Walling v. A. H. Belo Corp., 316 U.S. 624 (1942) (discussed below).

[299]Missel v. Overnight Motor Transp. Co., 126 F.2d 98, 101 (4th Cir. 1942).

[300]Missel v. Overnight Motor Transp. Co., 126 F.2d at 106.

asserted: "That the overtime provisions of the Act are aimed at re-employment and designed for economic and social purposes, as well as to protect the health or welfare of the employees, seems obvious from the omission of any absolute limitation upon weekly hours of work if properly compensated, and the absence of any limitation upon daily hours."[301] On the contrary, all of these goals would be more straightforwardly achievable if the 40-hour-week were rigidly enforced.

When employers finally appeared in the forum they had been seeking, the U.S. Supreme Court, the United States had already entered World War II and the work-sharing purposes born of the Depression had become largely irrelevant. The defendant and the American Trucking Associations as amicus curiae made the most of this turn of economic events. The association attacked the claim that premium overtime was designed to spread work for "all classes" by pointing out that although the FLSA was permanent legislation, Congress could not have "contemplated a permanent unemployment problem with respect to all classes of employees" as opposed to the unskilled.[302] Overnight Motor Transportation Company argued that the chief legal question was whether the Fourth Circuit had erred in ascribing "dual class coverage" to the FLSA by concluding that the overtime provision "went beyond the class scope of the minimum wage provisions and was intended to spread employment and raise wages among all classes of employees regardless of income."[303] The employer's overriding claim was that the FLSA without any doubt "was intended to be a 'poor man's' law."[304] (Ironically, the heads of the AFL and the CIO had also favored a FLSA bill that would have covered only low-paid and nonorganized workers.)[305] The employers association, too, harped on the theme that the FLSA was directed at "the underprivileged," but also tried out the ad absurdum argument that Congress could not possibly have meant to require employers to pay overtime to highly paid employees because such an obligation would perversely discourage them from paying more than the minimum wage.[306]

When asked by Justice Hugo Black, one of the authors of the FLSA, what his claim was, counsel for the association at oral argument responded that the overtime provision "'applies only to employees who do not receive the 30-cent minimum and 45 cents for overtime as declared in the Act. Section 7 is not

---

[301]Missel v. Overnight Motor Transp. Co., 126 F.2d at 104.

[302]Brief of American Trucking Associations, Inc., Amicus Curiae, at 22, Overnight Motor Transp. Co. v. Missel, 316 U.S. 572 (1942).

[303]Petition for Writ of Certiorari at 6, Overnight Motor Transp. Co. v. Missel, 316 U.S. 572 (1942).

[304]Brief for Petitioner at 21, Overnight Motor Transp. Co. v. Missel.

[305]Jonathan Grossman, "Fair Labor Standards Act of 1938: Maximum Struggle for a Minimum Wage," 101 (6) *Monthly Lab.Rev.* 22-30 at 25-26 (June 1978).

[306]Brief of American Trucking Associations, Inc., Amicus Curiae, at 11 (quote), 9.

meant to apply to employees who are paid more than the minimum rates. If Section 7 were applied to all upper bracket white-collar employees it would bring the Act into a field for which Congress never intended to legislate. Section 7 is to be construed in the light of Section 6 which refers primarily to the submerged classes....'"[307]

The Supreme Court then ruled with one only dissent that the regular rate did not mean the minimum wage. Its supporting analysis has survived and flourished as the locus classicus of congressional intent on the overtime provision. In refutation of the employer's claim that it was unconstitutional to regulate the wages of workers whose pay equaled the minimum or whose hours were not injurious to health, the Court used the opportunity to hold constitutional the regulation of hours for purposes other than health:

> Long hours may impede the free interstate flow of commodities by creating friction between production areas with different length workweeks, by offering opportunities for unfair competition through undue extension of hours, and by inducing labor discontent apt to lead to interference with commerce through interruption of work. Overtime pay probably will not solve all problems of overtime work, but Congress may properly use it to lessen the irritations.[308]

Thus, although the Supreme Court agreed with the Fourth Circuit that work-sharing and combating unemployment was one of the law's main purposes, it did not share the appellate court's erroneous notion of the comparative efficacy of overtime penalties and absolute hours caps: "The existence of such a purpose is no less certain because Congress chose to use a less drastic form of limitation than outright prohibition." The Court, perhaps inadvertently, then revealed the specific conditions under which the premium might function adequately: "In a period of widespread unemployment and small profits, the economy inherent in avoiding extra pay was expected to have an appreciable effect in the distribution of available work."[309]

The Supreme Court may have squelched employers' quest for a minimalist overtime premium[310]—nevertheless, more than thirty years later a federal judge

---

[307]"Argument Before High Court on Overtime Rate," 5 *Wage and Hour Reporter* 265, 267 (Apr. 13, 1942).

[308]Overnight Motor Transp. Co. v. Missel, 316 U.S. 572, 576 (1942).

[309]Overnight Motor Transp. Co. v. Missel, 316 U.S. at 578.

[310]Despite the clear holding in *Overnight Motor Transportation Company*, another employer raised the same defense before the Supreme Court later in 1942, which the Court ruled "merits but slight consideration." Warren-Bradshaw Drilling Co. v. Hall, 317 U.S. 88, 93 (1942).

dismissed an overtime suit filed by the DOL on these same grounds[311]—but it approved their other favored construction of the statutory term "regular rate" on which the overtime premium was due. Where firms paid a fixed weekly wage for variable or fluctuating hours, the hourly regular rate was to be determined by dividing the wage by the total number of hours worked (rather than, for example, by 40 hours)—a procedure of which the WHD had approved since 1939.[312] The Court conceded that under this method "the longer the hours, the less the rate and the pay per hour," but, without offering reasons, it asserted that this outcome "is not an argument...against" the method.[313] In particular, the Court failed to justify a definition that "does not fully effectuate the legislative policy of making overtime cost half as much again per hour as straight time."[314]

In the other outstanding overtime test case of 1942 the employer, A.H. Belo Corporation, expressly argued that it had "never urged the interpretation many times put forward,...and sometimes sanctioned,...that 'regular rate' means the minimum legal rate specified in Section of the Act...."[315] Instead, the case involved the narrower issue of whether employers violated the FLSA when they paid workers far in excess of the minimum wage, but set a fictitious hourly wage for variable hours, and guaranteed a fixed weekly amount so that the overtime penalty did not kick in until workers had worked more than 54 hours. Belo, publisher of the *Dallas Morning News* and other periodicals, had been paying almost all of its employees as much as or more than the FLSA minimum wage for a long time before 1938. Like many other employers, however, it too wished to avoid having to pay additional wages without violating the FLSA. The regional WHD office took the position that Belo's arrangement violated the act because the regular rate, on which overtime was due, by law had to be calculated by dividing the guaranteed weekly wage by the number of hours worked, whereas Belo failed to pay such overtime.[316]

The trial judge, as was not uncommon in the early years of the FLSA, was openly hostile to the anti-contractarian underpinnings of the statute and

[311]In Brennan v. Lauderdale Yacht Basin, Inc., 493 F.2d 188, 189 (5th Cir. 1974), the court of appeals had to reverse a judge who had held: "These people are not the people that [the FLSA] was designed to protect.... If Mr. Johnson had been paid the minimum wage, assuming he worked 50 hours a week, [for] 42 weeks out of the year, he was paid so far in excess of any standard hourly wage, at twice the minimum. His overtime was way over what the minimum overtime would be."

[312]WHD, Interpretative Bull. No. 4, § 12, in BNA, *Wage and Hour Manual* 95, 97 (1940 ed.).

[313]Overnight Motor Transp. Co. v. Missel, 316 U.S. at 580.

[314]Dodd, "The Supreme Court and Fair Labor Standards, 1941-1945" at 356.

[315]Brief for Respondent 32 n.14, Walling v. A. H. Belo Corp., 316 U.S. 624 (1942).

[316]A. H. Belo Corp. v. Street, 35 F. Supp. 430 (N.D. Tex. 1940).

aggressively ideological: "I cannot conceive of a law...that would unsettle amicability between employer and employees by interfering with their agreement, provided such agreement is equal to, or, in excess of, the legal requirement with reference to pay." The judge justified his single-minded focus on the minimum wage by stripping the FLSA of its hours regulation aspect: "[T]his statute does not prevent overtime. It does not say that a full-grown man or woman employee shall not work overtime. It...merely pretends to be and is a statute against less than a minimum wage."[317] His syntax already frayed, the judge then descended into an at times incomprehensible rant without ever identifying the substance of the dispute between Belo and the WHD:

> I don't know that the court is concerned with this, but when...the government has a right to go and figure, even to go into the office of the employer and find out whether the employer is treating his employee correctly..., if and when that results, in an almost endless burden, to seek to put into effect a plan that has been detailed to the court, and which disappears if carried to excessive length, I cannot believe that that construction should be indulged in. It emasculates the right of contract. ... It makes vassals of employee and employer and leaves us hanging by the thumbs at the mercy of the construction of the government as to what we mean when we contract....
>
> These two suits spark from a clash in systems. Neither is perfect. One fixes the independent week for the sine quo [sic] non. The other fixes the will of the contracting parties, provided, such will is above the denials of the law, as the summum bonum. One includes the right to say when payrolls shall be made. The other views the regularity of pay checks as the most important. One is cumbersome and irregular. The other is simple and regular. One is the child of unauthorized regulation. The other is the child of liberty. One deals only in dollars and cents. The other with happiness of employer and employee, vacations, pay when sick, or, absent, as well as with dollars and cents. Neither system is fixed by statute.[318]

It was not until the case came before the Fifth Circuit, which agreed with the trial court that Belo's payment plan carried out the letter and purpose of the statute, that the precise nature of the dispute became clear. The appellate judges appeared irritated by the WHD's hardline stance toward an employer which, if it merely "changed the form of its employment contracts to conform to [the WHD's] view,...could have paid its employees considerably less than it did, and still have been within the law...." Instead, the WHD "has brought this case and has stood throughout, upon the bold proposition, that where weekly salaries are paid, no matter how large the salary or how it was arrived at or agreed to, the 'regular rate'...must always, and can only, be determined, by dividing the weekly

---

[317]Fleming v. A. H. Belo Corp., 36 F. Supp. 907, 908 (N.D. Tex. 1941).

[318]Fleming v. A. H. Belo Corp., 36 F. Supp. at 908-909.

compensation, by the total number of hours the employee actually works during each week, and employer and employee cannot contract otherwise." Likewise, the Fifth Circuit looked askance at the WHD's inability to identify "words in the act" which prohibit employers from doing what Belo did, and at the WHD's insistence on supporting its position only by reference to the FLSA's purpose of penalizing and limiting overtime. The appeals court was offended by the administrator's view that Belo's pay scheme must be unlawful if it enabled the employer to continue to work its employees overtime without increasing wages above their pre-FLSA levels. For this very reason the court could not agree with the WHD that Belo "must be required to pay more than it agreed to pay and its employees agreed to receive, because the pay which by the agreement was fixed to cover both regular and overtime, must...be considered as covering only regular time, and for the overtime worked, there must be additional compensation."[319]

In contrast, the appellate court found that, because the statutory term "regular rate at which he is employed" was not ambiguous, it was unnecessary to examine the FLSA's purposes or legislative history. Rather, the Fifth Circuit thought the term straightforward: the WHD's approach was acceptable only in the absence of an express hourly rate within an agreement for a weekly salary; but when the contract established such a rate, it was erroneous to assume that the wage was not intended to cover the overtime as well. But even if the statutory term were ambiguous, resort to underlying policy would not aid the WHD's position because the FLSA's policy statement in section 2 "says nothing about spreading the work or reducing hours of working." The Fifth Circuit then virtually drained the overtime provision of any significance by asserting that

> the complete absence from the act of any prohibition against or limitation upon working extra hours, any prohibition against or limitation upon the making of agreements by employers with their employees, the expressions in Section 2, and particularly the provisions of Section 8, would compel us to conclude, that the purpose of the act is to establish and gradually raise minimum wages, that the overtime provisions in it are inserted not at all to discourage or limit overtime work but as a part of the scheme to raise substandard wages by providing a definite pay for overtime work when such work is required; and that nothing in it purports to or does at all impair the right of employer and employee to contract as they have done here.[320]

Ultimately the Fifth Circuit lapsed back into the libertarian rhetoric of the trial judge, accusing the administrator of construing the FLSA so as to place employers and employees in tutelage vis-à-vis him:

---

[319]Fleming v. A. H. Belo Corp., 121 F.2d 207, 210-11 (5th Cir. 1941).

[320]Fleming v. A. H. Belo Corp., 121 F.2d at 211-12.

> It may be admitted that there is a section of opinion in this country and in the Congress, sufficiently collectivistic to prefer the tutelary system for which the administrator contends, and that if they had had sufficient voting power, they would have so provided in the law. It must be conceded however on the other hand that there is another section of opinion both in the nation and in the Congress, which is not so collectivistic and still believes in reasonable freedom of contract. It is just because of this fact, that legislation is compromise, that the views of the proponents and of the opponents, as to the purposes and effect of the legislative act, are never regarded as of value in a construction of it, and that it is settled law that statutes must be construed in accordance with the intent of the legislature as expressed in the language of the act as a whole. Its meaning may not be sought by the courts in the vague penumbrae of the wishes and desires of its proponents or its opponents as these are expressed in debates.[321]

When the Supreme Court docketed the case, Colonel Philip Fleming, the Wage and Hour Administrator,[322] calling it the most important test yet of the FLSA, warned that if Belo prevailed, employers all over the United States would use the arrangement to evade overtime obligations.[323] Before the Supreme Court Belo sought to contextualize the purposes of the overtime law during world war. The employer accused the WHD of seeking to achieve an objective "square in the face of the needs of national defense upon which our very existence as a free people depends. Such supposed objective is to discourage or prohibit work over 40 hours a week, with design to 'spread' employment, although the nation's interest cries out for more production, more work and longer hours, to the fullest extent consistent with the maintenance of the standards of health and pay prescribed by the Act...."[324]

Moreover, even in the depressed economy of the 1930s, Belo argued, Congress expected work-spreading to be "kept within very modest limits" and to

> take place principally in the lowest paid and unskilled employments, where the labor product in dollar value is so low that the employer cannot afford the added overtime wage.

---

[321]Fleming v. A. H. Belo Corp., 121 F.2d at 213.

[322]Fleming, who had been a district engineer in the U.S. Army working on the construction of locks and dams, "had not been in any way active, or even interested, to be frank about it, in the long legislative fight that led to the enactment" of the FLSA prior to his appointment in 1939. *Minimum Wage Standards and Other Parts of the Fair Labor Standards Act of 1938: Hearings Before Subcommittee No. 4 of the House Committee on Education and Labor,* 80th Cong., 1st Sess. 751-52 (1947). After leaving the WHD in 1941, Fleming (1887-1955) was federal works administrator until 1949. 3 *Who Was Who in America (1951-1960)* at 288 (1966).

[323]"Wage-Hour Loses," *Bus. Wk.*, June 13, 1942, at 88.

[324]Position of Respondent with respect to the Petition for Certiorari Herein at 5, Fleming v. A. H. Belo Corp., 316 U.S. 624 (1942).

> It was known that in the skilled employments...overtime rates would be paid in lieu of curtailing hours. Indeed, it was known that in the skilled employments overtime pay, and even the precise formula of time and one-half, had already become a traditional policy.[325]

The Supreme Court's five to four decision was the first to explain precisely what Belo had done. In anticipation of the FLSA, Belo informed its employees that "[i]n order to conform our employment arrangements to the scheme of the Act without reducing the amount of money which you receive each week, we advise you that from and after October 24, 1938, your basic rate of pay will be" 67 cents per hour for the first 44 hours and not less than time and a half for additional hours, "with a guaranty on our part that you shall receive weekly, for regular time and for such overtime as the necessities of the business may demand," not less than $40. Belo thus set the hourly rate at 1/60th of the guaranteed weekly wage, as a result of which employees had to work more than 54.5 hours before their wages would exceed the guarantee. The Supreme Court conceded that the point of Belo's plan was to "permit as far as possible the payment of the same total weekly wage after the Act as before. But nothing in the Act bars an employer from contracting with his employees to pay them the same wages that they received previously, so long as the new rate equals or exceeds the minimum required by the Act."[326]

After in effect rejecting the WHD's position that Congress had intended to require employers to pay more for exercising their privilege to work their employees overtime than they had before the FLSA went into effect, the Court relegated to a footnote its relegation of section 18 to the dustheap of legal history: "Whatever the legal effect of this language, it is certainly not a prohibition and the Administrator does not rely upon it." The court then further tweaked the administrator by asserting that the Fifth Circuit's finding that Belo's effort to maintain their employees' weekly incomes (or, more realistically, Belo's wage costs) at its pre-FLSA levels "gains support" from the fact that Belo was formulating the plan at the very time that Andrews made his ill-fated Birmingham faux pas.[327]

The focus of the Court's statutory interpretation was "the regular rate" for overtime purposes, which Congress had failed to define. Whereas Belo argued that the regular rate was clearly 67 cents per hour, the WHD called that rate meaningless; instead, it viewed the agreement as one for a fixed weekly salary of $40 regardless of fluctuations in hours (up to 55 hours). The WHD therefore argued that the regular rate in fact had to be recalculated weekly by dividing the

---

[325]Brief for Respondent at 29, Fleming v. A. H. Belo Corp., 316 U.S. 624 (1942).

[326]Walling v. A. H. Belo Corp., 316 U.S. 624, 628-30 (1942).

[327]Walling v. A. H. Belo Corp., 316 U.S. at 630 n.6.

$40 guaranty by the number of hours worked; for any hours worked beyond 44, employees would then be entitled to 150 percent of that rate. Belo's $30,000 to $60,000 back overtime wage liability can be exemplified this way: if a worker worked 50 hours, his regular rate that week would be 80 cents; for the first 44 hours, his wage would have amounted to $35.20, while his six hours of overtime would have entitled him to an additional $7.20, for a total of $42.40, leaving him underpaid by $2.40. The Court agreed that the difficulty in the case stemmed from the guarantee, but it rejected the WHD's argument that the guarantee was inconsistent with and overrode the 67-cent hourly calculation. The majority reasoned, first, that indisputably real overtime kicked in again after 55 hours; and second, even with regard to the hours between 44 and 55, when wages were determined by the guarantee, if 67 cents was considered the regular rate, then the worker was actually being paid more than 150 percent overtime; however, neither such overpayments nor fluctuations in the overtime premium were prohibited by the FLSA provided that the rate never fell below 150 percent. The Court did not deny the force of the WHD's view that the 67-cent wage was artificial, but the parties may well have intended the "flexibility" that it generated in the overtime rate "[i]f it was the only means of securing uniformity in weekly income." Moreover, since weekly hours fluctuated drastically, the "regular rate" would always have been "'irregular'" both arithmetically and with respect to the parties' ability to foresee or plan on it.[328]

Ultimately, the majority was swayed by the perception that the arrangement was "mutually satisfactory" to Belo and its employees, whereas the WHD's approach "as a practical matter eliminates the possibility of steady income to employees with irregular hours." Presuming that Congress had intentionally refrained from defining "the regular rate" precisely because employment relationships were so manifold and "unpredictable," the majority revealed its bias in favor of promoting consumer instalment buying and against the statute's anti-contractualism:

> Where the question is as close as this one, it is well...to afford the fullest possible scope to agreements among the individuals who are actually affected. This policy is based upon a common sense recognition of the special problems confronting employer and employee in businesses where the work hours fluctuate from week to week and from day to day. Many such employees value the security of a regular weekly income. They want to operate on a family budget, to make commitments for payments on homes and automobiles and insurance.[329]

---

[328]Walling v. A. H. Belo Corp., 316 U.S. at 631-33.

[329]Walling v. A. H. Belo Corp., 316 U.S. 634-35.

Little wonder that Belo received 10,000 inquiries for copies of its contract the month the Supreme Court handed down its decision.[330]

The four dissenters regarded the contracts as agreements for weekly wages for variable hours with additional hourly compensation once the employees worked more than an ascertainable number of hours—namely, the number needed for the wages to reach the weekly guarantee, which was the "dominating feature," without which "the adoption of a low hourly rate would encounter the full weight of employee bargaining power. The guaranty avoids this conflict by fixing the minimum weekly wage." In effect, Belo paid 73 cents an hour for hours up to 54.5 and $1.00 an hour thereafter "expressed in the circumlocution of time and a half 67 cents...." So long as the weekly guarantee and the real overtime rate remained unchanged, the base hourly rate, the hours for which that rate was paid, and the alleged overtime premium were mere bookkeeping conveniences that could vary without affecting total earnings. Consequently, the number of hours that employees had to work to earn the guarantee could be increased by manipulating the other variables: "By such a verbal device, astute management may avoid many of the disadvantages of ordinary overtime, chief of which is a definite increase in the cost of labor as soon as the hours worked exceed the statutory workweek. If the intention of Congress is to require at least time and a half for overtime work beyond a fixed maximum...40, 42 or 44 hours..., that intention is frustrated by today's holding. ... Because there is no increase in labor cost between the statutory maximum and the hours contracted for (54 ½), the employer has a financial inducement to require hours beyond the statutory maximum."[331]

Commenting on the inconsistencies between *Overnight Motor Transportation* and *Belo*, the editors of *The New York Times* once again lambasted the law for creating absurdities by extending to higher-paid employees an overtime provision "designed to protect submarginal workers" and called for revision of the FLSA.[332] In the wake of these twin decisions, some defendant-employers sought to justify their overtime practices of paying fixed weekly wages for fluctuating hours as governed by *Belo*, while the WHD and aggrieved workers argued that *Overnight Motor Transportation* was controlling. Only employers that failed to include an hourly rate or to indicate an upper limit on the length of the work week and to repeat the talismanic words that the employee was to be paid time and a half the regular rate (or stated a contractual regular rate "completely unrelated to the

---

[330]*Fair Labor Standards Act Amendments: Hearings Before a Subcommittee of the Senate Committee on Labor and Public Welfare*, 80th Cong., 2d Sess., Pt. 1 at 506 (1948) (testimony of Irving Levy, counsel, UAW).

[331]Walling v. A. H. Belo Corp., 316 U.S. at 637-39 (dissent).

[332]"Wage-Hour Interpretations," *N.Y. Times*, June 12, 1942, at 30, col. 3, 4.

payments actually and normally received each week") for overtime wound up owing back overtime wages.[333]

In 1947, in the midst of congressional turmoil over making significant revisions to the FLSA, the Supreme Court upheld the vitality of *Belo* against another challenge by the WHD. The Halliburton Oil Well Cementing Company, which before enactment of the FLSA had paid its oil well service workers fixed monthly salaries, adopted a weekly guarantee like Belo's, which the Wage and Hour Administrator pressured it to abandon in 1942 , but which it reinstated later that year after the Supreme Court upheld Belo's plan. Halliburton issued contracts agreeing to pay the workers a regular basic hourly rate for the first 40 hours, and guaranteeing a specified weekly amount for regular time and such overtime as the business required. Although the regular rate exceeded the minimum wage, it "was always so related to the guaranteed flat sum that the employee became entitled to more than the guarantee only in weeks in which he worked more than 84 hours."[334]

Despite the fact that the wage plan was more egregious than Belo's not only because the real overtime threshold was 30 hours higher, but because in 20 percent of the workweeks, the employees worked more than 84 hours, the Court upheld Halliburton's arrangement because it did not differ materially from Belo's and Congress had never intervened to modify the overtime provision during the five years since that case had been decided.[335]

7. The Workers: From the Struggle Against Overtime Work to the Struggle for Overtime Premiums

[I]n the past...say 15 years ago, we didn't have any cases of suspensions or discharges for refusal to work overtime. In the past I'm told, and I find it hard to believe, but overtime at Chevron U.S.A. was a privilege.

---

[333]E.g., Walling v. Stone, 131 F.2d 461 (7th Cir. 1942); Seneca Coal & Coke Co., v. Lofton, 136 F.2d 359 (10th Cir. 1943); Walling v. Youngerman-Reynolds Hardwood Co., 325 U.S. 419, 425 (1945) (quote). In this last case, the employer contractually specified an hourly rate above the statutory minimum, but below the workers' actual regular rate based on their guaranteed piece rates. James Durkin, national representative of the United Office and Professional Workers of America, testified at a FLSA hearing in 1945 that under a "monstrous formula" sanctioned by WHD Interpretative Bulletin No. 4, an office worker with a fixed weekly salary of $40 for a fluctuating work week would find his hourly rate plummeting from $1 to 66.6 cents when his hours rose from 40 to 60. *Proposed Amendments to the Fair Labor Standards Act: Hearings Before the House Committee on Labor*, 79th Cong., 1st Sess. 413 (1945). This outcome was lawful only if the employer placed an upper limit on the number of weekly hours.

[334]Walling v. Halliburton Oil Well Cementing Co., 331 U.S. 17, 19 (1947).

[335]Walling v. Halliburton Oil Well Cementing Co., 331 U.S. at 21 n.8, 25.

> If they had an employee that they felt was abusing sick time, had an absentee problem, they would tell him he couldn't work any more overtime. Now, it's reversed. Overtime is looked on by the company more or less as a duty. If you want to get out of it, you better have a damned good reason....[336]

Ironically, the onset of the reversal of the secular decline in the length of the workweek coincided with the enactment of the FLSA and advent of World War II: "The goal of the 40-hour week had not yet been attained by 1940...when the defense program got underway"[337] and working hours increased again. In this most tangible sense, the FLSA did not live up to the standard set by the nineteenth-century British factory laws, which, as even Karl Marx admitted, by forcibly limiting the working day, curbed capital's urge for boundless draining of labor power.[338]

Whereas relatively few—and almost no organized—workers actually found their wages increased by the minimum wage provision of the FLSA, many workers began receiving overtime pay by the time the militarization of the economy extended the normal work week beyond forty hours. Of the more than twelve million employees covered by the FLSA in April 1939, the DOL estimated that fewer than 700,000 were receiving less than the statutory minimum (thirty cents); but of the 2,400,000 working overtime (then more than forty-two hours), 1,664,000, or slightly more than two-thirds, were not receiving time and one-half. By far the largest industry that had to reduce hours or pay overtime was sawmills (with more than 100,000 such employees), followed by foundry and machine shops, and furniture manufacturing.[339]

Indeed, while the statutory minimum wage of thirty to forty cents per hour became moot during the war, when a tight labor market made fifty cents the de facto minimum,[340] it was the longer workweek that largely sustained the increase in real weekly earnings.[341] Thus the average workweek for production workers in

---

[336]2 [Califormia] Senate Committee on Industrial Relations, *Interim Hearing on AB 1295—Mandatory Overtime* 350 (testimony of Ruth Bennett, Local 1-5, Oil, Chemical, and Atomic Workers, Chevron U.S.A. Richmond, Cal. refinery).

[337]J. Frederic Dewhurst et al., *America's Needs and Resources* 568 (1947).

[338]1 Marx, *Das Kapital* at 253.

[339]*See First Annual Report of the Administrator of the Wage and Hour Division, United States Department of Labor, For the Calendar Year 1939*, at 36-43, 158-60 (1940).

[340]*See Amendments of the Fair Labor Standards Act of 1938: Hearings Before the Senate Comm. on Education and Labor*, 79th Cong., 1st Sess. chart V at 860 (1945) (statement of Chester Bowles showing straight-time hourly rates of factory workers in the summer of 1945). Whereas in 1942 7,500,000 employees were being paid forty cents or less per hour, by the end of the war the National War Labor Board "automatically approved increases first up to 40 and later to 50 cents and hour." Joel Seidman, *American Labor from Defense to Reconversion* 129 (1976 [1953]).

[341]"Because most factory wage workers are working more intensely and for longer

manufacturing industries rose by one-fifth, from 37.7 hours in 1939 to 45.2 hours in 1945.[342] Overtime compensation peaked at $12 billion in 1943, $3.6 billion of which represented premium rates. In the machinery industry, overtime wages accounted for 27 percent of total wages. At the end of the war it was estimated that if the 40-hour week were restored with no change in wage rates, overall wages would fall by 16 percent and by more than one-third in war industries with the longest hours.[343]

The transition from depression to a full-capacity war economy, characterized by the conversion to continuous, 168-hour per week production,[344] also transformed the functioning and socio-economic purposes behind mandatory overtime payments. Whereas until 1940 the primary purpose of penalty premium rates was to discourage overtime, labor relations scholars have concluded that since World War II they "have come to be regarded by most workers as a special form of compensation offering an attractive form of compensation for additional income rather than as a protection against long or undesirable hours." Automobile industry management before the war, for example, had felt that workers were "becoming more eager for a chance to increase their annual earnings by working longer hours" and that they would "eventually be pressing for a mitigation of the restrictions on hours in the agreements and the act," but that the UAW's policy of permitting the unemployed to retain membership created strong rank-and-file pressure for shorter hours and work-sharing.[345] After the war, automobile collective bargaining agreements even came to safeguard a worker's right to overtime.[346] This transformation of overtime pay "into a means of increasing workers' earnings...took place during World War II, when workers started to rely on premium pay to keep pace with inflation."[347]

Perversely, the very "form of the limitation on hours" that Congress adopted "opened the way to hours far in excess of the standard...." Consequently, during

---

hours, they have been able to maintain their spendable earnings and to save." N. Arnold Tolles, "Spendable Earnings of Factory Workers, 1941-43," 58 *Monthly Lab. Rev.* 477, 478 (1944).

[342]4 *Minimum Wage Standards and Other Parts of the Fair Labor Standards Act of 1938: Hearings Before Subcomm. No. 4 of the House Comm. on Education and Labor*, 80th Cong., 1st Sess. 2618 (1947) (supplementary statement of the Wage and Hour Administrator). *See also* H. M. Douty, "Review of Basic American Labor Conditions," in *Labor in Postwar America* 109, 117-18 (Colston Warne ed. 1949).

[343]Labor Research Association, *Labor Fact Book 7*, at 137-38 (1945).

[344]"'Round the Clock," *Bus. Wk.*, Jan. 10, 1942, at 61-64.

[345]McPherson, *Labor Relations in the Automobile Industry* at 71.

[346]Robert Macdonald, *Collective Bargaining in the Automobile Industry: A Study of Wage Structure and Competitive Relations* 62 (1963).

[347]Ronald Schatz, *A History of Labor at General Electric and Westinghouse 1923-60*, at 159 (1983).

the 1940s and 1950s, as George Brooks, the research director of the International Brotherhood of Pulp, Sulphite and Paper Mill Workers, explained to the Conference on Shorter Hours of Work sponsored by the AFL-CIO in 1957, "the basic meaning and purpose of the law was twisted and changed. It no longer was a standard for hours worked, but a means of increasing income through premium rates." The use of cost-plus contracts during World War II and the progressive reduction of labor costs as a proportion of total costs in the wake of capital intensification of manufacturing conspired to deprive premium rates of their deterrent effect: "Employers did not care. The war-time experience and collective bargaining...have combined to change the whole concept of overtime rates from the idea of a penalty to the idea of privilege. The typical senior worker or the worker 'fortunate' enough to get extra hours regards them as a plum.... In all industries...there has been a concerted effort to increase the...penalty payments, not with the idea of preventing longer hours...but...of increasing income during prosperous times." Indeed, Brooks reported that in his own industry, where paper mills established 36-hour schedules, employees worked 42 hours including six at overtime rates.[348]

Not surprisingly, some in Congress during the war sought to curtail the right that millions of workers had recently secured to premium pay for over-hours.[349] Statutory overtime could no longer fulfill the function of sharing work as full employment approached during rearmament in 1940-41, but the Wage and Hour Administrator devoted an extraordinary amount of space in his annual report for 1940 to refuting claims that the forty-hour week was inconsistent with national defense preparedness,[350] and two years later continued to defend the overtime provision as "attracting labor in a democratic way, without compulsion, to the war industries where it was needed."[351] President Roosevelt's insistence during one of his fireside chats in 1940 that the emergency did not "justify making the workers of our nation toil for longer hours than now limited by statute"[352] was unintentionally ambiguous since, as Secretary Perkins explained in 1942 to a congressional panel considering a wartime ban on overtime rates for naval

[348]George Brooks, "Historical Background," in AFL-CIO, *The Shorter Work Week* 7-19 at 16-17 (1957).

[349]For a rhetorical description and denunciation of the anti-FLSA drive, see 93 *Cong. Rec.* 2266 (1947) (statement of Sen. Thomas, D. Ut.).

[350]U.S. DOL, WHD, *Annual Report for the Fiscal Year Ended June 30, 1940*, at 1-72.

[351]U.S. DOL, *Fair Labor Standards in Wartime: Annual Report, Wage and Hour Division, Public Contracts Division, For the Fiscal Year Ended June 30, 1942*, at 3-4 (1943).

[352]Fireside Chat of May 26, 1940, in *The Public Papers and Addresses of Franklin D. Roosevelt: 1940 Volume: War—And Aid to Democracies* 230-40 at 237 (1941).

contractors, the FLSA "permits unlimited hours per day and per week...."[353] Little wonder that the *Times* was amused by the flip-flop executed during the war by liberals who, in response to proposals for a longer 48-hour week, argued that the overtime provisions did not regulate or limit hours at all, but merely prevented exploitation.[354]

Ideologically, then, the war was a propitious time for employers to urge that "'the penalty for overtime should be canceled during the emergency to encourage a longer work week.'" The chairman of General Motors, Alfred P. Sloan, Jr., advocated this course: "'[I]f we increase the work week and pay a penalty, the result is to increase wages about 8 per cent. We get nothing for this 8 per cent because efficiency, manifestly, is not increased, therefore the result is a step toward inflation. ... Frankly, I do not believe in "something for nothing"....'" The Wage and Hour Administrator heaped ridicule on Sloan's proposal by focusing on the ratio between GM's most recent annual profit of $183,000,000 and payroll of $386,000,000: "'Which is the more inflationary, an 8 per cent increase for the workers or profits almost half as large as total payroll?'"[355]

A number of bills were introduced in 1942 to relieve employers (and ultimately the Treasury, which was paying the bills submitted by war contractors) of the burden of premium pay.[356] Senator O'Daniel of Texas seized the initiative in March with a bill that would have eliminated all restrictions on hours of labor and provided the same wage for all hours.[357] In explaining a later version of the bill, the senator may not have been indulging in hyperbole when he stated: "The change would please practically every employer of labor in America. They would rejoice at having the legislative shackles of premium pay for so-called overtime removed."[358] O'Daniel's explanation of the effect of the elimination of premium pay was novel: while the bill neither compelled workers to work overtime nor dealt with hourly wages at all, it did

> embrace the age-old, time tested, true economic philosophy that an employee should be paid the full amount per hour that his services are worth for each and every hour that he works, instead of being paid less per hour for earlier hours of the day when he is most efficient and productive, and more per hour for the later hours, when he may be fatigued

---

[353]*Hearings on H. R. 6790, to Permit the Performance of Essential Labor on Naval Contracts Without Regard to Laws and Contracts Limiting Hours of Employment* at 2627.

[354]"The Forty-Hour Week," *N.Y. Times*, June 14, 1942, sect. IV, at 10, col. 2 (editorial).

[355]"Fleming Defends Overtime Pay Rate," *N.Y. Times*, Jan. 9, 1941, at 17, col. 7.

[356]For a brief and uninspired account, see Roland Young, *Congressional Politics in the Second World War* 59-61 (1956).

[357]88 *Cong. Rec.* 2380 (1942) (S. 2373).

[358]88 *Cong. Rec.* 8705 (1942) (S. 2884).

and less productive, as our present 40-hour workweek law provides.[359]

Decades earlier, Alfred Marshall, who codified Anglo-American neoclassical economics, had offered an inverted subjectivist last-hour fable: "[M]ost persons...are glad when the hour for stopping arrives: perhaps they forget that the earlier hours of work have not cost them as much as the last: they are rather apt to think of nine hours' work as costing them nine times as much as the last hour; and it seldom occurs to them to think of themselves as reaping a producer's surplus or rent, through being paid for every hour at a rate sufficient to compensate them for the last, and most distressing hour."[360]

O'Daniel failed to explain why workers would willingly work overtime hours when their productivity was lower and thus employers should have paid them less or why employers prior to the FLSA voluntarily paid premium wages to induce workers to work additional hours during which both knew that their productivity declined. As a stevedoring company president observed just a few years later, although he "quite assuredly" would work his employees more overtime if the premium were only five cents an hour, "we basically want to work the maximum amount of straight time.... [I]f we are working men for eight hours and have to lap into overtime, we get less work performed. There is a fatigue proposition which you cannot escape. The productivity after a certain number of hours is on the downhill."[361]

Labor relations realpolitik under the special balance of forces created by world war compelled employers to approach the issue of overtime undogmatically. After all, as *Business Week* noted, even nonunion employers "might hesitate to abandon policies shaped by the 40-hour law" because they feared that such a reversion to longer hours without premium pay would merely provoke unionization efforts.[362] While testifying in 1942 before the House Naval Affairs Committee on these FLSA bills, William Witherow, the president of the NAM, "the most influential ideological holding company for American industry,"[363] revealed what was at stake if equilibrium were disturbed:

One provision of the bill...would deal with one of the Nation's most vexing

---

[359]88 *Cong. Rec.* 8705 (1942).

[360]Alfred Marshall, *Principles of Economics* 438 (8th ed. 1969 [1890]).

[361]Testimony of Frank W. Nolan, in Bay Ridge Operating Co. v. Aaron, Transcript of Record at 124.

[362]"40-Hour Fight?" *Bus. Wk.*, May 17, 1941, at 45, 47.

[363]Clark Kerr, "Employer Policies in Industrial Relations, 1945 to 1947," in *Labor in Postwar America* 43, 47 (Colston Warne ed. 1949). A sampling of radical contemporary opinion about the NAM may be gleaned from "Messiahs of Feudalism," 52 *Christian Century* 1615 (1935); "The NAM through the Ages," 93 *New Republic* 184 (1937); Alfred Hirsh, "What is Big Business Up to?" *Forum*, July 1938, at 3.

problems—one that has caused the most vehement, spontaneous outpouring of public resentment for many years—the questions of overtime pay after 40 hours of work.

It is obviously impossible to reconcile the spirit of the law that admittedly was designed to discourage utilization of manpower for more than 40 hours each week with a Nation-wide demand for all-out production effort. All the rhetoric in the world cannot disguise the fact that the two ideas just do not "jibe" with each other. ... And there is no question that of the two the public prefers the all-out production effort....[364]

Nevertheless, Witherow had to concede that, given "the practical realities of employment relations," neither he nor anyone else could unambiguously answer the question as to whether abandoning the overtime premium would speed production.[365] The NAM president finally fleshed out the reason for his reluctance to attack overtime pay:

For many months employees in many industries have been used to weekly pay checks considerably higher than before, primarily because of high overtime rates. To decrease this weekly pay check by the amount of overtime in it—without simultaneously freezing wage rates at their existing levels—would have one definite tendency. In all probability, there would be a widespread demand by unions throughout the country for an increase in basic hourly rates to a point off-setting the loss of overtime. This would normally stimulate increased labor difficulties and even if it did not increase strikes, it would increase the time management would be forced to take from our all-important projection job in order to sit around the negotiation table. I cannot believe that this would help production.[366]

The NAM's forthright acknowledgment that the campaign to suspend overtime premiums might easily turn into a Pyrrhic victory—an acknowledgment which the chairman of the War Production Board and the president of the CIO also made, albeit indirectly[367]—was in large part dictated by the fact that Congress rather than millions of individual consumers was footing the bill for war production. That employers did not, however, intend to play dead was obvious from Witherow's remark that "abandoning the 40-hour overtime is far less important at this time as a step to speed up production than several other constructive measures" before the Naval Affairs Committee chief among which was eliminating the closed shop.[368] Large corporations' reluctance to force the issue of overtime was probably also dictated by the realization that premium overtime payments were more than

---

[364]*Hearings on H.R. 6790* at 2843.

[365]*Hearings on H.R. 6790* at 2843.

[366]*Hearings on H.R. 6790* at 2844.

[367]*Hearings on H.R. 6790* at 2576, 2770 (statement of Donald Nelson and testimony of Philip Murray).

[368]*Hearings on H.R. 6790* at 2845.

compensated for by the savings inherent in operating expensive capital equipment longer workweeks. Eighty years after Karl Marx had recognized this positive impact of longer hours, even at higher overtime wages, on the rate of profit,[369] the BLS published the results of its study of large corporations producing war-related output revealing the profit-enhancing effect of overtime.[370]

The NAM's logic also implicitly raised the larger inverse question: Does the introduction of overtime work and pay tend to depress basic wage rates? This same question was raised at the same hearings by Secretary of Labor Perkins, whose testimony impressively resembled Witherow's. She argued that if Congress eliminated overtime premiums and thus reduced total weekly wages, "[i]t will be just as natural as getting up in the morning to increase basic wage rates if this little extra, which comes in the form of overtime pay and which has been just about enough to meet the increases in the cost of living, is taken away from them at this time." Indeed, Perkins went far beyond employers in her idiosyncratic praise of overtime, warning that if labor markets and unions reacted by pushing up basic wage rates, "the country would be left with a rigid structure of high wages...instead of the present flexible system which now exists where a man makes more money if he works longer, and less when he works less." Perkins saw overtime premiums as stabilizing wartime employment and combating dysfunctional turnover by enabling workers with "rather comfortable incomes" to reassure themselves: "'Well, I make out pretty well where I am with the overtime.'" The Labor Secretary's testimony culminated in her inadvertent confirmation of the nineteenth-century labor movement's critique of systematic overtime's Sisyphean character: "It is unfortunate for those workers who are able to maintain a subsistence sub-standard of living only by virtue of getting some overtime pay, if the trend to inflation is attacked primarily by eliminating those premium rates for overtime."[371]

Perkins's 1942 testimony was astounding in another respect: while *Belo* and *Overnight Motor Transport* were pending before the Supreme Court, she furnished employers with high authority for their campaign to downgrade the FLSA to a statute in aid of marginal workers. When asked whether the theory behind the law was work spreading, she replied that her congressional testimony in 1937 "was primarily that it was a minimum-wage law. It was a minimum-wage law which had features which regulated the hours, in order that your minimum wages might not become maximum wages." Secretary Perkins went on not only to emphasize that "we all were very careful to urge Congress not to put any absolute daily or weekly

---

[369]3 Karl Marx, *Das Kapital: Kritik der politischen Ökonomie*, in 25 Karl Marx [and] Friedrich Engels, *Werke* 87 (1964 [1894]). See also Karl Marx, *Ökonomische Manuskripte 1863-1867*, in 2:4, Pt. 2 Karl Marx [and] Friedrich Engels, *Gesamtausgabe (MEGA)* 50, 111 (1992).

[370]"Overtime Pay in Relation to Costs and Profits," 53 (1) *Monthly Lab. Rev.* 9-17 (July 1941).

[371]*Hearings on H.R. 6790* at 2631-32.

limitation upon the number of hours,"[372] but to refabricate an entirely new economic policy basis for this effort to avoid undue rigidity that in fact she had never articulated at the 1937 hearings:

> We also pointed out that this type of legislation, providing only for time and a half for overtime, and not limiting the hours of labor, would be extremely useful in case we had one of those high production periods by which American industry has been characterized, where there was a shortage of labor; and that it would be stabilizing because of the fact that it would permit for those brief periods working overtime and paying extra money, and at the same time would provide a natural ladder through which to ascend from the high income levels to the lower income levels that were necessary in a depressed period.[373]

After hearing this claim for the first time, Carl Vinson, chairman of the House Committee on Naval Affairs, reminded Perkins that "the theory upon which we enacted the bill was that that would penalize the employer and spread employment, and therefore if he did not spread the employment, he would be penalized to the extent of time and a half for overtime," and added that she "was proceeding on a different theory, in that the time and a half overtime supplements the weekly pay envelope." Trapped by her own ad hoc opportunistic support for overtime premiums at a time when they could no longer help spread work, the Secretary of Labor sought refuge in feigned ignorance of congressional intent: "I do not know, of course, what was the prevailing view in the mind of the Members of Congress who voted for the bill," and asseverated ("I am sure that I presented that point of view at that time") that even in 1937 she had advocated passage also on the grounds that the bill would "increase wages in proportion to the increase in work without creating a rigid wage structure."[374]

For wholly unrelated reasons *The New York Times* editors persisted in attacking overtime premiums during the war:

> What possible defense, other than a cynically political one, can be made for retaining the legally mandatory time-and-a-half rates beginning at forty hours, now that employers are virtually ordered to work men a minimum of forty-eight hours? The present time-and-a-half provisions cannot be defended even on grounds of "social justice." ... Their result is to give the smallest increases to those who already have the smallest wages, and the biggest increases to those who already have the biggest wages.[375]

---

[372]*Hearings on H.R. 6790* at 2637-38.

[373]*Hearings on H.R. 6790* at 2638.

[374]*Hearings on H.R. 6790* at 2638. For Perkins' 1937 statement and testimony, see *Fair Labor Standards Act of 1937: Joint Hearings* at 173-211.

[375]"Inflation Wins Again," *N.Y. Times*, Feb. 13, 1943, at 18, col. 1, 2.

Ultimately neither O'Daniel's proposed amendment of section 7 of FLSA[376] nor any competing proposal was adopted in 1942[377] or later,[378] but in 1942 President Roosevelt did issue an executive order, which did not affect the overtime provision of the FLSA, banning premium pay for work performed on Saturday or Sunday "except where such work is performed by the employee on the sixth or seventh day worked in his regularly scheduled workweek."[379] And in early 1943 he issued another order stating that no place of employment would be deemed making an effective utilization of manpower if its workweek was less than 48 hours.[380] Despite the fact that the order required employers faced with labor shortages not to hire new workers when they could meet their labor needs by working their current employees 48 hours,[381] the federal government enforced an overtime law originally designed to spread employment.[382] Looking back in 1946, ex-Secretary of Labor Frances Perkins was completely justified in remarking that the overtime provision had been "flexible enough to make it possible to work more than forty hours when necessary, as it was during the war."[383]

8. On the Waterfront: Overtime on Overtime?

[T]he profit motive doesn't seem to be working to prevent the...use of a great deal of

---

[376]*See* 88 *Cong. Rec.* 8706 (1942) (text of proposed S. 2884).

[377]Under S. 2232, submitted by Senator Reed of Kansas, premium pay would not have been mandatory until after forty-eight hours. 88 *Cong. Rec.* 1328 (1942). Many of the other bills introduced in 1942 would have suspended all hours limitations for the duration of the war. H.R. 6616 (Smith, Va.); H.R. 6823 (Peterson, Ga.); H.R. 7731 (Ramspeck); H.R. 6689 (Lambertson); H.R. 6795 (Boren); H.R. 6796 (Wickersham); H.R. 6826 (Colmer); H.R. 6835 (Thomas, Tx.); H.R. 7054 (Cole, N.Y.).

[378]Senator O'Daniel continued to introduce his bill for several sessions as did other Congressmen. In the first session of the Seventy-Eighth Congress (1943) the following bills were offered: S. 190 (O'Daniel); S. 237 (Reed); H.R. 992 (Colmer); H.R. 1804 (Smith); H.R. 2071 (Russell); H.R. 2107 (Curtis); in the first session of the Seventy-Ninth Congress (1945): S. 369 (O'Daniel); H.R. 1194 (Russell); in the second session of the Seventh-Ninth (1946): H.R. 6647 (Dondero); and in the first session of the Eightieth Congress: S. 160 (O'Daniel).

[379]Exec. Order No. 9240 (Sept. 9, 1942). For a discussion of the conflict over non-statutory premium time for weekend work, see Lichtenstein, *Labor's War at Home* at 96-108; "Premium Pay Provisions in Selected Union Agreements," 65 *Monthly Lab. Rev.* 419 (1947).

[380]Exec. Order No. 9301 (Feb. 9, 1943), in 8 *Fed. Reg.* 1825 (1943). President Truman revoked this order by Exec. Order No. 9607 (Aug. 30, 1945), in 10 *Fed. Reg.* 11191 (1945).

[381]War Manpower Commission Reg. 3, § 903.1, in 8 *Fed. Reg.* 7225 (1943).

[382]Harold Metz, *Labor Policy of the Federal Government* 218-19 (1945).

[383]Perkins, *The Roosevelt I Knew* at 266.

overtime....[384]

A third Supreme Court decision, issued in June 1948, was inflated by employers in certain industries, but especially longshore, stevedoring, and shipping, into another financial apocalypse of portal-pay magnitude.[385] In *Bay Ridge Operating Company v. Aaron* the Court held that the statutory regular rate on which time-and-a-half overtime had to be paid included time-and-a-half premium wages that longshoremen were paid for working shifts outside the core daytime hours regardless of how many hours they worked.[386] The International Longshoremen's Association (ILA) joined forces with employers to denounce the lawsuits for overtime that had been brought by individual members of the ILA. As ILA president-for-life Joseph Ryan testified at trial, "our Council went on record as being opposed to trying to get time and a half on time and a half, as it might wipe out all of the gains we had made for our men over a period of 25 years."[387]

About 400 longshoremen and ILA members filed two test suits in October 1947 against two stevedoring companies (one of which, Huron Stevedoring Corporation, was a subsidiary of Grace Lines) for $800,000 in back overtime. The nub of the complaint was that during World War II they had worked 66- to 70-hour weeks on the night shift in the Port of New York without receiving any overtime premium because the employers had taken the position that the $1.875 night shift rate was 150 percent of the regular (day-shift) rate of $1.25. A secondary issue involved day workers who worked a standard 44-hour week with no overtime for the last four hours.[388]

---

[384]1 [California] Senate Committee on Industrial Relations, *Interim Hearings on AB 1295—Mandatory Overtime* at 180 (statement of Sen. Alan Sieroty).

[385]See below chapter 3.

[386]Bay Ridge Operating Co. v. Aaron, 334 U.S. 446, *reh'g denied*, 335 U.S. 838 (1948).

[387]Testimony of Joseph B. Ryan, Transcript of Record at 183, Bay Ridge Operating Co.

[388]"Dock Workers Sue for $800,000 Pay," *N.Y. Times*, Oct. 5, 1945, at 14, col. 6. Intriguingly, the plaintiffs' lawyers were members of the firm of Goldwater and Flynn; Edward J. Flynn was leader of the Bronx Democratic Party (1922-53), chairman of the Democratic National Committee (1940-42), and President Roosevelt's long-time confidant, while Ryan, the ILA president, had long been a leading figure in Tammany Hall. 1 *Amendments to the Fair Labor Standards Act of 1938: Hearings Before the House Committee on Education and Labor*, 81st Cong., 1st Sess. 619 (1949) (testimony of Julius Bagley, attorney representing plaintiff-ILA members); Alfred Clark, "Monroe Goldwater Is Dead at 95," *N.Y. Times*, Nov. 24, 1980, at D11, col. 1 (Lexis); Harold Faber, "Papers of Flynn Go to Hyde Park," *N.Y. Times*, May 20, 1984, sect. 1, pt. 2, at 48, col. 4 (Lexis); Daniel Bell, "The Racket-Ridden Longshoremen: The Web of Economics and Politics," in *idem*, *The End of Ideology: On the Exhaustion of Political Ideas in the Fifties* 175-209 at 194 (rev. ed. 1966 [1960]). Much of Bell's essay, but not the material on the overtime issue, was taken from Daniel Bell, "Last of the Business Rackets," 43 *Fortune* 89-91, 194-

Initially the stevedoring companies prevailed at trial before federal judge Simon Rifkind, himself a New Deal insider.[389] The trial was notable both for the extensive testimony of two prominent scholars about the history of overtime work and for the fact that U.S. government lawyers represented defendant-employers because it would ultimately have been liable for any judgments since the longshoremen had loaded and unloaded ships operating under wartime cost-plus contracts. The federal government's interest in the outcome was intensified by the more than 200 additional suits that had been filed in the interim.[390] At issue was the collective bargaining agreement between the ILA and the defendant employers, which provided for two classes of pay: a straight-time hourly rate of $1.25 for all work performed between 8 a.m. and noon and from 1 p.m. to 5 p.m., Monday through Friday, and from 8 a.m. to noon Saturday, and a so-called overtime rate of $1.875 for work performed at any other time regardless of how many hours the employees worked during those other times. This arrangement had been in effect for decades; the only change that the parties made after the FLSA went into effect was relabeling: wages for the core hours were called "straight time" and all others "overtime rates."[391]

Ryan testified at trial that:

> we did not need the Fair Labor Standards Act. We were able to collective [sic] bargain, and by that bargaining made an eight-hour day and time and a half for overtime. ... We have that without the Fair Labor Act. The only place it helped us was if a fellow was fortunate enough to work eight hours a day, Monday, Tuesday, Wednesday, Thursday and Friday, that before the Fair Labor Act he had to work Saturday morning for four hours at the single rate of pay. After the Fair Labor Act came in, if a man could work those times—it is very seldom a man works five straight days of eight hours, but if we worked five days, previous to last October [1945], before the Fair Standards Act came in, Saturday morning, due to our 44-hour contract, we had to work four hours on Saturday at the straight pay. When the Fair Standards Act came in, if we worked one hour on Saturday morning..., we got time and a half, provided we had the 40 hours in the previous five days.[392]

---

203 (June 1951).

[389]Rifkind had been legislative secretary to and later law partner of Senator Wagner. Eric Pace, "Simon Rifkind, Celebrated Lawyer, Dies at 95," *N.Y. Times*, Nov. 15, 1995, at D20, col. 1 (Lexis). For a report on the decision, see "20 Longshoremen Lose Base-Pay Suit," *N.Y. Times*, Jan. 8, 1947, at 47, col. 4.

[390]Aaron v. Bay Ridge Operating Co., 162 F.2d 665, 668 n.5 (2d Cir. 1947); Petition for Writs of Certiorari at 16.

[391]Aaron v. Bay Ridge Operating Co., 162 F.2d at 672 (Finding of Fact No. 33).

[392]Testimony of Joseph B. Ryan, Transcript of Record at 189-90, Bay Ridge Operating Co.

In fact, however, as Ryan was forced to admit on cross-examination, for seven years the ILA had acquiesced in employers' refusal to pay such Saturday morning overtime.[393] And the plaintiffs were also correct in charging that all that the ILA and the employers had "sought to do...from 1938 on was to perpetuate the prestatutory wage pattern without adjusting their employment relations in any wise to the statutory requirements."[394]

The plaintiff-workers—whom the ILA president mischaracterized at trial as "non-union members who do not know anything about how our organization was built up"[395]—argued that since the higher rate was merely a shift differential for inconvenient night and weekend work, they were entitled to time and a half for any hours above 40. ILA president Ryan sought at trial to characterize the wage-hour structure as driven by anti-overtime sentiments:

> Our objective was to de-casualize longshore work as much as possible, to have the work done in the daytime as much as possible, and make it as expensive for the employers as possible on Sunday. ... We wanted to work in the daytime. We figured we lived only once. We want the daytime when every man who wants to work wants it done in the daytime and not during overtime. The employers would say it cannot be done in the steamship industry. I think we have proven for them that after 30 years of negotiating many of the things they said could not be done in the industry, when they found it too expensive to do it any other way, have been done.[396]

Rifkin saw a "certain plausibility" in both positions: on the one hand, workers who worked only nights received no premium pay after 40 hours; on the other hand, the agreement established a regular rate, of which the employers paid time and a half both for hours beyond 40 and, although the FLSA did not even require it, also for certain shift work. In seeking to reconcile three national policies (the NLRA, FLSA, and the wartime need for maximum production), Rifkind put great store by Ryan's testimony about the ILA's goals as well as by his statement that the suit "'might wipe out all of the gains we have made for our men over a period of 25 years,'" during which there had been no strikes.[397]

Rifkind's decision was driven by his perception that the collectively bargained wage system was the "natural development of a long history" and "not an artificial rearrangement of pre-F.L.S.A. rates of compensation in order to

---

[393]Testimony of Joseph B. Ryan, Transcript of Record at 190-95, Bay Ridge Operating Co.

[394]Brief for Respondents at 76-77.

[395]Testimony of Joseph B. Ryan, Transcript of Record at 177, Bay Ridge Operating Co.

[396]Testimony of Joseph B. Ryan, Transcript of Record at 173, Bay Ridge Operating Co.

[397]Addison v. Huron Stevedoring Corp., 69 F. Supp. 956, 957, 958 (S.D.N.Y. 1947).

avoid additional compensation."[398] He offered examples of superior terms of employment embodied in other collective bargaining agreements to buttress his claim that application of the plaintiffs' approach "would create havoc with established labor relations, put collective bargaining in the category of a device for obtaining money under false pretenses and probably strain the resources of a substantial proportion of American industry."[399] The first example involved a regular contractual workweek of 36 hours although the actual workweek was longer than 40 hours. The workers therefore received time and a half for all hours beyond 36, although the FLSA overtime requirement did not kick in until they had worked 40 hours. Because the average rate for 40 hours included time and a half for four hours, the workers' overtime rate, which was calculated as 150 percent of the straight-time rate for 36 hours, did not include the contractual overtime for hours 36 to 40. Nevertheless, Rifkind saw nothing in the FLSA to foreclose such "bona fide" union contracts. In the other example, a collective bargaining agreement provided for daily time and one-half overtime for hours beyond eight regardless of whether the workers worked 40 hours during that week. In weeks in which they worked five ten-hour days, they therefore received overtime for eight hours included within the first 40 hours, and the rate for hours in excess of 40 (all worked on the fifth day) was less than 150 percent of the average rate for the first 40 hours because it was calculated on the basis of the straight-time rate excluding the contractual overtime premium. Again, Rifkind concluded that applying plaintiffs' approach would merely deter employers from entering into such agreements in the first place.[400]

Finally, Rifkind was persuaded by the voluminous expert testimony that the premium was not merely a shift differential, which traditionally ran to only 5 to 15 cents per hour and was not designed to deter employers from operating, but to attract workers to work during less desirable hours without inhibiting the work. The longshoremen's 50 percent premium was designed to deter and largely succeeded in "curtailing...abnormal hours."[401]

The judge was misled by the trial testimony of the eminent labor historian and economist Philip Taft. Testifying on behalf of the defendant employers, Taft, in response to a question as to whether "overtime" had had a generally accepted meaning before the FLSA, stated that it described "excess time...." After the judge sustained plaintiffs' objection to a follow-up question on the grounds that it was unclear, Rifkind himself intervened to help clarify the concept. Taft

---

[398]Addison v. Huron Stevedoring Corp., 69 F. Supp. at 959-60.

[399]Addison v. Huron Stevedoring Corp., 69 F. Supp. at 959.

[400]Addison v. Huron Stevedoring Corp., 69 F. Supp. at 958.

[401]Addison v. Huron Stevedoring Corp., 69 F. Supp. at 961. Philip Taft testified to this effect about shift premiums; Transcript of Record at 332, 338, Bay Ridge Operating Co.

bluntly denied that "the idea of excessivity [was] an essential element of overtime" before the FLSA. Instead, he argued that it was "made up of two specific ideas, one arising in excess of a particular sequence, and the other may be a specific enumeration of hours." When Rifkind then asked him whether he meant that overtime had meant before 1938 "time in excess of a stipulated period, or...any time, whether in excess of not in excess, which was penalized...in the method of payment," Taft replied that the "two concepts were usually joined together." Yet when the judge asked whether the second concept was ever found without the first, Taft could not recall. But when Rifkind asked the logical follow-up question as to whether after all "excessivity was always an element of the overtime," Taft's replied incoherently: "Only in the sense that the definition was there."[402] Rifkind nevertheless adopted Taft's opinion in his findings of fact, which stated that although "excess time" had generally been the meaning of "overtime" before the FLSA, the "idea of excessivity...was not an indispensable element of the concept of overtime as understood," which also included "hours outside of a specified clock pattern."[403]

The plaintiffs identified the self-contradictory structure of the employers' and the ILA's rhetoric by underscoring that Ryan's testimony concerning the union's purpose in demanding higher rates for night and weekend work "contemplate[d] no deterrent against working long or excessive hours; it merely reflects the natural human desire to work by day and retire at night. But petitioners, following the line of their experts' testimony, urge that overtime as understood in American industry has always included, as an alternative concept, hours outside a basic clock pattern." But, the plaintiffs noted, contrary to Taft's testimony, "virtually all collective contracts include excessivity as an essential element in the computation of overtime."[404] Although the workers argued forcefully that the 50-percent premium for night work was compensation for its "general undesirability" and not for excessivity of hours, they failed, as far as Judge Rifkind was concerned, to rebut the quantitative argument that 50 percent was otherwise never found as the hallmark of a mere shift premium.[405] In fact, a BLS survey of collective bargaining agreements in effect in the second half of 1946 revealed no shift differentials remotely approaching those at issue in the longshore case: many amounted to only a few cents, and none exceeded 15 percent.[406]

---

[402]Bay Ridge Operating Co., Transcript of Record at 325-27.

[403]Findings of Fact 28 (a), Transcript of Record at 604-605, Bay Ridge Operating Co.

[404]Brief for Respondents at 66-67.

[405]Brief for Respondents at 76.

[406]"Premium Pay Provisions in Selected Union Agreements," 65 (4) *Monthly Lab. Rev.* 419-25 at 423-24 (Oct. 1947).

The unanimous Second Circuit decision in June 1947 reversing the district court, though written by the premier realist judge, Jerome Frank, oddly refrained from addressing any of Rifkind's real-world concerns about the potential for undermining collective bargaining and the negotiation of terms superior to those required by the FLSA. Instead, it bloodlessly ruled that the regular rate could not be determined by collective bargaining agreements, but only as an "'actual fact'";[407] the regular rate was therefore to be calculated by dividing total compensation by total hours worked.[408]

After the Second Circuit panel handed down its decision, the workers' lawyers estimated that total back overtime claims for the industry could range between $25 million and $50 million.[409] Two months later, in October 1947, the same lawyers filed two additional suits against 60 stevedoring companies listing 3,000 stevedores as plaintiffs. They deviated from the usual procedure of waiting until the Supreme Court had ruled on the test cases because the Portal-to-Portal Act, which would go into effect in September, had cut the statute of limitations to two years and would have excluded all the world war claims.[410] In its amicus brief in *Bay Ridge Operating Company* before the Supreme Court, the NAM had asserted that if plaintiffs prevailed, the ensuing litigation might exceed that spawned by the *Mt. Clemens Pottery Company* portal-pay decision.[411]

In June 1948, the Supreme Court upheld the workers' claims and rejected the position advocated by the United States and the ILA. The majority, agreeing with the Second Circuit on the regular rate as an actual fact, ruled that it can be calculated by dividing weekly compensation by hours worked unless the compensation includes an overtime premium since "Congress could not have intended" a pyramiding of overtime on overtime, which would have "expanded extravagantly" the scope of liability contemplated by Congress.[412] Without any reasoning, the Court rejected Rifkind's conclusion that the night premium was too large to have been merely a shift premium; it found that the size of the differential "cannot change the fact that large wages were paid for work in undesirable hours...or because the contracting parties wished to compress the regular working days into the straight time hours as much as possible." They

---

[407]Aaron v. Bay Ridge Operating Co., 162 F.2d at 668 (citing 149 Madison Avenue Co. v. Asselta, 331 U.S. 199 (1947)).

[408]Bay Ridge Operating Co. v. Aaron, 334 U.S. 446, 458 (1948).

[409]"Pier Men Upheld on Overtime Pay," *N.Y. Times*, June 8, 1947, at 27, col. 1.

[410]"3,000 Stevedores Sue for Millions," *N.Y. Times*, Aug. 17, 1947, at 16, col. 7. See also below chapter 3.

[411]Brief of the National Association of Manufacturers as Amicus Curiae at 7, Bay Ridge Operating Co. v. Aaron, 334 U.S. 446 (1948). See also "Overtime-on-Overtime—Administrative Interpretations," 10 *N.A.M. Law Digest* 57 (1948).

[412]Bay Ridge Operating Co. v. Aaron, 334 U.S. at 464, 465.

therefore did not fall under the rubric of overtime premium, which the majority held to be "an additional sum received by an employee for work because of previous work for a specified number of hours in the workweek or workday" whether specified by statute or contract.[413]

In an adroitly argued dissent, Felix Frankfurter, joined by Justices Jackson and Burton, provided the sociological underpinning for Judge Rifkind's view that employers should not be deterred from entering into legitimate collective bargaining agreements that offered workers terms superior to those of the FLSA by fears of back overtime liability for wages neither party had ever contemplated paying. Having learned the recent lesson of the portal-pay dispute, Frankfurter warned that Congress would not suffer yet "another doctrinaire construction by the Court of the Fair Labor Standards Act in disregard of industrial realities." Accusing the majority of abstractly treating the FLSA's words "as though they were parts of a cross-word puzzle" rather than "the means by which Congress sought to eliminate specific industrial abuses," Frankfurter charged that the Court had totally disregarded the struggle of a "strong union" against "anarchic exploitation of the necessities of casual labor...." Instead, the majority, getting an arithmetical answer to its own arithmetical question, "substitute[d] an arrangement rejected both by the union and the employers as inimical to the needs of their industry and subversive" of collective bargaining.[414]

Frankfurter argued that since the collective bargaining agreement's objectives of discouraging overwork and underemployment were congruent with the FLSA's, Congress did not authorize the courts to weaken a strong union by undermining its contracts. The dissent also criticized the majority for subjecting collective contracts "to the hazards of self-serving individualism" of a few union members in the absence of any judicially established evidence that the union officials had ignored or betrayed their responsibility and negotiated a sham contract that did not serve the interests of the union as a whole.[415]

These barbs resembled the reproach that the ILA's amicus brief had directed at the plaintiffs for wanting to repudiate what the collective bargaining agreement had established as regular and overtime rates, which were "far higher than those required" by the FLSA. The plaintiffs were then cast in the role of selfish and self-destructive ingrates: "Without collective bargaining these very plaintiffs who now seek overtime and overtime rates ranging up to $3.75 per hour...might, like millions of other American workers, still be working at the $.40 per hour

---

[413]Bay Ridge Operating Co. v. Aaron, 334 U.S. at 469, 475, 471.

[414]Bay Ridge Operating Co v. Aaron, 334 U.S. at 478, 479, 484 (Frankfurter, J., dissenting).

[415]Bay Ridge Operating Co v. Aaron, 334 U.S. at 485-87, 492-93 (Frankfurter, J., dissenting).

minimum provided by the Act."[416]

Curiously, neither Frankfurter nor the majority nor the Second Circuit judges ever alluded to the ILA's extremely undemocratic structure. The entire sociological edifice of Frankfurter's critique should have collapsed under revelation of the fact that the ILA was autocratically run by Joseph Ryan—also known as "King Ryan" after he had himself made president for life in 1943[417]—a corrupt right-winger in cahoots with mobsters and employers.[418] Only the plaintiffs in their Supreme Court brief, and even then only indirectly, hinted at the ILA's less than militant democracy. But even while citing secondary authorities that criticized the central institution of longshore industrial relations, the shape-up, as propagating "'favoritism, bribery, and demoralization,'" the plaintiffs rushed to disavow any "purpose...to advance social reform...."[419]

Evidence establishing the ILA's undemocratic structure and policies was abundantly available. Daniel Bell, later a world-famous sociologist, studying the ILA for *Fortune* in 1951, concluded that the union was one of few in the United States to "encourage cutthroat competition among men for jobs or tolerate a condition of job insecurity."[420] From World War I until the end of World War II, the ILA engaged in a "pattern of economic accommodation...which worked to the benefit of the shipowners and the union barons and against the interest of the men." Ryan could truthfully boast at trial that there was "never a strike since 1907 until 1945,"[421] but the collective bargaining agreements that the union secured "brought few benefits other than miniscule [sic] hourly wage increases for the men. ... The few rebellions...where the Communists sought to gain a foothold...were dealt with summarily."[422] Rebellious members often "get conked on the head."[423] The ILA, as a sociological study of the longshore unions found, "distinguished itself as one of the least effective unions in the country. Judged

---

[416]Brief on behalf of ILA as Amicus Curiae in Support of Petitioners' Petition for Writs of Certiorari at 8-9.

[417]"Longshoremen Plan Fight on Labor Bill," *N.Y. Times*, July 12, 1947, at 2, col. 6; 95 *Cong. Rec.* 1446 (1948) (Rep. Vito Marcantonio). On Ryan's dictatorial methods, see 1 *Amendments to the Fair Labor Standards Act of 1938: Hearings Before the House Committee on Education and Labor*, 81st Cong., 1st Sess. 605-608 (1949) (testimony of Julius Bagley, attorney representing plaintiff-ILA members in overtime suits).

[418]Walter Galenson, *The CIO Challenge to the AFL: A History of the American Labor Movement 1935-1941*, at 436, 448 (1960).

[419]Brief for Respondents at 18-19.

[420]Bell, "The Racket-Ridden Longshoremen," at 181.

[421]Testimony of Joseph Ryan (1946), Transcript of Record at 174, Bay Ridge Operating Co.

[422]Bell, "The Racket-Ridden Longshoremen" at 197.

[423]Matthew Josephson, "Red Skies over the Water Front," 118 *Colliers* 17, 88-90 at 89 (Oct. 5, 1946).

even by the minimal standards of business unionism, the ILA was an abject failure...."[424]

This cozy relationship was threatened, according to Bell, by the overtime lawsuits, which "scared the steamship operators" not only on account of the potentially large back wage liability, but because the need to open the books to determine who was owed how much in wages "might reveal the extent of payroll padding, duplicate hiring, and other practices which, since the government was paying all bills during this period on a cost-plus basis, could only have been conducted on a collusive basis. The shipping companies demanded, therefore, that the union waive all claims for overtime pay." After several twists and turns, including the first strike in the ILA's history in 1948, the union and the employers agreed to urge Congress to overrule the Supreme Court's *Bay Ridge Operating Company*: "It was a rare act of 'sacrifice' on the part of a union: abandoning several millions of dollars of legally entitled back pay...to ensure labor-management 'harmony.'"[425] A few years later even the conservative AFL could no longer ignore the overwhelming record and expelled the ILA for its connections to mobsters and acceptance of bribes from employers.[426]

Representative Angier Goodwin (R. Mass.) quickly became the chief congressional sponsor of amending the FLSA to wipe out any liability for the shipping companies. In July 1947, just a few weeks after the Second Circuit had issued its decision, Goodwin introduced a bill whose long preamble was taken verbatim from the Portal-to-Portal Act, which had been enacted two months earlier, replete with references to "immense" liabilities, serious impairment of capital resources, "financial ruin of many employers," "windfall payments," "champertous practices," and "Nation-wide industrial conflict."[427] Without making any reference to longshoremen, Goodwin's bill would have disposed of "pyramided overtime compensation" simply by entitling "employers and their employees" to fix regular and overtime rates "individually" or through collective bargaining and then prohibiting the use of such a contractual overtime rate in computing the FLSA regular rate.[428] Goodwin also wiped out liability

---

[424]Howard Kimeldorf, *Reds or Rackets? The Making of Radical and Conservative Unions on the Waterfront* 15 (1988).

[425]Bell, "The Racket-Ridden Longshoremen" at 199-201. For a more benign account of the ILA's position, stressing that the contract gave longshoremen more than the FLSA would have given them, and that the ILA's cooperation with employers in opposing the suits and urging congressional amendment of the FLSA merely constituted an effort to preserve the integrity of its collective bargaining agreements along the same lines pursued by other unions, see Vernon Jensen, *Strife on the Waterfront: The Port of New York Since 1945*, at 54-64 (1974).

[426]Kimeldorf, *Reds or Rackets?* at 15.

[427]H.R. 4387, § 1, 80th Cong., 1st Sess. (1947).

[428]H.R. 4387, § 2.

retroactively by depriving the courts of jurisdiction over any actions not in conformity with the new definition of "regular rate" even if those cases had been filed before the new law's effective date.[429]

After Congress had taken no action on Goodwin's bill in the first session of the Eightieth Congress, on April 20, 1948, before the Supreme Court had decided the case, Goodwin, conjuring up exactly the same astronomical figure that he and others had bandied about a year earlier during the portal-pay hysteria,[430] declared to the House of Representatives that (unnamed) "[s]tatisticians have calculated" that a potential liability of "$6,000,000,000. I repeat, $6,000,000,000" loomed like a "monstrous and destructive Frankenstein," bringing with it "ruin and bankruptcy for management in many lines of business." Certifying the correctness of each other's figures, he and Representative Rankin (D. Miss.) engaged in a colloquy forging the "astounding" factoid that $6 billion exceeded the value of the entire wheat and cotton crops.[431]

At a joint conference in New York two weeks later, which urged Congress to intervene to ward off a "'catastrophe of national proportions,'" Representative Goodwin announced that more than fifty industries were threatened by the $6-billion liability. The ILA's lawyer, Louis Waldman, sermonized that the "whole commercial and social structure of the country...was based upon the concept of freedom of contract, which could not be had without good faith. ... He contended that 'the good faith of American labor in dealing with its employers has been thwarted as a result'" of WHD interpretations and court decisions.[432]

Even before the Supreme Court published its *Bay Ridge Operating Company* decision, legislators had initiated the process to relieve employers of past and future liability. Although Senator Ball's omnibus FLSA revision bill, which included an anti-overtime-on-overtime provision, had been introduced earlier in the session,[433] on May 12, 1948, Goodwin introduced a bill devoted exclusively to this issue. It would have redefined "regular rate" to exclude any overtime premium, which was defined to include payment "because the employee has previously worked a specified number of hours during a specified period or

---

[429]H.R. 4387, § 4.

[430]93 *Cong. Rec.* 1497 (1947).

[431]94 *Cong. Rec.* 4652-54 (1948).

[432]"Overtime Revision by Congress Urged," *N.Y. Times*, May 4, 1948, at 51, col. 1.

[433]S. 2386, 80th Cong., 2d Sess. (Mar. 25, 1948). Ball's bill inserted a very lengthy definition of "regular rate" into the definitions section of the FLSA, which would have excluded from "normal, straight-time compensation and...credited to overtime compensation...overtime premiums paid for work performed in excess of the normal weekday or workweek scheduled in good faith by established practice or a collective-bargaining agreement" as well as overtime premiums for work performed on weekends and holidays. *Id.* § 2(n). Ball's bill never got out of committee, and Ball, a Republican from Minnesota, lost his seat in the 1948 election.

because of the time of day or the day of the week or year the work is performed."[434] A week later Goodwin availed himself of yet another forum at a hearing on his bill before a subcommittee of the House Judiciary Committee apparently attended only by Representative John Gwynne, the leading House figure in the previous year's enactment of the Portal-to-Portal Act. Having learned the value of rhetorical overkill in winning that battle, Goodwin, who stressed the "disturbing parallel" to the portal-pay litigation, declared: "There is no more important problem facing American industry today than that raised by a recent judicial interpretation" of the FLSA.[435] Senator Wiley, who had played a leading role in the portal-pay legislation in 1947, filed the companion bill in the Senate.[436]

Pro-labor congressmen belittled Goodwin's legal analysis, predictions, and data. On May 20, Representative Francis Walter (D. Pa.)—just beginning his career as a leading red hunter with the House Committee on Un-American Activities[437]—expressed surprise before the House that anyone could argue that longshoremen's wages fell under the overtime rubric. Moreover, the Portal Act, which the Congress had just passed the previous year, would considerably reduce any liabilities by virtue of its short statute of limitations and the defense it offered employers who relied in good faith on the Administrator's interpretation. In addition to pointing out that since the longshoremen's wage system was unique, other industries were unaffected, Walter stressed that Goodwin's bill and others were in reality designed to "stampede[]" Congress into adopting legislation that "would deprive 20,000,000 workers of the overtime benefits" of the FLSA by permitting employers to "select...anything you wish to be called the regular rate of pay so long as it is 40 cents or more an hour."[438]

In July 1948, employers "breathed a little easier" when the WHD issued an official interpretation indicating that *Bay Ridge Operating Company* "wasn't as far-reaching as many had feared at first." Under the new interpretation—good-

---

[434]H.R. 6534, § 4, 80th Cong., 2d Sess. (1948). The overtime rate also had to be at least one and a half times any lower rate "not proved to be a fictitious rate established by custom or individual labor contract, payable for the same work at other hours of the day or on other days, and includes any other true overtime rate."

[435]Transcript of Proceedings, House Committee on the Judiciary, Subcommittee No. 2, H.R. 6534, at 10, 6-7 (May 20, 1948) (unpublished).

[436]S. 2728, 80th Cong., 2d Sess. (May 24, 1948). Senator Butler filed an identical bill, S. 2832, on June 8.

[437]David Caute, *The Great Fear: The Anti-Communist Purge Under Truman and Eisenhower* 92, 377, 386 (1979) (discussing Walter's efforts to undermine the left-wing United Electrical Workers).

[438]94 *Cong. Rec.* 6204 (1948). Lawyers for the plaintiff-stevedores had stated at the time they filed two additional suits in 1947 that "virtually no overtime is accumulated by longshoremen during peace times." "3,000 Stevedores Sue for Millions."

faith reliance on which would protect employers under the Portal-to-Portal Act—if premium pay for weekend, holiday, or night work was paid only after workers had already worked a specified number of hours or days under some bona fide standard, it qualified as overtime compensation and could be excluded from the calculation of the regular rate.[439] By August 1948, Ryan, the ILA president, appeared even more eager to resolve the issue than the employers. Quoting Representative Fred Hartley, Jr., whose infamously anti-labor bill had just been enacted, he called for a special session of Congress to resolve the question of overtime rates for night workers.[440]

The CIO unions took a different approach than the ILA and the AFL to the "smear campaign...coined 'overtime on overtime,' which is deliberately designed to mislead and confuse the issue."[441] Whereas the AFL supported the proposed amendment of the FLSA as "forestall[ing] a chaotic situation in many industries,"[442] the UAW, though deciding not to file any suits, at the same time declared that it would contest any moves by employers to use *Bay Ridge Operating Company* as a pretext for eliminating premium pay for weekends or holidays or shift differentials.[443] The CIO also attacked AFL unions like the ILA by observing that "we do not believe that unions should be able to trade away time and a half for work after 40 hours in order to get some other benefit. ... We believe that the undermining of uniform overtime standards will again encourage chiselers to gain a competitive advantage at the expense of their employees' wages and living standards."[444]

During negotiations to settle the East Coast dock strike in late 1948, Secretary of Labor Tobin promised stevedoring employers that the Truman administration would submit legislation to Congress overruling the Supreme Court's decision.[445] Expediting its passage as a separate FLSA amendment ahead of enactment of a long overdue increase in the minimum wage, Democrats early in the Eighty-First

---

[439]"New Premium-Pay Rules," *Bus. Wk.*, July 24, 1948, at 94.

[440]"Pier Pay Dispute May Go to Truman," *N.Y. Times*, Oct. 2, 1948, at 31, col. 5.

[441]1 *Amendments to the Fair Labor Standards Act of 1938: Hearings Before the House Committee on Education and Labor*, 81st Cong., 1st Sess. 260 (1949) (resolution adopted by the CIO, Portland, Ore., Nov. 1948).

[442]1 *Amendments to the Fair Labor Standards Act of 1938: Hearings Before the House Committee on Education and Labor*, 81st Cong., 1st Sess. 260 (1949) (328) (statement of Walter Mason, national legislative representative, AFL).

[443]"Easy on Overtime," *Bus. Wk.*, Nov. 13, 1948, at 108.

[444]*Fair Labor Standards Act Amendments: Hearings Before a Subcommittee of the Senate Committee on Labor and Public Welfare*, 80th Cong., 2d Sess., Pt. 2 at 1026 (1948) (statement of Food, Tobacco, Agricultural and Allied Workers of America, CIO).

[445]"Help on Overtime," *Bus. Wk.*, Dec. 18, 1948, at 112; *Amendments to the Fair Labor Standards Act of 1938: Hearings Before the House Committee on Education and Labor on H.R. 2033*, 81st Cong., 1st Sess. at 16.

Congress, control of which had passed back to them with Truman's election, filed a bill in the House to overrule *Bay Ridge Operating Company.* Limited to longshore and construction work, and also purely prospective, H.R. 858 was passed by the House in February.[446] Executing the Truman administration's position that quick action was necessary "to remove serious difficulties in the maintenance of desirable labor standards arrived at through collective-bargaining agreements, and in order to prevent labor disputes,"[447] the Senate Labor Committee, amended the bill both to extend its reach to all of industry and to make it retroactive,[448] as Congress had done with the portal-pay claims two years earlier.[449]

Significantly, one of the reasons Congress adduced for treating the two disputes similarly was the fact that "in both cases, the filing of suits was deplored by responsible A. F. of L. officials...."[450] The electricians unions, for example, declared that it would not oppose employers' efforts to override *Bay Ridge Operating Company* "because it is not our policy to seek gains beyond our agreements."[451] Indeed, the ILA's general counsel coyly testified before Congress that the union did not sponsor retroactivity, but "if the employers can persuade Congress to incorporate retroactivity...we do not oppose it."[452] The CIO, in contrast, did not support the bill because "there was no reason why this overtime problem should be dealt with in advance of modernizing the Wage and Hour Act generally to give relief to the millions of workers who were denied adequate wage and hour protection." The CIO would not have objected to a purely prospective bill limited to longshoring, but it also stressed that the impact of *Bay Ridge Operating Company* had been vastly exaggerated: the Portal-to-Portal Act would wipe out some claims, while others would not stand up because relatively few workers were employed for more than 40 hours by the same employer.[453]

---

[446]H.R. 858, 81st Cong., 1st Sess. (1949).

[447]*To Clarify the Overtime Compensation Provisions of the Fair Labor Standards Act of 1938, as Amended: Hearings Before a Subcommittee of the Senate Committee on Labor and Public Welfare*, 81st Cong., 1st Sess. 2 (1949) (letter from Secretary of Labor Maurice Tobin to Sen. Elbert Thomas, Feb. 18, 1949).

[448]S. 336, 81st Cong., 1st Sess. (1949), from the beginning had applied to all industries, but not retroactively.

[449]See below chap. 3.

[450]S. Rep. No. 402, 81st Cong., 1st Sess., in U.S. Code Cong. Serv. 1949, at 1617, 1626.

[451]*To Clarify the Overtime Compensation Provisions of the Fair Labor Standards Act of 1938, as Amended* at 638 (letter from D. Tracy, pres., IBEW, to Sen. Elbert Thomas).

[452]*To Clarify the Overtime Compensation Provisions of the Fair Labor Standards Act of 1938, as Amended* at 40 (testimony of Louis Waldman).

[453]*To Clarify the Overtime Compensation Provisions of the Fair Labor Standards Act of 1938, as Amended* at 201-202 (statement of Irving Levy, general counsel, UAW,

The Senate passed the so-called overtime-on-overtime bill in May and the customarily choreographed bombastic debates were staged in the House. Proponents of the bill accused some of the lawyers behind the litigation of being communists and characterized the suits themselves as "one of the largest and most vicious rackets in the history of the country and the legal profession."[454] After differences were resolved in conference, President Truman signed it into law in August.[455] The amended FLSA provided that with respect to overtime payable to an employee who is paid for work on weekends, holidays, or the sixth or seventh day of a workweek at a premium not less than time and one-half, "the rate established in good faith for like work performed in nonovertime hours on other days," or who is paid for work outside the basic, normal, or regular workday (up to eight hours) or workweek (up to 40 hours), at a premium rate at least one and one-half times the rate established for like work performed during such workday or -week, the additional compensation of such a premium rate does not count as part of the regular rate.[456]

Later in 1949, when the FLSA was comprehensively revised, this first amendment was repealed[457] and subsumed within the new subsection of the act defining "regular rate" for the first time. Henceforward employers could lawfully exclude from the regular rate and credit against their statutory overtime liability the following categories of premium wages:

> extra compensation provided by a premium rate paid for certain hours worked by the employee in any day or workweek because such hours are hours worked in excess of eight in a day or in excess of the maximum workweek applicable to such employee under subsection (a) or in excess of the employee's normal working hours or regular working hours...;
>
> extra compensation provided by a premium rate paid for work by the employee on Saturdays, Sundays, holidays, or regular days of rest, or on the sixth or seventh day of the workweek, where such premium rate is not less than one and one-half times the rate established in good faith for like work performed in nonovertime hours on other days; or
>
> extra compensation provided by a premium rate paid to the employee, in pursuance of an applicable employment contract or collective-bargaining agreement, for work outside of the hours established in good faith by the contract or agreement as the basic, normal, or regular workday (not exceeding eight hours) or workweek (not exceeding the maximum workweek applicable to such employee under subsection (a)[)], where such

---

representing the CIO).

[454]95 *Cong. Rec.* 9491-92 (1949) (Rep. Werdel, R. Cal.).

[455]See H. Rep. No. 121 and S. Rep. No. 402, 81st Cong., 1st Sess. (1949).

[456]Act of July 30, 1949, § 1, ch. 352, 63 Stat. 446, 446.

[457]Fair Labor Standards Amendments of 1949, Pub. L. No. 393, § 16(f) 63 Stat. 910, 920.

premium rate is not less than one and one-half times the rate established in good faith by the contract or agreement for like work performed during such workday or workweek.[458]

The longshoremen litigation and its congressional consequences raised the same issues that the portal-pay dispute had generated in 1947: what happens when highly paid unionized workers take the initiative in pushing back the outer limits of labor standards legislation the primary beneficiaries of which Congress had never intended them to be?[459] Like the workers demanding to be paid for the time they had to devote to their employers' enterprise in walking to and from their work benches, the longshoremen had a compelling case: they could plausibly argue that they were being deprived of their statutory premium for the double burden of working extra-long hours at night. Their "regular rate" was manifestly the night rate at which they worked and not the lower day rate at which they did not work; under the FLSA, therefore, they seemed squarely entitled to the overtime premium on the night rate.[460] Nevertheless, their congressional opponents had little rhetorical difficulty in lumping them together with portal-pay litigants as pursuing claims totally lacking in "moral substance."[461]

In contrast, the dispute over Belo plan wages for salaried employees working irregular hours did not appear politically misguided. It not only focused on a perceived injustice to overtime workers, but was not confined to union workers; moreover, the campaign to prohibit or at least limit such plans was undertaken primarily not by unions, but by the DOL, which supported the shipping employers (and the ILA) in the longshoremen cases. That the DOL and workers also lost this battle does not undermine the judgment that, unlike the portal-pay dispute, it was not a self-destructive contest.

What New Deal insider-judges Rifkind and Frankfurter were really saying was that the longshoremen and their lawyers underrated the importance of Realpolitik: not only had the Congress in 1937-38 not intended the FLSA to give such additional legislative leverage to strong unions, but neither the Republican Eightieth Congress nor, as it turned out, the Eighty-First governed by a Republican-Southern Democratic coalition would ever put up with such legalistic readings. Because a quasi-monopolistic (albeit undemocratic and corrupt) union

---

[458]Fair Labor Standards Amendments of 1949, § 7(d)(5-7), 63 Stat. at 914 (codified at 29 U.S.C. § 7(e) (5-7)).

[459]See below chapter 3.

[460]The Supreme Court faulted the U.S. government's argument for treating "of the entire group of longshoremen instead of the individual workmen.... The straight time hours can be the regular working hours only to those who work in those hours." Bay Ridge Operating Co. v. Aaron, 334 U.S. at 473.

[461]95 *Cong. Rec.* at 9493 (Rep. Werdel citing magazine article).

had cut a long-term and stable deal with employers to secure relatively high wages for their members, Rifkind and Frankfurter were willing to bend the FLSA to avoid a super-contractual wage their political sense told them Congress had never contemplated. They may also have speculated that the litigation strategy would have been futile in any event since employers, had they been forced to pay significant additional sums in the future for night-overtime, might merely have bargained for lower base rates to hold themselves harmless. Ironically, however, unlike the portal-pay plaintiffs, the longshoremen's judicial victory would have been less costly to their employers since night-overtime was largely a creature of World War II and did not represent a major future liability.

The most untoward consequence of the longshoremen's litigation was the political space that it fruitlessly occupied that could otherwise have been devoted to more vital struggles to expand the FLSA for workers for whom the FLSA was clearly designed. Two of the most important efforts that were crowded out of the legislative agenda in 1949 were raising the minimum wage to $1.00 (instead of 75 cents), for which, for example, the Americans for Democratic Action was lobbying,[462] and which Congress did not enact for another six years,[463] and extending minimum wage coverage to farmworkers in so-called industrial agriculture[464]—a measure that did not become law until 1966.[465]

9. Taking Care of Business: Congress Cuts Overtime Coverage in 1949

> Henry Ford announced yesterday that his contribution to the Wilson campaign would be a country-wide eight-hour day propaganda. This will be spread from every point where there is a Ford agency.... "I am in favor of the passage of a Federal law that will make eight hours the national working day. ... There is no business where the employes cannot be worked eight hours a day and no more," he said. "If they can't do it, then the business is not properly managed."[466]

The war and Democratic control of Congress frustrated employers' initial efforts to revise the FLSA overtime provisions. When Republicans gained

---

[462]2 *Amendments to the Fair Labor Standards Act of 1938: Hearings Before the House Committee on Education and Labor*, 81st Cong., 1st Sess. 1014-15 (1949) (testimony of Joseph Rauh, chairman of exec. comm., ADA).

[463]Fair Labor Standards Amendments of 1955, Pub. L. No. 381, § 3, 69 Stat. 711.

[464]1 *Amendments to the Fair Labor Standards Act of 1938: Hearings Before the House Committee on Education and Labor*, 81st Cong., 1st Sess. 435 (1949) (testimony of Lazare Teper, research director, International Ladies Garment Workers Union).

[465]Fair Labor Standards Amendments of 1966, Pub. L. No. 601, 80 Stat. 830.

[466]"Ford Plans Great Wilson Propaganda," *N.Y. Times*, Oct. 7, 1916, at 3, col. 1-2.

control of the Eightieth Congress in 1947, big business's priorities were legislative intervention to put a stop to the thousands of portal-pay suits that had been filed for travel and wash-up time under the FLSA,[467] and enacting the Taft-Hartley amendments to undermine union power under the NLRA. Once those missions had been accomplished, employers turned their attention to other restrictions on their ability to deploy labor as they saw fit. Thus despite widespread wartime coverage in the business press of findings that longer workweeks led to less than proportional increases in output,[468] demonization of the 40-hour week became a propagandistic priority among large employers in 1947.

Hearings on FLSA revision held by the House Labor Committee late that year give a good sense of what firms found restrictive about the law and how far they intended to roll back labor standards legislation. In the course of the FLSA hearings, Representative Owens (R. Ill.), taking up the cause that employers had lost in1942, suggested that premium overtime payments be calculated only on the basis of the minimum wage, leaving organized workers to bargain for any additional overtime.[469] The Wage and Hour Administrator devoted 10 small-print pages to criticizing various proposals by employers ranging from outright repeal of the overtime provision, reducing the regular rate to the statutory minimum wage, extending the non-overtime workweek to 48 hours, to excluding piece-rate workers from the overtime provision.[470] A submission by a group of nineteen manufacturing companies in Cleveland employing more than 50,000 workers reveals the depth of the resentment harbored by unreconstructed northern industrial employers:

> Unfortunately, many people have forgotten, and a large majority of people have never known, that the effect of the overtime-pay provisions of the Federal Fair Labor Standards Act was to place a limit on the number of hours that the productive facilities of this Nation might be worked. ...
>
> Whatever arguments might have existed in 1938 for sharing the work no longer exist now. With prices...already too high because of shortages of goods, and with many nations...in desperate circumstances and crying out for the goods we might produce, it outrages every economic law to continue with a Government-imposed penalty to prevent

---

[467]See below chap. 3.

[468]E.g., "Overtime Can Tell," *Bus. Wk.*, Mar. 24, 1945, at 98.

[469]4 *Minimum Wage Standards and Other Parts of the Fair Labor Standards Act of 1938: Hearings Before Subcommittee No. 4 of the House Committee on Education and Labor*, 80th Cong., 1st Sess. 2515-17 (1948).

[470]"Supplementary Statement of the Administrator, Wage and Hour and Public Contracts Division, United States Department of Labor, on Proposed Amendments to the Fair Labor Standards Act," in 4 *Minimum Wage Standards and Other Parts of the Fair Labor Standards Act of 1938* at 2594, 2609-19.

the operation of this Nation's productive facilities more than 40 hours a week.[471]

To underscore just how superfluous the FLSA overtime provision was, the Cleveland manufacturers told a tale of a golden age of bilateral negotiational harmony long before the FLSA had been enacted and "unions had attained their present great bargaining power." Even back then it was employers'

> practice to pay premium rates when they wanted work done after regular working hours.
> The custom began years ago when working hours were 10 or more a day. A rush order or an emergency situation would arise requiring work past the customary hours. The employer would ask an individual employee, or a group of employees, to work overtime to meet the situation. Frequently the men would say they wanted to go home. Then an informal bargaining process would begin, in which the employer attempted to induce the men to stay by offering a premium of time and one-tenth, or time and one-fourth. The point was thus voluntarily determined at which the disinclination of men to work was overcome by their desire for additional money.[472]

Since such voluntary premium rates had been "part of the fabric of custom throughout American industry" even in nonunion plants before 1938, it would be even more the case by 1947 when unions "had grown to be the power they are...." But the Cleveland manufacturers preferred bargaining to congressional imposition of premium rates because it was less arbitrary and more flexible. More importantly, they charged, the function of premium rates—"induc[ing] men to do that which they ordinarily would not want to do, namely work overtime"—had been turned on its head: building trades unions in Cleveland, using "duress and threat of strike," had negotiated double-time rates for Saturday work and "then turned around and informed the contractor that unless he scheduled the tradesmen to work Saturdays on a regular basis, the men would not work the other days of the week." The next step in this union plot was "obvious": "Assured of Saturday work at double time, some men then take a day off in the middle of the week, but still draw 6 days' pay for working only 5."[473]

But the Cleveland manufacturers did see a ray of hope in the silent compulsions of the labor market: "With today's high living costs, there are many workmen who would be glad to gain extra money by working five and a half or six-hour days at straight time. It is their right to so elect. This would give them

---

[471] 4 *Minimum Wage Standards and Other Parts of the Fair Labor Standards Act of 1938* at 2846.

[472] 4 *Minimum Wage Standards and Other Parts of the Fair Labor Standards Act of 1938* at 2846.

[473] 4 *Minimum Wage Standards and Other Parts of the Fair Labor Standards Act of 1938* at 2847.

extra money with which to pay bills...." Unfortunately, the FLSA stood in the way of such a consensual extension of the normal workweek to 48 hours. Why all of a sudden that ancient custom of paying more to induce men to work more than they cared to was no longer in play, the manufacturers did not reveal. All they knew was that the mandatory FLSA overtime premium "in...most cases...absolutely bars employers from scheduling their operations more than the statutory maximum without penalty. Thus, men lose wages, and the Nation loses goods."[474] How, when all U.S. manufacturers faced exactly the same overtime cost structure, and, as much of rest of the industrial world lay in ruins, they produced half of world manufacturing output,[475] a slightly higher wage bill could possibly generate such disastrous consequences, the Cleveland employers did not bother explaining.

Dubious, apparently, of the likelihood of direct repeal of the overtime provision, the Cleveland group sought a legislative second-best: it urged Congress to enact a special provision permitting 48-hour workweeks at straight-time rates in any establishment in which a majority of employees authorized such an extension. The manufacturers sought to ward off any claims that they were merely demanding longer hours at lower pay by observing that "large number of workmen already accept work outside of their employment after working hours and on Saturdays to augment their regular incomes." Since they were willing to work for a second employer at straight-time wages (which were probably lower than those of their primary job), why should they be deprived of this same opportunity for an additional eight hours with their primary employer? After all: "Large numbers of American workmen are thrifty and industrious. Why deny them the right to utilize fully their time in the establishment where unquestionably they are paid the most, and deny their regular employer the use of his best trained and most competent help?"[476]

Other employer groups were not so timid as the Clevelanders. An umbrella organization of 46 industrial associations, including numerous state, local, and manufacturing associations spread all over the United States, urged outright repeal of the statutory overtime premium. Denying any desire to "'chisel,'" the group asserted that the FLSA simply "does invade the right of employer and employee to arrive at a more satisfactory arrangement than the law requires...." And in the wake of the launching of the Marshall Program and "[o]ur crying need today...for production, more production, more production," it concluded that "the

---

[474]4 *Minimum Wage Standards and Other Parts of the Fair Labor Standards Act of 1938* at 2847.

[475]W. S. Woytinsky and E. S. Woytinsky, *World Population and Production: Trends and Outlook* 1004-1005 (1953).

[476]4 *Minimum Wage Standards and Other Parts of the Fair Labor Standards Act of 1938* at 2851.

whole problem of overtime can be approached more intelligently through employment contracts than by statute."[477]

During the second session of the Eightieth Congress in 1948, employers shifted their focus toward raising the threshold triggering overtime or eliminating the premium altogether.[478] The NAM urged the "very drastic change" that anything above the minimum wage exceeded "the field which...the statute should have anything to do with." It clearly voiced employers' increasing irritation that "[m]ost of the problems in the last 6 years have been concerned with employees who receive double, or three or four times" the minimum wage and "this hair-splitting" over whether overtime had to be paid on bonuses and other fringes.[479] Before those plans could succeed, however, President Truman's surprise victory over Dewey and the Democrats' majority in the Eighty-First Congress emboldened labor and its legislative supporters to push for higher FLSA standards and broader coverage. But labor unions overestimated their congressional strength and in the end their drive to "modernize" the FLSA in the wake of the transition of the U.S. economy from depression to international domination[480] fell victim to a pro-employer Republican-Southern Democrat coalition, which thwarted not only efforts to expand FLSA coverage, but also to undo Taft-Hartley.[481]

In March 1948, the management magazine *Modern Industry* published a debate between Secretary of Labor Lewis Schwellenbach and a right-wing economist, Lewis Haney, over suspension of the statutory overtime premium. Noting that "[m]any employers are emphatically in favor of tossing it into the ashcan," the magazine asked whether Joe Worker and management would benefit from a reduction in overtime pay.[482] Conjuring up an "inflation emergency," Haney's diatribe culminated in the assertion that a 40-hour week with time and a half thereafter was "the essence of inflation." Reluctant to advocate a "disastrous deflation in dollar wages," he viewed increased output without a wage

---

[477]4 *Minimum Wage Standards and Other Parts of the Fair Labor Standards Act of 1938* at 2852-53, 2855 (quote).

[478]"Wage-Hour Changes Coming?" *U.S. News & World Report*, Nov. 28, 1947, at 22-23.

[479]*Fair Labor Standards Act Amendments: Hearings Before a Subcommittee of the Senate Committee on Labor and Public Welfare*, 80th Cong., 2d Sess., Pt. 2 at 938 (1948) (testimony of Raymond Smethurst, counsel, NAM).

[480]*Amendments to the Fair Labor Standards Act of 1938: Hearings Before the House Committee on Education and Labor on H.R. 2033*, 81st Cong., 1st Sess. 262 (1949) (statement of Solomon Barkin, chairman, CIO Committee on Revision of the FLSA).

[481]James Gross, *Broken Promise: The Subversion of U.S. Labor Relations Policy, 1947-1994*, at 42-57 (1995) (on the NLRA).

[482]"Should the 40-Hour Week Be Suspended?" 15 (3) *Modern Industry* 110-18 at 110 (Mar. 15, 1948).

increase as the only solution: "all laborers who can do so" had to be "allow[ed] and encourag[ed]...to work longer hours at their regular rate of pay. ... It took over 45 hours a week to win the war.... It will take much more than 40 hours to win the peace."[483]

The seriousness with which capital was pursuing a rollback of the FLSA was signaled by the forceful advocacy by the president of General Motors, Charles E. Wilson, of the 45-hour week. Delivering a talk entitled, "Can We Win the Peace with the Forty-Hour Week?" to the Cleveland Chamber of Commerce in April 1948, he reproached labor for having "made a 'sacred cow' of the forty-hour week when it was meaningless, when the welfare of the country was at stake." Wilson insisted that he was not "'advocating a plan that would reduce the compensation workmen are now receiving for forty-five hours. ... I am not advocating more work for the same pay. I am advocating more pay for more work.'"[484] Since the FLSA's much ballyhooed flexibility already permitted workweeks of any length provided that employers paid time and a half, Wilson's rhetoric made little sense. Lesser capital demanded even more. The National Small Business Men's Association proposed outright repeal of the FLSA.[485]

While capital was demanding more work, the AFL returned to its Depression-era theme of work-spreading. In January 1949, its Shorter Work-day Committee warned that when the Marshall Plan and rearmament no longer sufficed to "'carry us along,'" it would press for the thirty-hour week.[486] By September, the AFL Executive Council reported to the organization's annual convention that a shorter standard work day and week were needed. Viewing the long-term and postwar sweep of U.S. economic development as shaped by a persistent gap between strong productivity increases and lagging (working-class income) resulting in debilitating periodic unemployment, the AFL argued: "'While shorter hours alone cannot perform the full task of the expansion of job opportunities that will be needed in an ever-growing degree, it can make a very important contribution to the achievement of that aim. It is furthermore an entirely worthwhile end in itself, and a historic one for labor.'"[487]

The pro-labor Democrats expeditiously held hearings at the end of January and beginning of February 1949 on the administration's bill, H.R. 2033,[488] and

---

[483]Lewis Haney, "Should the 40-Hour Week Be Suspended? Yes," 15 (3) *Modern Industry* 111-16 at 113, 111 (Mar. 15, 1948).

[484]"C. E. Wilson Renews 45-Hour-Week Plea," *N.Y. Times*, Apr. 21, 1948, at 24, col. 3.

[485]"Want Labor Act Changed," *N.Y. Times*, July 1, 1948, at 40, col. 2.

[486]"AFL for 30-Hr. Week in Event of Slump," *N.Y. Times*, Jan. 3, 1949, at 6, col. 3.

[487]Joseph Loftus, "Fewer Hours with Same Pay Urged on AFL Convention," *N.Y. Times*, Oct. 3, 1949, at 1, col. 6, at 10, col. 2.

[488]*Amendments to the Fair Labor Standards Act of 1938: Hearings Before the House*

reported out a revised bill, H.R. 3190 (introduced by the chairman of the House Labor Committee, Representative Lesinski) in March. The bill, which was never enacted and failed even to reach the House floor, revealed unions' overoptimism. The committee's point of departure was the conviction that employers had succeeded in frustrating the attainment of the overtime provision's three objectives—shortening the workweek for workers' health, efficiency, and well-being, spreading work, and compensating workers for the burdens of long weeks—"by the use of two devices which have been held by the courts not to violate the present act, although their effect is to deny to an employee the full 50 percent premium for overtime work.... This bill would outlaw these devices." The Belo plan was defective in the committee's view because the "fact that the employee is paid time and one-half this [contractually assigned] rate...when he works in excess of the number of hours covered by the guaranty does not...justify failure to pay full time and one-half for each hour after 40, based on the pay to which the employee is entitled when he works only 40 hours."[489]

The other device, which the Supreme Court upheld in *Overnight Motor Transportation Co. v. Missel*, had, according to the House Labor Committee report, "been variously described as 'Chinese overtime,' the galloping rate,' or the 'fluctuating workweek.'"[490] The name "coolie or Chinese overtime," the president of the Office Employees International Union (AFL) explained to Congress, derived from the fact that the more hours an employee worked during a week, the lower his hourly pay.[491] Under this arrangement, workers were paid a fixed straight-time weekly salary regardless of how many hours they worked so that their regular rate, on which the overtime rate was based, decreased as the workweek increased. As the House Labor Committee noted: "The curious result of this method of calculation is that this employee, who would earn $1.25 an hour at straight time if he worked only 40 hours, can average only 78 cents an hour for the entire workweek, including overtime pay, if he works twice as long. It is apparent that the objectives of the act's overtime provisions are defeated by such a scheme."[492]

The Wage and Hour Administrator, William McComb, attacked such wage payment practices. He testified before the committee that "under such agreements, an employee may be worked for 50, 60, 70, or more hours a week

---

Committee on Education and Labor on H.R. 2033, 81st Cong., 1st Sess. 262 (1949).

[489]H. Rep. No. 267, 81st Cong., 1st Sess. 19 (1949).

[490]H. Rep. No. 267 at 19.

[491]3 *Minimum Wage Standards and Other Parts of the Fair Labor Standards Act of 1938: Hearings Before Subcommittee No. 4 of the House Committee on Education and Labor,* 80th Cong., 1st Sess. 1572-73 (1947) (testimony of Paul Hutchings).

[492]H. Rep. No. 267 at 19.

without any premium pay being paid for the excess hours." He urged Congress to correct the situation because the Supreme Court had upheld these plans on the grounds that the legislature had failed to prohibit them.[493] The AFL joined the attack on "Chinese overtime, under which salaried employees are systematically deprived of their rightful overtime compensation." To "correct this injustice," the AFL proposed that salaried workers' regular basis be calculated by dividing their weekly salary by no more than 40 hours and their monthly salary by no more than 173 hours.[494] The CIO also supported an amendment to remove the "injustice" caused by *Belo*, which had opened the way to "tricky evasion of the overtime provisions."[495]

The committee bill would have adopted the AFL's proposal by providing that "any salaried employee...employed in excess of forty hours in any workweek shall be paid for each such hour in excess of forty, in addition to his salary for forty hours of work, at a rate not less than one and one-half times the hourly rate obtained by dividing his weekly salary by not more than forty...."[496] The proposal, however, was not enacted, and the WHD promulgated an interpretative regulation, sustained by the courts, approving of this practice, which three business school professors later characterized as "for all purposes, negat[ing] the intent of the FLSA."[497]

The original House and Senate administration omnibus FLSA revision bills contained no amendment dealing with Belo plans.[498] But the next version of the Democratic House bill would have authorized Belo plans if they paid a regular rate of $1.50 an hour—that is, twice the proposed minimum wage of 75 cents.[499] The committee would have permitted the Labor Secretary to authorize "bona fide

---

[493] 1 *Amendments to the Fair Labor Standards Act of 1938: Hearings Before the House Committee on Education and Labor*, 81st Cong., 1st Sess. 55 (1949).

[494] 1 *Amendments to the Fair Labor Standards Act of 1938: Hearings Before the House Committee on Education and Labor*, 81st Cong., 1st Sess. 328-29 (1949) (statement of Walter Mason, national legislative representative, AFL).

[495] 1 *Amendments to the Fair Labor Standards Act of 1938: Hearings Before the House Committee on Education and Labor*, 81st Cong., 1st Sess. 276 (1949) (statement of.Irving Levy, general counsel, CIO).

[496] § 7(c), in H. Rep. No. 267 at 5. The provision would not have applied to workers paid at least $1.50 per hour pursuant to a collective bargaining agreement.

[497] 29 C.F.R. § 778.114 (1998); Condo v. Sysco Corp., 1 F.3d 599 (7th Cir. 1993); Dufrene v. Browning-Ferris, Inc., 2000 U.S. App. Lexis 4271 (5th Cir. Mar. 20, 2000); Christopher Martin, Robert Aalberts, and Lawrence Clark, "The Fair Labor Standards Act and the Fluctuating Workweek Scheme: Competitive Compensation Strategy or Worker Exploitation?" 44 *Labor L.J.* 92-100 at 100 (Feb. 1993) (quote).

[498] H.R. 2033, 81st Cong., 1st Sess. (Jan. 31, 1949) (introduced by Rep. Lesinski); S. 653, 81st Cong., 1st Sess. (Jan. 27, 1949) (introduced by Sen. Thomas).

[499] H.R. 3190, § 7(c), 81st Cong., 1st Sess. (Mar. 3, 1949) (introduced by Rep. Lesinski).

agreements for a guaranteed weekly wage in limited circumstances where the committee believes that collective bargaining and the payment of a genuine and sufficiently high rate of pay (at least $1.50 an hour) will obviate evasion and circumvention of the overtime provisions."[500] Consequently, the bill approved by the House Labor Committee was intended to prevent the use of these devices, which the Office Employees International Union—itself "part of the free enterprise team"—testified that Bank of America, the country's largest, still used.[501] Pro-business legislators derided this move as designed to make Belo-type wage plans "virtually unusable."[502]

As a result of complicated parliamentary procedures, a bill sponsored by a coalition of Republicans and Southern Democrats prevailed.[503] As enacted, the 1949 FLSA amendments wrote the Belo plan directly into the FLSA as an approved form of overtime payment. Under the new section it is lawful for an employer to employ an employee more than 40 hours a week pursuant to a "bona fide individual contract" or collective bargaining agreement, if the employee's duties necessitate irregular hours, and the contract specifies a regular rate not less than the statutory minimum wage and compensation of not less than time and a half that rate for all hours beyond 40 and "provides a weekly guaranty of pay for not more than sixty hours based on the rates so specified."[504] As the DOL notes in its regulations, such an approved guaranteed wage plan entitles an employer to work employees overtime "without increasing the cost to the employer, which he would otherwise incur under the Act."[505]

At least one state took notice: the Alaska Department of Labor issued a regulation that expressly makes the Belo plan's guaranteed weekly pay for variable hours, as approved by the FLSA, one of the "not acceptable methods of complying" with that state's overtime law.[506] In upholding the validity of the regulation, the Alaska Supreme Court agreed with the state's argument that the result of the Belo plan—that a worker's average hourly wage decreases as his overtime hours rise—"contravenes the policies of requiring increased compensation and promoting the spreading of employment."[507]

---

[500]H. Rep. No. 267, 81st Cong., 1st Sess. at 19.

[501]3 *Minimum Wage Standards and Other Parts of the Fair Labor Standards Act of 1938: Hearings Before Subcommittee No. 4 of the House Committee on Education and Labor* at 1577, 1575.

[502]95 *Cong. Rec.* at 11892, A5233.

[503]BNA, *The New Wage and Hour Law* 5-10 (1949).

[504]Fair Labor Standards Amendments of 1949, Pub. L. No. 393, § 7(e), 63 Stat. 910, 914 (codified at 29 U.S.C. § 7(f)).

[505]29 CFR § 778.404 (1999).

[506]Alaska Admin. Code tit. 8, § 15.100(d)(1) (2000).

[507]Dresser Industries, Inc., v. Alaska Dept. of Labor, 633 P.2d 998, 1006 (Alaska

10. Unsuccessful Efforts to Raise the Overtime Premium or Lower the Overtime Threshold: The 1960s and 1970s

"In the long run," warns Inland Steel Vice President William Caples, "anything that becomes expensive, we eliminate—we engineer it out." The risk is that such [increased overtime] penalties might provide the impetus for new breakthroughs in automation that would make unemployment even worse.[508]

Whether the premium is 200 or 500 percent does not make more people with the necessary abilities available for employment.[509]

In spite of these legislative cutbacks, by the early 1950s, the business press began taking a positive view of "Premium Pay Fattening Take-Home Wage,"[510] which had "helped to prop up consumer buying for a long time." Indeed, as firms cut workweeks "back to the peacetime standard of 40 hours" after the Korean war, the accompanying decline in income not only presented workers with "a new problem: how to live without overtime pay in the manner to which they have become accustomed," but also became "a business factor to be watched."[511] By the mid-1960s, it was reported that in "many companies overtime has been so much prized by workers that it has had to be allocated by some rationing device such as seniority."[512]

If the overtime provision was originally designed as a work-sharing mechanism to combat unemployment, as the social wage rose from 5 percent in 1938 to 20, 30, and 40 percent of payroll costs in the postwar decades,[513] the 50

1981), *cert. denied*, 455 U.S. 1019 (1982). Daniel Friesen, "Judicial Review: Challenging Alaska's Ban on the Fluctuating Workweek," 12(1-2) *U.C.L.A.-Alaska Law Review* 183-200 at 193 (Fall 1982-Spr.1983, assumes that "[o]ver-time hours are not bad per se...." Skyline Homes, Inc. v. Dept. Indus. Rels, 165 Cal. App.3d 239 (1985) and Goodrow v. Lane Bryant, Inc. 1999 Mass. Super. Lexis 94 (Apr. 1, 1999) follow Alaska.

[508]"The Debate About Overtime," *Time*, Jan. 24, 1964, at 61, 62.

[509]*Amendments to the Fair Labor Standards Act: Hearings Before the Subcommittee on Labor of the Senate Committee on Labor and Public Welfare*, Pt. 2, 89th Cong., 1st Sess. 1094 (1965) (written statement of General Electric Co.).

[510]"Premium Pay Fattening Take-Home Wage," *Bus. Wk.*, Aug. 5, 1950, at 78.

[511]"Problem: Life Without Overtime," *U.S. News & World Report*, Sept. 25, 1953, at 90-95 at 90.

[512]Neil Chamberlin, *The Labor Sector: An Introduction to Labor in the American Economy* 520 (1965).

[513]*Oversight of the Fair Labor Standards Act: Hearing of the Senate Committee on Labor and Human Resources*, 104th Cong., 2d Sess. 58-59 (1996) (prepared statement of the Flexible Employment Compensation and Scheduling (FLECS) Coalition). See also *Overtime Penalty Pay Act of 1964: Hearings Held Jointly Before the General Subcommittee on Labor and Select Subcommittee on Labor of the House Committee on*

percent premium became less effective in deterring firms from relying on overworking current employees in preference to hiring additional ones. (However, the 50 percent premium was and remains higher than the rates established by law or collective agreements in most European countries, which rely more heavily on mandatory norms than financial disincentives to prohibit overwork.)[514]

The diminished impact of the 50 percent overtime penalty in the wake of the increasing nonwage share of the social wage is illustrated by the steel industry. In 1940, when the hourly wage was 84 cents and social wage benefits only 7 cents, the overtime premium of $1.26 strongly encouraged steel companies to hire new workers at 91 cents per hour. By 1993, when the hourly wage had risen to $15.78, overtime wages of $23.67 served to deter firms from hiring new permanent workers at an hourly cost (including benefits) of $31.73. Despite the $5 an hour overtime penalty that the United Steelworkers negotiated with employers to be paid into a career development fund for every hour in excess of 56 per week, overtime accounted for 15 to 20 percent of all working hours in 1994.[515] Even an employer adamantly opposed to the 1977 California anti-mandatory overtime bill conceded that with weekly fixed costs of $97.12 per employee, a straight-time hourly wage rate of $6.20, and overtime of $9.30, "it is cheaper for us to work a regular employee 30 overtime hours a week than it is to hire an additional employee to do that work."[516] Yet others insisted that at union time and a half and double-time rates, "overtime is largely self-policing."[517]

Education and Labor, 88th Cong., 2d Sess. , Pt. 1 at 14 (1964) (statement of Sec'y of Labor Willard Wirtz) (benefits rose from 5 percent in 1938 to 20 percent in 1964); John Zalusky, "Discussant Remarks," in *Work Time and Employment: A Conference Report* 339-42 at 340 (Nat. Comm'n for Manpower Policy Spec. Rep. No. 28, 1978) (benefits rose from 5 percent in 1938 to 36.1 percent in 1975); [California] Senate Committee on Industrial Relations, *Interim Hearing on AB 1295—Mandatory Overtime: Appendices* 163 (1977) (prepared testimony of M. Walters, IBEW, Local 1245, stating that fringe benefits in utility industry exceed 40 percent of straight-time pay).

[514]*Hours of Work: Hearings Before the Select Subcommittee on Labor of the House Committee on Education and Labor*, 88th Cong., 1st Sess., Pt. 1, tab. 31 at 95 (1963); see also below section 13. In the People's Republic of China, the overtime premium amounts to 300 percent of regular wages when workers are required to work on statutory holidays such as Spring Festival. Láodòngfǎ [Labor Law], § 44 (July 5, 1994); *Gōngmín láodòng qúanyí bǎohù zhī shi shǒucè* 56-67 (Jǐng Tāo and Zhèng-xiāo Yuán, 1999); "Chūnjié jiābān gōngzī yǒu biāozhǔn," *Yangze Wǎnbào*, Feb. 19, 2000, at C4.

[515]Jim McKay, "Working More, Liking It Less," Pittsburgh *Post-Gazette*, Oct. 9, 1994, at C1 (Lexis).

[516]2 [California] Senate Committee on Industrial Relations, *Interim Hearing on AB 1295—Mandatory Overtime* 565 (testimony of Dale Zechar, dir., ind. rels. Davis-Walker Corp.).

[517]1 Senate Committee on Industrial Relations, *Interim Hearing on AB 1295—Mandatory Overtime* at 260 (testimony of James Watson, vice pres., Hunt-Wesson Foods). According to Watson, in the food processing industry fringe benefit costs such

Periodically unions' concern with the sharp increases in unemployment has given rise to new drives for a shorter workweek. Yet employers in the United States and elsewhere have long suspected that shorter-hours campaigns were "merely a pretense for raising wages by applying overtime rates earlier."[518] As long ago as 1786, employers charged that London bookbinders' willingness to work overtime contradicted their claims of fatigue and revealed that behind the demand for reduced hours lay a desire for greater income.[519] Perhaps the most startling post-World War II example of what a union with a strong labor market position can achieve in terms of short hours cum overtime was Local 3 of the International Brotherhood of Electrical Workers in New York City, whose members in 1961 were working under a 30-hour per week contract not including five hours of guaranteed overtime, when they demanded a 20-hour week as part of a spread-the-work campaign to ward off the labor-saving consequences of the introduction of automatic machinery. Although the union leadership denied that it was fighting for overtime pay, some electricians admitted that if the standard daily work schedule fell to four hours, they would still work seven hours. Ironically, the electricians and union officials themselves feared that, since it was "'only human nature'" to take a second job just to keep occupied,[520] the intensified job competition caused by such moonlighting might require government intervention "'protecting people from these moonlighters'" and to "'restrict men from looking for second and third jobs.'"[521]

Skeptics in the 1950s and 1960s could hardly be reassured by the best-known example of short hours—the 36-hour week of unionized rubber workers in Akron, of whom 10 to 20 percent held a second full-time job and another 30 to 40 percent a part-time job.[522] Because moonlighting by short-week workers

---

as life insurance and vacation were paid on the basis of number of hours worked in the sense that they were a percentage of gross earnings including overtime. *Id.* at 260-61.

[518]Gary Cross, *A Quest for Time: The Reduction of Work in Britain and France, 1840-1940*, at 187 (1989) (referring to France in the early twentieth century). In the 1930s, too, it was "sometimes alleged that the real objective of the short work week is not so much to reduce actual working hours as to place labor in a position to extract extra pay for overtime, computed on a shorter standard week." Brookings Institution, *The Recovery Problem in the United States* 521 (1936).

[519]M. Bienefeld, *Working Hours in British Industry: An Economic History* 215 (1972).

[520]Stanley Levey, "2 Unions Insisting on Shorter Week," *N.Y. Times*, Dec. 22, 1961, at 14; Laurence O'Donnell, "Demand by a New York Local Spotlights Drive to Cut the Work Week," *Wall St. J.*, Dec. 26, 1961, reprinted in Chamber of Commerce of the United States, *A Shorter Workweek? An Information Manual on Key Questions* 97, 98 (n.d. [ca. 1962]) (quote).

[521]"Union Men Say Shorter Work Week Would Counter Automation; Fear Moonlighting," *Wall St. J.*, Dec. 26, 1961, reprinted in Chamber of Commerce of the United States, *A Shorter Workweek?* at 98, 99.

[522]Woodrow Ginsburg and Ralph Bergmann, "The Worker's Viewpoint," in AFL-CIO,

undermined not only other workers' labor market position,[523] but also the legitimacy of the campaign for reduced working time, the AFL-CIO quickly asserted that the issue had been "grossly exaggerated. The basic reason for dual jobholding stems from a desire for added income and—this is most important—it is hardly at all related to a reduction in working hours without a cut in weekly pay."[524] And the admission by Harry Bridges, president of the International Longshoremen's and Warehousemen's Union and arguably the country's most prominent left-wing union official, to the *Wall Street Journal* that "'large numbers of our members, especially younger men who've accustomed themselves to a six or even seven-day week' and the fat paychecks it brings 'would certainly disagree with'" Bridges' preference to raise overtime rates to induce employers to hire more workers, cast doubt on grassroots support for the AFL-CIO's campaign.[525]

The basis for some automobile workers' resistance to the UAW's efforts to reduce overtime was not difficult to grasp: loss of premium wages was "actually worse than a layoff." Whereas the union contract secured workers 95 percent of their take-home pay for up to a year—during which they were "free to loaf or pickup temporary work"—eliminating overtime could bring about wage reductions of as much as 50 percent for those working 70 hours a week and being

---

The Shorter Work Week 36-42 at 38 (1957); Gabriel Kolko, "High Pay and a 'Six-Hour Day' in Akron," 134 (7) *New Republic* 10-11 (Feb. 13, 1956); "Akron Rubber Union Gives Up Short Day," *Bus. Wk.*, Apr. 21, 1956, at 45; Harvey Swados, "Less Work—Less Leisure," 186 (8) *Nation* 153-58 at 156 (Feb. 22, 1958); Sebastian de Grazia, *Of Time, Work, and Leisure* 64-65 (1964 [1962]). Benjamin Hunnicutt, *Kellogg's Six-Hour Day* 137 (1996), characterizes moonlighting as merely "the media 'take' on the shorter-hours story during the fifties, as reporters copied each other's explanation that workers wanted to work six hours so that they could work another job as well. The wildest reports...asserted that 33 percent of the workers on the short shift had second jobs in Akron...." Nevertheless, Hunnicutt fails to offer empirical evidence refuting the reports. several of which were written by the United Rubber Workers itself or leftists.

[523]John Lawrence, "Many Workers Who Have It Spurn Leisure, Take Two Jobs," *Wall St. J.*, Sept. 13, 1957, at 1, col. 6, at 7, col. 3-4.

[524]*Amendments to the Fair Labor Standards Act: Hearings Before the Senate Committee on Labor and Public Welfare*, Pt. 1, 89th Cong., 1st Sess. 115 (1965) (statement of Andrew Biemiller, dir., Dept. of Legislation, AFL-CIO).

[525]"Firms Say Double Time Pay for Extra Hours Wouldn't Boost Hiring," *Wall St. J.*, Jan. 23, 1964, at 1, col. 6, at 16, col. 5. A similar split between union leaders and members arose two years later when many workers agreed to employers' requests to give up some of their vacation for double-time wages. Unions opposed such arrangements because they feared that employers would resist demands for longer vacations in the future on the grounds that workers did not really want all the vacation they already had; in addition, since long vacations, like overtime premiums, were intended to spread work, trading them in for overtime was self-defeating. Frederick Klein, "Fims Offer Employes [sic] Double Wages If They Give Up Some Vacation," *Wall St. J.*, May 24, 1966, at 1, col. 6, at 14, col. 2.

paid double time on Sundays and triple time on contractual holidays.[526]

Although none of the shorter-hours campaigns bore fruit, the 1963-65 push during the Kennedy-Johnson administrations came closest to marshalling executive and congressional support. Without any backing from President Kennedy, who saw a reduction in worktime as a distant goal, several bills were filed in the House in early 1963 to lower to 32 or 35 hours the threshold at which the overtime premium was triggered.[527] Another bill would have lifted the overtime premium to 100 percent in industries "of major economic importance," including mining, communications, public utilities, wholesale trade, construction, and manufacturing.[528] The House Select Subcommittee on Labor held more than two weeks of hearings on the various bills.[529] While *Business Week* correctly predicted that the debate over a short work week would be the merest "chin music,"[530] unions welcomed the initiative, but were skeptical of the efficacy of the proposed overtime penalty: after all, the UAW Skilled Trade Conference had passed a resolution in December 1962 calling for double-time for the first two hours, triple-time thereafter, double-time for Saturday work, triple-time for Sunday work, and triple-time plus holiday pay on holidays.[531]

The drive to update the overtime provision of the FLSA received strong support from a BLS study conducted in May and published in August 1963. The timing was hardly coincidental as BLS commissioner Ewan Clague had testified before Congress in June on the "seeming paradox" of the coexistence of large volumes of overtime and unemployment.[532] The unprecedented study revealed that only 4.5 million or 29.4 percent of 15.2 million wage and salary workers working 41 hours or more at one job reported receiving premium pay for overtime. Interestingly, across the board, the longer the hours worked, the lower the proportion of workers reporting premium pay—even when "exempt" professional, technical, managerial, and sales workers were excluded. In construction fully 61 percent of these "nonexempt" workers failed to receive

---

[526]George Nikolaieff, "Lack of Overtime Hits the Auto Workers Hard As Detroit Cuts Back," *Wall St. J.*, Dec. 9, 1969, at 1, col. 6.

[527]H.R. 355 (Holland, 32 hours), 3102 (Powell, 35 hours), 3320 (Libonati, 35 hours), 9075 (Roosevelt, 35 hours), 88th Cong., 1st Sess. (1963). Two years earlier, Rep. Holland and Rep. Powell had already introduced a 32- and 35-hour amendment, respectively; H.R. 1940 and H.R. 5123, 87th Cong., 1st Sess. (1961).

[528]H.R. 1680, 88th Cong., 1st Sess. (1963).

[529]*Hours of Work: Hearings Before the Select Subcommittee on Labor of the House Committee on Education and Labor*, 88th Cong., 1st Sess., Pt. 1 and 2 (1963-1964).

[530]"Overtime in Midst of Job Famine," *Bus. Wk.*, Nov. 2, 1963, at 54.

[531]"Unions Mount Attack on Overtime," *Bus. Wk.*, Jan. 26, 1963, at 64.

[532]James Blackwood and Carol Kalish, "Long Hours and Premium Pay," 10 (2) *Employment and Earnings* iii (Aug. 1963).

premium pay as did 26.4 percent of their manufacturing counterparts. Viewed occupationally, 48.8 percent of all blue-collar workers, including 60.4 percent of nonfarm laborers were not paid for their overtime hours.[533] The rather lengthy article that *The New York Times* devoted to the survey quoted DOL officials as "surprised" by the findings, which they conceded could not be fully explained by exemptions from the FLSA, although they declined to conclude that the act "was being violated on any widespread basis" without further information.[534]

By the time the hearings were over in December 1963, a new phase had begun with the intervention of President Johnson. As 1964 opened, Secretary of Labor Willard Wirtz floated the notion to the press that raising the overtime premium might be a partial solution to the problem of unemployment since the volume of overtime equated to almost a million full-time jobs.[535] In his State of the Union address to Congress five days later, President Johnson bluntly rejected the 35-hour week as a way of reducing unemployment (then numbering 4 million) because it would increase costs, lower competitiveness, and share rather than create jobs. But he was "equally opposed to the 45- or 50-hour week in those industries where consistently excessive use of overtime causes increased unemployment." He therefore recommended legislation creating a tripartite industry committee to determine in which industries an increased penalty overtime rate would spur job creation without unduly increasing costs.[536] Modest as the recommendation was, *The New York Times* called it "by far the most radical" of Johnson's anti-poverty proposals.[537] A few days later in his *Economic Report*, Johnson repeated his opposition to "forcing the standard work week down to 35 hours."[538] Then on January 31, identical administration bills were introduced in both Houses of Congress mandating double overtime for hours beyond the number (but not fewer than 40) specified by the tripartite committees in industries affected by substantial and persistent overtime. The enhanced penalty did not apply if the overtime resulted from an extraordinary emergency or "usually compelling need...."[539]

Despite massive amounts of overtime at automobile plants in 1963 and unions' loudly declared intention to make excessive overtime a major point in

---

[533]Blackwood and Kalish, "Long Hours and Premium Pay," tab. 5 and 3 at x, viii.

[534]"Overtime Is Paid to Less Than 33%," *N.Y. Times*, Aug. 16, 1963, at 25, col. 5. The DOL apparently never did a follow-up study to generate the requisite data.

[535]"Wirtz Suggests Way to Make Jobs," *N.Y. Times*, Jan. 4, 1964, at 1, col. 7.

[536]"Annual Message to the Congress on the State of the Union," in *Public Papers of the Presidents of the United States: Lyndon B. Johnson 1963-64*, at 112, 115-16 (1965).

[537]Eileen Shanahan, "President Seeks a Cut in Overtime," *N.Y. Times*, Jan. 9, 1964, at 1, col. 7.

[538]*Economic Report of the President* 13 (1964).

[539]S. 2486 and H.R. 9802, § 3, 88th Cong., 2d Sess. (Jan. 31, 1964).

1964 collective bargaining, the business-oriented press reported that "[u]ntil President Johnson put overtime in the headlines, many people were not aware that it was developing into an issue."[540] And despite Johnson's rejection of labor's demands for a lower weekly threshold for overtime, employers let it be known that they intensely resented Johnson's indirect support for the UAW's and other unions' demands for double overtime in upcoming negotiations.[541] More threatening to the automobile manufacturers was a UAW bargaining proposal giving workers the option not to work overtime. As one GM production worker explained to *U.S. News & World Report*: "'If they left it up to us...they'd never get enough guys to get the line moving. As it is now, they can barely get enough on Saturday nights.'"[542]

Other employers such as David Rockefeller, unsurprisingly, opposed the whole proposal.[543] The president of the NAM, who told a Congressman that "[i]f your daddy wanted to work 72 hours I should not deny him," objected to any statutory overtime premium, though he was constrained to admit that "[o]ne and half times is what we have learned to live with."[544] During 1964 the House Labor Committee held three weeks of hearings, which triggered intense national debate, on which the press extensively reported.

The UAW, which stood at the forefront of the campaign to modernize the "antiquated" overtime penalty deterrent by increasing it to 100 percent,[545] also insisted on working class solidarity as the driving force behind it.[546] (Ironically,

---

[540]"Why the New Worry About Overtime," *U.S. News & World Rep.*, Jan. 20, 1964, at 89.

[541]"Business Is Cool to Overtime Pay Plan," *U.S. News & World Rep.*, Feb. 8, 1964, at 76; "Overtime-Pay Plan: Ending LBJ's 'Honeymoon with Businessmen," *U.S. News & World Rep.*, Feb. 24, 1964, at 113; "The Fight over Double-Time Pay," *U.S. News & World Rep.*, Mar. 2, 1964, at 88; "New Push for Double Overtime," *U.S. News & World Rep.*, Aug. 3, 1964, at 62.

[542]"Where Workers Complain About Too Much Pay," *U.S. News & World Report*, Jan. 27, 1964, at 92, 93.

[543]John Pomfret, "Wirtz Opens Fight Against Overtime," *N.Y. Times*, Feb. 18, 1964, at 24, col. 3.

[544]*Overtime Penalty Pay Act of 1964: Hearings Held Jointly Before the General Subcommittee on Labor and Select Subcommittee on Labor of the House Committee on Education and Labor*, 88th Cong., 2d Sess. , Pt. 1 at 57, 65 (1964) (testimony of W. Gullander).

[545]*Overtime Penalty Pay Act of 1964: Hearings Held Jointly Before the General Subcommittee on Labor and Select Subcommittee on Labor of the House Committee on Education and Labor*, 88th Cong., 2d Sess. , Pt. 2 at 780 (1964) (testimony of Leonard Woodcock, vice president, UAW). For illustrative calculations of the cost of overtime and hiring additional workers, see *id.* Pt. 1, tab. 6 at 24 (data furnished by Secretary of Labor Wirtz).

[546]For an argument that in the 1950s and 1960s Walter Reuther, the UAW president, successfully deflected rank and file calls for shorter hours (specifically a 30-hour week

30 years later, modernizing the "[h]opelessly outdated" depression-era FLSA for "today's fast-paced, information-based society" became the watchword of employers seeking not to increase the overtime penalty, but to eliminate it altogether either through a 160-hour four-week pay period or time-off.)[547] Leonard Woodcock, UAW vice president and later president, testified about his own personal experience of working at the nadir of the Great Depression in 1933 when, as a result of the implementation of the National Recovery Act code in the automobile industry, he saw his weekly hours drop from 84 to 40, while his hourly wage rose from 45 to 60 cents: "Now it is true my total wage was sharply reduced, but I certainly had no feeling of compunction about that because of the fact that we put on in that plant some 200 additional workers." He also reported to the House Labor Committee how surprised and impressed he had been by a recent survey revealing "the substantial feeling of shame that our members had at being forced to work overtime when their neighbors were out of work."[548]

Woodcock's insistence that "the forcing of overtime work is immoral" provoked one Congressman to engage him in Socratic dialog concerning the complex and ticklish relationship between working-class morality and individual workers' self-interest in still larger overtime premiums:

MR. FRELINGHUYSEN. Would you mind a brief interruption...with respect to the immorality of overtime? If it is immoral to work overtime, if there are those unemployed who would be qualified to work, how does increasing the penalty make it moral or is it still immoral even though the penalty is doubled? I am not sure I follow your reasoning. If it is immoral I should think we might forbid it rather than increasing the penalty.

MR. WOODCOCK. The purpose of the penalty is to be a deterrent toward the working of overtime.

MR. FRELINGHUYSEN. But it still is immoral, is that right?

MR. WOODCOCK. It is immoral to require some Americans to work against their will beyond 40 hours when their neighbors and friends are totally without work and in want.

MR. FRELINGHUYSEN. Is it immoral if they want to work overtime?

MR. WOODCOCK. The record shows they do not want to work overtime when others are out of work.

MR. FRELINGHUYSEN. If it is immoral might we not consider forbidding it?

MR. WOODCOCK. I don't see how you could put industry in such a straitjacket. The testimony has been—and we concede some overtime on occasion is necessary and flat prohibition would put a straitjacket on—would be entirely impractical. This is why we

---

with 40 hours' pay), see Edsforth, "Why Automation Didn't Shorten the Work Week" at 160-75.

[547]141 *Cong. Rec.* 11787, 11788 (1995) (Sen. Ashcroft).

[548]*Overtime Penalty Pay Act of 1964: Hearings Held Jointly Before the General Subcommittee on Labor and Select Subcommittee on Labor of the House Committee on Education and Labor*, Pt. 2 at 834.

need an economic deterrent that will insure that the overtime that is worked is actually necessary and unavoidable, but wipe out the great excess of overtime which is unnecessary.[549]

A suspicion of evasiveness seemed to cling to Woodcock's responses. The failure of nerve to express support for the venerable model of a strict eight-hour day or 40-hour week (with exceptions for emergencies) and the surprising sympathy with employers' operational imperatives and support for a free-market financial incentive rather than use of the state's police powers left the impression that the UAW could not afford to deprive even some of the country's highest paid manufacturing workers of access to more work at yet higher wages. Much later in his testimony Woodcock was able to dispel that impression (objectively if not intentionally) by reminding Senator Taft that the UAW had long been on record as "willing to have the extra penalty deterrent, the difference between the time and a half and double time...used for other purposes." Woodcock refused, however, to include relief of employers' unemployment compensation payments among those purposes.[550] The UAW's credibility was, however, enhanced by a resolution that it passed at its nineteenth constitutional convention in 1964 condemning moonlighting: "As it is immoral for an employer to deny job opportunities to unemployed workers by scheduling avoidable overtime work, so it is equally immoral in a time of high unemployment for a worker who already has a full-time job to deny an unemployed worker his right to employment by working at a second job...."[551]

Automobile management also sought to hoist supporters of the monopurposive theory of the overtime penalty with their own petard. Ford Motor Company vice president Theodore Yntema asked why, if proponents assert that its purpose is not to compensate workers, but to discourage employers from offering overtime,[552] workers should receive the premium payment:

---

[549]*Overtime Penalty Pay Act of 1964: Hearings Held Jointly Before the General Subcommittee on Labor and Select Subcommittee on Labor of the House Committee on Education and Labor*, Pt. 2 at 780.

[550]*Overtime Penalty Pay Act of 1964: Hearings Held Jointly Before the General Subcommittee on Labor and Select Subcommittee on Labor of the House Committee on Education and Labor*, Pt. 2 at 834. Woodcock was referring to collective bargaining demands, but seemed amenable to extending the principle to statutory regulation.

[551]*Amendments to the Fair Labor Standards Act: Hearinge Before the Subcommittee on Labor of the Senate Committee on Labor and Public Welfare*, Pt. 1, 89th Cong., 1st Sess. 278 (1965) (statement of Leonard Woodcock).

[552]For example, Rep. Dent stated that "[o]vertime pay was never intended to be a bonus for the worker on the job...." *Overtime Penalty Pay Act of 1964: Hearings Held Jointly Before the General Subcommittee on Labor and Select Subcommittee on Labor of the House Committee on Education and Labor*, Pt. 1 at 27.

> Given the alleged objectives and premises of the bill, it was really illogical to frame a proposal making overtime less attractive to business, but at the same time making it more attractive to labor. A logical proposal would make overtime less attractive to both business and labor. This could be done by requiring that penalty pay for overtime should not be given to the worker, but should be used for the benefit of the unemployed.
>
> While we do not advocate such a proposal, it would coincide precisely with the stated objectives of the administration.... However, it would not provide the windfall that H.R. 9802 does for the workers continuing to be employed overtime at the higher penalty rate. I suspect there would be little enthusiasm for any proposal from which the windfall was missing.[553]

Representative O'Hara, one of the chief sponsors of the overtime initiative in the 1960s, responded that Yntema had a "terrific idea... that had not occurred to me. ... But, by George, there is not any good reason why the extra half should go to the worker. As a matter of fact, there might be some good reasons why it should not. [W]hen the time arrives, I am going to revive the Yntema amendment to H.R. 9082 to pay that extra half...[to] some sort of fund to provide for training or retraining of workers...."[554]

If the only purpose of the overtime penalty were in fact to encourage employers to absorb the unemployed rather than to overwork the already employed, Yntema's ironic logic would be unexceptionable. Employers had demonstrated its validity—if not its practical effectiveness—during World War II when they deployed it to contest the continued compulsory payment of overtime premiums when there were no more unemployed for firms to absorb. Oddly, its force failed to prompt supporters of an increase in the penalty rate in the 1960s to admit, even rhetorically, that the premium had also always served to guarantee workers' freedom from (alienated) labor, to preserve their health, and to compensate them for the shortening of their working lives. Such an argument would have helped deflate employers' claim that the amendment was merely a disingenuous covert attempt to raise wages, but perhaps its evocation of Marxist class struggle was too high a rhetorical price to pay. Unions' failure to develop this perspective was so much the more puzzling since such a taint did not deter Malcolm Denise, vice president in charge of labor relations at Ford Motor

---

[553] *Overtime Penalty Pay Act of 1964: Hearings Held Jointly Before the General Subcommittee on Labor and Select Subcommittee on Labor of the House Committee on Education and Labor*, Pt. 1 at 200.

[554] *Overtime Penalty Pay Act of 1964: Hearings Held Jointly Before the General Subcommittee on Labor and Select Subcommittee on Labor of the House Committee on Education and Labor*, Pt. 1 at 294. Intriguingly, an economic stabilization and unemployment compensation plan advocated by the president of the General Motors Holding Corp., Albert Deane, during the Great Depression would have required employers to pay double overtime, but the worker would have received only time and a half, with the remainder paid as a tax to a national employment fund. See Hunnicutt, *Work Without End* at 232-35.

Company, from supplying the missing historical testimony: "I do not think that it can be legitimately said that the sole purpose of the Fair Labor Standards Act of 1938 was to spread employment. The drive for shorter working hours in this country has a long history. Its history was concerned with the health and welfare of people and their working and living lives."[555] Since the labor movement in the nineteenth and early twentieth century had pressed for an absolute limit of eight hours of work per day and not for overtime premiums, the AFL-CIO's newfound preference for flexible financial incentives may have caused it to suppress the reality of its traditions.

After the bills failed to be enacted, Representative O'Hara and Senator McNamara, who had introduced them, introduced stripped down versions in 1965, which simply raised the overtime premium across the board to 100 percent.[556] The Johnson administration then supported a new imitative, which took into account the uniform opposition that "virtually all the witnesses" had directed at the previous bills. Armed with new data from 1964 showing that 3.5 million employees worked five or more hours of overtime weekly for a total of 19.6 million hours, and that much of the overtime was being performed on a "fairly standard recurring basis...in occupations in which there is presently a surplus of manpower" (that is, a higher proportion of low-paid workers in almost all industries worked overtime than of higher-paid workers), Secretary of Labor Wirtz, "acting...from a kind of hardheaded idealism," proposed a two-tiered overtime premium.[557] S. 1986 and H.R. 8259 would have phased in over three years a higher 100-percent premium applying to hours above 48, 47, 46, and finally 45 hours, below which the old 50-percent penalty would have applied. The impact of the double-time would have been further softened by a provision permitting employers to pay the lower rate when the overtime work (beyond 45 hours) was "required only by reason of a period of extraordinary emergency or unusually compelling need" as defined by the Secretary of Labor.[558]

Wirtz was even receptive to liberal Republican Senator Jacob Javits's suggestion—which would have tested unions' commitment to the underlying principle of work sharing—that some administrative machinery be created exempting employers from the higher penalty rate if they could prove that its

---

[555]*Overtime Penalty Pay Act of 1964: Hearings Held Jointly Before the General Subcommittee on Labor and Select Subcommittee on Labor of the House Committee on Education and Labor*, Pt. 1 at 296.

[556]H.R. 6574, 89th Cong., 1st Sess. (1965); S. 1741, 89th Cong., 1st Sess. (1965).

[557]*Minimum Wage-Hour Amendments, 1965: Hearings Before the General Subcommittee on Labor of the House Committee on Education and Labor*, Pt. 1, 89th Cong., 1st Sess. 21-22, 113 (1965).

[558]S. 1986, § 404(a), 89th Cong., 1st Sess. (May 18, 1965).

imposition would increase costs without leading to increased hiring.[559] Numerous firms and industries, such as General Electric and the telephone, paper and rubber industries, inundated the congressional labor committees with evidence purporting to prove precisely such futility.[560]

Both the House and Senate labor committees heard extensive testimony in 1965, much of which replicated what they had heard in 1963 and 1964. The threat that the amendment might be adopted was serious enough to prompt *U.S. News & World Report* to declare (hyperbolically as it turned out): "The day may not be too far away when employers will be required by law to pay double-time rates for overtime work. But before that day comes...the issue is sure to bring on one of the biggest fights in the history of labor legislation."[561] Many employers sought to portray the move for a higher overtime penalty both as a transparent grab for higher wages by well-paid union members and a singularly counterproductive mechanism for reducing unemployment. For example, the National Electrical Contractors Association (NECA), long a staunch advocate of collective bargaining, told the House Labor Committee that in the electrical contracting industry and generally in construction it was "a well-known fact that...overtime jobs attract skilled workers. Once these workers are employed on the job, they wish to work as much overtime as is possible and at the same time restrict the employer from employing additional workmen." Indeed, the association's public relations director testified that an electrician's double-time hourly wage of $9.42 "would seriously be personally attractive enough to me to make me want to enter the industry tomorrow, on the union side." From the NECA's perspective, the enhanced overtime penalty was doomed to failure because it prompted responses from labor and capital diametrically opposed to those presumed by the underlying policy: instead of showing solidarity by sharing work with their unemployed brethren, employed craftsmen would monopolize it, while firms, instead of hiring additional workers, would automate any labor task that could lent itself to automation.[562] Other industries, such as petroleum

---

[559]*Amendments to the Fair Labor Standards Act: Hearings Before the Subcommittee on Labor of the Senate Committee on Labor and Public Welfare*, Pt. 1, 89th Cong., 1st Sess. 54 (1965)

[560]*Amendments to the Fair Labor Standards Act: Hearings Before the Subcommittee on Labor of the Senate Committee on Labor and Public Welfare*, Pt. 1, 89th Cong., 1st Sess. 353-57, 386-407 (1965) (statements and testimony of Hubert Kertz, vice pres. of operations, Am. Tel. & Tel. Co., and Eugene Stewart, special counsel, Am. Paper Institute); *Amendments to the Fair Labor Standards Act: Hearings Before the Subcommittee on Labor of the Senate Committee on Labor and Public Welfare*, Pt. 2, 89th Cong., 1st Sess. 1089-1101, 1202-11 (1965) (written statements of Virgil Day, vice-pres., GE, and of the Rubber Manufacturers Assoc.).

[561]"The Big Debate About Double Pay for Overtime," *U.S. News & World Report*, July 26, 1965, at 73.

[562]*Minimum Wage-Hour Amendments, 1965*, at 1662-63 (statement of Randolph Hale).

refining (with above-average benefit costs), offered data to undermine the claim that the 50-percent penalty rate did not suffice to give them an incentive to prefer hiring additional workers to overtime.[563]

The industry widely viewed as the chief abuser of overtime went to great pains in its testimony to undermine the economic underpinnings of the demand for a higher penalty by emphasizing "why overtime is not readily convertible into more jobs."[564] First, however, the automobile manufacturing firms stressed that the three-year agreement they had just entered into with the UAW had been preceded by extensive negotiations over the union's demand for double- and triple-time, which it finally abandoned in favor of other demands, such as inducements to early retirement and more holidays, vacation, and relief time, designed to spread employment. The auto firms were not amused that the UAW was now seeking to achieve through lobbying what it had lacked the power to gain through negotiations.[565] The main burden of the Automobile Manufacturers Association's testimony was the assertion that the vast majority of overtime work resulted from emergencies, retooling and model changeovers, cyclical and seasonal production patterns, and changes in customer preferences, which were "[q]uite obviously...inherent rigidities...that cannot be legislated out of existence." Furthermore, in many instances the overtime was being performed by skilled craftsmen, of whom the firms complained of suffering a serious shortage. Moreover, that a considerable proportion of overtime work was already being compensated at 100 percent under the UAW contract demonstrated that "there is no practical alternative regardless of how high the penalty."[566] Indeed, John Bugas, a Ford vice president and former head of the FBI's office in Detroit who had helped make Ford's primitive red-baiting practices more sophisticated after World War II,[567] testified that, despite the focus of congressional attention on the allegedly increasing impotence of the overtime penalty to induce employers to hire additional workers in the face of the expanding quasi-fixed

---

[563]*Amendments to the Fair Labor Standards Act: Hearings Before the Subcommittee on Labor of the Senate Committee on Labor and Public Welfare*, Pt. 1, 89th Cong., 1st Sess. 134-41 (1965) (statement and testimony of John Post, chairman, ind. rels. comm., Nat. Petroleum Refiners' Assoc.).

[564]*Minimum Wage-Hour Amendments, 1965*, at 1755 (statement of John Bugas, vice pres., Ford Motor Co.).

[565]*Minimum Wage-Hour Amendments, 1965*, at 1758 (statement of John Bugas); *Amendments to the Fair Labor Standards Act: Hearings Before the Subcommittee on Labor of the Senate Committee on Labor and Public Welfare*, Pt. 1, 89th Cong., 1st Sess. 227 (1965) (testimony of Malcolm Denise, Ford Motor Co.).

[566]*Minimum Wage-Hour Amendments, 1965*, at 1765-71 (quotes at 1768, 1769) (statement of John Bugas).

[567]David Caute, *The Great Fear: The Anti-Communist Purge Under Truman and Eisenhower* 371-72 (1979); "John S. Bugas Is Dead at 74; Was Top Executive at Ford," *N.Y. Times*, Dec. 3, 1982, at A28, col. 4 (Lexis).

benefits, in fifteen years of attending monthly scheduling meetings, he could not recall a single instance in which Ford had opted for overtime because it was cheaper: "We make the decision on overtime on completely different bases."[568] And finally, Bugas claimed on behalf of the auto manufacturing employers that they "would run into tremendous resistance" if they tried to reduce overtime in favor of additional hiring because the "vast majority—almost an infinitesimal minority do not like overtime, but the vast majority likes overtime. ... In tribute to the American worker he is a pretty industrious character if he gets paid for it."[569]

To be sure, the UAW offered rebuttals of all these arguments in its own written submissions. Its counter-propaganda was most effective in establishing that most overtime was systematic and long-term and had nothing to do with emergencies, cyclicity, or shortages of skilled craftsmen, and least plausible in distancing itself from the overtime system and denying complicity by its own members in its survival.[570] But because the congressional committees, as is almost always the case in such hearings,[571] failed to arrange for direct confrontation between these diametrically opposed points of view, and, many of the underlying data were either uniquely within the firms' possession or interpretable only by reference to arcane details of collective bargaining agreement, the dispute remained practically unresolvable.

Following the lengthy hearings on the overtime issue, Congress decided not to enact the proposals. Insisting that their absence reflected not "a negative view towards their advisability," but a "prudent, cautious approach to an important proposal that deserves further serious consideration,"[572] Congress retained only a slight trace in the landmark FLSA amendments of 1966 of the fervor that had once attached to the issue. It instructed the Secretary of Labor to submit the following year a "complete study of present practices dealing with overtime payments for work in excess of forty hours per week and the extent to which such overtime work impedes the creation of new job opportunities in American industry."[573] Since congressional concern was directed at the flagging deterrence

---

[568]*Minimum Wage-Hour Amendments, 1965*, at 1790 (testimony of John Bugas).

[569]*Minimum Wage-Hour Amendments, 1965*, at 1800-1801 (testimony of John Bugas).

[570]*Amendments to the Fair Labor Standards Act: Hearings Before the Subcommittee on Labor of the Senate Committee on Labor and Public Welfare*, Pt. 1, 89th Cong., 1st Sess. 236-80 (1965) (comments of UAW).

[571]Congressional hearings were not always aseptic. In the late nineteenth and early twentieth centuries high-ranking representatives of labor and capital frequently cross-examined one another.

[572]H. Rep. No. 1366: *Fair Labor Standards Amendments of 1966*, 89th Cong., 2d Sess. 36 (1966).

[573]Fair Labor Standards Amendments of 1966, § 603, P.L. 89-601, 80 Stat. 830, 844.

generated by the overtime penalty, the legislature expected the DOL's study of excessive hours to enable Congress to judge whether a higher penalty rate would "curtail long workweeks and create additional jobs."[574] The DOL's agnosticism served to maintain the status quo. Despite the evidence that the overtime penalty had lost much of its deterrent value, the Secretary of Labor found it "difficult...to develop with any degree of certainty any reliable estimate of the number of jobs which could be created if the original effectiveness were restored. More important, it is difficult to insure that there would not be a temporary reduction in total productive potential during the transition period if a stricter standard were applied." Consequently Secretary Wirtz proposed no legislative changes.[575] And as the Vietnam war drove the unemployment rate (3.8, 3.6, and 3.5 percent in 1967-69) to its lowest rate since the Korean war,[576] unemployment and its possible exacerbation by overtime work drifted out of public consciousness and discourse—until the next depression phase of the business cycle.

In the midst of the overtime hearings, the *Wall Street Journal* devoted a long front page article to detailing employers' denials that the proposed double time would spread employment. While some firms conceded that even double time would be cheaper than "handing out fringe benefits new workers would have to be given," others asserted that double time might even motivate them to lay workers off. A construction association went so far as to doubt that even triple time would preclude the continued use of overtime. The only hint that human volition might be able to prevail over the compulsions of capital valorization came from a manager who stated that he would react to mandatory double time not by hiring additional workers, but by stretching out schedules and making customers wait longer.[577] Why then the world of widget production could not also be slowed down out of deference to workers's desire for more time away from alienated labor, was not mentioned.

Yet the very next year, in mid-1965, the *Wall Street Journal* reported that "many factory managers now believe the regular overtime they have long scheduled to keep production ahead of swelling orders is both costly and inefficient. Having discovered that overtime "is a heavy cost burden...breeds absenteeism and hurts production efficiency as workers tire," "bosses" suddenly found it possible to implement measures that employers had told the newspaper in 1964 were impossible. They included different scheduling methods, upgrading

---

[574]S. Rep. No. 1487, 89th Cong., 2d Sess., in 1966 *Code Cong. & Adm. News* 3002, 3025-26.

[575]DOL, WHD, *Premium Payments for Overtime Under the Fair Labor Standards Act* 3 (Nov. 1967).

[576]*Employment and Training Report of the President,* tab. A-22 at 172 (1977).

[577]"Firms Say Double Time Pay for Extra Hours Wouldn't Boost Hiring," *Wall St. J.*, Jan. 23, 1964, at 1, col. 6, at 16, col. 4.

unskilled workers, hiring new workers, expanding capacity, and buying labor-saving machinery. Moreover, all these efforts "'to wash out the premium-time problem'...would surely be much intensified if Congress" enacted the double-time amendment.[578] Two years later yet another front-page *Journal* piece chronicled the proliferation of overtime cutbacks motivated by the perception that fatigue and absenteeism were wasteful and inefficient.[579]

Renewed union interest in amending the overtime provision was in fact sparked by the next expansion of the reserve army of the unemployed during the recession of 1974-75,[580] which found expression in a congressional bill in the late 1970s sponsored by Representative Conyers from Detroit. The bill (H.R. 11784) that he introduced on March 22, 1978, sought to restore the work-spreading impact of the FLSA by normalizing the workweek at 37.5 hours by 1980 and 35 hours by 1982 and penalizing overtime at 100 rather than 50 percent. Of perhaps greater significance was the bill's ban on mandatory overtime: "No employer shall knowingly permit any employee to perform work for which the employee is entitled under this section to receive compensation at the rate of pay applicable for overtime employment unless the employee gives his or her consent to perform such work." To discourage employers from unlawfully compelling workers to work overtime, Conyers inserted a liquidated damages provision making employers liable for an amount equal to three times the regular rate at which the workers were employed.[581] To anticipate charges that the bill would place an straitjacket on enterprise, the bill also authorized the Secretary of Labor to issue regulations to permit such exceptions to the ban on mandatory overtime "as may be necessary to deal with emergency situations (as determined by such Secretary) in which the production in an establishment would be severely jeopardized if no such exceptions existed."[582]

Without explaining why it was not feasible or desirable to prevent workers from undermining their own labor standards by working 60 hours a week while millions were unemployed, Conyers himself acknowledged that to achieve the bill's objective—to dampen employers' tendency during the recession and early recovery phases of the business cycle—it was necessary to apply sanctions against employers because "[n]o one wishes to curb an individual's choice of how

---

[578]Joseph Mathewson, "Many Factories Find Extra Hours Costly, Try to Eliminate Them," *Wall St. J.*, June 23, 1965, at 1, col. 6, at 20, col. 2-3 (quoting a manufacturing company official).

[579]Gregory Schirmer, "More Companies Slash Overtime to Increase Efficiency, Cut Costs," *Wall St. J.*, Mar. 3, 1967, at 1, col. 6.

[580]"Unions Campaign to Shrink Work Times," *Bus. Wk.*, Apr. 24, 1978, at 30, 31.

[581]H.R. 11784, §§ 2(a), 3(a)(10) (quote), and 4(b)(2), 95th Cong., 2d Sess. (1978).

[582]H.R. 11784, § 3(a)(10).

much and for whom he or she works."[583] Conyers' pragmatism contrasted sharply with the startling proposal that the Teamsters president, James Hoffa, had made to Congress 15 years earlier. He had insisted that reducing the workweek or work year would not significantly redistribute work "unless there is a penalty imposed on moonlighting in the form of double time payments by the first and second employer after 32 hours or 1,600 hours per year." Hoffa did not bother to explain either how an employer would know whether an employee simultaneously worked elsewhere or why it would not be more efficacious to penalize moonlighting by penalizing moonlighters directly rather than offering them further incentives in the form of double overtime.[584] A rare note of candor in this context had been sounded in 1965 by Labor Secretary Wirtz, who conceded that the overtime premium "has always been realistically and analytically a proper figure only in terms of employer cost, not in terms of employee compensation."[585]

Three weeks later Conyers participated in a conference in Dearborn, Michigan, called by the All Unions Committee to Shorten the Work Week. Dissatisfied with longer vacations and more holidays and personal days as a means of spreading work, 700 union officials from 25 unions, led by UAW members, supported Conyers' bill to reduce the standard workweek to 35 hours by increasing the overtime penalty to 100 percent. What *The New York Times* called the "less-work ethic" was unacceptable to management, especially since the All Unions Committee proposal envisioned no pay cut. As one industrial relations manager observed: "'I don't mind paying a higher wage if I'm getting productivity for it, but we're standing strongly against this time not worked.'"[586] This adamance apparently impressed some AFL-CIO officials such as UAW president Douglas Fraser, who told the conference that the history of the American labor movement suggested that picket lines and not Congress would be the source of a shorter workweek.[587] What Fraser failed to acknowledge was that in an socioeconomy as balkanized and labor markets as heterogeneous as

---

[583]124 *Cong. Rec.* 10155, 10156 (Apr. 13, 1978) (Conyers' extended remarks).

[584]*Hours of Work: Hearings Before the Select Subcommittee on Labor of the House Committee on Education and Labor*, 88th Cong., 1st Sess., Pt. 2 at 456 (1964). James Carey, president, International Union of Electrical Workers, made the same proposal. *Overtime Penalty Pay Act of 1964: Hearings Before the Select Subcommittee on Labor of the House Committee on Education and Labor*, 88th Cong., 2d Sess. Pt. 2 at 729 (1964).

[585]*Amendments to the Fair Labor Standards Act: Hearings Before the Subcommittee on Labor of the Senate Committee on Labor and Public Welfare*, 89th Cong., 1st Sess., Pt. 1 at 46 (1965).

[586]Jerry Flint, "Unions Meet Resistance in Trying to Cut Workweek," *N.Y. Times*, Apr. 16, 1978, sect. 1 at 24, col. 3.

[587]Mark Lett, "Do Not Count on Congress for Shorter Week, Labor Told," *Detroit News*, Apr. 12, 1978, reprinted in 124 *Cong. Rec.* 10158-59 (1978).

those of the United States, reliance on unions' individual strength in preference to society-wide norms imposed on the employing and employed classes would merely widen the gap between the organized and atomized strata. The consequence would be various types of paid time-off, for example, for UAW workers that low-paid nonunion workers could scarcely imagine.

After Congress took no action on Conyers' bill in the 95th Congress, he reintroduced it essentially unchanged on February 1, 1979 as H.R. 1784 (the times at which the reduced workweeks became effective were moved back one year).[588] He again emphasized that the 50 percent overtime penalty had lost its effectiveness in encouraging employers to hire additional workers.[589]

The Labor Standards Subcommittee of the House Education and Labor Committee held three days of hearings in October 1979, but no further congressional action was taken. (When Conyers reintroduced the bill in 1985, this time proposing to phase in a 32-hour workweek over eight years, it prompted little resonance.)[590] More than a grain of truth lay in employers' later claims that "'[e]ven when the Democrats controlled the House and the Senate and the White House, the issue [forced overtime] was never even on their radar screen.'"[591]

The testimony at the 1979 congressional hearings was nevertheless enlightening. The UAW representative offered a friendly amendment to the bill that would have required employers to pay the entire increase in the overtime penalty as a tax into the Unemployment Insurance fund: "Besides the virtue of reducing the scheduling of overtime by employers without increasing its desirability to workers, such a procedure would also explicitly link the problems of overtime and unemployment. It would...make those employers whose actions increase joblessness bear a disproportionate share of the cost of maintaining the unemployed."[592] The UAW and employers had pointed to the rationality of such a suggestion during the hearings in the 1960s, but they had not highlighted its effectiveness in making the connection transparent.

Employers were very sensitive to the bill's deprivation of their power to force employees to work overtime. While the NAM tersely charged that the provision

---

[588]H.R. 1784, 96th Cong., 1st Sess. (1979).

[589]125 *Cong. Rec.* 7609 (1979).

[590]H.R. 2933, 99th Cong., 1st Sess. (1985).

[591]Kevin Galvin, "Some Workers Protest Rise in Forced Overtime," Chattanooga *Free Press,* Nov. 22, 1998, at A4 (Lexis) (quoting Randel Johnson, U.S. Chamber of Commerce vice president).

[592]*To Revise the Overtime Compensation Requirements of the Fair Labor Standards Act of 1938: Hearings Before the Subcommittee on Labor Standards of the House Committee on Education and Labor*, 96th Cong., 1st Sess. 43 (1980) (statement of Ken Morris, member, UAW International Exec. Bd.).

would "inhibit operations and scheduling,"[593] the representative of the Chamber of Commerce of the United States, its deputy chief economist, offered arguments that were both mutually inconsistent and unprecedented. First, Robert Landry asserted that congressional conversion of mandatory into voluntary overtime would be an "intrusion...into the system of individual agreements between the nearly 80 percent of the work force that is not organized and their employers." According to this logic of "individual agreements" between large corporations and its individual employees, it is puzzling that the Chamber chose not to reject the label "mandatory" altogether. Instead, Landry went on to charge that Congress would merely create antagonisms among workers by enabling one to hold an entire factory hostage: "Placing a voluntary overtime clause in the law means that one worker by refusing overtime may deprive perhaps 100 persons of overtime and the extra income that they desire if they are involved in an assembly-line operation where each person is essential to the task."[594]

The representative of 35 of the country's largest food and hotel companies seemed almost incensed over ignorant congressional meddling in his members' prerogatives: "Who knows when a busload of hungry people will pull into one of our restaurants unannounced? We are not going to turn them away. At those times, our staff must remain on the job, even though they might have worked more than 8 hours on that particular day. ... Do we have to obtain that person's permission to conduct our business?" Bruce Cotton, the president of the Food Service and Lodging Institute, not only found it part of the natural order of things that consumers' purchasing power imperiously overrode workers' conviction that the restaurant's posted hours should be taken seriously, but combined inconsistent arguments by claiming that "[i]f there is a valid reason for refusal, the employer will invariably accept it and look for someone else" and complaining that the FLSA amendment would make it necessary for employers to "obtain the employee's consent—and we would assume that would be in writing—before scheduling overtime."[595]

Conyers' proposal of a 100-percent overtime penalty was hardly un-

---

[593]*To Revise the Overtime Compensation Requirements of the Fair Labor Standards Act of 1938* at 236 (letter from Kimberly Johnson-Smith, labor relations director, NAM, Nov. 5, 1979).

[594]*To Revise the Overtime Compensation Requirements of the Fair Labor Standards Act of 1938* at 115 (statement of Richard Landry).

[595]*To Revise the Overtime Compensation Requirements of the Fair Labor Standards Act of 1938* at 167 (statement of Bruce Cotton). The president of the Southern California Restaurant Assoc. used similar rhetoric at the 1977 hearings in California when he asked: "if the second shift waitress...calls in sick just before the start of her shift, are we to tell waiting customers that we can't take care of them because the waitress didn't want to work a little overtime?" Senate Committee on Industrial Relations, *Interim Hearing on AB 1295—Mandatory Overtime: Appendices* at 284 (statement of Stanley Stockton).

precedented. As long ago as 1891, the Nebraska legislature had enacted a law that required employers working their employees beyond eight hours per day to "pay as extra compensation, double the amount per hour as paid for the previous hour."[596] This penalty was interpreted as pyramiding so that each overtime hour had to be compensated at double the rate of the previous one. Such progressive penalization of overwork offended the Nebraska Supreme Court, which promptly held the act unconstitutional as paternalistic interference with contracts.[597]

11. "We Didn't Think that the Legislature Would Be So Crazy": The Alternative Model of Maximum Hours Legislation—Territorial Alaska's Absolute Universal Eight-Hour Law

> The Government is contented with the eight-hour law; why can't we little people in this frontier, God-forsaken country, have it? We are here trying to make a country out of it and make a living. We don't want very much.[598]

> It is my deliberate opinion, based upon a wide experience in this Territory, embracing to some extent every known condition affecting either labor or capital, that if there is a country on earth where there is a logical and reasonable demand for a shorter work day, it is Alaska. This is because of climatic conditions, which are frequently extremely unfavorable..., together with the isolation of the workingmen; and added to this is the fact that the average wage paid labor...is in most instances below that paid for the classes of work in the western and Pacific coast states.[599]

The eight-hour statute—prohibiting overtime work except when life or property was in imminent danger—covering all workers (including adult men and business partners) enacted by the Alaska territorial legislature in 1917 is the most radical piece of hours regulation in the history of the United States. Workers, especially miners, in this frontier society had been agitating for the eight-hour day for a number of years in the face of mine owners' insistence on 10-hour days

---

[596]1891 Neb. Laws ch. 54, § 3 at 361, 362. The contemporaneous draft eight-hours bill of the Social Democratic Federation in Britain also proposed double time. Webb and Cox, *The Eight Hours Day* at 164.

[597]Low v. Rees Printing Co., 59 N.W. 362 (Neb. 1894).

[598]"Hearings Before the Governor of Alaska on the Eight-Hour Law (Chapter 55, Session Laws of Alaska, 1917)" at 31 (Feb. 5-21, 1918) (statement of Jesse Rice), in Record Group 101, Box 2616, Alaska State Archives.

[599]Letter from Alaska Territorial Governor J. F. A. Strong to the Secretary of the Interior at 7 (Feb. 25, 1918), in Record Group 101: Territorial Governor, Series 130: General Correspondence, Box 159, File Code 156: Eight-Hour Workday Law, Alaska State Archives.

on the grounds that short seasons (lasting from May to October) required full use of every day. Understandably, miners were not keen on exposing themselves to punishing long days on hands and knees in damp permafrost mining operations, and expressly made the argument that such long workdays would shorten their working lives.[600]

The gold rush of the late 1890s had made Alaska the last frontier that "attracted rugged individualists with no capital but their hands, their courage, and a winter's grubstake, to wring an independent fortune from the Territory's gravels." However, within a few years, large monopolies turned "these little men" into "sullen wage-workers...." The salmon trust, for example, "brought home to residents that corporation control meant Asiatic labor" by staffing its floating canneries anchored in the territory's harbors with Hindus, Filipinos, and Chinese. Supreme among these monopolies was the so-called Guggenmorgan or Morganheim syndicate.[601] The Guggenheim family and the House of Morgan, the owners of this combination, as James Wickersham, Alaska's leading politician and for many years its delegate to Congress,[602] explained to the House Committee on the Territories in 1913, "have thrown out their tentacles along the coast in Alaska, have secured a monopoly of our coal, copper, and transportation, and they are in control of the three principal gateways to the interior of Alaska. They control the transportation in Alaska; they control the situation with respect to railroad building in Alaska; they control the fisheries in Alaska; they control the copper of Alaska...."[603] Not surprisingly, the Guggenheim-Morgan syndicate also "wielded tremendous influence in Washington on all matters pertaining to Alaska

---

[600]James Foster, "Syndicalism Northern Style: The Life and Death of WFM No. 193," 5 *Alaska Journal* 130-41 (Summer 1975); James Foster, "The Western Federation Comes to Alaska," 66(4) *Pacific Northwest Q.* 161-73 at 167 (Oct. 1975). Foster, "Syndicalism Northern Style" at 132, asserts that by 1907 the eight-hour-day had become "almost universal" except in mining, but evidence presented below shows that the shorter workday did not prevail in the canneries, the other major employing industry.

[601]Harvey O'Connor, *The Guggenheims: The Making of an American Dynasty* 258-60, 257 (1937). See also John Davis, *The Guggenheims: An American Epic* 100-108 (1978).

[602]Although Wickersham was widely held to be the Syndicate's staunchest foe, in 1906 and 1907 the Guggenheim-Morgan interests asked him to be their general counsel in Alaska; he declined because he refused to be subservient to the Guggenheims' corporation general counsel in Seattle, but when asked whether he would consider that position, he said yes. Evangeline Atwood, *Frontier Politics: Alaska's James Wickersham* 137, 146 (1979) (not revealing why the deal was not consummated).

[603]*The Building of Railroads in Alaska: Hearings Before the House Committee on the Territories on Bills H. R. 1739, H. R. 1806, and H. R. 2145*, 63d Cong., 1st Sess. 411 (1913). For a contemporaneous study documenting and economically conceptualizing the position of the Guggenheim-Morgan syndicate, see Edgar Salin, *Die wirtschaftliche Entwicklung von Alaska (and Yukon Territory): Ein Beitrag zu Geschichte und Theorie der Konzentrationsbewegung* (1914).

and its business associates in the territory were influential in local politics."[604]

The eight-hour day had become such a mainstream demand among the monopolies' proletarianized workers on the last frontier—the vast majority of whom were unmarried men[605]—that during the 1908 election campaign for congressional delegate all candidates agreed on the need for it; similarly, during the run-up to the elections for the first territorial legislature in 1912, party platforms also endorsed an eight-hour day.[606] Wickersham and his followers saw the congressional grant of home rule as undermining the Syndicate's political power, but others took a jaundiced view of the legislature's limited taxing powers and lack of control over such key industries as railroads and fishing, for which the salmon canneries had successfully lobbied.[607] Despite its initial opposition to home rule, such restrictions meant that the Syndicate "existed quite comfortably under territorial government."[608]

Indeed, the "Alaska syndicate came out the winner in Alaska's first Senate" by virtue of the election of four "corporate-oriented candidates" who could "kill an undesirable piece of legislation" in that eight-member chamber.[609] Nevertheless, miners, who together with mine owners predominated among the legislators at that first legislative session in 1913,[610] succeeded in enacting an eight-hour law for employment in underground mines and smelters and related operations on the grounds that it was "injurious to health and dangerous to life

---

[604]William Cashen, *Farthest North College President: Charles E. Bunnell and the Early History of the University of Alaska* 28 (1972)

[605]In 1910, white males outnumbered white females five to one in the total population; 71 percent of white men over the age of 15 were unmarried. 3 Bureau of the Census, *Thirteenth Census of the United States Taken in the Year 1910: Population 1910*, tab. 11 at 1139, tab. 15 at 1142 (1913). See also John Whitehead, "Dan Sutherland: Gold Rush Pioneer and Politician," 10 (1) *Alaska History* 1-5 at 1 (Spr. 1995). The 1910 census counted 38,350 occupied males and only 1,723 occupied females over the age of ten; in 1920 the corresponding figures were 24,712 and 2,085. Only 12 female miners were returned at the 1910 census compared to 11,372 men; in 1920, the figures were 20 and 5,287. 4 Bureau of the Census, *Fourteenth Census of the United States Taken in the Year 1920: Population: 1920: Occupations*, tab. 2 at 1262 (1923).

[606]Foster, "Syndicalism Northern Style" at 140; Ernest Gruening, *The State of Alaska* 159 (1968 [1954]).

[607]Cashen, *Farthest North College President* at 42-43; Richard Bloedel, "The First Bloom of Alaska Statehood: 1915-1916," 2(1) *Alaska J.* 8-17 at 8 (Winter 1972).

[608]Robert Stearns, "The Morgan-Guggenheim Syndicate and the Development of Alaska, 1906-1915," at 354 (Ph.D. diss., U. California, Santa Barbara, 1967). See also Jeannette Nichols, *Alaska: A History of Its Administration, Exploitation, and Industrial Development During Its First Half Century Under the Rule of the United States* 385-91 (1924).

[609]Atwood, *Frontier Politics* at 267.

[610]Gruening, *The State of Alaska* at 160.

and limb."[611] The legislature also enacted an eight-hour law that year for all work performed by contract for the territory or any municipality; longer workdays were permitted only "in cases of extraordinary emergency such as danger to life or property...."[612] The strong presence in Alaska of the radical Western Federation of Miners and the Socialist Party, which inscribed the eight-hour day in its platform in 1912, may have helped drive the legislation forward.[613]

The territorial governor's message to the second session of the legislature in 1915—which, as the result of the departure of most of the corporate-oriented senators, Wickersham "could control"[614]—recommended extension of the eight-hour law to placer mines. Governor John Strong, himself a former Alaskan miner,[615] justified his view by reference to the general experience "that a man who works eight hours a day will do as much work as he who works ten hours, and he will probably do it better."[616] Contentious debate saw both a repetition of the mine employers' argument that shorter hours were incompatible with a short season and a testimonial by at least one of the legislators who had been a miner of his experience of spending 10 hours in the muck and mud.[617] Finally, the legislature amended the 1913 eight-hour law to include underground placer mining.[618]

Concurrently with this debate over miners the legislature was also considering a more general eight-hour law. The first such bill was timid: it would have limited the workweek in laundries to 48 hours and conferred the eight-hour day on female workers in hotels, restaurants, bakeries, and telephone and telegraph exchanges.[619] The House of Representatives then recommitted the bill

---

[611]1913 Alaska Sess. Laws ch. 29, § 1 at 35, 36. The statute included an exception for emergencies, urgent necessity, and days on which shift changes were made; it did not include within the eight hours travel to or from the face. *Id.* § 2 at 36.

[612]1913 Alaska Sess. Laws ch. 7, § 2 at 8.

[613]Joseph Sullivan, "Sourdough Radicalism: Labor and Socialism in Alaska, 1905-1920," in *An Alaska Anthology: Interpreting the Past* 222-37 (Stephen Haycox and Mary Mangusso eds. 1996 [1992]).

[614]Atwood, *Frontier Politics* at 286-87.

[615]Gruening, *The State of Alaska* at 166.

[616]"Strong's Message Vigorous, Virile and Progressive," *Alaska Daily Empire*, Mar. 2, 1915, at 1, col. 7, at 2, col. 4, at 3, col. 1.

[617]"One House Passes 8 Hour Bill," *Alaska Daily Empire*, Mar. 24, 1915, at 1, col. 2, at 2, col. 4. See also "Fight Begins for 8-Hour Law for Placers," *Alaska Daily Empire*, Mar. 9, 1915, at 1, col. 4; "8-Hour Day for All of Mine Work," *Alaska Daily Empire*, Mar. 10, 1915, at 1, col. 4; "Pensions Favored by the Senate," *Alaska Daily Empire*, Apr. 10, 1915, at 1, col. 3, at 6, col. 3.

[618]1915 Alaska Sess. Laws ch. 6 at 6.

[619]"Several Cases of Employment Affected," *Alaska Daily Empire*, Mar. 11, 1915, at 1, col. 3.

to the Labor, Capital, and Immigration Committee, instructing it to include all industries.[620] Just two days before the session was to end, the press reported that absent some unforeseen event, the House would pass a universal eight-hour bill,[621] but the next day the House defeated the bill 9 to 6.[622]

On the last day of the session, the legislature—which, the president of the Senate stated three years later, "decided that it did not wish to assume the responsibility of enacting so important a measure without first submitting the question...to the people"[623]—ordered that the question as to whether the electorate favored a general eight-hour day for "all wage earners and salary earners" in Alaska be submitted to the electors at the next general election. If they voted in favor of the eight-hour day, the next session of the legislature was required to enact implementing legislation.[624] Thus although the scope of the law was uniquely universal in covering adult males and all industries, it did not propose to include non-wage or salary earners such as profit-taking business owners. The wording of the legislative proposal, as employers would point out two years later, also failed to specify whether "eight-hour day" meant an absolute ban on overtime work or merely imposed a penalty wage premium. However, since the first two legislatures, to the accompaniment of considerable publicity, had just enacted two eight-hour laws for miners permitting no overtime work, there would have been little reason to assume that the proposed general eight-hour statute was to be a mere overtime law.

Workers and labor unions displayed considerable enthusiasm for the referendum. Even the Nome local of the Western Federation of Miners, whose *Industrial Worker* took a jaundiced view of capitalist political institutions,[625] carried a streamer at the top of the front page during the run-up to the election urging workers to vote Yes. For these socialists, an eight-hour law "means more leisure for the worker; it means more rest and more time to fit oneself for the

---

[620]"Hanging Abolished; 8-Hour Day for All Industries Favored," *Alaska Daily Empire*, Apr. 21, 1915, at 1, col. 1.

[621]"General 8-Hour Bill May Pass," *Alaska Daily Empire*, Apr. 27, 1915, at 3, col. 5. In the very next column to this report the main newspaper of the capital, Juneau, printed a restaurant advertisement dressed up like a news article which mocked the proposed eight-hour law: A pro-eight-hour legislator is arrested by the sheriff for working his servants overtime whom he had sent to take his sick mother-in-law to the doctor; when the dog sled breaks down, they have to work more than eight hours, but the mother-in-law is nevertheless stranded in the blizzard. "Legislative Doings," *Alaska Daily Empire*, Apr. 27, 1915, at 3, col. 4.

[622]"Universal 8-Hour Bill Lost," *Alaska Daily Empire*, Apr. 28, 1915, at 1, col. 3.

[623]"Argument and Statement of Senator O. P. Hubbard," in "Hearings Before the Governor of Alaska on the Eight-Hour Law" at 224-28 at 227 (Feb. 20, 1918).

[624]1915 Alaska Sess. Laws ch. 58 at 109-10.

[625]James Foster, "AFL, IWW and Nome: 1905-1908," 5(2) *Alaska Journal* 66-73 (Spring 1975).

struggle for existence, so that we may learn to work and act that this existence will be no longer a struggle...." The industrial democracy to which the organization aspired would "not be hastened by keeping men and women with their noses to the grindstone, so that they know little of actual happenings, less of themselves...."[626] The day before the election, the paper, while bemoaning that non-workers, who tended to accept employers' viewpoint, were entitled to vote, conceded that some employers had recognized that shorter hours were "a business proposition because they got more out of the workers." But the *Industrial Worker* added that workers had their own reasons for wanting the shorter workday, including the resulting reduction in unemployment and competition.[627]

Interest in the referendum was intensified when, just two weeks before the election, the district court for the Fourth Judicial Division sitting in Fairbanks, on formal-technical grounds barely comprehensible to non-lawyers, invalidated the 1915 act that had amended the 1913 eight-hour law for miners to cover underground placer mining.[628] The case arose when, at the request of the United States, a grand jury indicted Sylvester Howell and Jennie Cleveland in July 1916 for having employed a worker in April for ten hours per day in underground placer mining workings in the absence of any imminent danger to life or property. In their defense, the employers raised the constitutional claim that the act was void as special legislation (presumably because it applied only to mining), but the court chose not to reach this issue. Instead, the judge accepted the defendants' argument that the title and body of the 1913 act limited its scope to lode mining, and, since the title of the 1915 amendment failed to extend the scope of the act, it was not germane to the act's subject matter other than lode mining, and therefore placer mining had never been validly subject to the law.[629]

Despite sustaining the employers' position, the judge, Charles Bunnell, who would play an even more prominent part in the struggle over the general eight-hour law in 1918, stressed that it was only with "the greatest reluctance" that courts invalidated laws enacted to protect workers engaged in hazardous occupations. Nevertheless, they were "compelled" to do so because of the legislature's failure to formulate the title of the 1915 amendment to expand the scope of the law.[630] Two years later, in a speech during his congressional delegate campaign, Wickersham, who himself had for years been the district

---

[626]"Vote 'Yes,'" *Daily Nome Industrial Worker*, Nov. 1, 1916, at 2, col. 1.

[627]"The Eight Hour Law," *Daily Nome Industrial Worker*, Nov. 6, 1916, at 2, col. 1.

[628]United States v. Howell, 5 Alaska 578 (4th Div. 1916). The *Report of the Governor of Alaska*, in 2 *Report of the Department of the Interior for the Fiscal Year Ended June 30, 1916*, at 432 (1917), noted that a test case had also been filed in Bunnell's court under the 1915 mining law.

[629]United States v. Howell, 5 Alaska at 578-79, 581.

[630]United States v. Howell, 5 Alaska at 582.

judge sitting in Fairbanks, called Bunnell's decision "the silliest rot he had ever read in a judicial decision...."[631]

Public interest in the eight-hour law was signaled by the fact that on the same day that Bunnell read his decision aloud in court, the *Fairbanks Daily News-Miner*, under a screaming banner headline, "8-Hour Law Unconstitutional," reprinted virtually the entire text. In a somewhat smaller font, the newspaper added the more colorful sub-headline: "Not Worth the Paper It's Written On." In case readers failed to turn to the inside pages, the editors helpfully summarized the day's editorial at the top of the article in large bolded type: "After Balling Upp [sic] Mineowners and Mineworkers Alike for a Year and Making Nothing But Trouble, Submitted to the Courts It Is Discovered That Alaska's 8-Hour Law Was Never a Law In Fact and Never Binding Upon Anybody Unless They Thought So." Beyond expressing its glee about the law's demise, the newspaper astutely observed that the decision was of "the greatest importance" not just to the litigants, but to "the whole Territory, as it is likely that similar decisions will be rendered by other courts in the other divisions, if the matter ever comes up there."[632] (Curiously, two years later, in the aftermath of Bunnell's decision striking down an eight-hour law, almost none of its supporters raised the converse question—whether it was still valid in Alaska's other three judicial divisions.) Without offering any supporting examples, the *News-Miner* editorialized that the statute had proved "an undesirable restriction upon laboring man and employer...resulting in an entire season's loss and annoyance to all of them...."[633]

Despite telegraph and telephone, news of the ruling moved slowly across the tundra. A whole month elapsed before the main newspaper down in Anchorage printed long excerpts from the decision,[634] and six weeks before the *Industrial Worker* out in remote Nome could discharge its anti-capitalist bile. Throwing up its hands, the paper charged that it was

> no use a layman discussing the relative merits of a judicial decision. These later [sic] day judges have a theologian of the middle ages...beaten a city block when it comes to splitting hairs, and the only interesting feature...is that the successful hair splitting on the bench is generally performed when some labor law is to be thrown out. ...
>
> These decisions like Bunnell's, these foolishly drawn up laws which the Bunnells tear up so easily, serve to show the worker that such scraps of paper are just scraps of paper

---

[631] "Wick Opens Up G.O.P. Campaign," *Tri-Weekly Nome Industrial Worker*, Aug. 3, 1918, at 1, col. 4, at 4, col. 1-4 at 3.

[632] "8-Hour Law Unconstitutional," *Fairbanks Daily News-Miner*, Oct. 23, 1916, at 1.

[633] "Incompetent Legislation," *Fairbanks Daily News-Miner*, Oct. 23, 1916, at 3, col. 1.

[634] "Decision of Bunnell in 8-Hour Law," *Anchorage Daily Times*, Nov. 20, 1916, at 4, col. 1-3.

and no more, when the economic power behind the legislators and the judges will have them so act. But when a labor organization, exerting its economic might and through the legislation enacted in the Union Hall, passes its eight hour law, there is a cast iron code that all the judges from hell to breakfast cannot tear with their long lean claws, try they ever so hard.[635]

Despite, or perhaps because of, Bunnell's ruling, more than 85 percent of voters in the referendum, led by the miners, favored the proposition at the general election in November 1916.[636] The following March, Governor Strong, in his message to the legislature at the beginning of its third session, reminded its members to "give careful consideration to this important matter, and to take such action as will carry out the expressed mandate of the people."[637]

The legislature did consider the matter, but not with the alacrity that the socialist *Industrial Worker* thought appropriate in light of the fact that the minority in the referendum "was so small that one could almost say the eight hour day demand was unanimous...."[638] A steady stream of mockery about the "Solons" and how they "shirk eight hour day" appeared in the paper for weeks.[639] But the bill that the Senate began considering in March was identical to the one that labor organizations had sought to introduce, and even the cynical *Industrial Worker* gave little chance of passage to an amendment to exempt the all-important fish canneries,[640] whose association telegraphed the legislature urging exemption on the grounds of "absolute necessity for safety of the country" of salmon production during World War I, which the United States had just entered.[641] During the legislative debate dire predictions were made of "the great calamity that would result" especially with respect to the cannery interests and

---

[635]"Unconstitutional," *Daily Nome Industrial Worker*, Dec. 4, 1916, at 2, col. 1.

[636]The vote was 10,416 in favor and 1,782 opposed. "Complete Returns of November Election as Reported upon by Territorial Canvassing Board," *Alaska Daily Empire*, Mar. 2, 1917, at 2, col. 4. On the miners' leading role in the struggle for eight-hour legislation, see "Maloney on Eight Hour," *Alaska Daily Empire*, Feb. 9, 1918, at 4, col. 1 (reprinting editorial from *Nenane News*).

[637]"Message of the Governor," in *The Journal of the House of Representatives of the Third Legislative Assembly of the Territory of Alaska* 14, 19 (1917).

[638]"The Eight Hour Day," *Daily Nome Industrial Worker*, Mar, 23,1917, at 2, col. 1 (editorial).

[639]"Shirk Eight Hour Day," *Daily Nome Industrial Worker*, Mar. 23, 1917, at 4, col. 1; "Senate Still Continues Deadlock in Juneau," *Daily Nome Industrial Worker*, Mar. 14, 1917, at 1, col. 4.

[640]"Senate General Eight Hour Bill Is Read," *Daily Nome Industrial Worker*, Mar. 30, 1917, at 1, col. 2.

[641]"Canneries Say 8-Hour Law Is Very Dangerous," *Alaska Daily Empire*, Apr. 12, 1917, at 5, col. 3; "Canneries Say Law Is Dangerous," *Anchorage Daily Times*, Apr. 23, 1917, at 3, col. 4.

curtailing of the nation's food supply.[642]

Patriotism, however, was not the fishing industry's real motivation. Rather, the canneries were impelled by the need to ward off interference with their practice of requiring employees to work extraordinarily long hours. Just a few months before the legislative debates, William Kirk, the general secretary of United Charities of Rochester, had published an article in *Survey* exposing these patterns. At one salmon cannery he met a 10-year-old boy whose job was "to watch an interminable row of cans as they passed him on a traveling belt. Every minute or so he would take out a bent can. For 10 cents an hour, and usually for ten hours a day, and six days a week, he had his eyes fixed on the can chute. Sometimes, he said, he worked ten and a half hours a day and sometimes as many as thirteen." At another cannery, children 10 to 12 years old were working from seven in the morning until six and often nine in the evening, including Sundays.[643] Often men and boys worked seven days a week, 14 or 14 and a half hours daily. A group of Hawaiian workers were paid a fixed $180 for the season to work seven days a week, 11 hours a day, with overtime (work after 6 p.m.) paid at 15 cents an hour. The canneries were especially partial toward Chinese workers: "they are industrious and tractable. They have such a low standard of living that they are willing to work excessively long hours without grumbling...."[644] Better even than Chinese workers, however, was machinery that did the work of 20 workers disassembling salmon by hand; the machine was known as the "iron Chink."[645]

Salmon cannery owners, however, did not need to rely solely on their own telegrams: they were influential enough to secure intervention by higher power-holders. In the midst of the legislative deliberations, Territorial Governor Strong transmitted to the legislators a telegram that he had received from Interior Secretary Franklin K. Lane—who had jurisdiction over Alaska—requesting, on behalf of the salmon packing industry, inclusion in the law of a clause authorizing

---

[642]"Pro and Con of General 8-Hour Law," *Anchorage Daily Times*, May 3, 1917, at 6, col. 3 (discussing session of Apr. 18).

[643]William Kirk, "Labor Forces of the Alaska Coast," 36(14) *Survey* 351-57 at 351 (July 1, 1916). Alaska's child labor law applied only to mining, but after a 1919 federal child labor tax law had been interpreted as applying to canneries in Alaska, the territorial labor commissioner recommended that "steps be taken to free native Alaskan children from the operation of this act." *Biennial Report of the Labor Commissioner for Alaska, 1919-1920*, at 4 (1921), in Record Group 101, Ser. 130, Box 196, File 52 Reports, Folder 196-3, Alaska State Archives. Such steps were presumably unnecessary since the U.S. Supreme Court struck the law down as unconstitutional. Bailey v. Drexel Furniture Co., 259 U.S. 20 (1922).

[644]Kirk, "Labor Forces of the Alaska Coast" at 352-53. Cannery employers also used a labor contractor system in an effort to rid themselves of any liability for wages; the largely Chinese crew leaders often failed to pay the workers. *Id.* at 352, 356-57.

[645]Salin, *Die wirtschaftliche Entwicklung von Alaska* at 37.

waiver of the eight-hour provision by the governor if a national emergency were declared by the interior secretary or the Council of National Defense.[646] The Council, which was established by Congress in 1916 to coordinate resources, consisted of several cabinet secretaries and worked through a huge network of state and local organizations; it asked all state legislatures to delegate to the governors the power to suspend or modify state labor laws during the war when the Council requested such suspension or modification.[647] The local councils of defense in Alaska, whose members were commonly "leading citizens of the community" associated with fishing or mining, sought to combine their call for longer workdays with combating the influence of the International Workers of the World in those industries.[648] Two days after receiving Lane's telegram, the Alaska House of Representatives added the suspension provision to the bill.[649] Even on the eve of final passage, the Nome newspaper of the Western Federation of Miners pilloried the senators for "pulling off a good josh on their constituents" by considering yet another referendum despite the more than ten to one majority in the original referendum: "Anything to avert this labor legislation in the interest of the higher-ups."[650] A few days later the Senate did pass a bill providing for an expression of voter opinion on whether the general eight-hour law for all wage and salary earners should be amended to exclude industries operating only during the short summer seasons, such as placer mines, canneries, and agriculture (as well as clerks), but the House did not concur.[651]

The legislature, however, did act. First, after the Alaska attorney general had filed an opinion with the House that the legislature's power to limit miners' hours was "no longer a mooted question,"[652] the legislature enacted a new special eight-

---

[646]"Secretary of Interior Asks Law Changes," *Alaska Daily Empire*, Apr. 14, 1917, at 2, col. 1-4. See also "General Eight Hour Law Not Effective Now," *Fairbanks Daily News-Miner*, May 12, 1917, at 4, col. 3.

[647]Act of Aug. 29, 1916, ch. 418, § 2, 39 Stat. 619, 649-50; *First Report of the Council of National Defense for the Fiscal Year Ended June 30, 1917*, at 76 (1917); Paul Murphy, *World War I and the Origin of Civil Liberties in the United States* 88 (1979).

[648]John Stewart, "The Alaskan Home Front During World War I" at 5, 7, 16-17, 21 (quote) (unpublished paper presented at Conf. on Military History, Anchorage, Nov. 2-3, 1984).

[649]*The Journal of the House of Representatives of the Third Legislative Assembly of the Territory of Alaska* at 146.

[650]"Senate Joshers Want to Refer Eight Hour Again," *Daily Nome Industrial Worker*, Apr. 26, 1917, at 4, col. 2 (the 10 to 1 figure was incorrect).

[651]"Session of Alaska Legislature Ends Thursday," *Anchorage Daily Times*, May 2, 1917, at 1, col. 2; *The Senate Journal of the Third Legislative Assembly of the Territory of Alaska* 143, 211 (1917) (Senate Bill No. 75); *The Journal of the House of Representatives of the Third Legislative Assembly of the Territory of Alaska* at 315.

[652]*Biennial Report of the Attorney General of the Territory of Alaska for the Period March 1, 1917, to March 1, 1919*, at 57, 58 (1919) (Mar. 24, 1917). See also "Grigsby's

hour law for miners not vulnerable to the defects that had prompted Judge Bunnell to strike down the 1915 act.[653] Then the legislators, by a vote of 6-0 in the Senate and 14-2 in the House,[654] enacted an unprecedented universal absolute eight-hour law. In the House, the bill had been introduced by Philip Corrigan, the chairman of the Committee on Labor, Capital, and Immigration, and a former miner, socialist, and president of Nome Local 240 of the Western Federation of Miners; in the Senate, another former miner, Swedish-born John Sundback, filed the bill.[655] (After being informed by the Attorney General that such a bill would not affect the general eight-hour law, the House passed an eight-hour law for women in numerous industries, but refused to concur in the Senate amendment to exclude "Natives or mixed blood during the salmon canning season," and the bill died.)[656]

The new law's central provision read:

> That a period of employment for all wage earners, and salary earners in the Territory of Alaska shall not exceed eight hours (8) within any calendar day, except in cases when life or property is in imminent danger. Employment as herein used shall be construed as the performance of labor or services for any individual, partnership, association or corporation, whether the person performing such labor or service be a member of such partnership or association to stockholder or officer of such corporation or not.[657]

Each day's violation constituted a separate misdemeanor and was punishable by a fine of $100 to $500 and/or 60 days' to six months' imprisonment. Finally, the statute included the provision that the interior secretary had urged empowering the governor to suspend or modify the operation of the law, at the request of the interior secretary or Council of National Defense, during World War I.[658]

Opinion on 8-Hour Bill," *Anchorage Daily Times*, Apr. 5, 1917, at 2, col. 2

[653]1917 Alaska Sess. Laws ch. 4 at 3.

[654]*The Senate Journal of the Third Legislative Assembly of the Territory of Alaska* at 117; *The Journal of the House of Representatives of the Third Legislative Assembly of the Territory of Alaska* at 183.

[655]*Who's Who in Alaskan Politics: A Biographical Dictionary of Alaskan Political Personalities, 1884-1974*, at 20, 97 (Evangeline Atwood and Robert DeArmond comp. 1977); Sullivan, "Sourdough Radicalism" at 233-34.

[656]*The Journal of the House of Representatives of the Third Legislative Assembly of the Territory of Alaska* at 216-17, 227-28, 357 (House Bill 10); *The Senate Journal of the Third Legislative Assembly of the Territory of Alaska* at 217 (quote), 222, 239. Bizarrely, six weeks later the newspaper of the Alaska Labor Union erroneously reported that H.B. 10 had been enacted and would go into effect July 20. "Alaska's Eight-Hour Law for Miners Is Now in Operation," *Alaska Labor News*, June 16, 1917, at 3, col. 1.

[657]1917 Alaska Sess. Laws, ch. 55, § 1, at 116.

[658]1917 Alaska Sess. Laws ch. 55 at 116. The legislature also voted on May Day to appropriate funds to pay overtime wages to its own employees. House Concurrent Res.

"One of the most discussed provisions of the law" and one that made it unique was the ban on work beyond eight hours even by business partners. The *Anchorage Sunday Times*, focusing on the issue of unfair intra-capitalist competition, editorialized that since the law did not impose such a ban "where a man is sole owner of his business," he "alone will have the right to work as long as he wishes, while the one which is owned by two partners, even though both are not there, will be unable to work more than eight hours."[659] Despite almost unanimous votes in both chambers on final enactment, this particular provision was subject to considerable controversy.[660] The Committee of the Whole of the House had recommended adoption of a proviso "that the period of employment prescribed by this Act shall not apply to Superintendents, Managers, Bosses, Foremen, or other executives of any partnership, association or corporations when acting as such." After the House struck "Bosses," it did adopt this amendment, but the Senate did not agree to it. A further motion in the House to strike the language imposing coverage on partners and corporate officers failed by a vote of 4-12.[661] That even the senators were plagued by some doubts as to the bill's constitutionality was signaled by their having voted twice to defer consideration of it until they received the attorney general's opinion.[662]

Notably, employers undertook no public campaign to persuade Congress to exercise its power to repeal the eight-hour law.[663] Their low profile during the legislative debates may not have been irrational. First of all, firms, and especially canneries, may have been relying on the suspension mechanism during the war years. Second, the other large employing industry, mining, was already largely subject to a special eight-hour law. The new law did apply for the first time to surface placer mining and dredges, but the number of newly covered workers was

---

No. 7, in 1917 Alaska Sess. Laws at 226.

[659]"The Eight-Hour Law," *Anchorage Sunday Times*, Dec. 23, 1917, at 4, col. 1.

[660]Legislative history analysis is, unfortunately, impeded by the fact that not all of the bills and amendments from the 1913, 1915, or 1917 legislative sessions have survived. Telephone interview with Judy Skagerberg, Alaska State Archives, Juneau (March 2000).

[661]*The Journal of the House of Representatives of the Third Legislative Assembly of the Territory of Alaska* at 170-71 (House Bill No. 28); *The Senate Journal of the Third Legislative Assembly of the Territory of Alaska* at 183, 196, 222. The House acted in the same vein when it voted to narrow the scope of coverage by substituting "all wage earners and salary earners" for "all labor or services." This language was enacted, but a further House proviso "that this Act shall not be construed to prohibit extra hours of employment necessitated by a change of shift" was not. *The Journal of the House of Representatives of the Third Legislative Assembly of the Territory of Alaska* at 170.

[662]*The Senate Journal of the Third Legislative Assembly of the Territory of Alaska* at 81, 108 (Senate Bill No 13).

[663]In establishing a territorial legislature in Alaska, Congress reserved to itself the right to disapprove any statutes enacted there. Act of Aug. 24, 1912, ch. 387, § 20, 37 Stat. 512, 518.

"small as compared with the other mining industries."[664] And finally, some employers may have assumed that a judge sympathetic to their interests might declare the law unconstitutional.

The first possibility was highlighted in the governor's annual report for 1917, which reminded the interior secretary that the governor was authorized to suspend the law if the secretary requested him to do so.[665] Predictably, as January 1, 1918, the effective date of the law, approached, employers began urging the authorities to make use of this mechanism. On December 4, the Interior Department wired Strong that a lumber mill company in Wrangell had petitioned the secretary to suspend the law "alleging enforcement will necessitate doscontinuance [sic] of business...." The department instructed the governor to "take up matter with company, ascertain facts and submit your recommendation on application."[666] Three days later, Newton Baker, the Secretary of War and chairman of the Council of National Defense, requested that Strong suspend the law as to the salmon industry for the duration of the war. Enforcement of the eight-hour law, according to Baker, "would either materially increase the cost or decrease the output of canned salmon, a most essential article of diet of our army our navy our civilian population and our allies...."[667] The pressure on the governor mounted three days later when he received an almost identical telegram from Interior Secretary Lane, who added that Herbert Hoover of the U.S. Food Administration concurred in the request.[668]

On December 15, 1917, Strong issued a proclamation suspending the eight-hour law not only as to the salmon fisheries and canneries, as Baker and Lane had requested, but also to "any manufacturing industry...whose products are necessary to the proper preparation of salmon as a food supply...."[669] After this first suspension, the governor seized the initiative two weeks later, recommending that Lane request him to suspend the law as to taking, preparing, and curing all other

---

[664]*Report of the Territorial Mine Inspector to the Governor of Alaska for the Year 1917*, at 11-12 (1918).

[665]*Report of the Governor of Alaska*, in 2 *Indian Affairs Territories: Reports of the Department of Interior for the Fiscal Year Ending June 30, 1917*, at 439 (65th Cong., 1st Sess., [?] H. Doc. No. 915, 1918).

[666]From Meyer Asst. to the Secretary to Governor Strong, Dec. 4, 1917, in Record Group 101, File Code 156, Box 152, Alaska State Archives.

[667]Telegram from Newton D. Baker to Hon J F Strong Governor of Alaska, Dec. 7, 1917, in Record Group 101, File Code 156, Box 152, Alaska State Archives.

[668]Telegram from Secretary Lane to Governor Strong, Dec. 10, 1917, in Record Group 101, File Code 156, Box 152, Alaska State Archives.

[669]Territory of Alaska, Executive Dept., A Proclamation, Dec. 15, 1917, in Record Group 101, File Code 156, Box 152, Alaska State Archives. See also "Eight-Hour Act Will Not Apply to Fisheries," *Anchorage Daily Times*, Dec. 13, 1917, at 1, col. 1.

kinds of food fish.[670] Lane took a week to reply to Strong's telegram, stating merely that he had "no request [for] suspension" regarding those industrics, but asking for Strong's view regarding suspension of the law in mining.[671] One possible reason for the alacrity with which Strong complied with Lane's requests was the governor's knowledge that Alaska Democrats at that very moment were lobbying the Wilson administration not to reappoint him in 1918 because he had failed to side with the Democratic candidate in the aftermath of the contested election for congressional delegate against Wickersham.[672]

Nevertheless, and expressly legitimizing his action by reference to Lane's "request," the governor on January 7, 1918, issued an executive order suspending the law as to the rest of the fishing industry.[673] Two days later Strong, however, answered a telegram from Lane[674] to the effect that no exception should be granted one of Alaska's railroads because he believed that the eight-hour law's emergency provision covered longer hours caused by winter weather and that therefore "no prosecution would follow."[675]

Not until December 21, 1917, did Strong reply to Lane's telegram of December 4 concerning the lumber mill. In his five-page letter the governor defended his action regarding the salmon industry on the grounds that, as a seasonal business, it would experience lower output if subject to the eight-hour law. After conceding that labor was scarce throughout Alaska—a finding that he would negate just two months later—he nevertheless opposed suspension in mining, but admitted that if the lumber manufacturing industry's claims were true, "it probably would be advisable to suspend the operation of the 8-hour law" as to it as well as to logging. After offering this specific advice, Strong veered off into a sermon about the patriotic demands of self-denial and self-sacrifice that applied to the "employer and capitalist" as much as to the workman.[676]

---

[670]Telegram from Governor Strong to Secretary Interior, Dec. 28, 1917, in Record Group 101, File Code 156, Box 152, Alaska State Archives.

[671]Telegram from Secretary Lane to Governor Strong, Jan. 5, 1917 [sic; should be 1918], in Record Group 101, File Code 156, Box 159, Alaska State Archives. This curious exchange would be clarified if the telegram contained a typo: Lane's phrase, "I have no request suspension," should perhaps have read, "I have to request suspension."

[672]James A. Wickersham, "Diaries," Dec. 7, 13, 14, 28, and 31, 1917, Jan. 1, 1918, in Alaska State Archives.

[673]Territory of Alaska, Governor's Office, Executive Order, Jan. 7, 1918, in Record Group 101, File Code 156, Box 159, Alaska State Archives.

[674]Telegram from Secretary Lane to Gov. Strong, Jan. 9, 1918, in Record Group 101, File Code 156, Box 159, Alaska State Archives.

[675]Telegram from Governor Strong to Secretary Interior, Jan. 9, 1918, in Record Group 101, File Code 156, Box 159, Alaska State Archives.

[676]Letter from Governor to Secretary of the Interior, Dec. 21, 1917, in Record Group 101, File Code 156, Box 152, Alaska State Archives. Strong did not explain how

In December 1917 and January 1918 the governor was bombarded with telegrams from capital and labor. The Ketchikan Power Company was perhaps most vigorous in not only requesting total suspension during the war, but also "feel[ing] this is an unjust law for Alaska and should never have been placed on the records."[677] Workers, in contrast, were concerned about enforcement of the new eight-hour law: as early as December 3, 1917, the Alaska Labor Union wired Strong that 2,000 members had unanimously passed a resolution demanding that the statute not be rescinded.[678] Governor Strong, mindful of union opinion and that the legislature had unanimously passed a law strongly approved by the people in a referendum, decided not to heed the call by the Anchorage Chamber of Commerce for suspension of the law altogether during the war.[679]

Nevertheless, the future of the eight-hour law became dimmer on New Year's Day 1918, when Interior Secretary Lane telegraphed Strong that the Anchorage Chamber of Commerce and the Cordova Council of Defense had requested general suspension and asked the governor to "wire me your views as to whether or not necessity exist [sic] for such action."[680] Strong's negative reply the following day was firm: "[I]t is my opinion that no necessity exists for general suspension.... This office has received but few requests for such action, and many against it. Labor organization protests have been especially numerous."[681]

Strong's personal views about the law may have been accurately reflected in his assurance to a private correspondent in early January that it was his "honest conviction that nothing would be gained by the general suspension of the law, and that includes the mining industry of the Territory. A general 8-hour law is being adopted all over the country, and the people of the Territory might just as well make up their minds that the day of the 8 hours has come and is here to stay." He buttressed this belief by reference to his own observations in the printing and newspaper business (he had been editor of the *Nome Nugget* and *Alaska Daily*

---

seasonality was relevant if canneries could operate on two or three shifts.

677Telegram from Ketchikan Power Co. to Major Strong, Governor of Alaska, Dec. 15, 1917, in Record Group 101, File Code 156, Box 152, Alaska State Archives

678Telegram from W J Henry to Hon J F A Strong, Dec. 3, 1917, in Record Group 101, File Code 156, Box 152, Alaska State Archives.

679"Suspension of Eight-Hour Law Asked: Chamber of Commerce of Anchorage States Enactment Interferes with War Policy," *Anchorage Daily Times*, Dec. 19, 1917, at 1, col. 5; "Eight-Hour Law Supported by Labor Unions," *Anchorage Daily Times*, Dec. 27, 1917, at 1, col. 4; Letter from Governor Strong to Andrew Beck and Al Braten, Jan. 12, 1918, published in "Received from Governor Strong; Via Yesterday's Mail," *Daily Nome Industrial Worker*, Feb. 28, 1918, at 5, col. 1.

680Telegram from Franklin K. Lane to Hon. J F A Strong, Jan. 1, 1918, in Record Group 101, File Code 156, Box 159, Alaska State Archives.

681Telegram from Strong, Governor to Secretary Interior, Jan. 2, 1918, in Record Group 101, File Code 156, Box 159, Alaska State Archives.

Empire), which had taught him that printers became physically exhausted by ten hours of work and that they could do as much work and more cheerfully in eight hours.[682] To be sure, Strong's optimism may have been the result of his lack of familiarity with details of the various laws; in any event, contrary to his view, the absolute eight-hour day for adult males (including business partners) with no provision for overtime work had not yet come. Indeed, more than 80 years later it had still not arrived.

To some employers or local branches of the Territorial Council of Defense requesting a general suspension of the eight-hour law Strong sent pro forma replies in January 1918, stating merely that under the statute his authority to suspend could be triggered only by a request from the secretary of the interior or the Council of National Defense.[683] To others he offered substantive reasons, stressing that during the campaign from 1915 to 1917 "no public speakers or the press of the Territory [had] discussed the merits of this referendum, neither did they protest against the passage of the law by the legislature."[684]

In the meantime, one of the initial consequences of the eight-hour law was the decision by stores in Anchorage to close at 6 p.m.,[685] a proposal that the socialist *Alaska Labor News* had made a year earlier on the grounds that Anchorage—which originated in 1915 as a tent settlement for workers building the Alaska railway—had already passed through its founding years when late-night hours were a necessity, but "hard on the clerks, hard on the business men."[686] The *Anchorage Sunday Times* editorially welcomed this early closing as a "condition which long ago should have been in existence" since most workers in Anchorage left work at 4:30 or 5 p.m. so that shopping could be completed by 6 p.m.[687]

The new law was also sufficiently talked about to become the subject of everyday humor. Under the headline, "Harmony Actor Does Not Heed Eight-Hour Law," one paper reported that "[a]nybody...depressed over the fact that the law prevents more than eight hours' work in one day, should go" see a new funny

---

[682]Letter from Governor Strong to Dr. Aline Bradley (Jan. 9, 1918), in J. F. A. Strong Papers, Box 1 Folder 25, Alaska and Polar Regions Archives, Rasmuson Library, University of Alaska at Fairbanks ("personal and confidential").

[683]See, e.g., W. Whittlesey, Secretary, Seward Branch Alaska Territorial Council of Defense to Governor J. F. A. Strong, Dec. 22, 1917, in Record Group 101, File Code 156, Box 152, Alaska State Archives; Governor Strong to W. Whittlesey, Jan. 8, 1918, in Record Group 101, File Code 156, Box 159, Alaska State Archives.

[684]Governor to Local Council of Defense, Valdez, Jan. 12, 1918, in Record Group 101, File Code 156, Box 159, Alaska State Archives.

[685]"Stores Will Close at Six Every Night," *Anchorage Sunday Times*, Dec. 30, 1917, at 1, col. 1.

[686]*Alaska Labor News*, Jan. 27, 1917, at 4, col. 1 (untitled editorial).

[687]"The Eight-Hour Law," *Anchorage Sunday Times*, Dec. 23, 1917, at 4, col. 1.

film where he would have to "put in overtime laughing."[688]

On January 10, Lane returned to the issue of the lumber industry and Strong's letter of Dec. 21, this time requesting further investigation and a definite recommendation concerning the company's claim that it was unable to supply spruce for airplanes.[689] A week later Strong replied, tacitly reversing himself, now advising against suspension because he was convinced that Alaska mills did not manufacture lumber suitable for airplanes.[690] Despite his resistance to further suspensions, employers' demands for a free hand with regard to the length of the workday became more intense. On January 15, the Guggenheim Kennecott Copper Corporation, "the greatest copper trust in the world"[691]—which the previous summer had accomplished the difficult task of breaking a strike by recruiting miners in Alaska in the midst of an alleged labor shortage[692]—stressing the interest of the United States Government in its output, wired Strong that in the "present National emergency it does not seem advisable that our plant should be subject to a sixteen hour shutdown and production stopped simply because mechanics...are not allowed by law to work even an hour overtime...."[693] The copper trust's influence was magnified during World War I during which production in Alaska recorded huge increases and far surpassed gold mining in value.[694] Two days later, the manager of a large mining company sought to sway the governor by charging that only "certain of the unions or socialistic class" opposed the nationwide movement to suspend eight-hour laws for non-underground mining operations, while "all real Americans, whether laborers or otherwise" supported it.[695] Then on the January 19, Interior Secretary Lane wired

---

[688]"Harmony Actor Does Not Heed Eight-Hour Law," *Anchorage Daily Times*, Jan. 4, 1918, at 2, col. 5.

[689]Telegram from Secretary Lane to Gov. Strong, Jan. 10, 1918, in Record Group 101, File Code 156, Box 159, Alaska State Archives.

[690]Telegram from Governor Strong to Secretary Interior, Jan. 19, 1918, in Record Group 101, File Code 156, Box 159, Alaska State Archives.

[691]*The Building of Railroads in Alaska* at 407 (testimony of James Wickersham, Alaskan Delegate to Congress).

[692]*Report of the Territorial Mine Inspector to the Governor of Alaska for the Year 1917*, at 10-11.

[693]Telegram from E. T. Stannard, manager, to Governor Strong, Jan. 15, 1918, in Record Group 101, File Code 156, Box 159, Alaska State Archives.

[694]The value of copper produced in Alaska rose from $2.8 million in 1914 to $29.4 million in 1916, declining to $24.4 million in 1917 as a result of "labor troubles at the Kennecott-Bonanza mine." The value of gold production held steady in the range of $16-17 million. *Annual Report of the Territorial Mine Inspector to the Governor of Alaska: 1921*, at 77-78 (n.d. [1922]); *Report of the Territorial Mine Inspector to the Governor of Alaska for the Year 1917* at 6 (quote).

[695]Letter from B. L. Thane (Alaska Gastineau Mining Co.) to Hon. J. F. A. Strong, Jan. 17, 1918, in Record Group 101, File Code 156, Box 159, Alaska State Archives.

Strong, again conveying requests to suspend the law as to railroads and steamships based on claims of labor shortages and prohibitive increases in operating expenses.[696]

This flood of messages culminated in Lane's telegram of January 23, informing the governor that the Council of National Defense had advised the states that no action should be taken on requests to suspend their eight-hour laws until the governor had held a hearing and concluded that suspension was advisable. Lane therefore instructed Strong to hold hearings on the petitions from the lumber manufacturing, logging, railroad, steamship, and mining industries, to send him and the Council a brief summary of the facts and his advice.[697]

The next day Governor Strong announced that beginning February 5 he would hold public hearings on petitions by those named industries for suspension of the law as to them and authorization to work employees more than eight hours for extra compensation. The announcement sparked mass labor meetings in January and February in support of the new law.[698] Unions sought to refute claims by operators of copper mines, logging camps, and lumber mills that an alleged scarcity of workers would make it impossible to meet war production needs by arguing that it was "common knowledge" that all the requisite skilled and unskilled workers would be forthcoming if employers paid fair wages for an eight-hour day.[699] They also observed that double shifts would take care of any labor shortage resulting from an eight-hour shift.[700] In contrast, local councils of defense urged the governor to suspend the law entirely; the council in Ketchikan, for example, asserted that carpenters, machinists, electricians, loggers, and others "must be available at all hours to make up" for the impossibility of increasing the number of workers caused by the labor shortage.[701]

---

[696]Telegram from Franklin K Lane Secy to Governor Strong, Jan. 19, 1918, in Record Group 101, File Code 156, Box 159, Alaska State Archives.

[697]Telegram from Lane to Hon J F A Strong, Jan. 23, 1919, in Record Group 101, File Code 156, Box 159, Alaska State Archives.

[698]Governor Strong to All Concerned, Jan. 24, 1918, in Record Group 101, File Code 156, Box 159, Alaska State Archives; "Hearing to Be Held on 8-Hour Law," *Alaska Daily Empire*, Jan. 25, 1918, at 5, col. 5; "Mass Meeting Will Discuss Eight Hour Act," *Anchorage Daily Times*, Jan. 29, 1918, at 2, col. 2; "Mass Meeting Opposes Change in Labor Law," *Anchorage Daily Times*, Jan. 30, 1918, at 1, col. 5; "Pertaining to the Eight Hour Law," *Daily Nome Industrial Worker*, Feb. 2, 1918, at 1, col. 1; "Mass Meeting Is in Favor of Eight Hour Day," *Anchorage Daily Times*, Feb. 7, 1918, at 3, col. 2; Eight Hour Law Hearing Fixed on February 15," *Anchorage Sunday Times*, Feb. 10, 1918, at 1, col. 2.

[699]"Mass Meeting Is in Favor of Eight Hour Day," *Anchorage Daily Times*, Feb. 7, 1918, at 3, col. 2, 3.

[700]"Labor Shortage—Eight-Hour Law," 1 (3) *Alaska Labor Union Bulletin* 2 (Feb. 15, 1918).

[701]Telegram from Ryus to Governor J F A Strong, Feb. 3, 1918, in Record Group 101,

Thousands attended mass meetings under the auspices of the Alaska Labor Union to oppose abrogation of the law.[702] These protest meetings captured the prevailing sentiment concerning overtime work. At one meeting in Juneau the night before the hearings began, a petition was debated including a proposal to provide workers with the option of working more than eight hours. Although the meeting had "started off like an old maids' tea party," the optional overtime proposal "immediately brought out a storm of protest" and it was voted down. Equally interesting was the discussion of a proposal to petition the governor to mandate time and a half for overtime work by fishermen, who, as a result of the governor's suspension of the new law as to them, were "required to work as long as the employer deems necessary." A representative of the fishermen, however, urged those attending not to take any action that might confuse the two issues: "'If the workers of this and other sections will stand solidly behind the eight-hour law as it now stands, the fishermen will take other means of protecting themselves.'"[703]

The hearings, which extended over more than two weeks, received broad coverage in the territorial press, the opening day, for example, being reported in a banner headline in the Juneau paper.[704] Mining, fisheries, logging, and shipping employers were most heavily represented at the hearings.[705] Much more interesting than employers' and workers' predictably stylized and empirically unverifiable responses to Governor Strong's call to focus on the question of whether Alaska was suffering from a labor shortage were the class divisions on the issue of whether workers should be permitted to work overtime.[706] Employers favored antipaternalistic arguments. Ralph Robertson, one of the territory's leading corporate lawyers and acting as agent of several companies,[707] asserted:

File Code 156, Box 159, Alaska State Archives.

[702]"Eight Hour Law Mass Meeting Anchorage," *Daily Nome Industrial Worker*, Feb. 1, 1918, at 1, col. 4.

[703]"Action Taken Last Night at Mass Meeting," *Alaska Daily Empire*, Feb. 5, 1918, at 6, col. 3-4.

[704]"Hearings Begin on 8-Hour Law," *Alaska Daily Empire*, Feb. 5, 1918, at 1.

[705] For the list of the companies (including Kennecott Copper Co.) testifying in favor of suspension, see Letter from Governor Strong to Secretary of the Interior at 2; "Hearings Before the Governor of Alaska on the Eight-Hour Law (Chapter 55, Session Laws of Alaska): Feb. 5 to 21, 1918" [unpaginated].

[706]"Hearing on 8-Hour Law Continued," *Alaska Daily Empire*, Feb. 6, 1918, at 2, col. 4.

[707]Robertson was also a U.S. Commissioner in Juneau in 1913, territorial director of the U.S. Employment Service from 1917 to 1919, mayor of Juneau from 1920 to 1923, and president of the Juneau Chamber of Commerce, in addition to presiding over Juneau's leading corporate law firms into the 1960s. 4 Alaska Reports viii (1914); *The American Bar: A Biographical Directory of Contemporary Lawyers of the United States and Canada*, at 1166 (1926).

"If a man wants to work overtime, he is entitled to it, but this law prohibits them from working their men over eight hours or paying them for it, no matter what proportion of the profits they are willing to give."[708] Moreover, employers insisted that some "men want to work overtime; they demand the right to work overtime, and they do work overtime."[709] Ironically, in comparison with Alaska's absolute eight-hour law, a statute that forced employers to pay premium overtime began to look appealing. According to Robertson:

> If this law would permit them, like the Oregon law does, which has gone to the Supreme Court and been held valid,...to employ men for an hour or two hours or three hours and pay them overtime, double time, or one-half time, whatever is a fair basis, as agreed upon between the labor and the employer, it would be a different proposition. But this law cuts them off on the 8 hours. ... If they work their men overtime, they are violating the letter of the law, if it is only five minutes overtime, just as much as though they worked them three hours overtime; and the laboring man has no way of getting paid, or saying to the employer, "I am willing to work overtime. I realize you are at a disadvantage and I am willing to work overtime."[710]

Other employer representatives tried a different tack. P. E. Bradley, speaking on behalf of two gold mining companies and a local council of defense, reported that all of his principals agreed that "eight hours a day was long enough for any man to work. However, they all" also felt that during the war "it would not be asking too much" to modify the law to "protect the workingman against being compelled to work more than eight hours, if he didn't see fit," but "at the same time giving him the privilege of working overtime in case he would like to do so and was paid for that overtime."[711] Herbert Faulkner, another Juneau corporate lawyer-lobbyist representing mining companies and an influential force in the Republican Party,[712] urged permissive overtime and went so far as to assert: "There is no answer to that argument. [N]o laboring man can have any valid

---

[708]"Hearings Before the Governor of Alaska on the Eight-Hour Law" at 6. A typo in the transcript makes it appear as if Governor Strong made this statement, but it is clear from the context that Robertson's name was inadvertently omitted.

[709]"Hearings Before the Governor of Alaska on the Eight-Hour Law" at 192 (Robert Capers referring to longshoremen). For hearing testimony of longshoremen who worked 36 hours without any overtime, see *id.* at 201 (E. E. Allen).

[710]"Hearings Before the Governor of Alaska on the Eight-Hour Law" at 8 (Robertson).

[711]"Hearings Before the Governor of Alaska on the Eight-Hour Law" at 51.

[712]Faulkner, who had been a U.S. marshall in Juneau, also engaged in a long corporate law career. 3 Alaska Reports vi; *The American Bar: The Professional Directory of Leading Lawyers Throughout the World* 1529 (39th ed. 1957); *Who's Who in Alaskan Politics* at 28-29; Atwood, *Frontier Politics* at 303. Faulkner and Robertson were the leading business lawyers in Juneau. Pamela Cravez, "Seizing the Frontier: Alaska's Territorial Lawyers" 41 (MS, n.d. [1984]).

objection to that kind of a proposition for this reason: that if they don't want to work more than eight hours, they don't have to."[713] The credibility of his call for replacing mandatory labor standards with a consensual race to the bottom may, however, have been tarnished by his historically suspect claim that "the mining companies do not want to force the men to work more than eight hours. It would be a ridiculous proposition to say that they could force any man to work more than eight hours."[714]

When one of the workers at the hearing, E. E. Tracy, tried to explain to Bradley why enforcement of labor standards could not be based on individual workers' willpower, even Governor Strong seemed unable to grasp the point of a nonpermissive standard:

> MR. TRACY: ... We know, I know that there's lot of times I would like to work ten hours; maybe I would like to work 12 hours, but I can't do it because the law prevents you---it keeps you away from me. I am not making any personal reflections, but I mean that the people are protected against---
>
> GOVERNOR STRONG: Pardon me. You are opposed to the workingmen working overtime?
>
> MR. TRACY: Yes.
>
> GOVERNOR STRONG: Absolutely?
>
> MR. TRACY: Absolutely. Although I agree with Mr. Bradley---I believe there's times when it is absolutely necessary to work overtime, and then there's times when it's required---when it's absolutely necessary---that some of the boys would also like to put in a couple of extra hours. I know---at least, I feel that way about it, that if I don't work overtime, I am only causing myself a hindrance, but if I don't want to work overtime, with the 8-hour law, then I've got some protection, because just the minute there is plenty of men come into the country and we get a little overabundance, the boss comes along and says, "Here, we would like to have you work a couple of hours overtime." Well, maybe I have something special to do.... If I don't work that two hours overtime, I roll up my blankets and get out. That's the way it works every place I ever been.[715]

By the end of the hearings, however, Strong seemed to understand the basis of workers' resistance when one of their representatives explained to him that while they would be willing to work ten hours or more at time and a half if it was necessary to maintain the army, "they are not willing, even at time and a half overtime, to work overtime, to work ten hours because some corporations ask for it. It would be practically establishing a ten-hour day. That's the ground they

---

[713]"Hearings Before the Governor of Alaska on the Eight-Hour Law" at 68.

[714]"Hearings Before the Governor of Alaska on the Eight-Hour Law" at 72.

[715]"Hearings Before the Governor of Alaska on the Eight-Hour Law" at 57.

take."[716]

Even more revealing than the overtime debate, however, was the explanatory light that the testimony shed on the legislature's puzzling enactment of such a radical maximum hours law. The antagonistic colloquies between representatives of capital and pro-labor former and current state legislators finally brought to light what public debate had failed to articulate in 1916-17—namely, that participants in the legislative process had been fully aware of the radical and unique character of their universal absolute eight-hour law.

Already on the first day of the hearings an interrogation of a worker by two representatives of saw-mill, logging, fishing, steamship, and mining companies produced more understanding of the law than the previous three years of public discussion. When the worker, Jesse Rice, stated that workers were not "kicking so much about the wages, but they know they don't have to work more than 8 hours in the States and we haven't got it here," Robertson and Faulkner challenged him:

> MR. ROBERTSON: In what states do they have it?
> MR. RICE: I don't remember them all---Washington has an eight-hour law.
> MR. FAULKNER: One like this?
> MR. RICE: No---
> Mr. FAULKNER: Their 8-hour law applies to hazardous occupations. Isn't that it?
> MR. RICE: Well, I won't state.
> MR. FAULKNER: Do you know any state where they have a general 8-hour law like this[?]
> MR. RICE: No; there is no states, but the employers are giving their employees an 8-hour law.
> MR. FAULKNER: Do you know of any place where they have a law like this[?]
> MR. RICE: No, this law is very rigid, and it's for a good cause. The workingman doesn't need to work more than 8 hours a day. If he can't make a living in 8 hours, he might as well not live.[717]

Later, when Faulkner observed that the manager of a steamship company office would be violating the law if he worked more than eight hours in order to perform the work of other employees who had left and couldn't be immediately replaced, a labor representative asked him and the other employer representatives opposed to the law why they had not raised such issues before the legislature acted.[718] Faulkner did not respond immediately, but shortly afterwards tried to

---

[716]"Hearings Before the Governor of Alaska on the Eight-Hour Law" at 218 (S. E. Mandle).

[717]"Hearings Before the Governor of Alaska on the Eight-Hour Law" at 34-35.

[718]"Hearings Before the Governor of Alaska on the Eight-Hour Law" at 91-92.

seize the rhetorical initiative in a colloquy with the former president of the Alaska Senate, Oliver Hubbard, by suggesting that somehow the legislature had had no popular mandate to craft the statute that it did:

MR. FAULKNER: Governor, I might call your attention to this fact, that at the time the question of a general eight-hour law was submitted to the people by the legislature, no specifications were made as to what kind of a law it was to be and the people could not at that time, people who voted on the law, tell what kind of a law the legislature would pass. That is, they did not have this kind of a law in contemplation and could not have had at the time they voted upon it.

SENATOR HUBBARD: Don't you think that the act of 1915 settled it? The legislature had no power to pass any law except one that conformed exactly to what the people voted for.

MR. FAULKNER: I am referring to the question submitted to the people.

SENATOR HUBBARD: You refer to the referendum?

MR. FAULKNER: Yes; the ballot provided for or against a general eight hour law.

SENATOR HUBBARD: Well, isn't that plain enough? It was a general eight-hour law without any qualifications, restrictions, limitations or anything else, and the clause which was put in at the request of the Department of the Interior and the Council of National Defense at the time it was passed could not, in my opinion, have been put in there by the legislature for the reason that it was not in keeping with the instructions of the people.

MR. FAULKNER: I would also like to have this in the record: that there is not another State in the Union that has such a law as this, and this kind of a law has never been enacted in any other country and it has never been tested.

SENATOR HUBBARD: Well, some people or some state or territory have always got to pass the first law of any kind.[719]

When Senator Hubbard sought to legitimize the general eight-hour law by reference to the eight-hour laws for miners that the legislature had enacted in 1913 and 1915, Faulkner baited him, asking why, if labor was so sure of the law's validity, it did not seek a court test. (Those in Juneau demanding that their opponents arrest violators were apparently unaware that an arrest warrant had already been issued in the Northern Commercial Company case in Fairbanks despite the fact that a widely reported judicial hearing in the case would take place only several days later.)[720] A labor representative tried to avoid this

---

[719]"Hearings Before the Governor of Alaska on the Eight-Hour Law" at 100.

[720]See below. Two days after the close of the governor's hearings, Strong telegraphed the U.S. attorney in Fairbanks asking for the status of the case. Roth wired back the same day that after two days of constitutional argument the court said that the decision would rendered the following week. The evening of the day the decision was handed down, Roth wired Strong that the law had been held unconstitutional. Governor Strong to U.S. Attorney Roth, Feb. 23, 1918; Roth to Strong, Feb. 23, 1918; Roth to Strong, Feb. 27,

treacherous terrain by proposing to Faulkner that the law be left as it was until the next session of the legislature (in 1919), at which time, "if there's something in that law that the workmen are radically opposed to," it could be amended. Faulkner, in turn, preempted that offer (which presumably referred to permitting premium overtime work) by declaring that the law was obviously void because the legislature lacked any power to regulate the hours of labor absent some relationship to health or life: "The legislature of the Territory of Alaska nor of any other state has any right to tell me that if I want to employ a stenographer more than eight hours and I am willing to pay her for more than eight hours labor and she is willing and it doesn't interfere with her health, that they can tell me that she can't work more than eight hours." F. Harrison, the labor representative, apparently nonplussed by Faulkner's analysis, waxed sarcastic: "It is not very often that you find the best legal talent of the country talking for the workingmen."[721]

Senator Hubbard—who believed that it had been a "serious mistake" to suspend the law with respect to fishing because fish prices were high enough to enable employers "easily [to] meet any emergency in either wages or employees"[722]—was forced to reveal still more about the hidden legislative history in a colloquy with Robert Capers, the lawyer representing the Kennecott Copper Corporation and the Copper River & Northwestern Railroad. These two enterprises, together with the Alaska Steamship Company, were the key components of the Guggenheim-Morgan Alaska Syndicate. When Capers (who also represented all these companies in litigation)[723] complained on behalf of the copper trust's railroad that operating conditions in Alaska required it to violate the law, Hubbard seemingly lost his patience: "Why didn't you make your kick before? ... Where were you when this matter was being submitted and where were you when the legislature was passing upon it that you didn't come down here and show the necessity for changing it? You have had your opportunity." At first Capers tried to avoid the senator's rebuke by asking him "a question or two" about the legislative history. When Hubbard insisted that at the referendum the people had voted for "a general eight-hour law for all wage and salary earners," Capers asked whether the legislature would not also have enacted a general eight-hour law if it had provided, as did the Adamson law, "that eight hours shall constitute a basis for a day's pay and that overwork shall be

---

1918; in Record Group 101, File Code 156, Box 152-7, Alaska State Archives.

[721]"Hearings Before the Governor of Alaska on the Eight-Hour Law" at 100-103.

[722]"Argument and Statement of Senator O. P. Hubbard," in "Hearings Before the Governor of Alaska on the Eight-Hour Law" at 228.

[723]E.g., Thede v. Alaska S.S. Co., 5 Alaska 194 (3d Div. 1914); Harvey & Co. v. Copper River & N.W. Ry., 5 Alaska 371 (3d Div. 1915); Johnson v. Kennecott Copper Corp., 5 Alaska 571 (3d Div. 1916).

compensated for as overtime...." To Hubbard's lame protest that "[t]hat is not the law," Capers replied: "There isn't in the history of the United States a law like this." But when the senator insisted that the railroad and mining companies and all Alaskans knew what the law covered, Capers repeated that a "great many laws could be general eight-hour laws."[724]

When Capers expressed his belief that the people had thought they were voting for an eight-hour cum premium overtime law—his only evidence being that he himself had voted for the law having "no idea whatever that the legislature would pass a law of the class that it did"[725]—adding that any law that "says to you, or myself or to Mr. Faulkner that they shall not work overtime is invalid,"[726] he triggered a dialog that quickly elicited from him an astounding admission concerning employers' lobbying strategy:

> SENATOR HUBBARD: Well, why didn't make your kick before it was passed[?]
>
> MR. CAPERS: Well, because we didn't think that the legislature would be so crazy as it afterwards developed to be.
>
> SENATOR HUBBARD: Well, that's all right. I want to say to you on that question of craziness that the legislature had this matter under discussion for a good while...and everyone had an opportunity to come and be heard...but not a single person came before that legislature or before any committee and made any such suggestion as you are making here now[.]
>
> MR. CAPERS: What suggestion[?]
>
> SENATOR HUBBARD: That it's not valid and that there isn't another State that has such an eight-hour law and that we had no power to pass it, and that we should have passed a...law providing that eight hours shall constitute the basis of a day's wage and that overtime shall be allowed and that additional time may be worked and so on. ... I want to say to you that the members of that legislature, if they had passed a different law, would not have been keeping faith with the people. That's what I say to you, Mr. Capers, and you may think that is crazy or not crazy. We wrote a law as nearly conforming to the act of 1915 as it was possible for us to write and we passed it, and the people who are here now, claiming that it should be set aside almost a month after it...went into force...did not come here than and show any defects in it or why it ought not be passed as the people had voted it; neither did they go to the people of the Territory through their press and say to the people, "This law is inadvisable; it will not work. Do not pass it. ... This isn't the kind of law you want." ... I say to you that no member of the legislature could have done otherwise; if any member...would have voted any differently, he would have been a traitor to the people.[727]

---

[724]"Hearings Before the Governor of Alaska on the Eight-Hour Law" at 109-12.

[725]"Hearings Before the Governor of Alaska on the Eight-Hour Law" at 185.

[726]"Hearings Before the Governor of Alaska on the Eight-Hour Law" at 112.

[727]"Hearings Before the Governor of Alaska on the Eight-Hour Law" at 112-14.

Since employers regarded the eight-hour law as "crazy," when Capers asserted that employers nourished "no particular antagonism to the general principles of eight-hour legislation," and that "[w]e are not taking from them [workers] the principle of the eight-hour law,"[728] he manifestly meant the unprincipled eight-hour day extended by consensual overtime work.

Having elicited from Hubbard that he was a practicing attorney, Capers kept pressing him to explain why he had not investigated the constitutionality of the bill he had supported. The ensuing colloquy suggests that labor and capital might have known all along that the law would be held invalid:

SENATOR HUBBARD: I see. Your sarcasm is beautiful, but it isn't sound.... It wouldn't have made any difference, Mr. Capers, if I looked into it thoroughly. ... I suppose you think I should have look[ed] it up like a professional lawyer and come down here and sa[id] to the members of the legislature: "Boys, I have looked this thing up. It's not valid; it's not legal. We can disrespect the people and their votes and cast it aside, because I'm a lawyer, I'm a great lawyer, and I have looked it up and it isn't valid.["]

MR. CAPERS: No, but you could have inquired into it.

SENATOR HUBBARD: Well, if you had inquired into this question then...you wouldn't have to come down here now to beg the Governor to overturn a law that has only been in operation a month. Were you asleep?

MR. CAPERS: No, but I thought you were on the job.[729]

This debate about the law's validity had to be broken off at this point because Governor Strong had grown impatient with it as not germane to the purpose of the hearing. He did confirm, however, that no public discussion had taken place before or after the referendum: "Apparently it was accepted as a matter of course." Indeed, Strong observed that he had never heard anything about the law until 30 days before it was to go into effect, when he "began to be deluged with appeals to suspend the law."[730] To be sure, the governor's account may not have been accurate. In March he received a letter from a consulting mining engineer in Philadelphia stating that when he had called on Strong in the fall of 1917, the governor "indicated that there wa[s] a clause in the law, which permitted you to practically abrogate this section...altho you did not commit yourself at that time...."[731]

---

[728]"Statement of R. E. Capers," in "Hearings Before the Governor of Alaska on the Eight-Hour Law" at 185-196 at 185, 187.

[729]"Hearings Before the Governor of Alaska on the Eight-Hour Law" at 115. Hubbard may in fact have been regarded as a legal authority since he had held important positions in the Justice Department in Washington, D.C. in the 1880s and 1890s and later in the Interior Department. *Who's Who in Alaska Politics* at 47-48.

[730]"Hearings Before the Governor of Alaska on the Eight-Hour Law" at 116.

[731] Letter from H. W. DuBois to Governor Strong, Mar. 14, 1918, in Record Group

The failure of employers' representatives to contradict Hubbard's and Strong's charges that they had never protested against the bill before it was enacted is puzzling. After all, the *Anchorage Daily Times* had reported on the "pyrotechnics" that were touched off in the House of Representatives on April 18, 1917, when "Judge John Winn, practicing lawyer of Juneau, dramatically declared, holding high in the air the bill, 'It is pernicious from every standpoint and not a single plausible excuse can be given for the bill.'" He then foretold of the "great calamity" for the territory's cannery interests and the country's food supply if the bill were passed. Winn even claimed that if referred to the electorate, the bill would be voted down as heavily as the referendum had passed in 1916. Royal Gunnison, a Juneau lawyer representing the Pacific Fisheries Association, a former district judge, and Robertson's law partner,[732] also addressed the House, submitting an amendment that would have exempted the cannery industry.[733] At the very least, then, the fishing industry had loudly resisted inclusion.[734]

In spite of the governor's admonition, the issue arose again the next day when Joseph Murray, a miner-lawyer who had been a member of the House of Representatives when it passed the eight-hour law in 1917, spoke up on behalf of miners.[735] The information he presented was arguably even more startling than Hubbard's. He revealed that he and other legislators had tried "to figure out some scheme whereby we would have a legitimate eight-hour law and still give the labor [sic] the opportunity of working overtime, at his election, without any risk if he didn't so elect; but after giving it a good deal of thought and after talking to other members and the men around this town of judgment and skill and brains, we couldn't figure any system of overtime."[736] Murray's view that the law should not be suspended, but merely modified to provide for premium overtime wages,[737] inspired Capers to subject him to the same grilling that Hubbard had undergone the previous day. His responses suggested that a more cynical attitude toward the bill had prevailed in the House than in the Senate:

101, File Group 156, Box 159, Alaska State Archives.

[732]*Martindale's American Law Directory: January, 1918*, at 18; *Who's Who in Alaska Politics* at 38.

[733]"Pro and Con of General 8-Hour Law," *Anchorage Daily Times*, May 3, 1917, at 6, col. 3.

[734]Unfortunately, the lack of a transcript of the legislative debates makes it impossible to flesh out the full scope of what employers and legislators said about the law.

[735]*Who's Who in Alaskan Politics* at 70.

[736]"Hearings Before the Governor of Alaska on the Eight-Hour Law" at 135.

[737]Although his statement is not clear, it seems that Murray believed that the entire overtime debate was "only a question of mathematics as to whether that scale would be changed." "Hearings Before the Governor of Alaska on the Eight-Hour Law" at 135.

MR. CAPERS: You are an attorney, I believe?

MR. MURRAY: Yes.

MR. CAPERS: Did you ever consider the validity of this act before it was passed?

MR. MURRY[sic]: Oh, yes.

MR. CAPERS: What is your view?

MR. MURRAY: I think it is doubtful. No eight-hour act like this has ever been sustained.

MR. CAPERS: Do you think, Mr. Murray, that you could have passed an unquestionable and valid eight-hour law? Or could you have improved on it?

MR. MURRAY: Well, I don't think so. There has never been any general eight-hour law sustained in the United States. Every other law like it has been sustained under the police power....

MR. CAPERS: Do you think that you could have complied with the instruction given you and have passed a valid law that would have made those necessary exceptions?

MR. MURRAY: No; I tried that Mr. Capers.

MR. CAPERS: Wherein did you fail?

MR. MURRAY: Well, to begin with, there were other lawyers in the legislature besides myself. ... I consulted with the Attorney General and I took the floor, and I tried to have as many special bills passed under the police power as possible; for instance, the eight-hour act for women; the eight-hour act for underground placer mines, and the eight-hour act for surface work, and I stayed on the floor, and in talking with the attorneys around Juneau, none of them thought that the act would be sustained, and for that reason I wanted as many of them passed under the police power as possible.[738]

Although Strong finished his report to the interior secretary on February 25, four days after the hearings had ended, the Interior Department could scarcely wait. The very day he completed it, the department telegraphed: "can you not wire brief statement in code as to conclusions and recommendations...."[739] The next day Strong had to telegraph back that it was not feasible to wire his conclusions and recommendations "owing to varied interests represented at hearings and ramifications of statements and testimony," but advised Lane that it would be in the mail together with the stenographic transcript in two days.[740] The fact that the district court held the statute unconstitutional on February 27, the day after Strong had dispatched his telegram, may have lessened Secretary Lane's interest in the report.[741] Strong himself understood which way the judicial

---

[738]"Hearings Before the Governor of Alaska on the Eight-Hour Law" at 136-37.

[739]Meyer to Governor Strong, Feb. 25, 1918, in Record Group 101, File Group 156, Box 159, Alaska State Archives.

[740]Governor Strong to Secretary Interior, Feb. 26, 1918, in Record Group 101, File Group 156, Box 159, Alaska State Archives.

[741]A month after he had submitted his report, Strong responded to an inquiry from a firm of consulting mining engineers with offices in Philadelphia and Paris about the eight-hour law that he was not at liberty to disclose his hearing findings, which he assumed

wind was blowing: on receiving a telegraphic inquiry on February 27 as to the exempt status of mills manufacturing airplane spruce, Strong wired back instead that the law had been held invalid.[742]

Based on the hearings and his experience, Governor Strong believed that "there is some difference of opinion among the working people. Some are in favor of overtime while others are emphatically against it."[743] His forthright report to the interior secretary rested largely on his finding that, contrary to employers' claims, the labor shortage was no more acute in Alaska than elsewhere in the United States, and "that if an eight-hour day were guaranteed the workers in Alaska with a fair scale of wages, a sufficient supply of labor...will be available to meet the demands of the various industries."[744] The decline in Alaska's population—from 64,356 in 1910 to 55,036 in 1920[745]—was misleading in the sense that most of the cannery workers were "imported"[746] and thus not included in the census enumerations. In 1913, for example, 5,000 of the 13,000 cannery workers were Chinese and Japanese "brought up from Seattle, San Francisco, and Portland in the summer time...and then ship[ped] back...."[747]

Strong's seemingly prolabor stance must be gauged against the background of his prior suspension of the law as to fisheries, which by 1917 were the territory's largest industry, and the fact that the other major industry, mining,[748] was subject to a special eight-hour law not affected by the controversy surrounding the general eight-hour law. Strong also rejected opponents'

---

would be "made public in due course" by the interior secretary or the Council of National Defense. Governor to H. W. DuBois, Philadelphia, Mar. 28, 1918, in Record Group 101, File Group 156, Box 159, Alaska State Archives.

[742]J. J. Daley and H. Shattuck to Governor Strong, Feb. 26, 1918, and Strong to Shattuck, Mar. 1, 1918, in Record Group 101, File Group 156, Box 159, Alaska State Archives. For similar correspondence, see telegram from Ketchikan Iron Works to Governor Strong, Feb. 22, 1918, and Strong to Ketchikan Iron Works, Mar. 1, 1918, in Record Group 101, File Group 156, Box 159, Alaska State Archives.

[743]"Hearings Before the Governor of Alaska on the Eight-Hour Law" at 218.

[744]Letter from Governor Strong to Secretary of the Interior at 5.

[745]3 Bureau of the Census, *Fourteenth Census of the United States Taken in the Year 1920: Population 1920*, tab. 1 at 1158 (1922). In fact, after doubling during the gold rush between 1890 and 1900, the population declined between 1900 and 1930. U.S. Bureau of the Census, *Historical Statistics of the United States, Colonial Times to 1970: Bicentennial Edition*, Pt. 2, Ser. A-13 at 9 (1976).

[746]30 *The Encyclopædia Britannica: The New Volumes* 102-104 at 104 (12th ed. 1922), s.v. "Alaska."

[747]*The Building of Railroads in Alaska* at 15 (testimony of Alaska congressional Delegate James Wickersham). Into the 1920s, these groups continued to account for 30 percent of fisheries workers. "Biennial Report of the Territorial Labor Commissioner to the Governor of Alaska 1921-22" n.p. (1923), in Record Group 101, Ser. 130, Box 221, Alaska State Archives.

[748]Gruening, *The State of Alaska* at 208-10.

allegations that those voting in favor of the eight-hour bill in 1916 had not understood the referendum. On the contrary, during the eighteen months the matter was before the public, he wrote, "no opposition to the proposal was indicated by the newspaper press or politicians, or others. I have, therefore, to conclude that when the people voted for this measure, they knew exactly what they were voting for."[749] This assertion may have been somewhat facile since public discussion of an eight-hour law had not dwelt on what became the statute's two principal features—coverage of businessmen and the absence of a provision for overtime work and pay.

Strong's recommendation to the secretary of the interior that no further suspension of the law be authorized (except with regard to the infant agricultural industry) was largely rooted in his pragmatic attitude toward avoiding labor unrest during the war. He reported to Lane that employers' agitation in favor of suspending the law had sparked a unionization movement all over Alaska which, in Strong's view, "will not end until every town and hamlet where any considerable amount of labor is employed, is organized...." Conflating Alaska's unique law with other hours laws, he emphasized that suspension would bring about strikes and "chaotic conditions" in all industries.[750]

> Labor in Alaska knows that the demand for an eight-hour day is nation-wide, for the workers regard it as an accepted national policy. Therefore...labor professes to see in the effort being made to set aside the Territorial 8-hour law, a deliberate design on the part of the employers to demand in its stead a ten-hour work day or more, all under the cover of patriotism, but really that their profits may be increased at the expense of the country and of labor. I make no comment on this phase of the Alaska labor situation, but I know that the feeling exists. Alaska labor...states unequivocally that it is willing to serve the Government in any capacity, to work such hours and for such pay as the Government may justly determine, but it is unwilling to serve public corporations or private employers on terms dictated or influenced by them.[751]

The governor's hearings coincided with other important developments driving toward a denouement. On February 4, 1918, Thomas Riggs and William Edes, members of the federal Alaskan Engineering Commission (which was charged with oversight of the planning and construction of federally owned railroads in the territory),[752] submitted to the Interior Department, which had

---

[749]Letter from Governor Strong to Secretary of the Interior at 9.

[750]Letter from Governor Strong to Secretary of the Interior at 10.

[751]Letter from Governor Strong to Secretary of the Interior at 9.

[752]Thomas Riggs, Jr., "The Government Railroad in Alaska—What Two Years and Limited Funds Have Accomplished," 73(19) *Engineering Record* 600-603 (May 6,1916); Joshua Bernhardt, *The Alaskan Engineering Commission: Its History, Activities and*

jurisdiction over Alaska, their "Memorandum Regarding Effect of Territorial Eight Hour Law," stating their reasons for opposing the law, which overlapped with employers' views. Organized labor in Alaska, which considered Riggs anti-labor and opposed his appointment as governor, was informed of this letter in March by the chairman of the U.S. Senate Committee on the Territories and published it to support its position.[753] By February 6, the Interior Department had already sent a copy of the memorandum to Governor Strong.[754] The statute in their opinion "will practically destroy many industries in the territory" and exacerbate a scarcity of labor in a place where "the active working season...is practically only six to seven months, and work during that period should be 'speeded up' rather than 'slowed down'...." Riggs and Edes predicted impracticality of enforcement, especially on railroads, which would have to carry extra crews in case of delay since railway delays would not meet the statutory definition of putting life or property in danger. The labor shortage, in turn, might make it "extremely difficult to put on additional crews of stevedores." They also called attention to the fact that the statute made no provision for payment for overtime: "We venture the opinion that many of the people of Alaska when voting for such a law thought it would mean considerable extra pay for some extra hours, and would be considerably surprised to learn that such is not the case." Riggs and Edes also noted that the "humanitarian object of the law" would conflict with the work patterns of men who worked eight hours for the railways and additional hours elsewhere. Finally, they based their recommendation that the Interior Department suspend the law on their

> opinion that most of the laboring population of Alaska with the exception of those doing underground work in mines, would prefer to work over eight hours during the long days if by so doing they got additional compensation.
>
> The application of the law, especially at this time when supplies of copper and other ore are necessary for carrying on the activities of the war, would in our opinion be very disastrous....[755]

Organization (1922).

[753]"Labor Unions Wage War Against Riggs," *Anchorage Daily Times*, Mar. 11, 1918, at 1, col. 5; "Union Workers Oppose Riggs for Governor," *Anchorage Daily Times*, Mar. 12, 1918, at 1, col. 1; "Organized Labor Vigorously Oppose Riggs for Gov'," *Daily Nome Industrial Worker*, Mar. 13, 1918, at 1, col. 1.

[754]Letter from Assistant to the Secretary of the Interior to Governor Strong (Feb. 6, 1918), in Record Group 101, File Code 156, Box 159, Alaska State Archives.

[755]Wm. C. Edes and Thomas Riggs, Jr., "Memorandum Regarding Effect of Territorial Eight Hour Law," Record Group 101, File Code 156, Alaska State Archives (Feb. 4, 1918). The version published in the newspaper deviated slightly from the original; "Of Course He Is in Favor of Enforcing 8 Hr. Law 'Nit'," *Daily Nome Industrial Worker*, Apr. 8, 1918, at 1, col. 4-6.

After months of efforts devoted to promoting Strong's reappointment and undermining Riggs's appointment, Wickersham was "shocked" to read in the morning newspapers on March 7 that Wilson had nevertheless appointed Riggs.[756] In response to attacks by Alaska labor unions against him for opposing the eight-hour law, Riggs insisted to the Committee on the Territories, which was holding hearings on his nomination, that he favored the law with "price-and-a-half for overtime work."[757] In his diary, Wickersham sneered that Riggs, a "good Guggenheim Republican,"[758] "will do what the Big Interests want done."[759] Specifically, Riggs "will suspend the law—of course—if requested."[760] Despite the attacks on Riggs for being "too friendly towards the Guggenheims and other big concerns,"[761] his answer apparently satisfied the senators: Strong, who had incurred the enmity of fellow Democrats for having helped certify Wickersham as winner of the 1916 election for congressional delegate against the Democrat Charles Sulzer—in April 1917 the Democratic Party central committee had voted not to endorse Strong for reappointment—withdrew from consideration, and in April was succeeded by Riggs as territorial governor.[762]

More important than the Edes-Riggs memorandum was the fact that just weeks after the law had gone into effect, a test case had been argued and decided involving the Northern Commercial Company, a large and powerful quasi-monopolistic mercantile enterprise with stores and operations throughout Alaska, which was so widely resented that it had antagonized even many employers.[763] On January 22, 1918, just three weeks after the law went into effect, the Justice's Court[764] for the Fairbanks Precinct issued an arrest warrant to the U.S. marshall

---

[756]Wickersham, "Diaries," Mar. 7, 1918.

[757]"Riggs Case a Practical Joke," *Fairbanks Daily News-Miner*," Apr. 4, 1918, at 1, col. 6. See also "The Grilling Makes Riggs Say He Is in Favor of 8 Hour Law?" *Daily Nome Industrial Worker*, Apr. 5, 1918, at 1, col. 1.

[758]Wickersham, "Diaries," Apr. 13, 1918.

[759]Wickersham, "Diaries," Mar. 12, 1918.

[760]Wickersham, "Diaries," Mar. 11, 1918.

[761]"Senate Committee Investigating Riggs," *Daily Nome Industrial Worker*, Mar. 18, 1918, at 1, col. 4. Riggs had also married the daughter of Frederick Coudert, a very prominent New York international corporate lawyer. 2(19) *Alaska Railroad Record* 145 (Mar. 19, 1918).

[762]Territory ex rel. Sulzer v. Canvassing Board, 5 Alaska 602 (1st Div. 1917); *Alaska Labor News*, Apr. 14, 1917, at 7, col. 2 (untitled); "Strong Out of Race," *Daily Nome Industrial Worker*, Mar. 25, 1918, at 1, col. 1; Atwood, *Frontier Politics* at 320; Stewart, "The Alaskan Home Front During World War I" at 10-12.

[763]Foster, "Syndicalism Northern Style" at 137, 141 n.46. The Northern Commercial Co. was not represented at the governor's hearings. For an uncritical company history, see L. D. Kitchener, *Flag over the North: The Story of the Northern Commercial Company* (n.d. [ca. 1954]).

[764]On the Justice's Court, see Act of June 6, 1900, ch. 786, §§ 944-1014, 31 Stat. 321,

for the Northern Commercial manager in Fairbanks because one of its salaried employees had been hired to work more than eight hours per day and had in fact worked more than eight hours the previous day although neither life nor property had been in imminent danger.[765] The manager was arrested the next day, but the government dismissed the charges against him, and on January 24 the court, despite the company's plea that the statute was unconstitutional and void, found Northern Commercial guilty and fined it $250.[766] On appeal to the district court, the employer further alleged that the act was void because the legislature had not complied with the congressional Organic Act by virtue of failing to give the bill the requisite number of readings.[767]

In mid-February, in the midst of Governor Strong's hearings on suspension of the law, District Court Judge Charles Bunnell held two days of hearings in Fairbanks, which were closely followed and widely reported. Bunnell, who had come to Alaska in 1900 as a teacher, left that occupation to practice law and engage in business, owning a lumber company and sheet metal works, and serving as president of the Valdez Chamber of Commerce. He was also active in the Democratic Party, becoming its unsuccessful candidate for delegate to Congress in 1914 against Wickersham, who was not alone in his belief that President Wilson had appointed Bunnell as district judge of the Fourth Division in 1915 as a reward for having run against him. Wickersham, a Progressive, also believed that "Big Interests" (meaning the Guggenheim-Morgan syndicate) had lobbied the Attorney General on Bunnell's behalf.[768]

480-89.

[765]United States v. Northern Commercial Co. and George Coleman, Complaint, No. 934 Cr. (Commissioner's & Ex Officio Justice of the Peace Court, Fairbanks Precinct, 4th Judicial Div., Terr. Alaska, Jan. 22, 1918); Warrant of Arrest, in Nat. Archives, Pacific Alaska Reg., Record Group, No. 21, Box No./Location 34 (01/10/08(2)), File: Case # 762.

[766]United States v. Northern Commercial Co., Transcript, in Nat. Archives, Pacific Alaska Reg., Record Group, No. 21, Box No./Location 34 (01/10/08(2)), File: Case # 762.

[767]United States v. Northern Commercial Co., Second Amended Demurrer (D. Alaska, 4th Div., Feb. 13, 1918), in Nat. Archives, Pacific Alaska Reg., Record Group, No. 21, Box No./Location 34 (01/10/08(2)), File: Case # 762.

[768]Cashen, *Farthest North College President* at 29-30, 39-79, quote at 63; Atwood, *Frontier Politics* at 281. Wickersham mentioned among Bunnell's advocates Wilds Richardson, chairman of the Alaska Road Commission, whom he accused of being a Syndicate lobbyist. Stearns, "The Morgan-Guggenheim Syndicate" at 320. As a result of Judge Bunnell's involvement in certifying the results of the 1916 election for Alaska delegate to Congress, which was contested by Wickersham, the latter mobilized his supporters to induce the Judiciary Committee not to confirm Wilson's appointment of Bunnell (1878-1956) to a second four-year term in 1919, and he served as a recess appointee until 1921, at which time he became the founding president of the Alaska Agricultural College and School of Mines and then of the University of Alaska from its founding in 1935 to 1949. *Id.* at 93-103; In re Wickersham, 6 Alaska 167 (4th Div. 1919); Wickersham, "Diaries," Dec. 7 and 12, 1918; Subcommittee of the Senate Judiciary Committee, "Nomination of Charles E. Bunnell as United States District Judge for the

Bunnell, as already noted, was no stranger to eight-hour law adjudication, having just 16 months earlier held invalid, on the thinnest of formal-technical grounds, the 1915 act amending the 1913 eight-hour law to include underground placer mining. Why, given Bunnell's proven jurisprudentially narrow mind in eight-hours adjudication, the United States chose to bring its test case in the Fairbanks Division is puzzling, since it presumably could also have found violations by Northern Commercial or other employers in the other judicial divisions.

The press noted that the new eight-hours case "means more to the country than any put to the test in several years" and that it was believed that whichever side lost would take the matter to the U.S. Supreme Court.[769] The case was also "awaited with a great deal of interest, as almost everyone in the territory is anxious to learn whether or not the law will stand the test."[770] On February 27, in a decision that he read for 45 minutes to a "courtroom...well filled with spectators, men from all walks of life, all interested in the outcome of the case,"[771] and that was reported in a front-page banner headline in the territorial press,[772] Judge Bunnell struck the law down as "plainly and palpably beyond all question in violation of the Fourteenth Amendment to the Constitution...."[773] First, the judge denied that the law derived any validity from the majority referendum vote in its favor. Indeed, the very fact that the Alaska Organic Law did not provide for

---

Fourth Judicial Division of the Territory of Alaska" (unpub., Dec. 31, 1920-Jan. 5, 1921); 3 *Who Was Who in America (1951-1960)* at 121 (1966); "Biographical Outline: Charles Ernest Bunnell," in Alaska and Polar Regions Archives, Rasmuson Library, University of Alaska Fairbanks. In the 1914 election, Wickersham received almost twice as many votes as Bunnell in all of Alaska and almost three times as many in the Fairbanks Judicial Division, where Wickersham had been and Bunnell was about to become district judge. *Fairbanks Daily News-Miner*, Nov. 7, 1916, at 4, col. 3. Governor Strong apparently adopted a hands-off attitude toward appointment of a judge for the Fourth Division. Shortly after Bunnell's appointment he replied to a correspondent who had urged him to give favorable consideration to someone else that: "Mr. Bunnell is a young man of more than ordinary ability, a good lawyer, I understand, and a man of probity in every way, and I venture to predict that he will give general satisfaction." Letter from Governor to T. H. Deal, Jan. 8, 1915, in Record Group 101, Ser. 130, File 52, Box 129, Alaska State Archives.

[769]"Eight Hour Law Argument Today," *Fairbanks Daily News-Miner*, Feb. 14, 1918, at 1, col. 2.

[770]"Eight Hour Law Will be Argued Soon," *Fairbanks Daily News-Miner*, Feb. 11, 1918, at 4, col. 4.

[771]"Bunnell Rules Eight Hour Law Unconstitutional," *Fairbanks Daily News-Miner*, Feb. 27, 1918, at 1, col. 3.

[772]"Eight-Hour Law Held Unconstitutional," *Anchorage Daily Times*, Feb. 28, 1918, at 1.

[773]United States v. Northern Commercial Co., slip. op. at 17 (Decision on Demurrer, D. Alaska, 4th Div., Feb. 27, 1918), in Nat. Archives, Pacific Alaska Reg., Record Group No. 21, Box No./Location 34 (01/10/08(2)), File: Case # 762.

such referenda created a "suspicion" in Bunnell's mind that a legislature that attempted to act beyond its powers "was actuated by some undisclosed motive."[774]

With rhetorical flourish Bunnell portrayed the statute's uniqueness:

> Although ably assisted by counsel...I confess myself unable to find, and counsel are unable to produce any act of any legislative body in the United States which, from the standpoint of word use and word construction, belongs in a class with this act. It is fairly entitled to the unique distinction of being alone though in a multitude.[775]

Bunnell failed to document this uniqueness adequately, but he did emphasize that the law expanded the meaning of "employment" by construing it to include performance of labor or services even by a partner. He went on to locate the act's unconstitutionality in its indiscriminately limiting the hours of all wage and salary earners without showing that the working conditions of clerks, carpenters, and cooks made regulation of their hours as reasonable as those of miners; it was also defective because it failed to provide for overtime payment for emergency work. The court ruled that to use the state police power to deprive a carpenter of the right to work four hours on a neighbor's house after having worked eight hours that same day for a contractor directly violated the Fourteenth Amendment to the U.S. Constitution.[776]

Within days after Bunnell had handed down his decision, the government secured a new indictment against the Northern Commercial Company, this time for an eight-hours violation committed on March 4.[777] Later that month Bunnell disposed of the case in a reported decision adopted almost verbatim from the previous case.[778] On March 5, one of Lane's assistants requested Wickersham to prepare a brief in opposition to suspension of the law, which Wickersham filed with Lane on March 11 although he believed that Lane would nevertheless

---

[774]United States v. Northern Commercial Co., slip. op. at 4-5.

[775]United States v. Northern Commercial Co., slip. op. at 5. Curiously, this passage was absent from Bunnell's second opinion a month later, which largely recycled the first opinion.

[776]United States v. Northern Commercial Co., slip op. at 5, 14-15.

[777]United States v. Northern Commercial Co., Indictment, No. 764 Cr. (D. Alaska Terr., 4th Jud. Div. , Mar. 5, 1918), in Nat. Archives, Pacific Alaska Reg., Record Group, No. 21, Box No./Location 34 (01/10/08(2)), File: Case # 764. This time the same manager whom the government had dismissed as a defendant in the first case appeared not only as a defendant, but also as the employee whom the company had unlawfully employed more than eight hours. Possibly this modification was a response to Bunnell's ruling in the first case that "[o]bviously, under the law the one performing the labor or services is liable." United States v. Northern Commercial Co., slip op. at 8.

[778]United States v. Northern Commercial Co., 6 Alaska 94 (1918).

suspend the law.[779] In spite of Bunnell's decision, on April 4, Interior Secretary Lane requested that the governor suspend the law as to fertilizer oil and other fish industry by-products[780]; the next day Strong ordered the suspension under the law that had just been declared invalid.[781]

The ambivalence that purported supporters of the law displayed was captured by an editorial in the *Alaska Daily Empire* at this juncture that focused on the question of overtime. The newspaper, which proclaimed that it "has always observed the eight-hour day"—to be sure, paying for the extra work when employees worked more than eight hours—started from the proposition that Alaskans "are unequivocally committed to the principle that eight hours shall constitute a day's work in Alaska." However, the editor

> felt that the inhibitions against "over-time" in the present law are too drastic. In a country that is far away from centers where extra men can be secured to take care of a rush of work the only way that the output of a concern that depends upon skilled workmen can make its production elastic is to permit men to work "over-time" in cases of emergency. ... The Empire believes that the time has not arrived in Alaska for prohibiting skilled men from working "over time" for extra pay when it would be for the interest of both employer and employee for them to do so.
>
> In most of the States where they have passed laws limiting the "over-time" that men may work the limit applies to the week rather than the day. Under the present law in Alaska men are permitted to work eight hours a day for seven days a week. It would fit the situation better to make the week the unit, and prohibit more than 56 hours work in any one week.[782]

On April 12, the Alaska Labor Union requested that the Justice Department appeal the decision,[783] on April 22 the U.S. Attorney General Thomas Gregory directed Rinehart Roth, the U.S. District Attorney for the Fourth Judicial District, to seek a writ of error, and on May 4 Roth petitioned for and Bunnell issued an order allowing a writ of error so that the government could appeal the decision

---

779 Wickersham, "Diaries," Mar. 5, 6, 11, 1918.

780 Telegram from Franklin K. Lane to Governor of Alaska, Apr. 4, 1918, in Record Group 101, File Group 156, Box 159, Alaska State Archives.

781 Territory of Alaska, Governor's Office, Executive Order, Apr. 5, 1918, in Record Group 101, File Group 156, Box 159, Alaska State Archives. See also "Received from Governor Strong; Via Yesterday's Mail," *Daily Nome Industrial Worker*, Feb. 28, 1918, at 5, col. 1; *Report of the Governor of Alaska*, in 2 *Reports of the Department of Interior for the Fiscal Year Ending June 30, 1918: Indian Affairs Territories*, at 565 (65th Cong., 3d Sess., H. Doc. No. 1455, 1919).

782 "The Eight-Hour Question," *Alaska Daily Empire*, Apr. 6, 1918, at 2, col. 1.

783 "Supreme Court to Make Review Alaska 8 Hour," *Alaska Daily Empire*, May 8, 1918, at 2, col. 7.

to the U.S. Supreme Court.[784] But five days later the U.S. Solicitor General, John W. Davis, informed Roth that on further reflection he had convinced the Justice Department that the writ of error "could not be successfully prosecuted...."[785] The same day Gregory informed Roth that he was revoking his telegram of April 22, which had directed him to seek a writ of error.[786]

Riggs, who had become governor on April 12, also involved himself in the litigation on May 9, wiring Judge Bunnell for information about the status of the case.[787] On receiving word from Bunnell the next day of Gregory's revocation,[788] Riggs immediately wired to Interior Secretary Lane: "Desirable this question be settled. Shall we proceed in perfecting appeal?"[789] Three days later Lane's office replied rather dismissively to Riggs that, given the revocation, "no further action on the part of the Governor of Alaska or this Department is necessary on any of the applications presented to the Department for suspension of the operation of the act above-mentioned."[790] Riggs, however, driven by public and personal agendas, was not so easily dismissed. He informed the interior department that:

> The District Attorney of this Division holds that this case does not cover the whole question and is applicable only in this one special instance, and that any number of cases may still be brought under the law. This office is constantly in receipt of requests for advice regarding the legality of the law and I have even been threatened with prosecution by certain members of the local union owing to the fact that my household servants are on duty more than eight hours during the calendar day. [T]he District Attorney and...the Attorney General for the Territory...are positive in their statements that the law should be definitely settled one way or the other. In consequence, the Attorney General of the Territory has wired the Attorney General of the United States requesting that an appeal be entered.[791]

---

[784]Nat. Archives, Pacific Alaska Reg., Record Group, No. 21, Box No./Location 34 (01/10/08(2)), File: Case # 764. Roth had made the nominating speech for Bunnell as Democratic congressional delegate in 1916. Atwood, *Frontier Politics* at 281.

[785]Letter from Jno. W. Davis to R. F. Roth, May 9, 1918, in Charles E. Bunnell Papers, Box 1, Folder 5, Alaska and Polar Regions Archives, Rasmuson Library, U. Alaska Fairbanks.

[786]Telegram from Gregory to Roth, May 9, 1918, in Bunnell Papers, Box 1, Folder 5.

[787]Governor Riggs to Judge Bunnell, May 9, 1918, in Record Group 101, File Group 156, Box 159, Alaska State Archives.

[788]Judge Bunnell to Governor Riggs, May 10, 1918, in Record Group 101, File Group 156, Box 159, Alaska State Archives.

[789]Governor Riggs to Secretary Interior Lane, May 11, 1918, in Record Group 101, File Group 156, Box 159, Alaska State Archives.

[790]Letter from E. C. Bradley, Assistant to the Secretary, to Governor Riggs, May 14, 1918, in Record Group 101, File Group 156, Box 159, Alaska State Archives.

[791]Governor to E. C. Bradley, May 28, 1918, in Record Group 101, File Group 156, Box 159, Alaska State Archives. Based on the Justice Department's position, the Interior

Attorney General George Grigsby of the Territory of Alaska had indeed requested that the Justice Department not dismiss the appeal, but Solicitor General Davis rejected the request because the Department saw no basis to support the statute's validity:

> The statute...forbids the employment of all wage-earners and salary-earners for more than eight hours in any day except in cases where life or property is in imminent danger. It is not limited in any way to unhealthful, hazardous, or exacting occupations, nor to children, women, or other classes demanding special care or protection. It has no such ostensible relation to the public health as the statutes upheld in Holden v. Hardy...and Bunting v. Oregon.... That the right to earn a living is a property right and one which cannot be taken away without due process of law or adequate justification under the police power is axiomatic.[792]

In the pithier language of the *Nome Industrial Worker*, the Justice Department deemed the eight-hour law invalid because it "applies to all whether working for themselves or for others and it is this amnibus [sic] feature that is disliked."[793]

A few days later Davis disposed of the governor's request in a letter to the Interior Department: "We cannot concur in the suggestion of Gov. Riggs that the law can be definitely settled only by a submission of the matter to the Supreme Court of the United States. There are many questions, of course, which reach a final settlement without the adjudication of that tribunal."[794] By indirection the Justice Department appeared to be suggesting to Riggs that he would have to find other ways for putting the quietus on rambunctious labor unions than frivolous political appeals to the Supreme Court. Attorney General Gregory himself was preoccupied at the time with prosecuting the International Workers of the World and others for making remarks interpretable as claims that World War I was being fought "'for the so-called capitalist class....'"[795]

Arguably the most astute legal question at this time was posed by the socialist *Nome Industrial Worker*, the newspaper of Local 240 of the International Union of Mine, Mill and Smelter Workers (formerly Western Federation of Miners).[796]

Department informed Riggs that it was not "practicable" for it to do anything else. Letter from Assistant Secretary to Governor Thomas Riggs, Jr., June 15, 1918, in *id.*

[792]Letter from Jno. W. Davis to George B. Grigsby, June 8, 1918, in Bunnell Papers, Box 1, Folder 5.

[793]"Present Status Eight Hour Appeal," *Tri-Weekly Nome Industrial Worker*, July 4, 1918, at 1, col. 4.

[794]Letter from Jno. W. Davis to S. G. Hopkins, Asst. Sec'y of the Interior, June 12, 1918, in Record Group 101, File Group 156, Box 159, Alaska State Archives.

[795]Murphy, *World War I and the Origin of Civil Liberties* at 96 (quoting letter from Gregory to William Redfield, Feb. 20, 1919, Justice Dept. Archives).

[796]As of the issue of July 9, 1917, the paper's masthead stated that the local's parent

In a telegram to Attorney General Grigsby on May 15, the paper asked: "Is Bunnell's decision binding from legal point view other three divisions, Territory." Although Grigsby was presumably less impressed with the *Industrial Worker*'s self-inspiring observation that "[w]e realize most effective way to enforce eight hour law is for workers organize," the next day he did answer the question straightforwardly: "Improper for me to express opinion on validity, believe law should be tested on Bunnell's decision. Not binding on any other three Divisions. But in view of attitude of Department of Justice, Attorneys might regard it as authority."[797] Since Nome was located in the Second Judicial Division and thus outside of Bunnell's jurisdiction, workers there were free to consider the law still valid.

The radical labor movement's reaction to the judicial repeal of the eight-hour law can be gauged by the *Industrial Worker*'s stream of editorials over the following months directing a barrage of insults at "the ever accommodating Judge Bunnell one of the brightest ornaments of the democratic machine in the Fourth Division."[798] The newspaper espoused a countermodel of statutory and constitutional legitimation: "ORGANIZE AND YOU SHALL BE THE ONES WHO SHALL DECLARE SAID LAWS CONSTITUTIONAL."[799] In an editorial repeatedly using the key Marxist term, "labor power," the *Industrial Worker* put newly arrived miners on notice that the eight-hour law "HAS BEEN DECLARED CONSTITUTIONAL BY ORGANIZED LABOR."[800] An article hailing ditch men who had quit in solidarity with the eight-hour strike urged miners to "[t]ell the boss or anybody else that you intend to abide by the eight hour law which has been adopted by ORGANIZED LABOR. (Regardless of the opinion of the likes of Judge Bunnell...)."[801]

In spite of its insistence that placer miners had not gained the eight-hour day because instead of relying on themselves, they had "relied upon a legislature which is attached to the interests of the bosses,"[802] the paper declared:

---

union was the IUMMSW.

[797]"Miners Union Wired Grigsby-He Replied," *Tri-Weekly Nome Industrial Worker*, May 16, 1918, at 1, col. 5-6.

[798]"The Labor Situation," *Tri-Weekly Nome Industrial Worker*, Aug. 29, 1918, at 2, col. 1.

[799]"Mr. Working Man," *Tri-Weekly Nome Industrial Worker*, June 6, 1918, at 2, col. 1.

[800]"Welcome," *Tri-Weekly Nome Industrial Worker*, June 25, 1918, at 2, col. 1-2.

[801]"Several Ditch Men Quit Work," *Tri-Weekly Nome Industrial Worker*, May 16, 1918, at 1, col. 4 at 6.

[802]"Mr. Working-Man," *Tri-Weekly Nome Industrial Worker*, May 14, 1918, at 2, col. 1 at 3.

> Beyond anything that has occurred in recent years the enforcement of the general eight hour law is most correctly to be considered the most important one to the working class the population within the Territory has faced since Alaska was purchased from Russia. ...
>
> Bunnell's decision ought to be self evident to the working-class that the only way to enforce such a law is to thoroughly organize, and convince Bunnell and the likes of him that his decision is not worth the paper it is written upon.
>
> It challenges the standing of corporation satellites to attempt to legislate for the small minority as against the rights of the workers who perform the functions of producing for a bunch of a worthless parasites.[803]

Considerable light is shed on the fate of Alaska's eight-hour law by Governor Riggs's first annual report, in which he repeated publicly the fears he had expressed internally to the Wilson administration about the consequences for the political legitimation of the territorial government of failing to reach closure:

> An attempt was made to have an appeal perfected on writ of error. By order of the Attorney General of the United States the district attorney of the fourth judicial district was not permitted to enter the appeal and all district attorneys of the four judicial divisions instructed not to enter any suit under the act. Later the attorney general of the Territory essayed to appear for the United States...but this attempt was also denied by the Department of Justice. The striking miners' union at Nome contended that the Attorney General had no authority to deny an appeal and remained on strike throughout the entire placer mining season, at the same time expressing a determination to maintain the law until definitely expunged from the statute books by a decision of the highest court. A conciliator of the Department of Labor sent to Nome...was unable to arrange an agreement between the gold mining operators and the strikers, the strikers holding out for an eight-hour day...and the principal operators holding firm to a longer day on a straight hourly basis without the time-and-a-half overtime feature, on the ground that placer mining with all the additional war-time costs would be unprofitable. An expression from various Alaskan unions showed considerable variance of opinion. The sentiment for a straight eight-hour day and for an eight-hour day with time-and-a-half overtime...being about equally divided, as is the sentiment regarding the validity of the court's decision. It is to be regretted that an appeal was not allowed to be taken as, until the question is settled definitely for all time, there will be a recrudescence of labor disturbance. ... Unless the legislature of the Territory will voluntarily amend the law or unless the Department of Justice will allow an appeal, I look for continued labor unrest.[804]

---

[803]"Mr. Working-Man," *Tri-Weekly Nome Industrial Worker*, May 28, 1918, at 2, col. 1-2.

[804]*Report of the Governor of Alaska*, in 2 *Reports of the Department of Interior for the Fiscal Year Ending June 30, 1918: Indian Affairs Territories*, at 565 (65th Cong., 3d Sess., H. Doc. No. 145, 1919). For an almost identical account, see 1 *Reports of the Department of Interior for the Fiscal Year Ended June 20, 1918*, at 142 (1919).

Riggs's interest in Supreme Court review may also have been a function of his own desire for definitive repeal of the law, but he did not wait for that eventuality to begin conducting his wartime campaign against so-called idlers and slackers and the Wobblies. Thus after the Navy had dispatched four ships in June at his request to forestall I.W.W. agitation among cannery workers,[805] the governor received a telegram in July from the chairman of the Selective Service Board in Nome wanting to know whether he could reclassify the striking gold miners (whom Riggs had discussed in his annual report) and draft them for refusing work in an industry essential to the war effort. Without any mention of the eight-hour law that the miners were trying to enforce, Riggs instructed him to consult the district attorney if the situation required "immediate action" against "idlers."[806] The next day the governor wired the *Nome Industrial Worker* in the same matter that, since the eight-hour law had been "construed both by the courts and by the department of Justice...to be unconstitutional and District Attorneys instructed from Washington not to prosecute under it," gold miners "dissatisfied with existing conditions should sink personal grievances to assist the smooth running of industry from a patriotic standpoint."[807] That same day, however, Riggs was apparently sufficiently unsure of himself that his office telegraphed the Provost Marshal General in Washington asking whether he had been correct in advising the Nome Selective Service Board that gold miners striking for an eight-hour day under a law declared unconstitutional were "idlers."[808] Although Riggs promptly wired the board in Nome that a draft "registrant who ceases work on account of a strike for a declared cause must not be classed as an idler nor has [sic] classification changed,"[809] he conveniently failed to disabuse the *Industrial Worker* of his earlier erroneous interpretation.[810]

Amusingly, the governor's abiding concern with labor unrest prompted him to use the same law to pressure employers that he castigated striking gold miners for seeking to uphold. In June, he sent admonishing letters to fishing employers that were taking advantage of the suspension of the eight-hour law, which in the meantime had become unenforcible (but not in the First Judicial Division in

---

[805]"Naval patrol for Alaskan Coast," *Tri-Weekly Nome Industrial Worker*," May 28, 1918, at 1, col. 1; Stewart, "The Alaskan Home Front During World War I" at 16-17.

[806]Telegram from Governor Riggs to [Carl] Lomen, July 15, 1918, in Record Group 101, Ser. 440, Box 90, Alaska State Archives.

[807]Telegram from Governor Riggs to Industrial Worker, Nome, July 16, 1918, in Record Group 101, Ser. 440, Box 90, Alaska State Archives.

[808]Telegram from Finnegan, Executive Officer, to Crowder, July 16, 1918, in Record Group 101, Ser. 440, Box 90, Alaska State Archives.

[809]Telegram from Governor Riggs to [Carl] Lomen, July 19, 1918, in Record Group 101, Ser. 440, Box 90, Alaska State Archives.

[810]Stewart, "The Alaskan Home Front During World War I" at 18.

which their businesses were located), although Riggs, like the miners he was berating, was wont to inform correspondents that "the law as passed is still upon the statute books":[811]

It has been brought to my attention that the men in your employ are working ten hours a day without additional compensation for two hours' overtime. The intention of the Council of National Defense and the Secretary of the Interior was not to do away with the basic principle of an eight-hour day in connection with the fisheries, but to lessen the hardships entailed by the Territorial law. Your scale of wages should be at the rate of an eight-hour day, with time and a half for overtime.

Will you kindly advise me if my information is correct and, if so, if you will not take steps to amend your schedule to the eight-hour basis, as contemplated by the various proclamations.[812]

To be sure, it is unclear what proclamations Riggs meant since Governor Strong's proclamations suspending the law as to fisheries contained no such statements concerning overtime, while the proclamations issued by President Wilson in March and April 1917 applied only to government contracts.

In contrast, the *Nome Industrial Worker* at this time was heaping abuse on proponents of overtime. In an editorial, the miners union found it "amusing to hear those scab apologists insist that the eight hour day is all right, but a man should be let work overtime. In point of fact everyone is willing to concede the eight hour day 'in principle' but they want to work ten or twelve, with overtime at straight time."[813]

The most tantalizing evidence that Riggs had joined with other officials in an effort to deal with the aftermath of Judge Bunnell's decision is a letter that he received, on official stationery of the Department of Justice/Office of Clerk of the District Court for the Territory of Alaska, from Judge Bunnell's clerk, Joseph E. Clark. Since district court judges appointed their clerks and Bunnell had appointed Clark, who had previously been chief deputy clerk,[814] to the much sought after post in 1915,[815] he was presumably acting under Bunnell's instructions.[816] Dated August 20, 1918, this extraordinary letter raises many more

---

[811]Governor to Mrs. Alice M. Veatch, Aug. 1, 1918, in Record Group 101, File Group 156, Box 159, Alaska State Archives.

[812]Governor to Northland Dock Co. and New England Fish Co., Ketchikan, June 21, 1918, in Record Group 101, File Group 156, Box 159, Alaska State Archives.

[813]"The Eight Hour Day," *Tri-Weekly Nome Industrial Worker*, Aug. 13, 1918, at 2, col. 1.

[814]4 *Alaska Reports* ix (appointed July 1, 1913).

[815]Cashen, *Farthest North College President* at 69-70.

[816]Act of June 6, 1900, ch. 786, § 6, 31 Stat. 321, 323. On the clerk's duties and powers, see *id.*, §§ 7, 730, 31 Stat. at 324, 447. That a federal district court clerk was not

questions than it answers. Clark informed the governor that he had enclosed a copy of the decision and Davis's letter to Grigsby, which "[w]e" had intended but omitted to give Riggs before he left Fairbanks. (Clark was sufficiently prominent in Fairbanks that the local paper mentioned only him and his wife along with the mayor and his wife as having been in the receiving line at a reception for Riggs a few days earlier.)[817] The clerk then observed that it was "apparent" to him that Bunnell's decision, based on Supreme Court precedent, together with the Attorney General's position, "ought to settle for the time at least, the question of a General 8-hour law." In a puzzling non sequitur referring to the Adamson Act, which was merely an overtime law, Clark then added: "We all know that the Democratic [sic] party is on record as being in favor of the 8-hour law, as was proven by the 8-hour railroad law passed in 1916." Clark deepened the mystery by disclosing: "We are taking the meat of Judge Bunnell's decision, having the same published, together with letters of the Attorney General on this subject, and will mail to every voter in the Fourth Division and will send a supply to the Second Division." Finally, Clark told Riggs that "[w]e" would like to know what Charles Sulzer, Alaska's Democratic delegate to Congress, said in reply to Riggs before "the pamphlet is printed," but noted that they would proceed in any event, adding that he did not believe that Riggs had raised the eight-hour question in his letter.[818]

Who "we" were, who was paying for the pamphlet, whether it was ever printed and distributed, and, above all, what the purpose of this campaign was all remain unclear. Since newspapers had lavished front-page banner headlines on the law and Bunnell's opinion, and since Alaska workers and labor unions had been actively engaged in campaigns to enact and preserve the law, it seems unlikely that the pamphlet could have been designed to serve a purely informational purpose. After all, in Nome, the seat of the Second Division, the *Industrial Worker* had just lambasted Bunnell for having declared the law unconstitutional "by a piece of trickery"[819] in these terms: "Such a travesty of justice has often been observed as this parasitic decision of Bunnell's apparently

---

a menial servant was signaled by his substantial salary, which at $3,500 in 1918 was about half of Judge Bunnell's and 70 percent of the Fairbanks U.S. Attorney's. U.S. Dept. of Justice, *Register of the Department of Justice and the Courts of the United States* 55 (26th ed. 1918).

[817]"Reception Was Huge Success," *Fairbanks Daily News-Miner*, Aug. 19, 1918, at 4, col. 1.

[818]Letter from J. E. Clark to Thomas Riggs, Jr., Aug. 20, 1918, in Record Group 101, File Group 156, Box 159, Alaska State Archives. The Fourth Division, headquartered in Fairbanks, covered much of the interior, while the Second Division, with its seat in Nome, covered the western part of Alaska.

[819]"Mr. Wage Worker Organize," *Tri-Weekly Nome Industrial Worker*, June 11, 1918, at 2, col. 1, at 3.

given for the unsophisticated working class to take for granted if they are boneheads enough to so do."[820]

Did Bunnell and Riggs intend to convince voters of the constitutional hopelessness of any legislative intervention? Or, on the contrary, did they hope to persuade workers to support enactment of a watered-down, constitutionally valid, overtime law at the next legislative session in 1919? This latter possibility is consistent with an initiative that Riggs undertook two weeks after receiving Clark's letter, sending telegrams to labor unions, asking: "Is the sentiment of your union in favor of an eight hour day only or eight hour day with overtime at increased rate of pay."[821] According to an alternative interpretation, advanced by the chief archivist at the Alaska State Archives, Clark "slipped into a party voice and expressed his intentions to send the information regarding the law and judicial decision as a Democratic Party publication. Bunnell's opinion and decisions by the Department of Justice not to pursue an appeal would not have been popular among the party faithful in the division."[822] This scenario implies that Bunnell was not involved in the plan of his clerk, who might even have been engaged in an act of disloyalty toward his superior. However, in light of District Judge Bunnell's commanding position within the Democratic Party in dispensing political patronage jobs,[823] it seems unlikely that he could have been kept in the dark about this unconventional yet public project. Moreover, the fact that Clark did not resign his position until May 1919—and then only to enter the automobile business in Colorado—at which time the *Fairbanks Daily News-Miner*'s reports depicted him as a hail fellow well met, does not suggest that Bunnell had fired Clark.[824]

That Riggs and his associates were pursuing an accommodationist rather than

---

[820]"Mr. Working Man," *Tri-Weekly Nome Industrial Worker*, June 6, 1918, at 2, col. 1-2.

[821]Telegram from Riggs Governor, Sept. 8, 1918 (handwritten draft), in Record Group 101, File Group 156, Box 159, Alaska State Archives.

[822]Email from John Stewart to author, Apr. 10, 2000.

[823]Cashen, *Farthest North College President* at 63-70. As Governor Strong informed a correspondent who had sought his help in obtaining a position at the time of Bunnell's appointment: "I do not care to suggest the name of anyone for the positions mentioned by you, or for any other position within the gift of Judge Bunnell, as I feel that he should be given a free hand in the selection of the men who will serve under him. ... There should be a number of positions within the gift of Mr. Bunnell, both clerkships and commissionerships, and you ought to land one of them." Letter from Governor to B. J. McGinnis, Jan. 7, 1915, in Record Group 101, Ser. 130, File 52, Box 129, Alaska State Archives. See also Letter from Governor to L. F. Protzman, Jan. 14, 1915, in *id.*

[824]"Clerk of Court Resignations," *Fairbanks Daily News-Miner*, May 2, 1919, at 4, col. 3; "Master Clark Has Smallpox," *Fairbanks Daily News-Miner*, May 2, 1919, at 2, col. 2; "Clerk of Court Quitting Job," *Fairbanks Daily News-Miner*, May 4, 1919, at 4, col. 3.

a confrontational course is also strongly corroborated by the governor's public preoccupation with the anarchy that labor radicals might rain down on Alaska at any moment. In his second annual report to the Secretary of the Interior for 1918-19, Riggs lamented:

> The resident workingman is of the very highest type—capable, energetic, and thrifty—but unfortunately Alaska during the past year has received many immigrants of the most undesirable type. The I.W.W. and advocates of soviet rule have been most active in agitating disturbance. The lack of police protection is well known, and the radicals work openly in their efforts to disorganize industry. Unfortunately, there are very large numbers of ignorant, illiterate laborers of foreign extraction in the Territory, and in many places the seeds of sedition, skillfully sown, have fallen on fertile soil. Except for the mounting cost of living, there seems to be little dissatisfaction among the wage earners, practically all agitation emanating from that class who are denunciatory of all vested interests but whose hands show no signs of callus.[825]

In contrast, Wickersham, during his election campaign against Sulzer, enthusiastically supported the eight-hour law, attacked Bunnell for having "obligingly" declared it unconstitutional, and "paid his compliments to this moral cowardice upon the part of Sulzer" for refusing to take a stand on the grounds that it was improper to do so while the suspension was under consideration.[826]

As late as October 1918 Governor Riggs seemed tentative in informing an out-of-state lawyer who had inquired as to whether the eight-hour law was still in effect that an appeal of the decision holding it unconstitutional "to the present time...has been denied."[827] In the event, "no final test was had on this, the only enforceable universal eight-hour law covering private employment enacted in America" before or since the enactment of the FLSA.[828]

At the beginning of the next legislative session in 1919, Governor Riggs announced that he would submit the letter he had received from the U.S. solicitor general explaining why the Justice Department had concluded that an appeal of Bunnell's decision would be a "mere waste of time and money." Nevertheless, Riggs, who regretted having to observe that to a small part of the Alaskan population "the Red Flag and its teachings of tyrannical and chaotic Bolshevism represent an end to be attained, no matter through what means," declared that the

---

[825]*Report of the Governor of Alaska*, in 2 *Reports of the Department of Interior for the Fiscal Year Ending June 30, 1919: Indian Affairs Territories*, at 479 (1920).

[826]"Wick Opens Up G.O.P. Campaign" at 4, col. 2.

[827]Letter from Governor Riggs to Robert Welch, Oct. 14, 1918, in Record Group 101, File Code 156, Box 159, Alaska State Archives.

[828]John Commons and John Andrews, *Principles of Labor Legislation* 140 (4th ed. 1936 [1916]).

legislature should consider a new eight-hour bill that could pass constitutional muster "to the end that, if possible, the desire of the electorate at the election of 1916 may be complied with."[829]

In fact, five days later an eight-hour law was the very first bill introduced in that session of the Alaska House of Representatives. The *Alaska Daily Empire* underscored its importance by printing the entire text the next day.[830] Seeking to avoid the constitutional pitfalls that had tripped the 1917 law, its authors, Representatives John Dunn and George Pennington, chose to dilute it in several significant ways. First, although House Bill No. 1 still covered adult males, it was now restricted to persons who were "hired [or] permitted to work for wages," thus presumably excluding business partners. Second, the bill was careful to declare as interlocking Alaskan public policies that: no such workers were to work "for longer hours...or days of service than is consistent with his or her health and physical well-being and the ability to promote the general welfare by his or her increasing usefulness as a healthy and intelligent citizen"; and working any person more than eight hours daily "in any mill, sawmill, lumber yard, manufacturing, mercantile or mechanical establishment, or office, or store, or any express or transportation company, or telephone company, laundry, hotel or restaurant, is injurious to the physical health and well-being of such person, and tends to prevent him or her from acquiring that degree of intelligence that is necessary to make him or her a useful and desirable citizen." Third, the bill excepted from the eight-hours maximum "watchmen and employees when engaged in making necessary repairs or in case of emergency." And finally, the most radical element of the 1917 law was deleted by a proviso "that employees may work overtime conditioned that payment be made for such overtime at the rate of time and one-half the regular wage."[831]

Two days after the bill's introduction, a mass meeting at Labor Union Hall in Juneau unanimously voted in favor of the bill as well as one extending coverage to the canneries. That some workers were prepared to recede from their maximalist demands was clear from remarks made at the meeting. For example, a member of the Cooks and Waiters Union approved of the new overtime provision on the grounds that "limiting...men to an eight-hour day would not be practicable in Alaska." Even greater skepticism was expressed by former Senator

---

[829]"Message of the Governor," in *The Journal of the House of Representatives of the Fourth Legislative Assembly of the Territory of Alaska* 34, 36, 45 (1919).

[830]"8-Hour Bill Is Presented to Legislature," *Alaska Daily Empire*, Mar. 11, 1919, at 2, col. 1.

[831]House Bill No. 1, §§ 1-2, Territory of Alaska, Fourth Session, Alaska State Archives, Records of the Territorial Legislature, Record Group 34, 1919, Series 30, Box 5180; *The Journal of the House of Representatives of the Fourth Legislative Assembly of the Territory of Alaska* at 56-57.

Hubbard, who doubted the new bill's constitutionality although he supported the effort. The bill's co-author, Representative Dunn—a Denver lawyer who had been prospecting in Alaska since 1905[832]—seemed on firmer jurisprudential footing when he urged its constitutionality on the grounds that it followed the Oregon overtime law, which had been upheld by the U.S. Supreme Court.[833] The fact that a fishermen's representative who had supported the absolute eight-hour law at the governor's hearing a year earlier now called the Dunn-Pennington bill a "masterpiece"[834] suggests that at least part of the labor movement had abandoned hopes of combating a mandatory longer workday through state intervention. Although several locals of the Alaska Labor Union did endorse the Dunn-Pennington bill, the *Nome Industrial Worker* reported that "no union locals affiliated with the American Federation of Labor has [sic] given its endorsement to the bill in its present emasculated condition."[835]

That compromised condition appears to have corresponded to Representative Pennington's own politics. On the one hand, just the previous year he had joined a labor union at the age of 62, believing: "Capitalists are blind if they cannot see and understand the forces working about them." He warned employers that if they failed to recognize workers' "rights, backed by justice, then they are manufacturing the very kind of men which they so much seem to fear."[836] On the other hand, the day after introducing H.B. 1, Pennington, in conformity with the legal landscape of the lower 48 states,[837] also filed his anti-Bolshevik "Bill to Guard Alaska Against Unamericanism," which criminalized the use of any flag to symbolize a purpose to overthrow or to advocate overthrowing the government of the United States or Alaska "by the general cessation of industry...."[838] He had also agreed not to include canneries in the bill because he and Dunn believed that it was "possibly" just to do so since those employers had already made their

[832]"Legislative Candidates Division 4," *Fairbanks Daily News-Miner*, Oct. 19, 1916, at 3, col. 5.

[833]"Rising Vote on Labor Problems at Mass Meeting," *Alaska Daily Empire*, Mar. 3, 1919, at 8, col. 4.

[834]"Mass Meeting Is Held over Eight-Hour Law," *Alaska Daily Empire*, Apr. 1, 1919, at 8, col. 1, at 2 (R. C. Oliver).

[835]"Legislature Busy at Juneau," *Weekly Nome Industrial Worker*, Apr. 5, 1919, at 1, col. 4. See also "Eight Hour Law Is Discussed at Meeting Alaska Labor Union," *Alaska Daily Empire*, Mar. 11, 1919, at 8, col. 1. The Alaska Labor Union had been founded in 1916 as a socialist organization, but dropped that orientation by 1917. Sullivan, "Sourdough Radicalism" at 232.

[836]"Mass Meeting Is Held over Eight-Hour Law," *Alaska Daily Empire*, Apr. 1, 1919, at 8, col. 1, at 2.

[837]See, e.g., Murphy, *World War I and the Origin of Civil Liberties in the United States*.

[838]"Bill to Guard Alaska Against Unamericanism," *Alaska Daily Empire*, Mar. 12, 1919, at 2, col. 5; H.B. No. 3, §§ 1-2.

contracts; nevertheless, he told the mass meeting that if workers wanted to include the fishermen, he was "willing to go down to defeat with the bill on that proposition...."[839] Excluding the canneries was tantamount to gutting the law: in 1919 the fishing industry employed 28,500 workers (90 percent of them in salmon canneries) at a time when the entire population of Alaska was only 55,000.[840]

At the beginning of April, Dunn presented to the Committee on Labor, Capital and Immigration a telegram from laborers in Anchorage supporting his bill with amendments to include canneries, and the committee promptly adopted the amendment, which also provided for coverage of logging camps.[841] The Committee of the Whole issued a report recommending that the bill pass with these amendments. It also recommended that the chairmen of the Committees on Labor, Capital and Immigration and Judiciary and Federal Relations be required to submit the amended bill to Alaska's attorney general for his opinion on its legality and constitutionality.[842]

The day after receiving the chairmen's request, Attorney General Grigsby sent the chairmen a comprehensive 13-page legal analysis of the bill—the full text of which was published in the Juneau newspaper[843]—concluding that most of the bill could pass constitutional muster. Grigsby instructed the legislature that no hours law had "ever been upheld on the theory that the constitutional right of all persons to contract freely is subject to regulation at the hands of a legislative majority regardless of the character of the employment which is the subject of the contract."[844] Based on the U.S. Supreme Court's decision upholding the Oregon hours law in 1917,[845] Grigsby concluded that H.B. 1, which he regarded as

---

[839]"Mass Meeting Is Held over Eight-Hour Law."

[840]30 *The Encyclopædia Britannica: The New Volumes* 102-104 (12th ed. 1922), s.v. "Alaska."

[841]*The Journal of the House of Representatives of the Fourth Legislative Assembly of the Territory of Alaska* 118 (1919).

[842]"Report of Committee of the Whole" on H.B. 1 (Apr. 5, 1919), in Records of the Territorial Legislature, Record Group 34, Series 30, Box 5180, Alaska State Archives; *The Journal of the House of Representatives of the Third Legislative Assembly of the Territory of Alaska* at 126-28; "Eight-Hour Bill Reported in the House," *Alaska Daily Empire*, Apr. 3, 1919, at 2, col. 1; "Happenings in the Legislature," *Weekly Nome Industrial Worker*, Apr. 12, 1919, at 1, col. 4.

[843]"Attorney-General Grigsby Holds Eight-Hour Bill Not Valid As It Now Stands," *Alaska Daily Empire*, Apr. 11, 1919, at 2, col. 1.

[844]Letter from Attorney General George Grigsby to James Bogan and John Dunn at 3 (Apr. 8, 1919), in Records of the Territorial Legislature, Record Group 34, Series 30, Box 5180, Alaska State Archives.

[845]Bunting v. Oregon, 243 U.S. 426 (1917); see also the discussion above in section 4. Interestingly, Josephine Goldmark of the National Consumers' League, one of the leading advocates of labor standards legislation, had sent Governor a copy of that organization's

"practically a duplicate" except as to the occupations covered and limitation of hours, would be upheld if it were limited to mills, factories, and manufacturing, saw mills, fisheries, logging camps, laundries, and transportation companies. But as to lumber yards, hotels, restaurants, telephone companies, offices, and stores, he believed that "whatever degree of unhealthiness is attached to such occupations is too remote to justify the exercise of the police power."[846] By "including almost every known occupation, ranging from that of a logger in the woods to a lawyer's or doctor's clerk," the legislature ran the risk that "courts might say that it is an attempt, in the guise of a health and public welfare law, to enact a general eight hour law." Indeed, Grigsby speculated that "a general eight hour law such as passed by the Legislature in 1917, preceded by a like legislative declaration as to its intent and purpose would...stand as good as chance of being upheld" as H.B. 1. Consequently, the Alaska attorney general concluded that in order to avoid a court ruling that voided the entire bill, elimination of the aforementioned occupations bearing no direct relation to health or welfare "would leave the proposed Act unobjectionable."[847]

Three days after Grigsby responded, Territorial Governor Riggs informed the Labor Committee chairman that he had received the following message from the Attorney General in Washington, A. Mitchell Palmer (to whom the chairmen had telegraphed the bill at Grigsby's request)[848]:

> Department unwilling to express its opinion as to whether proposed eight-hour bill will be held constitutional, but is willing to assure you that if lower court holds it unconstitutional, it will direct an appeal to be taken to the Supreme Court of the United States and will make every effort to uphold constitutionality of statute.[849]

As constitutionally more tenable bills wended their way through the legislature, negative pro-business voices began to be heard. The *Alaska Daily Empire*, which a year earlier had attacked the law (after Bunnell struck it down)

---

brief in defense of the Oregon law. Letter from Governor Strong to Josephine Goldmark, Jan. 28, 1918, in Record Group 101, File Code 156, Box 159, Alaska State Archives.

[846]Letter from Attorney General George Grigsby to James Bogan and John Dunn at 11, 8.

[847]Letter from Attorney General George Grigsby to James Bogan and John Dunn at 12-13 [as a result of a typo, page 11 and the following page are both paginated as page 11].

[848]Report of Standing Committee (Apr. 12, 1919), in Records of the Territorial Legislature, Record Group 34, Series 30, Box 5180, Alaska State Archives; *The Journal of the House of Representatives of the Fourth Legislative Assembly of the Territory of Alaska* at 135.

[849]Letter from Governor Thomas Riggs, Jr. to J. J. Bogan, chairman, House Committee on Labor, Capital and Immigration (Apr. 11, 1919), in Records of the Territorial Legislature, Record Group 34, Series 30, Box 5180, Alaska State Archives.

for banning overtime work, now that the offending provision had been eliminated, discovered a new flaw: "where labor cost is the principal item in manufacturing cost, it is not practical to pay time and a half for overtime, because the cost of the manufactured article would thereby be forced so high that the selling price would have to be so advanced that the market would be destroyed."[850] Some Alaska capitalists joined the *Daily Empire* in attacking what they regarded as "straight-jacket laws."[851]

The substitute bill, as recommended by the Committee on Labor, Capital and Immigration and designed to accommodate Grigsby's criticisms and suggestions,[852] passed the House 14-2 in April.[853] Even this diluted bill, however, was defeated in the Senate 6-2, where some senators argued that it would destroy the fishing industry, "which pays most of the Territorial taxes."[854] Representatives Dunn and Pennington introduced a second eight-hour bill designed to cover those industries (lumber yards, mercantile establishments, logging camps, offices, stores, express companies, telephone companies, laundries, hotels, and restaurants) coverage of which had been deemed questionable.[855] It passed the House unanimously, but was defeated 6-2 in the Senate.[856]

The pressure to deviate from the absolutist law of 1917 was further evidenced by Senate Bill No. 19, which was even titled, "An Act to establish a general eight hour day and to provide for the payment of overtime." It made eight hours a day's labor (except for farming and domestic service and hazardous occupations

---

[850]"Eight-Hour Legislation," *Alaska Daily Empire*, Apr. 4, 1919, at 4, col. 1 (editorial).

[851]"Falcon Joslin Speaks Against 8-Hour Measure," *Alaska Daily Empire*, Apr. 19, 1919, at 8, col. 4; "We Are Not for Straight-Jacket Laws," *Alaska Daily Empire*, Apr. 26, 1919, at 4, col. 1 (editorial).

[852]Report of Standing Committee (Apr. 16, 1919), in Records of the Territorial Legislature, Record Group 34, Series 30, Box 5180, Alaska State Archives; "Last Day for Bills Brings Flood in House," *Alaska Daily Empire*, Apr. 11, 1919, at 1, col. 4..

[853]Substitute House Bill No. 1, Territory of Alaska - Fourth Session [no date], in Records of the Territorial Legislature, Record Group 34, Series 30, Box 5180, Alaska State Archives; *The Journal of the House of Representatives of the Fourth Legislative Assembly of the Territory of Alaska* at 196; "Eight-Hour Bill Is Passed by Lower House," *Alaska Daily Empire*, Apr. 21, 1919, at 2, col. 5.

[854]HB1, in Records of the Territorial Legislature, Record Group 109, 1919 Bill Docket, Alaska House of Representatives, Alaska State Archives; *The Senate Journal of the Fourth Legislative Assembly of the Territory of Alaska* 119 (1919); "8 Hour Law May Not Pass Senate," *Weekly Nome Industrial Worker*, Apr. 26, 1919, at 1, col. 4 (quote).

[855]House Bill No. 39, Record Group 01/03, Ser. 30, Box 5180, Alaska State Archives. At the time of the bill's second reading laundries were deleted. *The Journal of the House of Representatives of the Fourth Legislative Assembly of the Territory of Alaska* at 226.

[856]*The Journal of the House of Representatives of the Fourth Legislative Assembly of the Territory of Alaska* at 241; *The Senate Journal of the Fourth Legislative Assembly of the Territory of Alaska* at 130; "Legislature Moving Fast in Last Days," *Alaska Daily Empire*, Apr. 28, 1919, at 2, col. 1.

otherwise regulated) unless the employer and employee signed an agreement designating other hours as a day's labor, in which case an overtime premium was not statutorily required; only where they failed to sign such an agreement was time and one-half mandated for hours in excess of eight.[857] It too was defeated 6-2.[858]

Yet another Senate bill, S.B. 54, limited overtime work (to be paid at time and a half) to making necessary repairs and emergencies when life or property was in imminent danger. Finding that "the recent actual experience of mankind" showed that "in general employment, longer hours of work in any one day than eight hours does not increase the amount of work done, but tends to impair the health and happiness of the individual, and render him less fit as a citizen and elector," the bill declared it as the territory's public policy to "promote the general health, physical well-being, and happiness of laborers by limiting" the workday to eight hours. However, the bill stated that this policy did not apply to certain industries by reason of climate, seasonality, or occasional employment; they included some of the territory's biggest employers such as fishing and canning, longshoring, transportation, and placer mining.[859] The fact that the bill passed the Senate 5-3[860] reflected the influence of the fishing industry. Indeed, Senator James Heckman, who introduced the bill, was a "successful salmon packer" and merchant, who had been connected with the industry since 1888.[861]

The intensity of labor-capital conflict in the Senate was captured by its members' reaction to a telegram sent to its chairman on April 22 by the mayor of Alaska's leading fishing center, the extreme southern town of Ketchikan, the Deep Sea Fishermen's Union, and a local of the Alaska Labor Union: "If Victory Loan to be success here eight hour bill Dunn-Pennington must pass with no

---

[857]Senate Bill No. 19 (Sen. Hess), in Records of the Territorial Legislature, Record Group 34, Series 30, Box 5180, Alaska State Archives. The full text was published in "Hess Author of New 8-Hour Bill in Senate," *Alaska Daily Empire*, Mar. 26, 1919, at 2, col. 3.

[858]SB19, in Records of the Territorial Legislature, Record Group 109, 1919 Bill Docket, Alaska Senate, Alaska State Archives; *The Journal of the Senate of the Fourth Legislative Assembly of the Territory of Alaska at* 118; "Eight-Hour Bill Is Passed by the Senate Members," *Alaska Daily Empire*, Apr. 28, 1919, at 2, col. 4.

[859]Senate Bill No. 54, §§ 1-3 (Sen. Heckman), in Records of the Territorial Legislature, Record Group 34, Series 30, Box 5180, Alaska State Archives. The Senate and House Journals in places refer to this bill as having been introduced by Sen. Frawley. *The Senate Journal of the Fourth Legislative Assembly of the Territory of Alaska* at 173; *The Journal of the House of Representatives of the Fourth Legislative Assembly of the Territory of Alaska* at 248, 350.

[860]*The Senate Journal of the Fourth Legislative Assembly of the Territory of Alaska* at 117.

[861]"Legislature as It Will Be Made Up at Next Term," *Fairbanks Daily News-Miner*, Nov. 13, 1916, at 3, col. 2.

restrictions political suicide for senators opposing so far as concerns labor."[862] The Senate immediately adopted a report of its special committee, which first characterized the "threat" as "a direct offer to purchase the vote of this body," and then initiated criminal prosecution:

> We could overlook the efforts of the signers...to intimidate members of this body but when such an attempt at intimidation is accompanied with the intimation that the authors will oppose the success of the Victory Loan now offered by our Government, we cannot reach any other conclusion than that the parties thereto are making threats that very closely touch the border line of conspiracy or treason....
>
> And we further recommend that the above telegram be turned over to the United States District Attorney to deal with as the law may direct.[863]

In contrast, labor's political strength in the House may have been decisive in the failure of the House and Senate conferees to agree on a final version.[864] On the penultimate day of the legislative session, the House, by a vote of 12-4, amended Senate Bill No. 54 to reincorporate all the excluded occupations (except agriculture and domestic service),[865] "Dunn and Pennington refusing to budge an inch. 'We will not yield a word,' said Mr. Pennington. Nor a 'coma [sic],' added Mr. Dunn."[866] Thus ended the Alaska labor movement's attempt to achieve a state-enforced general eight-hour day.

In his annual report to the Interior Department Governor Riggs remarked that the eight-hour bills had failed to pass in 1919 because "too many toes were trodden" in an attempt to keep the bills as general as possible. The fish packers, for example, who were "the ones really aimed at," denied the possibility of an eight-hour day on the grounds that "when a run of fish is on plants must operate more hours to prevent the spoiling of the raw material; the fishermen themselves

---

[862]*The Senate Journal of the Fourth Legislative Assembly of the Territory of Alaska* at 106.

[863]*The Senate Journal of the Fourth Legislative Assembly of the Territory of Alaska* at 107.

[864]Senate Bill No. 54, in Records of the Territorial Legislature, Record Group 109, 1919 Bill Docket, Alaska Senate, Alaska State Archives; *The Journal of the House of Representatives of the Fourth Legislative Assembly of the Territory of Alaska* at 318, 321, 322, 326; *The Senate Journal of the Fourth Legislative Assembly of the Territory of Alaska* at 150; "Eight Hour Bill Is Passed by the Senate Members"; "Measures for 8-Hour Day in Hopeless Shape," *Alaska Daily Empire*, Apr. 30, 1919, at 2, col. 5.

[865]*The Journal of the House of Representatives of the Fourth Legislative Assembly of the Territory of Alaska* at 264, 300.

[866]"Fourth Legislature Comes to an End After Being in Session for 33 Hours, Making Record for Alaska Sittings," *Alaska Daily Empire*, May 2, 1919, at 1, col. 1, 2. Wickersham, who did not mention passage of the eight-hour law in 1917 in his diaries, happened to be in Juneau the day after the legislature adjourned and noted that it had "failed to pass any 8 Hour Law...." Wickersham "Diaries," May 3, 1919.

asserting their absolute inability to comply with an eight-hour law, for the reason that almost all of them are share workers." Ironically, the governor concluded his account by observing that many industries had voluntarily adopted the eight-hour day with success.[867]

The forces pushing for some kind of hours regulation did not abandon their efforts. At the fifth legislative session in 1921 they undertook a more cautious overtime initiative. Although it, too, applied to adult men, House Bill No. 6 from the outset confined its scope to any mill, saw mill, factory, laundry, manufacturing establishment, or open-cut or open-pit quarry or mine. It was also more circumspect in attempting to anticipate any judicially constructed constitutional obstacles to hours regulation. Unlike earlier bills, it stated that "climatic and living conditions" in Alaska made employment in the named industries for more than eight hours a day "injurious to the health of both men and women...and greatly increase the likelihood of injury...." The bill then characterized these facts as justifying the territory's "exercise of its police power...to discourage the employment" of men or women in those industries for more than eight hours.[868]

The bill sought to insure judicial approval by offering employers even more daily overtime than the Oregon law, which permitted three hours and was upheld by the U.S. Supreme Court. H.B. 6 permitted employees to work as many as four hours of overtime at time and one-half.[869] Finally, the bill made each violation of the act a misdemeanor punishable by a fine of between $100 and $500 or imprisonment in federal jail for a period of between 30 days and six months.[870]

In the course of further deliberations, the bill's scope was expanded by inclusion of surface placer mines. In addition, for the first time an Alaska overtime bill made payment of overtime wages a civil obligation enforcible in a contract action.[871] Immediately before the House of Representatives passed the bill with these amendments by a vote of 15 to 1, it received the attorney general's opinion as to its constitutionality. Despite the strong similarity to the Oregon law, he viewed the bill as "certainly very close to the line...." He thought that "the chances are that it will be upheld but we have nothing to spare, because it

---

[867]*Report of the Governor of Alaska*, in 2 *Indian Affairs Territories: Reports of the Department of Interior for the Fiscal Year Ending June 30, 1919*, at 480 (66th Cong., 2d Sess., H. Doc. No. 409, 1920).

[868]Territory of Alaska, Fifth Session, House Bill No. 6, § 1, in Record Group 01, Ser. 30, Box 5181 (Legislative Bills and Resolutions, 1921-25), Alaska State Archives. Rep. George Getchell, who introduced the bill, had been a mining engineer and became Juneau's chief of police after leaving the House. *Who's Who in Alaska Politics* at 34.

[869]House Bill No. 6, § 2.

[870]H.B. 6, § 3.

[871]*The Journal of the House of Representatives of the Fifth Legislative Assembly of the Territory of Alaska* 169 (1921).

must be remembered that we have the history of legislation on the eight hour question against us in this Territory in our effort to uphold the validity of thc law."[872]

In the Senate, Luther Hess, vice president of the First National Bank of Fairbanks and "one of the most extensive holders of mining ground in the whole territory,"[873] introduced as a substitute for H.B. 6 an even more permissive version of his unsuccessful overtime bill (S.B. 19) from the previous session. Whereas the earlier bill at least mandated time and a half for overtime work beyond eight hours daily where the employer failed to obtain its employees' signature to an agreement stipulating to a longer workday, Hess's new bill merely required employers, in the absence of such an agreement, to pay overtime wages "at the rate of wages agreed upon; or if there is no agreement as to wages, at the rate of wages paid for like service in the community where the labor was performed."[874] This watered down version of an already diluted overtime bill passed the Senate by an overwhelming 7-1 majority.[875]

Although even the House overtime bill was far removed from the radical intervention in the labor market embodied in the 1917 law, the Senate bill constituted such a meaningless labor standard that it was no surprise that the House voted 11-4 not to concur in it.[876] A conference committee was unable to reach agreement, but a free conference committee (of which neither the House nor Senate bill author was a member)[877] voted 5-1 in favor of the Senate substitute. The agreement, however, was short-lived: the whole House disavowed its own managers, voting 9-5 against the Senate substitute, thus bringing to a close eight years of efforts to legislate the eight-hour day in Alaska.[878]

After the defeat of the initiatives of 1917, 1919, and 1921, no eight-hour bill was introduced during the 1923 session. Not only did the Alaska legislature never again enact a general absolute eight-hour law, it did not even enact an

---

[872]*The Journal of the House of Representatives of the Fifth Legislative Assembly of the Territory of Alaska* at 179.

[873]"Legislature as It Will Be Made Up at Next Term," *Fairbanks Daily News-Miner*, Nov. 13, 1916, at 3, col. 2, at 4.

[874]Territory of Alaska, Fifth Session, In the Senate, Substitute for House Bill No. 6, § 2 (Rep. Hess), in Record Group 01, Ser. 30, Box 5181 (Legislative Bills and Resolutions, 1921-25), Alaska State Archives.

[875]*The Senate Journal of the Fifth Legislative Assembly of the Territory of Alaska* 173 (1921).

[876]*The Journal of the House of Representatives of the Fifth Legislative Assembly of the Territory of Alaska* at 242.

[877]Unlike a conference committee, a free conference committee is free to suggest new amendments that are clearly germane.

[878]*The Journal of the House of Representatives of the Fifth Legislative Assembly of the Territory of Alaska* 308-309, 360.

overtime law until 1955.[879] And so far removed from workers' and legislators' concerns of those early years is the state's current overtime law that—despite its unusual retention of Alaska's quondam tradition of mandating premium pay after eight hours per day[880]—its express public policy fails to make any reference whatsoever to the goal of a shorter workday. Instead, the legislature's policy has been diluted merely to a matter of money—namely, "to establish...overtime compensation standards for workers at levels consistent with their health, efficiency and general well-being...."[881]

12. The Right to Say No: State Laws Limiting Mandatory Overtime Work

Remember, the long struggle for the 8-hour day was not a struggle for 8 hours of work. It was a struggle for 16 hours away from work.[882]

[F]rankly, we would prefer that all overtime be voluntary, however, we don't believe that we can survive with that. That's basically what it boils down to....[883]

Later legislative initiatives in other states, only one of them successful, sought either to limit the extent of mandatory overtime or to entitle workers to refuse it without jeopardizing their employment. The most high-profile political struggle erupted in 1977 over a bill filed in the California Assembly that simply provided: "No employee shall be terminated from his or her employment for refusal to work overtime."[884] The bill was amended repeatedly over the following several months. First, workers were protected from any kind of adverse disciplinary actions, while businesses with five or fewer employees, much of agriculture, trains, and work performed in emergencies endangering public health and safety were exempted; overtime was defined as work performed "over and

---

[879]1955 Alaska Sess. Laws, ch. 185 at 372 (providing for time and a half for hours beyond 40 weekly or eight daily with numerous exclusions).

[880]Alaska Stat. § 23.10.060(b) (2000).

[881]Alaska Stat. § 23.10.050 (2000). When this policy was adopted in 1959, it appears to have been taken verbatim from a four-year old New Mexico statute. 1959 Alaska Sess. Laws ch. 171, § 1, at 248; 1955 N.M. Laws ch. 200, § 1, at 459.

[882]Maurice Sugar, "The Truth About 'Portal to Portal,'" 7 *Law. Guild Rev.* 23, 25 (1947).

[883][California] Senate Committee on Industrial Relations, *Interim Hearings on AB 1295—Mandatory Overtime* at 188 (testimony of Wayland Bonbright, ind. rels. mgr., Pac. Gas & Elec. Co.).

[884]Calif. Leg. A.B. No. 1295 (introduced by Assemblyman Tom Bates, Oakland, Mar. 31, 1977).

above...the normal hours in a working week...."[885] Then the agricultural and small-business exemptions were deleted, but a broad and amorphous exemption was added for "emergencies due to unavoidable and unforeseeable circumstances which cause significant disruption of usual operations."[886] This new exemption was then tightened somewhat by substituting "extreme" for "significant."[887] Finally, on June 23, the small-business exemption was written back into the bill, this time, however, raised 10-fold to exempt employers employing 50 or fewer employees, leaving only 5 percent of private employers and 65 percent of the employees covered.[888]

The following day the California Assembly passed this amended bill by a margin of 43 to 29, but employers and their representatives were outraged. As one Assemblyman, who regarded it as "'the most antibusiness bill that has been considered by this Legislature,'" put it: "'We might as well put up a sign that says, "Business not welcome. The Legislature of the State of California will run your business."'"[889]

When the Senate Industrial Relations Committee held a hearing in November 1977, the bill's author summed up the fundamental issue: "Simply, do people have the right to say no to an order that they have to work beyond the normal work day. Does an employee have the right to say, 'I'm exhausted.', or 'It's my son's birthday.', or 'I have to pick my kids up.'...without the fear of being fired? Should people be allowed to control their own time? [T]his legislation protects that basic right."[890]

One of the most telling objections that employers raised to the bill was its capacity to undermine their coercive authority. As the California Laundry and Linen Supply Association complained: "All employees who work five and one-half or six days, could literally 'go on strike' any time they had a real or imagined 'grievance.' They simply refuse to work on Saturday, and management could not, under AB 1295, discipline them! [T]hey can all refuse overtime work and literally 'shut down' our plants. This would not be a 'strike,' but our entire plant

---

[885]Cal. Leg. A.B. No. 1295 (amended in Assembly May 17, 1977).

[886]Cal. Leg. A.B. No. 1295 (amended in Assembly May 27, 1977).

[887]Cal. Leg. A.B. No. 1295 (amended in Assembly June 6, 1977).

[888]Cal. Leg. A.B. No. 1295 (amended in Assembly June 23, 1977); "Bill Banning Forced Overtime for Workers Okd by Assembly," *L.A. Times*, June 25, 1977, § 2 at 12, col. 1.

[889]"Bill Banning Forced Overtime for Workers Okd by Assembly," *L.A. Times*, June 25, 1977, § 2 at 12, col. 1 (quoting Daniel Boatwright); California Legislature, *Assembly Final History 1977-78 Regular Session* 825 (A.B. 1295).

[890]1 [California] Senate Committee on Industrial Relations, *Interim Hearings on AB 1295—Mandatory Overtime* 3-4 (Nov. 7, 1977) (statement of Assemblyman Tom Bates). See also Jerry Gillam, "Bill to Outlaw Forced Overtime Disputed," *L.A. Times*, Nov. 8, 1977, Pt. I, at 28, col. 1-3.

of employees exercising their 'right' not to work overtime, granted them by AB 1295."[891]

The industrial relations director of another large firm inadvertently specified workers' real grievance—namely, that the employer had violated the central norm establishing that the clock objectively determines when enough is enough: "It would be very difficult to operate the business if the threat existed that all employees could walk off the job at the end of a work day regardless of the amount of work which remains to be done." Where that work is shipping "toys and sundries to drug and discount stores in 13...states" from a distribution center, it is clear both that no emergency warranted compelling employees to work against their will and that entrusting to management the decision as to how much of an in principle endless "amount of work remains to be done" underwrites workplace autocracy.[892] A vice president of Hunt-Wesson Foods painted an even more disturbing scenario for management, which at the same time gave substance to workers' seemingly rhetorical lamentations about involuntary servitude: "For the most part, there are no replacements available for skilled employees. If overtime were not required, key skilled employees could easily shut down any one or more of our operating plants by refusing overtime work."[893] Viewed in this way, employers' intense opposition to the bill was self-explanatory: the proposed law would have overridden employers' economically coercive counterpower to nullify workers' superior labor market position.

Unionized employers also resented the fact that a mandatory overtime law, by creating a background institutional entitlement that unions would otherwise have to make collective bargaining concessions to secure, would enable unions to have their cake and eat it too.[894] (By this logic, the notion that "[i]f the Legislature begins removing items from the collective bargaining arena, the process itself is threatened,"[895] should have precluded Congress from enacting the

---

[891]Senate Committee on Industrial Relations, *Interim Hearing on AB 1295—Mandatory Overtime: Appendices* at 259, 260 (letter from David MacKenzie, Nov. 30, 1977). See also *id.* at 217, 220 (Dale Zechar, chairperson, Ind. Rels. Comm., Cal. Mfrs. Assoc., "Comments on the Effects of A.B. 1295 (Mandatory Overtime)").

[892]1 Senate Committee on Industrial Relations, *Interim Hearing on AB 1295—Mandatory Overtime* at 281-82 (statement of Thomas Colbert, ind. rels. dir., Foremost-McKesson).

[893]1 Senate Committee on Industrial Relations, *Interim Hearing on AB 1295—Mandatory Overtime* at 258 (testimony of James Watson).

[894]Senate Committee on Industrial Relations, *Interim Hearing on AB 1295—Mandatory Overtime: Appendices* at 220 (Zechar).

[895]1 Senate Committee on Industrial Relations, *Interim Hearing on AB 1295—Mandatory Overtime* at 281 (statement of Thomas Colbert, ind. rels. Dir., Foremost-McKesson).

FLSA three years after the NLRA.)[896] Indeed, employers were especially indignant that the proposed law went far beyond what unions demanded during collective bargaining. The manager of the Crown Zellerbach paper mill in Los Angeles praised the "responsible recognition" that the workers' union had displayed in the most recent bargaining by requesting merely that: "'No employee shall be required to work more than 11 consecutive days without a day off. No employee shall be required to work more than one double shift per week, 16 hours, nor more than three 12 hour shifts, or no more than a combined total of three overtime days in any one week.'" To be sure, the manager's characterization of what could be regarded more as a plea for mercy than a demand as "a far cry from the proposed legislation" elicited this barbed rejoinder from the committee chairman: "On that point, sir, that's also a far cry from what exists in that agreement which you currently have."[897]

Unions, in contrast, complained that employers sometimes used mandatory overtime to stockpile output before the expiration of collective bargaining agreements to undermine strikes.[898] However, unions also made themselves vulnerable to a serious objection from legislators by conceding that many workers relied on overtime pay. Thus after a CWA official representing telephone company workers observed that "[m]ost of our members...want the overtime because they've got themselves in that economic situation where it's now a necessity. It's their overtime, so they get it," the chairman of the Senate Industrial Relations Committee asked him why the legislature should impose a solution on employers "if the workers themselves cannot come to an acceptable agreement to the point of being able to have a united position in dealing with management...." The CWA's unresponsive answer urged the legislature to act on the grounds that the unionized business sector was reluctant to negotiate on this matter because it did not want to have to face competition from nonunion firms that operated with a free hand regarding overtime.[899]

Employers, too, were guilty of self-contradictory logic when they warned

---

[896]Indeed, the U.S. Supreme Court has ruled that even with respect to federal preemption and the NLRA, states are free to regulate employment conditions even though such a statute "gives employees something for which they otherwise might have to bargain. ... Both employers and employees come to the bargaining table with rights under state law that form a '"backdrop"' for their negotiations...." Fort Halifax Packing Co. v. Coyne, 482 U.S. 1, 21 (1987).

[897]1 [California] Senate Committee on Industrial Relations, *Interim Hearings on AB 1295—Mandatory Overtime* at 225 (testimony of Doug Bockstanz and Sen. Bill Greene).

[898]2 Senate Committee on Industrial Relations, *Interim Hearing on AB 1295—Mandatory Overtime* at 448 (testimony of John Irving, pres., Machinists Union, San Diego Cty).

[899]1 Senate Committee on Industrial Relations, *Interim Hearing on AB 1295—Mandatory Overtime* at 127-28 (Ken Major, Cal. area dir., CWA, and chairman Senator Bill Greene).

legislators that the proposed law, by making "overtime labor less reliable than it is right now," would cause "prudent businessmen to reduce their dependence on overtime labor. This means there would be less overtime available for workers who depend on it to meet their obligations." When this veiled threat to eliminate voluntary along with mandatory overtime made no impression on the committee, a Crown Zellerbach paper mill manager virtually accused workers of forcing them into requiring overtime, lamenting: "This is not my policy to work overtime. As a matter of fact, my policy is to work less and less overtime. However, there are a large number of people who depend on overtime wages because of the financial situations they've gotten themselves into."[900]

After 30 hours of hearings, the bill's author was forced to dilute the bill to keep it alive in the senate committee, thus turning what had originally been a 15-word bill into six pages of largely procedural safeguards for employers. In addition to limiting coverage to firms with more than 100 employees and sunsetting the provision after three years, Assemblyman Tom Bates reduced workers' self-empowerment to the right to file a complaint with the state labor commissioner if the workers had previously filed a grievance or complaint with the employer and the parties had made a serious effort to resolve it. The commissioner was required to investigate complaints that workers had been "forced to work overtime by their employer on regular, recurring, and frequent bases as a term or condition of employment." At hearings the commissioner was authorized to hold he was required to take testimony and make findings on whether the employer had: made a serious attempt to create a voluntary overtime system and to find additional workers for overtime not coverable on a voluntary basis; used forced overtime in an arbitrary and capricious way; and taken his employees' personal concerns into account. After completing a lengthy administrative procedure saturated with due process for employers, the commissioner was authorized to grant an exemption from working overtime—and even this exemption might "permit the employer to work employees forced overtime under emergency conditions"—or issue a cease and desist order requiring the employer to give employees at least 48 hours advance notice of the requirement to work overtime, to create a voluntary overtime system, or to try to hire additional workers. A lengthy appeal process then became available to employers. But after business lobbyists argued that even this diluted provision would "interfere with management's right to require employes [sic] to work overtime when necessary," the senate committee rejected the bill four to two.[901] Thus

---

[900] 1 Senate Committee on Industrial Relations, *Interim Hearing on AB 1295—Mandatory Overtime* at 227, 230 (testimony of Doug Bockstanz).

[901] Jerry Gillam, "Senate Panel Rejects Bill to Forbid Forced Overtime," *L.A. Times*, May 19, 1978, § 1, at 3, col. 5-6; Cal. Leg. A.B. No. 1295 (amended in Senate May 8, 1978). The newspaper account stated that the business exemption threshold was 100

collapsed one of the major legislative efforts to offer a modicum of protection to workers against mandatory overtime.

In the wake of the defeat of the California overtime initiative, legislators in several other states sought to enact related legislation. On March 21, 1979, a bill, sponsored by 12 representatives, was introduced in the Wisconsin Assembly that would have prohibited employers from disciplining or terminating any employee for refusing to work more than eight hours of overtime in any week or more than 100 hours in a calendar year. Employers of fewer than 20 employees would have been exempt; the ban would also not have applied to emergencies endangering public health or safety or to those "due to unavoidable and unforeseeable circumstances causing a severe disruption of usual operations." The state Department of Industry, Labor and Human Relations was authorized to investigate complaints and issue enforcement orders.[902] In connection with a mandatory fiscal estimate submitted three weeks later, the department estimated that it was currently receiving 170 calls per month on this issue.[903] After a public hearing was held on the bill on April 24, 1979, the chief sponsor offered a substitute amendment that eliminated the weekly overtime standard and the small employer exemption, authorized the department to award reinstatement with back pay and to assess forfeitures against offending employers of not more than $100 (per day of continuing violations), but the bill nevertheless died in the Assembly on April 3, 1980.[904]

A related effort at the same time in neighboring Illinois received even shorter shrift: introduced on April 4, 1979, House Bill 1519 would have amended the state minimum wage and premium overtime law to prohibit employers from suspending, discharging, or otherwise disciplining any employee for refusing to work overtime hours (generally more than 40 per week). Though radical within the scope of its coverage, the bill would not have protected any of the large number of workers (including farm laborers, government employees, and executive, administrative, and professional employees) who were also excluded from the overtime premium provision.[905] However, the bill was tabled by a 15-0

---

employees, while the final amended bill (§ 570) specified 50 employees. On an effort two decades laters to limit mandatory overtime in unionized telephone companies, see Cal. Leg. A.B. No. 418 (1999-2000).

902State of Wisconsin, 1979 Assembly Bill 328.

903State of Wisconsin, 1979 Assembly Bill 328, Fiscal Estimate (Apr. 13, 1979) (provided by Wisconsin Legislative Reference Bureau).

904State of Wisconsin, Assembly Substitute Amendment 1, to 1979 Assembly Bill 328 (Sept. 12, 1979); *Bulletin of the Proceedings of the Wisconsin Legislature 1979 Session: Assembly* 189 (1981). Unfortunately, the Wisconsin legislature does not create hearing transcripts. Telephone interview with Richard Roe, State of Wisconsin, Legislative Reference Bureau (June 14, 2000).

905State of Illinois, House Bill 1519, 81st General Assembly (1979).

vote of the Labor and Commerce Committee three weeks later.[906]

An in some respects radical bill, very similar to the Wisconsin proposal, was introduced in the New Jersey Senate on January 24, 1980. Eugene Bedell's proposed law would have made it illegal for employers to terminate or discipline in any other manner any employee for refusing to work overtime. Senate Bill No. 887 broadly defined "overtime" as work over and above the employee's "normal daily hours of work...which in no event shall exceed eight hours per day, unless otherwise specified by a valid collective bargaining agreement." This expansive protection for nonunion workers was limited by several exceptions, the most important of which exempted all employers of 50 or fewer employees and excluded all executive, administrative, and professional employees. In addition, the law would not have applied to overtime work performed during emergencies in which public health or safety was endangered or those resulting from "unavoidabl[e] and unforeseeable circumstances which cause extreme disruption of usual operations." Finally, the bill would have provided for enforcement by conferring a private right of action on employees to sue employers for damages resulting from unlawful termination or disciplinary action; in addition to the greater of actual damages or $1,000 in statutory damages, Senate Bill. No. 887 would have awarded costs and reasonable attorneys' fees to employees who prevailed.[907] Thus, significantly, the bill did not directly enjoin employers from firing employees for refusing to work overtime, but merely sought to impose financial disincentives on firms.

The Senate, Labor, Industry and Professions Committee held a hearing on the bill in the industrial city of Linden in May 1980.[908] Despite the deference paid by the bill to collective bargaining agreements, many large unionized employers vigorously testified against state intervention, adamantly insisting "that it is absolutely necessary that management retain the right to take action for refusal to work overtime whenever it is necessary."[909] General Motors took an especially hard-line position, asserting at every turn the quasi-natural inevitability of its overtime regime: "by the very nature of the entire process of building

[906]Illinois Legislative Reference Bureau, *Legislative Synopsis and Digest*: Final Volume 2: 1979, at 2028.

[907]New Jersey Senate Bill No. 887 (Jan. 24, 1980).

[908]*Public Hearing Before Senate Labor, Industry and Professions Committee on S-887 (An Act to prohibit employers from terminating or otherwise disciplining employees for refusal to work overtime and providing penalties therefor, and supplementing Title 34 of the Revised Statutes): held May 8, 1980, City Hall, Linden, New Jersey* ([1980]); Robert Misseck, "Unions, Industry Clash on Overtime Measure," (Newark) *Star-Ledger*, May 9, 1980, at 32, col. 5.

[909]*Public Hearing Before Senate Labor, Industry and Professions Committee on S-887* at 63 (William Saller, general manager, governmental affairs, Public Service Electric & Gas Co.).

automobiles, overtime is inherent, it is unavoidable...."[910] Consequently, state intervention to make overtime voluntary with each individual employee was "unrealistic. It must be done, it cannot be optional. ... Half an assembly line cannot elect to work and the other half elect not to work, and both have their way." Moreover, General Motors alleged that such a law "would place the power in the hands of very few individuals to thwart the will and desire of the vast majority of their fellow employes [sic] who do want to work the premium hours, and in many instances to work even full straight time." It perversely sought to support its implausible claim that there was "no evidence showing that overtime has been a hardship on employes any more than has the requirement to report during regular working hours" with the argument that overtime enabled the many workers whom GM put on short-time and lay-off to work a 2000-hour year; in this way, the corporation sought to turn compulsory overtime work against its opponents by arguing that overtime served "the important function [of] accomplish[ing] precisely what has been frequently urged..., that is to stabilize employment...."[911]

In contrast, the New Jersey Business and Industry Association complained that the bill was "extremely discriminatory" because it left management in unionized firms "free to make such [overtime] assignments," whereas similar arrangements between nonunion employers and their individual employees would be "null and void," thus placing "the employer and the operation of his business at the discretion of the employee."[912] The largely nonunion hotel and restaurant industries sought to justify legislative inaction by suggesting parity between overtime rules laid down by management and individual workers. Just as any agreement by an employee at the time of hire to work the overtime that employer may "from time to time" call on him to perform should be honored, so, too: "If the prospective employee tells the employer that under no circumstances will he ever work more than eight hours a day, or more than 40 hours a week...and if the employer agrees to that, then that understanding should prevail. We don't think that New Jersey needs a state law to interfere with...such agreements...."[913] Conjuring up the best of all possible worlds, the New Jersey State Chamber of Commerce deployed an assertion that by logical extension would pooh-pooh the

---

[910]*Public Hearing Before Senate Labor, Industry and Professions Committee on S-887* at 28x (statement of General Motors Corp.).

[911]*Public Hearing Before Senate Labor, Industry and Professions Committee on S-887* at 26x-27x (statement of General Motors Corp.).

[912]*Public Hearing Before Senate Labor, Industry and Professions Committee on S-887* at 49x (written statement).

[913]*Public Hearing Before Senate Labor, Industry and Professions Committee on S-887* at 72-73 (testimony of Clark Martin, representing New Jersey Restaurant Association, Hotel/Motel Association, and Milk Industry Association).

need for any labor standards legislation: "Poor [employer overtime] practices are self-correcting."[914]

In the midst of this barrage of employers' solid opposition, even the bill's chief sponsor got cold feet. Despite his conviction that something was "wrong" "if we have to force people to work overtime when they don't want to in order to stay competitive," Senator Bedell admitted: "I still don't know; I have not made up my mind yet whether this legislation is the way or not."[915] Apparently neither he nor his colleagues were persuaded by the refutation of the necessity of overtime work offered by one telephone company worker who explained that her employer mandated two-day service for customers who merely wanted a phone of a different color:

> But is it really important to force people to work overtime so that you can have an outside jack by your pool? Is it critical that you have one at your cabana at the beach club? These are the kinds of things that we are forced to work overtime for....[916]

Unsurprisingly, the bill died in committee without any further legislative action.

Public recognition of the persistent resentment of mandatory overtime resurfaced at the turn of the millennium as several states took tentative and largely unsuccessful steps toward restraining employers from imposing super-normal workweeks on unwilling workers. In January 1999 a bill was introduced in the West Virginia legislature amending the time and a half for overtime provision in the state minimum wage and maximum hours law to provide "that an employee has the right to decline to work longer than the forty hours in any workweek."[917] A management-side law firm warned employers that the bill "takes away your right to require an employee to work overtime even when the request is crucial to productivity and overall business success."[918] In the event, the legislature adjourned in June without having taken any action on the bill; the bill was reintroduced in January 2000, but no action was taken.[919]

A more timorous bill introduced a week later in January in Maine made more

---

[914]*Public Hearing Before Senate Labor, Industry and Professions Committee on S-887* at 34 (testimony of James Morford, director, governmental relations, N.J. State Chamber of Commerce).

[915]*Public Hearing Before Senate Labor, Industry and Professions Committee on S-887* at 36.

[916]*Public Hearing Before Senate Labor, Industry and Professions Committee on S-887* at 47 (testimony of Barbara Brenner).

[917]West Virginia House Bill 2018, 74th Legislature, 1999 (Lexis).

[918]Steptoe & Johnson, "Do Employees Have the Right to Decline Overtime?" *West Virginia Employment Law Letter*, Feb. 1999 (Lexis).

[919]West Virginia House Bill 2018, 75th Legislature, 2000 (Lexis).

progress. The concrete occasion for the legislative initiative was the exasperation by workers with the Poland Springs bottling plant in Poland, Maine, who for four months or more in 1997 had been required to work 12- and 16-hour shifts seven days a week without any days off. The plant was organized by the United Food and Commercial Workers, but the collective bargaining agreement "allows workers to log more than 100 hours in a week...."[920]

The bill that was promptly introduced in the Maine Senate—by the senator representing the county in which the Poland Springs plant was located—amended the state maximum hour and overtime law so that an "employer may not require an employee to work overtime in violation of the following limitations: A. An employer may not require an employee to work more than 32 overtime hours in any one calendar week; and B. An employer may not require an employee to work overtime on more than 6 days in a calendar week." The bill excluded seasonal workers, but defined "overtime" to include more than eight hours in a day as well as more than 40 in a week.[921] This extraordinarily generous treatment of employers may be contrasted with similar regimes in Western Europe, where employers are permitted to employ workers during very limited overtime hours over a week, month, or year. For example, in Germany, the new working time law permits employees to work only two hours' overtime for 30 days a year.[922]

Three weeks later, the Joint Standing Committee on Labor held a hearing on the bill. The director of the state Bureau of Labor Standards testified that his agency "often receive calls...from workers who want to know if their employer can fire them if they refuse to work mandatory overtime, even mandatory overtime that to most people would seem extreme. The answer at present is YES...." The director reported that while the workers might consider their situation "unfair," the agency was also concerned "from a workplace safety perspective" because workplace injuries increase as the result of fatigue caused by "excessive hours on the job." The agency supported the bill, but suggested an "exemption for essential workers in public emergency situations."[923] Much of the testimony furnished by employers focused on the need for exemptions for emergency state work such as snowplowing. Surprisingly, even the submission of the National Federation of Independent Business, while not supportive, did not

---

[920]Jonathan van Fleet, "Overworked Workers Look for Relief," Lewiston *Sun-Journal*, Aug. 6, 1997, at 1B, col. 1.

[921]An Act to Limit Mandatory Overtime, Leg. Doc. No. 2116, S.P. 789, 118th Maine Legislature, 2d Reg. Sess. (Jan. 20, 1998).

[922]J. Rojot and R. Blanpain, "General Report," in *Legal and Contractual Limitations to Working Time in the European Union* 3, 46-47 (2d rev. ed.; R. Blanpain et al., eds., 1997). See also below section 13.

[923]Testimony of Alan Hinsey (Feb. 12, 1998) (furnished by Maine Law and Legislative Reference Library from the Labor Committee files).

denounce the bill as the end of the world for free enterprise.[924]

In committee, the amendatory process quickly watered down an already modest bill and accommodated many of the aforementioned concerns. The limit on overtime was stretched to 96 hours over three weeks, and that on daily overtime was deleted. Exemptions were added for public emergencies, essential services, and health and safety considerations.[925] It is unclear whether a newspaper was speaking tongue in cheek when it reported that under the bill "Maine workers will be limited to 96 hours of mandatory overtime within any three-week period...."[926] Another amendment enabled employers to request emergency waivers for up to three weeks for unforeseen or uncontrollable circumstances that would otherwise harm their firms.[927]

Basic criticisms of the bill made during the Senate floor debates were directed at the effort to "micromanage business" and "dictate" to manufacturers and labor: "The employees' overtime provides them an opportunity of an income that is not part of an annual salary and that they can purchase the extras in life that they couldn't have. ... Why don't we let them [manufacturers] run their business the way they feel is most efficient and is in the best interests of both their employees and their financial standings."[928] Another senator, after confessing that "[i]t sort of boggled the imagination as to why any sane, rational, economically motivated employer would continue that practice [of paying time and a half for long hours instead of hiring additional workers] for any great length of time particularly against the will of those who were employed," answered that benefit packages made it cheaper or at least competitive vis-à-vis hiring additional workers. But the senator's opposition to the bill rested on the calculation that "we are not yet at the point where the fringe benefit packages...customarily made available to employees will induce employers to exploit this situation to a degree that it requires us to take legislative action to correct the vice." Moreover, even where such expensive benefits are available, intervention would probably not be called for since those firms are likely to be unionized.[929]

The bill's sponsor, John Cleveland, made a crucial point that he apparently did not need to draw out for the members: "it puts no limitation whatsoever on voluntary overtime. An individual may work as many hours as they choose in a

---

[924]Letter from David Clough, state director, NFIB (Mar. 10, 1998).

[925]Leg. Doc. 2116, Filing No. S-518 (Mar. 16, 1998).

[926]"Bill Limiting Workers' Overtime Receives Initial House Approval," Portland *Press Herald*, Mar. 31, 1998, at 4B (Lexis).

[927]Leg. Doc. 2116, Filing No. S-627 (Mar. 26, 1998).

[928]*Legislative Record*, S-2177 (Sen. Mitchell, Mar. 27, 1998).

[929]*Legislative Record*, S-2176 (Sen. Mills, Mar. 27, 1998).

voluntary situation and many individuals choose to do that for a number of reasons."[930] Such a provision would be so open to abuse as to be unimaginable in any modern labor-protective statute. It would make it possible for employers, for example, to pressure workers into waiving their rights under minimum wage, overtime, safety and health, and social insurance laws. It was precisely the kind of provision that doomed nineteenth-century protective laws to meaninglessness. In this so-called pre-enforcement stage, maximum hours statutes were "unenforcible because they set standards which were to prevail only in the absence of an agreement to the contrary between the employer and the employee." Such laws might forbid employers to "'compel'" women to work beyond a certain number of hours, but the 'woman who wished to hold her job must perforce express willingness to work longer hours. But in the eyes of the law she was under no compulsion."[931]

After having made such crucial concessions, Cleveland finally responded to the aforementioned call for continued laissez-faire: "I think we have to recognize that these employees are human beings. They have families. They have children. They have community responsibilities. ... Is that the kind of society, at the end of the 20th century that we really want from people who work for a wage. That employers ought to be able to demand from them anything that they want? That they ought not to be able to live a life to help raise their children, to participate in their community but rather to be used more as slaves to meet the production schedule...?"[932] The Senate then passed the bill 22 to 13.[933] A smaller majority, 76-68, prevailed three days later in the House,[934] where the debate was more attentive to employers' complaints that the bill "would put such a string around them that there are occasions when they wouldn't be able to get essential work completed...."[935]

The governor's veto was curious in that he criticized the bill both for denying employers flexibility and making Maine less attractive to high-wage employers—an argument he perversely used the same day in vetoing an increase in the state minimum wage to $5.40 an hour—and for still permitting employers to require employees to work as many as 96 overtime hours every three weeks. When the Senate fell one vote short of the two-thirds majority needed to override the veto, employers survived their closest brush ever with even the feeblest of

---

[930]*Legislative Record*, S-2176 (Sen. Cleveland, Mar. 27, 1998).

[931]Brandeis, "Labor Legislation" at 625, 626.

[932]*Legislative Record*, S-2178-79 (Sen. Cleveland, Mar. 27, 1998).

[933]*Legislative Record*, S-2180 (Mar. 27, 1998).

[934]*Legislative Record*, H-2024 (Mar. 30, 1998).

[935]*Legislative Record*, H-2023 (Rep. Treadwell, Mar. 30, 1998).

interferences with their unfettered control over the length of the working day.[936]

But the more than century-long struggle for a general limit on overtime work finally took "a very small step" on May 5, 2000, when the governor signed an even weaker bill prohibiting employers from requiring employees to work more than 80 overtime hours every two weeks—a burden described by one senator as the limit beyond which workers are "probably dead on their feet." In addition to excluding farm and seasonal workers and even low-paid executive employees, the law exempted annual maintenance work to propitiate the paper industry.[937]

Pennsylvania joined the ranks of states considering anti-overtime legislation in October 1999, when 28 legislators introduced the Restricted Overtime Act in the House. This short and modest bill would afford employees not subject to a collective bargaining agreement the right to refuse to work more than 16 hours of overtime (beyond 40 hours) per week.[938] Employers declined to testify at the hearings in January 2000, but the Pennsylvania Chamber of Business and Industry submitted a letter that rejected such "unwarranted intrusions into employee/employer relationships," and disin-genuously suggested that the issue be addressed at the federal level to avoid causing Pennsylvania firms a competitive disadvantage.[939] Without identifying or justifying the philosophy, the antiunion Associated Builders & Contractors insisted: "As a philosophical matter, employees who want to work overtime should be encouraged to do so."[940]

Several union officials and members did testify. Like their counterparts elsewhere, workers focused on family values, expressing resentment at not being able to attend skating parties with or to tuck their children in bed.[941] AFL-CIO union officials and rank-and-file members stressed that they did not wish to restrict voluntary overtime.[942] Indeed, one long-year GTE telephone installer and

---

[936]*Legislative Record*, S-2497-98 (Apr. 8, 1998); A. Jay Higgins, "3 Labor Bills Fall in Legislature: Democrats' Support Not Enough to Override Governor's Veto," Bangor *Daily News*, Apr. 9, 1998 (Lexis).

[937]An Act to Limit Mandatory Overtime, 1999-2000 Me. Legis. Serv. ch. 750; *Legislative Record*, S-1969 (Mar. 31, 2000) (Sen. Douglass) (quotes).

[938]House Bill 1941 (Oct. 6, 1999).

[939]Letter from Fred Sembach, vice president, government affairs, Pennsylvania Chamber of Business and Industry, to Joseph Gladeck, Jr., chairman, House Labor Relations Committee, Jan. 18, 1999 [sic; should be 2000]. See also "Bills Would Limit Overtime and Require Breaks," Pittsburgh *Post-Gazette*, Jan. 23, 2000, at B3 (Westlaw).

[940]Letter from Duane Feagley, executive director, Assoc. Builders & Contractors, Inc., Keystone Chapter, to Joseph Gladeck, Jan. 18, 2000.

[941]House of Representatives, Commonwealth of Pennsylvania, [Hearing on] House Bills 1940 and 1941, House Labor Relations Committee 37-39 (statement of Homer Beard, GTE employee and IBEW member).

[942]House of Representatives, Commonwealth of Pennsylvania, [Hearing on] House Bills 1940 and 1941, at 8, 52 (testimony of Teresa Ruhl, regional COPE director, Penn. AFL-CIO, and Linda Sanders, UNITE member).

repairman, who in the previous eight months had worked the maximum number of overtime hours (12) permitted by the union contract every week and during seven weeks had been "forced" to work beyond the cap, testified that he and his co-workers would change their plans if the company just asked them as they formerly had done. "But when you're told as a slave that you will do it...it's a click in the switch."[943] Although no hostile legislator asked whether unions would support a bill that merely required employers to ask employees politely to work overtime, the Republican chairperson of the House Labor Relations Committee raised the same question that had arisen at the hearings in California in the 1970s: if overtime "is that big of a problem, then perhaps maybe this issue should take precedence over some of the other issues that are negotiated on behalf of the workers."[944]

Since the bill excluded places of employment under union contract, union witnesses raised the issue on their own, one rightly pointing out that even where unions do bargain over the issue, unionized employers still had to compete against nonunion firms that can work their employees "excessively...." Thus what both union workers and employers needed was "a fair and even field" where "across the state everybody could only work 16 hours overtime...."[945] The other explanation offered by unions as to why legislation was necessary, even in the unionized sector, to eliminate compulsory overtime was the failure of collective bargaining to resolve the matter to workers' liking. The president of the United Steelworkers (USW) local at a Bethlehem Steel plant explained that "[e]ven in a long and historic contractual relationship between the steel industry and my union," in the course of which the USW had negotiated overtime penalties, voluntary overtime preferences, overtime rotations, and temporary transfer programs,[946]

> no matter what level of relief or flexibility we have provided the steel industry, the demand for complete and total authority to be able to require unlimited overtime as the boss desires never recedes and is insatiable. ...
>
> If the management['s]...quest for unfettered overtime assignment rights exists in this kind of industry with a powerful and well-established union, what do you imagine is the situation for people in nonunion, management-dominated work places?
>
> I can tell you that my direct experience in working with people trying to organize a

---

[943]House of Representatives, Commonwealth of Pennsylvania, [Hearing on] House Bills 1940 and 1941, at 38, 58 (quote) (testimony of Homer Beard).

[944]House of Representatives, Commonwealth of Pennsylvania, [Hearing on] House Bills 1940 and 1941, at 47 (Rep. Joseph Gladeck).

[945]House of Representatives, Commonwealth of Pennsylvania, [Hearing on] House Bills 1940 and 1941, at 47 (testimony of Teresa Ruhl).

[946]House of Representatives, Commonwealth of Pennsylvania, [Hearing on] House Bills 1940 and 1941, at 12-13 (testimony of Ike Gitlen).

union is the situation has become a form of wage slavery.[947]

Despite this confessed impotence, the Pennsylvania legislature has neither amended the bill to include unions nor taken any other action toward enactment.

A much more ambitious initiative to curtail overtime began occupying the Washington State legislature in the year 2000. Senator Darlene Fairley, the Democratic chair of the Labor Committee, introduced a bill whose underlying legislative intent finds that employers' practices of requiring workers to work long days and even longer weeks

> hurt working families, make affordable child care difficult to find, and lead to higher stress levels and industrial injury and occupational disease rates. These practices limit employment opportunities to a smaller number of workers rather than extend employment opportunities to a larger number of workers. Thus, it is the intent of the legislature that workers not be required to work overtime.[948]

As recommended by the Labor Committee, the bill would have prohibited employers from requiring employees to work more than eight hours a day or 40 hours per week unless they work on a four-day, 10-hour schedule. Among the bill's numerous exceptions are workers performing emergency work (such as utility, fire, police, and medical personnel), and those packing or processing perishable agricultural products. The bill would also have permitted employers to petition for a variance if more than 80 percent of their affected employees voted in a secret ballot to approve a written proposal to work longer hours, but in no event more than 12 hours per day or 42 hours per week for four consecutive weeks. The bill would also have excluded the many workers already excluded from the state's overtime law, including farm workers, executive, administrative, and professional employees, news carriers, seamen, and workers on state-operated ferries. Finally, the bill would also have offered a closely hedged-in exemption for continuous production operations in two important industries in Washington—primary metal processing and paper products. Firms would have been permitted to require employees to work part of the next shift if: the need arose as a result of an unanticipated event such as employee sickness or emergency repair of machinery (but not because of a need to increase production to meet increased market demand), and the unanticipated event halted or may halt

---

[947]House of Representatives, Commonwealth of Pennsylvania, [Hearing on] House Bills 1940 and 1941, at 13-14 (testimony of Gitlen).

[948]Washington, Sen. Bill 6120, § 1 (Jan. 28, 2000). A companion bill introduced at the same time to provide overtime pay for software developers and engineers and related workers self-contradictorily uses the same language in its preamble to justify imposition of overtime compensation. Washington, Sen. Bill 6165 (Jan. 10, 2000).

the continuous production operation; the employer in good faith exhausted reasonable attempts to find volunteers from thc ncxt shift; the employees in question had critical skills and expertise required for the work; and the employer, pursuant to the employees' request, helped them get safe transportation home after the shift and to address child care or other family obligations successfully. A final limitation on the continuous operation exemption would have prohibited employers from requiring employees to work more than 12 consecutive hours or two straight shifts, or from requiring more than 16 overtime hours in any calendar month.[949] Again, workers at the hearings focused on overtime work's interference with their families, while employers bemoaned that the bill would deprive them of taking advantage of the "edge" they had in access to the world's best workforce.[950] The bill died in February 2000 in the Rules Committee.

13. Europe—You Have It Better, But Not Much

> In our plant...an employee gets three hours pay just for coming to work on short notice. Most overtime situations make an employee eligible for a meal paid for at the company's expense. ... I can assure you that this penalty by itself is enough to make even the most generous plant manager shudder when he considers the need for overtime. This is adequate incentive to discourage businesses from working unnecessary overtime. In other words, gentlemen, I can assure you that we work overtime only when we believe the work must be done, and overtime is the only way to achieve it. ... I believe we are reasonable men, and we conduct our businesses accordingly.[951]

Employers throughout the capitalist world prize the multidimensional flexibility that overtime work permits, but workers in European countries with strong or quasi-universal organization have been somewhat more successful than their U.S. counterparts in preventing employers from imposing it. For most of the twentieth century collective bargaining agreements and legislation in many European countries have capped the number of hours that an individual employee may work during a certain period (day, week, month, or year). By the end of World War I, Czechoslovakia, Finland, Greece, Great Britain, Norway, and Switzerland had instituted such statutory overtime caps, while Czechoslovakia,

---

[949]Washington, Sen. Bill 6120 (introduced Jan. 10, 2000, and recommended by committee Jan. 28, 2000). The bill was pre-filed on Dec. 8, 1999.

[950]Karen Gaudette, "Workers Seek Ban on Mandatory TO," *Columbian*, Jan. 14, 2000, at A1 (Westlaw).

[951]1 [California] Senate Committee on Industrial Relations, *Interim Hearings on AB 1295—Mandatory Overtime* at 224 (testimony of Doug Bockstanz, resident mgr., Crown Zellerbach Los Angeles mill).

Finland, the Netherlands, Poland, and Switzerland required employers to secure permits from state authorities.[952] The Netherlands, for example, began requiring employers in 1919 to obtain the permission of the labor inspectorate to work overtime.[953] This policy was strengthened after World War II when rigid controls became part of a centralized wage policy; the labor inspectorate issued permits only for short periods and "only if there is a convincing reason why overtime cannot be avoided."[954]

Statutory limits in Austria, Finland, Norway, Spain, and Switzerland ranging from 60 to 220 hours made "extensive and continuous recourse to [overtime] impossible." The former socialist countries, including the Soviet Union and the German Democratic Republic, created the strictest regimes, which prohibited economic overtime and permitted only emergency overtime.[955] In some countries, such as Portugal, overtime is paid on a progressive scale with the penalty rate increasing with the number of daily overtime hours. The new Labor Time Law in Germany permits workers to work 2 hours of overtime a day on 30 days during the year with a maximum work day of 10 hours.[956]

In the United Kingdom, which has witnessed a decline in the strength of its unions and until recently had been the only country in Western Europe (other than Denmark) with "no legislative hindrances to overtime for men," it had become so "popular with the workers" that employers feared that if they failed to offer enough overtime, many of their workers would move to firms that did. Consequently, "many firms in their advertisements for workers, emphasise the weekly earnings secured with customary overtime...."[957] Case law provided British workers with very meager protection against overwork by prohibiting employers from working employees hours so long that their health was injured.[958]

---

[952]League of Nations, *Report on the Eight-Hours Day or the Forty-Eight Hours Week* 40-47 (1919)

[953]Wet von den 1sten November 1919, §§ 29-30.

[954][U.K.] National Board for Prices and Incomes, *Hours of Work, Overtime and Shiftworking* 44 (Report No. 161, Cmnd. 4554, 1970).

[955]Archibald Evans, *Hours of Work in Industrialised Countries* 103-104 (ILO 1975) (quote); Arbeitsgesetzbuch der Deutschen Demokratischen Republik vom 16. Juni 1977, §§ 172-79, Gesetzblatt der DDR, Teil I, 185, 210-11.

[956]Rojot and Blanpain, "General Report" at 49, 46-47.

[957]Evans, *Hours of Work in Industrialised Countries* at 106, 100. For an ethnography of British industrial overtimers, see Ferdynand Zweig, *The Worker in an Affluent Society: Family Life and Industry* 70-76 (1961). See also "The Canker of Overtime," (London) *Times*, Oct. 26, 1954, at 9, col. 6-7.

[958]J. Rojot and R Blanpain, "General Report," in *Legal and Contractual Limitations* at 3, 47. The only such decision seems to be Johnstone v. Bloomsbury Health Authority, [1991] ICR 269 (C.A.), which found that a hospital was under a duty not to injure a resident physician's health by working him excessively long hours beyond his normal workweek.

To be sure, the alleged popularity of overtime in Britain is largely a function of low wages—with the highest incidence of overtime found in the lowest-paid industries and occupation[959]—as overtime pay remains "a major factor in family budgets," just as real wage losses in the United States since the 1970s have been found to explain the lack of pressure by workers to reduce the workweek.[960] These interrelationships replicate the causality that Marx, building on the factory inspectors' reports from the 1840s to the 1860s, uncovered: "the low price of labor during the so-called normal working time forces the better-paid overtime on the worker if he at all wants to wangle a sufficient wage." Enactment of free-market overtime laws (as opposed to maximum-hours laws) undermined Marx's conclusion that state limitation of the working day "put an end to such fun."[961]

Although Denmark, too, until recently lacked state regulation of overtime work,[962] most collective agreements deal with the question; unless a contract specifies otherwise, employees are obligated to work overtime if the employer requests it. If an agreement fails to specify limitations, employees are obligated to work according to the employer's directions, but case law holds employers in breach if they systematically use overtime; as a result, employers are not permitted to base their production plans on overtime. Provisions in many agreements entitling workers to 24 to 48 hours' notice merely entitle them to a bonus if employers fail to furnish proper notice. The overtime premium ranges from 50 to 100 percent, but many employers fail to pay anything at all for overtime work.[963] In April 1981 the government introduced a bill in parliament to limit overtime to 100 annual hours per worker. Despite a provision for modification by collective bargaining agreements, the employers association thwarted enactment.[964]

---

[959]E. G. Whybrew, *Overtime Working in Britain: A Study of Its Origins, Functions and Methods of Control* 60-63; (Royal Commission on Trade Unions and Employers' Associations, Research Papers 9, 1968); H. Clegg, *The System of Industrial Relations in Great Britain* 183-84 (1973 [1972]).

[960]Jill Rubery, Simon Deakin, and Sara Horrel, "United Kingdom," in *Times Are Changing: Working Time in 14 Industrialised Countries* 261-87 at 280 (Gerhard Bosch et al. eds., 1994) (quote); Gerhard Bosch, Peter Dawkins, and François Michon, "Working Time in 14 Industrialised Countries: An Overview," in *Times Are Changing* 1-45 at 38.

[961]1 Marx, *Das Kapital* at 569-70.

[962]An older temporary overtime law was generous to employers. Lov om Forbud mod Overarbejde, Act of May 7, 1937, in ILO, Legislative Series, 1937—Den. 3.

[963]P. Jacobsen, "Denmark," in *Legal and Contractual Limitation to Working Time in the European Union* 239, 254; Steen Scheuer, "The Impact of Collective Agreements on Working Time in Denmark," 37 (3) *British Journal of Industrial Relations* 465-81 (Sept. 1999).

[964]*Betænkning om begrænsning af overarbejde og om afspadsering fra udvalget af 1977 om fordeling af arbejdet* (Betænkning No. 865, 1979); R. A. Hart, *Shorter Working Time: A Dilemma for Collective Bargaining* 47-50, 52-53 (OECD 1984).

The promulgation by the Council of the European Union of its Working Time Directive on November 23, 1993 (with which member states were given three years to comply, although the United Kingdom, which opposed and challenged the Directive, did not issue implementing regulations until 1998) modified the legal regulation of overtime throughout Europe,[965] but especially in Britain, where the average workweek was longest,[966] the incidence of overtime highest, and state intervention absent. Article 6 of the Directive on maximum weekly working time provides:

> Member states shall take the measures necessary to ensure that, in keeping with the need to protect the safety and health of workers: 1. the period of weekly working time is limited by means of laws, regulations or administrative provisions or by collective agreements or agreements between the two sides of industry; 2. the average working time for each seven-day period, including overtime, does not exceed 48 hours.[967]

Although the 48-hour maximum still authorizes considerable overtime since the statutory workweek in many European countries is 40 hours and the average workweek has been reduced to fewer than 40, codifying the principle that overtime is legally limitable is, nevertheless, important.[968] The EU directive is additionally flawed by its exclusion of transport workers[969] and the considerable leeway it affords member states and employers. For example, it authorizes governments to establish a so-called reference period of up to four months during which an average of 48-hour weeks is formed,[970] and to derogate from Article 6 altogether when "the duration of the working time is not measured and/or predetermined or can be determined by the workers themselves, and particularly in the case of...managing executives or other persons with autonomous decision-taking powers...."[971] The 17-week reference period grants employers much greater flexibility than even the most capacious recent Republican congressional

---

[965]Claire Rankin, Annelise Phillips, and Martin Warren, *The Working Time Regulations 1998: A Practical Guide*, at 13-30 (1999).

[966]Michael Grisenthwaite and Carole Grant-Garwood, *Tolley's Practical Guide to the Working Times Directive and Regulations* 22-23 (1998).

[967]Council Directive 93/104/EC of 23 November 1993 Concerning Certain Aspects of the Organisation of Working Time, Art. 6.

[968]Mark Hall, Richard Lister, and Keith Sisson, *The New Law on Working Time: Managing the Implications of the 1998 Working Time Regulations* 81-83 (1998).

[969]Council Directive 93/104/EC of 23 November 1993 Concerning Certain Aspects of the Organisation of Working Time, Art. 1(3).

[970]Council Directive 93/104/EC of 23 November 1993 Concerning Certain Aspects of the Organisation of Working Time, Art. 16 (2).

[971]Council Directive 93/104/EC of 23 November 1993 Concerning Certain Aspects of the Organisation of Working Time, Art. 17(1)(a).

proposals, which dared not extend the period beyond four weeks.[972]

Even greater laxity has been introduced by the so-called opt-out provision—the scope of which had been insisted on by the U.K. government when the Directive was negotiated and of which only the U.K. has made use—which permits member states not to apply Article 6 for seven years (until 2003), when the Council must reexamine the issue. During this period, member states must, however, "ensure that: no employer requires a worker to work more than 48 hours over a seven-day period, calculated as an average for the reference period [of four months], unless he has first obtained the worker's agreement to perform such work, [and] no worker is subjected to any detriment by his employer because he is not willing to give his agreement to perform such work...."[973] Such language prompted the British Trades Union Congress to conclude that "bad employers will try and intimidate their staff."[974]

14. A Realistically Bleak Conclusion

The type of overtime...we're opposing is the oppressive type that goes far beyond the employee's obligation to his employer. ... The type of overtime that...makes the employee feel more like an indentured servant than a free man.[975]

At the conclusion of this historical overview of overtime work, it is chastening to realize that nothing remotely approaching a congressional majority exists for shortening the workweek or increasing the overtime penalty, let alone for protection against forced overwork even hedged with exceptions for employer emergencies.[976] These problems are so distant from public concerns or the AFL-

---

[972]See below section 14.

[973]Council Directive 93/104/EC of 23 November 1993 Concerning Certain Aspects of the Organisation of Working Time, Art. 18(1)(b)(I).

[974]"The 48 hour working week," http://www.tuc.org.uk/rights/wt_48.htm

[975]1 [California] Senate Committee on Industrial Relations, *Interim Hearings on AB 1295—Mandatory Overtime* 133 (Nov. 7, 1977) (statement of Ian McIntyre, Communication Workers of America, legislative and political chairman, Southern California).

[976]The leading leftist labor law scholar in Germany surprisingly considers a complete prohibition of overtime "illusory" since the situation may arise in almost all plants that suddenly additional work has to be performed and no additional workers are available or able to do it; he also believes that emergency clauses are no solution because employers would almost always find a way to construct an emergency together with a work force interested in overtime payments. He views as the only legal and economic solution making overtime "drastically" more expensive through collective bargaining, 120 per cent being a plausible penalty rate. 2 Wolfgang Däubler, *Das Arbeitsrecht: Ein Leitfaden für Arbeitnehmer* 84-85 (1979). Yet as long ago as 1913, Oregon prohibited a workday in excess of eight hours for governmental work except for "necessity, emergency, or where the public policy absolutely requires it," and then created a presumption that none

CIO's agenda that it has been years since even dead-on-arrival pro forma bills on these issues have been introduced in Congress.[977] The pendulum has swung so far to capital's side that the labor movement considers itself fortunate if it can stave off attempts to repeal the FLSA's existing overtime pay provisions. The limited legislative commitment to capping working hours is suggested by the fact that in the year 2000 eighteen states still lack an overtime law.[978]

Against this bleak political background, a lesson is to be learned from the Portal-to-Portal Act debacle. In enabling big business to trump the CIO's opportunistic litigation strategy in 1947, Congress wound up punishing the mass of unorganized workers who were and remain far more reliant on the FLSA for shoring up their weak labor-market power than unionists, who had merely opportunistically made use of the FLSA to gain bargaining leverage over large industrial firms.[979] Similarly, in the 1990s, the rhetorical animus of the anti-FLSA big business coalition is not directed against lawsuits by assistant managers in fast food restaurants working 70 hours a week for little more than the minimum wage. Rather, the Fair Labor Standards Act Reform Coalition's claim, strongly reminiscent of the rhetoric of 1947, is:

> Today's law unjustly enriches those at the top of the income scale. Disgruntled employees, with the help of the plaintiffs' bar, are taking advantage of these dated statutory provisions. Workers with incomes in the high five-figures or even greater—rocket scientists who train NASA mission control personnel and producers and writers of the NBC nightly news, to name just a few—have used the FLSA to demand time-and-one-half overtime premiums based on their already high rates of pay. The economic impact is staggering: billions of dollars of potential private sector liability for employee windfalls.... There are several changes that could bring the FLSA back in line with its original purpose of protecting those with inadequate bargaining power. First, employees above a certain income level should automatically be excluded from the FLSA's hourly wage and overtime mandates.[980]

---

of them existed "when other labor of like skill and efficiency, which has not been employed full time, is available." 1913 Or. Laws ch. 61, § 4 at 90, 91.

[977]Shortly after Clinton's election, stating that such legislation had a chance of enactment under an executive and legislature controlled by Democrats, the AFL-CIO announced that it would push the new administration to amend the FLSA to raise the overtime premium to 100 percent. David Francis, "Are Those Working Overtime Whistling?" *Christian Sci. Monitor*, Apr. 2, 1993, at 8 (Lexis). Nothing came of this initiative.

[978]U.S. WHD, "Minimum Wage Laws in the States," http://www.dol.gov/dol/esa/public/minwage/america/htm

[979]See below chapter 3.

[980]*Oversight of the Fair Labor Standards Act: Hearing of the Senate Committee on Labor and Human Resources,* 104th Cong., 2d Sess. 45, 47 (1996) (prepared statement of William J. Kilberg on behalf of the Fair Labor Standards Act Reform Coalition). The cases Kilberg referred to are Freeman v. National Broadcasting Co., 80 F.3d 78 (2d Cir.

Before a market-knows-best Republican president signs a FLSA dismantlement bill passed by a like-minded Republican Congress, the labor movement might consider compromising with big business: trading a single-criterion high salary-level ceiling for double overtime (one-half being designated for the Unemployment Insurance fund) for all remaining covered workers might be the biggest fraction of a loaf that an increasingly nonunionized labor force may be able to secure for a long time. Admittedly, however, even this reform, which would be far from optimal for workers and fail to satisfy employers, is very unlikely to be enacted.

Yet in the absence of such legislation, the potent employer lobby may get its way in extending the "revolution" of "total quality management" to the "one last bastion which remains untouched—the laws governing the workplace. Nowhere is this more devastating than the wage and hour laws that continue to impose mid-20th century strictures on a workplace racing into the next millennium."[981] The result may be the abolition of the 40-hour week even as an aspirational norm and its replacement by some variant of a 160-hour, 4-week pay period, during which firms would be privileged to employ workers as many or as few hours per week as fits the firms' production schedules without incurring any statutory overtime liability provided that they remained within the 160-hour limit for the four weeks.[982]

Whatever the shape of the next phase of the struggle over the length of the workday, so long as workers and unions accept profitability and consumer demand as the social economy's highest ordering principles, depriving capital of its status as the sole authorized interpreter of the market's commands will remain—to vary the Wage and Hour Administrator's 1938 dictum—an impious hope.

1996); Hashop v. Rockwell Space Operations Co., 867 F. Supp. 1287 (S.D. Tex. 1994).

[981]*Oversight of the Fair Labor Standards Act: Hearing of the Senate Committee on Labor and Human Resources,* 104th Cong., 2d Sess. 52, 59 (1996) (prepared statement of Flexible Employment Compensation and Scheduling (FLECS) Coalition).

[982]S. 1129, 104th Cong., 1st Sess. (1995). Juliet Schor's well-intentioned proposals to substitute time off for premium overtime wages ignores the political reality that if they could be enacted, the flexibility they would wind up promoting would be overwhelmingly employers' without securing workers real protection against coercion. Juliet Schor, *The Overworked American: The Unexpected Decline of Leisure* 143-44 (1991); Juliet Schor, "Worktime in Contemporary Context: Amending the Fair Labor, Standards Act," 70 *Chicago-Kent Law Rev.* 157-72 at 168 (1994).

2

Involuntary Overtime: The Case of Pseudo-Managers

Here again the power to define is the power to exclude.[1]

In a subtle way, the boom in working hours has also helped keep inflation down. Millions of salaried Americans...are clocking 50-, 60- and 70-hour work weeks even though on paper they officially work just 40 hours. These workers often do not put in for overtime pay, and the result is that they are making a quiet, below-the-radar contribution to the economy. ... This, economists say, has contributed to the recent rise in the nation's productivity rate.... This boost...has enabled American industry to keep profits high without having to resort to raising prices. ...

The overtime boom has created another source of tensions. Many corporate executives are unhappy about dishing out millions of dollars each week in time-and-a-half for overtime. As a result many companies are doing an end run around overtime laws by, for example, hiring thousands of workers as independent contractors who do not have to be paid time-and-a-half for every hour they work over 40.[2]

1. Neo-Chiseling

From the socialistic point of view, our entire industrial system might be made to appear as one of unconscionable exploitation, but it is obvious that such a view would be of no value for practical legislative or judicial purposes. Given our capitalistic system as it is, exploitation or oppression as a subject of legislation must have reference to things not implied in the prevailing economic constitution.[3]

In establishing the Department of Labor (DOL) in 1913, Congress stated that its purpose "shall be to foster, promote, and develop the welfare of the wage earners of the United States."[4] One significant example of the failure of the DOL

---

[1]*Twenty-Eighth Annual Report of the Secretary of Labor for the Fiscal Year Ended June 30 1940* at 236 (1940) (Wage and Hour Administrator Philip Fleming discussing the definition of executive employees under the FLSA).

[2]"Many Workers Not Sharing Good Times: U.S. Is the Leader in Hours Per Year," *Patriot Ledger* (Quincy, Mass.), Sept. 9, 1999, at 10 (Lexis).

[3]Ernst Freund, *Standards of American Legislation* 121-22 (1965 [1917]).

[4]An Act to Create a Department of Labor, ch. 141, § 1, 37 Stat. 736 (1913) (codified at 29 U.S.C. § 551 (1988)). The limited ambit of the federal Department of Labor at that time can be gauged by the fact that Woodrow Wilson, the first president to appoint a

during the Clinton administration to seize the opportunity to undo the damage done by a dozen years of de facto deregulation of labor standards by the blatantly pro-employer Reagan-Bush administrations involves employers' efforts to compel workers to work overtime without additional compensation merely by labeling them salaried managers.

In giving the notion of "free labor" a new dimension, employers have not limited themselves to this relatively subtle technique: "obsessed with profits in recent years,"[5] so many large firms have been engaging in the even more blatant but venerable[6] practice of requiring hourly employees to work overtime "off the clock" that "the fight over illegal overtime has become one of the most significant workplace issues of the 1990s" as "dozens of companies like Taco Bell, Nordstrom's, Food Lion, Longs Drug Stores and Electric Boat have been forced to pay millions to shortchanged workers."[7] As part of the settlement of

---

Secretary of Labor—after lame-duck President Taft had reluctantly signed the bill—took the dogmatic view (in a book he had published as a professor, but also reprinted several times during both of his terms) that Congress had no power to "regulate the conditions of labor in field and factory.... Back of the conditions of labor in the field and in the factory lie all the intimate matters of morals and of domestic and business relationship which have always been recognized as the undisputed field of state law...." The opposed view he called "absurd extravagancies of interpretation...." Woodrow Wilson, *Constitutional Government in the United States* 171, 179 (1917 [1908]); Jonathan Grossman, "The Origin of the U.S. Department of Labor," *Monthly Lab. Rev.*, Mar. 1973, at 3, 7.

[5]Alan Liddle, "Jury Finds Taco Bell Guilty in Wages Suit: Chain to Appeal Case's Class-Action Status," *Nation's Restaurant News*, Apr. 21, 1997, at 1 (Lexis). Workers have been able to file class-action lawsuits despite their prohibition under the FLSA by the Portal-to-Portal Act—see below chapter 3—by suing under state minimum wage and overtime laws.

[6]Almost from the FLSA's inception employers sought to evade it by having "workers punch out at the time required for apparent compliance and then...allow[ing] them to go on working 2 to 5 more hours...." Irving Dilliard, "United States Wage and Hour Law: Survey of 18 Months of Operation," *St. Louis Post-Dispatch*, May 12, 1940, reprinted in 86 *Cong. Rec.* A3293, A3294 (1940).

[7]Andrew Murr, "Pay? How About a Pizza? Cost-Cutting Companies Want Employees to Give Something for Nothing," *Newsweek*, Apr. 20, 1998, at 42 (Westlaw). The Food Lion supermarket chain required employees (some of whom it claimed were excluded from coverage as assistant managers) to perform their work in a certain number of hours and enunciated a no-overtime policy; because many workers could not complete their assigned tasks within the time allocated, they had to work off the clock for fear of being fired; local management suffered and permitted this performance of unpaid overtime. See Lyle v. Food Lion, Inc., 954 F.2d 984 (4th Cir. 1992); *Problems in the Labor Department's Enforcement of Wage and Hours Laws: Hearings Before the Employment and Housing Subcommittee of the Senate Committee on Government Operations*, 102d Cong., 2d Sess. (1993). For other cases finding or alleging that employers required employees to work off the clock, see Reich v. Waldbaum, Inc., 833 F. Supp. 1037 (S.D.N.Y. 1993), *rev'd on other grounds*, 52 F.3d 35 (2d Cir. 1995); Realite v. Ark Restaurants Corp., 7 F. Supp.2d 303 (S.D.N.Y. 1998); Harper v. Lovett's Buffet, Inc., 185 F.R.D. 358 (M.D. Ala. 1999); Frank Swoboda, "Nordstrom Settles Suit On Overtime; Employees to Receive More Than $ 20 Million," *Wash. Post*, Jan. 12, 1993, at C1

litigation involving as many as 150,000 current and former employees, Albertson's agreed to eliminate the hinge that made the scam possible—the "dollar-for-dollar reduction in managers' bonuses for exceeding the weekly allowable overtime amount."[8]

Mislabeling of workers as executives not entitled to overtime is particularly widespread in retail and service establishments such as grocery and convenience stores, and fast-food restaurants, which together employ a huge labor force of more than eleven million largely low-wage workers.[9] During the 1980s, eating and drinking places and grocery stores were ranked first and third, respectively, with respect to the increase in the number of employees.[10] The DOL's own *Career Guides to Industries* frankly observes that "[m]any workers" in restaurants earn the minimum wage "or less."[11]

Proliferating high-profile class-action litigation in the 1990s against Taco Bell, Wendy's, Albertson's, Shoney's, and other employers has underscored the prevalence of this unlawfully exploitative treatment of alleged managers.[12] For example, the plaintiffs—misclassified as assistant managers although they mostly performed routine production work—in a class action filed against 27 Wendy's

---

(Nexis); Steve Miletich, "Taco Bell Found Guilty of Worker Abuses," *Seattle Post-Intelligencer*, Apr. 9, 1997, at A1 (Westlaw); Steve Miletich, "Taco Bell Workers Win Back Wages: Chain Agrees to Pay 16,000 State Residents," *Seattle Post-Intelligencer*, Dec. 5, 1997, at B1 (Westlaw).

[8]"Albertson's, Employees Settle Wage Hour Dispute," 162 *Lab. Rel. Rep.* 466, 467 (Dec. 13, 1999).

[9]Grocery stores employ more than three million and eating and drinking places more than eight million workers. *Employment and Earnings*, June 1999, tab. B-12 at 97, 98; ftp://ftp.bls.gov/pub/special/requests/ee/ceseeb12.txt (data for September 1999). See also U.S. BLS, *Employment, Hours, and Earnings: United States, 1988-1996*, at 302-303, 315 (Bull. 2481, 1996); U.S. BLS, *Career Guides to Industries: 1998-99 Edition* 114-16 (Bull. 2503, 1998).

[10]Lois Plunkert, "The 1980's: A Decade of Job Growth and Industry Shifts," *Monthly Lab. Rev.*, Sept. 1990, at 3, tab. 5 at 12.

[11]U.S. BLS, *Career Guides to Industries: 1998-99 Edition* at 113.

[12]See Albertson's, Inc. v. United Food and Commercial Workers, 157 F.3d 758 (9th Cir. 1998); Belcher v. Shoney's, Inc., 30 F. Supp. 1010 (M.D. Tenn. 1998); Hoffmann v. Sbarro,Inc., 982 F. Supp. 249 (S.D.N.Y. 1997); Eugene v. McDonald's Corp., 1996 U.S. Dist. Lexis 10193 (N.D. Ill. 1996); Lyles v. K-Mart Corp., 519 F. Supp. 756 (M.D. Fla. 1981). Ilana DeBare, "Who's a Manager? Companies in California Are Facing a Growing Number of Class-Action Law Suits over this Complex, Far-Reaching Issue," *San Francisco Chronicle*, Oct. 20, 1997, at B1 (Nexis); G. Pascal Zachary, "Shortchanged: Many Firms Refuse to Pay for Overtime, Employees Complain," Wall St. J., June 24, 1996, at A1 (Westlaw); E. Scott Reckard, "Working Longer—For Less?" L.A. Times, June 11, 1997, at A1 (Nexis); Alan Liddle, "Wendy's Targeted in Lawsuit Tied to Calif. Overtime," *Nation's Restaurant News*, July, 27, 1998, at 3 (Westlaw); Alan Liddle, "Calif. OT Suits: Wendy's Settlement Seen, But Taco Bell Class Trial Looms," *Nation's Restaurant News*, Sept. 20, 1999, at 1 (Westlaw).

restaurants in California in 1998 complained that they worked six days a week often more than 12 hours a day and were even deprived of their statutorily mandated rest periods without receiving any overtime pay.[13] For the five years from 1993 to 1997, DOL compliance actions show that restaurants accounted for the greatest number of minimum wage and overtime violations (20,382 cases) followed by grocery stores and supermarkets (4,662): "Violators were concentrated in the fast-food industry: The Subway Sandwiches and Salads chain led the pack with 654 closed cases, followed by McDonald's (525), Burger King (441), Shoney's (395) and Taco Bell (322)." DOL records also revealed that 60.6 percent of restaurants it investigated had violated the wage and hour law; the industry ranked fourth (behind janitorial services, security guard services, and hotels and motels).[14] The retail and service industries accounted for 60-70 percent of all employees owed back minimum wages and half of those owed overtime wages according to DOL compliance actions for the years through 1996, the most recent year for which data are available.[15] In addition, retail and service employers are unique in lawfully employing as many as 80,000 full-time students at 85 per cent of the minimum wage.[16] Indeed, more than one-fourth of the almost eight million employees in eating and drinking places are 16 to 19 years old—five times the average for all industries.[17]

The imposition of mandatory unpaid overwork on restaurant workers who double as low-level supervisors is the paradoxical pendant to the proliferation of contingent employment in an industry whose "extraordinary profits...st[an]d like a giant inverted pyramid on the pinpoint of minimum wages."[18] Working side by

---

[13]Hawley v. Wendy's International, Inc., No. BC194235 (Los Angeles Superior Ct., July 14, 1998).

[14]Brian Tumulty, "Many Low-Wage Workers Getting Shortchanged on the Job," Gannett News Service, Dec. 20, 1997 (Nexis).

[15]U.S. Employment Standards Administration, Wage and Hour Division, *Minimum Wage and Overtime Hours Under the Fair Labor Standards Act: 1998 Report to the Congress*, tab. 6a at 34, tabs. D1a-d at 143-62 (1998).

[16]U.S. Employment Standards Administration, Wage and Hour Division, *Minimum Wage and Overtime Hours Under the Fair Labor Standards Act: 1998 Report to the Congress*, tab. 9 at 41, tab. 1a and 2a at 163, 165 (data for 1991-96); U.S. Employment Standards Administration, *Minimum Wages and Maximum Hours Under the Fair Labor Standards Act*, tab. 1 at 17, tab. 3 at 19 (n.d. [1991]) (data for 1980); 29 U.S.C. § 214(b) (1988). On McDonald's federal lobbying efforts on behalf of subminimum wages for its employees (the so-called McDonald's Amendment), see *Bill to Repeal Subminimum Wage Provisions for Full-Time Students: Hearing Before the Subcommittee on Labor Standards of the House Committee on Education and Labor*, 94th Cong. 2d Sess. 9-12 (1977) (Rep. O'Hara); George Lardner, Jr., "Business Gets Cold Feet on Subminimum Wage," *Wash. Post*, Mar. 20, 1981, at A1 (Nexis); John Love, McDonald's: *Behind the Golden Arches* 360-61, 369 (1986).

[17]U.S. BLS, *Career Guides to Industries: 1998-99 Edition* at 111

[18]Max Boas and Steve Chain, *Big Mac: The Unauthorized Story of McDonald's* 81, 95

side with upwards of 3,500,000 entirely nonunionized students and other largely young and female part-time employees who are paid the minimum wage for minimal hours without any additional non-statutory social wage supplements are so-called assistant managers.[19] "In many fast-food restaurants...sixteen-year-old employees are supervised by eighteen- or nineteen-year-old 'managers.'"[20] In exchange for a fixed weekly wage that may equate to less than the minimum wage and statutory overtime, assistant managers are required to perform both supervisory and "grunt" work for as many as seventy to eighty hours per week.[21]

How has the law come to condone and even facilitate such perverse

---

(1977 [1976]); *see also* William Alpert, *The Minimum Wage in the Restaurant Industry* (1986).

[19]*See, e.g.*, Marshall v. Burger King Corp., 504 F. Supp. 404, 407-408 (E.D.N.Y. 1980); Ivan Charner & Bryna Fraser, *Fast Food Jobs* 6, 35-36 (1984); "Employee Relations in the Fast Food Industry," *Retail/Services Lab. Rep.*, June 10, 1985, at CC-1 (Spec. Supp.); Ester Reiter, *Making Fast Food: From the Frying Pan into the Fryer* 159-61 (1991) (on sole successful union organizing effort in U.S. at one Burger King in Detroit); Chart House, Inc. d/b/a Burger King, 223 NLRB 100 (1976) (discussing collective bargaining agreement covering two Burger King restaurants in Peoria, Illinois); Greyhound Food Management Inc. d/b/a Burger King, 258 NLRB 1293 (1981); Burger King Corp., 265 NLRB 1507 (1982), *aff'd*, Burger King Corp. v. NLRB, 725 F.2d 1053 (6th Cir. 1983) (finding serious unfair labor practices committed by Burger King against employees trying to organize two Detroit restaurants and use of physical intimidation by workers against manager in effort to gain recognition); Alan Krueger, "Ownership, Agency, and Wages: An Examination of Franchising in the Fast Food Industry," 106 *Q.J. Econ.* 75, 82-83 (1991); Lawrence Katz & Alan Krueger, "The Effect of the Minimum Wage on the Fast-Food Industry," 46 *Indus. & Lab. Rel. Rev.* 6, 7 (1992); Robin Leidner, *Fast Food, Fast Talk: Service Work and the Routinization of Everyday Life* 44-85 (1993); *Daily Lab. Rep.*, Mar. 1, 1994 (Lexis) (no McDonald's unionized in U.S. or Canada); Michael Colton, "Big Mac Attack: Did Somebody Say Strike?," *Wash. Post*, Apr. 26, 1998, at F1 (Westlaw) (United Food and Commercial Worker's organization of McDonald's restaurant in Mason City, Iowa, for four years in 1970s only such success ever). Wage surveys in the early 1990s revealed that the minimum wage was the median wage in the fast-food industry. Even in such large non-southern urban areas as Philadelphia and San Francisco, the median wage was only marginally higher—$4.50 and $4.75 respectively. U.S. BLS, *Occupational Compensation Survey: Pay Only: Harrison County, MS—Fast Food Restaurants, January 1993* (1993); *Occupational Compensation Survey: Pay Only: Bell County, TX—Fast Food Restaurants, January 1993* (1993); *Occupational Compensation Survey: Pay Only: Philadelphia County—Fast Food Restaurants, November 1992* (1993); *Occupational Compensation Survey: Pay Only: San Francisco County—Fast Food Restaurants, January 1993* (1993).

[20]Ellen Greenberger and Laurence Steinberg, *When Teenagers Work: The Psychological and Social Costs of Adolescent Employment* 81 (1986).

[21]Managers at one chain—of combination gasoline station/convenience store/ restaurant—who were required to live on the premises, alleged that they worked as many as 120 hours per week, as a result of which their fixed salaries amounted to less than the minimum wage. Murray v. Stuckey's Inc., 939 F.2d 614, 616 (8th Cir. 1991). Even the BLS finally revealed in its *Occupational Outlook Handbook* that it "is common for restaurant and food service managers to work 50 to 60 hours or more per week." U.S. BLS, *Occupational Outlook Handbook: 1998-99 Edition* at 77.

compensation schemes, which, especially in the South and nonmetropolitan areas,[22] amount to "payment to supervisory personnel up to assistant manager levels [of] below subsistence-level income"?[23] This question becomes increasingly important as the evolution of corporate bureaucratic controls has made possible "a vastly greater stratification of the firm's workforce" as a consequence of which a "rapidly growing number of employees...supervise other workers....'"[24]

2. Origins of an Exclusion

The Fair Labor Standards Act was designed "to extend the frontiers of social progress".... Any exemption from such humanitarian and remedial legislation must therefore be narrowly construed.... To extend an exemption to other than those plainly and unmistakably within its terms and spirit is to...frustrate the announced will of the people.[25]

Ever since its enactment in 1938, the FLSA has excluded from its protection "any employee employed in a bona fide executive...capacity...(as such terms are defined and delimited by regulations of the [Wage and Hour] Administrator)."[26] The choice of the term "Exemptions" as the title of the exclusions provision of FLSA is curious. After all, an exemption is "[f]reedom from a general duty or service; immunity from a general burden, tax, or charge."[27] Exclusions, in contrast, refer to the denial of a benefit or other desirable goods. It is therefore the employer who is exempt—from the burden of paying the minimum wage or mandatory overtime. Conversely, the employee is excluded from these same protections. This Pickwickian sense of *exempt* may be a vestige of nineteenth-

---

[22]U.S. DOL, *Earnings Data Pertinent to a Review of the Salary Tests for Executive, Administrative and Professional Employees as Defined in Regulations, Part 541*, at 3, tab. 13 at 30, tab. 15 at 32 (1969).

[23]Christopher Gunn and Hazel Gunn, *Reclaiming Capital: Democratic Initiatives and Community Development* 27 (1991).

[24]Richard Edwards, *Contested Terrain: The Transformation of the Workplace in the Twentieth Century* 135 (1979).

[25]A.H. Phillips, Inc. v. Walling, 324 U.S. 490, 493 (1945) (quoting President Roosevelt's message to Congress on the FLSA bill).

[26]Fair Labor Standards Act, ch. 676, § 13 (a)(1), 52 Stat. 1060, 1067 (1938). The current version reads: "(as such terms are defined and delimited from time by regulations of the Secretary [of Labor]...." 29 U.S.C. § 213 (a)(1) (1988). For an analysis, based on archival research, of the New Deal origins of the treatment of managerial employees under the FLSA, see Deborah Malamud, "Engineering the Middle Classes: Class Line-Drawing in New Deal Hours Legislation," 96 *Mich. L. Rev.* 2212 (1998).

[27]*Black's Law Dictionary* 681 (4th ed. 1968 [1891]).

century American judicial contractarianism, which struck down, in the name of freedom of and to contract, labor-protective statutes as unconstitutional interferences with employees' "liberty to compete for employment upon unfavorable terms...."[28]

This commingling of premodern and modern terms is exacerbated by the fact that the regulations, administrators, employers, and commentators commonly speak of "nonexempt" and "exempt" employees.[29] However, despite massive exclusions of vulnerable workers such as migrant farmworkers,[30] most employees in the United States are nevertheless protected by the FLSA—in 1996 64.9 percent and 60.5 percent of wage and salary workers were "subject to and not exempt from" the minimum wage and overtime provision, respectively.[31] And since exclusions from coverage are to be construed narrowly in favor of inclusion,[32] use of the paired categories *nonexempt-exempt* to designate the universe of affected workers inverts the purpose and spirit of the FLSA.[33] To characterize covered, protected workers negatively as "nonexempt" suggests a statutory baseline of exclusion—as if workers had the burden of rebutting a presumption that employers are exempt from complying with the Act unless and until proven subject to its duties.[34] In fact, "an employer must prove that any

---

[28]Ernst Freund, *Standards of American Legislation* 124 (1965 [1917]). As an exemplar of such judicial views, see Godcharles v. Wigeman, 6 A. 354 (Pa. 1886).

[29]*See, e.g.*, 29 C.F.R. §§ 541.101-102 (1993); "Division Refuses to Redefine 'Executive,'" 4 *Wage & Hour Reporter* 509 (Sept. 22, 1941) (letter from Wage & Hour Adm'r to NAM assoc. Counsel, Raymond Smethurst (Sept. 4, 1941), referring to work as "non-exempt"); David Weeks, *Overtime Pay for Exempt Employees* 34 (National Indus. Conference Bd. Personnel Policy Study No. 208, 1967) (reproducing Allis-Chalmers salary policy); E. Gottlieb, *Overtime Compensation for Exempt Employees* 9 (Am. Management Assoc. Research Study 40, 1960); Sanford Cohen, *Labor Law* 61 (1964); Toby Parcel and Marie Sickmeier, "One Firm, Two Labor Markets: The Case of McDonald's in the Fast-Food Industry," 29 *Sociological Q*. 29, 42 (1988).

[30]See Marc Linder, "Farm Workers and the Fair Labor Standards Act: Racial Discrimination in the New Deal," 65 *Tex. L. Rev.* 1335-93 (1987); Marc Linder, *Migrant Workers and Minimum Wages: Regulating the Exploitation of Agricultural Labor in the United States* 125-75 (1992).

[31]The DOL's most recent estimate is that 79,422,000 and 74,044,000 of all 122,359,000 employed wage and salary workers in the civilian labor force were subject to the minimum wage and overtime provision, respectively, of the FLSA in 1996. U.S. Employment Standards Adm'n, *Minimum Wage and Overtime Hours Under the Fair Labor Standards Act: 1998 Report*, tab. 1 at 13, tab. 2 at 14.

[32]Phillips, Inc. v. Walling at 493.

[33]The universe is, strictly speaking, not exhausted by these two categories because in addition to "exemptions," the FLSA contains a definitions provision, which excludes other groups of workers from the statutory category of "employees." 29 U.S.C. § 203(e)(4) (1988).

[34]Edwards, *Contested Terrain* at 133, reports the linguistic usage but mistakenly attributes it to managerial practices rather than to the law itself.

exemption to the overtime provision applies. Proving the exemption is an affirmative defense; the statute assumes that an employee is covered."[35] And as a representative of Big Business employers and the former DOL Solicitor told Congress in 1995, the FLSA "is written now so that there is a presumption that all employees are non-exempt...."[36]

Ironically, the source of this distortion may have been mere sloppiness in drafting. The original administration bill as introduced by Senator Black provided in its definitions section that "'[e]mployee'...shall not include any person employed in an executive, administrative, supervisory, or professional capacity...."[37] These workers (together with agricultural laborers) constituted the totality of categorical exclusions. The bill also contained a provision titled, "Exemptions from Labor Standards with Respect to Wages and Hours," which required the proposed Labor Standards Board to issue a regulation providing that "any employer employing less than [blank] employees"shall not be deemed to be violating the law by paying "an oppressive or substandard wage...."[38] In other words, the bill exempted small employers from the obligations imposed on larger employers. The radically revised bill that Black introduced two months later and that much more closely resembled the actual enactment removed the named categories of workers from the definition of "employee" and transferred them to a section now titled simply, "Exemptions." Unlike its predecessor, however, this new provision referred only to employees and not at all to their employers.[39]

In spite of this infelicitous terminology, Congress did not intend to give employers free reign to deprive their employees of minimum wage and overtime rights by arbitrarily calling them *executives*.[40] It therefore required the DOL to issue regulations putting employers and employees on notice as to which groups of workers would be protected and which excluded. Since the word *executive*, which originated in the United States in the twentieth century,[41] is used "to designate anyone who holds a high-ranking management position" and thus "has

---

[35]Royster v. Food Lion, Inc., 1998 U.S. App. Lexis 11809 *13 n.9 (4th Cir. 1998).

[36]*Hearings on the Fair Labor Standards Act: Hearings Before the Subcommittee on Workforce Protections of the House Committee on Economic and Educational Opportunities*, 104th Cong., 1st Sess. 113 (Serial No. 104-46, 1996) (testimony of William Kilberg).

[37]S. 2475, 75th Cong., 1st Sess. § 2(a)(7) (May 24, 1937).

[38]*Id.* § 6(a).

[39]S. 2475, 75th Cong., 1st Sess. §§ 3(e) & 11(a) (July 6, 1937).

[40]On possible employer abuse of the classification, see "Industry Warned Not to Cut Corners on Pay Rules," *Nation's Restaurant News*, May 12, 1986, at 87 (Nexis).

[41]5 *The Oxford English Dictionary* 522 (2d ed. 1989).

status connotations,"[42] courts quickly concluded that "[d]oubtless the main purpose of the definition was to avoid evasion of the statute by merely colorable titles given to employees by nominal classifications having no substantial basis in reality."[43]

Because Congress expressly delegated to the DOL the authority to fill the definitional gap, that is, to issue so-called legislative regulations elucidating the meaning of "bona fide executive," they "have the force of law as much as though they were written in the statute."[44] Legislative regulations, however, "are as binding on the courts as if they had been directly enacted by Congress" only to the extent that they "are reasonable."[45] Thus if the DOL issues a regulatory definition that either is originally or, through the passage of time, becomes "arbitrary, capricious, or manifestly contrary to the statute,"[46] a federal court must declare it invalid, and cause the agency to begin afresh. In particular where "there is no longer a rational connection between the facts originally supporting the exclusion...and the regulation as it operates today[, t]he original purpose of the regulation...has become so detached from actual effect...as to make the current regulation arbitrary and capricious...."[47]

Exclusion of various executive, supervisory, professional, and clerical workers from state statutes limiting the hours of female employees had been widespread for decades before the FLSA.[48] The International Labour Organisation's 1919 eight-hours convention also excluded supervisory management and those working in a confidential capacity.[49] Even the version of Senator Hugo

---

[42]Dale Beach, *Personnel: The Management of People at Work* 171 (4th ed. 1980 [1963]).

[43]Jones v. Bethlehem-Fairfield Shipyard, Inc., 75 F. Supp. 86, 91 (D. Md. 1947).

[44]Helliwell v. Haberman, 140 F.2d 833, 834 (2d Cir. 1944).

[45]Fanelli v. United States Gypsum Co., 141 F.2d 216, 218 (2d Cir. 1944).

[46]Chevron, U.S.A., Inc., v. Natural Resources Defense Council, Inc., 467 U.S. 837, 843-44 (1984).

[47]Hazard v. Sullivan, 827 F. Supp. 1348, 1354 (M.D. Tenn. 1993), *rev'd sub nom.* Hazard v. Shalala, 44 F.3d 399, 404 (6th Cir. 1995). But see Gamboa v. Rubin, 80 F.3d 1338, 1343 (9th Cir. 1996) ("the Secretary's failure to adjust the automobile equity $1500 limit for inflation since its adoption almost 15 years ago has thwarted Congress's purpose in establishing the AFDC program and the Secretary's own rationale for adopting the $1500 limit"), vacated on other grounds sub nom. Gamboa v. Chandler, 101 F.3d 90 (9th Cir. 1996).

[48]Harry Millis and Royal Montgomery, *Labor's Progress and Some Basic Labor Problems* 531 (1938).

[49]Convention Limiting the Hours of Work in Industrial Undertakings to Eight Hours in the Day and Forty-Eight in the Week, art. 2(a) (1919). Even the rather stringent Labor Code of the former German Democratic Republic denied the overtime premium (of 25 percent) to managerial and professional workers, although the latter were entitled to corresponding time off, while the former were entitled to compensatory time off for

Black's thirty-hours bill that passed the Senate in 1933 excluded "officers, executives, and superintendents, and their personal and immediate clerical assistants...."[50] That approach conformed to the proposals of the president of General Motors, who urged Congress to exempt "[e]xecutives, managers, superintendents, and overseers, their assistants and staffs, also others engaged in a supervisory capacity...."[51] Exclusions of higher-paid white-collar employees had also been common in collective bargaining agreements covering them. For example, the agreement entered into just a few weeks after the FLSA was enacted between Time, Inc. and the Newspaper Guild of New York, a local of the leftist CIO-affiliated American Newspaper Guild, provided that the employer "shall not be required to compensate for overtime...in the case of writers, photographers, and executives earning one hundred dollars or more per week"; instead, such employees "shall be granted annual vacations of four...weeks with full pay."[52]

Some light is shed on the purpose of the exclusion of executive employees from the protections of the FLSA by its New Deal progenitor—the President's Reemployment Agreement (PRA) of 1933. The National Industrial Recovery Act (NIRA) authorized the President "to enter into agreements with, and to approve voluntary agreements between and among" workers, unions, firms, and industrial associations if he believed that the agreements would effectuate the NIRA's policy and were consistent with the industrial codes of fair competition required by the NIRA.[53] President Roosevelt used the PRA as a temporary blanket code until individual codes of fair competition were adopted for each industry.[54] The PRAs, which, unlike the codes of fair competition, were not legally enforcible, contained child labor, minimum wage, and maximum hours provisions. They specified that the hours provisions, which, in an effort to reemploy the unemployed, limited an individual worker's workweek to forty hours, did not apply to "employees in a managerial or executive capacity, who now receive more than $35 per week." This salary was more than twice the weekly minimum wage (of $15-$16) guaranteed by the PRAs.[55] Executives and supervisors were

---

Sunday and holiday hours. Arbeitsgesetzbuch der Deutschen Demokratischen Republik vom 16. Juni 1977, § 178, Gesetzblatt der DDR, Teil I, 185, 211.

[50]S. 158, 73d Cong., 1st Sess. (Apr. 7, 1933).

[51]*Thirty-Hour Week Bill: Hearings Before the House Committee on Labor*, 73d Cong., 1st Sess. 791 (1933) (statement of Alfred P. Sloan, Jr.).

[52]"A Labor Agreement for 'White Collar' Employees," 2 *Lab. Rels. Rep.* 749 (Aug. 8, 1938). The maximum paid vacation for employees entitled to time and one-half for overtime was three weeks.

[53]NIRA, ch. 90, § 4(a), 48 Stat. 195, 197 (1933). *See generally*, Bernard Bellush, *The Failure of the NRA* 48-52 (1975).

[54]"The President's Reemployment Agreement," 37 *Monthly Lab. Rev.* 262, 263 (1933).

[55]The President's Reemployment Agreement, ¶¶ 2-6, as published in *National*

also almost universally excepted from the hours provisions of the codes of fair competition on the ground that such limitations were "not appropriate" for them.[56]

Despite the PRA's "antisubterfuge" provision, which obligated employers not "to frustrate the spirit and intent of this Agreement which is...to increase employment by a universal covenant..., and to shorten hours and to raise wages for the shorter week to a living basis,"[57] employers sought to give "meaningless titles to minor employees to exempt them from the hours provisions...."[58] Consequently, Hugh Johnson, the National Recovery Administrator, soon found it necessary to issue a statement defining "manager" and "executive." He declared that in approving exceptions for such persons from the codes' maximum hours provisions, the National Recovery Administration did not intend "to provide for the exemption of any persons other than those who exercise real managerial or executive authority, which persons are invested with responsibilities entirely different from those of the wage earner and come within the class of the higher salaried employees." Johnson also used the opportunity to emphasize that paying less than the threshold $35 weekly salary created an irrebuttable presumption that the employee was not "exempt."[59]

Under the NIRA, then, both the salary level and the description of managerial duties established a clear divide between subordinate and superordinate employees. Although the PRA and the codes of fair competition, unlike the FLSA, did not expressly exclude managerial-executive employees from the minimum wage provisions, the high salary test functioned under both regimes as a superminimum wage vis-à-vis any employer wishing to take advantage of the exemption. Moreover, whereas the FLSA merely gave employers a financial incentive to hire additional workers rather than to pay premium overtime to existing employees, the PRA sought to expand employment more directly by obliging employers not to work their workers more than forty hours.[60]

Recovery Adm'n, What the Blue Eagle Means to You and How You Can Get It 5-8 (Bull. No. 4, 1933).

[56]Leverett Lyon et al., *The National Recovery Administration: An Analysis and Appraisal* 369, 382 (1972 [1935]).

[57]PRA, ¶ 8, in NRA, *What the Blue Eagle Means to You* at 8.

[58]U.S. BLS, *Handbook of Labor Statistics: 1936 Edition* 502 (Bull. No. 616, 1936).

[59]37 *Monthly Lab. Rev.* 1083 (1933). Johnson also issued an interpretation that so long as he was receiving more than $35 per week, the employee could act "primarily, although not wholly, in a managerial or executive capacity" without causing his employer to forfeit its exemption. Interpretation No. 15, in NRA, *What the Blue Eagle Means to You* at 17. For an example of a code that excepted all employees receiving more than $35 per week and executives and managerial and supervisory staffs from any hourly limitations, see Code of Fair Competition for the Automobile Manufacturing Industry, § III, in 1 NRA, *Codes of Fair Competition* 253, 255 (1933).

[60]Codes of fair competition did include premium overtime provisions. For a tabular

Nevertheless, freeing employers from this restriction with respect to their managerial employees had the same impact under both regimes—weakening the reemployment effect while ensuring that executive employees were sufficiently well-paid and closely allied with capital that they could be remitted to their own devices in warding off exploitation.

A similar regime would also have been established under the proposed National Textile Act, on which Congress held hearings in 1936 and 1937. In the 1936 bill, the flat ban on employing production employees more than 35 hours per week or more than 7 hours per day or clerical or office employees more than 40 hours weekly or 8 hours per day, did not apply to those engaged in a managerial or executive capacity at a salary of not less than $50.[61] The 1937 bill excepted employees engaged in a managerial or executive capacity and receiving $40 or more per week from the mandatory time and a half provision for hours in excess of 7 per day or 35 per week.[62] At one of the hearings on the bill, which took place just four days before the FLSA was introduced in May 1937, textile industry management informed the House Committee on Labor that it was "unalterably opposed" to the provision, which revealed the drafters' ignorance of "industrial mill management":

> In every mill there are large groups of persons in charge of certain departments covering minor operation [sic], as department managers or executives, where $40 per week would be excessively high, and yet the need for these department heads and managers working in excess of 40 hours per week must be apparent. The efficient department manager interested in his work and in the development of his department never quits when the whistle blows. In fact, very often his best work is done during the brief period after the other employees have left the mill. This is the period in which he plans his work and studies his operation.
>
> [I]t must be remembered that from these department managers and executives are frequently recruited the chief executives of the mills and their efficiency and development is controlled not by a desire to quit when the whistle blows, but to maintain contact with their work such hours as they find necessary for their own development.[63]

---

overview, see "Summary of Permanent Codes Adopted Under NIRA Up to November 8, 1933," 37 *Monthly Lab. Rev.* 1333 (1933).

[61]H.R. 9072, § 19, in *To Rehabilitate and Stabilize Labor Conditions in the Textile Industry of the United States: Hearings Before a Subcommittee of the House Committee on Labor on H.R. 9072*, 74th Cong., 2d Sess. 3, 7 (1936). Interestingly, the hours limitation applied even to proprietors doing production work. *Id.* § 3(5) at 3.

[62]H. R. 238, §§ 13(d) & (e), 75th Cong., 1st Sess. (Jan. 5, 1937).

[63]*To Regulate the Textile Industry: Hearings Before the Subcommittee of the House Committee on Labor on H.R. 238*, Pt. 6, 75th Cong., 1st Sess. 391 (1937) (testimony of Clement Driscoll, executive director, American Lace Manufacturers Association).

The industry witness requested that the salary cutoff be set at no more than $35—the level that had been established by the industry's NRA code.[64]

Representative William Connery, who introduced the FLSA bills with Black on May 24, 1937, had also been associated with him in promoting thirty-hours legislation. The thirty-hours bill that Connery introduced in 1937 excepted "officers, executives, and superintendents, and their personal and immediate clerical assistants" from the five-day, six-hour maximum.[65]

A cavalier attitude about the need to protect nonproduction workers against overreaching seemed particularly out of place in the 1930s when even *Personnel*, the magazine of the American Management Association (AMA), stressed that the Depression had gone a long way toward dismantling differentials that had favored salaried workers:

> Even social distinctions are disappearing with the increased number of high school and college graduates who voluntarily or under necessity have gone into manual labor. With this decline in class distinctions there has begun to grow up a community of interest between wage-earners and salaried employees. In some companies salaried workers have shown a desire for collective bargaining...either through their own organizations or by use of the same agencies that serve wage-earners.
>
> These circumstances have convinced many employers that there is need to restudy the working conditions of salaried employees, if for no other reason than to avoid serious depreciation of the loyalty, efficiency, and morale of this class of workers.... The question of overtime work is being given serious thought in many business organizations, and earnest efforts are being made to eliminate the exploitation of the salaried rank and file.[66]

The need for unionization or statutory intervention was suggested by a 1937 AMA survey, which found that only 7.5 percent of employers paid any of their salaried workers any type of premium overtime.[67] (A quarter-century later, it was still the case that fewer than a tenth of firms paid exempt employees time and one-half for overtime.)[68] As Congress was preparing to debate the scope of FLSA coverage for white-collar workers, an industrialist inadvertently revealed in *The New York Times* precisely why the purposes of the overtime provision applied to them: employers would use labor-saving bookkeeping and accounting machines to counteract the overtime penalty.[69]

---

[64] *To Regulate the Textile Industry* at 391.

[65] H.R. 1606, §1, 75th Cong., 1st Sess. (Jan. 5, 1937)

[66] "Overtime Work by Salaried Employees," 14 *Personnel* 90, 91 (1937).

[67] Calculated according to "Overtime Work by Salaried Employees" at 91.

[68] U.S. BLS, *Supplementary Compensation for Nonproduction Workers, 1963*, tab. 28 at 63 (Bull. No. 1470, 1965).

[69] *N.Y. Times*, Mar. 6, 1939, at 14, col. 6 (letter from Industrialist, Pittsburgh).

On the eve of Pearl Harbor, another management magazine, *Modern Industry*, warned employers that white collar workers had objectively and subjectively been incorporated into the working class:

A few years ago it could be fairly stated that white-collar jobs were preferable to factory jobs because of higher earnings, shorter working hours, modern working conditions, greater stability of employment, better chances of promotion.

Unionization and defense have reversed conditions. Today there is little question that the highest wages are paid to production workers. Working conditions—in terms of air conditioning, better lighting, washrooms, eating facilities, etc.—are better in some new factories than in the general offices of the same companies.... Union agreements assure greater security in employment and regular promotion. With the exception of hours—and for overtime work most production employees receive adequate compensation—there is little choice for the young person weighing his future between a factory job and a white-collar job. Improved working conditions and obvious economic advantages have seriously battered old prejudices against "hard work" as opposed to "soft jobs" in the office force. ...

Another significant trend is the growing unionization white-collar workers. Actual mechanization of clerical work, growing realization of a mutuality of interest, "de-classing" of white-collar and professional workers during years of depression unemployment, the example of economic gains won by factory workers through unionization, and very genuine dissatisfaction with present wages, hours, and working conditions, all have given impetus to union organization of these employees.[70]

Elmer Andrews, the first Wage and Hour Administrator, hazily alluded to class alignments when, on September 29, 1938, in a sneak preview of the regulations that would be issued a few weeks later, he answered a question about the definition of executive, administrative, and professional "folks" at a meeting of the Southern States Industrial Council in Birmingham, Alabama, by noting that he had "had that in mind more than anything else.... I am very sympathetic toward your problem there, because I know a superintendent is not a clock watcher, nor does he punch a time clock. Certainly if he was the sort of fellow that you would take care of if he is sick or knicked out, if you think enough of him for that, I think that really indicates he is a part of the executive family."[71]

The regulations that the DOL issued several days before the FLSA went into effect on October 24, 1938[72]—and which had generated so much interest that *The*

---

[70]"The White Collar Worker: Industry's Forgotten Men and Women," *Modern Industry*, Nov. 15, 1941, at 25, 26.

[71]"Some Employers' Questions Answered," 3 *Labor Relations Reporter* 194 (Oct. 17, 1938).

[72]James Prozzi, "Overtime Pay and the Managerial Employee: Still a 'Twilight Zone of Uncertainty,'" 41 *Lab. L.J.* 178, 179 (1990), erroneously states that the salary and

New York Times published them in full in the center of its front page[73]—specified that a bona fide and hence excluded executive employee is engaged primarily in management, directs other workers, has authority to hire and fire, has discretionary powers, and does no substantial amount of work of the same kind as the employers' covered employees. In addition to these criteria, the DOL prescribed a fixed salary level test, which the employer also had to satisfy. At $30 per week, it was a little less than three times the minimum wage for a full workweek.[74]

With the law barely in effect and despite the Wage and Hour Administrator's "Christmas gift" to the first violators—Andrews had postponed prosecutions until after the holidays[75]—efforts were already underway to seek regulatory or statutory changes.[76] At the end of November, Representative Ramspeck (D. Ga.), criticizing the hours provisions as inflexible, "suggested that it might be advisable to exempt all persons in higher wage brackets." He recommended that the House Labor Committee review the FLSA to determine where the line should be drawn.[77] A week later, Representative Fred Hartley (who in 1947 would gain abiding fame for his role in radically amending the National Labor Relations Act [NLRA]) told the Toy Manufacturers' annual convention that he would urge amending the FLSA to "eliminate the provisions on hours...on the ground that the hours regulations have an 'adverse effect upon salaried employees.'"[78] A few days later, *The New York Times* reported that on his cross-country tour Andrews had heard employers frequently refer to the overtime provision and "not understand why men who might be earning as much as $300 a week should receive

---

duties tests were not introduced until 1940.

[73]"Andrews Defines Exempt Employees," *N.Y. Times*, Oct. 20, 1938, at 1, col. 4. In general, Andrews found that the press had done a good job of acquainting the public with the FLSA. "Andrews Praises Press on Pay Law," *N.Y. Times*, Nov. 9, 1938, at 26, col. 2.

[74]29 C.F.R. § 541.1, as published in 3 *Fed. Reg.* 2518 (Oct. 19, 1938). Early on, the Wage and Hour Administrator emphasized to employers that because the regulations were conjunctive, they could not secure the exemption merely by paying salaries in excess of the regulatory threshold. "Limits Exemption Under Wages Act," *N.Y. Times*, Oct. 15, 1940, at 47, col. 1. The DOL ultimately also extended identical exclusions of executive employees to public contracts under the Walsh-Healey Act. 41 U.S.C. § 35, 38 (1988); Supplement to Rulings and Interpretations No. 2, Jan. 24, 1944, in BNA, *Wage and Hour Manual* 1117, 1181 (1944-45 ed.); 18 *Fed. Reg.* 1831 (1953).

[75]"May Ease Wage Act on Well-Paid Jobs," *N.Y. Times*, Dec. 23, 1938, at 40, col. 4, at 5.

[76]The extended congressional debates during the Seventy-Sixth Congress (1939-40) on the exclusion refute the claim that "[t]he legislative history of the Act contains no explanation for the managerial-professional exemption." Peter DeChiara, "Rethinking the Managerial-Professional Exemption of the Fair Labor Standards Act," 43 *Am. U.L. Rev.* 139, 160 (1993).

[77]*N.Y. Times*, Dec. 1, 1938, at 18, col. 6.

[78]"Toy Makers Seek Spread in Orders," *N.Y. Times*, Dec. 9, 1938, at 38, col. 1.

time-and-a-half pay after forty-four hours of work in a week.... 'Business men...see no reason why the men in the higher range of income should be classed with those who punch the time clock.... They say that these men can go fishing when they like and have other advantages.'" The amendment that employers had most frequently proposed to him was that "salaried employees guaranteed $150 a week or more and who have vacations with pay should be excluded from the overtime provisions...." The intensity of employers' objections was sufficient to prompt Andrews to conclude that they "'may lead to a suggestion to Congress' that employees be classified by income."[79] Andrews also recounted that businessmen also wondered why "a fellow not actually an executive or a professional, but perhaps engaged to the Boss' sister" should be treated like time-clock punchers.[80] The following day it was reported that the figure Andrews had heard on his trip was $150 per month, not per week.[81]

A few days later the Wage and Hour Administrator announced that he was "inclined to favor exempting" "permanent and comparatively well-paid workers...earning $300 to $400 a month...if it could be done 'without causing any harm.'" The harm Andrews had in mind was clear: "'Certainly no class of workers needs the protection of this law more than the low-paid white-collar group.... But I am talking about the worker with a guaranteed monthly wage of $300 to $400 a month who has a certain amount of discretion and who does not have to punch a time clock.'" Andrews announced that he had asked his legal staff to "determine whether well-paid groups...might be exempted from the overtime provisions by amending the definition of 'administrative' and 'executive' employees." If it was found that the definitions were too narrow, excluding many who should have been covered, he might hold hearings.[82] After Andrews had announced in late January 1939 that he would schedule hearings within a few weeks, the apparent momentum receded in February when he stated that he was putting off the scheduling because he interpreted a lack of interest in the hearings as an absence of any need for the exemption of high-salaried employees.[83]

But at the beginning of March Andrews was again reported as favoring congressional change in the coverage of highly paid white-collar employees,[84] and after a closed session of the House Labor Committee on March 14, he

---

[79]"May Bar Overtime for High Pay Group," *N.Y. Times*, Dec. 14, 1938, at 4, col. 2.

[80]"Proposal to Amend FLSA to Exempt Salaried Aides," 1 *Wage and Hour Reporter* 410 (Dec. 19, 1938).

[81]"A Correction," *N.Y. Times*, Dec. 15, 1938, at 19, col. 1.

[82]"May Ease Wage Act on Well-Paid Jobs," *N.Y. Times*, Dec. 23, 1938, at 40, col. 4, at 4-5.

[83]"Salaried Employees," 2 *Wage and Hour Reporter* 104 (Feb. 20, 1939).

[84]"Andrews Favors Wage-Hour Change," *N.Y. Times*, Mar. 3, 1939, at 19, col. 3.

announced that he was prepared to recommend several amendments including exemption from the overtime provision of all salaried employees with salaries in excess of $200 or $250 per month. House Labor Committee chairman Representative Mary Norton, who regarded the FLSA as one of her greatest achievements[85] and was personally opposed to opening the statute to the amending process, drafted an omnibus FLSA amendment bill to make the law successful and popular and to ward off the emasculation she feared from its enemies and a repetition of the attacks that had been directed at the NLRA.[86] Norton displayed no reluctance at all to amend one aspect of the FLSA:

> "Take for instance, the inclusion under the hours provisions of the so-called white-collar workers, regardless of the wages or salaries they receive. Who thinks the Congress intended that white-collar workers receiving $2,000 or $2,400 a year be covered into [sic] this law. I don't think so and I know it didn't.
>
> "When an office or other worker commands a salary of $2,000 or $2,400 a year, he should not be compelled to demand overtime at time-and-one-half pay if the exigencies of his work require him to remain on the job more than the allotted 44 hours.... On the contrary, he should expect to have to work overtime sometimes."[87]

Norton added that a majority of her committee favored a $2,000 white-collar exemption threshold, while the next day Andrews said that a $200 per month threshold might be too low, declaring his preference for a $3,000 annual threshold for salaried employees, a level familiar from the Social Security Act.[88] But two weeks later he endorsed the $200 figure.[89]

Employers had objected to paying overtime to employees with weekly incomes of $150 to $300, which amounted to 14 to 27 times the new minimum wage for a forty-four hour week, while Andrews referred to a weekly threshold of $75 to $100 or seven to nine times the minimum wage. Yet the House Labor Committee reported out an amending bill that would have given employers far more than they had asked for by writing "a guaranteed monthly salary of $200 or more" directly into the Act. That sum was chosen because any lower amount "would undoubtedly exempt a considerable number of salaried workers to whom

---

[85]On Norton's lack of stellar pro-labor or at least pro-CIO credentials, see George Paulsen, *A Living Wage for the Forgotten Man: The Quest for Fair Labor Standards 1933-1941*, at 98 (1996).

[86]"Eight Changes for FLSA," 2 *Wage and Hour Reporter* 147, 148 (1939); "House Group Talks Wage Law Change," *N.Y. Times*, Mar. 16, 1939, at 7, col. 4.

[87]"Eight Changes for FLSA" at 148.

[88]"Eight Changes for FLSA" at 148; "Wages-Hours Law Due to Be Changed," *N.Y. Times*, Mar. 17, 1939, at 36, col. 6.

[89]"Endorses Changes in Wage-Hour Law," *N.Y. Times*, Apr. 1, 1939, at 6, col. 8.

the overtime benefits of the act should extend."[90] In addition, as Norton explained on the House floor: "Of course, you gentlemen realize there is nothing in this act which limits the application of this exemption to clerical or so-called 'white collar' workers. If a ditch digger received $200 a month he would be similarly exempt under this provision."[91] Even this weekly salary level of $50, or four and half times the weekly minimum wage, would have been more protective of alleged executive workers than the $30 that the Wage and Hour Administrator had incorporated into the regulations.

Much more radical amendatory bills introduced in early 1939 would have excluded "any clerical employees, such as bookkeepers, stenographers, pay-roll clerks, auditors, cost accountants, purchasing agents, statisticians, or other office help regularly employed on a straight salary basis and given vacations with pay."[92]

After meeting with President Roosevelt on March 29, Norton filed the omnibus FLSA amendments bill exempting from the overtime provision employers with respect to those employed on a monthly basis and guaranteed a monthly salary of at least $200.[93] The Wage and Hour Administrator offered illuminating background data on the need for the change in a memorandum to Norton on the bill. Andrews sought to justify the higher income threshold by reference to the administrative problems of "numerous protests from employers" caused by the fact that the regulatory exemption was not applicable to many higher-salaried employees whose functions were not "clearly managerial or supervisory" or professional. The administrator found that it might be "an annoyance to all persons concerned, without contributing to any of the purposes which the Act was designed to achieve," to require overtime payments to highly paid nonsupervisory employees who worked long hours during emergencies, but who were free to leave early or absent themselves altogether during slack periods, and

---

[90]H.R. Rep. No. 522, 76th Cong., 1st Sess. 8-9 (1939). Norton's bill was H.R. 5435, § 5, 76th Cong., 1st Sess. See also H.R. 7133, § 5(a), 76th Cong., 1st Sess. (Rep. Barden, July 11, 1939) (guaranteed monthly salary of $150 or more or yearly salary of $1,800 or more "if such employee is not required by his employer to work any specific minimum number of hours in any workday, workweek, or other period"); H.R. 7349, § 5(a) 76th Cong., 1st Sess. (Rep. Ramspeck, July 24, 1939) (guaranteed monthly salary of $200 or more). Barden's earlier bill, H.R. 5374, in the same session, included no amendment concerning the white-collar exemptions.

[91]84 *Cong. Rec.* 5459 (1939). Norton delivered exactly the same explanation the following year. 86 *Cong. Rec.* 5122 (1940).

[92]H.R. 4363, 76th Cong., 1st Sess. (1939) (Rep. Cox). Identical language appeared in S. 2022, 76th Cong., 1st Sess. (1939) (Sen. Miller). H.R. 4645, 76th Cong., 1st Sess. (1939) (Rep. Thomas), would have excluded similar groups provided they were employed on an annual salary of at least $1,200.

[93]"The Wage-Hour Act Amendments," 2 *Wage and Hour Reporter* 167 (1939); H.R. 5435, § 5, 76th Cong., 1st Sess. (1939).

whose health and efficiency were "seldom jeopardized by poor working conditions." Andrews rejected revision of the regulatory definitions of the duties tests as unsatisfactory:

> Among the types of employees as to whom it is most frequently urged that subjecting them to a time clock is irritating and undesirable [are] private secretaries, executive assistants, cashiers, buyers, and, in general, higher paid clerical workers. Any form of description used in an administrative definition, which would exempt such persons would also probably exempt the great mass of clerical workers or else the definition would be impossible to interpret in any given case. Thus, a relaxation of the existing definition might seriously undermine the broad coverage of the Act intended by the Congress.[94]

The administrator highlighted the importance of retaining coverage of the mass of clerical workers by reference to censuses conducted in 1934 in Pennsylvania and Michigan. In the latter, half of the clerical workers earned less than $1,000, while in the former, 42 percent, including 56 percent of all female clerical workers, earned less than $17.50 per week. Since salaries were above average in those states, a large proportion of all clerical workers nationally fell below the $16.00 per week standard that the FLSA would provide for when the minimum wage reached 40 cents. And since many clerical workers worked very long hours, "ordinary clerical workers" needed the protections of the law as any other covered group. Andrews estimated that in Michigan the $200 threshold would have exempted less than 3 percent of non-executive, non-professional clerical employees (5 percent of males and one-half of one percent of females), while less than one percent would have been excluded by a $250 threshold. With respect to individual occupations in Michigan, the $200 figure would have exempted one-third of male secretaries, less than one-twentieth of male stenographers, less than 2 percent of female secretaries, and hardly any female secretaries.[95]

The new industrial unions' umbrella organization, the CIO, immediately protested the pro-employer bias of the bill as a whole. The elimination of overtime protection for salaried workers was, in its view, objectionable both because the FLSA already excluded so many of these employees and because even those earning more than $200 monthly needed and deserved legal protection.[96]

At this point in the legislative process, the momentum in favor of excluding

---

[94]"Administrator's Explanation of FLSA Changes," 2 *Wage and Hour Reporter* 168, 172, 173 (Apr. 3, 1939).

[95]"Administrator's Explanation of FLSA Changes" at 172-73.

[96]"Reaction to Norton Amendments," 2 *Wage and Hour Reporter* 183, 184 (Apr. 10, 1939).

a broad swath of white-collar workers from the overtime provision was halted by the complex forces shaping the 1939 amendments, which focused primarily on vastly expanding the scope of agricultural processing exemptions and was driven by southern representatives. The FLSA amendments proposed by them were too radical for Norton, Andrews, and the Roosevelt administration.[97] Norton declared that the president "will veto any bill that emasculates the law," which she believed had "brought greater relief to the underprivileged than any other law on the books." Andrews—who characterized all the amendments in the original Norton bill as "non-controversial"—expressed the fear that if agricultural packing and canning employers could establish the precedent of excluding large numbers of workers from the FLSA by sheer lobbying pressure "without a factual basis...no worker covered by this Act can long expect to receive its benefits. Such a legislative reward is an invitation to other employer pressure groups to secure a similar exemption for their workers." (To be sure, Andrews' apprehensions concerning exclusions driven by effective employer lobbying appeared a tad late in the day given the extensive list of such exclusions that employers had lobbied directly into the original FLSA..)[98] Finally, the Wage and Hour Administrator argued that codifying "intolerably long hours...would handicap labor unions in securing reasonable hours in their collective bargaining agreements."[99]

Specifically with regard to the white-collar amendment in the more radical bill sponsored by Graham Barden, an extreme anti-labor southern congressman, which would have lowered the exclusionary salary threshold to $150 per month, Andrews observed that if workers earning between this amount and the $200 figure that he had supported "may be worked an unlimited number of hours without overtime compensation, the purpose of the bill to spread employment in this group will be defeated." The Barden amendments, in addition to depriving hundreds of thousands of clerical workers of their right to overtime compensation—the majority of whom would presumably have been excluded by the Norton bill as well—would have excluded "all craft and skilled workers paid on a piece-rate or hourly scale where it would be to the employer's advantage to guarantee the employee $150 a month."[100]

---

[97]Paulsen, *A Living Wage for the Forgotten Man* at 139-43.

[98]FLSA, § 13, 52 Stat. at 1067.

[99]"Receding Prospect of FLSA Change," 2 *Wage and Hour Reporter* 283, 284 (June 12, 1939).

[100]"Status of FLSA Amendments," 2 *Wage and Hour Reporter* 343, 344 (July 24, 1939). In fact, the WHD could not furnish precise estimates on the number of workers who would be excluded from the FLSA if the various bills were enacted because it had abandoned a study to work up such data after discovering that they were unavailable. "Action on FLSA Changes," 2 *Wage and Hour Reporter* 351, 352 (July 31, 1939).

The controversy that employers successfully had unleashed as soon as the FLSA went into effect focused on the scope of the overtime penalty in general—did it apply only to minimum wage workers and minimum wages or also to higher-paid employees?—and its applicability to white-collar workers in particular.[101] Employers seized the upper hand in this struggle by implanting in public discourse the notion of the FLSA as merely "the Magna Charta of marginal workers in America...."[102] Even liberal newspapers, such as the *New York Post*, lent credence to this image by characterizing the FLSA's purpose as "put[ting] a floor under wages in some of the most shockingly underpaid industries...and...fix[ing] a limit to impossibly long hours."[103] In contrast, no counter-discourse succeeded in forging an equally compelling image conveying universal coverage. Consequently, the forces advocating broader applicability often fell back on legalisms, which were distinctly second-best rhetorical weapons.

One who rose above legalisms was Colonel Philip Fleming. During the short period between the time the FLSA went into effect in late 1938 and the accelerated military build-up in 1941, the Wage and Hour Administrator, who was responsible for enforcing the act, became a high-profile political-economic figure. Trying to propitiate law-abiding employers, while intimidating scoff-laws and energizing workers to file complaints against "chiselers"—as Roosevelt and others were wont to call them—he was continually engaged in "'Selling' Wage-Hour Law to Public" as "one of countless restrictions on free enterprise" and on a "market that always has functioned, and always must function, under a large number of restraints imposed by custom, voluntary organization, and law." In particular, Fleming sought to justify state intervention in the labor market as merely applying the principle of the "reservation price" to human labor that had guided businesses. In addresses to two employers organizations and a union in June 1940, he observed that during the depression:

> The sale of new automobiles would have been greatly stimulated if they had been priced at $10. But such a price would have been far below the cost of the materials used in their manufacture. The result of a $10 price simply would have been the transfer of capital from Henry Ford, General Motors and others who manufacture automobiles, to those who use them.
>
> Similarly, if all restrictions upon the labor market had been removed—if all labor legislation had been repealed and labor unions wiped out—much more labor might have been employed. But it is quite curious, I think, that while no sensible person expects

[101]See above chapter 1.

[102]Dilliard, "United States Wage and Hour Law" at 3293.

[103]"To Destroy Labor Standards," *N.Y. Post*, Apr. 15, 1940, reprinted in 86 *Cong. Rec.* at 2202 (App.).

automobile manufacturers to sell their wares at $10, many did advocate, and continue to advocate, that labor should be sold for any price it will bring, even though the result should be slow starvation. The worker's "capital" is his ability to produce, which is directly related to his health. And many people, who seem to think it is all right to destroy the worker's capital, would be horrified at the suggestion that the employer's capital should be wiped out. A seller's 'reservation price'—a price below which he will not sell—is wholly acceptable to common sense where material goods are concerned. It is no less sensible where human labor is concerned.

The Wage and Hour Law introduces such a "reservation price" into the labor market. The "reservation price" can be maintained here only by legislation strictly enforced, because in periods of widespread unemployment the worker could be forced to accept a wage below the minimum needed to maintain his "capital"—his health and efficiency—and far less than his requirements as a participant in a democratic order.

To make a reservation price for labor effective, an alternative to starvation must be provided, else many workers will ignore the Act and accept any wage, however low. A socially acceptable alternative to starvation is provided in the form of relief, unemployment insurance and other forms of social security.

The Wage and Hour Law...has the immediate social utility of preventing "capital-destroying" sales of labor, and the long run utility of shifting the employment of labor to economically justifiable enterprises—from those that cannot exist without subsidies provided by the public in the form of charity or relief....

[T]he Wage and Hour Law is a restriction...upon the "free enterprise system as a way of life" for the employer. It is also a restriction upon the "free enterprise system as a way of life" for the employee. It very drastically interferes with his freedom to work for ten cents an hour. It limits his freedom to work 60 hours a week for $5.[104]

Fleming's position could not have appealed to many newspapers—which were hardly dispassionate observers since publishers themselves were contesting coverage of numerous employees such as reporters and news carriers[105]—which were early and zealous propagandists of employers' constricted conception. *The New York Times*, for example, in July 1939 argued that even most congressmen who had voted for the FLSA thought it applied "only to submarginal labor. But by a combination of the so-called hours provisions with a joker inserted at the last minute by the conference committee the bill lent itself to a possible interpretation under which it fixed the hourly wages of all employes, no matter how high their compensation, except a few classes specifically exempted."[106] A year later the

---

[104]"'Selling' Wage-Hour Law to Public," 3 *Wage & Hour Reporter* 257, 258 (June 24, 1940). The legislative alternatives to starvation Fleming mentioned did not exist during the first several years of the depression.

[105]See Malamud, "Engineering the Middle Classes" at 2297, 2300-2301; Marc Linder, "From Street Urchins to Little Merchants: The Juridical Transvaluation of Child Newspaper Carriers," 63 *Temple L. Rev.* 829, 845-49 (1990).

[106]"Mr. Andrews Changes His Mind," *N.Y. Times*, July 22, 1939, at 14, col. 2.

newspaper was still complaining that the hours provision "brought under the act the overwhelming mass of all workers."[107] The New York *Herald Tribune* agreed that Congress intended to apply the act "only to sweatshop labor incapable of effecting through organization proper standards of its own devising."[108]

Not coincidentally, the claim that the law was designed to protect only "marginal labor" was coupled with undisguised hostility toward the statute altogether. Thus the *Times* repeatedly raised the issue of whether minimum wage regulation was the proper province of the federal government and would not be better left to the states. Since the whole point of federal intervention was to avoid a competitive race to the bottom and to act on behalf of workers in (especially southern) states whose legislatures would never enact any minimum wage legislation for men, the newspaper's argument made little sense that devolution to the states would terminate "the effort to force a procrustean uniformity on wage rates throughout the nation regardless of great differences in local conditions." The *Times* urged reexamination of the "so-called hours provisions" also on the grounds that "they are really disguised wage provisions which apply not merely to marginal or low-paid labor but to the overwhelming bulk of all labor. They have, moreover, been interpreted in such a way as in effect to set a different minimum wage for each employer."[109]

The *Herald Tribune*'s call for repeal or devolution to the states was more concrete and incendiary and more accurately reflected non-sweatshop employers' impatience with a statute they had not realized would cost them anything. Though designed to "prevent sweatshop conditions in the so-called marginal trades," the law had been interpreted by the Wage and Hour Division in such a "fantastic" manner as to "govern all industry, marginal or other...." The editors illustrated what they viewed as the Labor Department's perverse enforcement policy by reference to a test case it had brought against a commercial building

---

[107]"Wage-Hour Rulings," *N.Y. Times*, Oct. 16, 1940, at 22, col. 3. The original FLSA bill reflected the interpretation favored by the *Times*, but that language failed to survive enactment: "it shall be the policy of the Board to establish such minimum wage standards as will affect only those employees in need of legislative protection without interfering with the voluntary establishment of appropriate differentials and higher standards for other employees in the occupation to which such standards relate." S. 2475, § 12(6), 75th Cong., 1st Sess. (May 24, 1937).

[108]"Wage-Hour Absurdities," N.Y. *Herald Tribune*, Apr. 26, 1940, reprinted in 86 *Cong. Rec.* 2458 (1940) (Appendix).

[109]"Amending the Wage-Hour Law," *N.Y. Times*, Apr. 12, 1940, at 22, col. 2, 3. Even the *Washington Post*, which did not promote devolution to the states, agreed editorially that a "great mistake was made initially in providing for comprehensive coverage of industries in all parts of the country. The establishment of uniform minimum-wage rates and maximum-hour standards was likewise a blunder." It therefore urged revisions aimed at a "more workable and less rigid" law. "The Barden Bill," *Wash. Post*, Apr. 18, 1940, reprinted in 86 *Cong. Rec.* at 2202, 2203 (App.).

owner in New York City, which paid, pursuant to a union contract, its building service employees an average weekly wage of $29, "far above the minimum required" by the law, for a 48-hour week. Since the FLSA at the time set 42 hours as the threshold for overtime premiums, the DOL demanded back overtime wages: "'to blazes with the fact that these toilers are not engaged in a marginal industry, that by collective bargaining they have made their own terms....'" As written and administered, the FLSA, in the *Herald Tribune*'s view, would soon rival the NLRA in its destruction of free enterprise.[110]

The pro-states-rights stance of the metropolis's most respected dailies was puzzling since they were aligning themselves with the most reactionary opponents of the New Deal's modest intervention into capitalism's dysfunctionality—southern racists—who viewed the FLSA's main object as "overcom[ing]the splendid gifts of God to the South."[111] What was odd about this overlap was the fact that southern opponents correctly "charged that the business interests of the industrial East were responsible for enactment of the law because they hoped it would kill off competition from the South and West."[112] Yet these northern corporations were otherwise the New York newspapers' constituents.[113]

After more legislative wrangling between the House Labor and Rules Committees, Representative Ramspeck's so-called compromise bill deleted the $200 salary threshold from the Norton bill. Instead, it inserted a blanket exemption for all industries from the overtime provision with respect to employees not worked more than 160 hours per month..[114] On July 27, 1939, Norton's House Labor Committee reported another bill containing this provision, which would simply have excluded "any employee employed at a guaranteed monthly salary in excess of that required by this Act who does not work more than one hundred and sixty hours per month."[115] However, legislative efforts to reach a compromise on amending the FLSA in 1939 broke down in July when Andrews announced withdrawal of his support for the salary definition of excluded white-collar employees on the grounds that the unions (especially the Newspaper Guild) that supported him and his enforcement efforts opposed it.[116]

---

[110]"Wage-Hour Absurdities."

[111]81 *Cong. Rec.* 7882 (1937) (Sen. "Cotton" Ed Smith, D. S. Car.).

[112]"Confused Procedure," *Wash. Post*, reprinted in 86 *Cong. Rec.* 2507 (Apr. 29, 1940) (Appendix) (date of editorial unidentified).

[113]For an overview of *Times* editorial opinion on the minimum wage through World War II, see Richard McKenzie, *Times Change: The Minimum Wage and the New York Times* 13-23 (1994).

[114]"Action on FLSA Changes," 2 *Wage and Hour Reporter* 351 (July 31, 1939).

[115]H.R. 6406, § 5, 76th Cong., 1st Sess. (July 27, 1939); H. Rep. 1376, 76th Cong., 1st Sess. 5 (1939).

[116]"Andrews Shifts on 'White Collar,'" *N.Y. Times*, July 21, 1939, at 5, col. 1; Paulsen,

In 1940 Congress again took up the issue of excluding higher-paid workers from the premium overtime provision together with other amendments that would have constricted coverage, excluding many agricultural processing workers.[117] Supporters of these amendments were derisively known as "the dime-an-hour bloc."[118] Of the three principal bills, both Norton's administration bill (H.R. 5435)—viewed by labor as "the 'least obnoxious'"[119]—and Representative Ramspeck's compromise bill (H.R. 7349) would have excluded all employees employed at a guaranteed monthly salary of at least $200, while Barden's openly pro-employer bill (H.R. 7133) would have excluded all white-collar employees with salaries of at least $150 monthly if they were not required to work any specified number of hours. The WHD conservatively estimated that the Norton and Ramspeck bills would exclude an additional 125,000 employees from the hours provision, while 325,000 would be excluded under Barden's bill.[120]

As blatantly restrictive and antilabor as Barden's white-collar provision was, *The New York Times* speculated that it might perversely expand the law's scope. Since the newspaper asserted "almost universal agreement" that the FLSA was not intended to apply to "highly paid workers," it feared that by "'[r]estricting'" the FLSA to workers earning less than $150 monthly, Barden's bill had "the incidental effect of extending the application to all persons getting up to that amount. Instead of applying merely to the lowest paid workers, the act would then definitely cover much the greater part of our whole working population."[121] "The most important needed amendment," from the perspective of the *Times*, was "removal...of the mandatory blanket 'maximum hour' provisions...."[122]

The renewed legislative wrangling in April 1940 augured success for the anti-labor southern congressional coalition that "seemed able to dictate terms to the New Dealers...."[123] But by the end of the month, with the knowledge that

---

A Living Wage at 142. Nevertheless, when Andrews resigned two months later the *Times* speculated that his administration had not greatly pleased some unions. "Andrews Out, Fleming In," *N.Y. Times*, Oct. 19, 1939, at 22, col. 2.

[117]"House to Consider Wage Act Changes Early Next Week," *N.Y. Times*, Apr. 9, 1940, at 1, col. 1.

[118]"Here's That Bloc Again," *Washington Daily News*, Apr. 16, 1940, reprinted in 86 *Cong. Rec.* at 2202 (App.).

[119]Henry Dorris, "Wage Law Revision Nears House Test," *N.Y. Times*, Apr. 22, 1940, at 1, col. 5.

[120]The Wage and Hour Administrator's useful section-by-section comparison of the bills was published by Representative Norton in 86 *Cong. Rec.* at 2260-64 (App.). The estimates are explained at *id.*, 2264 n.g.

[121]"Wage-Hour Amendments," *N.Y. Times*, Apr. 25, 1940, at 22, col. 3 (editorial).

[122]"Wage-Hour Amendments," *N.Y. Times*, Apr. 29, 1940, at 14, col. 2 (editorial).

[123]Henry Dorris, "House Opens Way to Wide Changing of Wage-Hour Act," *N.Y. Times,* Apr. 26, 1940, at 1, col. 3. On the complex agricultural-sectional forces behind

Congress would be unable to override a certain presidential veto of the drastic Barden amendments, neither side could muster a majority even in the House, and having recommitted the original Norton bill, "[t]here was a rush for the doors, many hastening to catch trains for Louisville to see the Kentucky Derby."[124]

Although Norton's amendment failed in 1939 and 1940,[125] it and other legislative proposals setting the salary threshold as high as $350 per month[126] underscored the importance that Congress attached to "comparatively high" market-generated salaries as a guarantee against exploitation that rendered legislated protection against (unpaid) long hours unnecessary.[127] To be sure, proemployer proponents like Representative Barden preferred the nonsensical argument that without the amendment, those "who have responsible jobs, and sometimes like to go to a baseball game, play golf, or take an afternoon for fishing, either must forego [sic] this pleasure or violate the act."[128]

Even part of the press that in 1940 supported the FLSA in principle, such as the *Washington Star*, editorialized that "the basic purpose of the act would not suffer if white-collar workers, earning $150 or $200 a month, were exempted...."[129] The *St. Louis Post-Dispatch*, which opposed "emasculatory amendments," agreed that the law unfairly penalized "employers who pay their employees well over the minimum scale, perhaps as much as several times the

---

congressional alignments, see Henry Dorris, "Rural-Urban Split Looming in House in Wage Act Fight," *N.Y. Times*, Apr. 27, 1940, at 1, col. 1. See generally, James Patterson, *Congressional Conservatism and the New Deal: The Growth of the Conservative Coalition in Congress, 1933-1939* (1967); Richard Bensel, *Sectionalism and American Political Development: 1880-1980*, at 147-74 (1987 [1984]).

[124]"Andrews Criticizes Plans on Wage Cuts," *N.Y. Times*, Apr. 28, 1940, sect. III, at 6, col. 6; Henry Dorris, "Wage Bill Beaten; Republicans Join with New Dealers," *N.Y. Times*, May 1, 1940, at 1, col. 1; Henry Dorris, "Wage Act Changes Killed for Session by a Recommittal," *N.Y. Times*, May 4, 1940, at 1, col. 1 (quote).

[125]84 *Cong. Rec.* 6620-22 (1939); 86 *Cong. Rec.* 5500-5501 (1940).

[126]See Frank Cooper, "The Coverage of the Fair Labor Standards Act and Other Problems in Its Interpretation," 6 *Law & Contemp. Probs.* 333, 348 (1939).

[127]H.R. Rep. No. 522 at 8-9. The Minimum Wage Study Commission thus erred in asserting: "The current salary test as a basic criterion used to identify exempt workers implicitly introduces a minimum wage type concept in the administration of this provision which is counter to the original intent of the exemption." The Commission immediately contradicted its own position by conceding that Congress excluded these workers because "they were believed to be typically earning salaries well above the minimum wage level" and that "[a] relatively low salary test...defeats the 'good faith' aspects of the test." Conrad Fritsch & Kathy Vandell, "Exemptions from the Fair Labor Standards Act: Outside Salesworkers and Executive, Administrative, and Professional Employees," in 4 *Report of the Minimum Wage Study Commission* 235, 240, 244 (1981).

[128]86 *Cong. Rec.* at 4925 (Rep. Barden). The argument is specious because employees cannot violate the FLSA.

[129]"Wage-Hour Law," *Wash. Star*, Apr. 28, 1940, reprinted in 86 *Cong. Rec.* at 2508 (App.).

minimum" by requiring them to pay overtime to boot. Indeed, the newspaper believed that the law also unfairly placed many employees "in an unfortunate position": "They must either turn in memorandums for extra pay which they would prefer not to ask for or blink the time beyond the maximum which they may work in a week. ... In any case, persons earning approximately $2,000 a year are not those for whom Federal wage-hour legislation was intended. They may not be in the upper brackets, but they are not the bottom-rung workers in whose behalf the law was passed."[130]

The year 1940 also witnessed extensive DOL hearings on the exclusions of executive, administrative, and professional employees, culminating in the so-called Stein Report, which contains the most detailed official explanation of the purpose of the exclusion and the crucial function of the salary test in distinguishing between protected and unprotected employees. The DOL took as its point of departure that it "does not have the power to exempt *all* salaried workers" since "there is little advantage in salaried employment if it merely serves as a cloak for long hours [and] may well conceal excessively low hourly rates of pay."[131] Indeed, the DOL heard testimony in 1940 "that, as a result of the exemption from overtime payments accorded executives, employees in non-executive positions working the same number of hours and being paid at a lower rate will frequently surpass the executives in total compensation received."[132] Neglect of the need to protect non-bona fide executive employees was rooted in "a serious misreading of the Act [that] assume[d] that Congress meant to discourage long hours of work only where the wages paid were close to the statutory minimum. Living conditions can be improved and work spread even where wages are comparatively high." Moreover, the Stein Report concluded, "an astonishingly large percentage" of salaried white collar workers, many of whom were women, received low wages.[133]

Finally, and most centrally, the Stein Report observed:

> The term "executive" implies a certain prestige, status, and importance. Employees who qualify under the definition are denied the protection of the Act. It must be assumed that they enjoy compensatory privileges and this assumption will clearly fail if they are not

---

[130]"The Wage-Hour Battle," *St. Louis Post-Dispatch*, May 2, 1940, reprinted in 86 *Cong. Rec.* at 2721, 2722 (App.).

[131]U.S. DOL, *"Executive, Administrative, Professional...Outside Salesman" Redefined: Report and Recommendations of the Presiding Officer at Hearings Preliminary to Redefinition* 8, 7 (1940).

[132]*Id.* at 7 n.25.

[133]*Id.* at 8, 9. A survey conducted by the New York State Department of Labor in 1937 revealed that the average weekly earnings of male office workers in factories ($44.76) were double women's ($22.41). "Earnings of Office Workers in New York State Factories, October 1937," 46 *Monthly Lab. Rev.* 480 (1938).

paid a salary substantially higher than the wages guaranteed as a mere minimum under Section 6 of the Act. In no other way can there be assurance that Section 13 (a)(1) will not invite evasion of Section 6 and Section 7 for large numbers of workers to whom the wage and hour provisions should apply. Indeed, if an employer states that a particular employee is of sufficient importance to his firm to be classified as an "executive" employee and thereby exempt from the protections of the Act, the best single test of the employer's good faith in attributing importance to the employee's services is the amount of money he pays for them.[134]

In October 1940, on the same day that the Wage and Hour Administrator made the Stein Report public, he also published a revised set of white collar regulations, which again merited coverage in the center of the front page of *The New York Times*.[135] While declaring that "white-collar workers would continue to be protected from exploitation as to minimum wages and working hours," and especially from "long hours without overtime payment to make up for managerial inefficiency or to keep down payrolls," Administrator Philip Fleming stressed that "the new regulations were written under the belief held by him and his associates that the Wage and Hour Law was not to cover people like Hollywood stars or types of business administrators earning high salaries."[136] Although the major revisions dealt with the exclusion of so-called administrative employees (and resulted in the exclusion of an additional 100,000 of them),[137] the change made in the definition of executive employees is basically still in effect today.

In December, Fleming virtually boasted to the NAM of how accommodating he had been:

> [I]ndustry kept asking us about the important fellow in large organizations who didn't boss people—the assistant to the president, the personnel adviser, the purchasing agent. He is considered an executive. He eats in the executive dining room. Anyway, his salary is so high that he were paid time and half for overtime, he would have serious doubts he earned it.
>
> We took care of that fellow in our new definitions. We termed him an administrative employee. We accepted the idea that his work is too important to measure in hours. But we asked that that importance be measured on the pay check. We required that the pay

[134]U.S. DOL, *"Executive, Administrative, Professional"* at 19.

[135]Louis Stark, "Wage Head Revises White Collar Pay," *N.Y. Times*, Oct. 14, 1940, at 1, col. 4.

[136]Stark, "Wage Head Revises White Collar Pay" at 1, col. 4, at 11, col. 1.

[137]Stark, "Wage Head Revises White Collar Pay" at 1, col. 4. Two weeks later Fleming claimed that "the exemptions from the maximum hour limitations would not be so extensive as had at first been thought." "Wage Law Terms Put in New Light," *N.Y. Times*, Oct. 28, 1940, at 19, col. 1.

check be at least $200 a month.[138]

The provision in the 1938 regulatory definition, under which an excluded executive employee could engage in "no substantial amount of work" of the same kind as covered employees, had "caused more questions than any other requirements."[139] Fleming did relax this "exceedingly troublesome phrase"[140] to read: "whose hours of work of the same nature as that performed by nonexempt employees do not exceed twenty percent of the number of hours worked in the workweek by the nonexempt employees under his direction." In addition, a proviso made even this limitation inapplicable to "an employee who is in sole charge of an independent establishment or a physically separated branch establishment."[141] (The accommodation failed to satisfy the NAM, which in 1941 unsuccessfully requested that the WHD change its interpretation by using the employer in question rather than the industry as the standard by which to judge how much work putative managerial employees were performing of the same nature as that performed by nonmanagerial employees. The WHD rejected the proffered interpretation because it would have exempted many non-executive employees.)[142] Fleming also rejected criticism of the $30 weekly threshold as too high because he believed that it was incorrect to describe anyone paid less than that amount as an executive; moreover, the new regulations no longer permitted exclusion of any hourly paid employee no matter how high his or her wages.[143]

Employers in the wholesale distributive trades had been particularly eager to "convince the Wage-hour Administrator that the boss' secretary is an executive in her own right...." The "rub" arose from the "does no substantial amount of

---

[138]Philip Fleming, Address before the NAM, New York City, Dec. 12, 1940, in 86 *Cong. Rec.* at 6693, 6694 (App.).

[139]Stark, "Wage Head Revises White Collar Pay" at 11, col. 1.

[140]Letter from Philip Fleming to Sen. Elbert Thomas (Nov. 19, 1940), in 86 *Cong. Rec.* at 6613, 6615 (App.).

[141]29 C.F.R. § 541.1 (f), as published in 5 *Fed. Reg.* 4077 (1940). Currently, after the incorporation of retail and service employment, the provision reads: "Who does not devote more than 20 percent, or, in the case of an employee of a retail or service establishment who does not devote as much as 40 percent, of his hours of work in the workweek to activities which are not directly and closely related to the performance of the [supervisory] work described in paragraphs (a) through (d) of this section." 29 C.F.R. § 541.1 (e) (1999).

[142]"Division Refuses to Redefine 'Executive,'" 4 *Wage and Hour Reporter* 509-10 (Sept. 22, 1941). The WHD gave as an example of an unjustified exemption an employee who performed supervisory work 1 or 2 hours daily and bookkeeping the rest of the day in a firm that had no other bookkeeper. H.R. 8624, 76th Cong., 3d Sess (1940), would have written the language suggested by the NAM directly into the definition of an employee employed in a bona fide executive capacity.

[143]Letter from Fleming to Sen. Thomas, in 86 *Cong. Rec.* at 6615 (App.).

work" clause: "The boss' secretary could meet all the other requirements, but by taking dictation or typing letters—work similar to that done by nonexempt employees—she must come under the act. Wholesalers urged that this clause be stricken from the definition...." [144] Fleming, in an effort to pressure employers not to work low-paid secretaries overtime, did not accommodate this particularly outlandish request. As he explained to the NAM:

> [I]f there are employees in factories or offices who need the protection of an overtime penalty, the girl clerical worker is one of them.
>
> We all know her. We all like her. We know the sound of her high heels clicking in at 9 o'clock. ... Your wife approves of the way she dresses and you know that is the highest compliment your wife can pay another woman. ... She decorates the office and makes it a pleasanter place to work.
>
> There isn't much in the game for her. Yet she's as loyal and as willing to work long hours as the most ambitious of your junior executives.
>
> And our inspections reveal that she frequently does work long hours. Usually because of inefficient supervision, and sometimes because some ambitious executive wants to make a record. She is unorganized and she was unprotected until the wage and hour law went into effect.
>
> Well, now when she works more than 40 hours a week, she is paid time and a half for overtime. [C]ompliance is spreading and time and a half for overtime means that she is not going to work long hours often. Management is going to regard such overtime charges in the same light as demurrage on freight cars that could just as well have been unloaded. And I think this will make for greater efficiency. Your executive who gets going around 3 o'clock in the afternoon will have to get started closer to 9 a.m.[145]

More recently, employers' efforts to excuse their extraction of payless overwork from secretaries has stood the entire policy underlying the FLSA on its head by blaming the victim. Inverting and perverting the importance that the Stein Report attributed to "prestige," employers have sought to explain away their violation of the overtime provision by claiming: "Despite working overtime, many secretaries insist on being exempt because they view it as a sign of prestige...."[146]

These struggles over whether white-collar workers would be subject to wage

---

[144]"Who's an Executive?" *Bus. Wk.*, Apr. 20, 1940, at 34.

[145]Philip Fleming, "Two Years of the Wage and Hour Law," in *Wage and Hour Manual* 70, 72 (1941 ed.) (address delivered Dec. 12, 1940 to the American Congress of Industry of the NAM).

[146]This comment was made by the president of a firm that conducted a survey of 600 companies finding that 46 percent "exempt one or more of their secretarial levels from overtime pay" even though "27% of this group believe some exemptions wouldn't stand up to Labor Department scrutiny." Christopher Conte, "Labor Letter," *Wall St. J.*, Mar. 9, 1993, at A1, col. 5 (Westlaw).

and hour regulation can be understood only in connection with the more fundamental campaign, analyzed in Chapter 1, that broad segments of the employing class were conducting against the premium overtime payment provision in the FLSA. Their principal objective was limiting time and a half liability to the minimum wage, thus relieving firms of any obligation to pay overtime on wages and salaries in excess of this largely sub-market rate. Even as employers pressed this position, the business press itself undermined their claims that exempt white collar workers neither needed nor expected overtime payments. For example, *Nation's Business* reported in 1941 that "until recently" the lack of overtime had been offset by advantages such as annual vacation, sick leave without deductions, holiday pay, time off to take care of personal matters, job security, and good chances for promotion:

> But in recent years these differentials in favor of the salaried man have been gradually diminishing. ... This narrowing of the differentials between salaried employees and wage earners has been an important factor in fostering the growth of unions among foremen, clerical workers and other groups formerly considered distinct from manual labor.
>
> It is natural, therefore, that many exempt employees question the fairness of putting in unlimited overtime without extra compensation....[147]

The magazine went on to recommend payment of time and a half to "office workers in the lower exempted positions—those who are closest to the rank and file and whose duties differ only slightly from those of the non-exempts.... It is true that employees are closely related to management, but they may be even closer to labor. In the matter of compensation, they are likely to be more interested in the size of their pay checks than in the maintenance of their status in the managerial ranks. These employees have been subject to much exploitation in some companies."[148] (By the 1950s, voluntary payment of overtime to "exempt supervisors," designed in part to "maintain adequate differentials between supervisors and the supervised," was common though by no means universal.)[149]

Despite such insights, many employer associations continued adamantly to urge a vast expansion of the category of excluded white-collar workers. After World War II, some proposed elimination of the salary test altogether and complete reliance on a much broader definition of executive and professional employees taken from the recently enacted Taft-Hartley amendments to the

---

[147]Edward Cowdrick, "When the Boss Works Late," *Nation's Business*, May 1941, at 17, 18-19.

[148]Cowdrick, "When the Boss Works Late" at 114-15.

[149]"Overtime Pay Practices for Exempt Supervisors," 21 *Management Record* 110-13, 134-38, at 110 (Apr. 1959).

NLRA. At FLSA hearings in 1947, an umbrella organization of 46 industrial associations (which grew to 57 organizations by 1948 when it submitted the same testimony under the name National Industrial Council, an arm of the NAM)[150] recommended adopting Taft-Hartley's definition of "supervisor" for executive employees under the FLSA. The increased scope is obvious from the wording: "any individual having authority, in the interest of the employer, to hire, transfer, suspend, lay off, recall, promote, discharge, assign, reward, or discipline other employees, or responsibility to direct them, or to adjust their grievances, or effectively to recommend such action, if...the exercise of such authority is not of a merely routine or clerical nature, but requires the use of independent judgment."[151] These employers stressed that adoption of the NLRA definition also admirably served another purpose—"permit[ting] employers freely to manage their enterprises without outside interference, in order to produce the great quantities of goods now needed not only for domestic consumption but for the entire world."[152] The Chamber of Commerce of the United States also urged adoption of the NLRA definitions.[153] However, after the WHD heard testimony on this issue in connection with proposed revisions of the regulation in 1947 and 1948, it concluded that the different purposes that the definitions served in the two statutes did not warrant adoption of a single definition, especially since the result would be denial of FLSA protection to supervisors already deprived of collective bargaining rights.[154]

After employers had successfully prevailed upon Congress to eliminate the portal-pay suits in the first session of the Eightieth Congress,[155] Senator Joseph Ball introduced the Republicans' abortive omnibus FLSA revision bill in March 1948, which would have excluded from the overtime provision any employee employed on a salary basis amounting to $100 or more per week.[156] At the end

---

[150]*Fair Labor Standards Act Amendments: Hearings Before a Subcommittee of the Senate Committee on Labor and Public Welfare*, 80th Cong., 2d Sess., Pt. 2 at 1203-13 (1948).

[151]29 U.S.C. § 152(11) (1994).

[152]4 *Minimum Wage Standards and Other Parts of the Fair Labor Standards Act of 1938: Hearings Before Subcommittee No. 4 of the House Committee on Education and Labor*, 80th Cong., 1st Sess. 2859 (1948).

[153]*Fair Labor Standards Act Amendments: Hearings Before a Subcommittee of the Senate Committee on Labor and Public Welfare*, 80th Cong., 2d Sess., Pt. 1 at 542 (1948) (statement of H. Ramel, member of labor-relations committee of Chamber of Commerce).

[154]DOL, Wage and Hour and Public Contracts Divisions, *Report and Recommendations on Proposed Revisions of Regulations, Part 541 Defining the Terms "Executive" "Administrative" "Professional" "Local Retailing Capacity" "Outside Salesman"* 3-6 (1949).

[155]See below chapter 3.

[156]S. 2386, § 13(b)(3), 80th Cong., 2d Sess. (1948).

of 1949, the DOL reinforced the Stein Report's concerns when, in response to a petition filed by the left-wing United Electrical, Radio and Machine Workers to raise the salary test to $500 per month[157]—a standard that the American Newspaper Guild supported and publishers and editors denounced as "'utterly fantastic'" for small newspapers in 1948 at hearings on reporters' status as professionals[158]—it introduced, "for administrative convenience," a so-called short test in association with a higher ("upset") salary floor of $100 per week. The sole non-monetary requirements attached to it were (and remain) that the employee's primary duty be management and that he customarily and regularly supervise at least two other employees.[159]

3. Obsolescence of an Exclusion

[W]here a regulation's rationality is dependent on current socioeconomic conditions periodic review is essential to preserve that rationality.[160]

In the wake of inflation caused by World War II, the WHD realized in the late 1940s that "more realistic" salary levels had to be set: "A $30 a week test for 'executive' is obviously obsolete, when office boys, for example, earn an average of $30.52 in New York City, $28.27 in Atlanta and $37.85 in San Francisco."[161] By periodically raising the mandatory minimum salary test level in tandem with increases in the statutory minimum wage itself between 1940 and 1975, the DOL adhered to the principle—which "has been recognized administratively and approved judicially" and which most employer groups also originally supported—that "the weightiest test is the amount of compensation paid by the employer."[162] During the first Nixon Administration, for example, the DOL noted

---

[157]12 *Fed. Reg.* 6896 (1947). The UE petition was filed on Oct. 18, 1946. DOL, Wage and Hour and Public Contracts Divisions, *Report and Recommendations on Proposed Revisions of Regulations, Part 541* at 2.

[158]"Reporters' Hours Argued at Hearing," *N.Y. Times*, Jan. 14, 1948, at 15, col. 1.

[159]DOL, Wage and Hour and Public Contracts Divisions, *Report and Recommendations on Proposed Revisions of Regulations, Part 541* at 22-24; 29 C.F.R. § 541.1, as published in 14 *Fed. Reg.* 7705, 7706 (1949); 40 *Fed. Reg.* 7092 (1975).

[160]Hazard v. Sullivan, 827 F. Supp. at 1353.

[161]DOL, Wage and Hour and Public Contracts Divisions, *Report and Recommendations on Proposed Revisions of Regulations, Part 541* at 10. See also DOL, Wage and Hour and Public Contracts Divisions, *Report and Recommendations on Proposed Revision of Regulations, Part 541 Under the Fair Labor Standards Act Defining the Terms "Executive" "Administrative" "Professional" "Local Retailing Capacity" "Outside Salesman"* 4-10 (1958).

[162]Jones v. Bethlehem-Fairfield Shipyard at 91 (quotation); Fritsch & Vandell,

that:

> If the salary tests are set at a level where virtually everyone who meets the other requirements for exemption has earnings in excess of that amount, and many nonexempt workers also have earnings in excess of that amount, then the tests are no longer a useful tool for separating those who are clearly nonexempt from those who are probably exempt.[163]

Similarly, in justifying an increase in the executive salary threshold in the wake of increases in the minimum wage and the cost of living, the Ford Administration DOL stated that an interim increase was needed—pending completion of a study of salaries after which a further increase would be implemented—to insure that the test remain "realistic and effective as qualifying requirements for exemption from the Act's monetary provisions...."[164]

By 1978, after the ratio between the executive long-test salary and the weekly minimum wage had fallen to its second lowest level ever (1.5:1), President Carter's Wage and Hour Administrator announced that the interim salary test "no longer provide[s] basic minimum safeguards and protection for the economic position of the low paid executive...employees as contemplated by section 13(a)(1)" of the FLSA and current regulations.[165] Because neither the proposed increase to $225 in 1978 (which would have raised the ratio to 2.1:1) nor any other increase has ever again been implemented, by the time the minimum wage reached $4.25 in 1991, the ratio fell below 1:1. In other words, employers could perversely yet lawfully pay long-test executive employees salaries lower than the minimum wage, while requiring them to work overtime gratis.

Table 2-1 shows the course of the relationship between the minimum wage and the executive long- and short-test salaries from 1938 to the present.

Precisely such mathematical relationships expressly underlay the DOL's calibration of the salary level during the thirty-five-year period of its uncontested validity. Thus in 1963, the Wage and Hour Administrator stated that setting the long-test salary at eighty times the hourly minimum wage was "not unreasonable," but that a multiple of only sixty-four, that is, a ratio of 1.6:1,

> which is no more than the minimum wage employee will earn for a 56-hour week, will not...be truly descriptive of the wages of executive...employees in retail and service establishments, nor will it serve as a useful criterion in identifying those who are

---

"Exemptions from the Fair Labor Standards Act" at 243.

[163]DOL, *Earnings Data Pertinent to a Review of the Salary Tests* at 3.

[164]39 *Fed. Reg.* 29,603 (1974); 40 *Fed. Reg.* 7091 (1975).

[165]43 *Fed. Reg.* 14,688 (1978).

employed in a bona fide executive...capacity.[166]

Table 2-1: Ratio of Salary Tests to the Minimum Wage, 1938-97					
Year	Long-test salary ($/week)	Ratio to minimum wage	Short-test salary ($/week)	Ratio to minimum wage	Minimum wage ($/ week)
1938	30	2.7	none	—	11
1939	30	2.4	none	—	12.60
1940	30	2.5	none	—	12
1945	30	1.9	none	—	16
1950	55	1.8	100	3.3	30
1956	55	1.4	100	2.5	40
1959	80	2.0	125	3.1	40
1961	80	1.7	125	2.7	46
1963	100	2.0	150	3.0	50
1967	100	1.8	150	2.7	56
1968	100	1.6	150	2.3	64
1970	125	2.0	200	3.1	64
1974	125	1.6	200	2.5	80
1975	155	1.8	250	3.0	84
1976	155	1.7	250	2.7	92
1978	155	1.5	250	2.4	106
1979	155	1.3	250	2.2	116
1980	155	1.25	250	2.0	124
1981	155	1.2	250	1.9	134
1990	155	1.0	250	1.6	152
1991	155	0.9	250	1.5	170
1996	155	0.8	250	1.3	190
1997	155	0.75	250	1.2	206

Sources: 29 U.S.C. § 206 (a)(1) (various years); U.S. Department of Labor, *Earnings Data Pertinent to a Review of the Salary Tests*, tab. 1 at 11.[167]

---

[166] 28 *Fed. Reg.* 7002, 7005 (1963).

[167] The table includes every year in which either the minimum wage or the salary test was increased; the short-test salary was not introduced until 1950. The weekly minimum wage is computed as the product of the statutory hourly minimum wage and the maximum weekly number of sub-overtime hours (which was 44 in 1938-39, 42 in 1939-40, and 40 thereafter). The proposed increases that the Reagan Administration suspended indefinitely would have raised the long-test salary to $225 in 1981 and $250 in 1983; the ratio to the minimum wage would have risen to 1.7 and 1.9 respectively. Similarly, the proposed

The following example shows how a regulation that may once have been reasonably designed to protect supervisory employees against inordinate overreaching, has, through the mere passage of time, become irrational. In 1975, when the minimum wage was $2.10 per hour, an "exempt" assistant manager earning $155 per week had to work twenty-two hours of overtime before her salary failed to cover the minimum wage plus overtime (on the basis of the minimum wage). By 1997, the same "bona fide executive" already reached this point after 30 hours of straight time. Seen from a different perspective: by 1991, only a weekly salary of $319.30, or more than double the salary test level, would have held her harmless against twenty-two hours of overtime (at the minimum wage). Indeed, by 1997, even the short-test salary, which is supposed to be high enough to avoid ambiguity in distinguishing bona fide from mala fide executives, had fallen to a mere 20 per cent above the minimum wage.

In spite of the manifest dysfunctionality of the 1975 interim salary test, which had already "become obsolete" by 1978, the Carter Administration, "[a]s a result of unexpected delays," the cause of which it did not reveal, waited another three years before it issued a final rule.[168] In 1981 Donald Elisburg, the Assistant Secretary of Labor for Employment Standards Administration, stressed: "The purpose of the salary test has always been to prevent evasion of the FLSA by the designation of an excessive number of workers as executives..., with minimal duties designed barely to meet the duties and responsibilities requirements of the exemption." Repeating the DOL's forty-year-old position that the salary level is "the best single test" of employers' bona fides in classifying their employees as executives—a position that management itself has adopted in developing personnel criteria for the voluntary payment of overtime to certain upper-level "exempt" employees[169]—Elisburg observed that in order to fulfill that function, the salary test "ha[s] to be increased periodically to take into account the higher salary levels that...are in fact paid to bona fide executive...employees."[170] Because the exclusion of managers had always been based on the fact that they enjoy "compensatory privileges and benefits which are superior to those of other employees," the salary test level "must be periodically adjusted" to reflect not only increases in the minimum wage but also in average salaries of executive employees.[171]

---

increases in the short-test salary to $320 and $345 in 1981 and 1983 would have raised the minimum wage ratio to 2.4 and 2.6 respectively.

[168]46 *Fed. Reg.* 3011, 3012 (1981).

[169]Jerome Rosow, "Overtime Pay Policies for Executive, Administrative, and Professional Employees," 30 (2) *Personnel* 105-12 at 106 (Sept. 1953).

[170]46 *Fed Reg.* at 3011.

[171]46 *Fed. Reg.* at 3016.

In announcing a new executive long-test salary of $225 for 1981 and $250 for 1983 superseding the old salary test, which it variously described as "seriously outdated," "ineffective[]," and "virtually useless as a guide for employers and the Department of Labor in determining FLSA exemption status," the DOL urged employers to understand that the increase would enhance regulatory certainty: "Formerly, employers could rely on the salary test as a good indicator of whether an employee was likely to be exempt or not. Now that the test levels are lagging so far behind actual salaries, employers who do so could be misled into inadvertent noncompliance with the FLSA."[172] (The DOL apparently regards its own regulation as a guide for employers only, showing no concern for whether the test reliably instructs employees as to whether they are lawfully or unlawfully being "exempt" from the burden of being paid the minimum wage and premium wages for overtime.)[173] Whether disingenuous or merely self-delusional, the DOL's obfuscatory assertion makes no sense: by complying with an "obsolete" salary test, employers assumed and (continue to assume) no risk whatsoever of being deemed in violation of the FLSA by the DOL—so long as their employees perform the aforementioned "minimal duties designed barely to meet the duties and responsibilities requirements of the exemption."[174]

Instead, employers have gained the certainty of immunity from liability under the FLSA for extracting unpaid overtime hours from employees without alternatives. This employer overreaching vis-à-vis low-paid hybrid supervisor-grunts is documented, for example, by appellate litigation against Burger King Corporation. Its "deliberate corporate policy" of requiring "exempt" assistant managers to spend more than half of their fifty-four hour workweeks performing the same work as their supervisees was driven by the firm's desire to avoid paying premium overtime rates or any wages at all: "Were the Assistant Managers to abstain from production work, more hourly employees would be needed, 'thereby "blowing payroll"—that is, spending more than the store's budgeted amount for hourly labor.'"[175] Such practices directly subvert the mandatory overtime premium's goal of applying financial pressure on employers

---

[172]46 *Fed. Reg.* at 3016.

[173]Employers, in turn, prefer self-help: "It is not customary...to ask the [DOL] to classify all of a firm's employees, for...the agency is generally more liberal with overtime benefits than the average employer would be. Most employers classify their own personnel...." Gottlieb, *Overtime Compensation* at 7.

[174]46 *Fed. Reg.* at 3011.

[175]Donovan v. Burger King Corp., 675 F.2d 516, 518-19 (2d Cir. 1982) (citing the trial court opinion). *See also* Donovan v. Burger King Corp., 672 F.2d 221 (1st Cir. 1982); Marshall v. Erin Food Services, Inc. d/b/a Burger King, 672 F.2d 229 (1st Cir. 1982). As the DOL describes employers' choices after a higher salary test has gone into effect: employers will pay the new rate "*only* if the resulting cost would be no more than paying this worker on an hourly basis with premium pay for overtime." 46 *Fed. Reg.* at 3017.

"to spread employment to avoid the extra wage...."[176]

The niceties of the calculus entering employers' decisions as to whether to comply with the FLSA were made moot, however, by the Carter administration's waiting until the last week of its term to promulgate the new salary tests, which were scheduled to go into effect February 13, 1981. The three-year delay stemmed from opposition by the President's Council on Wage and Price Stability, which had "slapped down" the original proposal in 1978, and even in 1981 was arguing for a salary test of sixty times the minimum wage or $201. Despite employers' "outraged protests" and threats to sue to enjoin implementation of the regulation, Carter proceeded with the rule on January 7, the day after the Minimum Wage Study Commission (MWSC) had reported that employers violated the FLSA more often with regard to salaried than hourly-paid employees.[177]

Employers' "infuriat[ion] at this and other lame-duck decrees"[178] swiftly vanished as President Reagan, in one of his first official acts, issued as part of his overall deregulatory program a memorandum on January 29, 1981, postponing for sixty days all pending final regulations.[179] The same day, the DOL stayed the effective date of the regulation indefinitely, reopening the comment period.[180] The new Secretary of Labor, Raymond Donovan, himself a construction firm executive, justified the suspension by reference to the "devastating" impact the increased salary test would have had on small businesses.[181] Donovan's efforts to eliminate such "'unwarranted obstacles which cost the economy billions of dollars a year'" were applauded by the Chamber of Commerce of the United

---

[176]Overnight Motor Transport Co., v. Missel, 316 U.S. 572, 578 (1942).

[177]"A Raise for Low-Level Bosses," *Bus. Wk.*, Jan. 19, 1981, at 23. According to Elisburg, who was the main force behind raising the salary level, the White House and the Office of Management and Budget caused the initial delay; at the end of Carter's term, when the president finally agreed to the increase, there were so many last-minute regulations pending that in the rush it was not possible to insure that the regulation went into effect before Reagan took office. The AFL-CIO's lukewarm support for what it viewed to be an inadequate increase left Elisburg with little political strength to fend off Administration opponents of any raise. Telephone interview with Donald Elisburg, Washington D.C. area (carphone), Nov. 17, 1993, 6:15 p.m. CST. John Zalusky, an economist with the AFL-CIO, confirmed that unions were not satisfied with the proposed salary test regulation. Telephone interview, Washington, D.C., Nov. 18, 1993, at 9 a.m. CST.

[178]"Industry Is Infuriated by Lame-Duck Decrees," *Bus. Wk.*, Dec. 15, 1980, at 33.

[179]46 *Fed. Reg.* 11,227 (1981).

[180]46 *Fed. Reg.* 11,972 (1981). Because the DOL failed to give the proper notice period or to solicit public comment on its decision to stay indefinitely (or effectively to repeal) the regulation, the stay is arguably invalid. 5 U.S.C. §§ 551(5), 553(b) & © (1988).

[181]Drew von Bergen, "Labor Secretary Starts Erasing Predecessor's Slate," United Press International, Feb. 11, 1981 (Nexis).

States, which welcomed his "'play[ing] hardball on regulatory reform.'"[182] In March, the DOL, in the spirit of Reaganomic marketization that echoed employers' complaints about the alleged burdensomeness of the salary test,[183] specified that it was seeking public comments about "the probable economic impact of raising the salary tests to the revised levels...."[184]

Not until Reagan's second term did the DOL renew its interest in the salary tests. The trade press had reported in 1983 that "[u]pon reflection, the Reaganites concluded that the Carter-proposed salary test increases were not so unreasonable after all." DOL officials were said to be preparing a redraft by the end of the year "(probably containing several key concessions to restaurant industry lobbyists concerned over the Government's unwillingness to recognize more than one overtime-exempt manager per food-service unit)." But this proposal, too, was postponed as mysteriously as it had been initiated.[185] Deeming the intervening four years insufficient for a review of the regulations, the DOL once again reopened the comment period. This time it expressly solicited comments on whether the test should be eliminated altogether.[186] After the comment period was extended yet again in 1986,[187] employers' organizations were unable to formulate a united deregulatory program. In the face of union demands for a doubling of the long-test salary to $320-$325, the National Mass Retailing Institute urged outright elimination of the test. The Association of General Merchandise Chains, however, declined to support this position, in part for fear that the alternative would be "'far more detailed and burdensome inquiry [by DOL enforcement agents] into exempt employees' duties and responsibilities.'" Despite the retail trade press's reports of the DOL's accommodation of the employers' proposed relaxation of the duties test,[188] this clash of lobbyists, too, failed to produce any agency action.

Here the extremes met as the "if it ain't broke don't fix it" opposition to an

---

[182]Philip Shabecoff, "Swift Attack on Regulations," *N.Y. Times*, Feb. 12, 1981, at A15, col. 1 (Nexis) (quoting Donovan and Mark de Barnardo).

[183]46 *Fed. Reg.* at 3011-12.

[184]46 *Fed. Reg.* at 18,998-99.

[185]Ken Rankin, "Labor Dept. Quietly Shelves Plans to Rewrite Labor Practices Rules," *Nation's Restaurant News*, Nov. 7, 1983, at 6 (Nexis). Although only one employee per establishment may fall under the "in sole charge of an independent establishment" exemption, more than one may qualify under the general duties test. 29 C.F.R. §§ 541.1(e), 541.113(d) (1993).

[186]50 *Fed. Reg.* 47,696-97 (1985).

[187]51 *Fed. Reg.* 2525 (1986).

[188]"Labor Unions Press Feds for Higher Exempt Store Employee Wages," *Discount Store News*, June 23, 1986, at 2 (Nexis) (quoting AGMC president Edward Borda).

increase in the salary test mounted by Burger King and other employers[189] was matched by the relief expressed by the AFL-CIO that the dreaded "brutaliz[ation]" of the test by the Reagan Administration had never materialized.[190] Nevertheless, inaction systemically favored (and favors) employers: under the regulatory status quo the salary test is further eroded by inflation and minimum-wage increases, creating a de facto enforcement vacuum. By the end of the Bush Administration, which posted a "Next Action Undetermined" notice in its semi-annual DOL agenda,[191] proposed rulemaking was no longer even rumored.[192]

4. Consequences of an Exclusion

> There is probably nothing more disturbing in the world than being an assistant manager of a restaurant working 60 or 70 hours a week—working for really not much more than the minimum wage—and not having much hope of moving up.[193]

The number of "white collar" workers excluded from the FLSA is huge. The latest DOL estimates, for the year 1996, reveal that 32 million employees or 26 percent of all wage and salary employees fall under the excluded rubrics of executive, administrative, or professional employees.[194] By far the largest contingent—almost two-fifths—of excluded white collar employees worked in the service industries, followed by state and local government, manufacturing, and retail trade. At 36 percent, the service industry displayed the third highest proportion of excluded white collar employees behind the federal government and finance, insurance, and real estate. Table 2-2 breaks these data down by industry.

---

[189]*Nation's Restaurant News*, Mar. 10, 1986, at 46; *id.*, May 12, 1986, at 87 (Nexis).

[190]*Daily Lab. Rep.*, Mar. 4, 1987, at A-7 (Nexis).

[191]54 *Fed. Reg.* 44,366-67 (1989); see also *id.* at 16,443-44.

[192]All the DOL could muster was a buried footnote that consideration of the salary tests "will be undertaken in connection with any future rulemaking." 57 *Fed. Reg.* 37,666 n.1 (1992).

[193]*Restaurant Business*, May 1, 1981, at 175 (discussion contribution by Robert Emerson).

[194]Because bona fide executive employees are protected by the Act's prohibition of sex discrimination (the Equal Pay Act), their employers are required to make, keep, and preserve certain wage and hour records. 29 U.S.C. §§ 206(d), 211(c), 213(a); 29 C.F.R. §§ 516.2, 516.3 (1993).

Table 2-2: Excluded Executive, Administrative, and Professional Employees as % of All Employees, by Industry, 1996

Industry	All employees (000,000)	Excluded employees (000,000)	Excluded employees as % of all employees
All	122,359	31,729	26
Private sector	102,912	25,495	25
Agriculture/ forestry/fishing	1,907	252	13
Mining	574	95	17
Construction	5,400	736	14
Manufacturing	18,457	3,230	18
Transportation/ public utilities	6,261	1,413	23
Wholesale trade	6,483	1,580	24
Retail trade	21,625	3,049	14
Finance/insurance /real estate	6,899	2,706	39
Services	34,377	12,434	36
Private households	929	0	0
Public sector	19,447	6,234	36
Federal govt.	2,757	1,233	45
State/local govt.	16,690	5,002	30

Source: U.S. Employment Standards Administration, *Minimum Wage and Overtime Hours Under the Fair Labor Standards Act: 1998 Report*, tab. 3a at 16 (1998).

The number of executive employees is unknown, but if the MWSC's twenty-year-old estimate that two-thirds of the excluded white-collar employees are executive is accurate, they number upwards of twenty million.[195] The above-average rise in employment and in the proportion of excluded white collar employees in the service industry has in large part driven the economy-wide increase in the absolute and relative number of excluded white collar workers over the last two decades. Using a somewhat different data set—which produces a smaller universe of employment because it is restricted to full-time workers—the General Accounting Office (GAO) estimated that from 1983 to 1998, the number of excluded white collar workers rose from a range between 12 and 17 million to between 19 and 26 million. As a proportion of all full-time

[195]Fritsch & Vandell, "Exemptions from the Fair Labor Standards Act" at 245 (data for 1977).

wage and salary workers, excluded white collar employees increased from between 17 percent and 24 percent in 1983 to the 20 to 27 percent range in 1998.[196]

The GAO also found that while women's share in total full-time employment had remained stationary during this period, their share of excluded white collar employees rose from 33 percent to 42 percent, just about equal to their share in the work force.[197] Older data generated by the MWSC (from 1977 and 1980) had revealed that although women accounted for only 11 per cent of all executive employees, they constituted 26 per cent of such workers in the retail industry and 38 per cent of the lowest-paid retail executive employees; in the service industry, women accounted for 53 per cent of the lowest-paid "exempt" executives. Not surprisingly, these two industries also employed the largest proportion of low-paid "exempt" executives who worked overtime—rising in retail trade to two-thirds.[198]

The GAO also made the unsurprising discovery that a much larger proportion of excluded white collar workers work overtime than employees who are protected by FLSA's overtime provision. Whereas 35 percent of excluded white collar workers worked more than forty hours per week in 1983 and 44 percent in 1998, the corresponding figures for protected workers were only 15 percent and 19 percent, respectively. The gap among those working more than fifty hours was even greater: 10 percent and 15 percent for excluded white collar workers and only 4 and 5 percent, respectively, for protected employees.[199] Equally unsurprising was the MWSC's older finding of a "significant inverse relationship" between salary levels and the share of executive employees working overtime.[200]

The liberal protective purposes of FLSA require the courts to interpret exemptions narrowly and against employers[201] and the Secretary of Labor to restrict the exemption to those who are "truly executives and not [mere] employees."[202] The socioeconomic rationale for excluding "bona fide" executives is said to lie in the fact that they are sufficiently well compensated and have sufficient control over their hours that they should not be entitled to subject their

---

[196]GAO, *Fair Labor Standards Act: White-Collar Exemptions in the Modern Work Place* tab. 2 at 8 (GAO/HEHS-99-164, 1999).

[197]GAO, *Fair Labor Standards Act*, fig. 3 at 9.

[198]Fritsch & Vandell, "Exemptions from the Fair Labor Standards Act" at 246-48.

[199]GAO, *Fair Labor Standards Act*, fig. 4 at 12.

[200]Fritsch and Vandell, "Exemptions from the Fair Labor Standards Act" at 248, tab. C-5 at 262.

[201]*See, e.g.*, Arnold v. Ben Kanowsky, Inc., 361 U.S. 388, 392 (1960).

[202]Ralph Knight, Inc. v. Mantel, 135 F.2d 514, 517 (8th Cir. 1943).

employers to an overtime penalty for hours worked at their own discretion.[203] If, as the Wage and Hour Administrator who promulgated the executive employee regulations based on the Stein Report in 1940 noted, the essence of an exempt employee is that his "salary is so high that if he were paid time and a half for overtime, he would have serious doubts that he earned it,"[204] the extraordinarily capacious category that the DOL's inaction has irrationally created sweeps in millions of workers whose salary and autonomy are far removed from that model.

According to a 1990 survey by the National Restaurant Association (NRA), one-quarter of all assistant managers at fast-food restaurants earned less than $15,000.[205] The NRA's 1998 survey revealed that the salary of one-quarter of assistant managers at fast-food restaurants fell below $18,600; at all types of restaurants with annual sales below $500,000 and between $500,000 and $1,000,000, one-fourth of assistant managers received salaries below $16,600 and $19,035, respectively.[206] Night managers at fast-food restaurants were paid even less: their median salary was only $16,250, with one-fourth of them earning less than $14,000 and three-fourths receiving salaries below $18,388.[207] Even the BLS *Occupational Outlook Handbook* observes that in 1996 the lowest 10 percent of restaurant and food service managers earned $240 a week or less.[208]

---

[203]*See, e.g.*, Brock v. Claridge Hotel & Casino, 846 F.2d 180, 184 (3d Cir. 1988); *Hearing on Fair Labor Standards Act: Hearing Before the Subcomm. on Labor Standards of the House Comm. on Education & Labor*, 102d Cong., 2d Sess. 76 (Serial No. 102-122, 1992) (statement of Jonathan Hiatt, general counsel, Service Employees International Union); Gottlieb, *Overtime Compensation* at 5-6 ("'exempt personnel are paid for their long-term contribution to the company not directly measurable in hours'") (quoting company response to questionnaire).

[204]Fleming, "Two Years of the Wage and Hour Law" at 72.

[205]National Restaurant Association, *Compensation for Salaried Personnel in Food Services*, Exhibit 38 at 32 (1991) (as disclosed by NRA, Information Services, Washington, D.C., telephone interviews, Nov. 22-24, 1993). The annual salaries for assistant unit managers in fast-food restaurants ("limited menu no table service") for the upper quartile, median, and lower quartile (defined as the median of the lower half) were $19,731, $18,236, and $15,000 respectively for 1990.

[206]National Restaurant Association, *Compensation for Salaried Personnel in Restaurants—1998*, Exhibit 42 at 37 (1999). For fast-food restaurants, the upper quartile, median, and lower-quartile salaries of assistant managers were $24,875, $21,500, and $18,600 respectively; for restaurants of all types and sizes, the figures were $30,000, $25,000, and $20,800, respectively; for restaurants of all types with annual sales below $500,000, the salaries were $24,000, $20,000, and $16,600, respectively; for restaurants of all types with annual sales between $500,000 and $1,000,000, the salaries were $25,000, $22,000, and $19,035, respectively. Unfortunately, the report does not cross-tabulate type and size of restaurant. There may be no enterprise coverage for employees in restaurants with annual revenues below $500,000; see below chapter 4.

[207]National Restaurant Association, *Compensation for Salaried Personnel in Restaurants—1998*, Exhibit 43 at 38.

[208]U.S. BLS, *Occupational Outlook Handbook: 1998-99 Edition* at 77.

These $200-$380/week overtime workers[209] are precisely the employees whom President Clinton's Wage and Hour Administrator had in mind when she conceded that "there's something wrong with" excluding from the FLSA workers who are just "one step above the cashier."[210]

Ironically, the DOL's failure to keep the definition current also privileges employers to subject mala fide executives to a greater degree of exploitation than their supervisees. In the sanitized language of personnel relations, when "faced with a problem of resolving a conflict between compensation theory and economic reality," some firms are forced "to overcome the reluctance to treat exempt staff in the same manner as those who are nonexempt." (But retail employers, the prime abusers of the exemption, succumb much less frequently to these pressures than do firms in other industries.)[211] This legal privilege may, however, make it difficult for firms to maintain motivation and discipline where the "optimum salary differential"[212] between first-line supervisors and their subordinates becomes deranged. For management "'[i]t's an awful situation when you have a man supervising 15 or 20 people and they are making more than he is.'"[213] This inadvertent result of agency inaction gives a literal albeit unintended meaning to the MWSC's claim that the executive exclusion was rooted in the fact that these employees receive "compensatory privileges which made up for the lack of premium pay for overtime"—including the privilege of exercising "authority over others."[214] In the real world, however, as Ronald Coase has observed, it is not necessary for managers to pay "to exercise control over others" because they are paid to do so.[215]

Even in the economic boom of the late 1960s, a DOL study revealed that in 19 per cent of establishments, "the lowest paid exempt executive received a weekly salary that was below that of the highest paid nonexempt employee he supervised." And 41 per cent of exempt executives who were being paid exactly the long-test salary received lower earnings than their covered supervisees.[216]

---

[209]For examples of salaries as low as $10,000, see Parcel & Sickmeier, "One Firm, Two Labor Markets" at 39; Leidner, *Fast Food* at 53. Susan Aylward, Information Services, National Restaurant Ass'n, confirmed that salaried assistant managers work up to eighty hours per week. Telephone interview, Nov. 24, 1993, at 8 a.m. CST.

[210]Telephone interview with Maria Echaveste, Washington, D.C., Nov. 22, 1993, 10 a.m. CST.

[211]Burton Teague, *Overtime Pay Practices for Exempt Employees* vi, tab. 2 at 8 (Conference Bd. Rep. No. 797, 1981).

[212]Weeks, *Overtime Pay for Exempt Employees* at 9.

[213]Gottlieb, *Overtime Compensation* at 13 (quoting large defense products firm).

[214]Fritsch & Vandell, "Exemptions from the Fair Labor Standards Act" at 243.

[215]Ronald Coase, "The Nature of the Firm," 4 *Economica* (n.s.) 386, 390 (1937).

[216]U.S. Department of Labor, *Earnings Data Pertinent to a Review of the Salary Tests*

Again, in 1981, *Business Week*, which reported that employers were "incensed" about being required to pay overtime to "trainee managers," confirmed that "some hourly employees...do make more than some assistant managers who work long hours."[217]

The vast expansion of fast food restaurants and convenience stores, two major employers of so-called assistant managers, may have intensified this pattern of compensation inversion.[218] Thus in the 1980s, "eating and drinking places" added almost two million new jobs, one-tenth of all new jobs in the United States and twice as many as any other industry, becoming the largest private-sector employer.[219] From 1964 to 1995, supervisory employees in eating and drinking places rose by 474 percent—from 126,000 to 723,000—compared to 285 percent among nonsupervisors.[220]

McDonald's alone may employ upwards of 100,000 assistant managers.[221] With 284,000 employees in 1998, it was the eighth largest employer among the

---

at 26, tab. 16 at 33.

[217]"A Raise for Low-Level Bosses" at 24.

[218]According to a 1977 DOL survey, only 5 per cent of the lowest-paid executives supervised employees earning more than they did. This survey may have been skewed by the fact that it excluded executives who were (unlawfully) paid less than the long-test salary. Fritsch & Vandell, "Exemptions from the Fair Labor Standards Act" at 246, 253. At Food Lion, "a full-time stocker's maximum weekly pay is eighty percent of an assistant manager's minimum weekly salary." Royster v. Food Lion, Inc., 1998 U.S. App. 11809, *15 Lexis (4th Cir. 1998)

[219]Plunkert, "The 1980's: A Decade of Job Growth and Industry Shifts," tab. 5 at 12, 13; U.S. BLS, *Career Guides to Industries* 106 (Bull. 2403, 1992).

[220]Calculated according to data in 2 U.S. BLS, *Employment, Hours, and Earnings, United States, 1909-90*, at 803-805 (Bull. 2370, 1991); U.S. BLS, *Employment, Hours, and Earnings: United States, 1981-93*, at 394-95 (Bull. 2429, 1993); U.S. BLS, *Employment, Hours, and Earnings: United States, 1988-96*, at 315 (Bull. 2481, 1996) The figures for supervisory employees were calculated as the difference between "all employees" and "nonsupervisory workers." The BLS did not begin publishing data on nonsupervisory employees in this industry (SIC 58) until 1964. For an alternative estimate of 557,000 restaurant and food service managers in 1990 and 493,000 in 1996, see U.S. BLS, *Occupational Outlook Handbook* 58 (Bull. 2400, 1992); U.S. BLS, *Occupational Outlook Handbook: 1998-99 Edition* 77 (Bull. 2500, 1998).

[221]In 1993, McDonald's stated that four to five assistant managers worked at each of the 9,200 McDonald's restaurants in the United States, which employed on average 55-60 workers; 85 per cent of these restaurants were franchises. Telephone interview with Ann Connolly, McDonald's Corp., Oak Brook, Illinois, Nov. 22, 1993, at 4 p.m. CST. Six years later, when the number of restaurants had risen to 12,529, McDonald's stated that an average of seven to nine assistant and swing managers worked in each restaurant, which employed about 50 workers. Telephone interview with Customer Service representative, McDonald's Corp., Oak Brook, Illinois (Nov. 19, 1999); http://www.mcdonalds.com. On the unsuccessful attempt by the manager of a fast-food restaurant to sue the franchisor for failure to pay overtime, see Howell v. Chick-Fil-A, 127 Lab. Cas. (CCH) ¶ 33,051 (N.D. Fla. 1993).

Fortune 500,[222] and boasts that it "has replaced the U.S. Army as the organization that trains most of our country's young people—700,000 teens each year." The company that claims that "one-eighth of the current American workforce has worked for" it[223] was in 1992 the most profitable retail firm in the United States and in 1997 and 1998 the first and second most profitable food service firm, respectively, in the Fortune 1,000 with annual profits in excess of 1.5 billion dollars.[224] What was true of a hotel in a small town in Washington State underpaying a chambermaid during the Great Depression applies with much greater force to McDonald's: the most general legislative intent underlying the imposition of a wage floor, as the Supreme Court observed, remains that "[t]he community is not bound to provide what is in effect a subsidy for unconscionable employers."[225]

As a former assistant manager at Pizza Hut described the working life of one of these "exempt" executives:

> "[T]he glow of being a manager and being in charge fades as you're mopping the floor at two o'clock in the morning. ... As an assistant manager I was on a salary of $175. The cooks were paid by the hour. You had a manager who scheduled you. He had a profit line to work out with his district manager. He could either put on the cook and pay him the minimum wage plus overtime, or he could schedule the assistant manager who had to work all those crazy hours without any overtime. I usually worked about fifty hours, but there were people working sixty or seventy hours because their manager scheduled them that way. The assistant managers were making less than the minimum wage. ... As an assistant manager I generally spent the whole shift cooking. Late at night you generally just had a cook and a waitress. Somebody would have to mop the floor so I would do it. ... It didn't matter who did it. The manager's job was to assign someone to do it, including himself. When you're young you have this concept of a manager. You sort of see him as a miniature Lee Iacocca, walking through the plant with his suit and tie on, directing people. After a while you realized you were a glorified cook."[226]

Despite the fact that the duties test is already more lenient for the retail trade and service sectors—permitting "executive employees" to spend as much as 40

---

[222]"Fortune 5 Hundred Ranked by Performance," *Fortune*, Apr. 26, 1999, at F-28, F-32.

[223]McDonald's Corporation, "Welcome to McDonald's" 14, 23 (1998). See also Koepp, "Big Mac Strikes Back" at 59; Ben Wildavsky, "McJobs: Inside America's Largest Youth Training Program," *Policy Rev.*, Summer 1989, at 30.

[224]"The Service 500," *Fortune*, May 31, 1993, at 199, 220-21; "Fortune 1 Thousand Ranked Within Industries," *Fortune*, Apr. 27, 1998, at F-44, F-51; "Fortune 1 Thousand Ranked Within Industries," *Fortune*, Apr. 26, 1999, at F-51, F-58.

[225]West Coast Hotel v. Parrish, 300 U.S. 379, 399-400 (1937).

[226]Stan Luxenburg, *Roadside Empires: How the Chains Franchised America* 173 (1985) (quoting former Pizza Hut assistant manager).

per cent of their time on grunt work before they forfeit their bona fides[227]—and that the judiciary has interpreted short test's requirement that an executive employee's primary duty consist of management so limply that it was met even where Burger King assistant managers devoted more than half of their time to non-exempt work,[228] employers complain that this restriction is discriminatory because their managerial employees, such as the one just quoted, must perform the same routine "nonexempt" work as their own subordinates[229] while they are engaged in supervising the latter.[230]

Advocates of this hybrid supervisor-worker model, which contravenes Tayloristic scientific management's principle of the "strictly executive" work of "functional bosses,"[231] must overcome a categorical obstacle in the form of the rigidly hierarchical division of labor associated with capitalism and labor standards legislation: "Doing routine menial labor is not acting in an executive capacity."[232] Many assistant managers "roll up their sleeves and help with the cooking, clearing of tables, or other tasks" and not only "[d]uring busy periods"[233] or "[u]nder certain occasional emergency conditions."[234] But because they "'spend most of their time doing the same duties as the crew: making burritos, waiting on customers and mopping the floor,'"[235] the DOL and the courts have frequently found that as nonexempt employees they are entitled to back overtime wages.[236] The pay and working conditions of supervisor-workers undermine employers' claims that the duties-salary test "does not affect poor people. We are

[227]When Congress brought the bulk of retail and service employees under the FLSA in 1961, it permitted the executives among them to devote as much as 40 per cent of their time to "activities not closely directly or closely related to the performance of executive...activities," whereas all others are subject to the 20 per cent limit. Fair Labor Standards Amendments of 1961, Pub. L. No. 87-30, § 9, 75 Stat. 65, 71 (1961) (codified at 29 U.S.C. 213(a)(1) (1988)). On Senator Williams's unsuccessful effort to reduce the limit to 20 per cent, see S. 1861, § 7(a)(2), in Subcommittee on Labor of the Senate Committee on Labor & Public Welfare, 92d Cong., 2d Sess., *Background Material on the Fair Labor Standards Act Amendments of 1972*, at 27, 55 (1974).

[228]Donovan v. Burger King, 675 F.2d at 520-22.

[229]29 C.F.R. § 541.111(b) (1993).

[230]"Stage Is Set for Overtime Pay Rules Struggle," *Chain Age Store Executive*, Aug. 1986, at 35.

[231]Frederick Taylor, *Shop Management* 98-100 (1911).

[232]Wilkinson v. Noland Co., 40 F. Supp. 1009, 1011 (E.D. Va. 1941).

[233]U.S. BLS, *Occupational Outlook Handbook* 56 (1990-91 ed., Bull. 2350, 1990).

[234]29 C.F.R. § 541.109 (1993).

[235]Greg Hernandez, "Taco Bell Dispute Widens," *L.A. Times*, Sept. 3, 1999, at C3 (Westlaw) (quoting Diane Ritchie, lawyer representing plaintiff-assistant managers in suit against Taco Bell under California labor law).

[236]*See, e.g.*, Dole v. Papa Gino's of America, Inc., 712 F. Supp. 1038 (D. Mass. 1989).

talking about executives."[237]

What employers in fact are talking about is fending off a test that "would force" them to pay overtime.[238] What they in fact got after the Burger King case was such an extraordinary relaxation of the duties test that a GAO study of 32 federal cases decided between 1994 and 1998 dealing with the executive duties test found "hardly any instances in which a court overturned an employer's classification of a lower-income supervisor as an exempt executive." The GAO also discovered that the Burger King decision had intimidated the DOL into requiring its investigators to consider percentage limitations as only one factor in determining the worker's primary duty.[239]

At the same time, this kind of unstructured, unregulated, and often unpaid work schedule means that employers are able to preempt greater blocks of an employee's time, leaving an "exempt" executive with less time that he can "effectively use for his own purposes. It belongs to and is controlled by the employer."[240] This trend parallels a pattern that has become increasingly prevalent among hourly production and service employees whose employers require them to remain "on-call" at all times outside of their scheduled working hours, tethered to pagers or telephones, "not far removed from a prisoner serving a sentence under slightly relaxed house arrest terms."[241]

As the owners of fast-food chains and their franchisees have grown more concerned that the demographic changes limiting the pool of teenagers available for low-wage work will reduce profits,[242] Wall Street believes that managers become increasingly "crucial for success in fast food."[243] But

> managers of most fast food companies cannot be paid what they are really worth to their stores. Surely the entrepreneurial young person who works 80 or 90 hours per week for a salary of $10,000 or $12,000 per year is not receiving his or her full deserts. Enduring the gaff of dealing with the public, motivating teenage ingrates among his or her own employees, scrubbing the rest room floors, and receiving a wage that amounts to little

---

[237]*Labor Standards Amendments of 1973: Hearings Before the Subcommittee on Labor of the Senate Committee on Labor & Public Welfare*, 93d Cong., 1st Sess. 107 (1973) (statement of Marjorie Geerlofs, senior vice-president, Bambergers Dept. Store).

[238]*Fair Labor Standards Amendments of 1971: Hearings Before the Subcommittee on Labor of the Senate Committee on Labor & Public Welfare*, 92d Cong., 1st Sess. 594 (1971) (statement of John Mahaney, exec. dir., Ohio State Council of Retail Merchants).

[239]GAO, *Fair Labor Standards Act* at 29-30.

[240]29 C.F.R. § 785.15 (1993).

[241]Bright v. Houston Northwest Medical Center Survivor, Inc., 888 F.2d 1059, 1064 (5th Cir. 1989), *rev'd*, 934 F.2d 671 (5th Cir. 1991) (en banc). *See also* Owens v. Local No. 169, Ass'n of Western Pulp & Paper Workers, 971 F.2d 347 (9th Cir. 1992).

[242]Robert Emerson, *The New Economics of Fast Food* 98-104 and *passim* (1990).

[243]Luxenburg, *Roadside Empires* at 172.

more than the minimum wage when weekend and overtime hours are taken into account is not much of a job. However, some of the chains are still able to attract such people. How?

Much of the answer lies in the chains' ability to promise the hungry new store manager the opportunity to grow with the chain. In effect, the manager is told: "We'll pay you peanuts and make you work like a slave for now. But if you produce for us, in two years we'll have enough stores open to be able to make you a district manager, then a regional overseer, and then finally a statewide warlord or whatever." The young store manager is paid with promises, so to speak. This is fine for everyone involved so long as the chain continues to grow and advancement remains possible.[244]

"But when the chain stops growing the manager is left without any motivation."[245] The partial collapse of this huge and profitable pyramiding transaction in the wake of the oversupply of fast-food restaurants may alter the structure of low-level managerial compensation and hasten re-regulation of "exempt" managerial employees.[246] Such a shake-out may also inject greater realism into entry-level quasi-supervisors' career path self-assessments, dissuading them from acquiescing in what the trade calls paying their "dues" in the hope of "ris[ing] to the chief executive's slot"[247] or transmogrifying their $12,000 annual salaries into the more than half-million dollar initial investment required to open a franchise restaurant.[248] If front-line supervisors' so-called delayed-payment/bonding contracts[249] are massively perceived as camouflaged exploitation, there may be fewer assistant managers like the one at McDonald's, who, ruefully agreeing that one of his hourly subordinates needed to work only forty-five hours to surpass his salary for as many as sixty-two hours, nevertheless justified the disparate treatment on the ground that as a management trainee he

---

[244]Robert Emerson, *Fast Food: The Endless Shakeout* 188 (1979).

[245]Luxenburg, *Roadside Empires* at 172.

[246]Krueger, "Ownership, Agency, and Wages" at 79.

[247]"The Management Merry-Go-Round," *National Restaurant News*, Dec. 7, 1987, at F3 (Nexis).

[248]Stephen Koepp, "Big Mac Strikes Back," *Time*, Apr. 13, 1987, at 58, 59; *McDonald's 1992 Annual Report* 6 (1993). In keeping with the industry's apparent preference for unpaid labor, prospective franchisees are also required to work at a McDonald's fifteen to twenty hours per week for two years as "volunteers." Lisa Bertagnoli, "McDonald's: Company of the Quarter Century," *Restaurants & Institutions*, July 10, 1989, at 32, 38; Eric Berg, "An American Icon Wrestles with a Troubled Future," *N.Y. Times*, May 12, 1991, § 3, at 1, col. 2 (Nexis); McDonald's Corp. v. Miller, No. 92-4811 (AMW) (D.N.J. filed Nov. 17, 1992) (declaratory judgment action by McDonald's against prospective but terminated franchisee demanding back minimum wages); McDonald's Corp. v. Miller, 1994 U.S. Dist. Lexis 13243 (D.N.J. 1994), *aff'd*, 60 F.3d 815 (3d Cir. 1995).

[249]Krueger, "Ownership, Agency, and Wages" at 75-76.

would "soon be earning a good deal more."[250]

In spite of this history of overreaching, even the most learned judge in the United States has opined that, if the original purpose of the overtime provision of FLSA "was to prevent workers willing...to work abnormally long hours from taking jobs away from workers who prefer to work shorter hours," it is "no longer very likely" that workers do so "out of desperation."[251] Yet the Wage and Hour Administrator in the Ford Administration increased the short-test salary level (to $250) precisely because "certain employers are utilizing the high salary test to employ otherwise nonexempt employees (i.e., those who perform work in excess of the 20 percent tolerance for nonexempt work or the 40 percent tolerance allowed in...retail and service establishments) for excessively long work-weeks."[252]

Moreover, corporate "shedding" of older workers in recent years has created additional cohorts of vulnerable labor market applicants.[253] Unlike their teenage competitors who still live at home, they are unable to survive on the income generated by the minimum wage at forty (or fewer) hours per week at McDonald's, which is "inadequate to support one person, much less a family."[254] Yet "[o]lder workers who compete with students for jobs cannot demand much more."[255] When fast food chains such as McDonald's, Burger King, and Kentucky Fried Chicken perceived a shortage of teenagers in the late 1980s, they "rapidly recogniz[ed] the benefits of hiring older workers...."[256] Their diminished opportunities compelled many of them to acquiesce in low-paid "exempt" executive jobs precisely because the mandatory long hours were associated with salaries in excess of $170 (that is, the weekly minimum wage), even though they included no overtime premium and may not even have amounted to the minimum wage for every hour worked. In this regard, their "irrational" labor market

---

[250]"A Raise for Low-Level Bosses" at 24.

[251]Mechmet v. Four Seasons Hotels, Ltd., 825 F.2d 1173, 1176 (7th Cir. 1987) (per Posner, J.).

[252]40 *Fed. Reg.* 7092 (1975).

[253]*See, e.g.*, "They've Got to Eat, So Let Them Work," *Economist*, Sept. 16, 1989, at 17, 18; Isabel Wilkerson, "Refugees from Recession Fill Hotel's Payroll," *N.Y. Times*, Mar. 1, 1992, at 1, col. 2 (nat. ed.).

[254]Koepp, "Big Mac Strikes Back" at 59.

[255]Peter Kilborn, "For Forlorn Millions: The Recession Goes On," *N.Y. Times*, July 28, 1991, § 1, at 1, col. 1 (Nexis).

[256]Diane Duke, "Fast Food Firms Find Seniors Fit Recipe," *Austin Bus. J.*, Sept. 21, 1987, § 1, at 5 (Nexis). *See also* Kevin Klose, "McDonald's Woos Older Workers," *Wash. Post*, Feb. 9, 1987, at A3 (Nexis); "Food Service Industry Representatives Explore Ways to Employ Older Workers," *Daily Lab. Rep.*, July 29, 1987, at C-1; "McDonald's Seeks Retirees to Fill Void, *N.Y. Times*, Dec. 20, 1987, § 1, at 54, col. 4 (Nexis).

behavior uncannily resembled that of migrant farm workers.[257]

For these older workers, many of whom may have lost health-care benefits, the need for additional income supplants the desire to avoid long hours. In other words, fear of unemployment or lower-waged employment causes even those who "are not the marginal, non-unionized workers for whom" alone, in Judge Richard Posner's mind, "the overtime provisions were designed,"[258] to acquiesce in employers' drives "to exploit[] employees in a transitional stage in their promotion from hourly worker to executive function by obliging them to work both as an extra hand and as lower echelon management."[259]

An Acting Assistant Secretary for Employment Standards and Deputy Wage and Hour Administrator in the Clinton administration conceded the "absurdity of having a salary test that's lower than the minimum wage."[260] Another high-ranking national DOL official characterized as "totally embarrassing" his agency's having permitted the test-salary to become obsolete. Taken together with the acknowledgment that "we're not out there looking for section 541 violations,"[261] the DOL's admissions against interest underscore the invalidity of the current version of the salary test.

As a result of long-term agency neglect and/or political stalemate, the justification for what may once have been a reasonable regulation has, through the mere passage of time, "long since evaporated."[262] The fact that the minimum

---

[257]*See* Marc Linder, *Migrant Workers and Minimum Wages: Regulating the Exploitation of Agricultural Labor in the United States* 16-20 (1992).

[258]Mechmet v. Four Seasons Hotel Ltd., 825 F.2d at 1177. In private correspondence, Judge Posner stated that the original article of which this chapter is an updated revision "is very interesting but I am not persuaded by your argument that assistant managers of fast-food outlets are being exploited. If one-quarter are being paid $15,000, three-quarters are being paid more and if they are mainly young people for whom the assistant manager's job really is the first step on the corporate ladder, albeit a ladder that does not lead to a corporate presidency or even a franchise, I don't see why they should complain. The effect of applying the overtime provisions of the FLSA to them might be actually to reduce their pay, as they would cost more to employ. If someone who works 50 hours a week is worth only $15,000, someone who work 40 hours a week must be worth less." Letter from Richard Posner to Marc Linder (Apr. 10, 1995). Judge Posner did not reply to the response that "it would be very difficult to enforce labor standards based on the principle implicit in your view that assistant managers have nothing to complain about. That principle seems to be that no unlawful exploitation exists where an employer self-servingly predicts that some relevant proportion of its employees are merely going through a corporate rite of passage on the other side of which they will reappear as highly paid real managers." Letter from Marc Linder to Richard Posner (Apr. 13, 1995).

[259]Marshall v. Burger King Corp., 504 F. Supp. at 411.

[260]Telephone interview with John Fraser, Washington, D.C., Nov. 19, 1993, at 9 a.m. CST.

[261]Telephone interview with Ray Kamrath, Wage and Hour Division, Office of Policy, Planning, and Review, Washington, D.C., Nov. 8, 1993, at 11:00 a.m. CST.

[262]Geller v. Federal Communications Comm'n, 610 F.2d 973, 980 (D.C. Cir. 1979).

wage has more than doubled during the intervening quarter-century has rendered thc salary test a "clearly obsolete"[263] regulation so lacking in the requisite rationality and reasonableness as not merely to be "'unrelated to the tasks entrusted by Congress'" to the agency,[264] but to have turned them on their head. Other agencies' failure to adjust similar monetary indexes for inflation during shorter periods has prompted courts to declare welfare regulations invalid.[265] The Administrative Procedure Act's mandate that federal courts invalidate agency regulations found to be "arbitrary, capricious, [or] an abuse of discretion"[266] operates in such cases because, as here with regard to the salary test, they "are contrary to the intent of Congress."[267]

5. Future of an Exclusion

I am from the state of Florida where I work in a store as a manager. I was hired with the understanding that I would be required to work 45 hours/wk. Is there a limit to how many hours I am required to work without being compensated? During my tenure with this company, there have been weeks where I have been REQUIRED to work 70+ hours with weeks to months with no days off. When base rate is divided by hours worked, some of the managers are not even receiving minimum wage for the hours they work.

Rita Risser's Response:

Guess what—they got you. As a manager, you are exempt from the law requiring overtime. Minimum wage doesn't apply. Federal law defines a manager as someone whose primary duty is management and who receives at least $155 per week. And there's no limit on how many hours they can require you to work. ... I suggest you look for another job that pays better.[268]

Before his appointment as Secretary of Labor, Robert Reich realized that "'[c]ompared to the old blue-collar jobs that have been lost, these [minimum-

[263]*The Fair Labor Standards Act* 181 (Ellen Kearns ed., 1999).

[264]Walling v. Yeakley, 140 F.2d 830, 832 (10th Cir. 1944) (discussing the executive exemption and quoting Gray v. Powell, 314 U.S. 402, 413).

[265]Main Ass'n of Interdependent Neighborhoods v. Petit, 659 F. Supp. 1309, 1323 (D. Me. 1987) (141 per cent increase in inflation over fourteen-year period invalidated Medicaid resources regulation).

[266]5 U.S.C. § 706(2) (1988).

[267]Stewart v. San Francisco, 834 F. Supp. 1233, 1236 (N.D. Cal. 1993).

[268]http://www.fairmeasures.com/asklawyer/archive/fall96/ask27.html (Fair Measures Management Law Consulting Group).

wage fast-food] jobs represent a serious setback.'"[269] Together with the knowledge that his own department's regulations authorize employers to pay overtime workers even less than the minimum wage, he acquired the power, but lacked the civil courage, to terminate that subsidy by increasing the salary test to a level beyond which concern with exploitation is dissipated. Recent congressional action setting that level at 6.5 times the minimum wage (currently $33.48) for computer systems analysts, software engineers, and computer programmers is one relevant model.[270] Converted to weekly compensation based on forty hours, this $1,339 salary would be high enough to generate $20 per hour (straight-time) for executive employees working 57-hour weeks. Such a test might certify that the "noncommissioned officers of the industrial army,...the petty 'managers' of all sorts...enjoy...the privileges of exemption from the worst features of the proletarian situation...."[271]

Unlike the federal DOL, state agencies administering comparable state wage and hour laws at least purport to be trying to keep their salary test up-to-date. In New Jersey, for example, the weekly executive salary threshold is $400, while Iowa has set its long-test salary at $310 and short-test salary at $500.[272] California, which has conferred much greater attention and protection on assistant managers, in 1999 conditioned exclusion of executive employees from the state's overtime law on a monthly salary equivalent to twice the state minimum wage ($5.75 per hour) for full-time employment, which amounts to $1,978—far in excess of the previously effective thresholds of $900 and $1,150 in various industries.[273]

If there is a widespread social conviction that unlimited overtime even at such salaries constitutes intolerable overreaching, several corrective programs are available. One is the blanket elimination of the exclusion of executive, administrative, and professional employees from the overtime provision of

---

[269]Koepp, "Big Mac Strikes Back" at 59.

[270]Pub. L. No. 101-583, § 2, 104 Stat. 2871 (1990); 29 C.F.R. §§ 541.3(a)(4) & (e), 541.303 (1993); Andrew Pollack, "Computer Programmers to Lose Overtime Pay," *N.Y. Times*, Jan. 28, 1991, at C3, col. 1 (nat. ed.). For a similar proposal, see Robert Lipman, Allison Plesur, and Joel Katz, "A Call for Bright-Lines to Fix the Fair Labor Standards Act," 11 *Hofstra Lab. L.J.* 357, 383-88 (1994).

[271]Harry Braverman, *Labor and Monopoly Capital: The Degradation of Work in the Twentieth Century* 407 (1974).

[272]N.J. Admin. Code tit. 12, § 56-7.1(a)(6) (1998); Iowa Admin. Code r. 875-218.1(6) (1998).

[273]1999 Cal. Adv. Leg. Serv, ch. 134 (AB 60) § 9(a) (Deering); Cal. Admin. Code tit.8, §§ 11010.1 (A)(1), 11070.1(A)(1) (1999); Alan Liddle, "Calif. Lawmakers Reinstate Daily OT, OK Min. Monthly Manager Pay," *Nation's Restaurant News*, July 26, 1999, at 4 (Westlaw); Liddle, "Calif. OT Suits." Under California law, excluded executive employees must devote more than 50 percent of their work time to managerial duties.

FLSA.[274] Another is an across-the-board increase in the statutory overtime premium from 50 per cent to 100 per cent or more.[275] Finally, in the spirit of the recent worldwide resurgence of interest in shorter hours as a means of combating unemployment and/or increasing leisure,[276] a return to the pre-New Deal state maximum hours statutes prohibiting workweeks beyond a specified length becomes imaginable.[277] In contrast with these radical possibilities, a readjustment of the quarter-century-old obsolete salary test level is merely the rankest reformism—even if it is calculated, as the Wage and Hour Administrator declared in 1993, to "alienate the other interested parties" such as McDonald's,[278] which controlled one-sixth of the entire fast-food market and two-fifths of the burger business.[279]

However, the initial and continuing confusion or lack of forthrightness in explaining the policies underlying the FLSA overtime premium has also come back to haunt workers as courts have felt freer to deny overtime coverage for some relatively highly paid professional and managerial employees—whose status as excluded is grey—on the grounds that their high incomes alone disqualify them for protection.[280]

Big Business, eager to shed regulation of the duties of its putatively excluded white-collar employees and to avoid FLSA suits filed by "quite high level

---

[274]In enforcing the 39-hour week even for managers, French government agents "prowled garages to see what time people were actually leaving. Thousands of fines were issued and...some businesses...install[ed] time clocks even for managers...." Suzanne Daley, "A French Paradox at Work: 35-Hour Week May Turn Out to Be Best for Employers," *N.Y. Times*, Nov. 11, 1999, at C1, col. 2, at C27, col. 1-2 (nat. ed.).

[275]*See* above chapter 1; Ronald Ehrenberg and Paul Schumann, "The Overtime Pay Provisions of the Fair Labor Standards Act," in *The Economics of Legal Minimum Wages* 264, 267 (Simon Rottenberg ed., 1981); Ronald Ehrenberg, *Longer Hours or More Jobs? An Investigation of Amending Hours Legislation to Create Employment* 131-39 (1982).

[276]*See, e.g.*, Juliet Schor, *The Overworked American: The Unexpected Decline of Leisure* (1991); Roger Cohen, "Europeans Consider Shortening Workweek to Relieve Joblessness," *N.Y. Times*, Nov. 22, 1993, at A1, col. 4 (nat. ed.).

[277]*See* Elizabeth Brandeis, "Labor Legislation," in 3 John Commons et al., *History of Labor in the United States 1896-1932*, at 457-500, 540-63 (1935).

[278]Telephone interview with Maria Echaveste, Wage & Hour Administrator, Washington, D.C., Nov. 22, 1993, 10 a.m. CST.

[279]Barnaby Feder, "McDonald's Finds There's Still Plenty of Room to Grow," *N.Y. Times*, Jan. 9, 1994, § 3, at 5, col. 1 (nat. ed.).

[280]As a writer for the NBC Nightly News with a weekly salary of a thousand dollars observed: "'We're proud of the work we do.... We think it's very important work and we think we do it very well. But it's not brain surgery and it's not painting "Mona Lisas." We are just not creative artists. We are journalists.'" Alan Finder, "Are NBC News Writers Professionals? In Lawsuit, Writers Decline Honor," *N.Y. Times*, July 14, 1991, at 12, col. 1, at 3 (nat. ed.).

executives...well-to-do individuals,"[281] has shown some interest in setting a much higher salary test as the exclusive criterion for coverage. This initiative surfaced at a 1995 House Subcommittee on Workforce Protections hearing. William Kilberg, former DOL Solicitor, a corporate lawyer appearing on behalf of a coalition of "significant employers of white collar employees" such as accounting firms, computer companies, media outlets, and engineering consultants,[282] argued that "[i]f the rationale for protecting certain employees is that they lack the bargaining power to protect themselves, then the exemptions should be designed to separate those who possess adequate bargaining power from those who lack it. ... One promising solution would be to base exempt status for white collar employees...on the amount paid to each employee...."[283]

Appearing on behalf of the Labor Policy Association, "an organization of the senior human resource executives of 220 of the nation's largest corporations," which employed 11 million workers or 12 percent of the nonfarm private-sector work force,[284] Maggi Coil amplified and specified Kilberg's suggestion:

> We believe that the exempt/non-exempt rules need to be simplified. There should be some nexus between the amount of compensation earned by an employee and eligibility for the exemption. If an employee is highly paid, who cares whether he or she is engaged in production or management, or is exercising independent judgment or discretion. If an employee is being paid $40 per hour, to say that he or she must be paid $60 for each hour over forty because he or she is not being paid "on a salary basis" does not pass the common sense test.
>
> We realize that this is easier said than done. What is the magic number that divides a well-compensated employee from one who is on the "lower rungs" of the economic ladder? ... There are no easy answers and you can be sure that no matter what you come up with there will inevitably be anomalies at the margins.
>
> Despite these complexities, we believe the current crisis should compel you to pursue a solution because the current problems are well beyond "marginal."[285]

---

[281]*Hearings on the Fair Labor Standards Act: Hearings Before the Subcommittee on Workforce Protections of the House Committee on Economic and Educational Opportunities*, 104th Cong., 1st Sess. 67 (Serial No. 104-46, 1996) (statement of William Kilberg).

[282]*Hearings on the Fair Labor Standards Act: Hearings Before the Subcommittee on Workforce Protections of the House Committee on Economic and Educational Opportunities* at 66 (statement of William Kilberg).

[283]*Hearings on the Fair Labor Standards Act: Hearings Before the Subcommittee on Workforce Protections of the House Committee on Economic and Educational Opportunities* at 77-78 (statement of William Kilberg)

[284]*Hearings on the Fair Labor Standards Act: Hearings Before the Subcommittee on Workforce Protections of the House Committee on Economic and Educational Opportunities* at 18 (statement of Maggi Coil).

[285]*Hearings on the Fair Labor Standards Act: Hearings Before the Subcommittee on*

The following year the Flexible Employment Compensation and Scheduling Coalition—which includes a heterogeneous group of employers and association of large and small employers employing a large proportion of the workforce such as the Boeing, Eastman Kodak, General Electric, Hewlett-Packard, the NAM, NRA, National Federation of Independent Businesses, and the Chamber of Commerce of the United States—submitted Coil's statement verbatim at a Senate Labor and Human Resources Committee hearing on the FLSA.[286] The Labor Policy Association also submitted to the congressional subcommittee a paper that called for "chang[ing] the white collar exemption to a 'highly compensated employee' exemption defined solely by salary or wages paid. This would retain the current approach of covering all employees not excepted but would simply state that, once an employee's wages or salary reached a certain level, he or she no longer has a statutory entitlement to overtime premiums."[287]

With such proposals—Coil's $40 an hour figure would equate to an annual salary of $80,000—Big Business ran into Labor's open arms. Since Kilberg emphasized that "no one on our side of the table...is urging that the assistant deli manager be characterized as an exempt employee. We are concerned about accountants, engineers, paraprofessionals,"[288] the United Food and Commercial Workers International Union (UFCW) representative, assistant general counsel

---

Workforce Protections of the House Committee on Economic and Educational Opportunities at 23.

[286]*Oversight of the Fair Labor Standards Act: Hearing of the Senate Committee on Labor and Human Resources*, 104th Cong., 2d Sess. 57-58 (1996).

[287]LPA, "Reinventing the Fair Labor Standards Act to Support the Reengineered Workplace," in *Hearings on the Fair Labor Standards Act: Hearings Before the Subcommittee on Workforce Protections of the House Committee on Economic and Educational Opportunities* at 26, 52.

[288]*Hearings on the Fair Labor Standards Act: Hearings Before the Subcommittee on Workforce Protections of the House Committee on Economic and Educational Opportunities* at 120. A few weeks later, Kilberg published an op-ed in the *Wall Street Journal* summarizing Big Business's position. William Kilberg, "A 1938 Law that Hurts Workers More Than It Helps Them," *Wall St. J.*, May 10, 1995, at A19, col. 3. After having heard from Nick Clark, the UFCW attorney who testified at the hearing, about the testimony, the present author submitted a letter to the editor to the *Wall Street Journal* (with a copy to Kilberg) on May 10, 1995, responding to Kilberg and, tongue in cheek, calling on employers, if they were "seriously interested in deregulating labor relations," to "seize the opportunity" to reach agreement with unions on a higher, dispositive salary level. Although the *Journal* did not publish the letter, on July 31 and Aug. 3, 1995, the author received a telephone call from Sandra Boyd, assistant general counsel of the LPA. Stating that she had read and liked the letter, she asked whether the author might be interested in testifying at the counterpart Senate hearings in the fall or spring since congressional committees like to hear testimony from academics. Boyd stated that LPA members might be able to accept a salary level cutoff of $40,000 to $50,000, though she conceded that restaurant owners were not enthusiastic about such a proposal. Finally, she observed that although the AFL-CIO wanted the salary level increased, it did not want to open the FLSA up for fear of other changes.

Nick Clark, whose chief objective in testifying was to urge updating the obsolete salary level, perceived the common ground:

> this morning, the employer proposals seemed to coalesce for a bright-line test to solve many of these problems. In other words, if the salary levels were sufficiently high..., then workers above that salary level would not have to worry about the salary basis test regulations.
>
> Now that seems to be something we might be able to work with. Certainly, workers that are making over $100,000 a year, I think we can all agree, should be salaried and not have to worry about docking regulations. I think the figures that were floated out by Mr. Kilberg were six-figure incomes and things of that nature. ...
>
> What we are concerned about is workers who have had their wages and salaries eroded over 20 years of inflation, and who are on the low end of the scale, not the highly compensated workers that make six-figure incomes that Mr. Kilberg referred to.[289]

The UFCW was so conciliatory that when Representative Lynn Woolsey (D. Cal.) asked the obvious question as to whether it would not be "simpler just to pay everybody overtime, except for business owners," Clark declared: "we certainly are not suggesting that. We think that the salary exemption makes sense for a class of workers, and it's always been there in the Act, and certainly I'm on salary, and I don't have an objection to that."[290] Such acquiescence was remarkable since the MWSC had reported that on one view overtime exemptions had become "anachronistic" in light of the widespread approval of the 40-hour week; while the premium penalty's employment-spreading effect had become irrelevant, universalizing it would "reinforce the acknowledged public acceptance of the 40-hour workweek and...provide additional compensation for inconvenience and added risk of injury associated with overtime work."[291] When Clark

---

[289]*Hearings on the Fair Labor Standards Act: Hearings Before the Subcommittee on Workforce Protections of the House Committee on Economic and Educational Opportunities* at 100.

[290]*Hearings on the Fair Labor Standards Act: Hearings Before the Subcommittee on Workforce Protections of the House Committee on Economic and Educational Opportunities* at 118. Oddly, the chief characteristic that Clark used to explain why the overtime claims of workers with six-figure incomes were not a concern to the UFCW was not their high standard of living or the bargaining power that made possible the high salary; rather the income was an indicator of workplace autonomy and self-direction: "The reason the employer is paying these six-figure incomes to these workers is because they expect to exercise judgment as to how they allocate their time. They pay for a job to be completed. They don't tell the worker how to do the job, they say, here's the job, you get it done...and you work the number of hours it takes...." *Id.* 114, 115. These criteria are traditionally used to identify independent contractors, who are not covered by the FLSA or other labor-protective statutes, whereas executive and administrative employees, no matter how highly paid, are universally recognized as controlled by the employer and thus in an employment relationship.

[291]1 *Report of the Minimum Wage Study Commission* at 120.

repeated that "we, on the side of labor, would entertain" exempting from overtime everyone with a six-figure income, chairman Cass Ballenger (R. N.C.) ended the hearing by observing that, regardless of whether Clark or Kilberg had brought up the $100,000 figure, "there might be a point of discussion there...."[292]

But when Clark returned four years later to testify on a different aspect of the FLSA before the same House Subcommittee on Workforce Protections, he was reduced to observing that although in 1995 committee members and employer representatives had agreed that the salary levels were obsolete, neither the committee nor any employer had proposed a bill rectifying the inequity.[293]

The only congressional initiative even remotely embodying Clark's proposal was undertaken by Representative Thomas Petri (R. Wis.), who introduced identical bills in the 104th and 105th Congress in 1996 and 1997, which would have amended the exclusions and exemptions section of the FLSA to exclude from minimum wage and overtime coverage "any employee whose rate of annual compensation is not less than $40,000."[294] No action was taken on either of these bills—the first of which had no other supporters, and the second only three—which, like several bills in 1939-40, would have applied to all employees regardless of whether they fell into the three statutory white-collar categories. Ironically, Petri's purpose was not to protect workers from overreaching employers; on the contrary, his proposal was designed to

> create an income threshold that automatically exempts from FLSA scrutiny the highest paid strata of the workforce. This would directly reverse the trend toward questionable and irrational overtime awards for highly compensated employees. There is no reason that the FLSA, which was passed to protect laborers who "toil in factory and on farm," and who are "helpless victims of their own bargaining weakness," should ever be interpreted to protect workers making high five-figure or six-figure incomes.[295]

Even without correcting Petri's tendentious legislative history, it is clear from his own arithmetic as well as from reality that many workers with intermediate five-figure incomes lack the bargaining power to resist employer demands to overwork free of charge. Nevertheless, despite his biased motivation,

---

[292]*Hearings on the Fair Labor Standards Act: Hearings Before the Subcommittee on Workforce Protections of the House Committee on Economic and Educational Opportunities*, 104th Cong., 1st Sess. at 121.

[293]*Hearing on Rewarding Performance in Compensation Act: Hearing Before the Subcommittee on Workforce Protections of the House Committee on Education and the Workforce*, 106th Cong., 1st Sess. 12 (1999).

[294]H.R. 4266, § 2(a), 104th Cong., 2d Sess. (1996); H.R. 647, § 2(a), 105th Cong., 1st Sess. (1997).

[295]143 *Cong. Rec.* E 317, 318 (Feb. 26, 1997) (Lexis). For Petri's almost identical remarks, see 142 *Cong. Rec.* E 1789 (Sept. 27, 1996).

Petri's bills represent a step in the direction of drawing the coverage line on more rational, transparent, and easily administered bases.

The Clinton administration's failure to undertake any initiative to raise the salary test level contrasts sharply with the alacrity with which the president himself asked Congress to raise another long unchanged threshold—that for social security coverage for domestic workers. As soon as the $50 per quarter threshold became politically embarrassing for him, when a number of his prominent nominees were revealed to have violated the Internal Revenue Code by having failed to pay Federal Insurance Contributions Act taxes on behalf of their maids and nannies,[296] President Clinton informed Congress that "'[t]he financial threshold in the law is outdated, having remained unchanged for the past four decades. It is time to amend the law.'"[297] Congressional inaction since 1950 with regard to this threshold had favored domestic workers—at least those who worked for the fewer than one-quarter of employers who complied with the law.[298] Although it was on notice that tens of thousands of domestic workers would lose benefits,[299] no "conflicting interests of the many and differing constituencies" deterred Congress from quintupling the threshold and relieving many affluent recipients of maid services of employment tax liability.[300]

Similarly, when the DOL concluded that its regulation defining what it means

---

[296]26 U.S.C. § 3121(a)(7)(B) (1988); Michael Kelly, "Household Hiring Is Trickier with New Broom in Capital," *N.Y. Times*, Feb. 12, 1993, at A1, col. 5 (nat. ed.); Douglas Martin, "Illegal-Nanny Anxiety Afflicts Nation After Uproar over Baird and Wood," *N.Y. Times*, Feb. 15, 1993, at A7, col. 4 (nat. ed.); Richard Berke, "Judge's Friends Try to Save Candidacy for High Court," *N.Y. Times*, June 14, 1993, at A10, col. 1 (nat. ed.); Gwen Ifill, "Defense Nominee Didn't Pay Taxes for Housekeeper," *N.Y. Times*, Dec. 21, 1993, A1, at col. 3 (nat. ed.); "Statement of Bobby Ray Inman on Withdrawing His Nomination," *N.Y. Times*, Jan. 19, 1994, at A16, col. 1 (nat. ed.); Eric Schmitt, "Discussing Tax Stand, Inman Says Maid Was 'Contractor,'" *N.Y. Times*, Jan. 19, 1994, at A17, col. 1 (nat. ed.);

[297]Richard Berke, "Clinton Seeks Change in Tax Rule That Scuttled Baird Nomination," *N.Y. Times*, Apr. 24, 1993, at 7, col. 2 (nat. ed.) (quoting letter of Apr. 19, 1993, from Clinton to Sen. Biden, chairman of the Sen. Judiciary Comm.).

[298]*Hearing on Proposals to Simplify and Streamline the Payment of Employment Taxes for Domestic Workers Before the Subcommittee on Social Security and the Subcommittee on Human Resources of the House Committee on Ways & Means*, 103d Cong., 1st Sess. 5 (Mar. 4, 1993) (statement of Marshall Washburn, IRS) (mimeo 5); Michael Wines, "Panel Eases Employers' Tax on Domestic Workers," *N.Y. Times,* May 12, 1993, at C18, col. 3 (nat. ed.).

[299]"Not the Zoe Baird Problem," *Wash. Post*, May 3, 1993, at A18 (opinion editorial) (Nexis); "Ways and Means Outrage," *Wash. Post*, May 13, 1993, at A26 (opinion editorial) (Nexis); Michael Arnold, "Senate May Seek Different Solution on Tax Payments for Domestic Help," *Wash. Post*, June 20, 1993, at A16 (Nexis).

[300]Social Security Domestic Employment Reform Act of 1994, § 2(a)(1)(A), as published in 140 *Cong. Rec.* H11010 (codified at 26 U.S. Code § 3121(a)(7)(B) & (x)). See generally, Marc Linder "What Hath Zoe Baird Wrought? The New FICA Amendments on Domestic Service Employees," 66 *Tax Notes* 113 (1995).

for excluded white collar workers to be paid "on a salary basis" contradicted congressional intent as applied to public-sector employees, it promptly amended it to accommodate their employers.[301] Thus it should behoove an allegedly labor-friendly Democratic administration to arrive at the same conclusion regarding the salary-test level and to put an end to employers' efforts to appropriate unpaid labor in this particular manner by compelling workers to work supra-normal workweeks. As have many administrations before it, the Clinton Administration DOL repeatedly announced that § 541 is on its regulatory agenda.[302] In 1994, it announced that the salary level tests "are outdated and offer little practical guidance in the application of the exemption. ... Because the regulations are sorely out-of-date, a comprehensive rulemaking is necessary. ... Legal developments in court cases are causing progressive loss of control of the guiding interpretations under this exemption and are creating law without considering a comprehensive analytical approach to current compensation concepts and work-place practices."[303]

By 1999 even the GAO found the salary level to be universally regarded as "virtually meaningless" and in need of revision.[304] Yet the Assistant Secretary of Employment Standards in the Clinton administration made brutally clear how hopeless the prospect for raising the salary level had become when he trans-mogrified employers into "constituencies" of the Department of Labor: "any change in the current regulatory structure requires balancing the diametrically opposed, conflicting interests of the many and differing constituencies that would be affected. The views of interested parties are intractably held on opposite sides of the various issues under these regulations."[305]

---

[301]29 C.F.R. § 541.5d (1993). Under 29 C.F.R. § 541.118(a), an employer forfeits its exemption from the minimum wage and overtime provisions of FLSA if it docks salaried employees for absences from work for personal reasons of less than a day. State and local government employers complained that compliance with this regulation would require them to violate public accountability laws prohibiting payments to government employees for time not worked that is not covered by accrued leave. 57 *Fed. Reg.* 37,666-677 (1992); *Hearing on the Fair Labor Standards Act: Hearing Before the Subcommittee on Labor Standards, Occupational Health and Safety of the House Committee on Education and Labor*, 103d Cong., 1st Sess. (1993); 29 C.F.R. § 541.5d (1993).

[302]58 *Fed. Reg.* 24,569, 56,587 (1993).

[303]59 *Fed. Reg.* 57129-30 (1994). For similar or identical semiannual admissions, see 60 *Fed. Reg.* 23,544, 59,163 (1995); 61 *Fed. Reg.* 23,240, 62,087 (1996); 62 *Fed. Reg.* 57,094 (1997); 63 *Fed. Reg.* 61,289 (1998); 64 *Fed. Reg.* 21,499, 63,979 (1999).

[304]GAO, *Fair Labor Standards Act* at 33-34.

[305]Letter from Bernard Anderson to Cynthia Fagnoni, GAO, in GAO, *Fair Labor Standards Act* at 53. The Wage and Hour Administrator repeated these remarks in calling changes "extremely unlikely in the short-term." "Hearing on the Fair Labor Standards Act: Hearing Before the Subcommittee on Workforce Protections of the House Committee on Education and the Workforce on White-Collar Exemptions in the Modem Work Place" 106th Cong., 2d Sess. (May 3, 2000) (statement of T. Michael Kerr) (Westlaw).

3

How Working Off the Clock Came to Be Legal: The Portal-to-Portal Act of 1947

[M]oments are the elements of profit....[1]

1. Legal Amnesia

We are then confronted with the question of whether this court should lend its aid to a practice that deprives any working man of...the only thing he has to sell—his hours or minutes of labor.[2]

Should workers walk from the plant gate to their work stations on their own time? Or should employers who benefit from the economies associated with huge factories compensate employees for the five, ten, or fifteen-minute walk? More than half a century later, it is difficult to recapture the intensity of a conflict—over what was after all a minor aspect of the federal wage and hour law—which *The New York Times* called "one of the greatest legal-economic controversies in American history,"[3] while others, including a Supreme Court justice, compared it to the *Dred Scott* case in terms of the public attention it had generated.[4] In particular, the attention that employers and the press lavished on the trial of one such monetarily insignificant "portal-to-portal" claim in federal court in 1947 has

---

[1]*Reports of the Inspectors of Factories for the Half Year Ending 30th April, 1860*, at 56 (C. 2689, 34 Parl. Pap. 1860).

[2]Anderson v. Mt. Clemens Pottery Co., 60 F. Supp. 146, 149-50 (E.D. Mich. 1943).

[3]William White, "Government Asks Portal Case Ban: Origin 'Trifling,'" *N.Y. Times*, Jan. 24, 1947, at 1 col. 8.

[4]The author of the Supreme Court portal-pay cases, Frank Murphy, wrote his brother that "not even *Dred Scott*, the *Dartmouth College* case, and *Marbury v. Madison* had caused 'as much interest and excitement' as the Mt. Clemens opinion." 3 Sidney Fine, *Frank Murphy: The Washington Years* 332 (1984). In the same vein, a law review commentator noted: "Only occasionally does it occur that the subject matter of lawsuits in the courts becomes a matter of great public concern to the entire body politic. Among these in the past are the Dred Scott decision, the Gold Clause cases, and perhaps, the NRA case. [T]he course of the present cases on so-called portal to portal pay has attracted wide public attention and much daily comment in the press. These conditions bring to the fore the effect of political and economic conditions and relationships on judicial decisions in a much more forceful way than ordinarily occurs even in cases in which the court's decision between private litigants has a profound effect on political and economic history." Ralph Axley, "The Problem of Portal to Portal Pay," 1947 *Wisc. L. Rev.* 163, 163.

been unique in the post-World War II history of labor law.[5]

This dispute owed the fervor with which all parties invested it to the fact that it coincided with—and was a sideshow of—the campaign that capital conducted between 1945 and 1947 to reclaim the power, sovereignty, and control that it had been forced to cede to labor and the state during World War II.[6] When unions resisted,[7] "labor-management relations appear[ed] to be rushing toward a fateful climax."[8] Overshadowed historically, though not contemporaneously, by the debate over Taft-Hartley's incursions into the rights that workers had secured under the National Labor Relations Act,[9] the Portal-to-Portal Act of 1947 has receded into oblivion. Known today only to—and taken for granted by—specialist labor-law litigators, the Act's political-economic origins have become relegated to obscurity. Emblematic of this political amnesia is the fact that the major monograph devoted to labor problems during the first Truman administration never even alludes to the portal pay issue or legislation.[10]

---

[5]"It has been years since a Federal district judge, with one exception [the John L. Lewis contempt case], has found himself in a situation with such grave possibilities." Arthur Krock, "Picard in Portal Test," *N.Y. Times*, Jan. 29, 1947, at 6, col. 4.

[6]See Clark Kerr, "Employer Policies in Industrial Relations, 1945 to 1947," in *Labor in Postwar America* 43, 46-47 (Colston Warne ed. 1949); David Brody, *Workers in Industrial America* 173-204 (1981 [1980]); Howell Harris, *The Right to Manage: Industrial Relations Policies of American Business in the 1940s*, at 130 (1982); Nelson Lichtenstein, *Labor's War at Home: The CIO in World War II* 220 (1987 [1982]); Sanford Jacoby, *Employing Bureaucracy: Managers, Unions, and the Transformation of Work in American Industry, 1900-1945*, at 241-74 (1985).

[7]For an unusual portrait of the strikes of this period, see George Lipsitz, *Class and Culture in Cold War America* (1981).

[8]Louis Stark, "Portal Pay Issue Intensifies The Wage Dispute," *N.Y. Times*, Dec. 29, 1946, § 4, at 3, col. 3.

[9]When the Republican-dominated Eightieth Congress convened in January 1947, Senator Wiley, the chairman of the Senate Judiciary Committee, stated that his portal-pay hearing "was the first subcommittee hearing held under the auspices of the Republican Party since 1933 on a matter of national importance." *Portal to Portal Wages: Hearings Before a Subcommittee of the Senate Committee on the Judiciary*, 80th Cong. 1st Sess. 8 (1947).

[10]Arthur McClure, *The Truman Administration and the Problems of Postwar Labor, 1945-1948*, at 254, 257 (1969) (the bibliography includes a reference to a hearing and an article on the Portal-to-Portal Act). Indeed, Truman himself in his memoirs fails to refer to the issue. 1-2 Harry Truman, *Memoirs* (1955-56). Robert Donovan, *Conflict and Crisis: The Presidency of Harry S Truman, 1945-1948* (1977), not only never mentions the portal-to-portal dispute, but incorrectly asserts that "the Republican assault upon New Deal labor policy got off to a hot start April 17," *id.* at 299, when the House passed the Hartley bill, although the House had already passed the portal bill in February. The following major works on the Truman administration also fail even to mention the issue: Alonzo Hamby, *Beyond the New Deal: Harry S. Truman and American Liberalism* (1973); Bert Cochran,

This chapter presents a comprehensive political-economic legislative history of the Portal-to-Portal Act,[11] analyzing the unusual way in which litigation shaped the contours of the statute which the Portal Act amended, the Fair Labor Standards Act (FLSA). As part of a larger wartime and postwar labor conflict, the portal suits were both a calculated effort to maximize bargaining pressure on big business and a hapless venture by the Congress of Industrial Organizations (CIO) to secure large recoveries from employers without due consideration of the possible reactions by capital and the state or of the repercussions for the unorganized. In the event, the Portal Act's restrictive impact has not only fallen on the low-paid, but also extended far beyond the issue of walking time.

The analysis begins with an economic-historical discussion of the significance of the definition of compensable worktime under protective-statutory regimes (§ 2). The relevance for the portal controversy of the trends in overtime work, wages, and profits during and immediately after World War II is reviewed in § 3. Then follow studies of two mining cases that crucially shaped the political and jurisprudential contours of the portal-pay dispute (§ 4). Attention then shifts to the major industrial portal suit, the Supreme Court's decision in which set the stage for mass litigation and congressional intervention (§ 5). § 6 then offers a detailed legislative history of the Portal Act beginning with efforts at the state level to blunt the impact of the FLSA by shortening the applicable statutes of limitations. After a brief examination of the relationship between mandatory norms under the FLSA and consensual bargaining (§ 7), the ironic twists inhering in what turned out to be the most important achievement of the Portal Act, the elimination of class actions,

---

Harry Truman and the Crisis Presidency (1973); *The Truman Presidency* (Michael Lacey ed. 1989). A biography of the general counsel of the United Automobile Workers during the period under review fails to mention the portal struggle. Christopher Johnson, *Maurice Sugar: Law, Labor, and the Left in Detroit 1912-1950 (1988)*. None of the numerous articles on the controversy published by the *New York Times* was reprinted in an anthology including thirty pages of articles on labor from the reconversion period. *See Labor and Management* 164-97 (Richard Morris ed. 1973). A major exception is Joel Seidman, *American Labor from Defense to Reconversion* 259-61 (1976 [1953]). At the other extreme, a major history of the working day misunderstood the practical impact of portal-pay suits, claiming that "[b]y January 1947, workers had won nearly $6 billion in over 1,500 such cases," when in fact they had merely filed these cases, ultimately prevailing in none. David Roediger and Philip Foner, *On Our Own Time: A History of American Labor and the Working Day* 266 (1989). Absurdly ignorant is the assertion that "the Taft-Hartley Act effectively repealed...the Fair Labor Standards Act." Gerard Colby, *Du Pont Dynasty* 402 (1984).

[11]One aspect of the Portal-to-Portal Act that will not be analyzed is its constitutionality, which was upheld in Battaglia v. General Motors Corp., 169 F.2d 254 (2d Cir.), *cert. denied*, 335 U.S. 887 (1948). Among the numerous articles appearing on this issue is worth mentioning, Ray Brown, "Vested Rights and the Portal-to-Portal Act," 46 *Mich. L. Rev.* 723 (1948).

form the subject of § 8. The lessons to be learned from the portal litigation are summarized in § 9.

2. When and Where Does the Workday Begin and Who Decides?

[M]ost of these actions have been entered into...against employers always ready and willing to chisel a little free work from the men and women who work for them.[12]

Workers' demands to be compensated for travel and preparatory time is at first sight merely "[o]ne of the eternal conflicts out of which life is made up," namely "that between the effort of every man to get the most he can for his services, and that of society, disguised under the name of capital, to get his services for the least possible return...."[13] More particularly, it appears as "righteous"[14] resistance against efforts by employers to avoid an obligation to pay for all of their workers' time they have at their disposal. Thus rather than an example of higgling over terms, unions projected the portal pay issue as a type of theft. In this sense the controversy was a venerable one that differed little from that recounted by Karl Marx for Victorian Britain.[15]

Portal-pay disputes are especially liable to arise under wage and hour statutes; significantly, the most prominent portal-pay cases involved piece-rate workers. Before the advent of the FLSA, workers in the United States may have had relatively little interest in whether they were paid specifically for portal-type time: if they were members of the stronger trade unions, they may have succeeded in negotiating enhanced piece rates that reflected or somehow accommodated travel time and preliminary and postliminary activities.[16] If they did not have the bargaining power to achieve such adjustments, most had no other recourse. Ironically, in the pre-FLSA period many workers were less preoccupied with the

---

[12]93 *Cong. Rec.* 1488 (1947) (Rep. Sabath, Dem. Ill.).

[13]Vegelahn v. Guntner, 44 N.E. 1077, 1081 (Mass. 1896) (Holmes, J., dissenting).

[14]Senator Pepper used this word to characterize one of the portal cases. 93 *Cong. Rec.* 2301 (1947).

[15]1 Karl Marx, *Das Kapital* 206-11 (1867), republished in Karl Marx [and] Friedrich Engels, *Gesamtausgabe (MEGA)*, II:5 at 184-88 (1983).

[16]For examples from the late nineteenth and early twentieth century of demands by German workers for compensation for waiting and preliminary/postliminary activity time, see Richard Biernacki, *The Fabrication of Labor: Germany and Britain, 1640-1914*, at 362-82 (1995). Industrial collective bargaining agreements even in the 1940s typically contained numerous provisions mandating payments for various kinds of preliminary, postliminary, and waiting time. For a sample of such provisions, see *Regulating the Recovery of Portal-to-Portal Pay, and for Other Purposes: Hearings Before Subcommittee No. 2 of the House Committee on the Judiciary*, 80th Cong., 1st Sess. 93-101 (1947).

question of compensation for the walk between factory gate and bench and much more concerned with the reality of being fined or forbidden access to the plant for part or all of the day for having arrived even a few minutes late.[17] Underground miners in the United States as well as in Europe and Australia in the late nineteenth and early twentieth century were almost alone in having achieved a modicum of statutory protection against employer overreaching in an industry that imposed the longest and most brutal workplace travel-time and, not surprisingly, gave rise to the portal-to-portal controversy under the FLSA.[18]

Under the English Factory Acts, which regulated and specified the hours during which women and children could be employed, employers sought to jump the gun at the beginning of the day and to keep the workers at work after the end of the statutory working day. The factory inspectors in the 1850s reported how "snatching a few minutes" or the "petty pilferings of minutes"[19] could cumulatively result in impressive profits: "Five minutes a day's increased work, multiplied by weeks, are equal to two and half days produce in the year."[20] Under a similar Massachusetts statute the factory inspectors reported in 1886 that "where the engine is started several minutes before schedule time, complaints are made that the women...go to work five or ten minutes before the proper time, thus gaining one or two hours a week."[21] Then as now:

> The profit to be gained by it appears to be, to many, a greater temptation than they can resist; they calculate upon the chance of not being found out; and when they see the small amount of penalty and costs, which those who have been convicted have had to pay, they find that if they should be detected there will still be a considerable balance of gain.[22]

---

[17]1 Karl Marx, *Das Kapital* 416-17 (1867); *Fourth Biennial Report of the Bureau of Labor Statistics of Illinois: 1886*, at 501-26 (1886); Jeremy Atack and Fred Bateman, "Louis Brandeis, Work and Fatigue at the Start of the Twentieth Century: Prelude to Oregon's Hours Limitation Law" at 5 (Nat. Bur. Econ. Res. Working Paper No. 25, 1991); Biernacki, *The Fabrication of Labor* at 105-28.

[18]See below § 4.

[19]*Reports of the Inspectors of Factories for the Half Year Ending 31st October, 1856*, at 48 (C. 2153, 3 Parl. Pap. 1857 Sess. 2).

[20]*Reports of the Inspectors of Factories for the Half Year Ending 31st October, 1851*, at 5 (C. 1396, 23 Parl. Pap. 1852). "'If you will allow me,' said a highly respectable master to me, 'to work only ten minutes in the day over time, you put one thousand a year in my pocket.'" *Reports of the Inspectors of Factories for the Half Year Ending 31st October, 1856*, at 48 (C. 2153, 3 Parl. Pap. 1857 Sess. 1).

[21]*Report of the Chief of Massachusetts District Police, for the Year Ending December 31, 1886*, at 55 (Pub. Doc. No. 32, No. 32, 1887).

[22]*Reports of the Inspectors of Factories for the Half Year Ending 31st October, 1856*, at 34 (C. 2153, 3 Parl. Pap. 1857 Sess. 2).

The conflict over the compensability of workers' time in the United States intensified as firms, in order to take advantage of economics of scale and vertical integration, invested their capital in larger and larger plants, the layout of which required workers to walk long distances from the initial entry point to their individual work station. The mammoth military production facilities built during World War II reinforced this trend. In the metal products industries, for example, on which war production had its greatest impact, the number of establishments employing more than 2,500 wage earners increased sixfold from 1939 to1945, while their employment rose almost eightfold and their share of all metal products workers rose from 18.6 per cent to 48.8 per cent.[23] Even by 1947, when the effect of wartime concentration had in part been dissipated in the wake of demobilization, the number of all manufacturing plants in this largest category had increased by 186 per cent vis-à-vis 1939, while the number of workers employed in them had risen by 208 per cent. With the number of employees in manufacturing establishments serving as an indicator of plant size, Table 3-1 shows the employment trend in large plants (with more than 2,500 employees) between 1929 and 1992.

At the height of the portal controversy in 1947, more than two-thirds of all workers employed in these largest plants were concentrated in the transportation equipment, primary metals, machinery, and electrical machinery industries (in that order).[24] Indeed, almost one-third worked in steel mills and motor vehicle plants alone.[25] This industrial structure, in turn, geographically concentrated almost two-thirds of the large-plant workers in the six states of Michigan, Pennsylvania, Ohio, New York, Illinois, and Indiana (in that order).[26] By no coincidence, then, the bulk of the portal litigation arose in these industries and states.[27] As capital intensive and heavily organized plants, they formed the focus of an intense conflict between the CIO and large capital.

---

[23]U.S. Senate, *Economic Concentration and World War II: Report of the Smaller War Plants Corporation to the Special Comm. to Study Problems of American Small Business*, 79th Cong., 2d Sess., Sen. Doc. No. 206, Table C-6 at 337 (1946). The largest subgroups within this industrial classification were aircraft production and shipbuilding. For data on the subgroups, see *id.*, table C-4 at 330-36.

[24]Calculated according to data in U.S. Bureau of the Census, 1 *Census of Manufactures: 1947*, Table 1 at 97-98 (1950).

[25]U.S. Bureau of the Census, 1 *Census of Manufactures: 1947* at 125, 136.

[26]U.S. Bureau of the Census, 1 *Census of Manufactures: 1947* at 143-44.

[27]See S. Rep. No. 48: *Exempting Employers from Liability for Portal-to-Portal Wages in Certain Cases*, 80th Cong., 1st Sess. 2-4, 22-25 (1947).

Table 3-1: Employment in Manufacturing Establishments with 2,500 or More Employees (Large Plants), 1929-92

Year	Number of large plants	Total employees in large plants	Average number of employees in large plants	Employees in large plants as % of all mfg. employees
1929	195	910,740	4,670	11.5
1939	176	824,532	4,685	10.5
1947	504	2,541,700	5,043	17.8
1954	533	2,876,100	5,396	18.4
1958	533	2,654,500	4,980	17.2
1963	544	2,898,600	5,328	17.9
1967	674	3,628,800	5,384	19.6
1972	582	2,926,800	5,029	16.2
1977	581	2,911,100	5,010	15.7
1982	482	2,445,800	5,074	13.7
1987	421	2,304,300	5,473	13.0
1992	342	1,804,200	5,275	10.6

U.S. Bureau of the Census, *Sixteenth Census of the United States: 1940*. 1 *Manufactures: 1939*, at 119-21 (1942); U.S. Bureau of the Census, 1 *1967 Census of Manufactures*, tab. 1 and 2 at 2-4 and 2-5 (1971); U.S. Bureau of the Census, 1 *1972 Census of Manufactures: Subject and Special Statistics*, tab. 8 at 68 (1976); U.S. Bureau of the Census, 1 *1977 Census of Manufactures: Subject Statistics*, tab. 4 at 1-59 (1981); U.S. Bureau of the Census, *1982 Census of Manufactures, General Summary*, Pt. 2, tab. 1 at 1-3 (1985); U.S. Bureau of the Census, *1987 Census of Manufactures: Subject Series: General Summary*, tab. 4 at 1-99 (1991); U.S. Bureau of the Census, *1992 Census of Manufactures: Subject Series: General Summary*, tab. 1-4 at 178 (1996).

Contemporary liberal and leftist[28] commentators tended to argue that employers required an economic incentive to modify their plants so that workers might share in the economies of scale.[29] For example, Percival and Paul Goodman in *Communitas*, their well-known critique of city planning published in 1947, observed that the "universal and obvious assumption" that the huge wartime concentration of workers in mammoth industrial plants was technically efficient:

---

[28]That is, the part of the left that had not rejected FLSA as having shown the fallacy of trying to solve economic problems with social welfare measures because the Act did not thoroughly revalue wage-price relationships, redistribute national income, or deal with the root problems of technological, seasonal, and cyclical unemployment. *See, e.g.*, Herbert Burstein, "The Fair Labor Standards Act—A Legal and Economic Study," 6 *Law. Guild Rev.* 576 (1946).

[29]See, e.g., A.G. Mezerik, "Time Is Money," *The Nation*, Feb. 1, 1947, at 121, 122; Chandler Morse, "Economic Aspects of the Portal-to-Portal Pay Question," 7 *Law. Guild Rev.* 29, 32 (1947).

happens to be false, because it fails to consider what is by far the chief social expense in all large-scale production. This is labor time.

Let us regard the matter on its crudest level. Which is cheaper to transport, men or material?

Where the plant is concentrated, and a great many workers are employed in the same place the bulk of workers must live away and commute. But if the plant were scattered, the workers could live near their jobs, and it would be the processed materials that would have to be brought to several places for manufacture.... Which is cheaper to transport, living men twice daily or materials and mechanical parts...twice a week?

Which transport is easier to schedule so that there is no delay or interruption? The time of life of a piece of metal is not consumed while it waits for its truck: a piece of metal does not mind being compressed like a sardine. In a populated community, the supply trucks move at a convenient hour, but the fleet of trams and busses gorge and disgorge at 8:00-9:00 A.M. and at 4:00-5:00 P.M. Suppose that many of the workers travel by automobile; then there is mass parking, with one shift leaving while another is arriving, and the factory area must be still larger to allow for parking space. Next, after one gets to the area, there is the problem of walking to the work station: it is not unusual for the round trip to consume up to three-quarters of an hour. During part of the shifting, the machinery stands still.

To be sure, most of the consumption of labor time and nervous energy is not paid for by the capitalists, and the roads and franchises that make commutation possible are part of the social inheritance, paid for by the masses. But from the point of view of the social wealth, the expense must be added to the production, even though it does not technically appear in the price. From the point of view of the worker, his time is bound and useless even though it is not paid for. If parts of this expense, of time and effort, were made to appear as an item on the pay roll (as in the celebrated portal-to-portal demands of the mine workers), there would soon be better planning![30]

The conservative business press, however, rejected this position. As early as 1944, *Business Week* asserted that "time spent in travel or in changing clothes is not productive time. There is no way for alert management to absorb nonproductive costs. They can only be passed on to the consumer."[31] Without acknowledging the disconfirmation, two years later the magazine reported that in response to portal suits, employers were relocating gates and eliminating waiting

---

[30]Percival Goodman & Paul Goodman, *Communitas: Means of Livelihood and Ways of Life* 43 (1947). The authors, who exempted primary metallurgy and refining from this critique, deleted the Marxist language from the second edition. Percival Goodman & Paul Goodman, *Communitas: Means of Livelihood and Ways of Life* 83-84 (2d ed. 1960). Daniel Bell, "Work and Its Discontents: The Cult of Efficiency in America," in idem, *The End of Ideology: On the Exhaustion of Political Ideas in the Fifties* 227, 231 (rev. ed. 1966 [1956]), adopted this analysis.

[31]*Business Week*, Oct. 7, 1944, at 123. In the very next issue, Warner & Swasey, a machine manufacturer that later became a defendant in a portal-pay suit, published an advertisement on the inside front cover sounding the same theme. *Id.*, Oct. 14, 1944.

at time clocks.[32] From a somewhat different perspective, the *Wall Street Journal* editorialized on the subject repeatedly. Its basic insight was that since workers produced nothing while engaged in portal-to-portal travel:

> For the long run future it may make little difference in total wages whether they are reckoned on the basis of the time a man spends in the plant or on the basis of the time he actually spends handling the tools or running the machines.... [H]ourly rates reckoned on the longer period will for the long run be lower than those reckoned on a shorter period. If the union leaders think that they can fool their following into believing they are getting something for nothing, they have a low opinion of the intelligence of the followers.[33]

The implication was that the immediate result of the imposition of portal pay would be a redistribution of income from profit to wages, which, because the total income generated by the firm (or the economy) was not increased, would, through the mechanisms of equilibrium, work itself back to the status quo ante. With the wage-profit ratio relatively immutable, the unchanged wage bill would merely translate into a lower hourly rate for a longer workweek.

What this much-ado-about-nothing analysis overlooked was that, once travel time became compensable, the innovations that firms undertook to reduce such time would lower unit labor cost and result in productivity increases "as real as those due to the introduction of new labor-saving machinery."[34] Moreover, once those changes took place, the travel time saved could be devoted to directly productive labor, thus enhancing total output. In the alternative, workers could use the freed-up time as additional leisure. In effect, then, the half-hour they used to spend unnecessarily in portal-to-portal travel could be used in self-directed pursuits. In the latter case, to be sure, until the capital investment in these innovations was amortized, either the firm or the consumer would bear the costs of the workers' extra free time. In contrast, under the earlier regime, workers had disproportionately borne the costs of the inefficient layout of mines, mills, and plants in the form of curtailed leisure. Eventually, however, "the extra cost of portal-to-portal pay, spread over the entire wage bill, will be a small matter, as is now the cost of social security, which in its day, according to the N.A.M. [National Association of Manufacturers], promised revolution and bankruptcy."[35]

Northern manufacturing corporations had largely acquiesced in the FLSA so long as they believed that its minimal standards would have little or no impact on

---

[32]*Business Week*, Nov. 23, 1946, at 102, 104. *The Nation*, Dec. 28, 1946, at 759, included a similar report.

[33]"Portal-to-Portal," *Wall St. J.*, Dec. 18, 1946, at 6, col. 12. The same view was presented in "'Walking Time' Pay," *Wall St. J.*, Nov. 6, 1947, at 6, col. 2.

[34]Morse, "Economic Aspects of the Portal-to-Portal Pay Question" at 32.

[35]Mezerik, "Time Is Money" at 122.

their wage and hour policies or managerial prerogatives. Since they were already paying their employees higher wages than the new statutory minimum and premium pay for overtime, compliance did not initially loom as burdensome.[36] Nevertheless, as soon as the FLSA went into effect, employers of all sizes and in all regions began engaging in legal and extra-legal resistance to compliance with the premium overtime provision.[37]

In addition to this broad-based campaign to undermine the overtime provision altogether, a narrower dispute erupted over the compensability of the time that workers were engaged in certain activities. In order to determine the amount of wages owed, it was necessary to count the number of hours worked. Perhaps no worker had seriously urged that the FLSA clock started running the moment she walked out the front door of her house, but did it begin as soon as she walked through the employer's front door? Or did the employee have to make it all the way to her work station before her time was her employer's? And who had the final authority to make that determination? Was it within the sole discretion of the employer to set those bounds? Did pre-FLSA customs carry over? Did the agreement of the parties prevail—even where there was no bargaining because of the employer's overwhelming power?[38] Or did the new statute control the situation? And if so, who interpreted the law—the Wage and Hour Administrator or the courts? Such questions prompted the articulation of a labor-capital conflict in terms of whether the employer had breached a statutory obligation by failing to pay for all the hours worked or whether the employees had committed a breach of faith by abrogating long-standing customs in favor of demands for payment of time that traditionally was not separately compensated.

From the vantage point of large industrial capital, this entire line of inquiry seemed far more than it had bargained for in accepting the FLSA. By the time the postwar wave of portal-pay suits had acquired the status of a movement, such employers had lost their patience. The general counsel for Republic Steel Corporation, for example, declared to Congress that the "net effect" of the recent Supreme Court decisions had been

> to pervert the act from an instrument of righteous correction against sweatshop employers into an instrument to destroy the great majority of industrial employers in this country.... There is grim irony in the fact that the higher the wages paid by the particular employer,

---

[36]See Marc Linder, "Paternalistic State Intervention: The Contradictions of the Legal Empowerment of Vulnerable Workers," 23 *U.C. Davis L. Rev.* 733, 745-51 (1990).

[37]See above chapter 1.

[38]Frank Cooper, who represented the employer in the major industrial portal-pay case, stated "that the definition of the phrase 'hours worked' belongs at the bargaining table." Maurice Sugar and Frank Cooper, "Pro and Con—'Portal to Portal' Pay Suits," 26 *Mich. St. B.J.* 7, 11 (1947).

the more oppressive are the provisions of the act as interpreted by the Supreme Court.[39]

More emphatically and specifically still, the Business Advisory Council of the Department of Commerce, a group composed of representatives of the country's and world's largest industrial firms such as General Motors, Du Pont, U.S. Steel, Ford, Alcoa, and Standard Oil of New Jersey, informed Congress:

> Industry has felt from the beginning that the construction put upon the Fair Labor Standards Act by the Supreme Court was a complete misinterpretation of congressional intent.... Businessmen do not believe that Congress intended to make any radical change in the practice or customs regarding the relationship between employer and employee as to when his compensation started or how much it should be provided that the statutory minimum wage were paid and that employees received time and one half their usual rate when working more than 40 hours a week.[40]

As capital viewed the portal campaign, unions that were not strong enough to achieve additional wage advances on their own had appealed to the state to vindicate those claims for them. Ironically, argued capital, the statutory basis for this interference with the free operation of the labor market and the contest between labor and capital had not even been designed to aid unions, whereas the low-paid unorganized workers whom the FLSA was meant to bolster paternalistically[41] were not participants in the litigation.[42] Moreover, if labor prevailed on this claim, many employers would be compelled to restructure the layout of their plants in order to reduce their liability for portal wages. Not only had management not foreseen such an incursion into its sphere of dominion, but, depending on the technology of each factory and industry, such encroachment could lead to significant shifts in competitiveness among reputable employers. Yet

---

[39]*Portal to Portal Wages: Hearings Before a Subcomm. of the Senate Comm. on the Judiciary*, 80th Cong., 1st Sess. 52 (1947) (statement by Thomas Patton).

[40]*Portal to Portal Wages: Hearings Before a Subcomm. of the Senate Comm. on the Judiciary*, 80th Cong., 1st Sess. 615 (1947) (Statement by Subcommittee of Business Advisory on Attitude of Industry on Portal to Portal, as submitted by William Foster, Undersecretary of Commerce).

[41]For a clear statement of the motivations behind paternalistic labor legislation, see Robertson v. Baldwin, 165 U.S. 275, 287 (1897) (treating seamen "as deficient in that full and intelligent responsibility for their acts which is accredited to ordinary adults," Congress enacted a wage payment statute on their behalf).

[42]Lee Pressman, general counsel of the CIO and an organizer of the litigation campaign, testified before Congress that he knew of no portal suits brought by unorganized workers. *Regulating the Recovery of Portal-to-Portal Pay, and For Other Purposes: Hearings before Subcomm. No. 2 of the House Comm. on the Judiciary*, 80th Cong., 1st Sess. 166 (1947).

the FLSA was designed to suppress exclusively "unfair methods of competition."[43]

Workers, especially in the early days of the FLSA and in the context of organizing campaigns in the wake of the depression, may have tended to view statutory overtime claims as part and parcel of an overall bargaining process, which might have to be traded off for more important concessions from employers. The FLSA promoted such thinking because, when it was to their advantage, employees could decline to vindicate "a demand for the 'last measure of justice' to which [they] may be entitled."[44] But since, as the Supreme Court was to rule, employees could not waive their rights under the FLSA,[45] they could always[46] renege on such implied waivers and re-open the issue—even to the point of bankrupting the employer.[47] It was this class bias inherent in the logic of the FLSA that infuriated employers in the portal-pay controversy. In order to subvert this policy of unilateral rights, employers (and their dissenting supporters on the Supreme Court) sought to drive a conceptual and statutory wedge between unorganized and organized employees. Because it was undisputed that federally granted statutory rights preempted contractual agreements, unionized employers argued that Congress had really intended to confer such rights solely on low-paid and unorganized workers, whom they did not employ.[48] They argued that Congress had not granted similar entitlements to the unionized employees, with whom employers did enter into binding agreements. In the firms' view, so long as the workers received minimum wage and premium overtime, they could lawfully consent to any arrangements they wished—including customary practices as to when the workday began and compensable work time began. Such was the core of the portal-pay dispute.

This core, however, was not always on public display because unions failed to adopt or project a consistent and principled position on their members'—as contradistinguished from unorganized workers'—status under the FLSA. Stymied in their initial efforts through collective bargaining to secure wages for all the time their members placed at the disposal of their employers, unions appealed to the Wage and Hour Administrator and finally to the federal courts to vindicate these

---

[43]29 U.S.C. § 202(a).

[44]*Portal to Portal Wages: Hearings Before a Subcomm. of the Senate Comm. on the Judiciary*, 80th Cong., 1st Sess. 658 (1947) (testimony of Arthur Pettit, attorney, Winthrop, Stimson).

[45]See below § 7.

[46]That is, within the limitations period, which before the Portal-to-Portal Act, was rather long in some states. *See infra* § 6.

[47]See Marc Linder, "The Minimum Wage as Industrial Policy: A Forgotten Role," 16 *J. Legis.* 151 (1990). For a fictional representation of this policy from the standpoint of a trade unionist in Mexico, see B. Traven, *Die Baumwollpflücker* 124 (1983).

[48]See above chapter 1.

claims. Unless they were to win on a (legislatively reversible) technicality, unions had to legitimate their position by reference to socially recognized moral grounds. If they permitted their adversaries to stake out higher moral ground, the CIO should have anticipated ultimate defeat. Capital, in contrast, compelled to cast its postwar struggle to recover supremacy at the point of production as righteous resistance to judicial perversion of congressional intent and of employers' just expectations as well as to reneging labor unions, directed its appeal to the new Republican majority in Congress. It was this struggle between labor and capital over the possible new contours of their relationship in the postwar period, as displaced to the plane of legislation, interpretation, implementation, litigation, adjudication, and renewed litigation, that informed the portal-to-portal controversy.

The unresolved status of this conflict crystallized in November 1945 at the National Labor-Management Conference convened by President Truman. The committee on Management's Right to Manage was unable to reach agreement because the labor members, while conceding that "[t]he functions and responsibilities of management must be preserved if business and industry is to be efficient...and provide more good jobs," thought "it unwise to specify and classify" them or "to build a fence around the rights and responsibilities of management on the one hand and the unions on the other."[49]

3. Wages and Profits During Demobilization After World War II

We in the trade-union movement have always recognized that in reducing hours while we have not permitted a reduction of the hourly rates, we did not earn as much as we did when the hours were longer. However, we recognize that through organization we can step up the rate at another time. The reduction of hours is the most basic thing and the most worth-while thing for working men and women to fight for. It seems to me that the only answer to these men who find themselves in the position of having their earnings reduced by a cut in hours is that they must join a union.[50]

Because, with rare exceptions, the lowest hourly wage rate in the unionized industrial sector exceeded the statutory minimum by the end of World War II, the question of back wages for employees whose travel time did not extend their workweek beyond forty hours was "academic."[51] Portal litigation was therefore

---

[49] *The President's National Labor-Management Conference November 5-30, 1945: Summary and Committee Reports* 61 (U.S. DOL, Div. Lab. Standards, Bull. No. 77, 1946).

[50] *Proceedings of the Fifth National Conference on Labor Legislation: Washington, D.C., November 14, 15, 16, 1938*, at (DOL, Div. Lab. Standards, Bull. No. 25, 1939) (statement of Miss [Rose] Schneiderman).

[51] *Portal to Portal Wages: Hearings Before a Subcommittee of the Senate Committee on*

exclusively a creature of the overtime provision of the FLSA. Demobilization in 1945 brought about a significant reduction in the length of the workweek and, concomitantly, of real earnings. In the core sectors of military production, durable goods manufacturing, the organizing base of the CIO, average weekly hours plummeted by one-seventh from April 1945 (46.5 hours) to June 1946 (39.8). As a result of postwar inflation, real weekly earnings of workers in these industries declined during this period by one-sixth. Although the length of the workweek leveled off by the beginning of 1947, with inflation unabated, real earnings continued to decline, so that by the height of the portal-pay movement in February, real weekly earnings in durable goods manufacturing had dropped by 21.8 per cent since the end of the war in Europe.[52] While workers' real wages were falling and labor was unable to persuade either the Democratic-controlled Seventy-Ninth or the Republican-controlled Eightieth Congress to raise the minimum wage,[53] the Truman administration was reporting that "it is plain that business in general is receiving exceptional profits."[54]

When, in the wake of demobilization, the workweek was shortened but

---

the Judiciary, 80th Cong., 1st Sess. 191-94 (1947) (testimony of Lee Pressman).

[52]Milton Derber and Sidney Netreba, "Money and Real Weekly Earnings During Defense, War, and Reconversion Periods," 64 *Monthly Lab. Rev.* 983, tab. 1 at 987, tab. 2 at 989, tab. 3 at 996 (1947). For all manufacturing the corresponding decline was 16.6 per cent. A similar trend was reported for net spendable weekly earnings of manufacturing workers (a category which takes into account social security taxes). *See* Lenore Epstein and Eleanor Snyder, "Urban Price Trends," in *Labor in Postwar America* 137, 143-44 (C. Warne ed. 1949).

[53]A number of bills introduced in the Seventy-Ninth Congress proposed not only increasing the minimum wage to seventy-five cents, but also authorizing industry committees to set wage differentials for skilled workers. *Proposed Amendments to the Fair Labor Standards Act: Hearings Before the House Committee on Labor*, 79th Cong., 1st Sess. 1-20 (1945) (H.R. 3914, 3928, 4222, 4130, 3844, 3837, 3719); *Amendments of the Fair Labor Standards Act of 1938: Hearings Before the Senate Committee on Education and Labor*, 79th Cong., 1st Sess. 1-5 (1945) (S. 1349); 1 *Minimum Wage Standards: Hearings Before Subcommittee No. 4 of the House Committee on Education and Labor*, 80th Cong., 1st Sess. 21-25 (1947) (H.R. 40). For a summary of these failed legislative initiatives, see Harry Weiss and Robert Gronewald, "Wage and Hour Laws," in *Labor in Postwar America* 239, 240-45, 252-53 (C. Warne ed. 1949). For an impassioned and empirically supported plea for raising the floor, see U.S. DOL, *Annual Report of the Wage and Hour and Public Contracts Divisions, Fiscal Year 1946*, at 46-50 (1947). The Wage and Hour Administrator repeatedly urged these recommendations to Congress, in accordance with his duty under § 4 of the FLSA, until it finally amended the act in 1949 to raise the minimum wage to seventy-five cents. *See* U.S. DOL, *Annual Report of the Wage and Hour and Public Contracts Divisions, Fiscal Year 1947*, at 45-49 (1948); U.S. DOL, *Annual Report of the Wage and Hour and Public Contracts Divisions, Fiscal Year 1948*, at 57-61 (1949).

[54]*The Economic Report of the President: To the Congress, January 8, 1947*, at 5 (1947).

inflation accelerated, many workers were still eager for overtime premiums.[55] In this context it is therefore wrong to view the CIO's demand for portal pay as motivated by an interest "in shortening the working day by compelling employers to recognize that the day began from the moment the laborer came onto the premises until the moment he left."[56]

Of particular relevance to the labor movement was the Council of Economic Advisers' conclusion that in 1947 "profits on the whole were above the levels necessary to furnish incentives and funds for the expansion of business and to promote the sustained health of the economy."[57] These economic relationships fit well into the CIO's position that industry's increased profits could comfortably accommodate wage increases.[58] In the so-called first-round of postwar wage increases,[59] which extended from the end of the war in Japan to the spring of 1946, the pattern called for a rise of about 18 percent in weekly earnings.[60] But with the increase in the cost of living advancing more rapidly than the pattern increase of the first round,[61] pressure built up for a second round of increases in the spring of 1947,[62] which merely "offset advances in consumer prices that followed the lifting

---

[55]Ronald Schatz, *A History of Labor at General Electric and Westinghouse 1923-60*, at 159 (1983).

[56]William Swindler, *Court and Constitution in the Twentieth Century: The New Legality 1932-1968*, at 162 (1970).

[57]*The Economic Report of the President: To the Congress, January 14, 1948*, at 41 (1948).

[58]See [Robert Nathan], "A Wage Policy for 1947 Prepared for CIO," *Commercial and Financial Chronicle*, Dec. 19, 1946, at 3209, 3246-48. For industry's response, see George Terborgh, "Answering Mr. Nathan," *id.*, Dec. 26, 1946, at 3345, 3378-79.

[59]The stages of wage decontrol, which permitted a phased return to collective bargaining, can be tracked through the following executive orders: No. 9599, 10 *Fed. Reg.* 10,155 (Aug. 18, 1945); No. 9651, 10 *Fed. Reg.* 13,487 (Oct. 30, 1945); No. 9697, 11 *Fed. Reg.* 1691 (Feb. 14, 1946); No. 9801, 11 *Fed. Reg.* 13,435 (Nov. 9, 1946). For contemporary explanation, see U.S. DOL, *The National Wage Stabilization Board: January 1, 1946—February 24, 1947* (n.d. [ca. 1947]); H. Douty, "Wage Policy, and the Role of Fact-Finding Boards," 62 *Monthly Lab. Rev.* 537 (1946).

[60]H. Douty, "Review of Basic American Labor Conditions," in *Labor in Postwar America* 109, 121 (C. Warne ed. 1949). Forty per cent of manufacturing workers received increases in excess of the pattern, 40 percent received below-pattern increases, while 20 percent received no increase; the average for manufacturing as a whole was about 11 percent. When the final waves of the first round had spread out by October 1946, the aggregate average reached 16.5 percent. *Id.* at 122.

[61]*The Economic Report of the President: To The Congress, January 14, 1948*, at 39 (1948).

[62]According to John Dunlop, "The Decontrol of Wages and Prices," in *Labor in Postwar America* 3, 5, a wage increase had become "necessary both from considerations of politics

of price controls subsequent to the 'first round' of wage raises."[63]

In the interim between the first and second round, in late 1946, a time of sharply contested claims to postwar national income and of notable reductions in working class living standards,[64] the labor movement—especially the CIO—may have viewed the mass filing of portal-pay suits as furnishing additional bargaining strength.[65] Although the CIO publicly asserted that portal pay was a completely separate issue from general wage increases,[66] the press largely regarded the litigation as a bargaining lever positioned to buttress demands for second-round wage increases.[67] The CIO did not effectively project the principle at stake in its campaign.[68] In any event, the press failed to report on labor's explanations comparable to the pithy and easily comprehensible value-laden broadsides from employers denouncing portal claims as essentially parasitic.[69]

By the time the Supreme Court had disposed of its final FLSA-portal case in

---

and industrial relations" and "was essential, given the temper of wage earners and the facts of labor organizations." Barton Bernstein, "The Truman Administration and Its Reconversion Wage Policy," 6 *Lab. Hist.* 214 (1965), argues that the framework policy provided by the federal government was inept. *See also* Craufurd Goodwin and R. Stanley Herren, "The Truman Administration: Problems and Policies Unfold," in *Exhortation and Controls: The Search for a Wage-Price Policy 1945-1971*, at 9-48 (Craufurd Goodwin ed. 1975).

[63]"Trends in Urban Wage Rates, September 1947," 66 *Monthly Lab. Rev.* 45, 45 (1948).

[64]Significant light was shed on the class-differential impact of demobilization and inflation on the real standards of living of representative classes in an eight-part front-page series in the Wall Street Journal, which ran from December 18, 1946 to January 11, 1947.

[65]See, e.g., Joseph Loftus, "Portal Pay Claims Reaching Billions; A Boon to Unions," N.Y. Times, Dec. 22, 1946, at 1, col. 6.

[66]See, e.g., Joseph Loftus, "Portal Pay, Wages Separate, Says CIO," *N.Y. Times*, Dec. 25, 1946, at 1, col. 3; "Portal Pay Suits Asked By Electric Union," *N.Y. Times*, Dec. 31, 1946, at 12, col. 3.

[67]See, e.g., "The Portal-to-Portal Issue," *N.Y. Times*, Dec. 24, 1946, at 16, col. 1 (editorial) ("lever for one of the largest mass wage demands in the nation's history"); Albert Clark, "U.S. Has $5 Billion Stake in Limiting Back Wage Suits," *Wall. St. J.*, Dec. 17, 1946, at 6, col. 5.

[68]Philip Murray, the president of the CIO, thus engaged in understatement that the organization was "'interested in the application of portal-to-portal pay for all American industry. The C.I.O. intends to find out why the portal-to-portal provisions in the Fair Labor Standards Act which have long benefited the miners have not been made applicable to other wage earners.'" "Door-to-Door Pay," *Business Week*, Sept. 21, 1946, at 94, 95.

[69]The NAM, for example, saw portal pay demands as opening the way to new possibilities of "'obtaining more pay without more work.'" "NAM Group Seeks Labor Acts' Repeal," *N.Y. Times*, Dec. 23, 1946, at 1, col. 2, at 12, col. 4.

the fall of 1946,[70] even the NAM recognized that "[t]here [wa]s no question that time spent in a manufacturing establishment walking from a time clock to the place of employment, to the bench" was compensable.[71] Yet only one portal-pay settlement was prominently reported in the fall of 1946. Involving Dow Chemical in Michigan and District 50 of the United Mine Workers (UMW), it was reached without resort to litigation once it became "obvious to the company that the union could collect portal-to-portal pay for its members by going to court, if necessary, under the precedent set in the Mt. Clemens case."[72] *Business Week* expressly characterized it as "A Second-Round Solution," which, if widely applied, might "eliminate the threat of serious strikes without sharply boosting hourly rates."[73] Against the background of a six-year state statute of limitations, the agreement provided for $360 in back wages to each of 11,000 present and former employees. In addition to this retroactivity—which management generally found the most unacceptable aspect of portal-pay claims[74]—future relief was offered in the form of portal pay for walking from the clockroom to the lockers, clothes changing, and showering (if necessitated by chemical operations). In exchange for this almost half-hour per shift of future overtime pay, the union forwent its demand of a twenty-cent general wage increase.[75] Although by the end of 1946 *Business Week* reported that "[m]anagement recently learned with considerable interest" of the Dow-UMW settlement,[76] it appears to have served at best as a negative object lesson to employers.

Ironically, the Dow-UMW agreement interested unions—in particular, the CIO—a good deal more. Its general counsel, Lee Pressman, later told Congress that the fact that the UMW belonged to the AFL created a competitive situation, which the CIO unions felt compelled to match. When the CIO approached employers on the issue in the context of collective bargaining, however, they responded that negotiations had become unnecessary because Congress would soon amend the FLSA to overrule the prolabor decisions by the Supreme Court.[77]

Congressional proponents of strict anti-portal legislation insisted that the wave of portal litigation was a conspiracy carefully orchestrated by the CIO, verged on champerty, and was infiltrated by Communists. For example, Representative J.

---

[70]See below § 5.

[71]Raymond Smethurst, "The Portal-to Portal Issue," 13 *Vital Speeches of the Day* 204, 204 (Jan. 15, 1947) (NAM counsel delivering speech to NAM Congress on Dec. 5, 1946).

[72]"A Second-Round Solution," *Business Week*, Nov. 2, 1946, at 84.

[73]"A Second-Round Solution."

[74]*Business Week*, Sept. 21, 1946, at 84.

[75]*Business Week*, Nov. 2, 1946, at 84.

[76]*Business Week*, Dec. 14, 1946, at 98.

[77]Sen. Rep. No. 48: *Exempting Employers from Liability for Portal-to-Portal Wages in Certain Cases*, 80th Cong., 1st Sess. 20 (1947).

Parnell Thomas (who the following year was convicted of taking kickbacks from his staff and imprisoned) asserted: "As chairman of the Committee on Un-American Activities, I am in possession of certain information dealing with the inspiration of the original portal-to-portal pay suit.... The individual who is credited with concocting the idea of these suits, and the lawyer who brought the original action...both have long records of Communist affiliation."[78] Representative Rankin, another formidable member of that committee, charged that the portal litigation was a Communist plot to bankrupt the United States.[79]

Though protestations that the CIO unions were passively following their membership may, in light of the obvious tactical collective bargaining consequences, seem difficult to credit, some plausibility attaches to the claim that in fact once the inexorable logic of the Supreme Court portal decisions became widely disseminated by the very media that editorially fulminated against it, the pressure from the rank-and-file who "wanted theirs" became too great to resist. Indeed, one of the chief portal-pay litigators even suggested that union lawyers, apprehensive of precisely the sort of congressional backlash that eventually ensued, unsuccessfully tried to channel the discontent.[80]

4. Mine Owners Fail to Save Face-to-Face

In a way it is even humiliating to watch coal-miners working. It raises in you a momentary doubt about your own status as an "intellectual" and a superior person generally. For it is brought home to you...that only because miners sweat their guts out that superior persons can remain superior. You and I and the editor of the *Times Lit. Supp.*, and the Nancy poets and the Archbishop of Canterbury and Comrade X, author of *Marxism for Infants*—all of us *really* owe the comparative decency of our lives to poor drudges underground, blackened to the eyes, with their throats full of coal dust, driving their shovels forward with arms and belly muscles of steel.[81]

To grasp the seminal role that miners played in the struggle for portal pay it is necessary to gain a sense of the extraordinary travails that they undergo just getting to the face where they mine. No one has conveyed that sense more poignantly than

---

[78]93 *Cong. Rec.* at 538. Thomas was referring to Ben Riskin, the former research director of the International Union of Mine, Mill and Smelter Workers, and CIO counsel Lee Pressman. Forty years later Riskin was "in his own words, proudest of 'helping to win the "portal to portal" decision establishing the 8-hour day for all underground miners in the U.S.'" 2 *The Cold War Against Labor* 823 (A Ginger and D. Christiano eds. 1987).

[79]93 *Cong. Rec.* at 1511.

[80]Telephone interview with Ernie Goodman (April 2, 1990).

[81]George Orwell, *The Road to Wigan Pier* 31 (1966 [1937]).

George Orwell in *The Road to Wigan Pier*. Writing of his visits to British coal mines in the 1930s, Orwell noted that a nonminer would probably have to see several mines before understanding mining "because the mere effort of getting from place to place makes it difficult to notice anything else."[82] The descent itself was a disorienting experience:

> You get into the cage, which is a steel box about as wide as a telephone box and two or three times as long. It holds ten men, but they pack like pilchards in a tin, and a tall man cannot stand upright. The steel door shuts upon you, and somebody working the winding gear above drops you into the void. ... In the middle of the run the cage probably touches sixty miles an hour; in some of the deeper mines it touches even more. When you crawl out at the bottom you are perhaps four hundred yards under ground. That is to say you have a tolerable-sized mountain on top of you; hundreds of yards of solid rock...suspended over your head and held back only by wooden props as thick as the calf of your leg.[83]

Because Orwell had imagined that miners worked but a few yards from where the cage disgorged them, he was surprised by "the immense horizontal distances" that had to be traversed before they even got to work. Though a mine shaft was initially sunk near a coal seam, as the latter was worked out and others opened, the face of the mine would eventually be one to five miles distant from the pit bottom: "But these distances bear no relation to distances above ground. For in all that mile or three miles..., there is hardly anywhere...a man can stand upright."[84] Orwell then described the exertions necessary to move those three miles:

> At the start to walk stooping is rather a joke, but it is a joke that soon wears off. ... You have not only got to bend double, you have also got to keep your head up all the while so as to see the beams and girders and dodge them.... You have, therefore, a constant crick in the neck, but this is nothing to the pain in your knees and thighs. After half a mile it becomes (I am not exaggerating) an unbeatable agony. ... Your pace grows slower and slower. You come to a stretch of a couple of hundred yards where it is all exceptionally low and you have to work yourself along in a squatting position. [T]here is another low stretch of a hundred yards and then a succession of beams which you have to crawl under. You go down on all fours; even this is a relief after the squatting business. But when you come to the end of the beams and try to get up again, you find that your knees have temporarily struck...and refuse to lift you. ... But finally you do somehow creep as far as the coal face. You have gone a mile and taken the best part of an hour; a miner would do it in not much more than twenty minutes.
>
> [W]hat I want to emphasize is this. Here is this frightful business of crawling to and fro, which to any normal person is a hard day's work in itself; and it is not part of the miner's work at all, it is merely an extra, like the City man's daily ride in the Tube. The

---

[82]Orwell, *Road to Wigan Pier* at 21.

[83]Orwell, *Road to Wigan Pier* at 22.

[84]Orwell, *Road to Wigan Pier* at 22-23.

miner does that journey to and fro, and sandwiched in between there are seven and a half hours of savage work. ... A miner's working shift...doesn't sound very long, but one has got to add on to it at least an hour a day for "travelling," more often two hours and sometimes three. Of course, the "travelling" is not technically work and the miner is not paid for it; but it is as like work as makes no difference.[85]

Miners' ability to persuade legal decisionmakers that their deep conviction that this travel constituted work should also be the law under the FLSA was the question that triggered the portal-to-portal struggle. They had succeeded as early as 1912 in Arizona, when the state legislature enacted an eight-hours law for miners that included portal time.[86] In the version on the books at the time of the FLSA controversy, the Arizona law provided that for all persons engaged in work in underground mines the "period of employment...shall not exceed eight hours within any twenty-four hours, and the said eight hours shall include the time employed, occupied or consumed, in descending to and ascending from the point or place of work in any underground mine...."[87] The FLSA, however, was not a

---

[85]Orwell, *Road to Wigan Pier* at 24, 26.

[86]1912 Ariz. Sess. Laws ch. 28 at 59, 60.

[87]Ariz. Code § 56-115 at 634 (1939). This provision is still on the books. Ariz. Rev. Stats. Ann. § 23-282 (1995). Nevada's 1927 eight-hour law for miners included the time spent going from face to surface but not from surface to face. 1927 Nev. Stat. ch. 105 at 186. The legislature included all portal-to-portal time in the eight hours in 1949, and then excluded all portal time in 1993. 1949 Nev. Stat. ch. 126 at 197; 1993 Nev. Stat. ch. 273 at 821. As an early example of a state hours law excluding portal time, in 1913 Alaska's first territorial legislature enacted an eight-hour law for mines providing that the limit of eight hours referred only to work actually performed at the face. 1913 Alaska Sess. Laws ch. 29, § 2 at 35, 36. As early as 1884, Austria-Hungary enacted a portal-to-portal statute limiting the length of a miner's daily shift to twelve hours (of which the "real" work time was limited to ten hours), and defining the beginning and end of this shift as the descent into and completed ascent from the pit of the mine, respectively. Gesetz vom 21. Juni 1884, über die Beschäftigung von jugendlichen Arbeitern und Frauenspersonen, dann über die tägliche Arbeitsdauer und die Sonntagsruhe beim Bergbau, § 3, in *Reichsgesetzblatt für die im Reichsrathe vertretenen Königreiche und Länder* 367 (1884). The 1908 British eight-hours law for coal miners applied to a workman below ground "for the purpose of his work, and of going to and from his work, and measured the period by reference to the time at which "the last workman in the shift leaves the surface and the first workman in the shift returns to the surface." Coal Mines Regulation Act, 1908, § 1(1)-(2), 8 Edw. 7, ch. 57, at 320. The importance that miners attached to the portal-to-portal issue is reflected in the law's authorizing them to appoint and station someone "to be at the pit head, at all times when workmen are to be lowered or raised, for the purpose of observing the times...." *Id.* § 2(2) 322. According to E.H. Phelps Brown, *The Growth of British Industrial Relations: A Study from the Standpoint of 1906-14*, at (1974 [1959]), this statute failed to secure eight hours "'bank to bank'": it included travel underground, but excluded winding times, which added

maximum hours law: it merely prescribed minimum and overtime wages.

A. *Muscoda* and the Alabama Iron Ore Miners

Certain activities are plainly "work".... Other activities fall in the hazy penumbra; neither common understanding nor a priori reasoning will tell us whether they are work or not. [U]nderground travel in iron mines fell into the former category.... But walking to one's work place through a yard and factory cannot be said to be so plainly "work" that there is no room for a contrary understanding.[88]

Organized miners furnished a powerful initial impetus to the movement for portal-to-portal pay. Although accounts of this conflict have usually focused on the alleged wartime political machinations of John L. Lewis and the UMW designed to maneuver coal mine owners into raising wages outside the permissible limits of the so-called Little Steel formula (that is, wage increases designed to keep pace with cost-of-living increases since January 1, 1941),[89] in fact, iron ore miners in Alabama[90] were the portal-pay pioneers. The UMW did not achieve its organizing breakthrough in the Southern metal mines until the latter part of the 1930s,[91] when it succeeded in organizing the miners at the Tennessee Coal, Iron, and Railroad Company (TCIR).[92] By the beginning of World War II, the International Union of Mine, Mill and Smelter Workers had organized not only

---

a half-hour to the time spent below ground. In Parliament in 1993, "Shouts of 'shame' met Mr Eggar's [the Energy Minister's]disclosure that a 1908 Act limiting the time miners spend underground to 7.5 hours plus one hour 'winding time is to be repealed from 20 November." Stephen Goodwin, "Inside Parliament: Rebels Display Little Fight over New Threat to Mines," *Independent*, Oct. 21 1993, at 6 (Lexis). In the Australian state of Victoria, the eight hours also ran between the time when the miner began to descend and when he returned to the surface. Coal Mines Regulation Act 1928, § 7(1), Vict. Acts, No. 3657, at 514, 516.

[88]Archibald Cox, "The Influence of Mr. Justice Murphy on Labor Law," 48 *Mich. L. Rev.* 767, 807-808 (1950).

[89]Stabilization Act of 1942, Pub. L. No. 729, 56 Stat. 765 (1942); Executive Order No. 9250, 7 *Fed. Reg.* 7871 (1942); Exec. Order No. 9328, 8 *Fed. Reg.* 4681 (1943).

[90]The Red Mountain mines near Birmingham recorded the second largest production in the United States although the output was far inferior to that of the Mesabi range in Minnesota. Tennessee Coal, Iron, & Railroad Co. v. Muscoda Local No. 123, 321 U.S. 590 (1944), Record at 4023.

[91]Philip Taft, *Organizing Dixie: Alabama Workers in Industrial Era* 110-16 (Gary Fink ed. 1981).

[92]William Regensburger, "The Emergence of Industrial Unionism in the South, 1930-1945: The Case of Coal and Metal Miners," in *How Mighty A Force? Studies of Workers' Consciousness and Organization in the United States* 65, 90-92 (Maurice Zeitlin ed. 1983).

TCIR, but also the Sloss-Sheffield and Republic Steel mines.[93] These three companies, which owned the only substantial ore mines in Alabama,[94] were all components of still more powerful enterprises. TCIR had been acquired by the largest steel producer, U.S. Steel, in 1907, while Republic was the third largest steel producer in the United States; Sloss-Sheffield Steel & Iron Corporation was affiliated with Allied Chemical & Dye Corporation, one of the largest chemical producers.[95]

Precisely because the unions faced such strong opponents, they were unable to secure even partial travel time (for the trip out); the CIO union, for example, lost a strike over this issue against Republic Steel after one such failed effort between 1933 and 1935.[96] It was only in compliance with the "Modified Portal to Portal Wage-Hour Opinion" issued by the Wage and Hour Administrator on March 23, 1941, stating that effective May 1, 1941 the compensable workday began when the miner reported at the collar of the mine,[97] that the Southern iron ore companies began paying on a portal-to-portal basis. After the union again demanded back wages on behalf of 6,000 employees for such work (travel) time, which ranged from three minutes to forty minutes at the various mines,[98] the employers filed a declaratory judgment action[99] on April 1, 1941 in the federal district court for

---

[93]Regensburger, "Emergence of Industrial Unionism in the South," at 96-107. Before the FLSA went into effect, none of the mine owners had entered into contracts with the unions. TCIR's first contract took effect in October 1938, Sloss-Sheffield's a year later. Brief for Wage and Hour Administrator-Intervener, at 26, Tennessee Coal, Iron & Railroad Co. v. Muscoda Local No. 123, 321 U.S. 590 (1944). Republic had never executed a written agreement with the Smelters Union before the case went to trial. Brief for Petitioner Republic Steel Corp., at 8, Tennessee Coal, Iron & Railroad Co. v. Muscoda Local No. 123, 321 U.S. 590 (1944).

[94]Petition for Writ of Certiorari, at 10, Tennessee Coal, Iron, & Railroad Co. v. Muscoda Local No. 123, 321 U.S. 590 (1944).

[95]Ethel Armes, *The Story of Coal and Iron in Alabama* 517-24, 452-57, 356-57; *Poor's Financial Records: 1941 Industrial Manual* 2858, 3231, 2147, 2149. A union official stated in another context that TCIR was both "the single most profitable operation" of U.S. Steel and "the most profitable in the entire steel industry." *Amendments of the Fair Labor Standards Act of 1938: Hearings Before the Senate Committee on Education and Labor*, 79th Cong., 1st Sess. 1092 (statement of David McDonald, Sec'y-Treas. United Steel Workers).

[96]Tennessee Coal, Iron & Railroad Co. v. Muscoda Local No. 123, 321 U.S. 590, 611-12 (1944).

[97]"Overtime and Records for Miners," 3 *Wage & Hour Reporter* 466, 467 (Oct. 21, 1940); "Hours of Work in Metal Mines," 4 *Wage & Hour Reporter* 137 (May 24, 1941); Petition for Writ of Certiorari, at 12; Record at 76.

[98]Record at 121, 3587.

[99]In their original petitions the plaintiff-employers made the named-defendant employees

Northern Alabama to test the Administrator's ruling, which had formed the basis of an agreement into which the parties entered on May 5, 1941.[100]

In retrospect the plaintiff-employers may have made a tactical error in seeking "a rigid definition of working time favorable to them,"[101] but given the weight of the extraordinarily sympathetic facts in the miners' favor, the companies had little choice but to try to deflect the court's attention from those facts. The trial judge was, however, as he wrote not without a trace of irony, unable to oblige the employers' request for a declaration "without consideration of the actual conditions" of transportation "because transportation in the abstract might be construed to be a restful and pleasurable activity for passengers." The court then proceeded to describe those conditions in some detail: The crowded cars, otherwise used for transporting iron ore and bearing remnants of muck, were very crowded, causing the miners to crouch lying on top of one another; overhead dangers lurked in the humid and malodorous mines. The judge then promptly added that the recital was "not for the purpose of censure" of the employers, "for these conditions may well be the normal conditions in iron ore mines and practically inevitable."

---

class representatives of all their employees. Record at 34, 123, 183. This point does not appear to have been litigated. Ironically, the Portal-to-Portal Act banned opt-out class actions, although even earlier the courts refused to permit employees to prosecute such actions. See below § 8.

[100]Brief for Petitioner TCIR, at 5, 9; Muscoda, 321 U.S. at 592 n.3, 613. The Wage and Hour Administrator intervened in the action. Record at 304. In recounting these events, the dissent, citing the aforementioned "Modified Portal to Portal Wage-Hour Opinion," stated that, because portal-to-portal pay "was a complete change of opinion, the Administrator announced that he would not seek to compel restitution...." 321 U.S. at 613. Since Congress did not authorize the DOL to collect back wages under the FLSA until 1949, the Wage and Hour Administrator would not have been empowered to compel restitution. Ch. 736, § 14, 63 Stat. 919. Indeed, the Administrator urged Congress repeatedly to grant him such authority. *Proposed Amendments to the Fair Labor Standards Act: Hearings Before the House Committee on Labor*, 79th Cong., 1st Sess. 867 (1945) (statement by Metcalfe Walling); 4 *Minimum Wage Standards and Other Parts of the Fair Labor Standards Act of 1938: Hearings Before Subcommittee No. 4 of the House Committee on Education and Labor*, 80th Cong., 1st Sess. 2280 (1947) (statement by Metcalfe Walling, former Adm'r). Before 1949, the Administrator could seek to collect back wages (but not liquidated damages) by means of consent judgments into which employers were often willing to enter for fear of a more unpleasant alternative—namely, criminal process under § 16(a) or an injunction of the interstate shipment of goods under § 17. See Allan Tepper, Consent Judgments and Contempt Cases under the Fair Labor Standards Act of 1938," 22 *B.U.L. Rev.* 390, 391-92 (1942); G.W. Foster, Jr., "Jurisdiction, Rights, and remedies for Group Wrongs under the Fair Labor Standards Act: Special Federal Questions," 1975 *Wisc. L. Rev.* 295, 311-13.

[101]Tennessee Coal, Iron and R. Co. v. Muscoda Local No.123, 137 F.2d 176, 183 (5th Cir.1943) (denying reh'g).

Though of little comfort to employers whose capital was immobilized in iron ore mining, thc court underscored its narrowly fact-specific holding by referring to the conditions as "clearly...peculiar to the occupation of the men."[102] It then set forth as additional criteria for determining whether travel time was compensable the employer's strict control and supervision of the workers "clearly exercised in the interest of efficient operation of their mining business." That control manifested itself, for example, in the imposition of discipline for infractions committed during the trip. The court then summarized the three-part test as whether the transportation "bears in a substantial degree every indicia of worktime: supervision by the employer, physical and mental exertion, activity necessary to be performed for the employer's benefit...."[103]

The other contention pressed by the mine owners that was destined to become prominent in the debate over portal pay centered on the existence of a venerable tradition in the industry not to pay for such travel time. Ancillary to this claim was the argument that the custom was of a kind that Congress must have adopted in the FLSA overtime provision. The court disposed of this position on three levels. Empirically, it found no evidence of such a custom inasmuch as the workers were compensated on a tonnage or shift rather than an hourly basis.[104] In tension with this conclusion was the finding in the alternative that even if there were such a custom, "the methods of payment of wages were clearly dictated almost entirely by the employers. The employees worked on the best terms they could obtain and the fact that they could not obtain terms that would compensate them for time spent in travelling underground...does not indicate that they did not consider that time as working time." The negative inference that the court drew from the miners' pre-FLSA unsuccessful efforts to secure travel time pay as to their subjective attitude towards continued non-payment served to deny the existence of a valid custom as lacking "unhampered consent." Thus even if Congress had meant to exempt certain wage customs from the FLSA, its intent with regard to such unilaterally imposed wage schemes could not be divined. Finally, and potentially much more broadly, the trial judge suggested that it would be a mockery of an avowedly remedial statute if an occupational custom were permitted to avoid a congressional mandate.[105] Here the court came perilously close to committing a *petitio principii*

---

[102]Tennessee Coal, Iron & R. Co. v. Muscoda Local No. 123, 40 F. Supp. 4, 9 (N.D. Ala. 1941).

[103]40 F. Supp. at 10.

[104]40 F. Supp. at 7. Before the Supreme Court, Republic Steel made the ambiguous statement that although the wages were paid on a tonnage basis, "the rates of pay were fixed on evaluations made on the hourly basis." Brief for Petitioner Republic Steel Corp. at 7. TCIR also used a combination of tonnage, task, and incentive rates. Brief for Respondents at 12-15.

[105]Muscoda, 40 F. Supp. at 8.

since it had failed to demonstrate that Congress specifically intended to cover such travel time.

In a very brief affirmance, the Fifth Circuit rested its decision on the trial court's last point. More ominously, however, but with a possible nod to the controversy that was about to be unleashed, the appeals court stressed that its task was to limit itself to the facts and issues of the case without reference to any wider consequences.[106] Though perhaps also prescient, the majority was specifically responding to the dire predictions voiced by the vigorous dissent.

The dissenter stressed three equitable points in favor of the employers. First, even collective bargaining agreements with strong unions excluded travel pay. Second, the travel arrangements were "primarily for the benefit of the miner." And third, the danger and/or discomfort of the trip was reflected in the pay scales.[107] Against that background, awarding double liquidated damages for time and one-half for riding time would confer upon the miners three times the hourly rate for actual mining at the face. Finding this "injustice...shocking," the dissenter predicted that if triple back pay were imposed on all iron mines, "[m]any will go broke, or cease operations, causing a loss of jobs to their men." As an illustration of the hardship to be expected, one of the old mines owned by the defendants required 1.5 hours of travel time or nearly one-quarter of the seven-hour work day. A further specter was conjured up in the form of the inevitable application of the ruling to coal mines.[108]

In denying the employers' petition for rehearing, the Fifth Circuit rejected their claim that it was upholding the portal-to-portal theory as a matter of law. Rather, they were reaping what they had sown inasmuch as they requested a pro-employer "rigid definition of working time": "They now chide us for laying down such a definition against them."[109]

The Supreme Court decision written by Frank Murphy arguably represents the all-time high point of sympathetic FLSA jurisprudence—albeit one that did not pass unchallenged even at the time by part of the Court. Present-day mantra-like formulaic citations to key pithy passages of this opinion virtually never reveal their peculiar context. Thus Murphy, whom *Time* called "an eager beagle who is all heart-and-snuffles whenever the legal hunt picks up the scent of something human,"[110] described the miners as crowded into ore box cars "covered with muck" in which they are forced to ride "in a close 'spoon-fashion,' with bodies contorted and heads drawn in" to avoid the low mine ceilings: "Broken ribs,

---

[106]Tennessee Coal, Iron & R. Co. v. Muscoda Local No. 123, 135 F.2d 320, 322 (5th Cir.1943).

[107]135 F.2d at 324.

[108]135 F.2d at 325.

[109]137 F.2d at 183.

[110]*Time*, Feb. 17, 1947, at 23.

injured arms and legs, bloody heads often result; even fatalities are not unknown."[111] At 3,000 to 12,000 feet in the "malodorous shafts," produced by "human sewage resulting from a complete absence of sanitary facilities," the "subterranean walks are filled with discomforts and hidden perils" including "exposed high voltage electric cables and wires" and falling rocks.[112]

Justice Jackson, who concurred in Murphy's opinion on the grounds that the case posed no question of law or one "with a very obvious answer" because, absent a "very exceptional showing of error," the Supreme Court was bound to uphold the courts below, which had found that the travel was work for which no evidence of a custom excluded compensation,[113] regarded Murphy's rhetorical flourishes as unnecessary to the holding. Thus privately Jackson suggested to Murphy that the odor in the mines was irrelevant: "'Would it alter the rights any...if the mine smelled sweet as new-mown hay?'"[114]

Jackson's austere and sanitized view of the FLSA missed the point that Murphy was trying to give to the act. For the decidedly humanitarian tone and texture of the portal-to-portal decisions handed down by the Supreme Court are not coincidentally the product of Justice Murphy, who, his biographers agree, was guided by sympathy for the working class: "Faced with a choice, he simply could not square hazardous travel in coal mines with physical reality or Christian compassion."[115] Nor was it coincidental that hard upon the graphic depiction of the travel conditions in the iron mines followed the almost endlessly quoted affirmation of the FLSA as "remedial and humanitarian in purpose. We are not dealing here with mere chattels or articles of trade but with rights of those who toil, of those who sacrifice a full measure of their freedom and talents to the use and

---

[111]321 U.S. at 595 n.9 and 596. The employers, workers, and the intervener all submitted as exhibits photographs of the miners in the open-top cars that strongly convey the human-haulage aspects of the transportation. *See* Record at 4466-67, 4509-12, 4537, 4608.

[112]321 U.S. at 596.

[113]321 U.S. at 604-605.

[114]3 Sidney Fine, *Frank Murphy: The Washington Years* 323 (1984) (citing letter from Jackson to Murphy dated Mar. 2, 1944, in Jackson papers). That a plausible answer to Jackson's rhetorical question might have been Yes, emerges from a release by the Wage and Hour Administrator, who had not yet determined whether, because of the very unfavorable and hazardous conditions in the mines, the half-hour miners took to eat underground was compensable. Petition for Writ of Certiorari, at 42; Record at 397-98, 403-404. Later the Administrator determined that lunch periods of 30 minutes or more were not compensable even if taken underground. BNA, *Wage and Hour Manual* 241-42 (cumul. ed. 1944-45).

[115]J. Woodford Howard, Jr., *Mr. Justice Murphy: A Political Biography* 402 (1968). Richard Lunt, *The High Ministry of Government: The Political Career of Frank Murphy* (1965), also emphasizes the influence of the papal encyclicals. As mayor of Detroit in the 1930s, Murphy apparently bought and perhaps read Marxist literature. *See* Christopher Johnson, *Maurice Sugar: Law, Labor, and the Left in Detroit 1912-1950*, at 197 (1988).

profit of others. ... Such a statute must not be interpreted in a narrow, grudging manner."[116]

Beyond the lower courts' disposition of the employers' crucial claim of the existence of a contrary custom, Murphy did not go.[117] Murphy's innovation, which triggered considerable scholarly criticism, focused not on the existence of custom, but on its irrelevance: "But in any event it is immaterial that there may have been a prior custom.... The Fair Labor Standards Act was not designed to codify or perpetuate those customs and contracts which allow an employer to claim all of an employee's time while compensating him for only a part of it."[118] In an obituarial appreciation, Archibald Cox, echoing Jackson's concurrence, regretted that Murphy had added this principle of statutory construction.[119] And Murphy's principal biographer characterized the guideline as "a policy statement that went beyond the facts in *Muscoda* and was probably what provoked Frankfurter to send Murphy a cautionary note after he had read the slip opinion." Indeed, the biographer conjectured that Murphy himself "was not as certain about his policy as the opinion indicated" in light of his having written in the margin of the slip opinion opposite the passage in question: "'Regardless of well established understandings as to what constitutes compensable work?'"[120]

Such criticism is puzzling since Murphy answered his own question by carefully circumscribing the potential expansiveness of his ruling: "This does not foreclose, of course, reasonable provisions of contract or custom governing the computation for work hours where precisely accurate computation is difficult or impossible." Since the travel time in the iron ore mines could easily be calculated, however, *Muscoda* was not a hard case for Murphy. Nor was it one of those "borderline cases where the other facts give rise to serious doubts as to whether certain activity or non-activity constitutes work or employment."[121] Ironically, by virtue of his censured emphasis on the harsh conditions of the ore miners, Murphy furnished the very grounds for distinguishing this case from those in which employees encountered pleasant conditions of portal-to-portal travel.[122]

---

[116]321 U.S. at 597.

[117]His major addition consisted in what may have been an ironic citation of Blackstone to the effect that custom "'must have been peaceable and acquiesced in; not subject to contention and dispute.'" 321 U.S. at 602 n.17.

[118]321 U.S. at 602.

[119]Cox, "The Influence of Mr. Justice Murphy on Labor Law," 48 *Michigan L.Rev.* 767, 805 (1950).

[120]3 Sidney Fine, *Frank Murphy: The Washington Years* 322 (1984).

[121]321 U.S. at 603.

[122]For this reason Cox's stricture appears misplaced: "Even in the hands of the most pragmatic of judges the phrases used to explain one decision are apt to be applied as formulas in later cases, divorced from their practical background." "The Influence of Mr. Justice

In a lengthy and acerbic dissent, in which Chief Justice Stone concurred, Justice Roberts frontally attacked the opinion on several levels. To Murphy's compassion Roberts counterposed the argument that the compensability of travel time "should be approached not on the basis of any broad humanitarian prepossessions we may all entertain, not with a desire to construe legislation so as to accomplish what we deem worthy objects, but" in an effort strictly to divine congressional intent.[123] Thus "merely because the court thought that such activity imposed such hardship on him [the employee] or involved conditions so deleterious to his health or welfare that he ought to be compensated for them" did not empower it to treat as work what neither contract nor custom of the parties had ever so designated.[124]

If, however, Congress shared Murphy's humanitarian vision of the FLSA, his search for and application of that intent would be impeccably traditional. Here the confrontation between majority and dissent became pointed. Whereas Murphy viewed Congress as wanting "to achieve a uniform national policy of guaranteeing compensation for all work or employment engaged in by employees covered by the Act,"[125] Roberts insisted that the FLSA's "sole purpose was to increase employment, to require a fair day's pay for a fair day's work by raising the wages of the most poorly paid workers and reducing the hours of those most overworked, and thus correct inequalities in the cost of producing goods and prevent unfair competition in commerce."[126] The difference in emphasis bore significant public policy consequences. For as was to become clear in this dissent and other dissents in portal-pay and overtime cases, one wing of the Supreme Court, reflecting the views of large capital, took the position that the FLSA applied at best only marginally to unionized workers already protected by collective bargaining agreements.[127]

In the specific setting of the case, Roberts sought to reinforce his insistence that "Congress expected the provisions of the Act to be fitted into the prevailing practices and understandings as to what constituted work in various industries"[128]

Murphy on Labor Law," 48 *Mich. L. Rev.* at 809.

[123]321 U.S. at 606.

[124]321 U.S. at 617.

[125]321 U.S. at 602.

[126]321 U.S. at 606-607.

[127]For example, one of the petitioners had argued that the FLSA was not intended "to revolutionize conditions in industry which had been established by collective bargaining." Brief for Petitioner Sloss-Sheffield Steel & Iron Co. at 35-36. Justice Jackson clearly belonged to the pro-capital wing. *See* Eugene Gerhart, *America's Advocate: Robert H. Jackson* 245 (1958). Murphy sought to refute this claim by reference to specific provisions in the FLSA giving effect to two kinds of collective agreements. 321 U.S. at 603 n.18.

[128]321 U.S. at 608.

by reference to the parallel and related immunization of union contracts from scrutiny under FLSA. In the less successful part of his argument, Roberts circularly defined statutorily compensable work as "the actual service rendered to the employer for which he pays wages in conformity to custom or agreement."[129] The trouble with this framework is that where an unscrupulous employer had secured a vested right, through long years of acquiescence by its employees in superior power that then crystallized into custom, to require employees to perform uncompensated activities for its benefit: "To give controlling effect to custom or agreement in these situations would license the kind of 'sweating' the FLSA was intended to halt."[130] Even if an adjudicator were not concerned with the effect of such practices on the employees, elimination of their untoward competitive impact on non-sweating employers was indisputably congressional intent. In order to avoid this pitfall, the dissent was compelled to argue that the custom of face-to-face pay, that is, compensation only for work performed at the face of the mine to the exclusion of travel time, was the product not of naked power, but of the give-and-take of legitimate collective bargaining.[131]

Roberts' first step was to sanction the drawing of inferences for custom in iron ore mines from the experience in coal mining based on the similarity of physical conditions.[132] Although the next portal case to reach the Supreme Court would discredit Roberts' claim of better conditions in iron ore mines,[133] the important point elided by the dissent[134] was the vast difference in union strength between coal miners on the East Coast and ore miners in Alabama. Thus whereas some inference as to bargaining trade-offs might plausibly be drawn from the UMW's pre-FLSA acceptance of face-to-face compensation in coal mining,[135] the lack of

---

[129]321 U.S. at 608.

[130]Cox, "The Influence of Mr. Justice Murphy on Labor Law," 48 *Mich. L. Rev.* at 804.

[131]A Wall Street lawyer, a partner in the law firm of the former Secretary of War, Henry Stimson, who played an important part in giving shape to the Portal-to-Portal Act, later used precisely such language of "friendly and ungrudging relations" in arguing that even where an employee was not paid for nineteen minutes of what was indisputably preliminary or postliminary work, there was no injustice because "in most cases, nothing more is involved than the normal give and take which is required of normal life. Legislation should not be designed to bring out and develop the worst features in mankind. Mere picayuneness is not to be affirmatively developed by the holding out of a governmental shield to encourage and protect a demand for the 'last measure of justice' to which one may be entitled." *Portal to Portal Wages: Hearings Before a Subcommittee of the Senate Committee on the Judiciary*, 80th Cong., 1st Sess. 658 (1947) (testimony of Arthur Pettit).

[132]321 U.S. at 609.

[133]See below § 4.B.

[134]321 U.S. at 609-10.

[135]See below § 4.B. on how Murphy finessed this issue in granting portal pay to coal

pre-FLSA "bona fide collective bargaining" with recognized independent unions[136] by the powerful iron ore mine owners[137] rendered any comparison bctwccn the two unpersuasive.

The connection to the coal miners' claims for portal pay appeared particularly pernicious and unjust to the dissenters, who noted that the UMW had not raised such a demand until three days after the appeals court issued its decision in *Muscoda*. Glossing the UMW's announcement that it desired "'to take advantage of the law which, under the Alabama decision, grants them the right to be paid for the time they are in the mines,'"[138] Roberts saw it as proof that the union understood portal pay as a judicial declaration rather than a fact of industrial custom or agreement.[139] The dissent's approach reveals that a segment of the high judiciary, like a segment of the employing class, was still unreconciled to the state's incursion into private agreements between those of unequal bargaining power that FLSA represented. They did not understand or accept that the "FLSA is designed to defeat rather than implement contractual arrangements"[140] and to impose instead by societal fiat another standard, which the current structure of the labor market in that industry would not have produced.[141] In that sense, Roberts and Stone, the only pre-New Deal holdovers on the Supreme Court, confused judicial fiat with legislative directive.

B. *Jewell Ridge*: John L. Lewis and the Coal Miners

In every democratic country engaged in World War II, the coal mining industry was the center of bitter and prolonged labor dispute. The United States was no exception.[142]

Politically explosive conflict over portal-to-portal pay formed no small part of that wartime dispute. That this battle erupted in wartime was no coincidence. For "during World War II the insatiable demand for coal forced the reopening of older

---

miners in *Jewell Ridge*.

136 321 U.S. at 601.

137 Roberts obscured this fact with various euphemisms for so-called agreements with company unions. *See* Muscoda, 321 U.S. at 611-12.

138 321 U.S. at 617 (citing no source for the quotation).

139 321 U.S. at 618.

140 Secretary of Labor v. Lauritzen, 835 F.2d 1529, 1545 (7th Cir. 1987) (Easterbrook, J., concurring).

141 See Linder, "The Minimum Wage as Industrial Policy: A Forgotten Role."

142 Arthur Suffern, "The National War Labor Board and Coal," in 1 *The Termination Report of the National War Labor Board: Industrial Disputes and Wage Stabilization in Wartime, January 12, 1942-December 31, 1945*, at 1079, 1079 (n.d. [ca. 1946]).

mines whose tunnels stretched well back into the hills. Entrance-to-face time lengthened, lengthening in turn the work day of the miner by as much as two hours."[143] By 1944, the President's Committee on Portal to Portal Travel Time, which Roosevelt had created on November 8, 1943, to collect "more exact information as to the actual travel time" and the "possibility of reducing travel time" in bituminous coal mines,[144] reported that nationally coal miners averaged almost one hour of portal travel daily.[145] At the same time and to some extent relatedly, the UMW had launched an attack on the Roosevelt administration's imposition of a wage stabilization program.[146] Although the mine owners viewed the UMW's demand for portal pay in 1943 as "a subterfuge which would compel the operators to give 50 hours of pay for 35 hours of work—with time-and-one-half rates applicable to the extra fifteen"[147]—it was a subterfuge with a difference:

> The figure of two dollars a day that Lewis initially demanded at the beginning of negotiations was set by the January wildcatters, not by the union's economists after scrutiny of cost-of-living indexes. Indeed, Lewis called upon W. Jett Lauck, K.C. Adams and Percy Tetlow to develop a statistical justification for this sum. Likewise, when Lewis, following the advice of Lauck, decided to achieve the wage advance through the subterfuge of portal-to-portal pay, he stumbled on to a genuine rank-and-file grievance.[148]

Ironically, because the importance of portal pay in coal mining had virtually no counterpart elsewhere in the economy,[149] Lewis saw his portal-pay campaign as

---

[143]Robert Zieger, *John L. Lewis: Labor Leader* 139 (1988).

[144]Letter from President's Committee on Portal to Portal Travel Time to Mr. President [Roosevelt], at 1, 2, in Franklin D. Roosevelt Library, File: President's Committee on Portal to Portal Travel Time, 220.5.10 (Feb. 2, 1944).

[145]The average travel time amounted to 59.55 minutes for 152,575 coal miners engaged in production at the face, and 57.29 minutes for 220,417 UMW members in 1,430 mines producing 92.8 percent of the coal produced in UMW mines. President's Committee on Portal to Portal Travel Time ["Final Report"], tab. 4 & 5, in Franklin D. Roosevelt Library, File: President's Committee on Portal to Portal Travel Time, 220.5.10 (May 24, 1944). See also *Monthly Lab. Rev.*, July 1944, at 81.

[146]See Colston Warne, "Coal—the First Major Test of the Little Steel Formula," in 1 *Yearbook of American Labor: War Labor Policies* 278 (C. Warne ed. 1945); Carroll Daugherty and Milton Derber, "Wage Stabilization," in 1 *Yearbook of American Labor: War Labor Policies* 162; Seidman, *American Labor from Defense to Reconversion* at 109-30.

[147]Warne, "Coal—the First Major Test of the Little Steel Formula" at 284.

[148]Melvin Dubofsky and Warren Van Tine, *John L. Lewis: A Biography* 421 (1977).

[149]A possible exception was logging. *See Proposed Amendments to the Fair Labor Standards Act: Hearings Before the House Committee on Labor*, 79th Cong., 1st Sess. 240 (1945) (statement of Reuben Haslam, assoc. counsel, NAM, that travel time issue was pressing into lumber industry).

helping his membership without triggering the wave of inflationary wage demands that the Roosevelt administration feared.[150]

The dispute that arose when the UMW presented its demand for an across-the-board increase of two dollars per day at the wage conference with the mine operators in March 1943 was certified to the National War Labor Board (NWLB). The NWLB agreed in principle "that any payment for travel time should be so designated and paid for as an item separate and apart from hourly tonnage rates, in order that there may be no doubt that travel time has been included in the mine workers' compensation"[151] without issuing any concrete decision. After being directed by the NWLB to resume work under the terms of the old contract and negotiations, the union struck; the federal government then seized the mines, and work and negotiations were resumed—a cycle that repeated itself several times in 1943. In its next ruling, the NWLB conceded the UMW the right to demand portal pay, but rejected the specific demand for equal pay for unequal travel times as "plainly and unmistakably a demand for an 'indirect wage increase in violation of the wage stabilization policies'...."[152] Thwarted in its efforts with one group of operators, the union then negotiated a portal agreement for a flat $1.25 per day with another group. When the two sides submitted it to the NWLB for approval, the Board once again disapproved the portal-pay provision on the same grounds.[153] The Board finally approved a second agreement between the same parties that provided for an eight and one-half hour day inclusive of travel time; all these hours were to be compensated at straight-time rates with time-and-one-half for overtime. Although the NWLB characterized the provision as a "true" portal pay method, it seemed to have suspended disbelief, ultimately granting its approval "because we are convinced that when travel time is paid for the economic inducement imposed on the operators will lead them to reduce the travel time...."[154]

---

[150]Zieger, *John L. Lewis* at 140.

[151]Coal Operators' Negotiating Committee of the Appalachian Joint Wage Conference v. UMW, 8 *War Lab. Rep.* 502, 509 (1943).

[152]Coal Operators' Negotiating Committee of the Appalachian Joint Wage Conference v. UMW, 9 *War Lab. Rep.* 112, 118 (1943).

[153]Illinois Coal Operators Assoc. v. UMW, 10 *War Lab. Rep.* 684 (1943). The CIO and AFL members dissented; 10 War Lab. Rep. at 686, 770.

[154]Illinois Coal Operators Assoc. v. UMW, 11 *War Lab. Rep.* 687, 688 (1943). The AFL members of the Board dissented on the grounds that although the majority indicated that travel time was work time, the majority approved only half-time pay for the travel. *Id.* at 693-94. After another round of government seizure, the agreement concluded between Lewis and Secretary of Interior Ickes was adopted in December 1943 by operators accounting for two-thirds of coal output; the collective bargaining agreement provided for eight hours of productive work and forty-five minutes of travel time daily, with the latter compensated at two-thirds the rate of the former. The owners also agreed to pay each employee forty dollars in settlement of all portal claims that had accrued after April 1, 1943 in return for dropping

In the welter of these events, the second in the trilogy of portal-pay cases to reach the Supreme Court also originated as a declaratory judgment action—filed by an employer in July 1943 to test the legitimacy of the portal demand under the FLSA. The thousand employees at the Virginia mines travelled as much as eighty-eight minutes daily as far as five miles from portal to face.[155] Transportation of the miners by the mine owner not only within but also to the mine played a major part in the overall mobilization of the labor force; as described by management, this activity bore strong resemblance to the transportation of machinery or raw materials. Thus plaintiff-employer's superintendent testified at trial that "[w]e have busses that *haul* our employees from the surrounding country."[156] Absent an obligation to pay for the time spent in such travel, the company conceded both in its complaint and in trial testimony that it had not exhausted the possibilities for reducing the amount of travel time.[157] The underground travel, or "man trips"—as distinguished from coal hauling—were, the mine superintendent testified, for the convenience of the company; otherwise the miners would go work where coal was more easily mined.[158] The company was, even more to the point, "very much interested in how a man gets there. If a man has to walk there, he isn't worth anything when he gets there. The idea is to get him there able to work. ... It wouldn't be practical to try to operate the mine...having to walk from the driftmouth in."[159]

As to the level of exertion required of the miners during travel, a former miner who had risen to the presidency of the United Eastern Coal Sales Corporation[160] testified: "I don't think traveling is work. Because I elect to live in Scarsdale, New

---

all prior claims. *See* Colston Warne, "Coal—the First Major Test of the Little Steel Formula," in 1 *Yearbook of American Labor: War Labor Policies* 278, 297-99.

[155]Jewell Ridge Coal Corp. v. Local No. 6167 UMW, 53 F. Supp. 935, 937 (W.D. Va. 1943); Record at 6 (Complaint), Jewell Ridge Coal Corp. v. Local No. 6167, UMW, 325 U.S. 161 (1945).

[156]Record at 242 (emphasis added). Although the issue was not pursued on appeal, the district court inquired whether the 400 miners were entitled to portal pay for the time spent on the buses and trucks to the mine. 53 F. Supp. at 949.

[157]Record at 5, 245.

[158]Record at 256.

[159]Record at 157-58, 259.

[160]Since it was obvious that Jewell Ridge was a test case, other entities sought to intervene as plaintiffs in the proceedings. In ruling on the Southern Coal Producers' Association's motion, the district court conceded that as a matter of abstract fairness the employer's bargaining representative should be permitted to intervene because its counterpart, the UMW, was a defendant. But doubting its power to make the employees of intervenor's members in other jurisdictions parties defendant without their consent, the court denied the motion but permitted entry as amicus. Jewell Ridge Coal Corp. v. Local No. 6167 UMW, 3 F.R.D. 251, 253, 255 (W.D. Va. 1943).

York, and take the 8:22 every morning...isn't any reason why my salary should be raised above the fellow who lives in the apartment house right across the street from the Graybar building."[161] When challenged as to the differences between his mode of transportation and that of his erstwhile colleagues, he replied:

> There isn't any more difference relatively than to try to stand up in a coach train from New York to Washington and you sitting in your comfortable seat in a Pullman. ... You can't run Pullman trains in a coal mine, but there isn't any more discomfort in a ride in a trip of mine cars at the rate of six miles an hour than there is sitting in that chair.[162]

The trial judge recognized that the man trips were necessary for the successful operation of the mines and benefited the company by "promoting safety, orderliness and increased productiveness," but he found that they also benefited the workers themselves "by saving their time and energy, and thus increase their productiveness."[163] This reasoning cannot, at first sight, be denied a certain logic. There is virtually no facility that employers confer on their employees that does not simultaneously benefit both. But it is precisely that characteristic that points up the inherent untrustworthiness of "benefit" as a criterion of compensability. For employers could argue that the provision of machinery at the workplace also benefits the workers by saving their time and energy and increasing their productiveness; consequently, time spent working on the machine would not need to be compensated. Even Justice Murphy's eventual modification—"[e]xertion pursued necessarily and primarily for the benefit of the employer and his business"[164]—does not explain how to determine which party is benefited more.

Although this indeterminacy becomes particularly acute in the case of transportation furnished by the employer from the employee's permanent residence to the employer's door—it was precisely the slippery slope to "pillow-to-pillow" wage claims that opponents conjured up to discredit the narrower portal-pay demands[165]—it is dissipated considerably once the travel is confined to the

---

[161]Record at 164.

[162]Record at 164.

[163]53 F. Supp. at 939.

[164]Jewell Ridge Coal Corp. v. Local No. 6167, UMW, 325 U.S. 161, 165 (1945).

[165]93 *Cong. Rec.* at 1493 (Rep. Hobbs). *See also* "Topics of the Times," *N.Y. Times*, Jan. 3, 1947, at 20, col. 4 (an extended ad absurdum joke). Directly after the War a district court furnished the following socio-economic answer to the question of home-to-worksite travel: "The defendant then, if it did not furnish transportation, would have available to it as employees only those who had automobiles and thus [sic] able to furnish their own transportation. Necessarily then, in obtaining employees, the defendant, in place of having access to a restricted and unlimited labor market, would have access only to a restricted and limited labor market.... It cannot be said that...the facility was not provided primarily for the benefit of the defendant in carrying on its business, and without which it probably could not

employer's premises, as it is in the trilogy of portal cases decided by the Supreme Court. This consideration is not legalistic; rather, it reflects the employer's power to structure the arrangements and hence to reduce the time involved.[166] Thus it is not so much the fact that during the trip the employer controls the employee, but rather the transportation itself that is relevant.[167] For in terms of cost analysis, although the employee might have an incentive to reduce such idle—albeit unpleasantly spent—time, he is foreclosed from changing the distance travelled or the speed of the means of transport.[168] Conversely, only if the employer were

---

be carried on at all.... [A]ny choice the employees had was a 'Hobson's' choice." Walling v. Anaconda Copper Mining Co., 66 F. Supp. 913, 918 (D. Mont. 1946). In other words, the workers could either accept the facilities or not work for the company at all. With the same logic, however, "employee" and "employer" would be interchangeable. Thus workers without access to automobiles would have been participants in a restricted labor market, while the company was faced with a Hobson's choice of offering transportation or not operating a mine at all. This problem appears largely confined to infrastructurally underdeveloped areas that are further characterized by many low-income residents whose numbers exceed the opportunities for local employment. When a firm then seeks to exploit some natural resource there, the workers' penury would in the normal case presumably permit the employer to dictate whether travel time was paid. In the alternative, if the anticipated duration of the exploitation warranted it, the state, in an effort at community development, could either require such firms to build housing closer to the employment site or to establish public transportation or subsidize either or both.

[166]The time appeared long past in which mine owners contended that they could not control face workers, who set their own starting and stopping times and saw their "boss less often than once a day." Carter Goodrich, *The Miner's Freedom* 43, 41 (1925). Although mine operators do not appear to have challenged coverage under the FLSA on the grounds that miners were independent contractors, other employers were seeking to raise this claim in the 1940s. *See Regulating the Recovery of Portal-to-Portal Pay, and for Other Purposes: Hearings Before Subcommittee No. 2 of the House Committee on the Judiciary*, 80th Cong., 1st Sess. 236 (1947) (statement of Irving Richter, UAW); 4 *Minimum Wage Standards and Other Parts of the Fair Labor Standards Act of 1938: Hearings Before Subcommittee No. 4 of the House Committee on Education and Labor*, 80th Cong., 1st Sess. 2846-2848 (1947) (statement by group of Cleveland, Ohio firms). The Wage and Hour Administrator energetically opposed this effort; *id.* at 2621.

[167]To the extent, however, that management already places workers under its command even before the travel begins, this rationale supersedes the considerations discussed in the text. Thus it was held that the FLSA clock started running at the portal of a silver mine because that was "where the workmen are to appear at a specified time...under the control and direction of" the employer. Sunshine Mining Co. v. Carver, 41 F. Supp. 60, 66 (N.D. Idaho 1941).

[168]Even in the situation (described by Orwell for Britain) in which the miners are "permitted" to walk for hours from portal to face and back, although miners might be able to choose the speed at which they walked, they would not and could not determine where the

obligated to pay for the travel time, would it have an incentive to restructure the worksite in such a way as to reduce the time and hence the wage outlay. Indeed, the NWLB ultimately approved a portal-pay settlement in the coal industry precisely on these grounds.[169]

Finding that the transportation benefited the employees and the employer, the supervision during the trip was limited to enforcement of safety rules, and the travel was less hazardous than other coal mining operations, the trial judge concluded that none of the travel time met the criteria of compensability.[170] Of far greater consequence for the future course of portal pay, however, was the court's discussion of the role of custom and agreement, which had played a subordinate part in *Muscoda*. For not only had face-to-face been the universal mode of payment in the bituminous coal industry for a half-century, but plaintiff's employees, the defendants, had been organized and represented since 1933 by the UMW, all of whose post-FLSA collective bargaining agreements had been premised on face-to-face arrangements.[171] Weighty too in the judge's mind was the fact that the ore miners in *Muscoda* had, precisely in order to avoid the taint associated with a certain embarrassing historical problem in coal mining, conceded in their appellate brief that the UMW was a strong union with the power to paralyze production by strikes.[172]

It was precisely that embarrassing letter written jointly by the UMW and the mine owners to the Wage and Hour Administrator in 1940 disavowing portal pay that proved the miners' downfall before the district court. The story may be recounted briefly. Early in its existence, the Wage and Hour Division (WHD) had upheld portal-to-portal pay in the Cornucopia Gold Mine on the grounds that it had been a long-standing custom and tradition.[173] In 1940, a WHD investigation of a coal mine in Pennsylvania concluded that face-to-face compensation was proper, but added that if the Cornucopia rule were applicable, the coal mine would owe $70,000 in back wages. After the mine owner brought this information to President Lewis's attention, both the UMW and the mine operators told the WHD from time to time that they opposed any construction of the FLSA requiring travel pay. Then on July 7, 1940, the Appalachian Joint Conference Negotiating Committee and the director of the legal department of the UMW, Earl Houck,[174] sent Wage

---

portal and where the face were located. The same would be true, *mutatis mutandis*, of large factories.

[169]Illinois Coal Operators Assoc. v. UMW, 11 *War Lab. Rep.* 687, 688 (1943).

[170]53 F. Supp. at 939.

[171]53 F. Supp. at 939-40.

[172]53 F. Supp. at 948-49.

[173]Record at 683, 685.

[174]Houck's letter was approved by UMW vice-president Philip Murray while Lewis was sick. When the operators released this letter to embarrass Lewis in connection with the

and Hour Administrator Fleming a letter memorializing their joint position. The key portions of the letter stated:

> The uniform high rates of pay that have always been included in the wage agreement of the mining industry contemplate the employee's working day beginning when he arrives at his usual working place. Hence travel time was never considered as a part of the agreement or obligation of the employer to pay for since the eight-hour day was established in the industry—April 1, 1898.
>
> [A]ny ruling requiring such a change in the custom, tradition and contract provision so as to change the work day from "seven hours' work at the usual work places" to any new standard...and to the adjustment of wage rates made necessary thereby, would create so much confusion...as to result in complete chaos, and would probably result in a complete stoppage of work at practically all of the coal mines in the United States. Such a ruling...moreover would establish such diversity of time actually spent at productive work as between different bituminous coal mines and within each mines that there would be no basis on which any general wage scales would be predicated, collective bargaining would therefore be rendered impossible,...and the very purpose of the Fair Labor Standards Act would be defeated...[which] was passed...to aid workers in industries that had unreasonably long hours and unreasonably low rates of pay, as contrasted with the short hours and high rates of pay in the bituminous coal mines.[175]

In conclusion, the union and the operators urged the Administrator to issue a supplement to his Interpretative Bulletin No. 13 stating that the definition of working time set forth in the Appalachian Agreement, which embodied the custom and traditions of the industry, complied with the FLSA and Bulletin No. 13 on the grounds that "'reasonable standards agreed upon between the employer and the employee will be accepted for the purposes of the Act.'"[176] The Administrator replied to Houck on July 18, 1940, that face-to-face compensation "would not be unreasonable," repeating this position in a public statement a few days later.[177]

Jewell Ridge litigation, "Lewis repudiated the letter, saying that neither Houck nor any other employee of the United Mine Workers was authorized to speak for the policy, principles, or purposes of the organization." Saul Alinsky, *John L. Lewis: An Unauthorized Biography* 352-53 (1949).

[175]53 F. Supp. at 940-41 (setting forth entire text of letter).

[176]53 F. Supp. at 941.

[177]53 F. Supp. at 941; the entire letter is reproduced at 53 F. Supp. 950-53 n.1. Fleming later characterized his decision, which had been reached with considerable difficulty, as having been dictated by the unique venerability and uniformity of face-to-face compensation. Transcript at 692-95 (reproducing Fleming, "Collar-to-Collar vs. Face-to-Face," 142 *Engineering & Mining J.* (April 1941)). See also "Mining Determination," 3 *Wage & Hour Reporter* 332, 333 (Aug. 5, 1940). In the memorandum submitted to the Supreme Court as amicus in *Jewell Ridge*, Fleming stated that his earlier distinction between metal and coal mining, which had not been guided by legal principles but by his reluctance to disturb

In first presenting its demand for portal pay at a wage conference in March 1943, the UMW, according to the trial judge, "only contended for it then as an additional basis for its demand for a general wage increase to all mine workers" of two dollars per day.[178] Lewis's biographers have explained his supra-individual approach to portal pay as rooted in the assumption "that travel time would have to be calculated on an individual basis for each miner. The union naturally wanted to avoid the divisiveness this would foster among the rank and file. The union also feared that in establishing travel time in line with the Fair Labor Standards Act, which also provided for the forty-hour week, the mine workers would weaken their claim to a seven-hour day."[179] What remains puzzling about this explanation is that the Houck letter had indicated that the man trips

> are scheduled to leave the...opening of the mine at a certain hour, so that all the employees will reach their working places by the hour at which work regularly begins at the working places throughout the mine, and these trips are also scheduled to leave the inside of the mine...at the conclusion of the seven-hour period of work at the working places.[180]

In other words, all miners worked seven hours at the face, but some were required to travel longer than others. Why should this differential in individual unpaid travel time be less divisive than the differential in individual paid travel time?[181]

The embarrassment to which divulgence of the Houck letter was designed to expose Lewis and the UMW was not confined to them. For in the course of the portal-to-portal controversy this incident, which appears to have been peculiar if not unique to coal mining, was transformed by management (and in part by the AFL) into the archetypical breach of contractual good faith and integrity by CIO unions that delegitimated collective bargaining. More important still, capitalizing on this account, employers were able to convince the press and a majority of Congress that they were the aggrieved party: wresting that role away from workers who alleged that they were being robbed of compensation for precious minutes of work, capital successfully projected an image of well-paid workers who were trying to snooker their employers into paying triple back wages for time that they had solemnly covenanted to be noncompensable. If much of the non-mining population regarded venturing into a coal mine as a harrowing prospect to be

---

collective bargaining practices, had become untenable in the light of *Muscoda*. His failure to intervene in the coal case resulted solely from his desire not to influence the litigation. Memorandum at 2-3, 5.

[178] 53 F. Supp. at 941-42.

[179] Dubofsky and Van Tine, *John L. Lewis* at 421-22.

[180] 53 F. Supp. at 940.

[181] Presumably miners did not rotate with regard to closer and more remote working places, for in that case there would have been no individuation problems in calculating portal pay.

avoided under any circumstances, management cannot be gainsaid a significant propaganda victory in having convinced some segment of the public that it was just for miners not to be paid for one hour a day they spent deep in the bowels of the earth.

The trial judge also made much of this alleged untrustworthiness in citing Lewis' testimony at the FLSA hearings in 1937, when he had opposed government interference with collective bargaining outcomes in excess of statutory standards.[182] Cast as apostates, the UMW defendants failed, finally, to impress the court with their amended answer, which contended that when their collective bargaining agreement expired at the end of March 1943, the FLSA (and portal-to-portal principles) began to control. Rejecting as irrelevant the union's disclaimer of any overtime that had accrued before April 1, 1943, the district judge pointed out the inconsistency: "If the Fair Labor Standards Act...required the inclusion of travel time as work time, it did so irrespective of contract, and if there was a contract to the contrary, the contract would be ineffective as against the Act."[183]

On appeal, the Fourth Circuit reversed what it otherwise found a convincing decision on the basis of the Supreme Court's supervening *Muscoda* decision, which it found indistinguishable.[184] Neither of the possible exceptions mentioned by Murphy—the impossibility of precise computation of time or borderline cases—applied to the coal miners' situation. Moreover, the appeals court appeared reassured by the fact that the "disturbing effect of the decision here will not be so great as it otherwise would, in view of the fact that, by agreement between the miners and operators, the portal to portal system...has now been adopted in the industry." Consequently, the overtime claims for the period between April 1, 1943 and June 20, 1943, which amounted to a mere $40 per miner, constituted what had been awarded other miners as a result of settlement of portal claims.[185]

---

[182]53 F. Supp. at 943-44 (citing *The Fair Labor Standards Act of 1937: Joint Hearings Before the Senate Committee on Education and Labor and the House Committee on Labor*, 75th Cong., 1st Sess. 281 (1937). To be sure, Lewis was testifying about the powers of a labor standards board to set wages in various industries, a provision that was ultimately not enacted.

[183]53 F. Supp. at 950.

[184]Local No. 6167, UMW v. Jewell Ridge Coal Corp., 145 F.2d 10, 11 (4th Cir. 1945). The district court decision had been handed down in January 1944, the Supreme Court decision in Muscoda in March 1944.

[185]145 F. 2d at 13, 15. The dissenter was considerably less persuaded by the voluntary nature of such settlements, pointing out that strikes had led to an agreement between Lewis and the Secretary of the Interior including portal-pay provisions to which the greater part of the industry yielded. *Id.* at 15. *Jewell Ridge* remained in litigation because the Southern Coal Producers' Association, of which Jewell Ridge was a member, refused to participate in the Ickes-Lewis agreement of November 3, 1943, which coal operators accounting for two-thirds of national output had accepted; the Southern Coal Producers' Association adhered to

Having achieved only two-thirds pay for travel time in 1943, Lewis demanded the full rate for all travel time (including time and one-half after seven hours in thc mine) when negotiations over renewal of the contract began on March 2, 1945. A week later the Supreme Court heard oral argument in *Jewell Ridge*. As the familiar scenario of walkouts by the miners and government seizure of the mines was replayed,[186] pressure, Justice Jackson later alleged,[187] was exerted on Justice Murphy to hand down an opinion quickly in order to influence the outcome of the negotiations in favor of the UMW.[188] Writing for the majority, Murphy framed the sole issue on appeal as whether *Muscoda* was controlling.[189] Making short shrift of the petitioner's and the district court's reasoning, he summarily found that underground travel in bituminous coal mines satisfied the three elements of compensable work set forth in *Muscoda*: 1. physical or mental exertion (whether burdensome or not); 2. exertion controlled or required by the employer; and 3. exertion pursued necessarily and primarily for the benefit of the employer and his business.[190] Thus, for example, though less burdensome than the conditions under which the iron ore miners travelled, those in the coal mines caused the workers to watch out for low and falling ceilings.[191] The lack of subtlety characteristic of the opinion, large parts of which consisted merely of quotations from *Muscoda*,[192] was most conspicuous in the resolution of the for-whose-benefit prong of the work test. Asserting that the answer was "too obvious to require extended discussion," Murphy noted that the workers "do not engage in this travel for their own pleasure or convenience" but only as "a necessary prerequisite to the extraction of coal...which is the prime purpose of petitioner's business."[193] In his zeal to vindicate the rights of the workingman, Murphy failed to think through this

---

the position that travel time was not work time. Because the Association refused to join the agreement, the United States Government continued to operate the member mines. *See* Warne, "Coal—The First Major Test of the Little Steel Formula," at 297 n.15, 299 n.18.

[186]Colston Warne, "Industrial Relations in Coal," in *Labor in Postwar America* 367, 368-69.

[187]See below § 7.

[188]See Eugene Gerhart, *America's Advocate: Robert H. Jackson* 247-51 (1958). The Chief Justice originally assigned the opinion to Jackson, but when Reed switched his vote, Black assigned it to Murphy. 3 Fine, *Frank Murphy* at 325. Although Murphy apparently did not expedite issuance of the decision, which was handed down May 7, 1945, the UMW achieved all its bargaining objectives later that month.

[189]Jewell Ridge Coal Corp. v. Local No. 6167, UMW, 325 U.S. 161, 162 (1945).

[190]325 U.S. at 164-66.

[191]325 U.S. at 164.

[192]The mechanical quality of the opinion raises the question as to why the Court did not merely deny the petition for certiorari or issue a summary affirmance.

[193]325 U.S. at 165, 166.

approach, which in its open-endedness might have been applicable to employees driving their own automobiles to work in heavy traffic on dangerous roads. What the opinion lacked in logic, it packed in the empathetic language that runs like a red thread through Murphy's FLSA opinions. Here Murphy effectively subverted the plausibility of any argument that such extraordinary travel on the employer's premises might nevertheless be noncompensable:

> Those who are forced to travel in underground mines in order to earn their livelihood are unlike the ordinary traveler or ordinary workman on his way to work. They must journey beneath the crust of the earth, far removed from the fresh and open air and from the beneficial rays of the sun. ... From the moment they enter the portal until they leave they are subjected to constant hazards and dangers; they are left begrimed and exhausted by their continuous physical and mental exertion.
>
> To conclude that such subterraneous travel is not work is to ignore reality completely.[194]

Once again Murphy rejected the defense of custom by citing *Muscoda*.[195] This time, however, he emphatically added that not even the best employers were immune from the Act's injunction to pay for all time worked: "Conversely, employees are not to be deprived of the benefits of the Act simply because they are

---

[194]325 U.S. at 166.

[195]In his dissent, Jackson criticized the majority for its neglect of a recent unanimous opinion by Jackson in which the Court had held that a determination of whether waiting time was compensable working time involved "'scrutiny and construction of the agreements between the particular parties'": "'The law does not impose an arrangement upon the parties. It imposes upon the courts the task of finding what the arrangement was.'" 325 U.S. at 192-93 (quoting Skidmore v. Swift & Co., 323 U.S. 134, 137 (1944)). Absolutized out of context, this principle is clearly a misstatement of the law. In a number of important respects the FLSA certainly does "impose an arrangement upon the parties." The parties cannot, for example, agree that the hourly wage will be less than the statutory minimum. It may, nevertheless, be reasonable, where employees are "on call" for such extended periods of time that they are permitted to sleep and to eat and otherwise to engage in "pursuits of a purely private nature which would presumably occupy the employees' time whether they were on duty or not," 323 U.S. at 139, to permit agreements to provide "compensation for a reasonable portion of time in addition to" the actual physical work insofar as the "employee gives more to his employer than actual physical labor. He gives his time—for he is not free to sell it elsewhere." U.S. DOL, *First Annual Report, Wage and Hour and Public Contracts Divisions, For the Fiscal Year Ended June 30, 1939*, at 13 (1940). Ironically, however, that principle was mere dictum in *Skidmore* because the agreement called for no compensation for pure on-call waiting time; had that arrangement been controlling, Jackson would not have reversed and remanded the cause. In any event, the majority in *Jewell Ridge* impliedly resisted Jackson's bid to extend the principle beyond the very narrow and unusual sphere of 24-hour on-call work.

well paid or...represented by strong bargaining agents."[196] Presumably because Lewis's wage demands never envisioned individualized portal pay, Murphy stated in dictum that the Court was not foreclosing "the validity of agreements whereby, in a bona fide attempt to avoid complex difficulties of computation, travel time is averaged or fixed at an arbitrary figure and underground miners are paid on that basis rather than according to their individual travel time."[197] Returning to the principle of the case before him, however, Murphy concluded: "Thus shall each of petitioner's miners receive his own reward according to his own labor."[198]

The dissenters (and scholarly commentary) pounced on the contradiction between these two approaches. Jackson, joined by Chief Justice Stone, Roberts and Frankfurter, wrote a dissent three times as long as the majority opinion, detailing the history of the portal pay controversy in coal mining. Pointing out that the industry now operated under a portal-pay scheme (as part of the Ickes-Lewis agreement), worked out as a result of the federal government's seizure of the mines in 1943, which in effect (prospectively) credited each miner with forty-five minutes of travel time regardless of his actual time so spent, Jackson noted that the collective bargaining agreements based on this scheme did not even purport to comply with the FLSA.[199] Consequently, the Court had brought "into question the validity of all existing mine agreements":[200]

> If it is illegal for the operators and the miners by collective bargaining to agree that there shall be no travel time, it is obviously equally illegal to agree that travel time shall be fixed at an arbitrary figure which does not conform to the facts. ... Moreover, the averaging means that a part of the travel time earned by one miner is taken away from him and given to another who has earned less than the average, a procedure utterly unwarranted in the statute.[201]

---

[196]325 U.S. at 167.

[197]325 U.S. at 170.

[198]325 U.S. at 170.

[199]325 U.S. at 188-91.

[200]325 U.S. at 188.

[201]325 U.S. at 191. Even a sympathetic labor law scholar could not discern "any intellectually satisfying basis" for the corner Murphy had argued himself into: "[T]he union and the operators have for some years mutually agreed that in this industry underground travel shall not be treated as work. These agreements have, since the effective date of the Act, been either valid or invalid. To say that they were invalid is to say that the Court would have been obliged to strike them down at the insistence of an individual employee even though both the union and the operators had been urging the Court to sustain them. ... It is difficult to believe that a majority of the members of the Court would have held the agreements invalid if the case had come before them prior to the date of the union's change of front." E. Merrick Dodd, "The Supreme Court and Fair Labor Standards, 1941-1945," 59 *Harv. L. Rev.* 321, 354-55 (1946).

Thus by unnecessarily suggesting that the Court might approve a pseudo-portal-pay arrangement that clearly contradicted the principle of individuation set forth in his opinion, Murphy unwittingly confirmed that there might after all be practical reasons for deviating from the FLSA in the coal industry.[202] He thereby made it easier for opponents of portal pay to attack its underpinnings.[203]

Jackson also devoted considerable attention to showing that both the legislative history of the FLSA and the contemporaneously enacted Bituminous Coal Act evinced an intent to stabilize the industry by collective bargaining.[204] While the dissenters conceded that Congress intended to invalidate collective bargaining agreements that failed to secure employees minimum wages or overtime in compliance with the standards set by the FLSA,[205] they did not join issue on the central claim raised by portal-pay demands—that the face-to-face method did not compensate the miners for all the hours they worked. To be sure, the dissent sought to undercut this argument by pointing out that counsel for the union had noted that "the wage scale was fixed at a level intended indirectly to compensate travel time."[206] But this response was irrelevant because its cogency was confined to minimum wage claims, whereas the portal-pay cases were all based on overtime.[207]

5. Mt. Clemens Pottery Company: The CIO Knocks at Industry's Door

---

[202]See Dodd, "The Supreme Court and Fair Labor Standards, 1941-1945" at 355.

[203]This outcome is puzzling is light of the fact that Murphy removed his initial statement that the Court was not adjudicating the validity of agreements to average rather than to individuate travel time "after Rutledge pointed out to him that this assertion seemingly contradicted his 'basic premise that contract cannot make work not work.'" 3 Fine, *Frank Murphy* at 326.

[204]325 U.S. at 175-82. For a sophisticated analysis of the peculiarities of competition among coal producers, which ends shortly before the period under discussion, see John Bowman, *Capitalist Collective Action: Competition, Cooperation, and Conflict in the Coal Industry* (1989).

[205]325 U.S. at 177.

[206]325 U.S. at 172.

[207]The reason that this issue was never joined may lie in the relatively abstract plane on which the Supreme Court disposed of the case, which did not require it to delve into the mundane empirical intricacies of the prevailing wage system at the Jewell Ridge mines. Some confusion may have enveloped the overtime issue as a result of the fact that although the 1940 Houck letter indicated that miners were paid eighty cents per hour for a thirty-five hour week, the miners at Jewell Ridge were paid according to piece (tonnage) rates. These rates were apparently designed to secure parity with the hourly guarantee, which may have operated as a floor. *See* Jewell Ridge, 325 U.S. at 184 n.9; Record at 63-64, 612-13, 624-26, 630.

After learning that the CIO would demand portal-to-portal pay in all American industries, the justice wrote his brother approvingly, "This case may be the turning point in the economy of the country. I did not write it to unstabilize conditions in this country, but I did write it to make secure the rights of man. ... History...will record that it has made a step forward for those who toil by the sweat of their brow for their bread."[208]

The portal litigation until this point had dealt with underground (mining) or outdoor (forestry) places of production, which created unusual problems of access and uncommonly extended and hazardous travel. Unable to discern a deeper or more encompassing principle at stake, industrial employers and their counsel paid relatively little attention to these earlier portal decisions.[209] The final case in the Supreme Court trilogy, however, involved a medium-size factory like thousands of others in the United States. Precisely because of this ordinariness and the near-universality of the compensation practices there, a ruling that the FLSA had been violated "would mean that nearly every plant in the country would be in violation of the law and that billions of dollars in retroactive payments and liquidated damages could now be assessed against thousands of companies."[210] The workers'

---

[208]3 Fine, *Frank Murphy* at 332.

[209]A significant exception was a memorandum from NAM's law department of Nov. 3, 1944—that is, after the Supreme Court's *Muscoda* decision but before it reversed the Fourth Circuit in *Jewell Ridge*—predicting that the Wage and Hour Administrator would use the miner cases "'to regard as work-time the time spent by employees traveling anywhere on company property.'" "'Portal-To-Portal' Wage-Hour Liabilities," 9 *N.A.M. Law Digest* 3 (Supp. No. 1, Dec. 1946) (quoting memorandum). With hindsight, a leftist lawyer saw a meaning to employers' general blindness: "Since the adoption of this Act industry not only has demonstrated concerted opposition to it, but has maintained a strikingly consistent record for guessing wrong on almost every legal issue the cases have presented. Perhaps this is understandable when one recalls the multitude of prior decisions of the federal courts effecting the invalidation or emasculation of practically every labor enactment which had come out of Congress." Maurice Sugar, "The Truth About 'Portal to Portal,'" 7 *Law. Guild Rev.* 23, 23 (1947). In contrast, Arthur Krock, a leading political columnist for *The New York Times*, found an excuse for lack of journalistic foresight in a similar judicial failing. Arthur Krock, "Even the Dissenters Didn't See It Coming," *N.Y. Times*, Dec. 26, 1946, at 24, col. 5. To be sure, counsel for Tennessee Coal, Iron & Railroad Co. had argued to the trial court: "Doesn't everyone know that for all times in all plants, almost without exception, men go to the gates of plants, and even punch the clock, but their time at work does not begin until they get to their work benches...no matter how far the gate is from the place of work?" Record at 3492, Tennessee Coal, Iron & Railroad Co. v. Muscoda Local No. 123, 321 U.S. 590 (1944).

[210]Brief for Respondent at 98, Anderson v. Mt. Clemens Pottery Co., 328 U.S. 680 (1946). It is in the nature of tactical posturing that in opposing the workers' petition for writ of certiorari, the respondent-employer had argued that "The Decision Is Not of Importance in the Administration of the Act." Brief for Respondent in Opposition at 15.

counsel was therefore hardly exaggerating when he asserted that it was "the most important case pending under the Wage and Hour law in the United States today."[211] Indeed, when the Supreme Court remanded the case to the district court, the trial in the winter of 1947 became and has remained the most intensively and extensively reported on in the entire history of the FLSA.[212] What turned out to be ironic was that six years of litigation through the entire federal judicial system never clarified whether this crucial case had ever raised a portal issue.

The Mt. Clemens Pottery Co., located a few miles north of Detroit, was "the largest manufacturer of dinner ware pottery in the United States."[213] Acquired by S.S. Kresge in 1920, it was at the time of the litigation a wholly owned subsidiary of Kresge, whose chain stores it supplied.[214] While the average pottery establishment employed 131 wage earners,[215] 1,250 worked at Mt. Clemens.[216] Significantly for the overtime issue, ninety-five per cent of production workers were paid on a (group) piece-work basis.[217] Pottery as a whole, though "a small and relatively unimportant industry...has considerable importance in the union-management relations field because nation-wide collective bargaining has been notably successful since 1905 in its major division, general ware...."[218] Mt. Clemens fell outside that framework as nonunion in the late 1930s, but in the summer of 1940 the CIO Federation of Glass, Ceramic and Silica Sand Workers announced plans to organize unorganized sections of pottery manufacture; by the next year, Mt. Clemens was the most important local CIO industrial union in

---

[211]Record at 1497.

[212]"The legal attention of the country...will be centered on Judge Picard's court...." Walter Ruch, "Picard to Decide Portal Time Issue," *N.Y. Times*, Jan. 26, 1947, at 2, col. 4. On remand, *The New York Times* published the text of the full opinion (including footnotes). *N.Y. Times*, Feb. 9, 1947, at 26-27. *Business Week* featured a picture of the trial judge, Frank Picard, on its cover the week he handed down his decision. *Business Week*, Feb. 8, 1947.

[213]Brief of Appellants at 6.

[214]*Poor's Financial Record: 1941 Industrial Manual* 2594; Philip Taft, "Appendix B," in *How Collective Bargaining Works: A Survey of Experience in Leading American Industries* 910 (Harry Millis ed. 1942). Kresge did not sell Mt. Clemens Pottery, which had been established in 1914, until 1965. *Moody's Industrial Manual 1971*, at 1332. The original complaint named Kresge as a defendant, but for reasons that are not clear from the record, plaintiffs voluntarily discontinued as to it. Record at 7; Anderson v. Mt. Clemens Pottery Co., 60 F. Supp. 146, 148 (E.D. Mich. 1943).

[215]In 1937, 251 establishments employed 33,000 wage earners. U.S. Bureau of the Census, *Biennial Census of Manufactures* 1937, Pt. 1, at 847 (1939).

[216]Record at 8.

[217]Record at 166.

[218]Taft, "Appendix B; Pottery," at 908. The standard study of that system is David McCabe, *National Collective Bargaining in the Pottery Industry* (16 Johns Hopkins U. Stud. in Hist. & Pol. Sci., new ser. 1932).

pottery.[219]

On April 16, 1941, a few days after an organizational strike began[220] in the midst of efforts by Mt. Clemens to form a company union,[221] suit was filed in federal district court in Detroit by seven employees on behalf of themselves and "in behalf of all others similarly situated" and by Local 1083, United Pottery Workers of America, which was designated a representative by various of its members.[222] The case came before Judge Frank Picard, who had been Justice Murphy's former campaign manager when Murphy was candidate for governor of Michigan and who owed his appointment to the federal bench in 1939 to Murphy.[223] Picard, who had unsuccessfully run for the U.S. Senate in 1934, was a sufficiently well-known political figure that he was named by respondents in Gallup polls in November 1937 and January 1938 in response to a question as to their preference for the Democratic candidate for president in 1938 if Roosevelt did not run.[224] The gravamen of the complaint was "that the defendant compels its employees to punch

---

[219]Taft, "Appendix B: Pottery," at 910-11.

[220]"Pottery Strike in Mt. Clemens," *Detroit Free Press*, Apr. 15, 1941, at 14, col. 4; Record at 26 (affidavit of Charles Doll, general manager); Mt. Clemens Pottery Co. v. Anderson, 149 F.2d 461, 461 (6th Cir. 1945).

[221]NLRB v. Mt. Clemens Pottery Co., 147 F.2d 262, 263-65 (6th Cir. 1945).

[222]Record at 7. Steve Anderson, the eponymous plaintiff of the case, was the president of the local. *Id.* at 119. The class allegations in the complaint did not track the statutory language precisely. The collective action prong of § 16(b) authorizes employees to sue on behalf of themselves and "other employees similarly situated," while the representative action prong authorizes employees to "designate an agent or representative to maintain such action for and in behalf of all employees similarly situated." Why representatives are called upon to represent "all" similarly situated is unclear. *See* Rufus Poole, "Private Litigation under the Wage and Hour Act," 14 *Miss. L.J.* 157, 164 n.43 (1942). The trial judge denied a motion to dismiss the class action on the grounds that if a narrow interpretation were given to such suits, few could be brought under the FLSA. He therefore permitted all those claiming back wages for overtime in one classification. Record at 29-30 (Order of June 13, 1941). Approximately 300 employees were permitted to file designations. Mt. Clemens Pottery Co. v. Anderson, 149 F.2d at 461.

[223]J. Woodford Howard, Jr., *Mr. Justice Murphy: A Political Biography* 403 (1968); 1 Sidney Fine, *Frank Murphy: The Detroit Years* 28 (1975); *Business Week*, Feb. 8, 1947, at 8.

[224]Respondents named a total of 53 and 66 persons, respectively, in the two polls; Picard, like most preferences, was named by fewer than 0.5 percent of the respodents. Gallup Poll—A.I.P.O., US Gallup.37-104, Q084 and US Gallup.38-108, Q07B; Roper Center at University of Connecticut, Public Opinion Online (Lexis). Picard remained a district judge until 1961, dying two years later. *Biographical Dictionary of the Federal Judiciary* 220-21 (Harold Chase et al. comp., 1976). On Picard's pro-government,, anti-communist bias during the red-hunt trials of the early 1950s, see David Caute, *The Great Fear: The Anti-Communist Purge Under Truman and Eisenhower* 140-41, 202-203 (1979).

a time clock and in such a procedure deliberately falsifies the records of the time worked by its employees. That the said employees work 14 minutes in advance of the time shown on the clocks in the morning of each working day."[225]

The workers further alleged that the company clocked them out before they actually finished working before lunch and repeated the same procedure after lunch and at the end of the workday. Consequently, the plaintiffs pleaded, they were owed back wages and liquidated damages totalling $100,000 for overtime for forty minutes per day or three and one-quarter hours per week since the forty-hour provision of FLSA had gone into effect on October 24, 1940.[226] Or as their lead counsel[227] phrased it at a hearing: "[T]his company gyps each employee out of approximately 56 minutes of pay a day. ... Almost $1,000 a day they are taking out of the payroll of these employees."[228]

The court appointed a special master, Donald Quaife, who heard extensive testimony in 1942 and issued a report in March 1943.[229] He expressed his unsympathetic attitude toward the action most clearly in his skepticism as to why

---

[225]Record at 10.

[226]Record at 10-12. The plaintiffs also made overtime allegations for the period from Oct. 24, 1938 to Oct. 24, 1939, when the overtime provision of FLSA was triggered after forty-four hours, and from Oct. 24, 1939 to Oct. 24, 1940, when it kicked in after forty-two hours. *Id.* at 8-9. Their allegation that they had worked forty-five hours weekly for the defendant contradicted their other claim that they had worked three and one-quarter hours beyond forty. Finally, allegations were also made for some employees for minimum wages. *Id.* at 9-11. The following calculation underscores how even minimal individual claims can over time cumulate to a considerable liability—just as they once constituted a considerable source of savings—for a large employer. If the sum requested, $100,000, included liquidated damages, then the underlying back wages amounted to $50,000, or $40 for each of 1,250 employees. For the entire two and one-half years (from the day the FLSA went into effect until the day the suit was filed), this sum equalled thirty-one cents per week per employee. At the initial minimum wage of twenty-five cents per hour, this amount represented 2.5 hours weekly; at the later minimum wage of forty cents per hour, 1.5 hours. If the workers' regular rate of pay was higher, then even fewer hours of back wages would have been at issue.

[227]Edward Lamb stated during the litigation that he practiced law for the fun of it in "'the largest non-paying practice'" in the United States. "Back-Pay Lawyer Advises Caution," *N.Y. Times*, Dec. 29, 1946, at 3, col. 1. J. Parnell Thomas, the chairman of the House Committee on Un-American Activities, alleged in one of the few outbursts of red-baiting during the portal debates that Lamb "has followed the Communist party line and has associated himself with numerous Communist fronts...." 93 *Cong. Rec.* 539 (1947).

[228]Record at 382. Discrepancies cropped up in the record as to the exact number of minutes involved. The complaint specified fourteen, ten, fourteen, and fifteen minutes at the four clock-ins and clock-outs, which add up to fifty-three minutes, although the complaint then spoke of forty minutes. Record at 10-11.

[229]Record at 143-217.

no worker had ever complained about the "cheating" before suit was filed.[230] While appreciating the intimidating force exerted by possible dismissal, he noted that the workers had complained about other practices. The master therefore concluded that "[p]erhaps the true explanation" was that it had "never occurred to" the plaintiffs before suit was filed that Mt. Clemens was deliberately underpaying them.[231] The implication here—that the union manufactured hypertechnical claims about which the workers had never articulated felt needs but which they cynically supported as a "'gravy train'"[232]—was then largely adopted by employers and the press in the course of the portal and anti-portal movements. This stance overlooked the fact that, because the FLSA had just been enacted, piece-rate workers were unaccustomed to having their time, let alone all their time, expressly kept track of and compensated. Because this employers' position implicitly underlay the master's report, which the Supreme Court found not to be clearly erroneous, it gained enhanced legitimacy as the debate proceeded.

The master reported that plaintiffs contended in the alternative—if their 56-minute claim was not sustained—that "at least the full time the employees were in the plant as shown by entries punched on the time clock cards should have been, but was not, credited to them, since they were required to go directly from the time clocks to their respective departments and immediately thereafter to work."[233] In contrast, in the company's version, "the employees were given a fourteen minute period to check in and out.... It is claimed, however, that while they were permitted to come in fourteen minutes early, they were under no compulsion to do so, the only requirement being that they be at their place of work, ready to work, at the established starting time, and their time being their own until then."[234] Mt. Clemens argued in the alternative that even if the master found in favor of the plaintiffs, they could have no judgment because the amount of working time that had not been credited to them could not be computed.[235]

The master found that after entering the production part of the plant, which encompassed more than eight acres,[236] the workers punched in at the rate of twenty-five per minute, after which they walked to their work place for distances ranging from 130 to 890 feet. Although the company did not permit the workers to punch in more than fourteen minutes before what it called the starting time,[237] in

---

[230]Record at 190.

[231]Record at 191.

[232]"Exit Mount Clemens," *N.Y. Times*, April 4, 1947, at 22, col. 3 (editorial).

[233]Record at 163.

[234]Record at 163.

[235]Record at 163.

[236]This area is the equivalent of a square with sides of 200 yards, although the plant was actually nearly a quarter-mile long. Brief for Respondent at 34.

[237]Record at 167.

computing the hours worked on the basis of the time-clock cards, Mt. Clemens figured the time "from the succeeding even quarter hour after employees ring in to the quarter hour immediately preceding the time they punch out. Thus, for example, an employee whose card is punched in at 6:46 A.M., out at 12:03 P.M., in at 12:50 P.M., and out again at 4:07 P.M. is credited with eight working hours."[238]

In this example, therefore, the employee was, as the master did not trouble to state, credited with a total of thirty-four minutes fewer than she was actually on the premises and clocked in. The parties agreed that the employer did not consider the time spent walking from the time clocks to the work place working time and that such walking took place before the regular starting time. The parties also agreed that the time spent walking to the closer departments was one or two minutes; to the more distant departments the employees' estimates ranged from one-half to three minutes, while the employer's varied between six and eight.[239]

This latter fact is crucial for two reasons. First, it shows how minimal the walking time was by any estimate; and second, it underscores the perverse underlying structure of the dispute before the trial court—one that would later be inverted and cause considerable confusion as to what the case was all about. Because the workers' central claim went to the issue of the compensability of pre-7:00 a.m. work at their individual work place and the parties agreed that the dispute involved a maximum of fourteen minutes, it was in the employees' interest to understate the amount of walking time in order to maximize the amount of time they could have devoted to such work; conversely, it was in the employer's interest to exaggerate the amount of walking time in order to minimize the amount of potentially compensable time spent in pre-7:00 a.m. work.

The master touched on, but never dispositively resolved the issue of walking time. The plaintiffs contended that the proper standard was that "all time spent by the employee on the employer's premises at the request of the latter" was compensable.[240] This formula tracked the guide articulated by the Wage and Hour Administrator.[241] The master rejected this formula solely by virtue of the fact that he believed that he had found an example that refuted its literalness—namely, that lunch time, even where it had to be eaten on the employer's premises, was not

---

[238]Record at 168.

[239]Record at 173-74.

[240]Record at 197.

[241]Interpretative Bulletin No. 13, ¶ 2 in BNA, *Wage and Hour Manual* 172 (cumul. ed. 1944-45 [July 1939]) ("all time during which an employee is required...to be on the employer's premises"). More pertinently, a WHD official testified that he had told Mt. Clemens in 1939 "that time spent on the premises by any employees who were required to be there by the company was to be considered as hours worked, regardless of whether they worked or not." Record at 1324.

compensable.[242] Yet this case makes little if any sense. For other than in the instance of those who live on the employer's premises, there would be a presumption that any order not to leave the premises for lunch was based on the employer's desire to keep the employee within hailing distance. Subject to such a restriction, the employee would have a valid claim to compensation for lunch time.[243] In any event, the master offered no principled resolution of the issue of walking time, merely stating that in view of the workers' knowledge of the custom and practice not to credit them for that time, "it would seem that defendant's practice...was not improper under the Act."[244]

As to the preliminary work, the master found that:

> Practically all of the workmen in the plant had certain duties to perform after arriving at their departments previous to the commencement of actual production.... Two kinds of activity are embraced under this heading: (1) personal preparations, such as putting on aprons or overalls, removing shirts, taping or greasing arms, putting on finger cots; (2) activity of a non-personal nature, involving the preparation of equipment for commencement of production work, such as turning on switches for lights and machinery, opening windows and assembling and sharpening tools.[245]

The plaintiffs testified that they performed two to three minutes of preliminary work each day "immediately upon arrival in the department." The company conceded that so-called personal preliminary activities did take place before the established starting time; the company denied that the so-called non-personal preparations were performed at all before starting time, or in the alternative, for more for than a minute.[246]

Even bracketing the factual dispute over its duration, resolution of the issue of the compensability of preliminary activity caused the master "more difficulty." For without benefit of pertinent case law, he was confronted with a WHD Inspection Field Letter that "ma[de] it clear that the Administrator considers such work [non-personal preliminary duties] as part of the employment time" and with conflicting industry customs.[247] Ultimately the master found it unnecessary to reach the issue "in view of another principle of law which is applicable here...which requires that in order for the Court to render a judgment for damages in favor of a plaintiff,

---

[242]Record at 197.

[243]See Lofton v. Seneca Coal & Coke Co., 2 Wage & Hour Cas. 669, 675 (N.D. Okla. 1942) (half-hour lunch period compensable where employee required to remain at his place of work "so that defendant received the benefit of his presence"), *aff'd*, 136 F.2d 359 (10th Cir. 1943), *cert. denied*, 320 U.S. 772 (1943).

[244]Record at 199.

[245]Record at 169.

[246]Record at 174.

[247]Record at 200.

evidence as to the amount of damages suffered must be reasonably definite and not based upon mere conjecture."[248] If the flat claim of fifty-six minutes per day or the contention that all the punched time on the cards constituted work time had been credible, then there would have been no impediment. Computing overtime, however, on the basis of a finding that the employees worked more time than credited to them but less than that shown on the time cards would be speculative and unreliable because the plaintiffs kept no time records and could not recollect—independently of the time cards—when they arrived at their departments or began preliminary work on any given day. The master therefore felt compelled to deny recovery on this claim. But even if the plaintiffs had been able to overcome this hurdle, he added, they would still have had to deal with "counterbalancing time not worked by employees when they quit and cleaned up in advance of the established quitting time."[249] Finally, the master cautioned that even if the plaintiffs had been able to avoid all these problems, the amount recovered "would be very small, inasmuch as such time under the most liberal estimates could not have aggregated over one-half hour per week, and in most instances there was a greater margin than that between the weekly working time credited to the employees and the statutory period for payment of straight time."[250] In other words, the master in dictum developed the issue of de minimis on which the case would ultimately hinge.

In order to gain some perspective on standard industrial practice, the master also devoted some attention to the testimony elicited by the parties from their expert witnesses. He concluded that all had agreed that it was a "practically universal[]" custom in manufacturing plants with time clocks[251] that:

> If an employee arrives early in his department, his time is his own until the regular starting time. The punched entries on the time cards show the time the employees enter and leave the production part of the plant, but do not show the time they commenced and stopped work; and the time worked is not computed directly according to these entries, since it is obvious that they will practically always show more time than is actually worked. Instead, if the punch-in time is prior to the beginning of the shift it is assumed that the employee started at the regular starting time....[252]

In fact, however, one of the plaintiffs' expert witnesses, the director of research of the UAW, had responded directly to a question by the master that in some plants

---

[248]Record at 200 (citing several appellate and district court FLSA cases).

[249]Record at 201. Both employers' representatives and the U.S. government later adopted this argument. See below.

[250]Record at 202.

[251]Record at 170.

[252]Record at 171.

workers punched time clocks directly in their departments to record the beginning of their work.[253] In other words, it would have been administratively possible for Mt. Clemens to record the actual starting times for workers who went directly to work.[254]

The master thus made four pertinent summary findings of fact. First, the workers had never objected to, but had acquiesced in, the practices over which they eventually sued. Second, the workers neither were required to work nor did they in fact work fifty-six uncredited minutes daily. Third, the workers were instructed to be in their departments "ready to work and with personal preliminary duties performed, by the established starting time." And fourth, the workers failed to prove that they were required to report in advance of the starting time, that they performed other than preliminary work before that time, "or that they worked continuously from the time they punched their cards in to the time they punched out."[255] The master also made three pertinent summary conclusions of law. First, the plaintiffs had the burden of proof to show that the company failed to compensate them for some of their work. Second, plaintiffs failed to carry that burden "with the possible exception of preliminary work." And third, a computation of the time spent in such preliminary work "cannot be made except upon a speculative basis, and accordingly forms no basis for recovery of overtime pay."[256]

The question that lay before district judge Picard was whether to approve the master's report.[257] If the workers' account were correct, Picard wrote, the court would be "face to face with a method of employer domination and unfairness that, to say the least, would be most reprehensible," whereas upholding the employer's version—that since the work was done by crews on a piece rate, it was important that the whole crew be at work on time—would lead to a conclusion that its procedures had been reasonable.[258] Although Picard agreed with the master "in the main," certain details merited closer scrutiny, in particular the fact that the time

---

[253]Record at 1460-61.

[254]To be sure, this arrangement would have eliminated the problem of non-payment for preliminary work, but would not have dealt with walking time from the gate. Since that distance would presumably have been fixed, however, it would not have been difficult to ascertain a reasonable amount of time to walk it and to factor that time into the computation of working time. In that case, then, it would not have mattered how early workers had arrived at the outside gate—they would have been paid only for the walking time to their work bench. This consideration is important inasmuch as Mt. Clemens conceded that workers had to punch in early in order to be in their departments by starting time. Record at 173.

[255]Record at 214-15.

[256]Record at 217.

[257]Anderson v. Mt. Clemens Pottery Co., 60 F. Supp. 146, 148 (E.D. Mich. 1943).

[258]60 F. Supp. at 148-49.

cards and calculations showed that

> [b]y eight minutes to seven but a few stragglers were left. [T]he preparation even after punching the clock wouldn't take more than one or one and a half minutes and to the farthest point in the plant from the time clock wouldn't take more than 2 minutes. It is apparent, therefore, that practically every member of the entire shift was ready to work at 5 to 7 minutes before the hour and it does not seem probable that with compensation set by piece work, and the crew ready...these employees didn't start to work immediately. In fact, it appears that this was encouraged by the company as being mutually beneficial.[259]

Or as Picard phrased it somewhat more informally at a hearing several months later:

> Now, I know what went on out there. I do think that if they got down there, the bunch of them, being on piece work, that they jumped the gun, and I do think that the people were as much a party to it as the management. The management encouraged it; and I would like to penalize the management for doing it. But I have got to go on your proof.[260]

Crucial here is that Picard, who clearly maintained strong sympathies for the workers, viewed their whole overtime claim as based on the practice, which presumably antedated the FLSA, of beginning piece work before the official starting hour. Before the wage and hour law went into effect, such practices mattered less. Perhaps in the welter of disputed issues surrounding the union's organizing campaign, the workers had had more pressing issues to stress. But since their claims were unwaivable within the statute of limitations, they were free to "sav[e] up these claims like Octagon soap wrappers."[261] But just as clearly, Picard was of the opinion that neither walking from the clock nor preliminary work was the real abuse in this case. Rather,

> when a crew was ready to work they might jump the gun. In the experience of this court that's just exactly what would happen 99 times out of 100 on piece work and it was one of the practices that the Wages and Hours Act sought to discourage both on the part of the employer and employee. To us it is obvious that...an attempt was made either by the company itself or by certain foremen in currying favor with the employer, to circumvent the spirit of the Wages and Hours Act.[262]

In other words, having decided that *Mt. Clemens* was not a portal-pay case at all, Picard ruled that the court would not "lend its aid to a practice that deprives

---

[259] 60 F. Supp. at 149.
[260] Record at 1506.
[261] 92 *Cong. Rec.* 1559 (1946) (Rep. Hobbs).
[262] 60 F. Supp. at 149.

any working man of...the only thing he has to sell—his hours or minutes of labor."[263] He therefore held to be compensable all the time shown by time cards over and above five minutes for punching in and two minutes for walking to the work place—a total of seven minutes, which he credited to the employer. Thus Picard expressly denied the walking time.[264]

In 1944, Judge Picard awarded the approximately 300 named plaintiffs and intervenors a de minimis recovery of $1,207.87 in overtime and an equal amount in liquidated damages in addition to $2,000 in attorney fees.[265]

On appeal, the Sixth Circuit reversed and dismissed.[266] The narrow ground of decision was the fact that the master's findings were all supported by substantial evidence, which the district court was required to accept unless they were clearly erroneous, just as an appeals must accept the findings of a district court. Instead, Judge Picard "applied an arbitrary formula," which "produced a judgment based upon surmise and conjecture" because the employees based their claims "on a mere estimated average of overtime worked."[267]

In their petition for writ of certiorari, the employees argued that all the time they spent after clocking in bore all the indicia of work—that is, exertion on the employer's premises controlled or required by the employer necessarily and primarily for the employer's benefit.[268] The question presented to the Supreme Court was, the plaintiffs implied, complicated by the fact that the district court

> did not base its judgment for the plaintiffs upon a ruling that the time spent by the employees in checking through the time clocks or in going to their work places was strictly working time. Instead the District Court indicated that time spent in these activities should be credited to the employer and deducted from the time shown on the time cards. The Circuit Court..., however, in treating this case as an ordinary travel time case, misconstrued the District Court's decision....[269]

The plaintiffs' formulation was, to say the least, disingenuous. First, Picard had expressly ruled that punching in and walking were not compensable. Second, given the procedural grounds on which the Sixth Circuit reversed the trial court, it was immaterial whether it viewed travel time as crucial or not. And finally, if *Anderson v. Mt. Clemens Pottery Co.* was not an "ordinary travel time case," then

---

[263]60 F. Supp. at 149-50.

[264]60 F. Supp. at 150. Picard also allowed the employer five minutes for punching in after lunch, but denied recovery for punching out.

[265]Record at 289, 297-305. One worker received as little as one cent in back wages.

[266]Mt. Clemens Pottery Co. v. Anderson, 149 F.2d 461 (6th Cir. 1945).

[267]149 F.2d at 464, 465.

[268]Petition for Writ of Certiorari at 6.

[269]Petition for Writ of Certiorari at 7-8.

why had plaintiffs been arguing "throughout these proceedings...that because of the impossibility of calculating travel time to the exact second the reviewing court should compel a modification of the trial court's decision [and give] the employees full recovery from the employer for the amounts shown on the time cards"?[270]

The answer to this rhetorical question appears to be that the workers had never argued that *Mt. Clemens* was a travel time case; instead, they had pleaded the case as involving actual production work before the clock started ("jumping-the-gun") and preliminary activities.[271] However, when the appeals court reversed Picard on the not-clearly-erroneous standard, plaintiffs' counsel may have believed that the easiest way to persuade the Supreme Court to grant certiorari was to assert that *Mt. Clemens* presented the question that the Court had left open in *Jewell Ridge* concerning "'the validity of agreements whereby, in a bona fide attempt to avoid complex difficulties of computation, travel time is averaged or fixed at an arbitrary figure....'"[272] Although this argument appears misguided since the "arbitrary" element had allegedly been introduced by Judge Picard—and not by the parties, as in *Jewell Ridge*—the Court did grant certiorari.[273]

In their brief, the workers offered a rather different view of the daily work routine than the decisions below had disclosed. Now they asserted that all their personal preliminary activities (including clothes changing) took place even before they clocked in.[274] After clocking in, it took only thirty to ninety seconds "to get into productive activities."[275] In understating the travel time, the workers sought to convince the Court that it was not being called on to work a revolution in industrial practices, for the "case reveal[ed] a curious and an unusual situation in employer-employee relations in the United States" in that the company required the employees to clock in "as much as fourteen minutes before the regular starting time" but paid them only from the succeeding quarter hour.[276]

The company, of course, took the opposite tack, emphasizing that, because its practice was "universal," any ruling that it was in violation of the FLSA would have equally broad consequences for all industry.[277] Mt. Clemens sought to buttress this argument by suggesting that the clock-in and payment arrangement was universal precisely because it was eminently reasonable:

---

[270]Petition for Writ of Certiorari at 8.

[271]Indeed, the plaintiffs argued to the Supreme Court that because the Sixth Circuit had misinterpreted the decision below, it had left "the law as to working time in our industrial plants in a state of uncertainty." Petition for Writ of Certiorari at 9.

[272]Petition for Writ of Certiorari at 8.

[273]Anderson v. Mt. Clemens Pottery Co., 326 U.S. 706 (1945).

[274]Brief for Appellants at 8, 23.

[275]Brief for Appellants at 8.

[276]Brief for Appellants at 9.

[277]Brief for Respondent at 27.

One of the practical realities of operating a factory is that it is impossible for a group of one thousand or more individuals to arrive at their places of work simultaneously. ... It is in recognition of this fact that all plants have developed a custom of opening their doors and permitting employees to enter fifteen or thirty minutes before starting time.

The objective is to have everyone in the plant ready to go to work at starting time. To do this the individuals who lead the parade must enter the plant earlier than others.[278]

Misrepresenting the nature of the employees' claim, the company then charged:

Any requirement that an employee must be paid for the time getting into the plant would be directly at odds with the practice that has prevailed in plants all over the country for many years. ... It would mean that nearly every such plant in the country would be in violation of the law and that billions of dollars in retroactive payments and liquidated damages could now be assessed against thousands of companies.[279]

Finally, the employer developed an argument designed to put unions on notice that if they pushed this game too far, capital could respond in ways that might make the recovery of portal wages very unpleasant and expensive for employees:

Bickering over such minutiae was not contemplated when the Fair Labor Standards Act was adopted. ... If employees were given a right to insist upon such a demand, employers would doubtless counter with requirements that employees must start work and become subject to strict control of management from the very moment they enter the company's promises. ... Any such requirement would retard the development of the beneficent practices of allowing rest periods, and time off for a "snack" on the job, and the privilege of quitting work a few minutes before quitting time when convenient....[280]

Such a retaliatory countermove was perhaps the only one still available to Mt.

---

[278]Brief for Respondent at 96-97.

[279]Brief for Respondent at 97, 98.

[280]Brief for Respondent at 98. Remarkably, on remand before Judge Picard a year later, the Department of Justice expressly adopted this argument. In seeking to save labor from the consequences of its own imprudence, the Assistant Attorney General told Picard that "'[o]n the facts of this case the play is not worth the candle.'" *Time*, Feb. 10, 1947 at 82 (quoting John Sonnett); *see also* Walter Ruch, "Picard Reopens Basic Portal Suit; U.S. Protests Pay," *N.Y. Times*, Jan. 31, 1947, at 1, col. 5, at 4, col. 3. The "minutiae" over which the CIO was "bickering," according to the NAM, included "(1) changing clothes, (2) checking equipment, (3) taking medical examinations, (4) figuring earnings from piece rate tickets, (5) preparing reports, (6) walking...to and from work on company premises, (7) waiting for work, (8) waiting to get paid, (9) eating meals "on duty," and (10) resting for periods not exceeding 20 minutes." "'Portal-to-Portal' Wage-Hour Liabilities," 9 *N.A.M. Law Digest* 3, 4 (Supp. No. 1 Dec. 1946).

Clemens once it had conceded both that performance of non-personal preliminary activities was compensable working time[281] and that the cost to it of computing how long an employee was in the plant would exceed the benefit to the workers.[282]

Viewed against the strongly empathetic descriptions of the conditions under which the miners travelled from portal to face in Justice Murphy's opinions in *Muscoda* and *Jewell Ridge*, the sharply contrasting language toward the beginning of *Mt. Clemens* immediately created the expectation of a different approach and outcome:

> The employees...walk to their working places along clean, painted floors of the brightly illuminated and well ventilated building. They are free to take whatever course through the plant they desire and may stop off at any portion of the journey to converse with other employees and to do whatever else they may desire.[283]

And indeed little else in the opinion recalls the humanitarian images of those earlier cases. Instead, the lever Murphy used to reverse the appeals court was its approval of the master's imposition on the workers of "an improper standard of proof...that has the practical effect of impairing many of the benefits of" the FLSA.[284] Although an employee had the burden of proving that he had performed the work for which he alleged underpayment: "The remedial nature of this statute and the great public policy which it embodies...militate against making that burden an impossible hurdle...."[285] This equitable readjustment of the evidentiary burdens was buttressed by the employer's obligation under § 11(c) of the FLSA to keep time records. The Court thus disapproved of the Sixth Circuit's solution of penalizing the employee for the employer's violation of the recordkeeping provision.[286]

For the future, whenever an employer failed to keep adequate and accurate time records reflecting when the employee began his preliminary activities, all the

---

[281]Respondent's Reply to Brief of Wage and Hour Division at 4. The Wage and Hour Administrator appeared as amicus in order to underscore its position "that both the 'personal' and 'non-personal' duties constitute employment compensable under the Act," a view as to which it had consistently "advised numerous employer associations and labor unions in various industries." Brief for L. Metcalfe Walling, Adm'r of the Wage & Hour Div., U.S. DOL, as Amicus Curiae at 3, 7. The Administrator also noted that he had not yet taken a position on the compensability of walking time from fences to working places in normal peacetime operations. *Id.* at 8 n.6.

[282]Brief for Respondent at 99.

[283]Anderson v. Mt. Clemens Pottery Co., 328 U.S. 680, 683 (1946).

[284]328 U.S. at 686.

[285]328 U.S. at 687.

[286]To be sure, this violation did not give rise to a private right of action; but the Administrator could seek criminal sanctions under § 215(a)(5) and § 216(a).

employee would be required to produce was "sufficient evidence to show the amount and extent of that work as a matter of just and reasonable evidence."[287] Such a showing—and the Court held that Picard's "arbitrary formula" did not meet that standard—sufficed to shift the burden to the employer either to produce counter-evidence of the real amount of work performed or "to negative the reasonableness of the inference to be drawn from the employee's evidence."[288] Failure to do so would justify recovery "even though the result be only approximate."[289] This procedural innovation is the only pro-employee proposition of *Mt. Clemens* that survived the congressional backlash.[290]

Having set forth this principle by way of prologue, the Court proceeded to eliminate most of the workers' claims. First, Murphy upheld the circuit court's ruling that Picard had erred in failing to accept the master's fact finding that the workers did not perform unpaid "actual productive work" before scheduled hours.[291] This ruling was crucial insofar as the only sympathy Picard had expressed for the workers was that the company made pieceworkers "jump the gun." With the guts of the case now ripped out, Picard's decision on remand was virtually preordained. Second, Murphy implicitly upheld the appeals court's characterization of Picard's judgment as based on an "arbitrary formula" by ruling that the workers had not proved "that they were engaged in work from the moment they punched in...to the moment when they punched out."[292] By this formulation the Court presumably meant, more specifically, that they had not proved how much of the maximum of fourteen minutes allotted to them to get from punch-in to the scheduled beginning of work was actually devoted to compensable activity.[293] Moreover, the Court rejected the argument that mere presence on the employer's premises, as reflected on time clock records, should start the FLSA clock absent

---

[287]328 U.S. at 687.

[288]328 U.S. at 687-88.

[289]328 U.S.. at 688.

[290]On the unsuccessful efforts to overturn this holding as well, see below § VII. Remarkably, the only authority the Supreme Court cited for this point was a student note. The student, in turn, had bottomed the proposed law reform on courts' "inherent equitable powers to draw from the refusal to keep records, consequences similar to those explicitly drawn, by the Federal Rules of Civil Procedure, from the refusal to produce them." Note, "Determination of Wages under Fair Labor Standards Act," 43 *Colum. L. Rev.* 355, 358 (1943).

[291]328 U.S. at 689.

[292]328 U.S. at 689.

[293]This conclusion flows from the Court's rejection of the assumption that it would be "unfair" to credit the first person past the clock with more compensable time than the last person. *Id.* at 690. Had the Court accepted the workers' claim that they went to work immediately, such a calculation would not have been unfair.

any requirement by the employer that the employee actually be there.[294] By the same token, Murphy implicitly declined the plaintiffs' invitation to avail himself of the opportunity to implement the dictum in *Jewell Ridge* concerning the possibility of permitting an arbitrary aggregate average fixing of travel time rather than requiring individualized accounts.

Only on one point of proof did the Court favor the plaintiffs—namely:

> that it was necessary for them to be on the premises for some time prior and subsequent to the scheduled working hours. The employer required them to punch in, walk to their work benches and perform preliminary duties during the 14-minute periods preceding productive work; the same activities in reverse occurred in the 14-minute periods subsequent to the completion of productive work. Since the statutory workweek includes all time during which an employee is necessarily required to be on the employer's premises...the time spent in these activities must be accorded appropriate compensation.[295]

Ignoring the time spent waiting to clock in as not having been pleaded,[296] the Court certified the time spent walking on Mt. Clemens's premises after clocking in as working time, estimated at "2 to 12 minutes daily, if not more," because it

> was under the complete control of the employer, being dependent solely upon the physical arrangements which the employer made in the factory. ... Without such walking...the productive aims of the employer could not have been achieved. The employees' convenience and necessity...bore no relation whatever to this walking time; they walked on the employer's premises only because they were compelled to do so by the necessities

---

[294] 328 U.S. at 690.

[295] 328 U.S. at 690-91.

[296] 328 U.S. at 691. In two cases, one decided before and the other after *Mt. Clemens*, recovery for clock-waiting time was denied on de minimis grounds. Cameron v. Bendix Aviation Corp., 65 F. Supp. 510 (E.D. Pa. 1946); McIntyre v. Joseph E. Seagram & Sons, Inc., 72 F. Supp. 372 (W.D. Ky. 1947). It is unclear why the workers did not assert a claim for this time since the Administrator had ruled "that if the employer requires the employees to punch a time clock and the employee is required to be present for a considerable period of time before doing so, such time will be considered hours worked." Interpretative Bulletin No. 13 at ¶ 3 in BNA, *Wage and Hour Manual* 173 (cumul. ed. 1944-1945 [originally issued July 1939]). Even the master had interpreted this provision to mean that "the employer would seem to be obligated to have sufficient clocks so the employees would not be required to wait an unreasonable time to punch in or out." Record at 197. Since the Supreme Court found that a minimum of eight minutes was needed for the workers to get by the clock, 328 U.S. at 683, and since all the indicia of work and control by and benefit for the employer spelled out by the court with regard to walking also applied fully to waiting to clock in, the employees would presumably have been entitled to recover. In the ensuing wave of litigation, the CIO did follow up this cue.

of the employer's business.[297]

According to the Court, however, the employees while walking from the clocks to their work benches at Mt. Clemens did attend to their own "convenience." The time consumed by such purely personal detours and frolics was to be deducted to arrive at the compensable time, which "was limited to the minimum time necessarily spent in walking at an ordinary rate along the most direct route" and should normally be easily calculable.[298] The Court, in other words, was not only instructing Picard to make such calculations on remand, but also issuing a guideline to all employers for establishing such standards for their employees.

With regard to preliminary activities, the Court invalidated the master's distinction between compensable non-personal and non-compensable personal ones. They were all compensable work because the employees undertook them "necessarily and primarily for the employer's benefit" rather than solely for their own convenience.[299]

Having given workers their only due, however, Murphy promptly took most of it back in the form of the other enduring holding of *Mt. Clemens*: time spent both walking and in preliminaries was subject to a de minimis rule so that "negligible" or "insubstantial and insignificant" periods of time need not be compensated.[300]

> The workweek contemplated by § 7(a) must be computed in the light of the realities of the industrial world. When the matter in issue concerns only a few seconds or minutes beyond the scheduled working hours, such trifles may be disregarded. Split-second absurdities are not justified by the actualities of working conditions or by the policy of the Fair Labor Standards Act. It is only when an employee is required to give up a substantial measure of his time and effort that compensable working time is involved.[301]

In *Mt. Clemens*, Murphy was certain that this de minimis rule could "doubtless be applied to much of the walking time," leaving it to Judge Picard to determine just how much.[302]

The dissent by Burton, with whom Frankfurter concurred,[303] sought to re-focus

---

[297] 328 U.S. at 691.

[298] 328 U.S. at 692.

[299] 328 U.S. at 693.

[300] 328 U.S. at 692, 693.

[301] 328 U.S. at 692.

[302] 328 U.S. at 692.

[303] Jackson, who was chief U.S. prosecutor at the Nuremberg trials at the time, did not take part. He attacked Justice Black publicly the day after *Mt. Clemens* was handed down. See below § 7.

the analysis on custom, contract, and collective bargaining. Instead of requiring employers to engage in the futility of recording small amounts of time spent in non-productive activities, he pointed out that "the obvious, long established and simple way to compensate an employee for such activities is to recognize those activities in the rate of pay for the particular job. These items are appropriate for consideration in collective bargaining."[304] Moreover, there was "no evidence that Congress meant...to set aside long established contracts or customs which had absorbed in the rate of pay of the respective jobs recognition of whatever preliminary activities might be required of the worker by that particular job."[305]

Workers could, it is true, try to secure portal pay or any other terms and conditions of employment through collective bargaining. The FLSA, however, was a recognition of the political and economic reality that many workers were not able to obtain certain levels of compensation by such methods; consequently, Congress compelled all concerned parties to comply with standards set by society at large. To remit employees to their own devices in defining as central a statutory term as compensable work would have marked a return to the pre-statutory period. Moreover, reliance on custom, contract, and bargaining would have reproduced precisely those conditions of unfair competition that enabled "chiseling" employers to underprice those employers who could not or did not wish to "sweat" their employees.[306] If what Burton really meant was that the FLSA was not designed to promote the marginal improvements in working conditions that strong unions had previously apparently preferred to trade off for other terms,[307] he failed to explain how that result could be achieved without harming the unorganized workers (and more law-abiding employers) whom Congress indisputably wanted to support.

The Court's decision unleashed an outcry. Representative Vorys (Rep. Ohio) called it "the most outrageous and unconscionable instance of judicial usurpation of the law-making power that I have ever seen."[308] while Senator Wherry (Rep.

---

[304]328 U.S. at 697.

[305]328 U.S. at 698.

[306]"I think the opportunity for evasion in the Fair Labor Standards Act comes...in determining the amount of time that shall be put in, in order to secure the minimum wage. The opportunity for chiseling there, is an opportunity to chisel upon the hours worked...." 93 *Cong. Rec.* 2251 (1947) (Sen. McGrath). For the use and meaning of these terms in the various FLSA congressional debates, see Marc Linder, "The Minimum Wage as Industrial Policy: A Forgotten Role," 16 *J. Legis.* 151, 160-62 (1990). Even what may appear to the individual worker to be negligible unlawful deductions from compensable time can, when spread out of over thousands of workers for long periods of time, aggregate to significant cost advantages. See above § 2.

[307]Since the work-spreading goal of premium pay for overtime was macroeconomic, it was designed to apply to all workers including members of the strongest unions.

[308]93 *Cong. Rec.* at 1514.

Neb.) declared that the effect of *Mt. Clemens* had been "to pervert the act from an instrument of righteous correction into an instrument to destroy those very employers who have attempted conscientiously to obey the mandates of the act."[309] Roscoe Pound, the director of the National Conference of Judicial Councils, former dean of the Harvard Law School, and arguably the most prominent law professor in the United States, who had turned to the right in the 1930s, charged that decisions such as *Mt. Clemens* threatened to transform the United States into an "autocracy." *The New York Times* quoted Pound as contending that the "'Supreme Court's handling of the portal-to-portal case was an example of spurious interpretation in which judicial statesmanship was conspicuously exhibited.'"[310] Frances Perkins, Roosevelt's Secretary of Labor, called the Supreme Court's decision a "'doctrinaire'...one that could not have been made by any one with practical knowledge of working conditions."[311] Even Elmer Andrews, the first Wage and Hour Administrator, expressed surprise that his own portal interpretation for mining had been extended to less hazardous employment, though he concluded that "[t]here can be no moral disagreement with" the Supreme Court's decision because Mt. Clemens obliged its employees to work almost fifteen minutes "getting ready to do more work."[312]

Yet these denunciations appear strangely inappropriate. After all, the de minimis condition[313] imposed such narrow limits on recoveries that it would be difficult to sustain politically relevant sympathy for employers sued for any surviving claims for substantial periods of time. Given the individual nature of the rights created by the FLSA, the de minimis exception contained a very favorable twist for employers: "The walking time of some employees conceivably could be as little as two minutes a day and this might be disregarded under the de minimis

---

[309]93 *Cong. Rec.* at 2195. One of Murphy's biographers echoed these sentiments twenty years later in calling the portal-pay trilogy "Frank Murphy's closest brush with abuse." J. Woodford Howard, Jr., *Mr. Justice Murphy: A Political Biography* 405 (1968).

[310]"Pound Hits High Court for Its Interpretation," *N.Y. Times*, Feb. 11, 1947, at 20, col. 2.

[311]"Miss Perkins Urges Labor Pacts Providing Ways to End Disputes," *N.Y. Times*, Jan. 16, 1947, at 4, col. 4. Arthur Krock immediately seized upon this remark; Arthur Krock, "Miss Perkins Goes to the Root of the Decision," *N.Y. Times*, Jan. 17, 1947, at 22, col. 5.

[312]Alfred Zipser, Jr., "Many Portal Suits Held Unwarranted," *N.Y. Times*, Jan. 5, 1947, § 3 at 1, col. 2, at 8, col. 4.

[313]According to Eugene Gressman, who was Murphy's clerk from 1943 to 1948, the de minimis doctrine was injected into the opinion precisely because Murphy believed that there was a difference between conditions in mines and factories. Telephone interview with Eugene Gressman, April 9, 1990. Gressman, the longest-serving Supreme Court clerk in modern times, was so closely involved in writing Murphy's opinions that he was jocularly called "Mr. Justice Gressman."

rule. The fact that this would aggregate forty hours a day or more for all the employees would not enter into consideration."[314] Even the evidentiary adjustment that the Court made in favor of employees was arguably nothing more than a negative incentive to employers to comply with their recordkeeping obligations under § 11(c). In this sense, Archibald Cox may have been exaggerating when he speculated that the decision "would have caused radical changes in the payroll practices of American industry."[315]

Indeed, had the Court framed its ruling purely prospectively, it might have deprived employers and their congressional advocates of any moral basis for overturning *Mt. Clemens*. Intriguingly, the NAM counsel, in commenting on the organization's petition for amicus status on remand, observed: "Application of the principle of prospective rather than retroactive effect to this case and to all portal-to-portal cases would go a long way toward clearing up the great uncertainty and public concern created by the litigation. Our remedy is one which would reduce the portal-to-portal controversy, however it is finally decided, to dimensions which could be handled without danger of disrupting the whole national economy." [316] By the same token, had the CIO restricted its litigation campaign to enforcing the new ruling only prospectively, the financially fueled fervor that triggered impressive lobbying efforts on behalf of a portal amendment to the FLSA would have been seriously undercut. In the event, however, employers were disposed "to fight every portal pay suit...in the firm belief that the Supreme Court will change its mind."[317] In the meantime, critics of *Mt. Clemens* tried to rework the salient points of the dissent into the language of amendatory bills.[318]

After the Supreme Court's denial of a rehearing to Mt. Clemens on October 10, 1946,[319] events unfolded on two tracks. First, attention focused on the

---

[314]"Clark Asks a Hand in Key Portal Suit," *N.Y. Times*, Jan. 3, 1947, at 1, col. 6, at 5, col. 6.

[315]Cox, "The Influence of Mr. Justice Murphy on Labor Law" at 807.

[316]"NAM Gives Basis for Entering Portal Case; Says Back-Pay Plan Could Wreck Economy," *N.Y. Times*, Jan. 11, 1947, at 7, col. 5.

[317]Anthony Leviero, "Bill to Wipe Out Portal Pay Suits Ready in Capital," *N.Y. Times*, Jan. 2, 1947, at 1, col. 4, at 6, col. 5. Employers hoped that the Court would change its mind in part through a change of personnel. *Id.*

[318]The notions of contract and custom found their way into virtually all of the bills. Several incorporated Burton's phrase concerning the absorption of preliminary activities in the rate of pay. *See, e.g.*, H.R. 1041, 80th Cong., 1st Sess. (1947) (Rep. Fernandez).

[319]Anderson v. Mt. Clemens Pottery Co., 329 U.S. 822 (1946). In January 1947 Arthur Krock noted that lawyers suggested that before Congress acted, it would be best for the Supreme Court to rehear *Mt. Clemens*. Arthur Krock, "The Long Trail to the Portal-to-Portal Suits," *N.Y. Times*, January 10, 1947, at 20, col. 5. Krock did not explain on what grounds a second petition for rehearing might have a greater chance of success. Krock also failed to state that by (unnamed) "lawyers" he in fact was referring to Justice Jackson, with whom he

proceedings on remand before Judge Picard. Second, employers and their associations awaited the outcome of the congressional elections in November to determine whether legislative overruling of *Mt. Clemens* might be feasible. Once the magnitude of the Republican victory became clear, employers were less inclined to work out settlements with unions and more inclined to wait for the new Congress to take care of the matter. Thus a Wall Street lawyer urged that it "is not recommended that actions be brought by the employer for declaratory judgments to determine its liability. [T]he new Congress may well rectify the inequities which presently exist. The employer might do well just prayerfully to sit tight...."[320] Conversely, the pace of litigation accelerated as unions began to fear that if they did not file promptly, their claims would be cut off.[321]

All of this strategic behavior must be seen against the backdrop of the contemporaneous second round of postwar wage negotiations, which made it clear to all concerned that if the employees ultimately prevailed in the litigation, unions could use the pressure of out-of-court settlements to bargain for larger wage increases.[322] Nevertheless, Edward Lamb, counsel for the employees in *Mt. Clemens*, warned unions that they risked restrictive congressional action if they

had a private conference on January 7, 1947. The contents of the memorandum Krock made of Jackson's remarks at that conference are virtually identical with that of his article. *See* Eugene Gerhart, *America's Advocate: Robert H. Jackson* 274 (1958).

[320]George Cotter, "Portal to Portal Pay," 33 *Virg. L. Rev.* 44, 67 (1947). The president of Packard Motor Co. appears to have adopted this fatalistic-reverential pose: "There is nothing we in industry can do or say. The issue is now a legal fact and the answer to it all is in the hands of Congress. We can only wait to see what they will do." "Portal Pay Demands, If Awarded, Would Wipe Out Auto Industry, Warns Christopher of Packard," *Wall St. J.*, Jan. 11, 1947, at 2, col. 1.

[321]Lee Pressman, CIO general counsel and one of the architects of the portal-pay legal campaign, testified before Congress that filings mounted "when some Congressmen started making statements that 'As soon as we get into Washington, there is going to be a law wiping out past claims.'" *Regulating the Recovery of Portal-to-Portal Pay, and For Other Purposes: Hearings Before Subcommittee No. 2 of the House Committee on the Judiciary*, 80th Cong., 1st Sess. 174 (1947).

[322]See Joseph Loftus, "Portal Pay Claims Reaching Billions; A Boon to Unions," *N.Y. Times*, Dec. 22, 1946, at 1, col. 6; "UAW to Ask Pay Rises Plus Portal Demands," *N.Y. Times*, Dec. 24, 1946, at 10, col. 4; Joseph Loftus, "Portal Pay, Wages Separate, Says CIO," *N.Y. Times*, Dec. 25, 1946, at 1, col. 3; "Portal Pay Asked By Electric Union," *N.Y. Times*, Dec. 31, 1946, at 12, col. 3. *But see* Clayton Sutton, "Rubber Union, Seeking Pay Raise, Tells Local 'Go Slow' on Law Suits," *Wall St. J.*, Jan. 9, 1947, at 1, col. 6; "Portal-to-Portal," *Wall St. J.*, Jan. 22, 1947, at 4, col. 2 (editorial) (Inland Steel proposes that base wage rates be reduced to finance nonproductive time Inland may be obligated to pay for under FLSA).

filed suits for "'fabulous and reckless'" amounts.[323]

Not until January 1947 did the proceedings on remand resume in Judge Picard's court. Out of court, however, the general and business press as well as the law reviews joined in the campaign to educate and mobilize their various audiences for capitalist law reform. Throughout December 1946, *The New York Times* and *Wall Street Journal* kept readers informed of the latest portal suits, highlighting the maximum but, in the reality of litigation, infeasible[324] recoveries,[325] and furnished a running account of employers associations' initiatives to overturn *Mt. Clemens*.[326] For example, the *Times* front page declared on December 29: "Portal Pay Suits Exceed a Billion."[327] More important, however, in manufacturing public opinion and the "hysteria"[328] that might galvanize Congress into action, however, was the newspaper's constant and unswerving editorial promotion of management's position. Thus the *Times*, ignoring the fact that the whole point of the FLSA was to negate contract in favor of uniform standards, editorialized that the portal-pay suits, which were "apparently to be used as a lever for one of the largest mass wage demands in the nation's history," were "a peculiarly disturbing and harassing type of wage demand" because they retroactively inserted provisions into agreements never intended by the parties and were "capricious" because they were related not to intent but to the nature of the industry and its geographic location.[329] Conveniently ignoring that tucked away in a *Times* article was the account that, having been put on notice by advisory opinions from the Wage and Hour Administrator since 1940, "[s]ome employers protected themselves accordingly but

---

[323]"Back-Pay Lawyer Advises Caution," *N.Y. Times*, Dec. 29, 1946, at 3, col. 1; "Picard Hits Hysteria," N.Y. Times, Dec. 24, 1946, at 10, col. 3.

[324]See, e.g., "Industry Payment on Portal Suits Seen Fraction of Vast Union Claims," *Wall St. J.*, Dec. 30, 1946, at 2, col. 2.

[325]See, e.g., "Asks $120,000,000 in Portal Pay Suit," *N.Y. Times*, Dec. 10, 1946, at 24, col. 5 (suit by USW members against U.S. Steel); "6 Billion Possible in Portal Claims," *N.Y. Times*, Dec. 22, 1946, at 3, col. 4 (suit by UAW members against Ford for $270,000,000); "Portal Pay Suits Pass $900,000,000," *N.Y. Times*, Dec. 28, 1946, at 2, col. 4; "Bethlehem Sued for $200,000,000," *N.Y. Times*, Dec. 29, 1946, at 3, col. 4.

[326]See, e.g., "Business Confused by Wage Decision," *N.Y. Times*, Dec. 18, 1946, at 47, col. 3; "Business Starts Campaign To Limit Portal Suit Costs," *N.Y. Times*, Dec. 24, 1946, at 1, col. 5 (U.S. Chamber of Commerce drafts four amendments); John Morris, "Republicans Back Quick Bill To Curb Suits for Portal Pay," *N.Y. Times*, Dec. 27, 1946, at 1, col. 2; "GOP Drive Grows to Curb Pay Suits," *N.Y. Times*, Dec. 28, 1946, at 2, col. 2.

[327]"Portal Pay Suits Exceed a Billion," *N.Y. Times*, Dec. 29, 1946, at 1, col. 6.

[328]"Picard Hits Hysteria," *N.Y. Times*, Dec. 24, 1946, at 10, col. 3.

[329]"The Portal-to-Portal Issue," *N.Y. Times*, Dec. 24, 1946, at 16, col. 1 (editorial). See also "Retroactive Relief?" *N.Y. Times*, Dec. 28, 1946, at 14, col. 2 (editorial on reopening government contracts).

the majority of them apparently did not do so,"[330] the *Times*'s chief editorial page columnist, Arthur Krock, secretly echoing the sentiments of Justice Jackson, warned that "the largest sum of money ever transferred from one pocket to another in this country will have changed hands without a word or a line of authorization by Congress in the statute thus interpreted."[331]

The *Wall Street Journal* tended to glide off into its wonted histrionic tone:

If anyone were to assert that the motive behind these numerous suits to collect from employers some billions of retroactive pay was the overthrow of private ownership and its replacement by communism, the charge would be indignantly—though perhaps not unanimously—denied by organized labor's spokesmen. Few unionists, we take it, have that purpose in mind. But the fact is that, whatever their aim, the general success of these suits could help mightily to bring about that result.[332]

Even before Picard reopened the proceedings he had already become something of a press celebrity, granting frequent interviews, presumably to absolve himself of any responsibility for the "hysteria" caused by *Mt. Clemens*.[333] His primary message was that he was amazed at what had become of his original ruling, which did not deal with portal issues at all, but with a claim for overtime for actual productive work.[334] Before the trial resumed, Picard dealt with a number of motions, all of which were dutifully reported by the *Times*. Thus he granted the motion of the United States to enter an appearance as an amicus, which Attorney General Tom Clark had filed to represent the government in its capacity as administrator of the FLSA and as an affected party where cost-plus war contractors

---

[330]Joseph Loftus, "Portal Pay Claims Reaching Billions; A Boon to Unions," *N.Y. Times*, Dec. 22, 1946, at 1, col. 8.

[331]Arthur Krock, "The Long Trail to the Portal-to-Portal Suits," *N.Y. Times*, Jan. 10, 1947, at 20, col. 5. For evidence that these remarks were actually Jackson's, see Gerhart, *America's Advocate* at 274. The generally conservative positions that underlay Krock's indefatigable editorializing against portal pay may be gleaned from Arthur Krock, *Memoirs* (1968).

[332]"Portal Pay," *Wall St. J.*, Dec. 24, 1946, at 4 col. 1 (editorial). The reasoning behind this dire prediction ran this way: Because the smaller firms would not be able to pay, "a real concentration of 'economic power'" would result leading to greater governmental control and even nationalization. The *Journal*, however also published several more sober editorials on the possible economic consequences of portal pay. See "'Walking Time' Pay," *Wall St. J.*, Nov. 6, 1946, at 6, col. 2; "Portal-to-Portal," *Wall St. J.*, Dec. 18, 1946, at 6, col. 1.

[333]"Picard Hits Hysteria," *N.Y. Times*, Dec. 24, 1946, at 10, col. 3.

[334]"Overtime Is Basis of Portal Claims," *N.Y. Times*, Dec. 23, 1946, at 11, col. 1. The president of the Michigan CIO Council agreed. *Id.* Howard, Jr., *Mr. Justice Murphy* at 403, incorrectly regarded Picard's apologia as "comic relief." It may have been self-serving, but it was nevertheless accurate.

might seek reimbursement for additional wages awarded through portal-pay litigation.[335] Picard also prompted objections from the defendant by appearing *sua sponte* at the Mt. Clemens plant with a stop-watch to compute travel time.[336] The NAM was also permitted to enter as an amicus, its chief position being that the court should deny retroactive force to any ruling.[337]

In the days before Picard reopened the hearing, the United States also began adopting a harder line as amicus, urging dismissal of the claims unless the workers could show that they were really substantial and "not against the public interest."[338] The Government reinforced its role by successfully petitioning the court for status as an intervenor, which would then permit it to appeal any ruling.[339]

Picard, well aware of the attention being focused on him, prefaced his opinion of February 8, 1947 with an apologia. The case, he noted, did not originate as a claim for walking time or preliminary activities, but solely for unpaid overtime for actual production labor, which Picard believed the workers had been required to perform before and after their scheduled hours. When the Supreme Court sustained the Sixth Circuit's ruling that he was bound by the master's conclusion to the contrary, "[o]rdinarily this would have ended the case then and there."[340] But the parties had inserted into the record evidence about walking and preliminary activities in order to bolster their contrary positions on the issue of productive

[335]"Clark Asks A Hand in Key Portal Suit," *N.Y. Times*, Jan. 3, 1947, at 1, col. 6, at 5, col. 5; Walter Ruch, "Portal-Pay Judge Allows U.S. Brief," *N.Y. Times*, Jan. 4, 1947, at 17, col. 8. Arthur Krock characterized the attorney general's intervention as "a precedent in the legal history of the United States." Krock, "Portal-To-Portal Case Brings Rare Reaction," *N.Y. Times*, Jan. 26, 1947, § 4 at 3, col. 1.

[336]Walter Ruch, "$400,000,000 Asked of Auto 'Big Three,'" *N.Y. Times*, Jan. 3, 1947, at 5, col. 1; Walter Ruch, "Portal-Pay Judge Allows U.S. Brief," *N.Y. Times*, Jan. 4, 1947, at 17, col. 8.

[337]"Portal Pay Suits Entered by NAM," *N.Y. Times*, Jan. 10, 1947, at 14, col. 3; "NAM Gives Basis for Entering Portal Case; Says Back-Pay Plan Could Wreck Economy," *N.Y. Times*, Jan. 11, 1947, at 7, col. 4.

[338]William White, "Government Asks Portal Case Ban: Origin 'Trifling,'" *N.Y. Times*, Jan. 24, 1947, at 1, col. 8. Lamb, the workers' attorney, charged that the Department of Justice's "'vendetta against organized labor'" had put it in conflict with the Wage and Hour Administrator. Although Walling denied the charge, he did state that he had long taken the position that employees should be paid for make-ready time required by the employer. Walter Ruch, "U.S. Row Charged over Portal Case," *N.Y. Times*, Feb. 1, 1947, at 7, col. 5.

[339]See Walter Ruch, "Government Seeks Portal Case Role," *N.Y. Times*, Feb. 5, 1947, at 16, col. 1; Walter Ruch, "Picard Lets U.S. Enter Portal Suit," *N.Y. Times*, Feb. 7, 1947, at 13, col. 1. Indeed, Picard even asked the government attorney whether the latter could expedite review by the Supreme Court. Walter Ruch, "Truman Supports U.S. In Portal Case," *N.Y. Times*, Feb. 6, 1947, at 15, col. 1.

[340]Anderson v. Mt. Clemens Pottery Co., 69 F. Supp. 710, 712 (E.D. Mich. 1947).

overtime; that is to say, the company overstated walking and preliminary activity time in order to undermine the workers' claim to wages for actual work, whereas the workers understandably minimized that time. But it was not the Supreme Court that raised the portal issue; rather:

> It's here because defendant company oversold its defense before the master four years ago in explaining why its employees reported 14 minutes before starting hours. This was quickly taken advantage of by plaintiffs in the interim between the Court of Appeals and the Supreme Court. [W]hen the Supreme Court held that this Court was wrong in granting overtime for what we believed was real production labor, it found itself in the position where it must in all fairness at least inquire into the extent of walking time and preliminary activities to which defendant company was apparently admittedly subjecting its employees....[341]

Because Picard had never instructed the master to compute the time spent walking and engaged in preliminary activities, he heard new testimony on this point, which, as he had anticipated, was not credible since each side now had an incentive to reverse its position with regard to exaggerating or understating the time consumed. The judge concluded from this conflicting testimony that walking time was maximally three minutes.[342] With regard to preliminary activities, Picard found that they amounted to less than three minutes per day.[343] Based on his review of the meager precedents, Picard concluded that the walking time and preliminary activities, taken together, were de minimis.[344] In a largely incoherent analysis Picard sought to deal with the Supreme Court's reference to two to twelve minutes of walking time. But his conclusion that even the maximum individual daily walking time of 6.2 minutes was de minimis appeared dictated instead by his perception that precisely because the FLSA was "above all aimed to prevent exploitation of the laborer who under dire requirement of providing necessities of life...might make any kind of a [sic] bargain in order to get a job,...how can anybody claim that...[under *Muscoda* or *Jewell Ridge*] walking time of the type and amount involved in this case can be considered compensable...?"[345] Picard's resolution of the de minimis issue based on this interpretation of the Supreme Court's portal trilogy was misguided in the sense that the Court had been well aware not only of the vast difference in conditions between the halls at Mt.

---

[341]69 F. Supp. at 713.

[342]69 F. Supp. at 714-15.

[343]Contrary to the Supreme Court's opinion, Picard did not consider what the master had called personal activities (such as putting on aprons) as preliminary; similarly, the nonpersonal preliminary or make-ready activity was "part of the job and was considered in the rate of pay." 69 F. Supp. at 715.

[344]69 F. Supp. at 716-19.

[345]69 F. Supp. at 719.

Clemens and the mine shafts, but also of the minimal dimensions of the portal time at stake in the case. Had these factors been dispositive, Murphy would not have bothered to remand the case.[346]

In dictum, Picard granted the NAM (amicus curiae) its most urgently pleaded point: a rule of non-retroactivity. But it was not so generally formulated as the NAM would have wished: Picard bottomed it on the company's reliance on the results of a WHD compliance inspection.[347] Adding dictum to dictum, Picard came much closer to accommodating the NAM's position by insisting that "any industry" in "the general field of manufacture" would have been warranted in ignoring "such a narrow, picayunish, meager" amount of portal time before the Supreme Court had spoken in *Mt. Clemens*.[348] In virtual disregard of the clear holding of the trilogy, Picard seemed almost overeager to make amends with the business world that had castigated him: "Custom and usage should be considered. ... Otherwise there can be no stability in an industrial world when tomorrow may see some new interpretation of the workweek that would disrupt our entire economic structure."[349] To adhere to such a position even with regard to the underlying back wages without liquidated damages where, by his own admission, "a holding to the contrary would not be calamitous,"[350] seemed even to Picard so harsh that he justified it by absurdist metaphor: "we should look upon labor and industry as...husband and wife where the give and take is not all on one side."[351] In a final act of self-defense he also expressed "some regrets for the original plaintiffs," whose version of not having been paid for jumping the gun he still accepted, although the Supreme Court had precluded him from awarding them a recovery.[352] And while these plaintiffs might not have been worthy of portal pay, Picard held out the prospect that somewhere sometime some portal suit might prevail.[353]

Reactions to Picard's ruling were predictable. Plaintiffs' counsel, Lamb,

---

[346]This cavalier attitude was also at odds with a colloquy that Picard had with the NAM's counsel at the remand proceedings in which he "wormed from" the attorney "the statement that the segments of employees' time that he did not want counted as meriting payment might amount to $75 a year. 'Is $75 de minimis to you?' asked Picard. And when Crow replied, 'No, I don't think so,' Picard added, 'I'd like that in the record.'" "Drama of the Stopwatches," *Business Week*, Feb. 8, 1947, at 17, 18.

[347]69 F. Supp. at 720. The record factually contradicted Picard's statement.

[348]69 F. Supp. at 720.

[349]69 F. Supp. at 720.

[350]69 F. Supp. at 721.

[351]69 F. Supp. at 722.

[352]69 F. Supp. at 722.

[353]69 F. Supp. at 722. If so, it would not be in Picard's court. *See* Bateman v. Ford Motor Co., 76 F. Supp. 178 (E.D. Mich. 1948) (per Picard, J.).

immediately announced that they planned to appeal, adding however, that in several respects Mt. Clemens was not a true portal case; consequently, the facts did "not justify compensation comparable to that which" existed in heavy industry.[354] If shortly before Picard handed down his decision, Representative Hartley was of the opinion that the Supreme Court decision "'threatens the structure of our free-enterprise system,"[355] as soon as Picard's ruling became public, Senator Taft and others, supported by employers, announced the Republicans' intention of legislating an end to the suits.[356] Undeterred, the CIO, viewing Picard's decision as inconsistent with the Supreme Court ruling, filed new suits.[357]

The New York Times, which made the dismissal its lead article[358] and published the entire text of the opinion (including footnotes),[359] exulted in three editorials. Expressing great relief, it hoped that organized labor had learned its lesson "that wages ought to be adjusted by collective bargaining, not by fantastic proceedings at law."[360] The next day it offered further reflection on the matter:

> As a legal exercise this case will probably fascinate students of jurisprudence for years to come. ... But as a symbol it will serve its purpose. It should lead to a legislative clarification of the Fair Labor Standards Act and to a decision by the unions to fix wages by fair negotiation and not by gymnastics in the courts.[361]

Several days later the newspaper of record praised Picard for "having done much to abate the portal-to-portal hysteria and to restrict that principle to its fair and proper sphere."[362] *Business Week* best captured the mood in the wake of Picard's failure to convince any of the parties to abandon the fight: "in the portal-to-portal cause celebre, how and what the formerly obscure Detroit judge ruled was itself de minimis. The stock market's reaction to his decision seemed appropriate. It sold off. There was a widespread recognition that the portal-to-portal issue was still far from settled."[363]

---

[354]"Appeal is Planned on Portal Decision," *N.Y. Times*, Feb. 9, 1947, at 16, col. 4.

[355]*U.S. News and World Report*, Feb. 7, 1947, at 34.

[356]"GOP Sets Priority on Pay-Suits Curb," *N.Y. Times*, Feb. 10, 1947, at 1, col. 3. *See also* A. Leviero, "Backers of Portal Pay Curb Will Push Bills in Congress," *N.Y. Times*, Feb. 9, 1947, at 1, col. 6.

[357]"UAW Sues Again Despite Portal Ban," *N.Y. Times*, Feb. 11, 1947, at 20, col. 5.

[358]Walter Ruch, "Picard Dismisses Portal Pay Case, Hits 5 Billion Suits," *N.Y. Times*, Feb. 9, 1947, at 1, col. 8.

[359]*N.Y. Times*, Feb 9, 1947, at 26-27.

[360]"Judge Picard Reconsiders," *N.Y. Times*, Feb. 9, 1947, § 4 at 8, col. 1 (editorial).

[361]"Mt. Clemens As A Symbol," *N.Y. Times*, Feb. 10, 1947, at 28, col. 2 (editorial).

[362]"Mount Clemens in Retrospect," *N.Y. Times*, Feb. 14, 1947, at 20, col. 2 (editorial).

[363]*Business Week*, Feb. 15, 1947, at 86.

The appeal was filed with the Sixth Circuit in March, but two weeks later, when the CIO realized that further prosecution of the case was becoming counterproductive,[364] the plaintiffs moved to dismiss.[365] That realization was promoted by Attorney General Clark's announcement that he would seek expedited review by the Supreme Court before the appeals court acted.[366] As grounds for his action he alleged that the district court portal cases "threaten[ed] to embarrass court procedure, and to interrupt industrial relations while the nation is passing from war to peace manufacture."[367] The Sixth Circuit quickly dismissed the appeal per curiam,[368] and a week later the Supreme Court dismissed the government's petition on Clark's motion.[369] If the unions believed that voluntary dismissal would appease the anti-portal-pay forces, or if the Truman administration believed that strong government intervention before the Supreme Court would make possible a new decision accommodating employers' concerns about "'the expense, difficulty and possible disruption of industrial peace incident to the keeping of records of short intervals of time,'"[370] Representative John Gwynne promptly declared that it would have no effect on the legislative process.[371]

6. "Wait for That Nice New Republican Congress to Come Riding to the Rescue"[372]

You are advised...that travel time has been reduced in recent months. The proposal to measure it and the possibility of having it paid for in wages appears to operate automatically to reduce it.[373]

---

[364]The plaintiffs' attorney, Lamb, stated that the Attorney General was "'seeking to scuttle the entire Wage and Hour Act by a savage attack'" on the case. "Exit Mount Clemens," *N.Y. Times*, Apr. 4, 1947, at 22, col. 3 (editorial).

[365]"Workers Abandon Mt. Clemens Suit," *N.Y. Times*, Apr. 3, 1947, at 21, col. 1.

[366]"Government Seeks Portal Case Speed," *N.Y. Times*, Mar. 19, 1947, at 17, col. 3 (pursuant to 28 U.S.C. § 347(a)).

[367]Lewis Wood, "High Court Action on Portal Asked," *N.Y. Times*, Mar. 21, 1947, at 8, col. 5.

[368]Anderson v. Mt. Clemens Pottery Co. (United States, Intervenor), 162 F.2d 200 (6th Cir. 1947).

[369]United States v. Mt. Clemens Pottery Co., 331 U.S. 784 (1947).

[370]Wood, "High Court Action on Portal Asked at 8, col. 6 (quoting Clark's petition).

[371]"Workers Abandon Mt. Clemens Suit," *N.Y. Times*, Apr. 3, 1947, at 21, col. 1.

[372]John Cort, "The Labor Movement: Boxed in a Portal-to-Portal Suit," *Commonweal*, Feb. 14, 1947, at 447, 447.

[373]Letter from President's Committee on Portal to Portal Travel Time to Mr. President [Roosevelt], at 2, in Franklin D. Roosevelt Library, File: President's Committee on Portal

A. Precursors of the Portal-to-Portal Act

1. State Statutes of Limitations

Because Congress had failed to provide for a specific statute of limitations in the FLSA, courts had to apply what they considered the most analogous state statute of limitations of the state. In the absence of a uniform national standard, a patchwork of limitations—and hence of rights and liability—arose not only among the states, but even within a state, as courts disagreed over the applicable state statute. As of the date of enactment of the FLSA in 1938, these periods of limitation varied from one year to twelve years.[374]

The legislative genesis of the core of the Portal-to-Portal Act can be traced back to a movement to shorten the limitations period; during World War II several states enacted statutes of limitation that discriminated against wage claims in general and FLSA overtime and liquidated damages in particular.[375] Overtime was the special animus of employers simply because the vast majority of all FLSA violations involved premium pay rather than minimum wages or child labor.[376] As early as 1943, the Wage and Hour Administrator warned of the adverse enforcement impact of such laws, which he characterized as "State Efforts at Nullification" aimed at the FLSA's "defeat in practice."[377] And shortly before the war ended in Europe, the press reported that a "successful and little-known behind-the-scenes campaign is well under way in many states to hamstring time-and-a-half payment for overtime work...."[378] These efforts had been made possible by

---

to Portal Travel Time, 220.5.10 (Feb. 2, 1944).

[374]U.S. DOL, *Annual Report, Wage and Hour and Public Contracts Divisions, For the Fiscal Year Ended June 30, 1946*, Table H at 86 (1947).

[375]Harry Weiss, "Minimum Labor Standards," in 1 *Yearbook of American Labor: War Labor Policies* 198, 209, conjectured that "[i]ncreased liability of employers under the Act may have been responsible for" the wave of state legislation.

[376]See, e.g., U.S. DOL, *Fair Labor Standards in Wartime: Annual Report Wage and Hour Division, For the Fiscal Year Ended June 30, 1942*, tab. III (1943); U.S. DOL, *Annual Report of the Wage and Hour and Public Contracts Divisions, Fiscal Year 1946*, tab. 3 at 20, tab. D at 74-76 (1947).

[377]*Fair Labor Standards in Wartime, 2nd Year: Annual Report Wage and Hour and Public Contracts Division For the Fiscal Year Ended June 30, 1943*, at 4 (1944). *See also Fair Labor Standards in Wartime, 3rd Year: Annual Report Wage and Hour and Public Contracts Division For the Fiscal Year Ended June 30, 1944*, at 7 (1945); *Annual Report Wage and Hour and Public Contracts Division For the Fiscal Year Ended June 30, 1946*, at 62-65, 86 (1947).

[378]Victor Riesel, "Labor News and Comment: Time-and-a-Half Payment for Overtime Threatened," *N.Y. Post*, Mar. 21, 1945, at 39, col. 1. Riesel noted similarities between this

Congress's omission of a limitations period in the FLSA itself.[379]

It is instructive to review the most prominent state laws, which imposed the shortest limitations period. In Oregon the legislature, citing an "emergency," acted in March 1943 to limit "[r]ecovery for overtime or premium pay...required or authorized by any statute...to...work performed within six months" before the suit for future claims and only ninety days for past claims.[380] In contrast, actions to recover regular wages, which could be brought for six years after accrual,[381] remained unaffected. Employees promptly challenged the statute in state and federal court. The Oregon Supreme Court struck down the statute in 1945 on the grounds that "legislation manifestly hostile to the exercise of rights granted by a federal statute cannot stand."[382] In reliance on this decision, the Ninth Circuit affirmed the judgment of a federal district court that the law "unreasonably interferes with the normal operation" of the FLSA and hence with Congress's commerce power.[383] In 1947 the legislature amended the statute to extend the limitations period to one year for future and past claims.[384] Enactment of the Portal-to-Portal Act with its own limitations period several weeks later made moot the state law's constitutionality as to future claims.

The Iowa legislature, which acted a week after Oregon's in 1943, took a different tack. It imposed the six-month limitations period on "all cases wherein a claim...has arisen or may arise pursuant to the provisions of any Federal statute wherein no period of limitation is prescribed...."[385] The law was held invalid as to the FLSA and discriminatory against federally granted rights.[386] In the midst of

---

campaign and a contemporaneous one for state "right-to-work" laws organized by the Christian America Association and Fight For Free Enterprise, Inc., both of which were designed to circumvent a federal legislature deemed impervious to anti-labor initiatives.

[379]The first bill to establish a limitations period appears to have been introduced only a few months after the FLSA went into effect. In the first session of the Seventy-Sixth Congress (March 13, 1939) Senator Wiley offered S. 1765, which would have provided for a four-year period within which to recover double liability (that is, liquidated damages) for minimum wage or overtime. Some irony attaches to this sponsorship inasmuch as Wiley was the chief Senate supporter of the portal bill with its much shorter limitations period in 1947.

[380]1943 Or. Laws ch. 265.

[381]§ 1-204 O.C.L.A.

[382]Fullerton v. Lamm, 163 P.2d 941, 945 (Or. 1945), *reh'g denied*, 165 P.2d 63 (1946), *rev'g* Fullerton v. Lamm, 9 Lab. Cas. ¶62,495 (Or. Cir. Ct. 1944).

[383]Kurth v. E.H. Clarke Lumber Co., 9 Lab. Cas. ¶ 62,494 at 67,261 (D. Or. 1944), *aff'd*, E.H. Clarke Lumber Co. v. Kurth, 152 F.2d 914 (9th Cir. 1945).

[384]1947 Or. Laws ch. 492.

[385]1943 Iowa Acts ch. 267 § 1.

[386]Kappler v. Republic Pictures Corp., 59 F. Supp. 112 (S.D. Iowa 1945), *aff'd*, Republic Pictures Corp. v. Kappler, 151 F.2d 543 (8th Cir. 1945), *aff'd per curiam*, 327 U.S. 757,

these judicial proceedings, the Iowa legislature, too, repealed its earlier statute, enacting a new one with a two-year period for future claims for wages without reference to federal statutes.[387] After a federal district court upheld the statute,[388] it too was preempted by the new Portal-to-Portal Act.[389]

Although a number of states continued to enact such statutes of limitations[390] even while Congress was debating and after it passed the Portal-to-Portal Act,[391] the rude judicial reception accorded them[392] induced the NAM to curtail these efforts during 1946 in favor of a congressional campaign.[393] Now that labor, capital, and the executive and legislative branches of the federal government agreed that a uniform national limitations period was a desideratum,[394] the primary stumbling block, as the failure to enact any of the legislative initiatives in the Seventy-Ninth Congress showed,[395] was disagreement over the appropriate length

---

reh'g denied, 327 U.S. 817 (1946).

[387]1945 Iowa Acts ch. 222. Already existing claims had to be brought within six months of enactment.

[388]Reid v. Solar Corp., 69 F. Supp. 626 (N.D. Iowa 1946).

[389]This preemption applied to future claims; under § 6 of the Portal-to-Portal Act, which provided for the possible applicability of state statutes of limitations for already existing claims, the Iowa statute was upheld in Kendall v. Keith Furnace Co., 162 F.2d 1004 (8th Cir. 1947).

[390]For an overview see, U.S. Department of Labor, *Annual Report, Wage and Hour and Public Contracts Divisions, For the Fiscal Year Ended June 30, 1946*, Table H at 86 (1947); Note, "Limitations of Actions Under Section 16(b) of the Fair Labor Standards Act," 45 *Colum. L. Rev.* 444 (1945).

[391]Perhaps the most remarkable such statute was a Massachusetts act that provided that recovery of back wages "based upon any judicial interpretation of a state or federal statute differing from or overruling a previous interpretation of the same" had to be brought within one year after that interpretation or, if it was an already existing interpretation, within one year after enactment. 1947 Mass. Acts ch. 333. The Idaho Hours Worked Act, though not applicable to FLSA, declared it to "contrary to the public policy of the State of Idaho for persons now to sue for attorneys' fees, liquidated damages, and alleged overtime for non-productive work performed during the war...." 1947 Idaho Sess. Laws ch. 267, § 1. The act then set forth a checklist of noncompensable activities to be excluded from the definition of "hours worked." § 2.

[392]For example, a South Carolina statute imposing a one-year limitation on federal wage claims was held invalid. Rockton & Rion Ry. v. Davis, 159 F.2d 291 (4th Cir. 1946), *aff'g* Davis v. Rockton & Rion R.R., 65 F. Supp. 67 (W.D. S. Car. 1946).

[393]*See* "Retroactive Penalties under Federal Law: The 'Gwynne' Bill—HR 2788," 9 *N.A.M. Law Digest* 1, 3 (1946); *Business Week*, Dec. 7, 1946, at 76, 78.

[394]*E.g., Thirty-Third Annual Report of the Secretary of Labor for the Fiscal Year Ended June 30, 1945*, at 10-11 (1945).

[395]Earlier Representative Costello (Dem. Cal.) repeatedly undertook unsuccessful efforts

of that period.

2. A Federal Statute of Limitations

After the "'dime-an-hour' bloc"[396] failed to gut the FLSA with a six-month statute of limitations before the war,[397] the drive for a uniform but quick federal cutoff for FLSA claims started in earnest in 1945. The chief advocate of such an abbreviated period of limitations in the Seventy-Ninth Congress was Representative Gwynne, a Republican from Iowa, who feared that the United States was "becoming a socialistic nation."[398] On March 28, as the U.S. and Red Armies were approaching each other in Germany, he introduced H.R. 2788, which would simply have amended the Judicial Code so that, absent a specific limitations provision, an action to recover damages would have to have been brought within one year "unless a shorter time be fixed in any applicable State statute."[399] H.R. 2788 was interesting for two reasons. First, it was not limited to the FLSA, but would have applied to numerous federal commercial statutes.[400] Second, brevity, not uniformity, was its goal. Gwynne himself underscored this point by reference to the need to protect employers against double damages "for events which were lawful when they occurred but unlawful in retrospect" by virtue of the fact that "the concepts of work time, over-all coverage, and the Administrator's authority

---

to insert a short period of limitations into FLSA. H.R. 10446, 76th Cong., 2d-3rd Sess. (1940) (six months); H.R. 2660, 77th Cong., 1st Sess. (1941) (six months); H.R. 6791, 77th Cong., 2d Sess. (1942) (one year); H.R. 835, 78th Cong., 1st Sess. (1943) (one year).

396 Wage and Hour Administrator Elmer Andrews applied this term to the forces that were seeking to exclude groups of workers from FLSA coverage following its enactment. "Andrews Shifts on 'White Collar,'" *N.Y. Times*, July 21, 1939, at 5, col. 1.

397 E.g., H.R. 7133, § 10(b), 76th Cong., 1st Sess. (1939) (introduced by Rep. Graham Barden, Dem., N.C.).

398 John Gwynne, "Shall Victory's Fruits Be Lost, or Representative Government Be Saved?" *Waterloo Courier*, July 10, 1944, at 4 (guest editorial). Gwynne served in the House from 1935 to 1948, when he lost the Republican primary. In 1953 President Eisenhower appointed him to the Federal Trade Commission, of which he served as chairman from 1955 to 1959, when he retired. *See* "Ex-Congressman John Gwynne, 82," *Waterloo Courier*, July 5, 1972, at 5.

399 91 *Cong. Rec.* 2927 (1945). Two other bills were offered with a six-month period of limitation. S. 760, 79th Cong., 1st Sess. (1945) (Johnson); H.R. 3079, 79th Cong., 1st Sess. (1945) (Chenoweth). Both sponsors represented Colorado, one of the states that had enacted a short statute of limitations designed to apply solely to federal statutes.

400 *See* 91 *Cong. Rec.* 2927-29 (setting forth applicable laws). The bill provided for a two-year period in public actions.

are constantly being enlarged by new interpretation."[401] Since "a legal right is a law suit won, and a legal duty, a law suit lost,"[402] Gwynne's animus is difficult to locate systemically. He sought to motivate his legislation by way of a case, "beg[ging] for correction," from Iowa, in which an employer was sued under the FLSA for overtime wages and liquidated damages three years after the employment had been terminated and six years after the cause of action had accrued. Characterizing Iowa's six-month statute of limitations—without revealing its length—as "reasonable," Gwynne was disturbed that, despite the employee's laches, the court instead applied Iowa's five- or ten-year statute of limitations for contracts.[403] Why wage contracts should be treated differently than other contracts, Gwynne did not explain. Moreover, although it may be uncommon for employees to wait three years after the termination of the employment relationship before filing, the purpose and effect of the bill was to shorten the period for current employees who were intimidated by the possibility of retaliation.[404]

In June and July 1945, a subcommittee of the House Judiciary Committee held hearings on H.R. 2788.[405] The first witness was the NAM counsel, Raymond Smethurst, whose statement was not confined to complaints about the limitations period or even portal-pay issues under FLSA.[406] He also expressed employers' concerns about the expansion of coverage resulting from judicial interpretations of the statutory term, "commerce," as well as about the Supreme Court's recent ruling that employees' waivers of their damages claims pursuant to an agreement with an employer were void.[407] The NAM took the position that during the coming "difficult period of reconversion" a statute of limitations would promote "an

---

[401]91 *Cong. Rec.* 2927.

[402]Jerome Frank, *Courts on Trial: Myth and Reality in American Justice* 9 (1973 [1949]).

[403]91 *Cong. Rec.* 2926.

[404]The case Gwynne was referring to was Keen v. Mid-Continent Petroleum Corp., 58 F. Supp. 915, 63 F. Supp. 120 (N.D. Iowa 1945). Since the employer was a Delaware corporation operating a refinery in Oklahoma and merely distributing oil products in Iowa (and represented by Oklahoma counsel), it seems improbable that Gwynne was merely engaged in energetic constituent service.

[405]*Limiting the Time for Bringing Certain Actions under the Laws of the United States: Hearing Before Subcommittee No. 4 of the House Committee on the Judiciary*, 79th Cong., 1st Sess. (1945). The chairman of the subcommittee, Representative Hobbs of Alabama, was arguably the most vociferous opponent of the FLSA at the time of the portal-pay hearings in 1947.

[406]*Business Week* later commented that the NAM's testimony "did take on a significant propaganda aspect." "Shorter Weeks," *Business Week*, June 16, 1946, at 98, 102.

[407]*Limiting the Time for Bringing Certain Actions under the Laws of the United States* at 21-22.

important and needed stimulant to postwar business venture and risk taking."[408] The NAM was therefore grateful for the "partial corrective" that Gwynne's bill provided as to future claims. But:

> The Bill does not meet the equally serious need for reducing liabilities which may already have accrued under recent administrative rulings and judicial decisions.
>
> 4. It is recommended, therefore, that the bill be amended (a) to include actions for penalties or wage adjustment not now clearly covered; (b) to reduce the period within which such...actions must be brought; (c) to provide the same treatment for actions which have already accrued...as is provided for future claims....
>
> 5. If the committee decides...that a reasonable time should be allowed for filing of accrued actions, we urge that such period should not exceed 90 days, and as to such actions, that a maximum period of recovery be provided not to exceed a period of 1 year prior to the effective date of the limiting statute.[409]

In light of the recent portal-to-portal decisions by the Supreme Court in favor of miners, it came as no surprise that the representative of the National Coal Association supported the NAM's proposals.[410]

Of considerable interest was the testimony of the Wage and Hour Administrator, Metcalfe Walling, who sharply criticized the bill's permissive provisions with regard to state statutes of limitations as undermining nationally uniform standards.[411] Walling himself suggested a three-year limitations period.[412] He also used the opportunity to urge Congress again to confer authority on him to define the FLSA's terms and issue interpretations with the force of substantive law subject to judicial review. The Administrator shrewdly couched this plea in such a manner as to address employers' concerns about retroactive liability. For an enforcement agency, the WHD had been peculiarly handicapped by Congress:

> The year 1938—that in which the Fair Labor Standards Act was enacted—was a year in which the tide of hostility to so-called "administrative absolutism"...was already rising. It is not surprising, therefore, that in the Fair Labor Standards Act Congress confined the powers of the Administrator of the Wage and Hour Division within very narrow limits.

---

[408] *Limiting the Time for Bringing Certain Actions under the Laws of the United States* at 32.

[409] *Limiting the Time for Bringing Certain Actions under the Laws of the United States* at 32

[410] *Limiting the Time for Bringing Certain Actions under the Laws of the United States* at 38-40 (statement of James Haley).

[411] *Limiting the Time for Bringing Certain Actions under the Laws of the United States* at 149.

[412] *Limiting the Time for Bringing Certain Actions under the Laws of the United States* at 155.

He has no rule-making power except with respect to minor matters, no power to hear and decide cases, and no power to initiate litigation except in injunction cases.[413]

Since Walling conceded that even with such powers, he might be overruled by a court, in which case an employer might be liable despite an initially favorable ruling by the Administrator, his "cure [wa]s to permit the Administrator to protect those employers who follow his interpretation in good faith."[414] If, in addition, Congress amended the FLSA to provide for "simple restitution of wages owed without liquidated damages where the violation is not willful" or the employer had followed the Administrator's interpretation, Walling argued, "justice would be served."[415] Walling's initiative turned out to be doubly ironic. First, this strongly pro-employer measure—after all, it was the penal aspect of the retroactivity that incensed employers—was not even offered by employers, but rather by the Administrator himself; and second, Congress ultimately adopted Walling's proposal as to good faith and willfulness—without conferring any additional powers on the Administrator.

In October, the House Judiciary Committee, through Representative Hobbs, reported favorably on H.R. 2788, amending it to incorporate the NAM's proposal on already existing claims. Indeed, much of the report's explanatory section was taken almost literally from Smethurst's testimony. The Judiciary Committee also inserted a more radical version of the Administrator's suggested provision on eliminating liability for good faith reliance on administrative rulings.[416] Specifically, the committee's bill read:

That causes of action which had accrued prior to the passage of this Act, and which had not become barred by any applicable statute of limitation may be maintained if commenced within six months after the date of enactment: *Provided further*, That no liability shall be predicated in any case on any act...committed in good faith in accord with any regulation, order, or administrative interpretation or practice, notwithstanding that such regulation, order, interpretation, or practice may, after such act or commission, be amended, rescinded, or be determined by judicial authority to be invalid or of no legal effect.[417]

Whereas Walling had merely proposed excusing employers from liability for

---

[413]E. Merrick Dodd, "The Supreme Court and Fair Labor Standards, 1941-1945," 59 *Harv. L. Rev.* 321, 370 (1946).

[414]*Limiting the Time for Bringing Certain Actions under the Laws of the United States*, at 146.

[415]*Limiting the Time for Bringing Certain Actions under the Laws of the United States* at 154.

[416]H. Rep. No. 1141: *Limiting the Time for Bringing Certain Actions under the Laws of the United States*, 79th Cong., 1st Sess. 1-5 (1945).

[417]H. Rep. No. 1141 at 1.

liquidated damages where they had followed the Administrator's ruling, the committee bill would apparently have abolished liability even for the underlying back wages. The Attorney General and the Secretary of Labor both expressed strong opposition to the committee's bill[418] as did several Democratic members of the committee.[419]

Although a rule was reported for H.R. 2788 providing for two hours of debate, the House leadership did not call it up.[420] In November 1945, however, Gwynne did have the opportunity to speak on the bill, at which time he assured his colleagues that there was "[n]ot the slightest reason" to consider the bill "antilabor."[421] On a more candid note, he kept his bill's chances alive by stating that he was "not quarreling with anyone who thinks the statute of limitations should be a little longer."[422] And the following March, the Senate Judiciary Committee, too, reported H.R. 2788 favorably, this time with a two-year limitations period.[423] Truman's new Attorney General, Tom Clark, found this period "somewhat brief," instead suggesting five years.[424]

At the same time that Gwynne's statute of limitations bill was wending its way through the Judiciary Committees, the Labor Committees in both chambers were also considering amendments to the FLSA. Indeed, a struggle was emerging over which committee should have jurisdiction over the bill.[425] Both major FLSA bills in 1945, which were largely designed to raise the minimum wage,[426] contained

---

[418]H. Rep. No. 1141 at 7-9.

[419]H. Rep. No. 1141, Pt. 2 and 3, 79th Cong., 1st Sess. (1945).

[420]91 *Cong. Rec.* at 10946 (statement of Rep. Gwynne).

[421]91 *Cong. Rec.* at 10947 (exchange between Representatives Gwynne and Horan).

[422]91 *Cong. Rec.* at 10947.

[423]S. Rep. No. 1395: *Limiting the Time for Bringing Certain Actions under the Laws of the United States*, 79th Cong., 2d Sess. 2 (1946).

[424]S. Rep. No. 1395 at 6. Clark also proposed an extended period for causes of action that had already accrued. *Id.*

[425]Two Democratic members of the House Judiciary Committee expressed minority views to the effect that it would be more appropriate for the House Labor Committee to consider the question "than to legislate in the blunderbuss manner proposed in this bill." H. Rep. No. 1141, Pt. 2, 79th Cong., 1st Sess. 2 (1945).

[426]In cautioning against "[a] too rapid increase in the minimum wage," Senator Taft made the important point that "[t]he difficulty is that the less efficient producers and the small industries are driven out of business and the industry is likely to be concentrated in the large mass production units and the monopolistic companies in the industry." 92 *Cong. Rec.* 2493 (1946). This argument echoed the largely forgotten criticism which the leading marginalist in the United States had directed at populist advocates of state minimum wage laws decades earlier. J.B. Clark, "The Minimum Wage," 112 *Atlantic Monthly* 289, 296 (1912).

provisions for a five-year period of limitations.[427] The Senate debated and, in April, passed S. 1349, the Fair Labor Standards Amendments of 1946, which included a two-year limitations period and conferred on courts discretion to reduce or to eliminate liquidated damages when the employer showed that its violation had not been willful and that it had acted in good faith.[428] In July, the Senate, at the request of a bipartisan group of Senators, briefly returned to H.R. 2788, amending it to provide for a three-year period.[429] In the meantime, in May, the House, after extended debate over the length of the limitations period,[430] passed H.R. 2788 with a two-year period.[431] When Representative Hobbs the next day sought unanimous consent by the House to concur in the Senate amendments, objections by three prolabor Congressmen effectively killed the bill.[432]

Since these early congressional bills were exclusively statutes of limitations with no reference to portal issues,[433] it was with some justification (and as much

---

[427]*Proposed Amendments to the Fair Labor Standards Act: Hearings Before the House Committee on Labor*, 79th Cong., 1st Sess. 4 (1945) (H.R. 3914); *Amendments of the Fair Labor Standards Act of 1938: Hearings Before the Senate Committee on Education and Labor*, 79th Cong., 1st Sess. 5 (1945) (S. 1349).

[428]92 *Cong. Rec.* 2245, 3205 (1946). For the debate over whether the period should be one, two, three, or five years, see *id.* at 3187-3189. Senator Cordon of Oregon sponsored a short period on behalf of lumber employers who had apparently been sued for unpaid travel time by employees whom they had transported to the woods during the war. The debate in the House brought out the fact that such workers had not been driven from home, but rather had first driven to company property before they were transported further. 92 *Cong. Rec.* 5296 (1946) (colloquy between Representatives Gwynne and Savage).

[429]92 *Cong. Rec.* 10372-10373 (1946). Causes that had accrued eighteen months or more before enactment were required to be filed within six months after enactment. The bill also eliminated liability for violations committed in good faith reliance on administrative rulings.

[430]92 *Cong. Rec.* 5290-5305 (1946). The supporters of a short period competed with one another in telling war stories about "outrageous suits...which shock our sense of justice." *Id.* at 5293 (Representative Hancock). Among the new arguments offered, the most interesting stemmed from Representative Feighan, who pointed out that if the short limitations period made it impossible for employees to bring suit (because "the poorly paid, unorganized workers...who would not get their 40 cents an hour and overtime if it were not for this law" would not normally file suit until they had been laid off or found a new job), they could not act as private attorneys general, thus imposing on the taxpayer additional expenditures for enforcement of the FLSA. *Id.* at 5297-5298.

[431]92 *Cong. Rec.* 5305-5306 (1946).

[432]92 *Cong. Rec.* 10487 (1946).

[433]Conversely, in 1941 bills were introduced in both houses providing that the FLSA shall not be interpreted to require employers to pay employees amounts greater than those agreed on, but these bills contained no limitations period. S. 1015, 77th Cong., 1st Sess. (1941) (Sheppard); H.R. 5268, 77th Cong., 1st Sess. (1941) (Patton).

Schadenfreude as hindsight would permit) that the NAM could later assert that the Portal-to-Portal Act would have been unnecessary had an earlier bill been enacted.[434] By the same token, since even in the latter part of 1946 unions' demand for retroactivity was more important to "a large segment of management" than for portal pay as such,[435] it was not a foregone conclusion that congressional action would necessarily go beyond achieving a compromise on a limitations period.

B. The Portal-to-Portal Act of 1947

> Of course, Mr. Speaker, I am sorry that this remarkable law [FLSA] may be utilized against those unfortunate companies...which made millions during the war, and barely succeeded in accumulating profits, surplus, and reserves amounting to 26 billions of dollars; and I know it would cost them something if that law...were to remain in force.[436]

1. Preliminary Skirmishes

Even before the Eightieth Congress convened on January 3, 1947, Republican Congressmen, reacting to employers' complaints that "'invisible bankruptcy'" hovered over industry,[437] began floating specific proposals to amend the FLSA. Thus already on December 27, Representative Hoffman of Michigan was reported to have drafted two amendments designed to make only "productive" work compensable. Tracking the language descriptive of precisely the preliminary activities at issue in *Mt. Clemens*, Hoffman would also have excluded from the workweek any time spent walking from the time clock.[438] Hoffman motivated his bill as a means of dealing with a situation which was "'an invitation to unscrupulous lawyers and racketeering labor leaders'" and "'unscrupulous

---

[434] *Regulating the Recovery of Portal-to-Portal Pay, and For Other Purposes: Hearings before Subcommittee No. 2 of the House Committee on the Judiciary*, 80th Cong., 1st Sess. 419 (1947) (statement by Raymond Smethurst, NAM counsel).

[435] "Door-to-Door Pay," *Business Week*, Sept. 21, 1946, at 94.

[436] 93 *Cong. Rec.* 1002 (1947) (Rep. Adolph Sabath, Dem. Ill., dean of the House).

[437] "Wolman Predicts One More Pay Rise," *N.Y. Times*, Dec. 6, 1946, at 3, col. 5 (statement by Raymond Smethurst, counsel to NAM). Monsanto Chemical Co., a defendant in a portal suit, wrote a letter to the Senate Judiciary Committee stating that portal legislation was the first problem the new Congress should attack. *Portal to Portal Wages: Hearings Before a Subcommittee of the Senate Committee on the Judiciary*, 80th Cong., 1st Sess. 801 (1947).

[438] "GOP Drive Grows to Curb Pay Suits," *N.Y. Times*, Dec. 28, 1946, at 2, col. 2. Hoffman then introduced this bill as the first portal bill in the House on January 3, 1947 as H.R. 89.

blackmailers.'"[439] *The New York Times*, for which no anti-portal-pay legislation was too radical, placed its imprimatur on Hoffman's proposal as "the most forthright," while warning unions that the further filing of suits "would play into the hands of the reactionary element."[440]

Beginning on the opening day of the Eightieth Congress, a flood of anti-portal bills was introduced. Most embodied provisions similar to what eventually became the principal House and Senate bills.[441] Perhaps the most extraordinary piece of legislation was proposed by Texas Senator O'Daniel in the form of an amendment to the Internal Revenue Code. It would have imposed a 100 per cent income tax on all portal suit recoveries and entitled payors to deduct such amounts from their income taxes.[442] By January 15, the Senate Judiciary Committee[443] was already holding hearings—the first, boasted chairman Wiley, "held under the auspices of the Republican Party since 1933 on a matter of national importance."[444] The accelerated pace of congressional action went hand in hand with the stepped-up portal litigation. After workers had filed 727 portal suits in federal courts during the last six months of 1946, alone in January 1947 an additional 1,186 were

---

[439]Anthony Leviero, "Bill to Wipe Out Portal Pay Suits Ready in Capital," *N.Y. Times*, Jan. 2, 1947, at 1, col. 4. Even before the formal House debates on the portal bill began, Representative Hoffman expressed strong animus against "Judge" Murphy, recalling his role as Governor of Michigan at the time of the sit-down strikes at General Motors, when he "left the sit-down strikers in possession of private property...." 93 *Cong. Rec.* 298 (1947). During the debates he called Murphy the "CIO's Santa Claus." *Id.* at 1562.

[440]"The Portal-to-Portal Issue," *N.Y. Times*, Jan. 4, 1947, at 14, col. 2.

[441]*See* S. 307 (Wilson); S. 557 (Wilson); H.R. 89 (Hoffman); H.R. 233 (Dondero) (providing for thirty-day limitations period in actions for overtime and liquidated damages and no liability for violations of FLSA pursuant to a collective bargaining agreement); H.R. 477 (Smith, Va.); H.R. 613 (Price, Fl.); H.R. 776 (Buck); H.R. 957 (Jennings); H.R. 1041 (Fernandez); H.R. 1046 (Hoffman); H.R. 1194 (Hoffman); H.R. 1277 (Hartley); H.R. 1440 (Fernandez).

[442]93 *Cong. Rec.* 414 (1947). A bill in the Massachusetts legislature likewise proposed to impose a 100 per cent tax on portal pay. "Bills Would Bar Portal Suits," *N.Y. Times*, Jan. 9, 1947, at 10, col. 8.

[443]The bills were apparently referred to the Judiciary rather than to the Labor Committee because they provided for limitation of courts' jurisdiction. *See* Jeter Ray, "The Portal to Portal Act of 1947," 20 *Tenn. L. Rev.* 151, 153 (1948) (associate solicitor, U.S. DOL). Some bills were referred to the labor committees, but never advanced. *E.g.*, H.R. 1041. Sen. Taft, the chairman of the Labor and Public Welfare Committee, stated that the Senate bill was initially referred to his committee, but that he had not objected to its having been placed under the jurisdiction of the Judiciary Committee since it seemed to involve constitutional issues rather than questions directly related to the FLSA. 93 *Cong. Rec.* 2369.

[444]*Portal to Portal Wages: Hearings Before a Subcommittee of the Senate Committee on the Judiciary*, 80th Cong., 1st Sess. 8 (1947).

recorded.[445] The closer Congress appeared to be moving to closing the portal permanently, the more actions were filed.[446] And as reports circulated that the defendants' total liability was approaching $6 billion,[447] Congress, in turn, felt that much more obliged to act quickly to stave off the purportedly looming mass bankruptcies that would halt the postwar reconversion process. Thus Senator Capehart, who filed the first Senate portal bill on January 6,[448] declared at the outset of the Senate hearings:

> This problem might not be so urgent if it were merely a question of an economic struggle between two parties, one of which wants the money and the other of which has the money. But these so-called portal-to-portal suits in fact...threaten the very existence of thousands of businesses....[449]

The Truman administration in December 1946 and January 1947 undertook to exert some influence over the eventual shape of the Republicans' amendatory legislation in two ways. First, as noted, it entered the *Mt. Clemens* proceedings on remand in order to persuade Picard to dismiss the suit on de minimis grounds.[450] Second, reports began appearing that the Treasury would provide partial financial

---

[445]S. Rep. No. 48: *Exempting Employers from Liability for Portal-to-Portal Wages in Certain Cases*, 80th Cong., 1st Sess. 2 (1947). During the remaining five months of the fiscal year ending June 30, 1947, only 326 more portal suits were filed, producing a total of 2,239. Enactment of the Portal-to-Portal Act in May radically reduced filings; in the following four years 44, 13, 5, and 13 portal suits were filed respectively. These data are taken from the corresponding *Annual Report of the Director of the Administrative Office of the United States Courts*, Table C 2. The Administrative Office, which until then had not published more detailed data on FLSA cases, calculated these figures by asking the district clerks "to include cases brought under Sections 7 and 16 of the Fair Labor Standards Act seeking compensation for unpaid minimum wages or unpaid overtime compensation in which the question is raised as to whether the employee's compensation has included pay for all the time during which he was necessarily required to be on the employer's premises or at his prescribed work place." S. Rep. No. 48 at 2.

[446]*Regulating the Recovery of Portal-to-Portal Pay, and For Other Purposes: Hearings Before Subcommittee No. 2 of the House Committee on the Judiciary*, 80th Cong., 1st Sess. 174 (1947) (testimony of Lee Pressman, general counsel, CIO).

[447]S. Rep. No. 48 at 2. This sum was presumably calculated from the amounts alleged under the rubric "amount demanded" on the civil cover sheets. Interestingly, more than a month earlier *The New York Times* quoted "[i]ndustry leaders" as citing the same figure. "6 Billion Possible in Portal Claims," *N.Y. Times*, Dec. 22, 1946, at 3, col. 4.

[448]S. 49 was referred to the Labor Committee, but when it was later decided that the Judiciary Committee would have jurisdiction over all portal bills, Capehart was compelled to offer it as an amendment to Senator Wiley's bill, S. 70. *Portal to Portal Wages* at 11-12.

[449]*Portal to Portal Wages* at 17.

[450]See above § 5.

relief to affected employers. In late December *The New York Times* editorialized (without attribution) about "[t]wo possible avenues" of such relief. One involved re-opening back corporate income tax statements for the years of high wartime taxation so that refunds could be made to recapture the retroactive wage payments compelled by portal litigation (or settlements). The other was the renegotiation of government war contracts to take into account the new state of facts.[451] The next day the *Times* reserved the lead-article column of its Sunday business section for "an authority on taxation," who explained how the carry-back provisions of the wartime excess profits tax might work.[452] Then, as if by coincidence, two weeks later the Treasury Department issued a ruling in reply to an inquiry by the "M. Company," which had agreed to pay its employees back portal wages, that it could recalculate its tax liability in effect by writing off both back portal wages and liquidated damages against the war years of high profits and taxes in which the labor was performed.[453]

Corporations, to be sure, were "greatly pleased" by this ruling,[454] but the *Times* warned that the resulting decline in federal revenues by two to three billion dollars "would make it virtually impossible to reduce income tax rates, as the Republicans have proposed."[455] Although these steps by the Truman administration have been interpreted as part of its effort to forestall portal legislation,[456] the contemporary view is much more plausible that the Treasury ruling was "likely to...[s]pur congressional action to block further portal-to-portal pay suits...in order to save the Government from raids on the Treasury."[457] Why, in light of the fact that such action by the Republican congressional majority seemed a foregone conclusion in any event, the Truman administration found it necessary to apply this indirect pressure, remains unclear.[458] For the Attorney General's intervention in *Mt.*

---

[451]"Retroactive Relief?" *N.Y. Times*, Dec. 28, 1946, at 14, col. 2 (editorial).

[452]Godfrey Nelson, "Portal Pay Raises Tax Implications," *N.Y. Times*, Dec. 29, 1946, § 3 at 1, col. 6. The same author estimated that employers might ultimately shift almost three-fifths of the financial burden to the Treasury. Godfrey Nelson, "Treasury to Lose in Portal-Pay Suits," *N.Y. Times*, Jan. 5, 1947, § 3 at 1, col. 4.

[453]I.T. 3836, 1947-1 C.B. 33; Charles Hurd, "Grants Tax Refund in Portal Actions," *N.Y. Times*, Jan. 23, 1947, at 1, col. 7.

[454]"Treasury Rules Industry Can Charge Funds Paid in Portal Suits Against Federal Taxes," *Wall St. J.*, Jan. 23, 1947, at 3, col. 2.

[455]"The Budget and Portal Pay," *N.Y. Times*, Jan. 24, 1947, at 20, col. 2 (editorial). Godfrey Nelson, "Treasury Sharing Portal Pay Suits," *N.Y. Times*, Jan. 26, 1947, § 3 at 1, col. 5, provided further estimates of the Treasury losses.

[456]*See* Susan Hartmann, *Truman and the 80th Congress* 41 (1971).

[457]"Treasury Rules Industry Can Charge Funds Paid in Portal Suits Against Federal Taxes," *Wall St. J.*, Jan. 23, 1947, at 3, col. 1.

[458]Still more puzzling for its indirectness was that the government was, according to a

Clemens had already suggested to large industrial capital—which was the primary object of the suits[459]—where the Administration's sympathies lay with regard to the future of portal claims, while management presumably understood that Truman could not afford to jeopardize the electoral support of organized labor by additionally associating his administration with retroactive antilabor legislation.

2. The House De Facto Repeals Fair Labor Standards

Although the House began holding hearings on the portal issue on February 3, several days after the Senate had already concluded its hearings, it had issued its committee report, debated, and voted on its bill before the Senate opened floor debate. The bill on which Subcommittee No. 2 of the House Judiciary Committee, of which Gwynne was chairman, held hearings was Gwynne's H.R. 584, "A bill to define the jurisdiction of the courts, to regulate actions arising under the laws of the United States, and for other purposes."[460] The findings and purposes section of H.R. 584, which applied to the FLSA, the Walsh-Healey Act, and the Davis-Bacon Act,[461] emphasized that because the administration and interpretation of these statutes had disregarded custom, practice, and agreement, they interfered with collective bargaining and created "windfalls of unearned compensation to employees."[462] To eliminate such "inequities and hardships," H.R. 584 limited actions by:

Senate investigation, forcing war contractors to settle for full payment of all portal claims, with the resulting liability passed on to the government under cost plus fee contracts. William White, "Federal Policy Under Fire In War-Job Portal Pay Suits," *N.Y. Times*, Jan. 9, 1947, at 1, col. 6.

[459]The defendants in the largest suits included U.S. Steel, General Motors, Bethlehem Steel, Ford, International Harvester, Chrysler, A.T.& T., and Standard Oil of New Jersey. See "Treasury Rules Industry Can Charge Funds Paid in Portal Suits Against Federal Taxes," *Wall St. J.*, Jan. 23, 1947, at 3, col. 2; S. Rep. No. 48 at 22-25.

[460]*Regulating the Recovery of Portal-to-Portal Pay, and for Other Purposes: Hearings Before Subcommittee No. 2 of the House Committee on the Judiciary*, 80th Cong., 1st Sess. 1 (1947) (hereinafter *Regulating the Recovery of Portal-to-Portal Pay*). For Gwynne's explanatory remarks when he introduced the bill on January 7, 1947, see 93 *Cong. Rec.* 153-54 (1947). Also subject of the hearings was H.J. Res. 91, "To prohibit suits for recovery of portal-to-portal pay." Introduced by Representative Knutson, it would have applied retroactively and prospectively, defining "portal-to-portal pay" as "pay for the time during which an employee is required to be on the employer's premises...and is not engaged in productive work" unless contract or industry custom provided otherwise. *Regulating the Recovery of Portal-to-Portal Pay* at 4.

[461]§ 4.

[462]§ 1.

1. creating a one-year statute of limitations (§ 2(a));[463]
2. prohibiting actions based on any act done or omitted "in good faith consistent with or in reliance on any administrative regulation, order, ruling, interpretation, enforcement policy, or practice notwithstanding that after such act or omission" any of the foregoing "is modified, rescinded, or declared by judicial authority to be invalid" (§ 2(e));
3. prohibiting actions based on an employer's failure to pay an employee for activities other than those "which at the time of such failure were specifically required to be paid for either by custom or practice of such employer at the plant...or by express agreement" (§ 3);
4. permitting all claims to be "waived, compromised, adjusted, settled, or released" (§ 2(f));
5. limiting attorneys' fees, which were made permissive rather than mandatory, to five per cent of the amount recovered, subject to a maximum of $5,000 "to be paid out of but not in addition to the amount of the judgment" (§ 2(g));[464]
6. placing the burden of proof on the plaintiff, whereby "the failure of the defendant to produce records not required, at the time the transactions...occurred, by published regulations authorized by statute shall give rise to no prejudicial inference affecting liability or the measure...of damages" (§ 2(h));
7. withdrawing from the courts jurisdiction to "entertain, proceed with, impose liability, or enter judgment" on any actions already filed "except in accord with the Act's conditions" and except with regard to "actions upon which final judgment" had been entered prior to the Act's effective date "and from which no appeal had been or could be taken" (§ 3(a)); and
8. making the award of penalties or actual, liquidated, or compensatory damages contingent on an express judicial finding that the underlying violation "was in bad faith and without reasonable grounds," in which case the court was granted discretion to award penalties or damages (§ 3(c)).

This comprehensive catalog of amendments,[465] though packaged as merely

---

[463]Claims that had already accrued had to be filed within ninety days of the Act's effective date unless the action would have been barred by any other applicable (presumably state) state statute of limitations. § 2(b).

[464]Attorneys who charged or received fees beyond these limits were guilty of a misdemeanor and subject to fine and imprisonment.

[465]Included in the House hearings is a document entitled, "Appendix to Statement Before Subcommittee of the House Committee on the Judiciary [Committee Print]," dated February —, 1947, which is labelled H.R. 584 as introduced by Gwynne on January 7, 1947, but includes a number of specifically marked omissions and insertions. *Regulating the Recovery of Portal-to-Portal Pay* at 334. The status of this version and the role it may have played in the legislative process are unclear. It did make a number of significant changes the language of which is puzzling. In a separate definitions section it defined "'work,' 'employment' or 'hours of labor'" to mean only activities for which custom, practice, or express agreement required payment. *Id.* at 335. Yet a new section entitled, "Additional Provisions With Respect to Actions Based upon Activities or Time Not Constituting Work," which imposed

undoing the effects of several Supreme Court decisions, not only transcended the portal issue, but effectively eliminated the mandatory and uniform character of the FLSA's standards. The bill's linchpin in this respect was § 3, which both retroactively and prospectively relieved employers of all liability for any wages that they did not agree or were not accustomed to pay. Thus to take an extreme example that would have comfortably fit within the words and intent of Gwynne's bill: if an employer's practice was not to pay his employees for their first hour's work and he had never expressly agreed to do so, that flagrant violation of the FLSA would no longer be actionable. In a feat of legislative overkill, the bill's other provisions served to wipe out any claims that for any reason whatsoever might have slipped through the principal barrier. The NAM's designation of Gwynne's bill as the most favorable to employers[466] was therefore scarcely surprising.

Testimony at the hearings was predictable, with employers offering strong support[467] and unions vehement opposition. Of interest were the nuances separating the positions of the AFL and CIO. Earlier in January, both the president of the AFL, William Green,[468] and the president of its Metal Trades Department, John Frey, denounced portal suits as dishonoring collective bargaining agreements:

> To inject now the question of back pay for portal-to-portal time would be an admission that when wage agreements were signed by trade union representatives, they had been insincere during negotiations and had held mental reservations....
>
> Our trade union movement has no assets more valuable than its agreements with employers and the integrity which is involved.[469]

Perhaps the most pointed rejection came from the Amalgamated Meat Cutters and Butcher Workmen of North America, whose president and secretary-treasurer announced in the union's monthly magazine:

---

very severe evidentiary burdens on plaintiffs, seems supererogatory since such claims would by definition not have been actionable. *Id.* at 337.

[466]*See* "Pending Labor Legislation: 'Portal-To-Portal' and Other Retroactive Liabilities," 9 *N.A.M. Law Digest* 3, 4 (Supp. No. 2, Jan. 1947).

[467]Interestingly, the NAM denied its support to the "effective though drastic course" of totally repealing FLSA in order to avoid any constitutional defects arising from retroactively nullifying portal claims. *Regulating the Recovery of Portal-to-Portal Pay* at 419 (statement of Raymond Smethurst, counsel, NAM).

[468]*Regulating the Recovery of Portal-to-Portal Pay* at 74 (testimony of Walter Mason, national legislative representative, AFL, citing Green's statement of Jan. 14).

[469]John Frey, "No Fair! Portal-to-Portal Suits Violate a Basic Principle of Collective Bargaining," *Am. Federationist*, Feb. 1947, at 17. The dispute between the AFL and CIO escalated to the level of physical violence in Alabama. *See* "AFL Members Raid CIO 'Portal' Office," *N.Y. Times*, Jan. 17, 1947, at 16, col. 2.

> When we decided that we were entitled to extra pay for changing into and out of clothes, for the sharpening of tools and for many other so-called "portal-to-portal" issues, we negotiated for them in good faith. Our employers conceded these "portal-to-portal" issues reluctantly, but the fact remains that a bargain had been made. ... Each agreement specifically defines the understanding reached. Law suits against employers who acted in good faith in...signing contracts with our organization ought not now, in our opinion, suffer the embarrassment of long legal controversy in matters which neither side could foresee....
>
> We are not unmindful that there are certain gentlemen of the legislature in our nation's capital and in our several states that have in mind to curb the present rights of organized labor. ... Large corporations whose interests are more in profit than in the advancement of human welfare will fight side by side with those legislators who are anti-labor. ...
>
> Our International Union, therefore, WILL NOT and our local unions SHOULD NOT engage in "portal-to-portal" suits against our friendly employers which might cause them, perhaps in retaliation, to also join the forces of those who would enslave us.[470]

This position, which echoed the moral indignation expressed by employers, had secured the AFL editorial praise.[471] Yet at the hearings, the AFL representative, largely avoiding the claim that portal suits had "struck 'below the belts' of employers,"[472] stressed the inequity stemming from the physical expansion of plants, which required workers to walk up to a half-mile for fifteen or twenty minutes. That the AFL opposed not only H.R. 584 but any portal legislation,[473] derived in part from its fear that such innovations would grandfather in customs and practices in violation of the FLSA that unorganized workers would be powerless to overcome.[474] The radically abbreviated limitations period, which obviously affected all the FLSA claims and claimants adversely, also troubled the AFL.[475]

The star witness for the CIO[476] was its general counsel, Lee Pressman.[477] His

---

[470]Earl Jimerson & Patrick Gorman, "Portal-to-Portal: An Editorial," 33(2) *Butcher Workman* 4, col. 1 (Feb. 1947).

[471]*See, e.g.*, "Portal-to-Portal Pay," *N.Y. Times*, Jan. 18, 1947, at 14, col. 3 (editorial).

[472]*Commercial and Financial Chronicle*, Jan. 23, 1947, at 494 (quoting Earl Jimerson, president, Amalgamated Meat Cutters). Jimerson & Gorman, "Portal-to-Portal," stated that the union could "look back with pride that we have never struck below the belt."

[473]*Regulating the Recovery of Portal-to-Portal Pay* at 78, 83 (testimony of Walter Mason, national legislative representative, AFL). *See also Report of the Proceedings of the Sixty-Sixth Convention of the American Federation of Labor* 220-22 (1947).

[474]*Regulating the Recovery of Portal-to-Portal Pay* at 79.

[475]*Regulating the Recovery of Portal-to-Portal Pay* at 81.

[476]The representative of the United Steel Workers-CIO offered such a vivid picture of the long and dangerous walk that steelworkers were required to take—across railroad tracks and under overhead cranes—from the plant gate to the open hearth that he even succeeded in prompting Gwynne to acknowledge that he advocated payment for many of the activities.

responses were as aggressive as the committee members' questions were belligerent. In order to deflate the bathos surrounding employers' complaints, Pressman opened by remarking that the "profits of not a single American corporation have been diminished by any judgment so far rendered in any [portal] lawsuit."[478] If the committee were really interested in dealing with portal problems, Pressman suggested, it would investigate "the hardships imposed upon working people" in large industrial plants such as steel mills. It would, moreover, discover that where portal-pay obligations are imposed on employers, as in iron ore mining, it had proved possible for them to reorganize their operations more efficiently to increase employees' leisure as well as to reduce their own liabilities.[479] Pressman also provoked Gwynne by pointing out to him that his bill was so capacious that logically it would absolve an employer from liability who customarily turned back the clock so that his employees were never recorded as or paid for working overtime.[480]

By the same token, the CIO representative displayed a willingness to accommodate employers and congressmen on a number of portal issues. This more conciliatory attitude may have been dictated by the recognition that since the litigation had insured that some version of an antilabor portal bill would pass both houses,[481] the CIO was "seeking a way out of this muddle without losing face."[482] Thus, for example, he thought worthy of consideration Gwynne's offhand suggestion to permit settlements of the FLSA claims subject to approval by the Wage and Hour Administrator.[483] That non-hazardous walking time as in *Mt.*

Id. at 103-105, 109-10 (testimony of David McDonald, sec'y-treasurer, USW). McDonald stressed that in such large and highly integrated plants companies "have wrung from the workers an increased contribution to the companies' profits." *Id.* at 112.

[477]See generally, *Current Biography 1947*, at 528-30 (1948). According to Nelson Lichtenstein, *Labor's War at Home: The CIO in World War II* 143 (1987 [1982]), during World War II the legitimacy of the Communist Party among the highest echelons of the CIO was such that Pressman was an open fellow traveler. Pressman himself stated in 1950 that he had joined a Communist group for one year in 1934. "Lee Pressman, Labor Lawyer, and Ex-C.I.O Counsel, Dies," *N.Y. Times*, Nov. 21, 1969, at 47, col. 1-2.

[478]*Regulating the Recovery of Portal to Portal Pay* at 115.

[479]*Id.* at 131.

[480]*Id.* at 141.

[481]*Time* quoted Pressman as saying: "'They are fantastic, local lawyers have gone hogwild. Suits for these incredible sums have fanned the flames of antiunionism.'" *Time*, Jan. 27, 1947, at 83.

[482]"Steel Wage-Price May Set Pattern," *N.Y. Times*, Feb. 2, 1947, § 3 at 1, at 9, col. 5. *See also* S. Scheibla, "CIO Portal Pay Strategy Backfires; Union Abandons Out-of-Court Settlement Hopes," *Wall St. J.*, Jan. 28, 1947, at 3, col. 2.

[483]*Regulating the Recovery of Portal-to-Portal Pay* at 160. The 1949 FLSA amendments included such a provision. See above § IV. At the Senate hearings, Pressman testified that

Clemens was not the CIO's highest priority emerged from another colloquy between Pressman and Gwynne in which the congressman pressed the CIO lawyer to concede that there was "quite a jump" from not paying blast furnace workers for time spent changing clothes to the practice at Mt. Clemens. Pressman retorted: "I will be glad to draft an amendment to take care of that situation, if you will agree with me that these things are times worked. Your bill does not do that."[484]

Following the House hearings, the subcommittee prepared another draft, after which the full House Judiciary Committee wrote the bill, H.R. 2157, which it reported to the House.[485] The principal changes vis-à-vis H.R. 584 were as follows: 1. the grace period during which already accrued portal claims could be brought was extended from ninety days to six months (§ 2(b)); 2. the statute of limitations was not tolled as to any individual claimant (in a class or representative action)[486] until he was named as a party (§ 2(c)); 3. the good-faith reliance provision was clarified as an employer's affirmative defense (§ 2(e)); 4. the limitation on the employer's liability for the employee's attorneys' fees was eliminated; and 5. the imposition of the burden of proof on the employee was eliminated.

Although somewhat less radical than the previous bill, H.R. 2157, like H.R. 584, was most prominent for its undifferentiated applicability retroactively and prospectively. This feature, taken together with the sharp restrictions of numerous enforcement and recovery provisions having nothing to do with portal issues, led the minority members of the committee to accuse the majority of "emasculat[ing]" the FLSA: "Why do not the proponents of the bill honestly say they want to kill the Fair Labor Standards Act?"[487] In particular, the use of "custom or practice" as a guide to compensability the minority saw as enabling the new employer "to write the law for himself" and undermining uniformity of standards among already existing employers.[488] An especially poignant example of this generous legislative conferral of self-help power upon employers emerged inadvertently in the course of the House debates. Representative Francis Walter, a Democratic supporter of

---

it would be proper for Congress to amend the FLSA to permit compromises of all portal-to-portal back wages through collective bargaining. *Portal to Portal Wages: Hearings Before a Subcommittee of the Senate Committee on the Judiciary*, 80th Cong., 1st Sess. 218 (1947). During the debates, Senator Pepper echoed this position. 93 *Cong. Rec.* at 2301.

[484]*Regulating the Recovery of Portal-to-Portal Pay* at 170.

[485]93 *Cong. Rec.* at 1489 (statement of Rep. Michener, chairman of Judiciary Comm.). The bill that the committee reported on February 25 as H.R. 2157 was identical with the H.R. 2157 that Gwynne had introduced the previous day.

[486]93 *Cong. Rec.* at 1491 (statement of Rep. Gwynne).

[487]H. Rep. No. 71: *Regulating the Recovery of Portal-to-Portal Pay, and For Other Purposes*, 80th Cong., 1st Sess. 9, 18 (1947).

[488]H. Rep. No. 71 at 16.

a portal bill, in responding to a question as to whether "custom or practice" that was "bad or in error...would be a defense,"[489] granted that the issue had "caused the committee a great deal of trouble":

> [C]ustom and practice...means a custom and practice not in violation of the law. Certainly no employer could, for example, compel an employee to get to this place of his business an hour before he punches the clock and because he had done that for a while relieve himself of his responsibility to comply with the law by saying, "That is the custom and practice of my business." No court would uphold any arrangement of that sort. Certainly that is work under any of the definitions of the courts and we have to rely on a common-sense interpretation of that language.[490]

In fact, as Walter was constrained to concede, the "custom or practice" language was so capacious that it literally encompassed the aforementioned sham, thus remitting workers to the courts for an interpretation that would have comported better with the spirit behind the language that Walter himself was unable to express. Unfortunately for the employees, the legislative history was so replete with vindictiveness, that the literal interpretation in fact coincided with the spirit of the bills.

The minority members took the position that, because most of the existing claims would be subject to de minimis dismissals, Congress should leave their resolution to the courts. Instead of succumbing to the "great hysteria" over portal suits,[491] Congress should deal with the issue prospectively either by writing into the FLSA a definition of work[492] or by empowering the Wage and Hour Administrator to issue binding regulations.[493]

The committee recommended passage on February 25, and the bill was referred to the Committee of the Whole House for four hours of debate on February 27 and 28.[494] The extremes were stated at the outset by two representatives from Illinois. The Republican Leo Allen denied that the bill was antilabor,[495] while the Democrat Adolph Sabath, who had served since 1907, called

---

[489]93 *Cong. Rec.* at 1497 (Rep. Miller).

[490]93 *Cong. Rec.* at 1497.

[491]H. Rep. No. 71 at 9.

[492]The minority proposed language tracking that of Murphy's opinions: "in order to be deemed compens-able...activities must be conducted under the control, direction, or requirement of the employer and must be primarily for the benefit of the employer." H. Rep. No. 71 at 17.

[493]H. Rep. No. 71 at 17, 15.

[494]*House Journal*, Feb. 26, 1947, at 159.

[495]93 *Cong. Rec.* at 1494.

it "as vicious as any other antilabor bill ever brought to this House."[496] A number of Democrats excoriated the bill as a direct attack on the FLSA itself,[497] but others would not have opposed legislation confined to the portal issue if a longer limitations period had been inserted.[498]

All ten amendments to H.R. 2157 as well as a motion to recommit were rejected by large majorities.[499] Among the more significant ones,[500] two would have extended the limitations period to two and three years respectively.[501] Representative Javits's amendment to focus relief from portal claims to employers on collective bargaining agreements also failed.[502]

The voting patterns of the Eightieth Congress were deeply impressed with two interrelated facts of the party and sectional results of the 1946 congressional elections that sealed the demise of the New Deal coalition.[503] It was the first Congress since the Hoover administration in which the Republican Party controlled both chambers by a significant majority; the influence of the South on the Democratic delegation reached a high point as a consequence of the fact that Democratic candidates gained their largest share of Southern seats since 1921, while, in the wake of massive Republican victories in recently Democratic districts in the North,[504] Southern Democrats represented the largest share of Democratic representatives since 1921.[505] Of the 188 Democrats who faced 245 Republicans in the House, 103 (or fifty-five per cent) represented the South and accounted for all but two seats in the eleven Southern states.

---

[496]93 *Cong. Rec*. at 1495.

[497]Representatives Norton and Welch, for example, took this position. 93 *Cong. Rec.* at 1503, 1513.

[498]Representative McCormack, the minority whip, typified this group. 93 *Cong. Rec*. at 1558. Representative Celler appeared to fall between these two groups of Democrats. 93 *Cong. Rec*. at 1495.

[499]The motion to recommit with instructions to report the bill back with a two-year limitations period was defeated on a division vote 219 to 42. 93 *Cong. Rec*. at 1573.

[500]For a description of the less significant ones, see 3 *Cong. Q*. 44-45 (1947).

[501]The first was defeated on a division 124 to 73, the second 145 to 40. 93 *Cong. Q*. at 44.

[502]The division vote was 131 to 53. 93 *Cong. Rec*. at 1571. Although Javits explained the purpose of his amendment in such language, its text contained the same reference to "custom or practice" as the principal bill. *Id*. at 1565.

[503]*See* James Boylan, *The New Deal Coalition and the Election of 1946*, at 151-77 (1981); Robert Garson, *The Democratic Party and the Politics of Sectionalism, 1941-1948* (1974).

[504]*See* Joseph Loftus, "House Labor Bloc Nearly Destroyed," *N.Y. Times*, Nov. 7, 1946, at 1.

[505]*See* Richard Bensel, *Sectionalism and American Political Development 1880-1980*, at 381-85 (1982)

The roll-call vote on February 28 in the House on H.R. 2157[506] revealed a rigid party-section pattern.[507] While the Republican majority may have functioned as the transmission belt for implementing the agenda articulated by large corporate employers, the entire Southern delegation, but virtually no other Democrats, joined them.[508] Overall, more than six times as many representatives voted yea as nay (345-56). Of the 241 Republicans who voted, 236 or ninety-eight per cent supported H.R. 2157.[509] Although 109 or sixty-eight per cent of the Democrats who voted supported H.R. 2157, ninety of those supporters were Southerners; an additional thirteen represented Border states. No Southerner opposed the bill while only three Northern Democrats voted yea. The fifty-one Democrats who opposed the bill[510] were geographically concentrated, thirteen representing New York City alone.[511] Five Democrats each from Illinois and California voted nay, as did three each from Massachusetts, Michigan, Ohio and Pennsylvania, and two each from New Jersey and Rhode Island.[512] Not surprisingly, this Democratic opposition roughly coincided with the geographic concentration of the portal litigation.[513]

3. The Senate Lets Bygones Be Bygones

More persons than the employer and the employee are interested in a labor contract; public interest is also involved.[514]

---

[506]93 *Cong. Rec.* at 1573.

[507]In this regard it outdid the votes a few weeks later on Taft-Hartley. See Harry Millis and Emily Clark Brown, *From the Wagner Act to Taft-Hartley* 371-92 (1950) (chapter written by Seymour Mann).

[508]On Southern Democratic-Republican congressional voting alliances in the 1930s and 1940s, see V.O. Key, Jr., *Southern Politics in State and Nation* 345-82 (1949).

[509]The five who opposed the bill were Javits of New York, Brophy and Hull of Wisconsin, Meade of Kentucky, and Welch of California. Neither Brophy, who had been a mechanic, nor Meade was reelected, while Hull had previously been elected as a Progressive. *See Biographical Dictionary of the United States Congress 1774-1989*, Sen. Doc. No. 100-34, 100th Congress, 2d Sess. 678, 1230, 1487 (Bicentennial ed. 1989).

[510]Vito Marcantonio, the American Labor Party member from New York City, also voted nay.

[511]No member of the nine-person delegation from Brooklyn, all of whom were Democrats, voted yea. Seven voted nay, one (Delaney) was paired against, and one did not vote. Similarly, all of the Democratic representatives from Manhattan and the Bronx voted nay.

[512]The other ten Democratic votes each represented a different state.

[513]See above § 2.

[514]93 *Cong. Rec.* at 2178 (Sen. Donnell).

The Senate hearings, which lasted from January 15 to January 30, concerned S. 70, which Senator Wiley, the chair of the Judiciary Committee, had introduced. A relatively short piece of legislation, it chiefly took the form of an amendment of the overtime provision of FLSA. The bill defined "work week" to include "only the time during which an employee is engaged in productive work" unless it is compensable pursuant to agreement or custom. It then prohibited all future claims for back wages for time spent in other than productive work. In addition, S. 70 offered an affirmative defense to employers against liability for liquidated damages if they could show that their failure to pay was "a bona fide error made in good faith." Wiley's bill, finally, also permitted employees to release their employers from their liability for liquidated damages.[515] Although this bill was marred by a serious drafting defect inasmuch as it failed to define "productive work,"[516] it otherwise introduced relatively modest changes into FLSA. Its key provision was purely prospective, while the good faith and waiver provisions were confined to liquidated damages.

Senator Capehart, a manufacturer,[517] offered an amendment to S. 70 in the form of a substitute.[518] Capehart's bill was much longer and detailed. It contained a preamble of findings[519] similar to that which was ultimately adopted in the Portal-to-Portal Act. It went far beyond Wiley's bill in a number of crucial respects. In particular, Capehart's bill: 1. was retroactive as well as prospective; 2. applied to minimum wages as well as to overtime; 3. excluded from custom or practice any payments made by an employer in order to conform to any judicial decisions or administrative rulings; 4. made an award of liquidated damages contingent on a finding that the violation was in bad faith and without reasonable grounds, thus reversing the burden of proof; 5. offered relief from liability for any act or omission done in good-faith reliance on any act of the Wage and Hour Administrator even if the latter were held invalid; 6. extended the waiver or release provision to cover back wages in addition to liquidated damages; and 7. inserted a one-year limitations period for future claims together with a three-month grace period for existing claims insofar as the latter were not barred by any other applicable statute

---

[515]*Portal to Portal Wages: Hearings Before a Subcommittee of the Senate Comm. on the Judiciary*, 80th Cong., 1st Sess. 3 (1947) (hereinafter *Portal to Portal Wages*).

[516]Unlike H.R. 89, which listed very specific activities. *Id.* at 5.

[517]*Cong. Directory*, 80th Cong., 1st Sess. 32 (1st ed. 1947).

[518]Capchart had introduced his bill, S. 49, before Wiley, but after it had been referred to the Labor Committee, it was decided that the Judiciary Committee would handle all the portal bills; he was therefore constrained by parliamentary rules to offer his bill as an amendment. *Portal to Portal Wages* at 11-12. In the midst of the Senate hearings, on January 18, Capehart introduced a modified version of his amendment. It is this second version that is discussed in the text. The two versions are at *id.* 3-5, 38-40.

[519]*Portal to Portal Wages* at 38, § 1.

of limitations.[520]

Though much broader in scope than Wiley's bill, Capehart's bill was less far-reaching than Gwynne's H.R. 584. First, whereas Gwynne permitted courts great discretion with regard to awarding liquidated damages, Capehart's bill required courts to award full liquidated damages if they awarded any. Second, Capehart's bill contained no provision comparable to the heavy burden of proof that Gwynne imposed on plaintiffs. And, third, Capehart did not limit the award of attorneys' fees. For these reasons, the NAM, while appreciative of Capehart's efforts, preferred the Gwynne bill.[521]

Employers did not present a completely unified or uniform position at the Senate hearings. In part because of doubts concerning the constitutionality of a retroactive ban on claims, there was "some difference of opinion between corporation lawyers" "[a]s to the remedies for the situation."[522] The NAM's counsel emphasized the need for a one-year limitations period, relief from liquidated damages for non-willful violations, and generally a rollback of the law to its state before the Supreme Court had decided *Mt. Clemens*, including a restoration of the customary rules of the burden of proof.[523] The Chamber of Commerce of the United States went even further, advocating a prohibition on class suits or the assignment of claims.[524]

Like the Chamber's representative,[525] the NAM's counsel opposed conferring expanded rule-making power on the Wage and Hour Administrator to define working time.[526] In contrast, the Business Advisory Council of the Department of Commerce, the members of which were largely the high-ranking officers and managers of the country's largest corporations,[527] believed that the Administrator "should be given power to issue authoritative definitions of the general terms used in the statute."[528] Although many employers may have instinctively objected to authorizing New Deal bureaucrats to interpret the intent of an antilabor Republican

---

[520]*Portal to Portal Wages* at 38-40.

[521]9 *NAM Law Digest* 3-4 (Supp. No. 2, Jan. 1947).

[522]*Portal to Portal Wages* at 616 ("Statement by Subcomm. of Business Advisory Comm. on Attitude of Industry on Portal to Portal").

[523]*Portal to Portal Wages* at 111, 114 (testimony of Raymond Smethurst).

[524]*Portal to Portal Wages* at 133. It was unclear whether ignorance or disingenuousness underlay the Chamber's contention that compromising claims was not problematic because employees did not bring suits alone but through a union lawyer. *Id.* at 135.

[525]*Portal to Portal Wages* at 127 (testimony of Thomas Howard, Manufacture Dept.).

[526]*Portal to Portal Wages* at 112.

[527]*See Portal to Portal Wages* at 609-14.

[528]*Portal to Portal Wages* at 620 (statement of William Foster, Undersecretary of Commerce, speaking on behalf of the Business Advisory Council).

Congress,[529] it is unclear that any fundamental principle was at stake in choosing between agency and judicial enforcement.[530] After all, even such binding regulations would have been subject to judicial review. Since the entire portal dispute erupted over unfavorable court—in particular Supreme Court—decisions, employers may have perceived themselves as facing a Hobson's choice. In this sense, the optimal solution for them may have been the one actually adopted: reliance on the relatively detailed catalog of excluded activities that this Republican Congress then and there could dictate to agency and courts.

Precisely such a step was suggested by Arthur Pettit, an attorney in the corporate law firm of Winthrop, Stimson, of which the former Secretary of War was an eponymous partner. Senator Capehart deemed his testimony so interesting that he asked Pettit to write down what he thought the bill should include.[531] Pettit offered an unusual amalgam of modest and radical proposals. On the one hand, he opposed using the individual plant as the standard for judging the existence of a custom or practice because it would merely favor bad employers, cause discontent among employees, and undermine FLSA's uniform standards.[532] On the other hand, in order to eliminate existing claims not based on custom or practice, he proposed repealing the minimum wage, overtime, and private right of action provisions of FLSA on the grounds that those claims constituted a burden on commerce. Should the Supreme Court then hold such a repeal unconstitutional, Pettit advocated as a fallback position a prohibition on collective and representative actions.[533] Although Congress ultimately chose not to adopt these more radical proposals, it did incorporate his recommendation for dealing with future claims by inserting specific exclusions into the act such as walking, riding, traveling, and incidental work activities before and after the scheduled work period.[534] In fact, Congress went even further by omitting Pettit's limitation of such noncompensable portal time to periods shorter than twenty minutes, which Pettit believed marked

[529]Senator Eastland unsuccessfully tried to elicit from Undersecretary Foster an acknowledgment that agencies invariably exceed their authority. *Portal to Portal Wages* at 620. Significantly, the CIO representative, Lee Pressman, did not oppose giving the Administrator rule-making power. *Id.* at 221.

[530]*But see* A. Mezerik, "'Time is Money,'" *Nation*, Feb. 1, 1947, at 121, 122, who speculated that management preferred the courts at least until a Republican administration came to power.

[531]93 *Cong. Rec.* 2131 (1947) (statement of Sen. Donnell). Donnell stated at the hearings that Pettit had also spoken to him personally after one of the hearings and interested him in Pettit's suggestions. *Portal to Portal Wages* at 637.

[532]*Portal to Portal Wages* at 645.

[533]*Portal to Portal Wages* at 645-48.

[534]*Portal to Portal Wages* at 655.

off the point at which employer overreaching began.[535]

H.R. 2157 was committed and recommitted to the Senate Judiciary Committee on March 3,[536] which issued its report on March 10 offering a much more detailed overview of the portal litigation and the legal issues surrounding the proposed legislation than the House report. It devoted a great deal of space to presenting data on the volume of litigation, documenting the orchestration of the portal campaign by the CIO, and sketching the worst-case financial impact of the lawsuits on firms and the federal government.[537] In justifying the need for intervention, the committee speculated that pending litigation would adversely affect labor-management relations; for if employers postponed entering into new collective bargaining agreements because of the threat of portal liability, employees would resent the delay, while employers would develop ill-will toward their employees on account of the unfounded portal claims.[538] The report also implied that Judge Picard's dictum to the effect that he was not holding all portal claims nonactionable had not obviated the need for congressional action.[539]

The Senate version of H.R. 2157, as reported by the committee, differed fundamentally from the House version in that it gutted the FLSA only retroactively. Like the House bill, it virtually wiped out all existing claims and not merely those related to portal issues, but left the FLSA intact, albeit impaired, for the future, by exempting from the portal ban future activities taking place during (as opposed to before or after) the normal workday (§ 6). The committee rewrote the bill in a number of other important ways that both favored and disadvantaged employees.[540] For example, it provided for a two-year limitations period (§ 9),[541] but banned representative actions and required the plaintiffs in collective actions to file written consents (§ 8). But more importantly, the Senate bill, unlike the House version, sharply distinguished between existing and future claims; specifically, it did not extend the pro-employer provisions regarding attorneys' fees, liquidated damages, the burden of proof, and the compromise and settlement of claims to future actions (§§ 2-6).[542]

---

535 *Portal to Portal Wages* at 658.

536 *Senate Journal*, Mar. 3, 1947, at 120-21.

537 S. Rep. No. 48: *Exempting Employers from Liability for Portal-to-Portal Wages in Certain Cases*, 80th Cong., 1st Sess. 1-39 (1947).

538 S. Rep. No. 48 at 39-40.

539 S. Rep. No. 48 at 42-43.

540 Senator Wiley presented a useful detailed point-by-point tabular comparison of the two bills during the Senate debates. Unfortunately, it contains a transposition making §§ 4(b) and 4(c) of the Senate bill appear as provisions of the House bill. 93 *Cong. Rec.* at 2084-86.

541 It also provided for a 120-day grace period to file accrued claims.

542 Like the House bill, the Senate version contained separability provisions (§ 4) that served to eliminate any existing claims that for any reason survived their intended destruction

In explaining this latter provision, the committee report furnished what would become very important pieces of legislative history with regard to specifying the types of portal activities for which employers were to be relieved of liability. Thus with regard to future—as contradistinguished from existing—claims, § 6 of the bill made the following portal-to-portal activities noncompensable (unless compensable on the basis of contract,[543] custom, or practice):

"(a) walking, riding or traveling to and from the actual place of performance of the principal activity or activities which such employee is employed to perform, and

"(b) activities which were preliminary to or postliminary to said principal activity or activities

which occur either prior to the time on any particular workday at which such employee commences, or subsequent to the time on any particular workday at which he ceases, such principal activity or activities...."[544]

The committee report, after noting that the bill did "not define what constitutes work," appended this nonexhaustive "list of noncompensable activities...outside the employee's workday":

(1) Walking, riding, or traveling to and from the actual place of performance of the principal activity or activities within the employer's plant, mine, building, or other place of employment, irrespective of whether such walking, riding, or traveling occur on or off the premises of the employer or before or after the employee has checked in or out. Examples of this are (a) walking or riding from the plant gate to the employee's lathe, workbench, or other actual place of performance of his principal activity or activities; (b) riding on busses from a town to an outlying mine; (c) riding on busses or trains from an assembly point to a particular site at which a logging operation is being conducted.

(2) Checking in or out and waiting in line to do so, changing clothes, washing up or showering, waiting in line to receive pay checks, and the performance of other activities

---

by § 3. The separability section included provisions on attorney's fees and burden of proof that were even more pro-employer than the corresponding provisions of H.R. 584, which had been eliminated from H.R. 2157. The first would have prohibited courts from awarding any attorney's fee (§ 4(b)), while the second deprived employees of the benefit of any inferences in proving the extent of their claims (§ 4(c)). The latter provisions was essentially an effort to overturn the Supreme Court's ruling on the burden of proof.

[543]Although the report expressly stated that § 6 relieved employers of liability for travel time from the portal to the face of a mine, the committee took notice of the fact that because the then effective UMW collective bargaining contract provided for such portal pay, the liability of employers party to that contract would not be affected by § 6. S. Rep. No. 48 at 48.

[544]93 *Cong. Rec.* at 2376. The bill used quotation marks to indicate that the provision was to be inserted as a new § 7A of the FLSA.

occurring prior and subsequent to the workday, such as the preliminary activities which were involved in the Mt. Clemens case....[545]

Since the above-cited provisions of § 6 of the Senate version of H.R. 2157 were adopted intact in the Portal-to-Portal Act,[546] these specifications made clear that the scope of noncompensable portal activities was meant to be very broad.[547] The drafters of the bill insisted on comprehensive exclusions because they believed that unions' portal suits had confronted employers with a slippery slope to bankruptcy:

[U]nless we draw a line and say, "Before this line items shall not be compensable unless by contract or custom," we are in constant danger of an ever-expanding application of the doctrine of portal-to-portal pay so as to run not merely from the portal of the employer's premises to the place of work, but from the portal of the employee's home, or perhaps from his dining table.[548]

In contrast, the committee indicated that it also intended to give the term "principal activity," which overlapped with the compensable "workday," a broad scope:

(1) In connection with the operation of a lathe an employee will frequently at the commencement of his workday oil, grease, or clean his machine, or install a new cutting tool. Such activities are an integral part of the principal activity....

---

[545]S. Rep. No. 48 at 47.

[546]Ch. 52, § 4(a), 61 Stat. 84, 87 (1947) (current version at 29 U.S.C. § 254(a)).

[547]The Wage and Hour Administrator incorporated them literally into the portal-to-portal interpretative bulletin that he issued on Nov. 18, 1947. 12 *Fed. Reg.* 7655 (1947) (codified at 29 C.F.R. § 790.7). For illustrations of the equally broad judicial interpretations holding travel time noncompensable, see Carter v. Panama Canal Co., 463 F.2d 1289 (D.C. Cir. 1972) (walk from check-in point to locomotives along canal); Ralph v. Tidewater Constr. Co., 361 F.2d 806 (4th Cir. 1966) (trip from shore out to work site in bay); Dolan v. Project Constr. Corp., 558 F. Supp. 1308 (D. Colo. 1983) (trip from main camp to construction site). To be sure, the last-cited case appears wrongly decided even under the Portal-to-Portal Act because the workers were required to check in at the camp and were not permitted to use their own transportation.

[548]93 *Cong. Rec.* at 2121 (statement of Sen. Donnell). Donnell was reacting to testimony by mining employers to the effect that potash miners in New Mexico had sued for portal pay for a twelve-mile trip to the mines during which they read and slept in buses the employer did not own. *Id.* Sen. Murray regretted that H.R. 2157 "would make noncompensable many burdensome activities performed for the employer by employees in the lumbering, smeltering, and petroleum-refining industries" in Montana; he mentioned in particular the more than one hour per day that loggers travelled through "trackless forests" with their saws and axes. 93 *Cong. Rec.* at 2238.

(2) In the case of a garment worker in a textile mill, who is required to report 30 minutes before other employees...and who during such 30 minutes distributes clothing...at the workbenches of other employees and get machines in readiness for operation by other employees, such activities are among the principal activities of such employee.[549]

Of overriding significance in the same context was the committee's declaration that the existing and unamended provisions of the FLSA would continue to control the compensability of all future claims for activities occurring within the workday. The report illustrated this intent by reference to rest and lunch periods; it then added the very important statement: "and the same will be true as to waiting periods during a production breakdown and a production break-down and to other waiting periods during the workday."[550] The retention of this protection under the FLSA allayed the worst fears that unions had expressed on behalf of unorganized workers.[551] The practice of not paying employees for the time they waited for work during the workday had been widespread before the enactment of the FLSA. For example, when future Teamsters president Jimmy Hoffa worked at a Kroger's warehouse in Detroit in 1931, loaders had to spend as many as 80 hours a week at the workplace to get their 48 hours because the employer paid only for the time they actually spent loading.[552]

The minority members of the Senate Judiciary Committee[553] agreed "that portal-to-portal relief was necessary," but objected to the majority's approach because it unnecessarily destroyed existing non-portal claims and lowered FLSA standards for future claims.[554] In particular the minority emphasized that the majority bill created the danger that contract would "supersede the statutory standards"; for "[a]s between employer and an unorganized employee at the lower end of the wage scale, who will influence the custom or practice or contract which will determine which is compensable and which is not?"[555] And even among strong unions, such as the UMW, H.R. 2157 would permit owners to renegotiate

---

[549]S. Rep. No. 48 at 48. In explaining the conference report to the House, Gwynne incorrectly asserted that even for the future the laying out of garments to work on would not be compensable. *See* 93 *Cong. Rec.* at 4389.

[550]S. Rep. No. 48 at 48. In explaining the conference report to the House, Walter incorrectly stated that even as to the future, claims for stand-by time would not be compensable. 93 *Cong. Rec.* at 4389-90.

[551]93 *Cong. Rec.* at 2132 (statement of Sen. Donnell). The unionists were unable to avert the withdrawal of such protection for existing claims.

[552]James Hoffa, *The Trials of Jimmy Hoffa: An Autobiography* 45 (1970).

[553]These included one Republican, Sen. Langer, who eventually voted against the bill. The two Southern Democrats did not join the minority.

[554]S. Rep. No. 48, Pt. 2: *Exempting Employers from Liability for Portal-to-Portal Wages in Certain Cases*, 80th Cong., 1st Sess. 1 (1947).

[555]S. Rep. No. 48, Pt. 2 at 6.

the portal wages they had already been compelled to pay through litigation.[556]

The minority members announced a four-point substitute amendment that would have: 1. barred recovery for portal claims that had already accrued but for other types of FLSA violations; 2. permitted compromise of existing portal claims; 3. established a three-year statute of limitations; and 4. relieved employers of future liability for acts occasioned by adherence to written regulations or interpretations of the Wage and Hour Administrator.[557] When Senators McCarran and McGrath introduced this substitute amendment during the debates, it included several additional elements: 1. the elimination of representative actions; 2. a requirement that any plaintiff to a class action file a written consent, at which time the action would have been deemed to have begun as to that claimant; and 3. a six-month grace period during which to file already accrued causes of action unless barred by applicable shorter periods of limitations.[558]

The Senate debates were much more extensive than those in the House, occupying six days between March 14 and March 21. Here, too, by large majorities all amendments were rejected. An interesting alignment of forces emerged in the course of debate over the effect of the majority and minority bills on existing claims. The minority contended that the majority bill "wiped out" not just existing portal claims, but all existing claims of violations of the FLSA.[559] This part of the debate was not contentious because the Republican floor leader, Senator Donnell, virtually boasted that in order to wipe out all existing portal claims, the majority had found it necessary to "wipe out some rights here and there" that should not have been eliminated.[560] While the subcommittee was preparing preliminary drafts, it took the position that no existing claims, unless based on contract or custom, should be compensable regardless of whether the time at issue took place before, during, or after the scheduled workday. But then Senator Donnell[561] invited several AFL and CIO officials to confer with him privately, at which time they brought to his attention the plight of garment factory workers who might have to wait two hours without compensation when the

---

[556]S. Rep. No. 48, Pt. 2 at 8-9.

[557]S. Rep. No. 48, Pt. 2. at 9.

[558]93 *Cong. Rec.* 2288.

[559]S. Rep. No. 48, Pt. 2. at 2. In a more alarmist charge, Senator McCarran asserted: "For the future...the language of the majority bill means that no employee has any rights under the Fair Labor Standards Act which his employer is not willing he should have." 93 *Cong. Rec.* at 2245. Although this assertion may have been true of portal claims (as well as of the House bill in its entirety), it was not true of other future claims. Senators Cooper and McGrath made this point at length. 93 *Cong. Rec.* at 2297-98.

[560]93 *Cong. Rec.* at 2130, 2125.

[561]Senators Donnell, Cooper, and Eastland were in charge of drafting the Senate bill.

production line was down.[562] If that practice was custom in the plant and no contract contradicted it, the proposed bill would have legalized the employer's policy. In order to deal with such problems, the subcommittee redrafted the bill to strike only (existing) portal claims involving periods before and after the normal workday. But then

> [a] gentleman by the name of Finlay, who is associated with the Standard Oil Co. of New Jersey...came to Washington and left a memorandum with us, followed by a letter, taking the position pretty generally that if we should not legislate with reference to the period...between whistle and whistle, we would still leave unattained our objective to wipe out the portal-to-portal suits.[563]

Therefore, in order to insure that claims for walking time back and forth to the cafeteria were wiped out, the subcommittee returned to its original twenty-four-hour per day conception, thus sacrificing the garment workers.[564] Senator Donnell then stated that he had recounted this private legislative history in such detail because it was important to show that when Congress wiped out non-portal claims, it was "not acting capriciously or arbitrarily, but within its sound discretion in...demolishing the portal-to-portal cases."[565] Although no Democrat had charged that the majority was acting arbitrarily when it did the bidding of any official of the Standard Oil Company who happened to drop off a memo, the monolog left no doubt about the intended effect of the majority bill on existing claims.

About the corresponding effect of the McCarran-McGrath bill much more doubt obtained—especially among Democrats. The authors asserted that by inserting the phrase "not compensable working time," their amendment wiped out all existing claims involving the issue of compensable working time (including portal claims), but would not "touch claims which do not in any way involve the question of whether the nature of the activities engaged in was such as to be considered work."[566] Thus, for example, whereas the majority bill would have eliminated a claim for minimum wage in connection with a piece-rate contract not

---

[562]At the Senate hearings, a representative of the Amalgamated Clothing Workers Union testified that, although there were no portal problems in garments factories where its members were employed, unorganized workers faced a problem with regard to "enforced unproductivity" or downtime where they worked on a piece rate. *Portal to Portal Wages* at 161 (testimony of John Abt, special counsel).

[563]93 *Cong. Rec.* at 2132.

[564]93 *Cong. Rec.* at 2132. Sen. Donnell stated later, however, that these union representations had persuaded the subcommittee to insure that "the compensation for the iniquitous practices of an employer" be preserved. 93 *Cong. Rec.* at 2362.

[565]93 *Cong. Rec.* at 2132.

[566]93 *Cong. Rec.* at 2290 (statement of Sen. McCarran).

specifying any hours, the McCarran-McGrath bill would not have.[567] Senator Barkley, the Democratic minority leader, offered a hypothetical situation in which an employer required employees to show up thirty minutes before starting time to sharpen tools, an activity for which neither contract nor custom mandated payment. He then asked McCarran whether, if the employer coerced the employees to obey him for fear that they would lose their job, they could recover under McCarran's bill. McCarran, agreeing that there were many such cases in the United States,[568] was constrained to concede that such workers would be left unprotected.[569] When Senator Cooper, a leading Republican supporter of the majority bill, asked McCarran how his bill then really differed from the majority's, the latter sought refuge, like Representative Walter, in the spirit of the FLSA.[570] At that point, Senators Cooper and McGrath joined to "make contribution [sic] to the legislative history" by emphasizing that the bill was intended not only to preserve all the protections of the FLSA for the future for activities during the workday proper, but also to create an expansive compensable universe of "principal activities."[571]

After this comforting exchange, the Senate rejected the McCarran-McGrath amendment 53 to 35.[572] In quick succession the chamber also defeated several other amendments, including one to raise the minimum wage to sixty cents per hour.[573] In an effort to prevent employers from reorganizing work activities in order "to throw all of the nonprincipal activities at the beginning or end of the day" so that "[j]anitorial...services, normally performed by other workers could be

---

[567]93 *Cong. Rec.* at 2290.

[568]Senator Pepper, perhaps the most radical opponent of portal legislation in the Senate, added that in the South, when "workers are required to be present 30 minutes ahead of time," economic compulsion reinforced the employer's demand—as evidenced by the fact that only forty per cent of families in the United States "had total liquid savings of as much as $40." 93 *Cong. Rec.* at 2303-2304. Senator Johnston (Dem. S.C.), who had worked in a cotton mill and represented workers in wage and hour suits, offered a concrete example. 93 *Cong. Rec.* at 2371.

[569]93 *Cong. Rec.* at 2291.

[570]93 *Cong. Rec.* at 2292. Senators Barkley and McCarran may also have been speaking past each other since their colloquy seemed to be based on the assumption that the inquiry concerned past and future claims whereas McCarran's amendment did not apply to future claims.

[571]*See* 93 *Cong. Rec.* at 2296-99.

[572]93 *Cong. Rec.* at 2366. Eight Southern Democrats voted with the Republicans against the amendment; the same two Republicans who ultimately voted against the majority bill, supported the amendment.

[573]It was defeated 57-32 on a vote to table. 93 *Cong. Rec.* at 2368-2369 (introduced by Sen Myers, Dem. Pa.). The Senate rejected by a vote of 50 to 39 Holland's amendment to exclude the Walsh-Healey and Bacon Act from the operation of the bill. 93 *Cong. Rec.* at 2367.

required of production workers" without compensation,[574] another unsuccessful amendment proposed language permitting portal suits covering preliminary or postliminary activities "normally engaged in during the working day."[575]

Further factional maneuvering emerged over the issue of the length of the limitations period. Holland, a Southern Democrat backing portal legislation, proposed an amendment permitting applicable state statutes of limitations with periods between one and two years to remain in force on the grounds that they had stifled portal litigation.[576] McGrath responded for the liberal Democrats by noting that the limitations issue was completely extraneous to the portal problem since the majority bill had effectively eliminated such claims for the past. He emphasized instead that a short period would undermine enforcement to the detriment especially of low-paid unorganized workers.[577] He then presented data showing that when FLSA was originally enacted, ninety-five per cent of covered employees worked in states with applicable statutes of limitations of at least three years; and even despite the movement toward shorter state limitations periods,[578] almost three-fifths of covered workers worked in states with periods of at least five years. Thus the two-year period in the majority bill would reduce the rights of eight-eight per cent of all covered workers, while under the House version of one year, ninety-five per cent would lose and none would gain.[579]

After Holland's amendment was defeated,[580] the liberals sought to maintain the status quo, which was more favorable to employees, by an amendment deleting the limitations period altogether and reinstating applicable state provisions. In an important test of labor's strength on an issue that related only to the viability of non-portal FLSA rights, more than two-thirds of those voting rejected the amendment.[581]

---

[574]93 *Cong. Rec*. at 2259.

[575]It was rejected 50-39. 93 *Cong. Rec*. at 2367 (introduced by Kilgore, Dem. W. Va.).

[576]93 *Cong. Rec*. at 2184, 2273-74.

[577]Since "the members of organized labor hardly need the protection of" the FLSA, McGrath coyly added that if the latter's protection were destroyed, "we will drive more and more Americans to the necessity of joining labor unions; not that perhaps any of us have any objection to that...." 93 *Cong. Rec*. at 2256.

[578]Interestingly, most of the states that shortened the limitations period, had no experience of their own with administering or enforcing minimum wage laws. 93 *Cong. Rec*. at 2256-57 (statement of Sen. McGrath).

[579]93 *Cong. Rec*. at 2257.

[580]40 to 23; McCarran, whose own amendment included a three-year period, voted yea. 93 *Cong. Rec*. at 2277.

[581]The vote was 61 to 28. 93 *Cong. Rec*. at 2367-68 (introduced by Sen. Magnuson). The yeas were artificially inflated by the votes of Holland and Wilson (Rep. Ia.), who were presumably swayed by the desire to preserve their states' very short limitations periods.

On the final roll-call vote in the Senate, where 51 Republicans faced 45 Democrats, and all twenty-two Southern senators, representing almost half of the Democratic contingent, were Democrats,[582] the sharp divide along party-sectional lines was only slightly less prominent than in the House. The Senate passed H.R. 2157 on March 21 by a 64 to 24 vote. Forty-six Republicans supported the bill and only two voted nay; all eighteen Democratic supporters were Southerners.[583]

4. Compromise in Conference: Flaying But Sparing the FLSA

Portal-Pay Ban as Finally Passed Is a Paradise for Chiselers[584]

The same day that the Senate passed its version of H.R. 2157, it informed the House that it wanted a conference, which the House on March 25 agreed to hold.[585] The committee of conference[586] issued its report on April 29 recommending a bill that represented an amalgam of each house's bill.[587] On May 1, 1947, both chambers agreed to the conference report.[588]

By far the most important product of the conference was the abandonment by the House of its undifferentiated treatment of existing and future claims. Had the House prevailed on the key provision in its bill, the FLSA would have been virtually repealed since H.R. 2157, which was not confined to portal claims, eliminated statutory standards in favor of contract, custom, or practice. Violations of the FLSA would then have been reduced to something akin to common-law

---

Wilson had introduced S. 307, which was the counterpart to the bill introduced by Gwynne, who also represented Iowa, a state whose legislature had pioneered in the field of short limitations periods for the FLSA.

[582]*Congressional Directory*, 80th Cong., 1st Sess. 145-66 (1st ed. 1947).

[583]Including one from Maryland. The two Republicans were Aiken of Vermont and Langer of North Dakota. 93 *Cong. Rec.* at 2375 (1947). Three Southern Democrats opposed the bill, while the most impassioned opponent of the anti-portal legislation, Pepper of Florida, did not vote. The three were Olin Johnston (S.C.), Lister Hill (Ala.), and John Sparkman (Ala.). On the backgrounds of these racist prolabor senators, see *Current Biography 1951*, at 310 (1952) (Johnston); *Current Biography 1943*, at 297 (1944) (Hill); *Current Biography 1950*, at 539 (1951) (Sparkman).

[584]*United Mine Workers J.*, May 15, 1947, at 7.

[585]*House Journal*, March 21, 1947, at 215; *id.*, March 25, 1947, at 221.

[586]The House managers were Michener, Gwynne, Goodwin (R. Mass.), and Walter; the Senate's were Wiley, Donnell, Cooper, and Eastland (D.. Miss.).

[587]See H. Conf. Rep. No. 326: *Portal-to-Portal Act of 1947*, 80th Cong., 1st Sess. (1947).

[588]The House agreed on a division, 173-27. *House Journal*, May 1, 1947, at 319; *Senate Journal*, May 1, 1947, at 226-27.

breaches of contract.[589] The Senate bill closely resembled the House bill with regard to existing claims,[590] but differed radically from the House version in restricting the relief that it granted employers from liability for future claims solely to portal claims, which it sought to identify through examples. By adopting the language of the Senate provision virtually intact,[591] the conference salvaged the FLSA.

Yet in incorporating the language of both bills that defined the "custom or practice" that would mandate compensation as that of the individual establishment,[592] the conference rejected testimony that such a criterion would favor bad employers and undermine the uniformity of the FLSA standards[593] and colleagues' recommendations that at the very least an industry-wide standard be applied in order to avoid rewarding unscrupulous employers in perpetuity either through grandfathering in their practices or encouraging them to create "dummy" entities that would be free to establish new practices.[594] Unless many firms in the industries that were the objects of portal suits actually were paying for portal

---

[589]The courts recognized that the all-encompassing nature of the relief that was carried over to § 2 of the Portal-to-Portal Act was not limited to portal claims. E.g., Steiner v. Mitchell, 350 U.S. 247, 255-56 (1956) (dictum); Cities Service Defense Corp. v. Dutton, 240 F.2d 113, 115-17 (8th Cir. 1957), *cert. denied*, 355 U.S. 828 (1957); Bauler v. Pressed Steel Car Co., 182 F.2d 357 (7th Cir. 1950); Seese v. Bethlehem Steel Co., 74 F. Supp. 412, 416 (D. Md. 1947), *aff'd*, 168 F.2d 58 (4th Cir. 1948); Miller v. Howe Sound Mining Co., 77 F. Supp. 540 (E.D. Wash. 1948); Kemp v. Day & Zimmerman, Inc., 33 N.W.2d 569, 591 (Iowa 1948). The only contrary opinion included in the national reporter system was Central Missouri Tel. Co. v. Conwell, 170 F.2d 641, 645 (8th Cir. 1948), which held that because the Portal-to-Portal Act did not repeal the overtime provision of the FLSA, plaintiffs were not required to plead a contract, custom, or practice to support a claim for compensation for nonportal normal worktime. The Eighth Circuit impliedly overruled this decision in *Cities Service Defense Corp.* The courts were swayed by § 2(d) of the Portal-to-Portal Act, which withdrew from the courts jurisdiction of actions for liability not authorized under § 2(a).

[590]Although § 2 of the Senate bill, unlike the House bill, referred to "[r]elief from portal-to-portal claims," § 5 circularly defined "'portal-to-portal activities'" as meaning "those activities which section 2...provides shall not be a basis of liability" under the FLSA. Since the more substantive illustrations of portal activities in § 6, which governed future claims, did not apply to past claims under § 2, the Senate bill appeared to offer employers relief from all liability for past claims. As the discussion in the text of the Senate debates indicates, the bill's supporters conceded that they had sacrificed existing nonportal claims in order to insure that all existing portal claims were wiped out. The conference report came to the same conclusion. H. Conf. Rep. No. 326 at 9.

[591]Ch. 52, § 4, 61 Stat. 84, 86-87.

[592]§§ 2(a)(2) and 4(b)(2), 61 Stat. at 85, 87.

[593]Portal to Portal Wages at 645 (testimony of Arthur Pettit).

[594]93 *Cong. Rec.* at 2237 (statement of Sen. Murray).

activities and thus created an industry-wide standard different from that to which "chiseling" employers adhered, it is puzzling why Congress elected to adopt establishment-based "custom or practice." Although the fact that the findings and policy section of the conference bill adopted the language in the Senate bill concerning the "gross inequality of competitive conditions between employers and between industries"[595] suggests that members had thought about the issue, its meaning is unclear. Senator Donnell, whose exposition of the bill alone occupied two and one-half days of the Senate's debate time, cast some light on the matter by stating that, unless Congress took action with regard to future claims,

> there is grave likelihood of continued inequality of competitive conditions as between employers, and between industries, due to the fact, as between employers, that one employer may have a plant physically so located that his portal time is greater than that of an employer across the street, who because of his physical location, does not find the same necessity for long walking spaces for employees.[596]

Underlying Donnell's analysis was a conception of plant layout as a kind of natural catastrophe or gift wholly independent of human intervention. If some firms built very large plants whose economies of scale were in part based on the uncompensated time workers had to spend walking across huge internal spaces, such construction design was a conscious investment decision by management.[597] The mere fact that employees could not muster the strength to compel compensation before the enactment of the FLSA, did not create any moral—let alone legal—entitlement on the part of employers to preserve such costless operations under the FLSA. Donnell's only justification of the employer's and Congress's position was a circular or vacuous one:

> [I]t is the view of well-informed individuals that there is compensation granted to every employee in the performance of his duties, if in computing the hourly figure or the price per piece of his product, the fact that he did the walking or did the preliminary activities had been taken into account....[598]

Donnell might have lent empirical support to his claims had he actually collected data on wages in plants "across the street" from each other with varying amounts of walking time. If, ceteris paribus, the similarly situated workers with greater portal time actually received higher hourly or piece rates, then the

---

[595]§ 1(a)(3), 61 Stat. at 84.

[596]93 *Cong. Rec.* at 2122.

[597]Even the AFL recognized this state of affairs. *See Portal to Portal Wages* at 145 (statement of Walter Mason, nat. leg. representative, AFL).

[598]93 *Cong. Rec.* at 2090.

proponents of portal legislation would have succeeded in cutting the moral ground from under the CIO's claims. If, as seems more in accord with the real workings of the labor market, such time was not compensated at either plant, then the moral and economic foundations of the employers' position would have collapsed.

The House conferees yielded on another important point—the one-year period of limitations—by accepting the Senate bill's provision of a two-year period for future claims.[599] In addition, the Senate ban on representative actions,[600] to which there was no House counterpart, was adopted in the act.[601] Despite the congressional uproar over the Supreme Court decisions making the compromise of any claims, including liquidated damages, very difficult,[602] the House conferees were also unable to persuade their Senate counterparts to extend the right to compromise to future claims.[603] But the House managers did achieve partial success on a related issue. While the Senate bill had had no provision concerning liquidated damages, the House bill had conferred discretion on a court that found that the employer's violation "was in bad faith and without reasonable ground" to award liquidated damages not to exceed the underlying back wages.[604] The compromise consisted in shifting the burden to the employer to show that his actionable act or omission was in "good faith" and "that he had reasonable grounds for believing" that it did not violate FLSA.[605]

Both bills had had provisions relieving employers of liability where the act or omission in question was in good-faith reliance on an administrative regulation, order, interpretation, or ruling even where such regulation was later judicially

---

[599]§ 6(a), 61 Stat. at 87-88. All existing claims had to be filed within the shorter of two years after the cause accrued or the period prescribed by the applicable state statute of limitations. § 6(b). This rule was subject to a grace-period proviso that, if a cause was filed within 120 days of the enactment of the Portal-to-Portal Act, the action could have accrued more than two years earlier if the applicable state limitations period extended that far back. § 6(c).

[600]§ 8(a).

[601]For analysis of the collective action provisions, see below § 8.

[602]See below § 7.

[603] § 3, 61 Stat. at 86. The Act contained a further limitation found in neither the House nor Senate bill: an existing claim could be compromised only "if there exists a bona fide dispute as to the amount payable" and if the compromise amounts to at least the minimum wage or time and one-half. *Id.* § 3(a).

[604]H.R. 2157, § 2(g).

[605]§ 11, 61 Stat. at 89. Congressional interest in this issue had been sparked by a judicial ruling that, although it would be "a keen injustice for employers bewildered by strange legislation and confused by divergent authority in the courts" to face additional liquidated damages where their violation had been committed in good faith, such "harshness" was mandatory. Missel v. Overnight Motor Transp. Co., 126 F.2d 98, 111 (4th Cir. 1942), *aff'd*, 316 U.S. 572, 581-84 (1942). On congressional interest, see H. Rep. No. 71 at 8.

invalidated.[606] The minor differences between them were compromised by not requiring the administrative ruling as to existing claims to be in writing or to be issued by the Wage and Hour Administrator.[607] The managers narrowed the scope of this relief by noting that an employer's reliance on the statement of an individual agency official that was not in fact the agency's interpretation would not affect his liability.[608] Moreover, one of the conferees explained to the House that the defense did not apply where the "employer had knowledge of conflicting rules and chose to act in accordance with the one most favorable to him."[609] A class bias inheres in this good-faith reliance provision since it in effect makes the Administrator's interpretations "binding on employees but not on employers." For while the employer is protected, no employee can "perform certain activities with the assurance that he will be compensated in accordance with the written opinions of the Administrator."[610]

5. In Lieu of a Veto: Presidential Legislative History

President Truman took the entire ten days granted him by the Constitution[611] to sign the bill during which he received conflicting advice from his advisers and cabinet members.[612] While his special counsel, Clark Clifford, urged him to veto the bill and to specify the kind of bill he wanted, the Senate Minority Leader, Barkley, convinced Truman that Congress would not approve more favorable legislation. While Secretary of Labor Schwellenbach and the vice chairman of the Council of Economic Advisers, Leon Keyserling, kept urging disapproval, Secretary of Commerce Harriman, Secretary of the Navy Forrestal, and Attorney General Clark all favored approval.[613] In finally signing the bill, Truman, an historian of the Eightieth Congress has argued, was motivated by the political judgment that

---

[606]The provision was contained in § 2(e) of the House bill and § 10 of the Senate bill.

[607]§§ 9-10, 61 Stat. at 88-89.

[608]*See* H. Conf. Rep. No. 326 at 16-17.

[609]93 *Cong. Rec.* at 4390 (Rep. Walter).

[610]Note, "Fair Labor Standards Act under the Portal to Portal Act," 15 *U. Chi. L. Rev.* 352, 357-58 (1948).

[611]Art. I, § 7, cl. 2.

[612]During this period a group of liberal reformers and academics, including Elizabeth Brandeis, Paul Douglas, Walter Gellhorn, and Hubert Humphrey, sent Truman a letter in which they couched their opposition to H.R. 2157 in terms of the adverse competitive impact it would have on scrupulous employers. *See* 93 *Cong. Rec.* at A2172.

[613]Susan Hartmann, *Truman and the 80th Congress* 44 (1971).

the issue was not one on which substantial public opinion demanded a veto. Unorganized workers were politically inarticulate, and a large part of the population, forgetting about the unorganized workers whom the bill affected, viewed the extravagant portal claims as another attempt by powerful unions to line their pockets at the expense of consumers. Thus Truman found no compelling reason to abandon his conciliatory posture.[614]

In signing the bill, Truman avoided antagonizing Congress at a time when his foreign policy initiatives were pending, and preserved his option to veto Taft-Hartley. In the event: "Truman's approval of the portal bill marked the end of his appeasement strategy."[615] That end was foreshadowed by what may have been a unique presidential exercise in creating legislative history. In his message to Congress transmitting his approval he instructed Congress (and the courts)[616] as to what Congress had meant by certain provisions. In particular Truman insisted that the legislative history of § 4, dealing with future claims,

> shows that the Congress intends the words "principal activities" are to be construed liberally to include any work of consequence performed for the employer, no matter when the work is performed. We should not lose sight of the important requirement under the act that all "principal activities" must be paid for, regardless of contract, custom, or practice. I am sure the courts will not permit employers to use artificial devices such as the shifting of work to the beginning or the end of the day to avoid liability under the law.[617]

Congress was not amused. Even Senator McGrath, a Democratic opponent of the bill and Truman's former Solicitor General and future Attorney General, found it necessary to inform his colleagues that presidential statements did not become part of the legislative history.[618] On a more specific note, Senator Donnell, answering on behalf of the Judiciary Committee, left no doubt that Truman was right about one matter—it was unorganized workers who would bear the brunt of the Act. Donnell observed that if an employee sewing in a factory prior to enactment had not been compensated for the time she spent waiting for the production line to start up again during the day and no contract or custom required

---

[614]Hartmann, *Truman and the 80th Congress* at 45-46.

[615]Hartmann, *Truman and the 80th Congress* at 46.

[616]One court actually took notice. In Mauro v. Slaughter & Co., 14 Lab. Cas. ¶ 64,299 at 72,720-21 (S.D.N.Y. 1948), the judge cited Truman's message as authority for the proposition that Congress did not mean to void existing nonportal claims not based on contract, custom, or practice. In fact, Truman did not even take that position.

[617]H. Doc. No. 247: *Portal-to-Portal Act of 1947: Message from the President of the United States Transmitting his Approval of H.R. 2157*, 80th Cong., 1st Sess. 2 (1947).

[618]93 *Cong. Rec.* at 6262.

payment, the employer would not be liable for back wages.[619]

7. The Unwaivability of Liquidated Damages: Statute Trumps Bargaining

[W]e hope that organized labor will realize that wages ought to be adjusted by collective bargaining, not by fantastic proceedings at law, and that this famous issue will be remembered only as a historical curiosity.[620]

One tension running throughout the congressional and judicial disputes over portal pay involved the relationship of the FLSA to collective bargaining. Although the FLSA was designed to preempt individual or collective adhesion contracts in favor of statutory standards in order to enable workers lacking a strong bargaining position to receive adequate compensation for their work, many member of Congress and the judiciary believed that organized workers were at best inadvertent and marginal beneficiaries of the FLSA.[621]

Justice Jackson was a prominent advocate of this position. As a coda to his dissent in *Jewell Ridge*,[622] two years later Jackson returned to the subject of the

---

[619]93 *Cong. Rec.* at 7541. He also contradicted Truman on another point that undermined enforcement of the FLSA; an employer did not have to show that he had relied on an affirmative action by an administrative agency: that ruling or policy "may consist solely of the absence of action." *Id.*

[620]"Judge Picard Reconsiders," *N.Y. Times*, Feb. 9, 1947, § 4 at 8, col. 1 (editorial).

[621]See above chapter 1.

[622]Jewell Ridge Coal Corp. had unsuccessfully petitioned the Court for rehearing on unusual grounds. It challenged Black's qualification to hear the case both because he had been the most active sponsor of the FLSA as a Senator and because he had been a law partner with respondents' chief counsel. Petition for Rehearing at 2-3. The chief counsel, Crompton Harris, had also represented the union in *Muscoda*. Although the Court denied the petition without a statement of the reasons, Jackson, concurring in the denial, wrote that since the Court was without authority to exclude a Justice from sitting in any case, the complaint was improperly addressed to the Court. Jewell Ridge Coal Corp. v. Local No. 6167, UMW, 325 U.S. 897 (1945). Jackson's irony became apparent a year later when, unable to repress his animus against Black any longer, Jackson, while on leave at Nuremberg as chief prosecutor for the United States, castigated Black for having judged his ex-partner's case as well as for having (unsuccessfully) tried to influence the outcome of a coal strike by urging Murphy to hand down the decision in favor of the miners without waiting for the opinion or dissent. The press prominently reported on the unusual eruption. "Jackson Attacks Black for Judging Ex-Partner's Case," *N.Y. Times*, June 11, 1946, at 1, col. 6; "Test of Jackson's Statement Attacking Black," *id.* at 2, col. 3; Lewis Wood, "Split of Jackson and Black Long Widening in Capital," *id.* at 2, col. 4.

relationship between the FLSA and collective bargaining in a non-portal case, insisting that the FLSA was not intended to regulate labor relations except as to minimum wages and overtime. Instead, under the National Labor Relations Act (NLRA), employers and employees could give expression to their needs and customs. This division of labor could best be effectuated without strife by giving decisiveness in borderline cases either to the NLRA or to the Wage and Hour Administrator's rulings. In *Jewell Ridge*, however, the Court, by rejecting both approaches, "foreclosed every means by which any claim, however dubious, under this statute or under the Court's elastic and somewhat unpredictable interpretations of it, can safely or finally be settled, except by litigation to final judgment."[623]

Jackson's irritation had been triggered by two decisions,[624] whose cumulative impact was to preclude employees from ever waiving their rights to liquidated damages under the FLSA by entering into a purely private settlement agreement with an employer for back wages releasing him from all other claims. In *Brooklyn Savings Bank v. O'Neil*,[625] the Supreme Court resolved "the question whether an employee subject to the terms of the Act can waive or release his right to receive from his employer liquidated damages under § 16(b)."[626] More than two years after termination of the employment, the employer computed the statutory overtime due the worker and offered it to him in exchange for a release of all his FLSA rights. After accepting the money, the worker sued for liquidated damages.[627] In the factually variant companion case of *Dize v. Maddrix*, the employer, after discharging the worker, tendered him back wages that both parties knew to be less than the minimum and overtime wages due. The worker accepted the money and signed a general release of all his rights under the FLSA. He then hired a lawyer to secure the balance. When the employer tendered that sum before suit was filed, the worker refused it because the offer did not include liquidated damages. In both cases the employers claimed that the release was a defense to the subsequent actions brought solely for liquidated damages.[628]

Before proceeding to the central issue, the Court examined the question of whether the releases were "given in settlement of a bona fide dispute between the parties with respect to coverage or amount due under the Act or whether it constituted a mere waiver" of FLSA rights. Because the Court decided that "the release was not given in settlement of a bona fide dispute between employer and

---

[623]Walling v. Portland Terminal Co., 330 U.S. 148, 154, 155 (1947) (Jackson, J., concurring).

[624]Jackson voted with the majority in the first and did not participate in the second.

[625]And the companion case of *Dize v. Maddrix*, 324 U.S. 697 (1945).

[626]324 U.S. at 699.

[627]324 U.S. at 700.

[628]324 U.S. at 701-702.

employee,"[629] it did not reach the issue of "what limitation, if any, § 16(b) of the Act places on the validity" of a settlement made "in consideration of a bona fide compromise...."[630]

The pertinent statutory language of § 16(b) read as follows:

> Any employer who violates the provisions of § 6 or § 7 of this Act shall be liable to the employee or employees affected in the amount of their unpaid minimum wages, or their unpaid overtime compensation...and in an additional equal amount as liquidated damages.

In the absence of specific consideration and resolution of the issue by Congress, the Court explored the broader legislative policy behind the provision. Generally the FLSA "was a recognition of the fact that due to the unequal bargaining power as between employer and employee, certain segments of the population required Federal compulsory legislation to prevent private contracts on their part which endangered national health and efficiency...."[631] The court was of the opinion that the same policy considerations that prohibited waiver of statutory wages by agreement on the grounds that it "would nullify the purposes of the Act," "also prohibit waiver of the employee's right to liquidated damages."[632] The Court then sketched a very expansive view of the congressional purpose behind the provision of liquidated damages as a

> recognition that failure to pay the statutory minimum on time may be so detrimental to maintenance of the minimum standard of living "necessary for health, efficiency, and general well-being of workers"...that double payment must be made in the event of delay in order to insure restoration of the worker to that minimum standard of well-being. Employees receiving less than the statutory minimum are not likely to have sufficient resources to maintain their well-being and efficiency until such sums are paid at a future date. The same policy which forbids waiver of the statutory minimum...requires that reparations to restore damage done by such failure to pay on time must be made to accomplish Congressional purposes. Moreover, the same policy which forbids employee waiver of the minimum statutory rate because of inequality of bargaining power, prohibits these same employees from bargaining with their employer in determining whether so little damage was suffered that waiver of liquidated damage is called for.[633]

The Court also emphasized that the "private-public character" of the right to liquidated damages precluded waiver, which would undermine the intended "deterrent effect": "Knowledge on the part of the employer that he cannot escape

---

[629]324 U.S. at 703..

[630]324 U.S. at 714.

[631]324 U.S. at 706.

[632]324 U.S.. at 707.

[633]324 U.S. at 707-708.

liability for liquidated damages by taking advantage of the needs of his employees tends to insure compliance in the first place." Finally, the Court recurred to the fact that one of the FLSA's functions is to protect employers that can maintain profitability without having to resort to certain kinds of exploitation from wage-chiseling competitors: "An employer is not to be allowed to gain a competitive advantage by reason of the fact that his employees are more willing to waive claims for liquidated damages than are those of his competitor."[634] Thus even where he has paid all back wages but in an untimely fashion, "the employer shall be liable for liquidated damages in an amount equal to minimum wages overdue; liability is not conditioned on default at the time suit is begun."[635]

The following term the Court seized the opportunity to revisit the issue that had been left open in *Brooklyn Savings Bank.* Making very short shrift of the employer's argument, it held that "the remedy of liquidated damages cannot be bargained away by bona fide settlements of disputes over coverage" or hours of work or rates of pay.[636] In support the Court cited the reasoning of *Brooklyn Savings Bank.* Specifically:

> the purpose of the Act, which...was to secure for the lowest paid segment of the nation's workers a subsistence wage, leads to the conclusion that neither wages nor the damages for withholding them are capable of reduction by compromise of controversies over coverage. Such a compromise thwarts the public policy of minimum wages, promptly paid...by reducing the sum selected by Congress as proper compensation for withholding wages.[637]

Extending that incompetence from individual workers to organized labor, did not, in Jackson's view, redound to the latter's benefit; as he had written in dissent in *Jewell Ridge*, it was "hard to see how the long-range interests of labor itself are advanced by a holding that there is no mode by which it may bind itself to any specified future conduct, however fairly bargained."[638] The subtext here was that while the pro-labor majority of the Court may have intended to confer a benefit on

---

[634]324 U.S. at 710.

[635]*Id.* at 711.

[636]*Schulte, Inc. v. Gangi*, 328 U.S. 108, 114, 115 (1946).

[637]328 U.S. at 116. In dictum the Court modified the absolute quality of the ineffectiveness of waivers by noting that "the requirement of pleading the issues and submitting the judgment to judicial scrutiny may differentiate stipulated judgments from compromises by the parties." *Id.* at 113 n.8. In a later case it was held that once a claim goes to final judgment, the employee can compromise by accepting his full back wages and attorney's fees but only nominal liquidated damages where the employer is insolvent. Bracey v. Luray, 68 F. Supp. 701 (D. Md. 1946), *aff'd*, 161 F.2d 128 (4th Cir. 1947), *cert. denied*, 332 U.S. 790 (1947).

[638]325 U.S. at 195.

unions by permitting them unilaterally to avoid collective bargaining agreements that did not comply with the overtime provisions of the FLSA, this one-sided flexibility would eventually provoke damaging countervailing measures by management.

Coming on the eve of congressional debate on the portal-to-portal bill in February 1947, Jackson's concurrence in *Portland Terminal* served to remind Democrats that it was now legitimate for New Dealers to question the pro-union bias of the Court. Such doubts were particularly apposite where the Court sought to clothe "a powerful group so plainly outside of the policy of the Act" with a "coat [that] ill fits the United Mine Workers."[639] The dissenters' tenaciously propagated position[640]—that organized workers were at best inadvertent and marginal beneficiaries of the FLSA whose statutory claims should be taken cum grano salis—underlay much of the advocacy by large capital and the Republican congressional majority of restrictive portal-pay legislation. Large northern manufacturing corporations, which had initially acquiesced in the FLSA in the belief that its minimal standards would have no impact on their wage policies or operations, had been organizing resistance to its overtime provision since 1938.[641] When the CIO began filing portal-pay overtime suits against them, these employers finally succeeded in teaching unions a lesson in expeditious legislative overruling.

The Portal-to-Portal Act eventually granted employers a limited defense against mandatory liquidated damages. Where an employer can show "that the act or omission giving rise to such action was in good faith and that it had reasonable grounds for believing that its act or omission was not a violation of" the FLSA, the court has discretion to award less than full liquidated damages.[642] In a suit solely for liquidated damages, the "act or omission" in question would refer to the failure or refusal[643] to pay liquidated damages. If the late payment of wages was unreasonable or not in good faith, then the award of liquidated damages would be automatic and ministerial. If, however, the employer could show good faith *and* reasonableness with regard to the late payment of wages, then he could a fortiori

[639]Jewell Ridge Coal Corp., 325 U.S. at 192 (Jackson, J., dissenting).

[640]And unwittingly confirmed by the Houck letter.

[641]See above chapter 1.

[642]Portal to Portal Act, ch. 52, §11, 61 Stat. 89 (1947) (codified as amended at 29 U.S.C. § 260 (1985)). The Act also made waivers permissible "with respect to activities engaged in prior to May 14, 1947." 29 U.S.C. § 253(b).

[643]Presumably demand for payment of liquidated damages would be no more a prerequisite for filing suit than demand for back wages. "A right to sue for compensation vests whenever the pay period passes and the employer fails to pay the amounts required by law. Thereafter nothing further need happen. The cause of action has matured." S. Rep. No. 48 Part 2: *Exempting Employers from Liability for Portal-to-Portal Wages in Certain Cases*, 80th Cong., 1st Sess. 5 (1947).

show them with regard to the failure to pay liquidated damages—although even then the court would have discretion to award full liquidated damages.

Even after enactment of the portal legislation, Congress remained concerned about the declining volume of voluntary restitution of back wages. Of the causes of this decline:

> Undoubtedly one of the most important...is the fact that an employer who pays back wages which he withheld in violation of the act has no assurance that he will not be sued for an equivalent amount plus attorney's fees under the provisions of section 16(b) of the act. One of the principal effects of the committee proposal will be to assure employers who pay back wages in full under the supervision of the Wage and Hour Division that they need not worry about the possibility of suits for liquidated damages and attorney's fees.[644]

Consequently, Congress again amended the FLSA in 1949 to provide for involvement by the DOL:

> The Secretary is authorized to supervise the payment of the unpaid minimum wages or the unpaid overtime compensation owing to any employee..., and the agreement of any employee to accept such payment shall upon payment in full constitute a waiver by such employee of any right he may have under subsection (b)...to such unpaid minimum wages or unpaid overtime compensation and an additional equal amount as liquidated damages.[645]

In the end, then, provided that workers avoid intercession by the DOL,[646] no waiver or release given in a purely private agreement with the employer can be effective.[647] Congress, then, contrary to Jackson's view, appears to have realized that statutory norms should take precedence over contract.

8. The Elimination of the Class Action That Never Was

> [I]f we were to enact this legislation...it would probably be the greatest boon to labor unions they have had in many years, because it would force the unorganized employees to

---

[644]S. Rep. No. 640, 81st Cong., 1st Sess., *reprinted in* 1949 U.S. Code Cong. Serv. 2241, 2249.

[645]Act of Oct. 26, 1949, ch. 736, § 14, 63 Stat. 919 (codified as amended at 29 U.S.C. § 216(c) (Supp. 1989)).

[646]Where a worker signed a receipt and accepted the check tendered by the employer for the amount determined by the DOL to be owed and then, on advice of counsel returned the check without having cashed it, it was held that the waiver was effective. Sneed v. Sneed's Shipbuilding, Inc., 545 F.2d 537 (5th Cir. 1977).

[647]Lynn's Food Stores, Inc. v. United States, 679 F.2d 1350 (11th Cir. 1982).

join a union in order to get a contract and therefore protect their rights.[662]

The Portal-to-Portal Act has exerted its most decisive and lasting impact on capital-labor relations in the unorganized sector by prohibiting the use of what today are called opt-out class actions. This result is ironic because the unions had not conducted the portal litigation in the form of such class actions—although congressional animus against that procedural form was based on the mistaken impression that they had done so. Moreover, the prohibition has not vitally injured unions, which can continue to resolve FLSA-type claims collectively through a grievance-arbitration system, whereas unorganized workers, deprived of the opt-out class action, are remitted to a very ineffectual means of pressuring employers to comply with the FLSA. Further irony inheres in the fact that this empirically unfounded congressional action laid the basis for excluding the FLSA claimants from the benefits of the expanded class action procedures introduced by the Federal Rules of Civil Procedure twenty years later.

The original FLSA of 1938 provided for two varieties of collective actions. For violations of the minimum wage or overtime provisions an action could be maintained

> by any one or more employees for and in behalf of himself or themselves and other employees similarly situated, or such employee or employees may designate an agent or representative to maintain such action for and in behalf of all employees similarly situated.[663]

The development of such actions under the FLSA was hampered by a judicial bias against this procedural innovation as well as by the courts' perplexity as to whether actions brought pursuant to § 16(b) were additionally subject to the limitations of Rule 23(a) of the Federal Rules of Civil Procedure,[664] which had gone into effect only the month before FLSA in 1938.[665] Rule 23 provided at that

---

[662]93 *Cong. Rec.* at 2374 (Senator Aiken).

[663]Ch. 676, § 16(b), 52 Stat. 1060, 1069 (1938).

[664]*See, e.g.*, Lofther v. First Nat. Bank of Chicago, 45 F. Supp. 986 (N.D. Ill. 1941). Smith v. Stark Trucking, Inc., 53 F. Supp. 826, 828 (N.D. Ohio 1943), was unusual in recognizing that "it would be purposeless to discuss the question whether this is a true class action as prescribed in Rule 23.... Confusion might arise from an unnecessary discussion of the applicability of Rule 23. The question for decision is: Does the instant suit follow the pattern delineated in the Act itself?"

[665]The Federal Rules of Civil Procedure went into effect three months after the adjournment of the second regular session of the seventy-fifth Congress. Fed. R. Civ. P. 86, as published in 308 U.S. 645, 766 (1939). The third session (which was the second regular session) of Congress adjourned on June 16, 1938. *See* 82 *Cong. Rec.* 3 (1937); 83 *Cong. Rec.* 9612, 9699 (1938). The Rules therefore went into effect Sept. 16, 1938. The minimum

time that, where the requirements of numerosity and adequacy of representation were met, so-called spurious class actions[666] could be brought "when the character of the right sought to be enforced for or against the class is...several, and there is a common question of law or fact affecting the several rights and a common relief is sought."[667] Because judgments in spurious class actions included only those who intervened before a trial on the merits, "no material advantage" would have accrued to employees from bringing the FLSA actions pursuant to Rule 23(a)(3).[668] Indeed, doubt attached to whether suits under the FLSA even rose to the level of spurious class actions inasmuch as the "common question" or "common relief" might be lacking; they might, it was said, merely be amenable to permissive intervention.[669]

In determining whether the FLSA expansively authorized the "virtual representation" of unnamed employees[670] or was merely designed to enable relatively impecunious workers to avoid unnecessary litigation costs by "join[ing] a series of separate law suits into one proceeding,"[671] courts were ostensibly guided

---

wage and maximum hours provisions of the FLSA went into effect on October 24, 1938, 120 days after its date of enactment (June 25, 1938). *See* ch. 676, §§ 6(b) and 7(d), 52 Stat. 1060, 1063, 1064 (1938). As late as March 1947, an employer, arguing that § 16(b) had gone into effect on June 25, 1938, moved to dismiss a representative action on the grounds that § 16(b) conflicted with and had been repealed by Rule 23(a). The motion was denied. McNichols v. Lennox Furnace Co., 7 F.R.D. 40, 41-42 (N.D.N.Y. 1947).

[666]Original Rule 23(a) distinguished among true, hybrid, and spurious class actions. The first is one in which "but for the class action device the joinder of all interested persons would be essential." James Moore and Marcus Cohn, "Federal Class Actions," 32 *Ill. L. Rev.* 307, 314 (1937). The second group involves a specific property, but the members' interests are several. In the spurious class action, a common question of law or fact unites the class, but the members' rights are several. Moore, who was the research assistant to the reporter for the Advisory Committee on Rules for Civil Procedure, drafted an unadopted version of Rule 23 that specifically provided that the judgment would be conclusive on the class in true class actions, but only on the parties in the other two. *See* James Moore, "Federal Rules of Civil Procedure: Some Problems Raised by the Preliminary Draft," 25 *Geo. L.J.* 551, 571 (1937); James Moore and Marcus Cohn, "Federal Class Actions--Jurisdiction and Effect of Judgment," 32 *Ill. L. Rev.* 555, 556 (1937).

[667]Fed. R. Civ. P. 23(a)(3), as published in 308 U.S. 645, 689 (1939).

[668]Rufus Poole, "Private Litigation under the Wage and Hour Act," 14 *Miss. L.J.* 157, 165 (1942) (ass't solicitor, DOL).

[669]*See, e.g.*, Saxton v. W.S. Askew Co., 35 F. Supp. 519, 521 (N.D. Ga. 1940); James Rahl, "The Class Action Device and Employee Suits under the Fair Labor Standards Act," 37 *Ill. L. Rev.* 119, 128-32 (1942).

[670]Kuligowski v. Hart, 2 Wage & Hour Cas. 931, 934 (Ohio C.P., Cuyahoga County, 1942).

[671]Lofther v. First Nat. Bank of Chicago, 45 F. Supp. at 988.

by their solicitude for the rights of employers and of unnamed plaintiffs. The more radical position rejected the legitimacy of any class action by denying Congress the power "to force one to become a plaintiff against his will or without his consent, or to select for him an agent or attorney to represent him."[672] The more moderate position merely denied that Congress intended to permit the adjudication or preclusion of claims without an employee's knowledge.[673]

The other due process barrier to judicial acceptance of class actions (whether under the FLSA or not) was the notion that it "just isn't cricket" "to afford the absentees all the benefits of winning but to impose upon them none of the burdens of losing."[674] In other words, it was not fair to the defendant to permit members to participate after a decree had been rendered "even though, had the suit been unsuccessful, they would not have been bound by it."[675] Despite the lack of "complete symmetry between binding the defendant to a favorable decree and binding the absentee to an unfavorable decree,"[676] the courts took a very dim view of such one-way intervention.[677] Consequently, even before the 1947 amendments, the courts limited participation in the FLSA actions to named plaintiffs, intervenors, and consenters who joined the action before the trial on the merits.

Possible movement toward a conception of class actions under the FLSA that might have transcended the scope of Rule 23(a)(3) emerged when an early

---

[672]Brooks v. Southern Dairies, Inc., 38 F. Supp. 588, 588 (S.D. Fla. 1941).

[673]Saxton v. W.S. Askew Co., 35 F. Supp. at 521.

[674]Harry Kalven, Jr. and Maurice Rosenfield, "The Contemporary Function of the Class Suit," 8 *U. Chi. L. Rev.* 684, 713 (1941).

[675]Kalven and Rosenfield, "The Contemporary Function of the Class Suit" at 711.

[676]Kalven and Rosenfield, "The Contemporary Function of the Class Suit" at 713. Kalven and Rosenfield explained the difference this way: "[T]he defendant has been afforded his day in court; he has had the opportunity to present his case fully in his own right, and he has lost. He has no more reason to relitigate the entire controversy against the absentee members than he has to do so against the immediate plaintiff. But it cannot be said that the absentee has had his day in court to a comparable degree. ... The defendant cannot properly complain about the way in which he is treated; he can complain only that the absentees are not subjected to the risk of losing the case. But to the extent that the risk of losing would be greater on them because they are merely represented, it is only fair that they are not equally subjected to that risk." *Id.* To the extent that the representation was adequate (and free), this argument appears to have justified the need for opt-out class actions rather than for one-way intervention. G.W. Foster, Jr., "Jurisdiction, Rights, and Remedies for Group Wrongs Under the Fair Labor Standards Act: Special Federal Questions," 1975 *Wisc. L. Rev.* 295, 325, supported the Kalven-Rosenfield position.

[677]Roberts v. Western Airlines, 425 F. Supp. 416, 419 (N.D. Cal. 1976) (one of primary purposes of 1966 amendments of the Federal Rules of Civil Procedure "was to eliminate this type of 'one way intervention' in spurious class actions"), indicates that this view has survived.

influential district court decision, *Shain v. Armour & Co.*, held that general principles of class actions that disqualified suits in which claims were distinct and the subject of independent suits, even though a common question of law was involved, did not govern the FLSA because they would have nullified § 16(b).[678] But the court quickly stifled such a possibility by holding that only where the interests of the named and unnamed plaintiffs were so common and united as to entitle the former to stand in judgment for the latter would constitutional due process requirements permit making the judgment res judicata for the whole class. FLSA cases, however, did not meet that requirement because "different members of a class are free to either assert rights or to challenge them as their individual judgments dictate and the interests of the representatives of the class are not necessarily or even probably the same as those whom they are deemed to represent."[679]

The cogency of this ruling was weakened by the observation that if fairness was the problem, the threshold requirement of adequate representation would have avoided it. For those not adequately represented would not have been bound.[680] The inability of the class representative to demonstrate typicality of claims would have compelled the same result. The *Shain* court's ruling on the unnamed class members' freedom to join or not could have formed the basis of a notice and opt-out procedure that would have addressed the judicial antipathy to one-way intervention. In the event, even before the Portal-to-Portal Act eliminated whatever expansive potential FLSA class actions may ever have had, the courts in non-portal litigation had almost unanimously[681] opted for this restrictive approach,[682] confining

---

[678]Shain v. Armour & Co., 40 F. Supp. 488, 489-90 (W.D. Ky. 1941).

[679]40 F. Supp. at 490.

[680]*See* Comment, "FLSA Class Action Limited to Employees Giving Assent," 55 *Harv. L. Rev.* 688, 689 (1942).

[681]Only one (semi-reported) decision appears to have approved the bringing of a FLSA action on behalf of other employees without naming them on the grounds that the "Act was intended to and does link together all employees who are not paid according to its provisions and as to them creates a question of common interest. Each is given the right to have his claim presented in the action of a fellow employee." Clint v. Franklin Bargain House, Inc., 1 Wage & Hour Cas. 1068, 1071, 20 Oh. Op. 196 (C.P. Lucas County, 1941). Intriguingly, the plaintiffs' counsel was Edward Lamb, who represented the workers in *Mt. Clemens Pottery Co.* Another semi-reported Ohio case in obscure language permitted a FLSA action to go forward on behalf of undisclosed others. Potts v. Stedman Co., 2 Wage & Hour Cas. 884, 22 Oh. Op. 488 (C.P. Athens County, 1942). In Cissell v. Great Atlantic & Pacific Tea Co., 37 F. Supp. 913, 914 (W.D. Ky. 1941), an individual plaintiff, who, though unnamed, had shared in a settlement in a previous case, sued the employer for an additional amount on the grounds that the previous judgment "was not binding as to him because he was not a party to that suit and...the settlement was agreed upon in fear of losing his job." The court held that the settlement was "binding upon him as one of the class for whom the plaintiff professed

and assimilating such actions to the mere device for permissive joinder[683] that spurious class actions had been designed as under the original Rule 23(a).[684] The most capacious gloss the courts were willing to put on workers' § 16(b) rights was the Third Circuit's holding that even subject to the aforementioned limitations, the spurious class action implemented an important statutory purpose insofar as "employees, if they wish, can join in their litigation so that no one of them need stand alone in doing something likely to incur the displeasure of an employer. It brings something of the strength of collective bargaining to a collective lawsuit."[685]

---

to act as authorized by the very statute which gives him the claim now sued upon. ... If he elects to take its benefits, he must accept its restrictions also." It is unclear whether *Shain*, which was decided by the same judge, was meant to overturn *Cissell*.

[682]For a comprehensive overview of the case law, see Pentland v. Dravo Corp., 153 F.2d 851, 853-56 (3d Cir. 1945).

[683]See Foster, Jurisdiction, Rights, and Remedies for Group Wrongs Under the Fair Labor Standards Act" at 324-27; Albert Gerber and S. Galfand, "Employees' Suits Under the Fair Labor Standards Act," 95 *U. Penn. L. Rev.* 505, 508-509 (1947); James Rahl, "The Class Action Device and Employee Suits under the Fair Labor Standards Act," 37 *Ill. L. Rev.* 119 (1942).

[684]*See* 2 James Moore and Joseph Friedman, *Moore's Federal Practice* § 23.04-(3) at 2241 (1938).

[685]Pentland v. Dravo Corp., 152 F.2d at 853. Zechariah Chafee, Jr., elaborated on this intermediary status of FLSA:

> In other types, it is usually not worth while to have a class suit at all unless everybody is bound. Here it may be. Congress has set up an easy way for starting a suit for each of a considerable number of people with rather small means to claim some money. It saves expenses to pool. But they might never sue if it were necessary to sign everybody up first. So a few can begin it. Once a bandwagon gets moving, others can jump on it if they want to. Still they may not want to. ... The very support Congress gives their claims indicates an unwillingness to let them be barred by what somebody else does.
>
> So a suit under the Fair Labor Standards Act is usually treated as an Invitation To Come In. This is the best opportunity I know for this type of class suit. ... The outsiders hear about the victory and come around asking for money too. Most of the decisions say they get nothing. It is too late. This is tough on them, but fairer than barring them if they stay out and the class is defeated. Coming in is somewhat like starting a new separate suit and probably will be barred after the period of the Statute of Limitations even if the class suit started in time. The proceeding is really an informal substitute for permissive intervention. ... Perhaps the Invitation To Come In should be confined to a few situations where a statute, like the Fair Labor Standards Act, expressly authorizes a class suit....

Zechariah Chafee, Jr., *Some Problems of Equity* 274-75, 283 (1950). Chafee does not appear to have been aware of the Portal-to-Portal Act and its consequences for class actions under the FLSA. For an earlier use of the notion of invitation in a non-FLSA context, see William

Against this precedential background it is scarcely surprising that

> a reading of the opinions in the period leaves one suspicious that attorneys for plaintiffs in these private representative actions lacked the resources or the time to frame up suggestions, built around available precedents, that could have led to effective implementation of the representative actions authorized in section 16(b).[686]

Employees' attorneys did indeed prosecute the portal litigation in a very conservative manner. One of the leading plaintiffs' attorneys indicated that, to the best of his knowledge, all the suits were filed as opt-in collective actions because counsel, uncertain how far the courts would let them push FLSA class actions, which were an innovation even under the Federal Rules of Civil Procedure, were reluctant to embarrass themselves.[687]

The opt-in approach may also simply have been dictated by the fact that virtually all of the portal suits were brought by unionized workers as representative actions naming a union official as the representative, who was not required to be an affected employee or a real party in interest.[688] Those members who wished to name the representative as their agent had to sign authorization cards, which were filed with the complaint.[689] Recovery then ran only to those filing authorizations.[690] The outright prohibition of these representative actions under the Portal-to-Portal Act,[691] even though they had been rather cumbersome procedural devices, was

---

Blume, "The 'Common Questions' Principle in the Code Provision for Representative Suits," 30 *Mich. L. Rev.* 878, 898 (1932).

[686]Foster, "Jurisdiction, Rights, and Remedies for Group Wrongs Under the Fair Labor Standards Act" at 324 n.103.

[687]Telephone interview with Ernie Goodman (Apr. 2, 1990).

[688]Lee Pressman, the CIO general counsel who coordinated the portal litigation, testified before Congress that he knew of no portal suits brought by unorganized workers. *Regulating the Recovery of Portal-to-Portal Pay, and For Other Purposes: Hearings Before Subcomm. No. 2 of the House Comm. on the Judiciary*, 80th Cong., 1st Sess. 166 (1947).

[689]Thus when Pressman filed a portal suit against Bethlehem Steel, he attached a 535-page "brief" containing the names of 13,000 workers. "Bethlehem Sued for $200,000,000," *N.Y. Times*, Dec. 29, 1946, at 3, col. 4. *See also* "Rules Individuals Must Sign," *Wall St. J.*, Feb. 1, 1947, at 2, col. 6 (court ruling that unless union submits signed declarations of 5,286 employees of Campbell Soup Co. within twenty days, they will be dismissed).

[690]*Regulating the Recovery of Portal-to-Portal Pay, and For Other Purposes: Hearings Before Subcommittee No. 2 of the House Committee on the Judiciary*, 80th Cong., 1st Sess. 175 (1947) (testimony of Lee Pressman).

[691]The Portal-to-Portal Act amended § 16(b) by eliminating the grant of authority to file representative actions. Ch. 52, § 5(a), 61 Stat. 84, 87 (1947). The repeal did not affect pending representative actions. *Id.* § 5(b).

clearly designed as an attack on union-organized litigation.[692]

The driving force behind the congressional animus against class actions in 1947 was expressed most clearly by the Senate floor leader, Senator Donnell, in explaining the Senate bill to the members. He justified the prohibition of representative actions on the grounds that an "outsider, perhaps someone who is desirous of stirring up litigation without being an employee at all," might create "unwholesome champertous situations."[693] To collective actions Donnell had no objections—provided that consents were filed. The need for consents he explained by way of a story involving an employee who files a suit on behalf of himself and all other employees of the United States Steel Corporation; three years later, after the statute of limitations has run, some of the employees come forward and say: "Now, we will ratify what this man did in filing suit for us 3 years ago, and although we would be barred by limitations if we filed our suit ourselves at the time we now come into court, nevertheless, since he instituted the suit for us 3 years ago, we now join in that suit."[694] Donnell found such a situation unfair because such employees would not have had any obligation before entering. Once the new consent provision became operative, it would no longer "be possible for 10,000 men to wait 3 years, with the employers not knowing how many thousands of dollars or millions of dollars...of claims will be asserted against them" and then to come forward after they would otherwise have been time-barred. For Donnell, then,

> [o]bviously...this is a wholesome provision, for it is certainly unwholesome to allow an individual to come into court alleging that he is suing on behalf of 10,000 persons and actually not have a solitary person behind him, and later on have 10,000 men join in the suit, which was not brought in good faith, was not brought by a party in interest....
>
> Certainly there is not injustice in that, for if a man wants to join in the suit, why should he not give his consent, in writing...?[695]

This entire line of argument makes sense only if interpreted as motivated by

---

[692]*See* Note, "Fair Labor Standards under the Portal to Portal Act," 15 *U. Chi. L. Rev.* 352, 360 (1948). The Supreme Court got this piece of history wrong when it recently stated that the Portal-to-Portal Act abolished representative actions in part in response to "excessive litigation spawned by plaintiffs' lacking a personal interest in the outcome" and required employees to file written consents. Hoffmann-LaRoche, Inc. v. Sperling, 110 S. Ct. 482, 488 (1989). It was not such bogus litigation that Congress meant to eliminate, but rather lawsuits in which unions all too diligently signed up all too many members.

[693]93 *Cong. Rec.* at 2182. Although Donnell did not state openly that he had unions in mind, Senator McGrath asked him whether the NAM engaged in champerty when it informed members of recent Supreme Court rulings entitling them to certain rights. *Id.* at 2093.

[694]93 *Cong. Rec.* at 2182.

[695]93 *Cong. Rec.* at 2182.

a general animus against what in 1966 became Rule 23(b)(3) class actions.[696] For discovery and the plaintiff's own affirmative duties to prove numerosity, typicality,[697] and adequacy of representation[698] in connection with the motion for class certification, would bring to light all the information about which, Donnell complained, the disingenuous litigant was intentionally keeping the employer in the dark. With such protections in place, the basis of the policy supporting the restrictions on opt-out class actions in the Portal-to-Portal Act collapses.[699]

In the event, the Portal-to-Portal Act outlawed opt-out class actions by inserting a requirement that written consents be filed:

The second sentence of section 16(b) of the Fair Labor Standards Act...is amended to read

---

[696]Thus Senator McGrath, whose knowledge appears to have been formed solely by newspaper accounts, charged that the portal suits were "representative of thousands or perhaps even millions of Americans who do not even know they are represented." 93 Cong. Rec. 2250 (1947). Although McGrath appears to have been misinformed, even if he had been correct, his accusation amounts to nothing more than a bias against Rule 23(b)(3) class actions. In her zeal to advocate an expansion of class actions under the FLSA, one author has misunderstood the radical character of the Portal-to-Portal Act. The amendments were not designed to address "[t]he confusion surrounding the binding effect of class actions judgments" or to clarify the procedures; nor is it the case that Congress did not intend to limit non-representative class actions. *See* Barbara McAdoo, "The Class Action Notice Under the FLSA: Denial is a Threat to Effective Remedies in ADEA Actions," 91 *Dick. L. Rev.* 357, 361, 369 (1986). On the contrary, Congress knew exactly how the CIO had used class actions and wanted to prevent any repetition. Elizabeth Spahn, "Resurrecting the Spurious Class: Opting-In to the Age Discrimination in Employment Act and the Equal Pay Act through the Fair Labor Standards Act," 71 *Geo. L.J.* 119, 129-30 (1982), similarly underestimates the restrictive political-economic motivations underlying introduction of the mandatory opt-in provision. This repressive intent is accurately depicted in Dolan v. Project Constr. Corp., 725 F.2d 1263, 1266-67 (10th Cir. 1984).

[697]Or as an early FLSA case held with regard to named class members: "If the evidence does not sustain the allegation that the other plaintiffs are similarly situated..., they will be dismissed...." McReynolds v. Louisville Taxicab & Transfer Co., 5 F.R.D. 61, 62 (W.D. Ky. 1942).

[698]*See, e.g.*, Saxton v. W.S. Askew Co., 35 F. Supp. at 521.

[699]Walter Gellhorn, a law professor at Columbia University, misunderstood the meaning of the prohibition on assignment of claims in the Gwynne bill, which he interpreted as barring the pooling of claims. N.Y. *Herald Tribune*, Feb. 28, 1947 (letter), *reprinted in* 93 *Cong. Rec.* A927-28 (1947). This provision, which reappeared as § 2(e) of the Portal-to-Portal Act as applied only to existing claims, was designed merely to make it "impossible for anyone (even though permitted to do so under State law) to buy existing claims which were not compensable under contract, custom, or practice, with the hope of compromising such claims at a profit...." H. Conf. Rep. No. 326: *Portal-to-Portal Act of 1947*, 80th Cong., 1st Sess. 11 (1947).

as follows: "Action to recover such liability may be maintained...by any one or more employees for and in behalf of himself or themselves and other employees similarly situated. No employee shall be a party plaintiff to any such action unless he gives his consent in writing to become such a party and such consent is filed in the court in which such action is brought."[700]

Ironically, employees might have been better situated had Congress totally abolished class actions under the FLSA in 1947.[701] For when the class action provisions of the Federal Rules of Civil Procedure were liberalized in 1966, an opportunity was lost to lay the groundwork for the rehabilitation of class actions under the FLSA. If the collective action provision of the FLSA had been repealed, Rule 23(b)(3) would have created parity between employees under the FLSA and other litigants. But the Advisory Committee made it clear that the amendments were not intended to affect § 16(b) of the FLSA.[702]

One scholar has taken the position that the Advisory Committee acted wisely "because the cumbersome procedure for determining the scope of judgment in advance of deciding...the employer's liability under the Act would be no improvement over the group remedies available now to the Secretary of Labor under section 16(c) and section 17 of the Act."[703] This judgment rests on an overestimation of the efficacy of enforcement by the DOL. Moreover, both the absolute and relative volume of DOL litigation has plummeted catastrophically since the early 1970s. As seen in Table 3-2, the number of FLSA cases filed by the DOL peaked at 1,721 in 1970; by 1997, it had shrunk by 92 percent to a mere 143. Since the overall volume of FLSA filings declined by only 25 percent (from 2,176 to 1,633) during those years, the DOL's share fell from 79 percent to 9 percent.[704]

---

[700]§ 5(a), 61 Stat. at 87. A separate rule governed the applicability of the new statute of limitations to pending collective actions was provided for in § 8 of the Portal-to-Portal Act.

[701]In explaining the new rule for determining when an action begins for purposes of the statute of limitations, the conference committee spoke of "a collective or class action" interchangeably, merely distinguishing "a collective action" as one "brought by an employee or employees for and in behalf of himself or themselves and other employees similarly situated" from "a class action" as "described in Rule 23 of the Federal Rules of Civil Procedure." H. Conf. Rep. No. 326 at 14. Such language misleadingly creates the impression that litigants could elect between the two procedures. In referring to "a collective or class action instituted under" the FLSA, however, § 7 of the Portal-to-Portal Act itself suggests that the two terms are used synonymously. The federal courts are in agreement that class actions brought under Rule 23 and the FLSA are "mutually exclusive and irreconcilable." La Chapelle v. Owens-Illinois, Inc., 513 F.2d 286, 289 (5th Cir. 1975).

[702]Advisory Committee's Note to Fed. R. Civ. P. 23, 39 F.R.D. 98, 104 (1966).

[703]Foster, "Jurisdiction" at 342.

[704]Calculated according to data in *Annual Report of the Director of the Administrative*

Gauged against this background of inaction, the warning that the Wage and Hour Administrator issued to the NAM in 1940 seems almost comic:

> The day I was sworn in...I issued a statement which was widely published. It advised employers to "put their houses in order" because this law was going to be enforced.
>
> I warned employers to straighten themselves out under this law before amounts due their workers accumulated to financially embarrassing sums. ...
>
> If you are not sure that you are in compliance with this law...my advice to you is make sure.
>
> Because our inspector will soon be around. ... Enforcement of this act is as certain as death or taxes.
>
> I commend this law to you. Its provision of a 40-hour week with an overtime penalty is enforcing the employment of America. And the minimum wage is filling many a Christmas stocking that otherwise would have hung empty.[705]

Experience in representing very low-paid employees with high turn-over rates such as migrant farm workers indicates that it is precisely such workers, whom the DOL fails to reach, whose peripatetic living conditions frequently disable them from opting in to class actions. Yet only if Congress—like some states[706]—makes opt-out class actions available to such workers, thereby overcoming the restrictive individualistic framework imposed by the consent requirement,[707] can the original vision of joint public-private enforcement of the FLSA[708] come into its own.

9. Lessons and Consequences

> In the field of wage legislation, the Portal-to-Portal Pay Act is as severe a blow to workers' rights as the Taft Hartley Act is in the field of industrial relations.[709]

What can be learned from the struggle over portal-to-portal pay? Was Senator Aiken, one of two Senate Republicans to vote against the bill, right in saying "that labor was extremely unwise in starting the portal-to-portal suits...for the purpose

---

Office of the United States Courts, Table C 2 (various years).

[705]Philip Fleming, Address Before the NAM, New York City, Dec. 12, 1940, in 86 *Cong. Rec.* at A6963, A6965 (1940).

[706]E.g., Alaska Stat. § 23.10.110(b) (2000); Webster v. Bechtel, Inc., 621 P.2d 890, 903 (Alaska 1980).

[707]Stephen Yeazell, "From Group Litigation to Class Action, Part II: Interest, Class and Representation," 27 *UCLA L. Rev.* 1067, 1103 (1980).

[708]Kalven and Rosenfeld, "The Contemporary Function of the Class Suit" at 721.

[709]*Final Proceedings of the Ninth Constitutional Convention of the Congress of Industrial Organizations* 92 (1947).

of embarrassing the employer, and with the mistaken idea that the union was going to make bargaining capital out of it"?[710] It is not clear that the CIO instigated the litigation campaign. It is just as plausible that unions, in response to a growing demand by industrial workers for back wages in the wake of the Supreme Court *Mt. Clemens* decision, sought to reshape an otherwise uncoordinated proliferation of suits[711] into a bargaining tradeoff for higher wages. But regardless of whether the unions' role was primary or mediatory, they bear the historical responsibility for failing to anticipate the outcome.

By offering employers, including the country's largest industrial corporations, a motive and a basis for attacking the FLSA frontally, the CIO unwittingly undermined whatever political-economic momentum had built up during the war for expanding the scope and coverage of the Act. Thus employers succeeded not only in delaying an increase in the minimum wage until 1950 and scuttling organized labor's more far-reaching amendments proposed during the 79th Congress,[712] but also in enacting their own agenda for defusing the FLSA's potential for inflicting significant financial losses on employers. Employers were able to achieve this end through the abbreviated limitations period and the effective elimination of class actions. The latter was particularly important because, in addition to their economic impact, class actions could have served as vehicles for politically mobilizing unorganized workers around issues of basic working conditions—including that of who controls the length of the compensable working day.

Even if it were unfair to categorize *Mt. Clemens* under the heading, Hard Cases Make Bad (Statutory) Law, union leaders and counsel should nevertheless have taken greater care to distinguish between the theatrical-symbolic and the monetary-redistributional goals of the litigation. Had they emphasized this distinction to employers, workers, legislators, and the public at large, unions could have exerted greater leverage over the early postwar wage-bargaining process. Such a campaign would, hindsight teaches, have benefited immensely from two tactical innovations. First, if the chief purpose was to improve working conditions in the long run, litigation should have focused on prospective relief. Not only would this approach have completely eliminated the basis of the financial hysteria and moral indignation that employers and legislators were able to project so effectively, it would also have sustained a much more sympathetic political movement. This focus on better working conditions could have been coordinated with the second tactic—bringing a test case, with facts considerably more egregious than those in *Mt. Clemens*, requesting prospective declaratory relief. The very lengthy and

---

[710]93 *Cong. Rec.* at 2372, 2098.

[711]Although the workers did not bring these suits on their own, the mere fact that the unions filed the suits for the workers does not resolve the issue of who induced whom.

[712]See above § 6.A.2.

hazardous walking time in the steel mills might have been the ideal vehicle. David McDonald, the then secretary-treasurer and later president of the United Steel Workers, painted such a vivid picture for the House Judiciary Committee of the long and dangerous walk that steelworkers were required to take, across railroad tracks and under overhead cranes, from the plant gate to the open hearth that he succeeded in prompting even Representative Gwynne to acknowledge that he advocated payment for many of the activities. Significantly, McDonald stressed that in such large and highly integrated plants firms "have wrung from the workers an increased contribution to the companies' profits."[713] In the end, without any congressional intercession on which to rely, large corporate employers might have been forced not only to acquiesce in future portal pay (or equivalent arrangements), but also to concede greater wage increases in exchange for an understanding that unions would bring no suits for back portal wages. In this connection, the CIO should have generously offered to sponsor the FLSA amendment that Lee Pressman had proposed—that FLSA compromises be permitted within the framework of bona fide collective bargaining.[714]

The opportunistically instrumental attitude that the CIO and its constituent unions adopted toward the FLSA deprived them of the long-term strategic perspective that could have contributed to a transformation of the FLSA from a minimally intrusive regime into one that might have intervened much more significantly into managerial prerogatives in the nonunion sector. Because they failed to recognize the ultimate stakes as the NAM and large industrial capital did, the unions were unable to structure the portal litigation in such a way as to raise the issue expressly of what was compensable work and who made that determination. The reason for this failure lay in the CIO's ambiguous attitude toward the FLSA. Like the large unionized employers, the industrial unions had viewed that statute as largely directed at aiding the low-paid in their struggles with their chiseling employers. Because the CIO either subordinated the portal suits to its postwar bargaining campaign or viewed them as an expeditious and relatively costless means of securing back wages to compensate for current inflation, it failed to develop a sustained interest in an incremental litigation strategy that would have

---

[713]See *Regulating the Recovery of Portal-to-Portal Pay, and For Other Purposes: Hearings Before Subcommittee No. 2 of the House Committee on the Judiciary*, 80th Cong., 1st Sess. 103-105, 109-10, 112 (quote) (1947). Senator Pepper stated that when he worked in a steel mill, he had had to walk three-quarters of a mile from the gate to the workplace, which he thought should have been compensable. 93 *Cong. Rec.* at 2306.

[714]See above § 6. In the continued absence of such a statutory provision, the Supreme Court has held that, because, even under a collective bargaining agreement, FLSA rights devolve on employees as individuals rather than as members of a labor union, they are neither waivable nor barred by previous unsuccessful submission to arbitration. Barrentine v. Arkansas-Best Freight System, Inc., 450 U.S. 728, 739-46 (1981).

tested the outer limits of the FLSA.

Had the unions proceeded in this fashion, confining themselves to prospective relief, they might have been in a position to settle the principle that the decision as to when and where the workday begins was not only not within the discretion of the employer, but was not even committed to agreement by both parties. Reserved for determination by the courts (and the Wage and Hour Administrator) as a mandatory norm and withdrawn from the bargaining process, the definition of worktime might have encroached upon the unchallenged power of nonunion employers unilaterally to establish working conditions beyond the statutory minimum wage and overtime. But the industrial unions showed little interest in the FLSA for its own sake (or for that of the unorganized work force that depended on it) precisely because they were confident that they were strong enough to achieve these goals, at least for their own members, through collective bargaining.

In the event, the initiators and intended beneficiaries of the inadequately thought-through portal-pay demands did not turn out to be the primary victims of the unanticipated legislative intervention. Unionized workers were the virtually exclusive supporters of portal pay, but low-paid unorganized employees have ultimately paid the price for the congressional reaction. Consequently, even under the Portal Act, unions can seek to achieve their goals through collective bargaining; atomized employees, however, have few statutory rights beyond an abridged FLSA on which to rely.

In fact, however, the large industrial unions in the forefront of portal litigation do not have portal-pay provisions in their contracts. Under the master contracts of the United Automobile Workers (UAW), United Electrical, Radio, and Machine Workers (UE), and United Steelworkers of America (USW), the employer does not pay for the time during which the employee walks from the outer gate of the plant to the work department. At least in the electrical industry, the problems may have been alleviated by a shift to smaller plants requiring less walking time. In the electrical machinery/equipment industry, employees working in the largest plants (establishments with 2,500 or more employees) as a share of all employees declined from 33.2 per cent in 1947 to 23.4 per cent in 1982, as the average number of employees in these largest plants declined from 5,325 to 4,389; by 1992, such establishments, with an average of 4,330 employees, accounted for only 13.2 percent of employees. The trend in primary metals was similar: establishments with 2,500 or more employees, which averaged 5,553 employees in 1947 and accounted for 37.4 percent of total industry employment, witnessed significant deconcentration; by 1982, they averaged 4,763 employees and accounted for 27.3 percent of employment; ten years later, the corresponding figures were only 4,130 and 16.8 percent. Automobile plants did not experience such deconcentration. In 1947, transportation equipment establishments with more than 2,500 employees employed on average 6,069 employees and accounted for 59.1 percent of industry employment; by 1982, such plants had grown to an average of 6,547 employees and accounted for 56.6 percent of employment; by 1992, such establishments, employing on average 6,806 employees, still accounted for 51.2 percent of all industry employment.[715] The UMW, by contrast, has preserved portal pay in all its contracts, including those controlling surface mining, despite periodic efforts by owners to eliminate portal provisions. Because travel time can consume as much as three hours daily roundtrip, miners feel so strongly about it that portal wages have become traditional even in nonunion mines.[716]

Ironically, even the untoward outcome itself has deviated significantly from the results that the CIO feared most. Generally, waiting time (including downtime) during the workday has remained compensable in the typical industrial setting,[717] as have certain so-called preliminary, preparatory, and postliminary activities to the extent that they are integral to the employees' principal activity.[718] But many

---

[715] Calculated according to data in U.S. Bureau of the Census, 1 *Census of Manufactures: 1947*, Table 1 at 98 (1950); U.S. Bureau of the Census, *1982 Census of Manufactures, General Summary*, Pt. 2, Table 1 at 1-5, 1-6 (1985); U.S. Bureau of the Census, *1992 Census of Manufactures: Subject Series: General Summary*, tab. 1-4 at 1-180, 1-181 (1996).

[716]Telephone interviews on June 18, 1990 with the following members of union research departments: Larian Angelo (UE); Michael Cannon (UAW); and Ed Ghering (USW); Don Wallace (UMW). For an example of travel time between a copper mine and the company office for which an arbitrator found that workers were entitled to an overtime premium under a USW collective bargaining agreement but not under the Portal Act, see Silver Bell Mining and United Steel Workers, Local 6705, 112 Lab. Arb. (BNA) 1175 (1999).

[717]*See, e.g.*, Mireles v. Frio Foods, Inc., 899 F.2d 1407, 1411-14 (5th Cir. 1990). To the extent that the court denied the workers compensation for waiting time during the workday in this case, the decision was based on considerations—namely, that the workers could use longer periods of time effectively for their own purposes—unrelated to the Portal-to-Portal Act.

[718]The Supreme Court has interpreted the principal-integral-preliminary-activity nexus broadly in favor of workers. *See* Steiner v. Mitchell, 350 U.S. 247 (1956); Mitchell v. King Packing Co., 350 U.S. 260 (1956). *See also* Barrentine v. Arkansas-Best Freight System, Inc., 750 F.2d 47, 50 (8th Cir. 1984) ("The legislative history of the Portal-to-Portal Act and decisions construing it...make clear that the terms 'principal activity or activities,' which must be paid for, are to be read liberally"). To be sure, the lower courts have not always interpreted the provision quite so expansively as the solicitor of the DOL had hoped shortly after the Portal-to-Portal Act went into effect. *See* William Tyson, "The Portal-to-Portal Act of 1947—Its Effect on Determination of Time Worked Under the Fair Labor Standards Act After May 14, 1947," in *Proc. of the N.Y.U. First Annual Conf. on Labor* 441, 472 (1948). For examples of such cases, see E.I. Du Pont de Nemours & Co., 227 F.2d 133 (4th Cir. 1955); Hodgson v. Katz & Besthoff, #38, Inc., 365 F. Supp. 1193 (W.D. La. 1973) (preliminary activities of cashiers not compensable). More recently, courts, while requiring meat slaughterhouses to pay workers for the time they spend sharpening knives, waiting for sharpened knives and donning personal protective equipment, have held that the Portal Act exempts these employers from liability for paying workers for donning clean white outer garments even though the employers required them to wear such clothing pursuant to U.S.

employers still demand more free labor. In one of the more comically disingenuous requests of this type, the Associated Builders and Contractors, a militantly antiunion organization, urged Congress to legalize such time filching:

> Hourly employees may sometimes desire to perform preparatory activities in anticipation of their normal duties, such as arriving at their work station early, getting their tools lined up for the day's work, reviewing the day's schedule, and so on. The current definition of "employ" discourages (indeed prohibits) self initiation by hourly workers who wish to put forth extra effort in furtherance of their own skills and careers.[719]

The most egregious cases have upheld employers' power to impose extraordinarily onerous noncompensable travel on workers. For example, Grand Union, a supermarket chain, was permitted by the Second Circuit to "make unreasonable travel time not compensable simply by making it a regular part of the employee's job."[720] Grand Union had required a refrigerator mechanic to travel five and one-half to nine and one-half hours daily between his house and its many stores in the New York-Connecticut area without compensation even though he transported company equipment and it reimbursed him for mileage and gasoline. Despite the fact that the worker would have faced these enormous distances regardless of where he had chosen to live, the court, while conceding that his "situation strikes us as inequitable," saw no way to generate a different outcome under the Portal-to-Portal Act.[721] Indeed, so strong was the Portal Act's ideological pull on the judicial mind that the appeals panel failed even to mention that the employer had made a mockery of the FLSA by requiring the worker to store hundreds of pounds of its equipment and materials at his house.[722] If the worker had picked up Grand Union's equipment anywhere except at his own house, the FLSA clock would have begun running as soon as he arrived at that pick-up location.[723] It is scarcely imaginable that any judge would have relieved Grand Union of liability if it had engaged in the analogously unlawful act of requiring its butchers to store company knife sharpeners at home so that they could sharpen

---

Department of Agriculture regulations. Reich v. IBP, Inc., 820 F. Supp. 1315 (D. Kan. 1993), aff'd, 38 F.3d 1123 (10th Cir. 1994).

[719]*Oversight of the Fair Labor Standards Act: Hearing of the Senate Labor and Human Resources Committee*, 104th Cong., 2d Sess. 61 (1996).

[720]Kavanagh v. Grand Union Co., 192 F.3d 269, 276 (2d Cir. 1999) (Korman, Dist. J., dissenting).

[721]Kavanagh v. Grand Union Co., at 272.

[722]Kavanagh v. Grand Union, Motion for Rehearing and Rehearing en Banc at 2 (Nov. 29, 1999); Telephone interview with attorney Tara Kavanagh and plaintiff David Kavanagh, Bellport, N.Y. (Nov. 7, 1999).

[723]29 C.F.R. § 785.38 (1999).

their knives at home off the clock.

In reaching a similar anti-worker conclusion, the Fifth Circuit[724] could not even discern inequity in relieving an employer of liability for the five hours daily that he "hauled" migrant farmworkers between El Paso and the chile pepper fields of New Mexico despite the fact that the workers could not have chosen to live close to the fields since the farmers refused to provide housing in this remote area lacking the population base for the peak needs of a seasonal harvest and the infrastructure for the requisite rental housing, which this subminimum-wage work force could not afford anyway. The unpaid traveling and waiting time that adds up to an eighteen-hour day[725] is made possible by the Portal-to-Portal Act, which makes a self-fulfilling prophecy of agricultural economists' claim that the farm labor market "is an open, ready access market for the salvage of zero and low opportunity cost time...."[726]

No matter how outrageous such overreaching may be, it is Congress's preclusion of the opt-out class action that has had the most enduring and deleterious impact on the minimum wage workers who continue to litigate under the FLSA. At the same time, the absolute prohibition of representative actions, which was manifestly directed against the industrial unions, has not prevented unions from pursuing their remedies through collective bargaining and arbitration. Because the Portal-to-Portal Act, unlike Taft-Hartley,[727] no longer serves this original vindictive anti-union purpose,[728] it should be repealed. Once that repeal

---

[724]Vega v. Gasper, 36 F.3d 417 (5th Cir. 1994). But see Morillion v. Royal Packing Co., 2000 Cal. Lexis 2061 (Cal. Sup. Ct., Mar. 27, 2000) (decided under California state law but holding that farmworkers who were required to meet at a certain place to be driven in employer's buses to fields and were subject to discipline if they failed to arrive at departure place on time or drove to fields in their own vehicles were subject to an employer's control and thus entitled to wages for the travel time).

[725]For a detailed discussion of the facts, see Marc Linder, *Migrant Workers and Minimum Wages: Regulating the Exploitation of Agricultural Labor in the United States* 6-11 (1992).

[726]Varden Fuller & Willem van Vuuren, "Farm Labor and Labor Markets," in *Size, Structure, and Future of Farms* 144-70 at 154 (A. Ball & Early Heady eds. 1972).

[727]"[T]he conclusion is inescapable that Congress was less interested in curing union abuses than in using them as an excuse for weakening the organized labor movement." Seidman, *American Labor from Defense to Reconversion* at 268. Barton Bernstein, "America in War and Peace: The Test of Liberalism," in *Towards A New Past: Dissenting Essays in American History* 289, 290, 303 (B. Bernstein ed. 1969 [1967]), cautions that neither businessmen nor Congress meant to destroy unions in 1946-47, but merely to weaken them. For a different perspective, which places more responsibility on Truman, see Harvard Sitkoff, "Years of the Locust: Interpretations of the Truman Presidency Since 1965," in *The Truman Period As a Research Field: A Reappraisal, 1972*, at 75, 85 (Richard Kirkendall ed. 1974).

[728]Ironically, Congress repeatedly heard that the unorganized would bear the brunt of the

has been accomplished, it may become possible to demarginalize the FLSA, restoring to it the potential that it once possessed for empowering low-paid workers to embark upon self-organization.[729]

amendments. *See, e.g.*, 93 *Cong. Rec.* at 2265 (statement by Sen. Thomas, Dem. Ut.). Rather than applaud this result, supporters of the bill suggested that in this instance part of the baby ("injustice") would have to be thrown out with the bath water. 93 *Cong. Rec.* at 2098 (Sen. Donnell). Thus when Senator Aiken asked Senator Donnell how a poor and unorganized worker would be able to go to the expense of showing the statutorily requisite custom or practice in order to prevail on a claim, Donnell replied that "any plaintiff in any case must make out his case, no matter how rich or how poor he may be." *Id.*

[729]Linder, "The Minimum Wage as Industrial Policy: A Forgotten Role" at 161.

Table 3-2: Civil FLSA Cases Commenced in U.S. Courts, 1941-98			
Year	U.S. plaintiff cases	Total cases	U.S. plaintiff cases as % of all cases
1998	150	1562	10
1997	143	1633	9
1996	168	1558	11
1995	213	1580	13
1994	270	1545	17
1993	333	1457	23
1992	399	1464	27
1991	473	1290	37
1990	564	1282	44
1989	618	1381	45
1988	633	1392	45
1987	705	1468	48
1986	589	1405	42
1985	655	1288	51
1984	772	1479	52
1983	809	1383	58
1982	939	1527	61
1981	1153	1762	65
1980	1378	1897	73
1979	1148	1706	67
1978	1160	1678	69
1977	1356	1990	68
1976	1401	2014	70
1975	1316	1836	72
1974	1505	1898	79
1973	1454	1840	79
1972	1700	2195	77
1971	1686	2182	77
1970	1721	2176	79
1969	1686	2164	78
1968	1529	2073	74
1967	1608	2256	71

1966	1459	2075	70
1965	1269	1806	70
1964	1436	1916	75
1963	1376	1756	78
1962	1252	1565	80
1961	1260	1554	81
1960	1206	1436	84
1959	1081	1290	84
1958	996	1215	82
1957	840	1014	83
1956	497	626	79
1955	491	644	76
1954	380	563	67
1953	645	863	75
1952	524	749	70
1951	511	763	67
1950	337	583	58
1949	364	642	57
1948	266	1062	25
1947	243	3772	6
1946	358	1524	23
1945	458	1081	42
1944	484	1148	47
1943	588	1532	38
1942	1249	2311	54
1941	1718	2581	67
Total	**51,522**	**90,432**	**57**

Source: Office of Public Affairs, Administrative Office of the United States Courts, *Judicial Business of the United States Courts,* tab. C 2 (in the Report for 1944 and 1943 the data were published at Table 6; for 1942 at Table 7) (1941-1998). This publication was formerly titled, *Annual Report of the Director of the Administrative Office of the United States Courts.*

Note: For the years 1947 to 1951, the private litigant cases included a separate rubric for portal-to-portal cases (which numbered 2239, 44, 13, 5, and 13 for the five years). They are combined here. From 1961 forward the cases are broken down according to U.S. plaintiff and defendant and private litigant cases, with a total of all cases specifically stated; from 1941 to 1960 the rubrics include only U.S. plaintiff and private litigant cases; these have been added here on the assumption that they encompass all the cases.

4

Exempting Small Business from Overtime Regulation: The "Original" Accumulation of Capital and the Inversion of Industrial Policy

A...self-respecting democracy can plead no...economic reason for chiseling workers' wages or stretching workers' hours. ... All but the hopelessly reactionary will agree that to conserve our primary resources of man power, government must have some control over...the exploitation of unorganized labor.[1]

President Franklin D. Roosevelt, 1937

By expanding and increasing the FLSA small business exemption, we have done much to preserve the admirable capacity of American entrepreneurs to grow from today's small employers into the larger employers of tomorrow. That is good for the economy; it is good for America's work force.[2]

President George Bush, 1989

1. This Overtime Is on the House

Another issue that has come to our attention is the concern of many small contractors that they will be placed at a competitive disadvantage against other contractors who are not complying with the rule and who may escape OSHA enforcement. What some contractors may not realize is that OSHA does not have jurisdiction over sole proprietorships or other companies where no employer-employee relationship exists. Unfortunately, this may mean that there is not a level playing field between these different types of companies in the residential construction industry, so the concern is understandable. It is not, however, a valid reason to deny needed fall protection to millions of workers.[3]

---

[1]"The President Recommends Legislation Establishing Minimum Wages and Maximum Hours," in *The Public Papers and Addresses of Franklin D. Roosevelt: 1937 Volume: The Constitution Prevails* 209, 210-11 (1941).

[2]George Bush, "Statement upon Signing H.R. 2710," in *Public Papers of the Presidents of the United States: George Bush: 1989*, at 1533 (1990).

[3]*OSHA Fall Protection Standards: Hearings Before the Subcommittee on Regulation and Paperwork of the House Committee on Small Business*, 104th Cong., 1st Sess. 73-74 (1995) (statement of Joseph Dear, Assistant Secretary of Labor for Occupational Safety and Health).

Hail as big as baseballs pounded Iowa City, Iowa, in the late afternoon of May 18, 1997.[4] In 15 minutes the storm damaged enough houses to qualify as the 1997 Full Employment for Roofers Act (of Nature). Because the damage outran the capacity of local roofing contractors to meet the vast increase in demand, "hail-stormers," migrating roofing contractors and their crews who follow storms around the country, "fill[ing] in labor vacuums," soon arrived and settled in for months of work.[5]

In June, a 24-year-old local unemployed man noticed a posting at the Iowa Workforce Development (aka unemployment) office in Iowa City for a job as a roofer. He had never worked as a roofer, but the $8 an hour wage exceeded the pay of the other listed jobs.[6] When he called, the employer hired him on the spot.

As the worker soon discovered, however, the conditions of employment left much to be desired. Despite the fact that Iowa City boasted a 2 percent unemployment rate, among the lowest in the United States, and had enjoyed such low rates for years,[7] the employer did not pay overtime (for hours in excess of 40 per workweek), maintain a workers compensation policy, or pay into the social

---

[4]"Rain, Hail, Tornadoes Hit Eastern Iowa," *Des Moines Register*, May 19, 1997, at 2 (Lexis).

[5]Kathleen Hughes, "Hailstormers '97: Transient Roofing Crews Invade Johnson County," *icon*, Aug. 7, 1997 (http://www.jeonet.com/icon/backs/1997/08-07-97/cover.htm).

[6]Nationally the mean hourly wage for roofers was $12.87 in 1996. The modal wage range—that is, the wage which the largest group of roofers (17 percent) received—was $5.75-$8.49. Roofing was the only construction trade characterized by such a low modal wage range. In 1997 the mean hourly wage rose to $13.38 and the modal range to $11.25-$13.24, but an above-average proportion of roofers continued to fall in the lowest-paid group. U.S. BLS, "Occupational Employment Statistics: 1996 National Occupational Employment and Wage Data" (http://stats.bls.gov/oes/national/oes87808.htm). The establishment-based and employment wage data collected by the Bureau of Labor Statistics (BLS) are flawed by virtue of being linked to employers' reports to state Unemployment Insurance systems. U.S. BLS, *BLS Handbook of Methods* 17-19, 32-34, 42-46 (Bull. 2490, 1997). Because employers who, like the one mentioned in the text, do not comply with their obligations to pay into that system also tend to pay lower wages, their absence from the sample distorts the average wage levels and wage range distributions. The BLS is aware of this flaw and suspects that this uncovered sector of construction has expanded during the 1980s and 1990s, but does not adjust for it. Telephone interview with George Werking, Assistant Commissioner, Office of Federal/State Programs, DOL, Washington, D.C. (Feb. 17, 1998).

[7]The unemployment rate was as low as 0.6 percent for 1989 and never exceeded 3.4 percent on an annual basis during the 1990s. Iowa Workforce Development (http://www.state.ia.us/government/wd/lmi/etables/cityiowa.txt and http://www.state.ia.us/government/wd/ris/lmi/files/etables/historic/cityiowa.txt).

security or unemployment insurance systems. The employer was also often weeks behind in paying wages. Roofing is very dangerous work—376 roofers in the United States were killed on the job from 1992 to 1998[8]—but the employer also failed to comply with the Occupational Safety and Health Administration's fall protection standards for residential roofing.[9]

Arrests throughout the spring and summer of "illegal aliens" working for "substandard wages" for out-of-state roofing contractors[10] pointed to another facet of the paradoxical coexistence of unfavorable working conditions and a very tight labor market.[11] Local observers were moved by the illegality of such conditions, including the failure to report wages to the Internal Revenue Service, when Mexican workers were involved:[12] "No disability, no social security, no insurance, nothing. It's not the way to...sub the work out."[13] But almost identical practices of local roofers vis-à-vis local or, in any event, U.S.-citizen workers, which had been quotidian for years, remained invisible and never prompted anyone to protest.

Unbeknownst to him, the worker was embarking upon a labor law odyssey in the course of which he would become the victim of the Fair Labor Standards Amendments of 1989, best known for having raised the minimum wage. By the time he was fired in November for attempting to assert his rights under various labor and social insurance laws, he would know more about one particular aspect

---

[8]U.S. DOL, "Census of Fatal Occupational Injuries" (1992-1998) (http://stats.bls.gov/oshcfoi1.htm). In 1995, when 60 roofers were killed, the fatality rate was 28 per 100,000 employed—more than twice as high as for all construction workers and more than five times higher than for all workers. U.S. DOL, "1995 Census of Fatal Occupational Injuries: Fatality Rates," tab. 2 (http://stats.bls.gov/oshcfoi1.htm). The National Roofing Contractors Association admits that roofing was one of "the five worst offenders, those with the highest injury and death rates" which OSHA targeted for policing at its inception in 1971. John Vogel and Theodore Karamanski, *One Hundred Years of Roofing in America* 147 (1986).

[9]29 C.F.R. § 1926.501(b)(13) & § 1926.502 (1997). Throughout this Article, "residential" does not include high-rise apartment houses.

[10]Dave Gosch, "Illegal Aliens Pouring In to Fix Hail-Damaged Roofs," *Cedar Rapids Gazette*, July 11, 1997 (http://www.gazetteonline.com/showcase/show934.htm). See also "Iowa," States News Briefs, May 30, 1997 (Lexis).

[11]In California, state labor agencies added construction (together with restaurants) to agriculture and garment manufacture as targeted industries. It was selected for investigation because it draws on the same (immigrant) labor base of "the 'most exploitable' workers." Andy McCue, "State to Expand Crackdown on Labor Law Violations," *Press-Enterprise* (Riverside, CA), Dec. 4, 1997, at D1 (Lexis) (quoting state labor commissioner)..

[12]Gosch, "Illegal Aliens Pouring In to Fix Hail-Damaged Roofs."

[13]Hughes, "Hailstormers '97" (quoting the president of the Eastern Iowa Building Inspectors).

of those amendments than virtually all the lobbyists who pleaded for them, the legislators who enacted them, and the employers' associations and labor unions that are supposed to monitor such laws.[14]

Dissatisfied because the employer was not withholding and paying in social security taxes, the worker spoke to a local labor law professor, who deposed him at length about various aspects of his employment. The professor suggested that the worker request time and one-half for the hundred hours of overtime that he had worked. At first the employer indicated that he would acquiesce in the demand. Later, however, he refused, saying that he had consulted an attorney, who had informed him that for two reasons he was not covered by the overtime law: he did not do $500,000 of business annually, and he was not engaged in interstate commerce. The professor, who fancied himself immensely learned in the Fair Labor Standards Act (FLSA), laughed. He knew that Congress, taking its cue from the U.S. Supreme Court's vindication of an extremely expansive concept of the congressional commerce power, had inserted precisely such a broad coverage provision into the FLSA. He also knew that, apart from farmworkers and a few other groups of marginal workers whose employers had successfully lobbied Congress for exemptions, "virtually every employer is covered under one or another of the law's coverage tests."[15] The labor law sage confidently informed the worker that no matter how small the employer's business, "if he's got you hammering one nail or laying down one shingle that was produced outside of Iowa, you're covered."

Thus, too, began a labor law professor's odyssey and acquaintanceship with an obscure provision of the Fair Labor Standards Amendments of 1989. His

---

[14]Two reporters who dealt with the small-business exemption debate concerning the minimum wage totally overlooked the significant impact on premium overtime. Jeanne Sadler and Albert Karr, "Minimum-Wage Exemptions Baffle Many: Congress May Act to Expand and Simplify Rules," *Wall St. J.*, Mar. 23, 1989 (Westlaw). The only dissertation devoted to the 1989 FLSA amendments presents itself as a Marxist class analysis, yet ignores the small-business exemption, the inter- and intra-class issue of overriding importance in the act. Paul Kamolnick, "The Minimum Wage Restoration Act of 1989: Wage Relation, Class Politics, and the Rhetoric of Wage Minimizers" at 215 (Ph.D. diss., Florida State U. 1990). In an article derived from the dissertation, the author mistakenly views the exemption as total, not understanding that as an exemption from enterprise coverage it still permits individual coverage of workers individually engaged in commerce. Paul Kamolnick, "American Workers and the Future of Minimum Wage Politics," 25 (2) *Rev. Radical Political Economics* 26-49 at 32-33 (June 1993).

[15]Lewin Joel III, *Every Employee's Guide to the Law* 68 (1993). Julie Athey, *Defusing the Overtime Bomb: How to Comply with the FLSA* 6 (1999), also states that the DOL's interpretation of "interstate commerce" is so broad that "the FLSA covers virtually every employee in every occupation unless the employer or employee is subject to a specific statutory exemption."

journey would prove to be a lonely and jarring one since virtually no one else who should have been familiar with Congress's handiwork expelling employees of small construction contractors from the minimum wage and overtime had paved the road.

This chapter will examine the origins, development, legislative reality and rhetoric, and economic policy behind and consequences of the alleged small-business exemption in the FLSA. It explains how a mandatory fair labor standards regime originally designed to benefit workers and law-abiding employers by putting an end to wage-cutting as a competitive tool, has, perversely, been refashioned to authorize and reinforce such sweatshop methods. During the first quarter-century of the FLSA, small businesses were exempt because they were, by and large, identical with local economic activity, which premodern constitutional jurisprudence deemed beyond the congressional commerce power. Today, when virtually no constitutional obstacle stands in the way of achieving universal minimum wage and overtime protection, Congress is, ironically, excluding more and more workers of small employers from the FLSA. This chapter explains that this exemption is dysfunctional because the new de facto industrial policy is based on a flawed theory of capital accumulation: freeing all of the smallest businesses from minimum wage and overtime obligations merely condemns the vast majority of their employees to working under substandard conditions without enabling more than a few of them to capitalize their wage-chiseling into job-generation. Exposing the juridical forms in which this transmogrification of public policy has been clothed is the purpose of Chapter 4.

In order to focus attention on the bizarrely unsystematic and even blind manner in which the national legislature of the world's leading economy can make and silently invert industrial policy, the analysis uses the construction industry, which was the most radically affected by the 1989 amendments, to illustrate the process. It should have come as no surprise to Congress that the establishment of an enclave of unfair labor standards encourages small construction employers—defined as doing less than $500,000 of business annually, but employing perhaps as many as 10 workers—to use their lawful exemption from the FLSA as a springboard to create a sector of outlawry in which they illegally exempt themselves from the rest of the federal and state labor-protective regime including social security, unemployment insurance, workers compensation, and occupational safety and health regulations. The fact that the roofing contractor mentioned at the outset had been failing to pay his employees time and a half for overtime long before a lawyer informed him that he was exempt underscores the seamlessness of this policy web: Congress was in large part merely legalizing or ratifying what had been rampant noncompliance among small employers,[16] the lawfulness of whose post-1989

[16]The Minimum Wage Study Commission found the highest incidence of overtime violations in establishments with 1 to 9 employees: 26.7 percent of covered/nonexempt

compensation practices was purely inadvertent. This regime of unlawfulness is underscored by the fact that between 1991 and 1995, special trades contractors, the focal point of construction small business, recorded the highest incidence of overtime violations of all industries.[17]

The chapter begins with an analysis of the congressional transvaluation of small businesses, which culminated in a revision of the FLSA largely exempting them from minimum wage and overtime obligations; this statutory change was designed to constrain their employees to subsidize their capital accumulation by depressing wage and hour standards. The chapter then proceeds to a detailed legislative history. First, it is shown that small business advocates' efforts to characterize the FLSA as having always embodied a general small-business exemption are misleading: to the extent that small firms' exempt status was a function of their local and non-interstate orientation, of which their smallness was an indicator, it was logical for Congress progressively to eliminate the exemption as the Supreme Court came to approve a vastly more comprehensive commerce power. The chapter then systematizes the legislative history of the creation of "enterprise coverage" in 1961, which implemented the Court's modernized understanding of the breadth of federal regulation of an increasingly nationalized economy. After tracing the seeds of reversal of this congressional policy of ever broader coverage in 1977, Chapter 4 offers a comprehensive analysis of the 1989 amendments, which is enriched by interviews with many of the crucial participants. A review of further efforts in the 1990s to convert the small-business exemption from enterprise coverage into a total exemption by eliminating coverage of workers individually engaged in interstate commerce or production of goods for such commerce is followed by an empirical analysis of the surprisingly broad impact of the 1989 coverage restriction on the employees and employers in the construction industry. The penultimate section is devoted to explaining how the national legislative process generated such a perverse outcome. In the final section the troubling possibility is raised that, if large capital and organized labor regard the markets in which they operate as immune to competitive wage-cutting from the small-business sector, they might become indifferent to more extreme efforts to deregulate labor standards.

---

establishments in 1979. Brigitte Sellekaerts & Stephen Welch, "Violations of the Fair Labor Standards Act: Inferences from the 1979 Noncompliance Survey," 3 *Report of the Minimum Wage Study Commission* 77, tab. 3 at 83 (1981).

[17]G. Pascal Zachary, "Shortchanged: Many Firms Refuse to Pay for Overtime, Employees Complain," *Wall St. J.*, June 24, 1996, at A1 (Westlaw). Special trades contractors victimized 2.11 percent of employees; apparel makers ranked second at 1.93 percent.

2. The Neo-Smithian Economic Policy Behind the Unfair Labor Standards Amendments of 1989

Senator [H. ALEXANDER] SMITH. I have had called to my attention that the minimum wage legislation in Great Britain and Australia was an outcome of a socialistic government....

Senator [PAUL] DOUGLAS. Historically...in Australia it was put into effect...by the Liberal Party. But in the state of Victoria, which is where minimum wages were tried most, it was by the so-called Conservative Party.

I would like to have the Secretary's statement as to whether he believes the minimum wage is a socialistic institution?

Secretary [of Labor JAMES] MITCHELL. No, sir.[18]

What context could possibly link Karl Marx, who spilled nothing but contemptuous bile on socialist demands for a statutory minimum wage,[19] with the U.S. national minimum wage and overtime law? After all, Marx's account of the 400-year history of Britain's "Blood Legislation...for Depressing Wages," which imposed a wage maximum in order to suppress workers' efforts to take advantage of temporarily favorable constellations of supply and demand in the labor market, but never a minimum wage to sustain their health and welfare, stressed that once the capitalist mode of production consolidated itself, such state-enforced measures were no longer necessary. On the contrary: at that point, refractory workers would be taken care of by capitalism's own "natural laws."[20]

The connection between Marx and the FLSA emerges in the exemptions and exclusions from that statute. The reason for this rather curious link is straightforward. The national minimum wage law fulfills a function analogous to the British maximum hours statutes—which workers in the United States generally still lack[21]—that Marx praised: it imposes limits on the exploitability of especially

---

[18]*Amending the Fair Labor Standards Act of 1938: Hearings Before the Subcommittee on Labor of the Senate Committee on Labor and Public Welfare*, 84th Cong., 1st Sess. 58-59 (1955).

[19]In 1880, leading French socialists asked Marx and Engels' help in drafting a labor party electoral program, which included a reformist demand for a statutory minimum wage, of which Marx said: "If the French proletariat is still so childish that it requires such bait, so is it not worth while drawing up any programme whatever." Letter from Karl Marx to Adolph Sorge, Nov. 5, 1880, in Karl Marx [&] Friedrich Engels, *Werke* 34:474-78 at 475-76 (1966) (the latter part of this quotation is in English in the original); see also letter from Friedrich Engels to Eduard Bernstein, Oct. 25, 1881, in *id.* 35:228-34 at 232 (1967).

[20]1 Karl Marx, *Das Kapital: Kritik der politischen Ökonomie*, in 23 Karl Marx [&] Friedrich Engels, *Werke* 761-70 (1962 [1867]).

[21]See above chapter 1.

vulnerable and unorganized workers.[22] Once such a statute protects the vast majority of a national working class and becomes an integral part of the institutional background of the labor market, those workers who are excluded from its protections are exposed to more palpable and brutal conditions of exploitation. Similarly, their employers, who are exempt from this law, become legal outlaws, free to impose on them the kinds of unfair labor standards that also make these employers unfair competitors vis-à-vis firms that are subject to and comply with the law.

What is the purpose of privileging the creation of these economic free-fire zones? Such a deregulatory program suited not only the rugged individualist rhetoric of the Reagan-Bush decade, but also the then new iconoclastic economic view that small businesses created most new jobs.[23] As presented by President George Bush, whose explanation on the occasion of signing into law the minimum wage increase in 1989 furnishes an epigraph to this chapter, the point of banishing the employees of small firms from the regime of entitlement to minimum and premium overtime wages is transparent enough: to empower small capitalists to use unfettered labor market forces to pay low wages so that they can accelerate their accumulation of capital and facilitate the breakthrough to large-scale operations.

Here Marx reenters. He presented a history of the "so-called original accumulation" of capital to puncture apologetic Adam Smithian fairy tales of a peaceful "previous" accumulation, which were supposed to make plausible the mystery of the concentration of masses of capital and labor power in the hands of commodity producers, which is the result, but also the prerequisite, of capitalist production. In Marx's account this prehistory of capital, by contrast, was a centuries-long bloody process of the violent expropriation of the immediate producers and their forced transformation into the modern proletariat.[24]

In explaining why he and the Congress decided to excuse small employers from paying the minimum wage and overtime, President Bush offered a new variant of the story of the previous accumulation of capital. Unlike the Smithian version, however, it was not set in "that rude state of society which precedes both the accumulation of stock and the appropriation of land...."[25] Instead of choosing a fictitious location, Bush unmistakably placed it in the real late-twentieth-century business world. Ironically, what is mythical about this type of previous accumulation is not its site, but its very existence: the typical effect of privileging a sector committed to unfair labor standards is not to catapult small employers into the ranks of large capital, but to enable already existing wage "chiselers" to survive

---

[22]1 Marx, *Das Kapital* at 279-320.

[23]David Birch, "Who Creates Jobs"? *Pub. Interest*, No. 65, Fall 1981, at 3.

[24]1 Marx, *Das Kapital* at 741-91; Adam Smith, *An Inquiry into the Nature and Causes of the Wealth of Nations* 259-60 (Edwin Cannan ed. 1937 [1776]).

[25]Smith, *Wealth of Nations* at 47.

and to encourage additional ones to start up.

In one ironic sense, however, the supposed basis for the exemption is, literally, set in a quasi-Smithian pre-accumulation state: one-fourth to one-third of all construction business owners report that they used no capital at all to start or become the owner of their business.[26] The ease with which would-be wage-chiselers can go into the construction business and take advantage of the exemption from coverage under the FLSA is even greater than these capital-less origins suggest. Many small special trade contractors, such as roofers, require their customers to pay for materials in advance. Moreover, in many cases the customers also pay the employees' wages: where contractors lack either assets or credit to meet their payroll, they, like the roofing contractor mentioned at the outset, unlawfully shifting their entrepreneurial risk, do not pay their workers until they themselves are paid.

By perpetuating the very conditions that it was the purpose of the FLSA to eliminate, Bush's approach undermines the law's underlying proto-industrial policy of driving such "parasitic" employers out of business and concentrating production in more efficient firms.[27] It also deflects attention from the fact that many construction employers who remain or choose to remain small can afford to pay high (union) wages and still make "a comfortable, if not luxurious living."[28]

It was precisely firms, small or large, that were unable to increase productivity in the wake of mandated wage increases that a wage and hour statute was designed to oust from business in favor of more productive entities. Senator Kit Bond recently illustrated the inversion of industrial policy that has occurred by adducing a small firm's very inability to adapt to external stimuli as the reason for keeping it alive: "If you increase the minimum wage for the smallest of the employers, there are real tradeoffs. The smallest of the small employers, American businesses

---

[26]U.S. Bureau of the Census, *1992 Economic Census: Characteristics of Business Owners*, tab. 14a at 118 (1997) (26.4 percent of all construction business owners needed no capital to start their businesses); U.S. Bureau of the Census, *1987 Economic Censuses: Characteristics of Business Owners*, tab. 15a at 98 (1992) (proportions ranged from 26.2 percent among women, to 32.3 percent among white men, to 40.0 percent among blacks). The start-up capital "includes assets and money that were your own, that were given to you, and that you borrowed." *Id.* at C-1. Since capital requirements in the specialty trades, which constitute the bulk of the smallest employers, are below average for construction, this cross-tabulation, if available, would presumably reveal an even higher percentage of capital-less business founders.

[27]Marc Linder, "The Minimum Wage as Industrial Policy: A Forgotten Role," 16 *J. Legis*. 151 (1990).

[28]Gay Miller, "Union Plumber Fights Nonunion Competitor and Barbs About Bills," *Wall. St. J.*, July 24, 1977, at 1, col. 1, at 17, col. 5 (plumbing contractor earns $29,000 a year on revenue of $279,000 paying $12.33 an hour including benefits to four union journeymen plumbers).

grossing under $500,000 per year, will, in my view, be forced to lay off workers. ... An increase in wages with no increase in productivity and revenues means lost jobs."[29] Moreover, exempting the very employers who are most likely not to pay the minimum wage turns into a farce the carefully orchestrated debates over raising a minimum wage that will not apply to those who need it most. (That farcicalness is underscored by the hopelessly obsolete level of the minimum wage setting: even after it was increased to $5.15 in 1997, it amounted, in real terms, to only 69.8 percent of its all-time highest value in 1968, and remained far below the level attained in all years between 1956 and 1984.)[30]

In an effort to enlist new sources of support for labor market deregulation, Republicans have more recently taken to suggesting that it is also a feminist policy: "Almost 8 million women-owned businesses exist in the United States, and many of those...are very small businesses just getting started. If they are getting started, if they are making a success, we do not want to penalize them and their workers by imposing on the smallest of the small businesses a burden that they cannot handle."[31] President Clinton's administrator of the Small Business Administration (SBA) went even further, suggesting that subminimum wages in small businesses were discounted, as it were, by the fee that workers there owed the owners for employing them in their first jobs, providing general skills, "hiring a large fraction of part time, seasonal and contingent workers," and "bearing the cost of turnover associated with minimum wage jobs."[32]

If these alleged "costs"[33] seem more like the conditions that enable employers to take advantage of workers with little labor market power, just how far national economic policy has regressed, at least rhetorically, since the New Deal can be gauged by Senator Borah's response in 1937 to Senator Pepper's question as to what would happen under the FLSA if an employer could not afford to pay a living wage: "he should close up the business. No business has a right to coin the very lifeblood of workmen into dollars and cents."[34]

Instead, by the 1990s, small firms and their congressional supporters believed that the overtime provision of the FLSA should be closed up. The National Federation of Independent Business's chief senatorial lobbyist—herself the spouse

---

[29]142 *Cong. Rec*. 7410 (1996) (Sen. Bond).

[30]Calculated according to U.S. DOL, "Value of the Federal Minimum Wage, 1938-1997" (http://dol.gov/dol/esa/public/minwage/chart2.htm). Gabriel Kolko, *Main Currents in American History* 326 (1984 [1976]), called the FLSA "irrelevant to human needs...."

[31]142 *Cong. Rec*. at 7464 (Sen. Bond).

[32]142 *Cong. Rec* at. 7465 (Sen. Bond citing from a letter from Phil Lader to the Secretary of Labor).

[33]142 *Cong. Rec* at. 7465 (Sen. Bond citing from a letter from Phil Lader to the Secretary of Labor).

[34]81 *Cong. Rec*. 7796 (1937).

of a small building contractor—testified in 1997 on behalf of an FLSA amendment that would have deprived workers of their entitlement to the overtime premium, permitting, instead, employers to use an 80-hour, two-week pay period and to give time and a half off from work on the grounds that: "Our members cannot afford to pay their employees overtime. This is something that they can offer in exchange that gives them a benefit. ... Let us say you are a building contractor and because of the seasonal nature of the work, you want your employees to work 30 hours 1 week and 50 hours the next because of the way it works. You do not want to have to pay in that second week 10 hours of additional overtime.... [T]he reason why a contractor...cannot...have them work for 50 hours is because he cannot afford to pay the overtime...."[35]

The economist Joan Robinson, adapting Oscar Wilde's bon mot, tweaked Marx by observing that the only thing worse than being exploited is not being exploited—namely, being unemployed. Late-twentieth-century employment policy in the United States appears to be based on a transvaluation of Robinson's dictum: it is not so much that the only thing worse than being superexploited is not being superexploited, but, rather, that being superexploited, that is, working in the unfair labor standards sector, is actually good not only for their hyper-accumulating employers and the economy as a whole, but for the workers themselves. In contrast, even in the midst of the enormous unemployment of the 1930s, the original proponents of the FLSA proceeded from a radically different set of values. Senator Borah, for example, recognized no exceptions to his principle that "American industry can pay its employees enough to enable them to live. ... [W]e have no right to work slaves in this country, either white or black. ... I start with the proposition that the right to live is higher than the right to own a business."[36]

Sixty years later, Senator Bond, seeking allies for an amendment excluding yet more workers from the minimum wage, seemed to suggest that software-billionaires owed their vertical take-off careers from their humble beginnings in a garage to an exemption from paying the minimum wage: "If they become successful, like a Microsoft, as soon as they hit $500,000 annual gross revenue, then the minimum wage goes up to the full amount provided in this bill."[37]

Amusingly, in the real world, even after Microsoft hit $1,000,000 in gross annual revenues: "When it came to the clerical help, Gates had been tightfisted beyond the bounds of the law. Overtime had been paid on a straight-time basis...."[38] Microsoft's first million-dollar year was 1978.[39] In 1980, Microsoft

---

[35]*The Family Friendly Workplace Act: Hearing Before the Subcommittee on Employment and Training of the Senate Committee on Labor and Human Resources*, 105th Cong., 1st Sess. 52 (S. Hrg. 105-12, 1997).

[36]81 *Cong. Rec.* at 7796.

[37]142 *Cong. Rec.* at 7464.

[38]Stephen Manes and Paul Andrews, *Gates: How Microsoft's Mogul Reinvented an*

office staffers

checked into the labor regulations and discovered that they deserved time and a half for overtime—currently and retroactively. When Steve Wood approached Gates about it, he agreed to start paying time and a half but insisted that back pay was out of the question. If the secretaries wanted to file a complaint, well let 'em.

They did. When the state notified Gates that the back pay was due, it wasn't long before Marla Wood got the news:

> Bill comes storming into my office saying he just had a phone call from these people, just livid. This was the one time I was really on the receiving end of one of his rages—I mean just screaming about this and how it was going to ruin his reputation. ...

But before she and her husband departed Microsoft, Marla saw to it that the issue was settled. Although it amounted to only $100 or so for her and as little as $20 for the others, "It was just a matter of principle."

The overtime issue remained a *bête noir* for Gates and his new lieutenant Ballmer.[40]

Implicit in Bond's Horatio Alger story is the admonition to those who work for the vast majority of would-be entrepreneurs who never grow into minimum wage coverage not to despair: their sacrifices make possible the Microsofts of the world. The severe employment-related disruptions associated with the typically brief lives and brutal deaths of small businesses also fed the new ideology of universal risk glorified by market-knows-besters in the wake of the demise of the post-World War II Keynesian boom. In the words of David Birch, the Reagan-era originator of the thesis that small businesses create most new jobs: "Those firms that insulate themselves from fluctuations appear to have cut off the very vitality that keeps their counterparts going. Just as failure appears essential to our system, so does instability."[41]

3. The Nexus Between the Antiquated Notion of Intrastate Commerce and Small Business

[A]n establishment that is under $500,000 in annual gross receipts probably would not be

---

Industry—and Made Himself the Richest Man in America 144 (1993).

[39]Manes and Andrews, *Gates* at 128. Even in its infancy the company was extraordinarily profitable: in 1977, when annual revenue amounted to $381,715, pretax net income reach $112,471. *Id.* at 118.

[40]Manes and Andrews, *Gates* at 144.

[41]Birch, "Who Creates Jobs" at 9.

substantially engaged in interstate commerce.[42]

Initially, the implicit exemption of small employers from the FLSA in 1937-1938 resulted from the trepidations of the legislative drafters in the Roosevelt administration and Congress that the Supreme Court might strike down the statute as an unconstitutionally broad exercise of the legislature's commerce power.[43] A cautious approach was especially prevalent in the wake of the 1936 decision in *Carter v. Carter Coal Company*—the Court's atavistically narrow interpretation of the commerce clause as applied to federal regulation of the coal industry in the midst of the greatest economic crisis in U.S. history:

> The relation of employer and employee is a local relation. At common law, it is one of the domestic relations. The wages are paid for the doing of local work. Working conditions are obviously local conditions. The employees are not engaged in or about commerce, but exclusively in producing a commodity. And the controversies and evils, which it is the object of the act to regulate and minimize, are local controversies and evils affecting local work undertaken to accomplish that local result. Such effect as they may have upon commerce, however extensive it may be, is secondary and indirect. An increase in the greatness of the effect adds to its importance. It does not alter its character.[44]

Based on this unambiguous rejection, the Solicitor of Labor informed the Secretary of Labor in early 1937 that any proposed labor legislation seeking to regulate "business enterprises of a purely local nature" "categorically possesses no constitutional validity."[45] Nevertheless, in April, just six weeks before the FLSA bill was introduced, the Supreme Court upheld the constitutionality of the National Labor Relations Act, which empowered the National Labor Relations Board (NLRB) to prevent any person from engaging in any unfair labor practice "affecting commerce."[46] *NLRB v. Jones & Laughlin Steel Corporation*, in effect overturning *Carter Coal,* finally made it possible to use an economically realistic concept of interstate commerce as the basis of federal labor standards legislation[47]:

---

[42]*Amendments to the Fair Labor Standards Act of 1938: Hearings Before the House Committee on Education & Labor*, 81st Cong., 1st Sess. 95 (1949) (testimony of Harold Nystrom, chief, Interpretation Branch, Office of the Solicitor, U.S. Dept. of Labor).

[43]On the drafters' preoccupation with the possibility that the Supreme Court would strike down the statute, see George Paulsen, "Ghost of the NRA: Drafting National Wage and Hour Legislation in 1937," 67 *Soc. Sci. Q.* 241 (1986).

[44]Carter v. Carter Coal Co., 298 U.S. 238, 308-309 (1936).

[45]Charles Gregory to Frances Perkins, Jan. 19, 1937, at 1, 4 (Subject: Constitutional Validity of Proposed Collective Bargaining Legislation), in Frances Perkins Papers, Rare Book and Manuscript Library, Columbia University Library.

[46]29 U.S.C. § 160(a) (1994).

[47]Robert Stern, "The Commerce Clause and the National Economy, 1933-1946: Part

"Although activities may be intrastate in character when separately considered, if they have such a close and substantial relation to interstate commerce that their control is essential or appropriate to protect that commerce from burdens or obstructions, Congress cannot be denied the power to exercise that control." The Court, however, did set limits: this power could not be extended to "effects upon interstate commerce so indirect and remote that to embrace them, in view of our complex society, would effectually obliterate the distinction between what is national and what is local and create a completely centralized government."[48] The decision galvanized the Roosevelt administration to push forward with a fair labor standards bill, but some of the drafters were still skeptical that the Supreme Court would find that low wages and long hours spawned labor disputes that obstructed commerce.[49]

In his message to Congress on May 24, 1937, the day on which the FLSA bill was introduced, President Roosevelt conceded that "there are many purely local pursuits and services which no Federal legislation can effectively cover."[50] Although the original administration FLSA bill was titled, "A Bill To provide for the establishment of fair labor standards in employments in and affecting interstate commerce," and its preamble or "legislative declaration" was phrased in terms of the "employment of workers in substandard labor conditions in occupations in interstate commerce, in the production of goods for interstate commerce, or otherwise directly affecting interstate commerce,"[51] the more expansive concept of "affecting interstate commerce" did not survive the conference committee.[52] The elimination of this wider scope was, as the Wage and Hour Administrator, who was to become increasingly frustrated by the limits of his enforcement jurisdiction, later observed, "primarily based on doubts as to whether coverage 'affecting commerce' would be sustained by the Supreme Court."[53]

Those small employers that became exempt from the statute did so by virtue of the design of its narrow interstate commerce coverage provision, which did not even dare to reach the constitutionally permissible limits: intended to regulate only

---

Two," 59 *Harv. L. Rev.* 883, 885 (1946).

[48]NLRB v. Jones & Laughlin Steel Corp., 301 U.S. 1, 37 (1937).

[49]George Paulsen, *A Living Wage for the Forgotten Man: The Quest for Fair Labor Standards 1933-1941*, at 74-75 (1996). The Supreme Court finally approved the "'labor dispute' theory" of coverage in Maryland v. Wirtz, 392 U.S. 183, 192 (1968).

[50]"The President Recommends Legislation Establishing Minimum Wages and Maximum Hours" at 214.

[51]S. 2745, 75th Cong., 1st Sess., § 1(a) (May 24, 1937).

[52]H. Rep. No. 2738: *Fair Labor Standards Act of 1938*, 75th Cong., 3d Sess. 13, 28 (1938); Fair Labor Standards Act of 1938, ch. 676, § 2(a), 52 Stat. 1060, 1060.

[53]U.S. DOL, Wage and Hour and Public Contracts Divisions, *Annual Report* 52 (1946).

those industries and firms most unassailably engaged in interstate commerce, it inevitably left uncovered small companies whose operations were deemed remote from the national market. Thus Senator Hugo Black, who introduced the administration bill and chaired the Education and Labor Committee, reported on behalf of the committee six weeks later, when its revised bill still included "affecting interstate commerce," that the bill "carefully excludes...business...of a purely local nature. [I]t is not even intended to include...those purely local and small business establishments that happen to lie near State lines, and solely on account of such location, actually serve a wholly local community trade within two States."[54] Black, who presided over the first set of hearings, clarified the link between small size and noninterstate commerce by observing that the bill provided "standards for those business units that are actually engaged in and substantially and materially affecting interstate commerce...[l]eaving to the States and the local communities...the power of regulating the small business units that affect the local community only."[55] Senator Black also emphasized that by limiting coverage to "goods which are actually manufactured for transportation and are transported in interstate commerce," the bill "eliminate[d]...any idea that this is an effort to regulate wages and hours in the various service employments...."[56] Assistant Attorney General Robert Jackson, the administration's chief spokesman at the hearings, whose task was to address the constitutional issues of the commerce power, added that as a result of administrative impracticalities, "perhaps it is best at the present moment not to attempt to regulate...[s]mall employers...."[57]

This legislative cautiousness, however, soon proved superfluous. As early as 1941—at a time when the Wage and Hour Division (WHD) of the U.S. Department of Labor (DOL) had already observed an incipient trend toward "balkanization" as some manufacturing firms began to localize their operations to avoid FLSA coverage and take advantage of cheaper labor[58]—the Supreme Court, in rejecting a commerce clause-based attack against the FLSA, signaled that an employer's size alone did not compel a constitutionally based exemption:

> Congress, to attain its objective in the suppression of nationwide competition in interstate commerce by goods produced under substandard conditions, has made no distinction as

---

[54]S. Rep. No. 884: *Fair Labor Standards Act*, 75th Cong., 1st Sess. 5 (1937).

[55]*Fair Labor Standards Act of 1937: Joint Hearings Before the Senate Committee on Education and Labor and the House Committee on Labor*, 75th Cong., 1st Sess. 36 (1937).

[56]81 *Cong. Rec.* 7648 (1937).

[57]*Fair Labor Standards Act of 1937* at 49.

[58]Rufus Poole, "Relationship of State and Federal Wage and Hour Legislation," 31 (1) *Am. Lab. Leg. Rev.* 18-21 at 19 (Mar. 1941). Poole was the assistant general counsel at the WHD.

to the volume or amount of shipments in the commerce or of production for commerce by any particular shipper or producer. It recognized that in present day industry, competition by a small part may affect the whole and that the total effect of the competition of many small producers may be great.[59]

Indeed, in 1948, when the WHD published data on the size-distribution of covered establishments, two-fifths employed three or fewer employees, including 18 percent that employed only one employee.[60] And in 1961, when Congress adopted the much more expansive enterprise coverage approach, the use of a dollar-volume exemption level was designed to "provide more than adequate assurance that the newly covered enterprises will be those plainly engaged to a substantial extent in interstate commerce and should make it abundantly certain that no small local business will be affected."[61] By the 1960s, after the Supreme Court had removed virtually all commerce-clause restraints on congressional power to regulate the economy,[62] Congress pushed coverage to small and local sites within the economic network of which the New Deal drafters of the FLSA could scarcely have dreamt. By the late 1960s, for example, the law required virtually all construction firms, regardless of size, to pay the minimum wage and time and one-half for overtime hours.

A few years later Congress was so confident of the reach of its commerce power that it could even "find[] that the employment of persons in domestic service in households affects commerce."[63] Indeed, the way in which Congress fashioned this finding in 1974 verged on a constitutional provocation:

The Committee found that domestics and the equipment that they use in their work are in interstate commerce. For example, vacuum cleaners are produced in only six States, and laundry equipment is produced in only seven States, creating a tremendous flow in commerce of these items used daily by domestics. Also it is common knowledge that every domestic handles such items as soap, wax, and other household cleaners which have

---

[59]United States v. Darby, 312 U.S. 100, 123 (1941).

[60]Calculated according to U.S. DOL, Wage and Hour and Public Contracts Divisions, *Annual Report*, tab. 16 at 85 (1948). The establishments for which no size distribution were available have been omitted from this calculation. The first such data (for 1950) to include construction revealed that 42 percent of the establishments employed three or fewer employees compared to 38 percent for all industries. U.S. DOL, Wage and Hour and Public Contracts Divisions, *Annual Report*, tab. 14 at 276 (1950).

[61]S. Rep. No. 145, 87th Cong., 1st Sess. 44 (1961).

[62]Even the Supreme Court's stunning reversal of its 60-year-old expansive and deferential commerce power jurisprudence in holding unconstitutional a statute that criminalized knowing possession of a firearm in a school zone expressly reaffirmed the broad reach of the FLSA. United States v. Lopez, 514 U.S. 549, 558 (1995).

[63]29 U.S.C. § 202(a) (1993) (added 1974).

moved in interstate commerce.... In addition, employment of domestics in households frees time for the members of the household to themselves engage in activities in interstate commerce.[64]

Yet three years later, a Democratic-controlled Congress set a precedent by increasing rather than decreasing the dollar-volume threshold below which employers were exempt from enterprise coverage. And in 1989, the Bush administration, by maneuvering congressional Democrats into acquiescing in an unprecedented retrograde curtailment of coverage (based on firm size) as the quid pro quo for an increase in the minimum wage, succeeded in excluding a large number of additional workers—potentially including 1.25 million or one-fourth of all construction employees—from the FLSA. In relieving tens of thousands of employers of the necessity of paying their employees the social wage, Congress has chosen to re-expose millions of workers to the bracing experience of total immersion in the sphere of unfair labor standards.

4. The Vicissitudes of Construction Industry Coverage

In my judgment, these people are in interstate commerce. They have been for the last 20 years. However, we have exempted them from the coverage of the act for economic reasons, not for constitutional reasons.[65]

From the outset, the FLSA was dysfunctionally flawed by the discrepancy between its broadly declared objectives and its narrow scope of coverage, intervention, and protection. The "Finding and Declaration of Policy" in the first section of the act announced that Congress sought to regulate interstate commerce in order to "correct and as rapidly as practicable to eliminate" "labor conditions detrimental to the maintenance of the minimum standard of living necessary for health, efficiency, and general well-being of workers" that existed in industries engaged in commerce and production of goods for commerce and were spread and perpetuated through interstate commerce.[66] However, instead of structuring the statute so as to encompass as many workers as possible in order to effectuate this policy, Congress imposed a very narrow conception of coverage and superimposed on this general framework a substantively irrational and scandalously extensive hodgepodge of exemptions of employers and exclusions of workers that made it impossible to block the ramifying effects of wage-cutting throughout an increasing-

---

[64]S. Rep. No. 690: *Fair Labor Standards Amendments of 1974*, 93d Cong., 2d Sess. 21 (1974).

[65]106 *Cong. Rec.* 16,678 (1960) (Sen. John F. Kennedy).

[66]Fair Labor Standards Act of 1938, ch. 676, §§ 2(a) & (b), 52 Stat. 1060, 1060.

ly national economy. In 1981, the Minimum Wage Study Commission (MWSC) determined that 10 percent of the employed workforce was not covered by the FLSA, but exemptions excluded a further 27 percent and 31 percent from the minimum wage and overtime provisions, respectively.[67] This "bewildering array"[68] of exemptions and exclusions, the products of efficacious employer lobbying, have become even more voluminous over time.[69] The commission calculated that "42 exemptions completely or partially exempt almost 30 million private-sector workers" from the minimum wage or overtime provisions.[70]

The construction industry is an important case in point. When the FLSA was enacted in 1938, it was generally believed that most construction workers would not be entitled to the minimum wage or overtime because few could meet the requirement of being personally and individually "engaged in commerce or in the production of goods for commerce...."[71] That year the Wage and Hour Administrator issued an interpretative bulletin stating: "The employees of local construction contractors generally are not engaged in interstate commerce and do not produce any goods which are shipped or sold across State lines. Thus it is our opinion that employees engaged in the original construction of buildings are not generally within the scope of the Act, even if the buildings when completed are used to produce goods for commerce." Some construction workers, however, the administrator ventured to speculate, might be covered. Employees of contractors engaged in the maintenance, repair, or reconstruction of highways, railroads, bridges, pipelines, and other "essential instrumentalities of interstate or foreign commerce would seem to be engaged in interstate commerce," while those employed to maintain, repair, or reconstruct buildings "used to produce goods for interstate commerce would seem to be engaged in a 'process or occupation necessary to the production' of such goods within Section 3(j) of the Act" and thus covered.[72]

---

[67]Stephen Welch, "FLSA Coverage, Exemptions and Violations: Some Institutional Considerations," 3 *Report of the Minimum Wage Study Commission* 1, 14 (1981).

[68]Welch, "FLSA Coverage" at 5.

[69]29 U.S.C. § 213.

[70]1 *Report of the Minimum Wage Study Commission* 107 (1981).

[71]Fair Labor Standards Act of 1938, ch. 676, §§ 6(a) & 7(a), 52 Stat. 1060, 1062, 1063. To be sure, many of the construction workers not covered by the FLSA were protected by the pre-New Deal Davis-Bacon Act, which required contractors on federal government projects to pay prevailing wages, thus protecting local wage levels from efforts by itinerant contractors to depress them by importing workers from other regions to work at lower rates. Act of Mar. 3, 1931, ch. 411, 46 Stat. 1494.

[72]U.S. DOL, Wage and Hour Administration, Interpretative Bulletin No. 5, in BNA, *1940 Wage and Hour Manual* 18, 23 (Dec. 2, 1938; rev. Nov. 27, 1939). See also "Building Workers Under the FLSA," 4 *Wage & Hour Reporter* 282-84 (June 2, 1941).

The Wage and Hour Administrator acknowledged to a committee of concerned employers in 1940 that the situation was a "'Chinese puzzle,'" but did not believe that the courts would apply the FLSA to workers engaged in the original construction of factories that would produce goods for interstate commerce. He added, ironically, that the situation would perhaps be less puzzling "if we disregarded judicial precedents and rendered opinions to the effect that all employees in the building construction industry are covered by the law."[73]

The first estimates of FLSA coverage that the WHD compiled in April 1939 did not even include construction workers among the 4,632,500 covered nonmanufacturing employees.[74] During World War II, the WHD estimated that only 200,000 of 1,500,000 construction workers were covered and subject to the act's minimum wage and overtime provisions.[75]

Despite the huge volume of large-scale industrial, military, and infrastructural construction activity during World War II, even after it ended, the Associated General Contractors of America complained to the Senate Labor Committee that "the greatest uncertainty" existed as to the FLSA's applicability to construction: "The extent to which various construction operations constitute engaging in interstate commerce, or producing goods for interstate commerce has not yet been determined...although the law was enacted in 1938."[76] The committee itself could do no better than offer its guess that construction was "[p]robably covered...."[77]

---

[73]Letter from Philip Fleming to J. S. Capper, president, Toro Mfg. Corp. (May 18, 1940), reprinted in 86 *Cong. Rec.* A3787, A3790 (1940).

[74]*First Annual Report of the Administrator of the Wage and Hour Division United States Department of Labor for the Calendar Year 1939*, at 40-41 (1940). A comparative estimate of coverage in 1939 and 1947 also listed none of the 1,150,000 construction workers as covered in 1939. U.S. DOL, Wage and Hour and Public Contracts Division, *Annual Report*, tab. 13 at 80 (1948). The accuracy of these and all later DOL coverage estimates mentioned is suspect. According to Allan Moss, the chief economist of the WHD, the DOL never even revealed the underlying methodology. Telephone interviews with Allan Moss, Washington, D.C. (Nov-Dec. 1997 and Jan. 1998).

[75]S. Rep. No. 1012, Part 2: *Amendments to the Fair Labor Standards Act of 1938: Supplemental Report of the Committee of the Senate Committee on Education and Labor*, 79th Cong., 2d Sess., tab. 44 at 87 (1946) (data for 1943).

[76]*Amendments of the Fair Labor Standards Act: Hearings Before a Subcommittee of the Senate Committee on Education and Labor*, 79th Cong., 1st Sess. 883-84 (1945).

[77]S. Rep. No. 1012, Part 2, at 91. The committee's uncertainty was in part a result of the fact that although the NLRA provided for coverage of activities affecting commerce, construction was "the only major industry over which NLRB has not asserted jurisdiction." *Id.* Prior to the enactment of Taft-Hartley in 1947: "Few cases were filed from the construction industry because of its widespread unionization and the nature of collective bargaining prevailing, and the Board had no desire to extend its operations into that field." Harry Millis and Emily Brown, *From the Wagner Act to Taft-Hartley: A Study of National*

That construction firms preferred undergoing the anxiety of "the greatest uncertainty" to paying their employees overtime voluntarily and thus avoiding any legal disputes, suggests that at least some construction workers lacked the labor market power to achieve such premium rates on their own—precisely the defect that the mandatory norm was designed to remedy.[78]

These early interpretations and speculations gave a premonition of the complex, narrow, and quasi-arbitrary judicial glosses that would follow as courts in the course of deciding coverage disputes strove to give meaning to cramped statutory language that increasingly conflicted with the FLSA's invasively anti-contractual orientation and the realities of a highly interdependent economy. As late as 1960, just a year before Congress expanded the act's commerce-based coverage, the Supreme Court, in yet another rearguard action denying overtime protection to employees of one of the country's largest construction firms who had built a dam to increase a city's water reservoir capacity, adverted to this tension:

> limits on coverage cannot be understood merely in terms of the social purposes of the Act, in light of which any limitations must appear inconsistent. For the Act also manifests the competing concern of Congress to avoid undue displacement of state regulation of activities of a dominantly local character. Accommodation of these interests was sought by the device of confinement of coverage to employment in activities of traditionally national concern.[79]

In upholding the FLSA against a commerce clause-based constitutional challenge in 1941, the Supreme Court made it clear that the congressional commerce power "extends to those activities intrastate which so affect interstate commerce or the exercise of the power of Congress over it as to make regulation of them appropriate means to the attainment of a legitimate end, the exercise of the granted power of Congress to regulate interstate commerce."[80] But the next year the Supreme Court made it equally clear that: "The history of the legislation leaves no doubt that Congress chose not to enter areas which it might have occupied. As passed by the House, the bill applied to employers 'engaged in commerce in any industry affecting commerce.' ... But the bill recommended by the conference applied only to employees 'engaged in commerce or in the production of goods for commerce.'..."[81]

Labor Policy and Labor Relations 401 (1950).

[78]By the early postwar period, the FLSA's unchanged minimum wage of 40 cents was so obsolete as to be economically irrelevant.

[79]Mitchell v. H. B. Zachry, Co., 362 U.S. 310, 316 (1960). On the company's size, see H. B. Zachry Co. v. Mitchell, 262 F.2d 546, 548 (5th Cir. 1959).

[80]United States v. Darby, 312 U.S. at 118.

[81]A. B. Kirschbaum Co. v. Walling, 316 U.S. 517, 522 (1942). The next year the

With the constitutional obstacles removed, it was up to Congress to enlarge the scope of coverage. The FLSA underwent no changes during World War II, but literally within days of the end of the war, President Truman accorded an important place to amending the statute in his program for the reconversion period. Starting from the position that the "foundations of a healthy national economy cannot be secure so long as any large section of our working people receive substandard wages," Truman proposed an extension of the act's scope. The basis for the proposal focused on avoiding a race to the bottom: "There now exists a twilight zone in which some workers are covered, and others, doing similar work, are not. Extension of coverage would benefit both workers and employers by removing competitive inequities."[82] Truman's State of the Union Message in 1946 repeated the recommendation, shifting the focus to the need for a "decent standard of living" for those who did not "happen to be covered by the act as it now stands."[83]

In 1946 the Wage and Hour Administrator, who was confronted with the problem of enforcing the FLSA, was still complaining of the "serious problem" resulting from the fact that firms operating on an intrastate basis in competition with interstate firms were lawfully able to avoid minimum wage and overtime payments. As a result, the statutory policy of "eliminat[ing] unfair competition in common is defeated." The administrator accordingly recommended that Congress amend the FLSA to reach the "activities affecting commerce" that the Supreme Court has already approved.[84]

That same year, the Senate Education and Labor Committee reported out a bill embodying the Truman administration's coverage recommendations. S. 1349 sought to exercise the congressional commerce power vindicated by the Supreme Court by affording minimum wage and overtime protection to employees of enterprises engaged in an "activity affecting commerce." This key term was, in turn, defined to include "any activity in commerce or necessary to commerce or competing with any activity in commerce or where the payment of wages at rates below those prescribed by this Act or where the employment of oppressive child labor would burden or obstruct or tends to burden or obstruct commerce or the free

---

Court reaffirmed that in the FLSA "Congress did not intend that the regulation of hours and wages should extend to the furthest reaches of federal authority." McLeod v. Threkeld, 319 U.S. 491, 493 (1943).

[82]Harry S. Truman, "Special Message to the Congress Presenting a 21-Point Program for the Reconversion Period," in *Public Papers of the Presidents of the United States: Harry S. Truman: 1945*, at 263, 269, 270 (1961).

[83]Harry S. Truman, "Message to the Congress on the State of the Union and on the Budget for 1947," in *Public Papers of the Presidents of the United States: Harry S. Truman: 1946*, at 36, 58 (1962).

[84]U.S. DOL, Wage and Hour and Public Contracts Divisions, *Annual Report* 51-52 (1947).

flow of commerce."[85] The standards of "competing with any activity in commerce," reminiscent of the extraordinarily broad commerce power approved by the Supreme Court in *Wickard v. Filburn*,[86] and of obstructing commerce, modeled after the NLRA,[87] made it perhaps the broadest scope of coverage ever proposed for the FLSA, especially since the NLRB had never asserted jurisdiction over many of the employers that S. 1349 would have covered.[88] The language would keep reappearing in FLSA bills for years. The bill also limited the exemption for retail and service employers to those with four or fewer establishments with a total annual sales volume of no more than $500,000.[89]

Despite this expansive amendment, the committee did not believe that most excluded workers would be brought into the act. For example, it estimated that the coverage of construction workers would be doubled; but since only one-fifth had been previously covered, three-fifths would remain uncovered. The committee was, however, also relatively unconcerned about the level of coverage: because a large proportion of the industry was unionized, wage rates below the minimum wage or time and a half did not appear to be a major problem.[90] Even the AFL lobbyist, in response to committee counsel Archibald Cox's question as to whether he was suggesting that the act's protection was "seriously needed" in construction, conceded: "Not so far as the minimum wage is concerned."[91] In the event, even

---

[85]S. 1349, 79th Cong., 2d Sess., § 2(d) (Mar. 5, 1946).

[86]317 U.S. 111 (1942).

[87]Ch. 372, § 1, 49 Stat. 449, 449 (1935), codified at 29 U.S.C. § 151 (1994).

[88]*Amending the Fair Labor Standards Act of 1938: Hearings Before the Subcommittee on Labor of the Senate Committee Labor and Public Welfare*, 84th Cong., 1st Sess. 7 (1955) (letter from Stuart Rothman, Solicitor of Labor, to Sen. Douglas) (discussing same language).

[89]S. 1349, § 9.

[90]S. Rep. No. 1012, Part 2, at 92. Calculating the degree of unionization among construction workers has always been made difficult by the extraordinary fluctuations in employment within a year and by the fact that construction unions represent many workers who are employed outside of the construction industry. In the late 1940s total building trades union membership amounted to about 2.4 million. Leo Troy, *Trade Union Membership, 1897-1962*, tab. A-1, A-2, A-3 (1965). In 1951, the president of the AFL-CIO Building and Construction Trades Department estimated the degree of organization at 90 percent, but this figure was unrealistically high. *To Amend the National Labor Relations Act of 1947, with Respect to the Building and Construction Industry: Hearings Before the Subcommittee on Labor and Labor Management Relations of the Senate Committee on Labor and Public Welfare*, 82d Cong., 1st Sess. 57-58 (1951) (statement of Richard Gray).

[91]*Fair Labor Standards Act Amendments: Hearings Before a Subcommittee of the Senate Committee on Labor and Public Welfare*, 80th Cong., 2d Sess., Pt. 1 at 128 (1948). Cox did not get a straight answer to his follow-up question about overtime.

without the amendment, the WHD estimated that in 1947 one-third of construction workers were entitled to protection under the act.[92]

Labor's weakness in 1946 was reflected in the fact that the full Senate passed the bill without the expanded coverage provision.[93] In the House, the Committee on Labor failed even to include expanded coverage in the bill it reported out.[94] This legislative failure prompted the Wage and Hour Administrator to reiterate his plea for expansion of coverage. In 1948, he declared that the "coverage provisions do not make possible the attainment" of the act's objectives of eliminating substandard labor conditions in industries producing goods for commerce or unfair competition in such industries resulting from such conditions. Moreover, the "unequal treatment of employees who work together in the same plant" resulting from individual worker-based coverage caused "dissatisfaction and friction." If, on the other hand, an employer voluntarily paid uncovered employees the same minimum or overtime wages as covered workers, it might be "at a disadvantage in competing with other plants producing for intrastate consumption which do not pay the minimum wage."[95]

During the Republican-dominated Eightieth Congress, the party's omnibus FLSA revision bill, which never got out of committee, would have radically shrunk commerce coverage. It would have amended the definition of "production" by adding one proviso excluding any employee from minimum wage and overtime coverage "if fewer than five and less than 20 per centum of the employees in the establishment in which he is employed are engaged in commerce or in the production of goods for commerce in occupations not exempted under...section 13 (a)...." Under yet another proviso, no employee would have been covered solely by virtue of being employed in a process or occupation necessary to the production of goods for commerce "if his employer (A) is not directly engaged in the production of goods for commerce and (B) less than 50 per centum of the business of such employer is necessary to the production of goods for commerce."[96]

Despite the Senate labor committee's cavalier attitude toward the problem, litigation in the 1940s and 1950s brought by construction workers complaining that they had not been paid the minimum wage and overtime in conformity with the FLSA was voluminous. The court rulings on the scope of interstate commerce coverage of the construction industry were tortuous—"matters," as the Supreme

---

[92]DOL, Wage and Hour and Public Contracts Divisions, *Annual Report*, tab. 13 & 14 at 80-81 (1948).

[93]92 Cong. Rec. 3205 (1946).

[94]H. Rep. No. 2300: *Increasing the Minimum Wage Rate Under the Fair Labor Standards Act of 1938*, 79th Cong. 2d Sess. (1946).

[95]DOL, Wage and Hour and Public Contracts Divisions, *Annual Report* 89 (1948).

[96]S. 2386, 80th Cong., 2d Sess. (1948) (amending § 3(j)) (Sen. Ball).

Court fastidiously put it, "of the nicest degree."[97] A few examples will suffice. During World War II, Brown & Root, Inc., a very large, profitable, anti-union, and—through its financing of the congressional election campaigns of Lyndon Johnson in particular and the Democratic Party as a whole—politically well-connected national construction firm,[98] built an ammunitions depot for the U.S. Navy in Oklahoma. A group of some 60 workers who had worked 10. 5 to 11.5 hours daily every day for a year and a half without receiving overtime wages was rebuffed by the Tenth Circuit, which hair-splittingly ruled in 1949 that:

> It is now well settled that employees engaged in the original construction of a new building or facility are not within the coverage of the Fair Labor Standards Act..., even though the building or facility, when completed, will be used for the production of goods for commerce or as an instrumentality of interstate commerce.
>
> The reason for this rule is that since the new building...has not yet been dedicated to use in the production of goods for commerce, although it may be intended to be so used when completed, such work does not have such a close and immediate tie to the production of goods for commerce as to bring such worker within the coverage of the Fair Labor Standards Act....[99]

The DOL not only accepted, but elaborated on this logic. In 1949 the chief of the Interpretations Branch of the DOL's Office of the Solicitor testified before Congress: "When the man is constructing a building in the first instance for a factory, that building may or may not be used for a factory. There is no way of telling."[100] The perception that such limiting interpretations of the FLSA's reach left little prospect of progressive enlargement of the universe of covered workers prompted the Democrats, after they regained control of the Congress in the 1948 elections, to seek to expand the FLSA's coverage statutorily. Viewing President Truman's re-election as a mandate to roll back the pro-employer policies of the Eightieth Congress, Democrats introduced bills not only to repeal Taft-Hartley,[101] but to modernize the FLSA. In January 1949 administration bills were introduced

---

[97]Mitchell v. H. B. Zachry, Co., 362 at 321. Later opponents of more expansive coverage argued that many judicial decisions upholding coverage had been "ridiculous." 106 Cong. Rec. 16,315-17 (1960) (Sen. Ellender).

[98]Marc Linder, *Projecting Capitalism: A History of the Internationalization of the Construction Industry* 119 (1994). Herman Brown, the owner, "hated Negroes and he hated unions"—the former because they were "lazy" and the latter because they "encouraged laziness in white men." Robert Caro, *The Years of Lyndon Johnson: The Path to Power* 469 (1982).

[99]McDaniel v. Brown & Root, Inc., 172 F.2d 466, 471 (10th Cir. 1949).

[100]*Amendments to the Fair Labor Standards Act of 1938: Hearings Before the House Committee on Education & Labor* at 61 (testimony of Harold Nystrom).

[101]R. Alton Lee, *Truman and Taft-Hartley: A Question of Mandate* (1966).

in the Senate and House creating enterprise coverage by extending the coverage of the minimum wage and overtime provisions so that "every employer who is engaged in any activity affecting commerce" had to pay to each of his "employees employed in or about or in connection with any enterprise where he is engaged" the requisite sums.[102] Once again, "activity affecting commerce," was defined to include "any activity necessary to commerce or competing with any activity in commerce or where the existence of labor standards below those prescribed by this Act would burden or obstruct or tend to burden or obstruct commerce or the free flow of commerce."[103]

With this formulation the administration was frankly trying to "define the scope to the furthest reaches of the commerce power." The provision was designed, as the solicitor of labor testified to Congress, to "reach employees in the States which unfortunately have no State laws to protect them."[104] Among the categories of construction workers whom the Truman administration intended to bring within the FLSA were those engaged in the original construction of new factories, airports, warehouses, office, loft, and other buildings or structures, "which will be used in commerce or production of goods for commerce although they will not become an integral part of existing facilities." In addition, employees constructing apartment houses, stores, and residences would have been covered "if a substantial portion of materials used come from other States."[105]

Pro-labor Democrats had, however, overestimated their legislative strength. In the end, a coalition of Republicans and southern Democrats was able not only to eliminate this approach, but to insert language, designed to roll back coverage of local business, restricting coverage of those engaged in the production of goods for commerce to employees working on such goods in closely related processes or occupations "directly essential" (in contradistinction to the previous "necessary" standard) to that production.[106]

---

[102]H.R. 2033, 81st Cong., 1st Sess., §§ 6(a) & 7(a) (1949); S. 653, 81st Cong., 1st Sess., §§ 6(a) & 7(a) (1949).

[103]H.R. 2033, § 3(n); S. 653, § 3(n). To be sure, the bills also excluded employees of retail and service establishments whose employer had neither more than four establishments nor a total sales volume of more than $500,000. *Id.* § 13(a).

[104]*Amendments to the Fair Labor Standards Act of 1938: Hearings Before the House Committee on Education & Labor* at 27, 26 (testimony of William Tyson).

[105]Tyson, "Memorandum: Scope of section 3(n)," in *Amendments to the Fair Labor Standards Act of 1938: Hearings Before the House Committee on Education & Labor* at 123.

[106]This language was added to § 3(j). For the legislative history, see Paul Sanders, "Basic Coverage of the Amended Federal Wage and Hour Law," 3 *Vand. L. Rev.* 175 (1950). For the Wage and Hour Administrator's realistic interpretation of the restriction, see U.S. DOL, Wage and Hour and Public Contracts Divisions, *Annual Report* 221-22

In the wake of Congress's failure to restructure coverage so as to harmonize the act's expansive socio-economic policy with the potentially almost limitless reach of the commerce power, the federal courts continued handing down decisions ordaining constricted and complex patterns of coverage. Even when construction workers prevailed—sometimes, to be sure, only after an appellate court overturned the trial court judge—the reasoning remained convoluted. The volume of reported federal litigation indicates that nonpayment of overtime compensation was a common practice even among large construction firms on large projects.

In 1952 the Sixth Circuit, in adjudicating another overtime claim, ruled that construction of a new intrastate highway, which after completion would carry interstate traffic, fell outside the scope of the FLSA. A ruling in favor of coverage would, the court observed, mean that "every passable country road is within the same classification for practically every country road, however isolated and however local, at some point carries passengers or freight to or from some interstate destination." Against the background of such slippery-slope logic, the court found that such a "sweeping contention is not sustained by the sound and applicable law."[107] In 1954, the Fifth Circuit chided the parties for even invoking the original construction doctrine in a case of "simply building housing units so that the people of the little town of Ville Platte, Louisiana, could have some place in which to live. Nothing...could be more local and less integrated in interstate commerce."[108]

The updated interpretive bulletin on FLSA coverage of the construction industry that the WHD issued in 1956 summarized several of the most important obstacles to individual employee coverage:

> Unless the construction work is physically or functionally integrated or closely identified with an existing covered facility it is not regarded as covered construction because it is not closely enough related to or integrated with the production of goods for commerce or the engagement in commerce. For this reason the erection, maintenance or repair of dwellings, apartments, hotels, churches and schools are not covered projects. Similarly the construction of a separate, wholly new, factory building, not constructed as part or as an improvement of an existing covered production plant, is not covered.[109]

(1950).

[107]Koepfle v. Garavaglia, 200 F.2d 191, 193 (6th Cir. 1952).

[108]Billeaudeau v. Temple Associates, Inc., 213 F.2d 707, 710 (5th Cir. 1954). The plaintiffs were watchmen on the site who received a little more than half the minimum wage; they argued that they had received building materials shipped interstate.

[109]21 *Fed. Reg.* 5439, 5440 (1956), codified at 29 C.F.R. § 776.26 (1997). This interpretation is still valid as applied to individual employee coverage. Thus where a small employer is exempt under enterprise coverage, its employees could still be individually covered under the jurisprudence developed by the courts under the pre-1961 FLSA and embodied at §§ 776.22b-.29.

The DOL experienced the difficulties in overcoming these obstacles in 1959, when it brought suit on behalf of 72 construction workers of a firm that built a new electronic organ factory that the Baldwin Piano Company of Cincinnati decided to locate in Arkansas in order to avail itself of "the favorable labor market and other advantages...." The federal district court rejected the Secretary of Labor's argument that the workers were engaged in the production of goods for commerce on the grounds that the new plant extended, enlarged, and improved the original plant so as to become integral and essential to the operation of the Ohio plant.[110]

Even after the Congress added expansive enterprise coverage to the FLSA in 1961, courts had to strain mightily to find that workers were entitled to overtime payments in disputes that had arisen under the pre-1961 act. The Secretary of Labor had to file suit on behalf of workers whose employer had failed to pay overtime compensation for work building a woolen fabric manufacturing plant for Burlington Industries in 1959 and 1960. After a detailed discussion of the relationship between the customer's old and new plant, the trial judge concluded that the construction of the new plant was "an integral part of the sequence of activities leading to the production of a different fabric that was to be placed in the channels of commerce, not a mere localized activity insignificantly related thereto. Consequently, the work was "so 'directly essential' and 'closely related' to actual production in or for commerce as to be within...that proximity to commerce which the Act demands as a predicate to coverage."[111] The DOL also sued a general contractor specializing in the construction of manufacturing plants for having violated the overtime rights of its employees who built a plumbing brass factory for Crane Company in Arkansas to replace two others in Chicago and Los Angeles. In 1963, the Eighth Circuit reversed the lower court's dismissal of the action, ruling that it could not "conceive of any new construction more 'closely related' and more 'directly essential' to production of goods for commerce than the relocation-replacement construction of this factory, designed and dedicated to take the place of existing plants and which was to operate as an integral part of Crane's nation-wide business."[112]

So deeply ingrained was the notion of individual engagement in interstate commerce as the basis of FLSA coverage that it was not obvious to all that the novel concept of enterprise coverage had displaced it. Even with regard to a case that had arisen after the 1961 had gone into effect, a federal appeals court found it necessary to instruct at least one trial court judge that he had erroneously failed to find coverage because he had overlooked the fact that Congress had added enterprise coverage in 1961.[113]

---

[110]Mitchell v. Tune, 178 F. Supp. 138, 140 (quote), 144 (W.D. Ark. 1959).

[111]Goldberg v. Barger Construction Co., 210 F. Supp. 752, 755 (W.D. N.C. 1962).

[112]Wirtz v. H. D. McDaniel, 325 F.2d 75, 83 (8th Cir. 1963).

[113]Childress v. Whitley Enterprises, 388 F.2d 742 (4th Cir. 1968).

5. Nationalizing the Interstate Commerce Scope of the FLSA: From Individual to Enterprise Coverage

The amendment would continue to exempt the small independent tradesman who employs his friends and neighbors and whose sense of responsibility for their welfare and his position in the community are the best safeguards against his exploiting his employees.[114]

Even when the DOL succeeded in persuading courts that construction workers were engaged in commerce or the production of goods for interstate commerce, the uncertainty of prevailing and the necessity of having recourse to strained interpretations not only made a mockery of the FLSA's objective of eliminating "labor conditions detrimental to the maintenance of the minimum standard of living necessary for health, efficiency, and general well-being of workers,"[115] but also made it impossible to establish nationally uniform enforcement standards. In view of these socio-economically, politically, and administratively debilitating prospects, it was not surprising that even the Eisenhower administration, joined by a Democratic congressional majority, set out to enlarge the class of covered workers and to reduce the volume of litigation over the interstate commerce basis of coverage. As early as 1955, the *Economic Report of the President* observed that "only" 24 million of 44 million private-sector employees were covered by the FLSA in addition to 3.5 million covered under 20 state wage and hour laws. The President's Council of Economic Advisers was not an enthusiastic supporter of "minimum wage laws, which do not deal with the fundamental causes of low incomes or poverty. However, minimum wage laws can assist the comparatively small number of workers who are at the fringes of competitive labor markets." Despite its fears of "lower production and substantial unemployment" and inflation, the Council, impelled by the recognition that both federal and state laws excluded the lowest-paid workers, concluded: "It would be well for both the Congress and the States to consider the question of bringing substantial numbers of workers excluded from the protection of a minimum wage, under its coverage."[116]

In 1955 the Subcommittee on Labor of the Senate Committee on Labor and Public Welfare, which was chaired by Paul Douglas, a former University of

---

[114]H. Rep. No. 2300: *Increasing the Minimum Wage Rate Under the Fair Labor Standards Act of 1938*, 79th Cong., 2d Sess. 10 (1946) (Democratic minority views of proposed amendment to impose coverage on retail and service firms owning five or more establishments with a total annual sales of $500,000 or more).

[115]FLSA, § 2(a), 52 Stat. at 1060.

[116]*Economic Report of the President* 58-59 (1955).

Chicago professor and internationally famous labor economist, held hearings on bills proposing to amend the FLSA by increasing the minimum wage and coverage. The subcommittee considered S. 662, which sought to expand coverage by defining, once again, as an "activity affecting commerce" "any activity in commerce, necessary to commerce or competing with any activity in commerce or where the payment of wages at rates below those prescribed by this Act would burden or obstruct or tend to burden or obstruct commerce or the free flow of commerce."[117] The bill operationalized this definition, which had been appearing in FLSA bills for years, by creating enterprise-based coverage: the amended minimum wage and overtime provisions required employers "engaged in any activity affecting commerce" to pay minimum wages and overtime premiums to all their employees.[118] The bill did not expressly include construction employees (who had never been expressly excluded),[119] but did cut back the exclusion of employees in retail and service establishments to those employed by an employer having four or fewer establishments with a total annual sales volume of not more than $500,000.[120]

That legislative movement would eventually occur was signaled by the testimony of President Eisenhower's Secretary of Labor, James Mitchell, who based his remarks on the recommendation in the *Economic Report*. Without redefining the FLSA commerce coverage, he testified that it would be possible to incorporate multistate enterprises and other firms engaged "to a major extent" in commerce or production of goods for commerce. But Mitchell also revealed the administration's recognition of the necessity to shift to enterprise coverage:[121] "No

---

[117]S. 662, 84th Cong., 1st Sess., § 3(d), in *Amending the Fair Labor Standards Act of 1938: Hearings Before the Subcommittee on Labor of the Senate Committee Labor and Public Welfare*, 84th Cong., 1st Sess. 2, 3 (1955).

[118]S. 662, 84th Cong., 1st Sess., §§ 5(a) & 6(a), in *Amending the Fair Labor Standards Act of 1938: Hearings Before the Subcommittee on Labor of the Senate Committee Labor and Public Welfare*, 84th Cong., 1st Sess. at 3-4.

[119]Vivien Hart, "The Right to a Fair Wage: American Experience and the European Social Charter," in *Writing a National Identity: Political, Economic, and Cultural Perspectives on the Written Constitution* 106, 117 (Vivien Hart and Shannon Stimson eds., 1993), incorrectly asserted that in the course of having "demolished specific exemptions" in 1966, Congress extended the definition of interstate commerce to include construction: first, construction was never exempt; second, it was not interstate commerce, but enterprise coverage that was defined to include construction; and finally, the year was 1961.

[120]S. 662, 84th Cong., 1st Sess., § 9, in *Amending the Fair Labor Standards Act of 1938: Hearings Before the Subcommittee on Labor of the Senate Committee Labor and Public Welfare*, 84th Cong., 1st Sess. at 5.

[121]*Amending the Fair Labor Standards Act of 1938: Hearings Before the Subcommittee on Labor of the Senate Committee Labor and Public Welfare*, 84th Cong., 1st Sess. at 45.

sound reason appears why the act should not apply throughout these businesses which are controlled on an interstate basis. The claim may rightly be made that industries of such interstate character are already covered under the present language of the act. However, coverage of these industries is spotty due to the fact that it is on an individual-employee basis rather than on an enterprise basis."[122] Mitchell's realism was in part driven by the insight that the "unequal treatment" inherent in the requirement that individual employees be engaged in commerce worked an "injustice" not only to the employees, but also to "the fairminded employer who treats all of his employees with evenhanded justice with respect to the act's requirements. He is placed at a competitive disadvantage with the employer who limits the benefits of the act to some of his employees."[123]

Although no legislation emerged from Congress in 1955, the flurry of similar bills introduced during the remaining legislative sessions of the first and second Eisenhower administration made it apparent that expanded coverage based on a more modern and realistic conception of national commerce was inevitable. Alone the fact that retailing was no longer local—supermarkets had increased their share of total food retail sales from less than one-fifth at the time of the FLSA's enactment in 1938 to more than one-half by 1960—necessitated a reorientation of commerce coverage.[124] Enterprise coverage was acceptable to the administration, but the question of how far the definition of interstate commerce could be pushed was still open. In 1957, when the chairman of the Subcommittee on Labor Standards of the House Committee on Education and Labor, Augustine Kelley, introduced H.R. 4575, which repeated the same expansive definition used by S. 662 two years earlier,[125] Secretary Mitchell rejected it as "broader than any language ever used by the Congress for application of the commerce clause...." Nevertheless, he proposed an administration alternative (enterprise "substantially engaged" in interstate commerce) accompanied by a very narrow wedge of inclusion for firms employing 100 or more employees and receiving more than $1 million in materials from out of state. These very modest changes would have added about 2.5 million covered workers including 200,000 in 100 construction

---

[122]*Amending the Fair Labor Standards Act of 1938: Hearings Before the Subcommittee on Labor of the Senate Committee Labor and Public Welfare*, 84th Cong., 1st Sess. at 43-44.

[123]*Amending the Fair Labor Standards Act of 1938: Hearings Before the Subcommittee on Labor of the Senate Committee Labor and Public Welfare*, 84th Cong., 1st Sess. at 47.

[124]H. Rep. No. 75: *Fair Labor Standards Amendments of 1961*, 87th Cong., 1st Sess. 8 (1961).

[125]H. R. 4575, 85th Cong. 1st Sess., § 3(c) (1957), in *Fair Labor Standards Act: Hearings Before a Subcommittee of the House Committee on Education and Labor*, 85th Cong. 1st Sess. 1565, 1566 (1957).

firms.[126] Although the AFL-CIO found the administration's approach disappointingly limited, the fact that even the unions were, at least verbally and tactically, "willing to support continued exemptions for small-business firms" on the grounds that "the Main Street grocery store" should not be subject to the same federal regulatory power as large chainstore betokened the possibility of eventual compromise.[127]

That the Kennedy administration would eventually engage the issue was prefigured by Senator Kennedy's prominent role in galvanizing support for such legislation in the Eighty-Sixth Congress. As the chairman of the Labor and Public Welfare Committee, he had introduced in the first session (1959) S. 1046, which proposed coverage that was in two respects significantly broader than the provision ultimately enacted. First, going beyond S. 662 of 1955, Kennedy's bill defined the key term, "activity affecting commerce," as including "any activity in commerce, necessary to commerce, or competing with any activity in commerce, or where the payment of wages at rates below those prescribed in the Act, or the employment of child labor prohibited by this Act, burdens or obstructs or tends to burden or obstruct commerce or the free flow of commerce."[128] Second, among the specifically enumerated categories of employers engaged in activity affecting commerce was that of construction enterprises whose annual gross sales volume was at least $50,000—a virtually nominal threshold.[129] A bill, identical in these respects, was introduced in the House of Representatives by James Roosevelt.[130]

These proposals for a significant expansion of coverage were driven by the data, which the DOL prepared periodically and were presented at the hearings, revealing the sectoral distribution of the included and excluded workers. In 1957, for example, overall, only 24 million or 55 percent of 44 million private-sector wage and salary workers were both covered by and not specifically excluded (on some other grounds) from the minimum wage provision of the FLSA. (This denominator excluded an additional 23 million proprietors, self-employed, unpaid farm family workers, government employees, and executive, administrative, and

---

[126]*Fair Labor Standards Act: Hearings Before a Subcommittee of the House Committee on Education and Labor*, 85th Cong. 1st Sess. at 3-4.

[127]*Fair Labor Standards Act: Hearings Before a Subcommittee of the House Committee on Education and Labor*, 85th Cong. 1st Sess. at 34 (statement of Andrew Biemiller, director of legislative dept., AFL-CIO).

[128]S. 1046, 86th Cong., 1st Sess., § 2(c) (1959), in *To Amend the Fair Labor Standards Act: Hearings Before the Subcommittee on Labor of the Senate Committee on Labor and Public Welfare*, 86th Cong., 1st Sess., 2, 3 (1959).

[129]S. 1046, 86th Cong., 1st Sess., § 2(c) (1959), in *To Amend the Fair Labor Standards Act: Hearings Before the Subcommittee on Labor of the Senate Committee on Labor and Public Welfare* at 3-4.

[130]H.R. 4488, 86th Cong., 1st Sess., §§ 3 (s) & (t) (Feb. 16, 1959).

professional employees.) This proportion varied from 99 percent in mining and 95 percent in manufacturing to 17 percent in services, 3 percent in retail trade, and 0 in agriculture and domestic employment. Of 2,909,000 construction workers, the DOL estimated that only 44 percent were covered and not excluded. Failure to meet the FLSA's definition of interstate commerce accounted for almost all the 1,616,000 excluded construction workers: 1,567,000 fell into this category, whereas only 49,000 were excluded on some other grounds.[131] The DOL also estimated that S. 1046 would have offered minimum wage protection to about 40 percent of all excluded workers. In construction, the low exemption threshold of $50,000 would have brought in about 85 percent of all excluded workers. To be sure, whereas almost one-half of all the additional workers entitled to the minimum wage had been receiving less than the proposed minimum of $1.25, only 10 percent of the newly covered construction workers would have fallen into that group. But a much larger proportion of construction workers would have become newly entitled to time and one-half for overtime.[132]

In a special legislative message in May 1960, during the last congressional session of his presidency, Eisenhower characterized an expansion of coverage (to include three million more workers) as the most urgently needed change in the FLSA.[133] After his nomination as the Democratic presidential candidate in the summer of 1960, Senator Kennedy successfully pushed S. 3758, which contained coverage based on an "enterprise engaged in an activity affecting commerce," through the Senate.[134] Kennedy's bill originally covered construction enterprises with annual gross sales in excess of $50,000, but after considerable and complicated legislative maneuvering, the threshold was ultimately set at $350,000.[135]

---

[131]In contrast, overall, 27 percent of all excluded workers were excluded for reasons other than a failure to meet the interstate commerce definition.

[132]Calculated according to *To Amend the Fair Labor Standards Act: Hearings Before the Subcommittee on Labor of the Senate Committee on Labor and Public Welfare*, Appendix A, tab. 1 & 2 at 56-57 (attached to statement of Stanley Ruttenberg, director of research, AFL-CIO). Charts 1-3, in *id.* at 17-19, present the tabular data in the form of graphs. The data on overtime coverage were not presented. For reasons that are not clear, although the aggregate data were similar four years earlier, the DOL estimated that in 1953 only 614,000 or 24 percent of all 2,565,000 construction workers were covered by the FLSA. *Amending the Fair Labor Standards Act of 1938: Hearings Before the Subcommittee on Labor of the Senate Committee on Labor and Public Welfare*, 84th Cong., 2d Sess., tab. 1 at 49 (1956).

[133]"Special Message to the Congress on the Legislative Program," in *Public Papers of the Presidents of the United States: Dwight D. Eisenhower: 1960-61*, at 385, 392-93 (1961 [May 3, 1960]).

[134]S. 3758, 86th Cong., 2d Sess., §§ 2(s) & (t); S. Rep. No. 1744, 86th Cong., 2d Sess. (1960); 106 *Cong. Rec.* 16,717 (1960).

[135]106 *Cong. Rec.* at 16,214 (explanation of Sen. Goldwater). Goldwater himself had

The corresponding House bill lacked the same expansiveness (the original bill did not even include construction among the enterprises engaged in an activity affecting commerce), and the congressional conference committee failed to reach a compromise, in large part, because the two strong labor standards advocates among the seven House conferees (Roosevelt and John Dent) were outnumbered by conservatives and southern Democrats.[136] Rather than attempt to reach an agreement under these unfavorable conditions, Kennedy preferred to wait until after the election.[137]

Barely two weeks after taking office, the Kennedy administration, through Representative Roosevelt, introduced H.R. 3935 to extend coverage to several million additional workers by including those employed in certain specified classes of enterprises in which employees handled, sold, or otherwise worked on goods that had been moved in or produced for commerce. Construction establishments were covered under this definition if their annual gross volume of sales amounted to at least $350,000; the sales-volume threshold for retail and service enterprises was set at $1 million.[138]

Conservatives, sensing the potential for eventual universal coverage, bitterly opposed the enterprise-coverage approach to interstate commerce. Senator Barry Goldwater, its most vociferous foe, already in 1960 had to "resist to my utmost the term 'activity affecting commerce'" because he could "see no end to the Federal Government's following through." The new basis of coverage was "probably the opening wedge...to completely negating" the Tenth Amendment to the constitution, "the keystone of our Republic. If that goes, we go."[139] Even under the guise of vindicating states rights,[140] the chief opponents in 1961 in the Senate, Goldwater and Everett Dirksen, were unable to mask the fact that despite their solicitude for small local businesses—"It does not take a very large construction business to do

---

unsuccessfully proposed to amend the bill to provide for a $500,000 coverage threshold. Amendment to S. 3758 (June 29, 1960).

[136]H.R. 12677, 86th Cong., 2d Sess., § 2(c) (June 15, 1960); H. Rep. No. 1933, 86th Cong., 2d Sess. 21-22 (1960); 106 Cong. Rec. at 17,673, 18,562.

[137]Robert Leiter, "Coverage Confusion Under the Fair Labor Standards Act," 13 *Lab. L.J.* 139, 145 (1962).

[138]H.R. 3935, 87th Cong., 1st Sess. § 2(b) (Feb. 7, 1961); 107 Cong. Rec. 1823-25 (1961).

[139]106 *Cong. Rec.* 16,212 (1960).

[140]Senator Goldwater asserted that he was "not sitting here as a complete advocate of States rights" because, although he believed that minimum wage regulation should be left to the states, he had "also told the States that if they did not act in this field, the Federal Government will have to act in this field." *To Amend the Fair Labor Standards Act: Hearings Before the Subcommittee on Labor of the Senate Committee on Labor and Public Welfare*, 86th Cong., 1st Sess. 30 (1959).

an annual volume of $350,000"[141]—what they were purportedly seeking to shelter such firms from was not so much federal regulation as precisely the unmistakable nationalization of the labor market and the economy overall:

> The dollar volume standards...are designed to create the impression that the minimum wage and overtime pay requirements are directed exclusively at "big business" and that "small business" falling below these dollar standards will continue to be free from the act's requirements and will thereby be unaffected by the economic effects of the extended coverage. Actually, this is mere surface appearance; the reality is otherwise. A small business, in all of its activities, competes directly with large enterprises in the same industry; it also competes with all other industries in the same labor market for the available supply of labor.
>
> If the larger enterprises are compelled by law to pay higher wages, small business operating in the same labor market must pay the same rates in order to secure or retain employees. Thus, the exemptions or the freedom from coverage the committee bill seems to extend to some small business is nothing but delusion.[142]

In other words, Goldwater was arguing a variant of the dictum that "[t]he laws of trade are stronger than the laws of men."[143] The twist here was that because covered and exempt sectors were communicating vessels, the laws of the market would in effect bring about the universalization of coverage that the legislature could not. Goldwater's concern seemed to lie with the alleged market-mediated impact of the legal regime on small businesses. In fact, however, Goldwater did not believe in the reality of the underlying economic model that he postulated. His real objective was to protect larger businesses from the "unfair and arbitrary" and "harshly discriminatory" dollar-volume criterion that would privilege the smaller competitor "across the street" not to pay the minimum wage and overtime premiums. Since Goldwater was himself the owner of a larger retail enterprise, his passion about the competitive disadvantage was not surprising.[144]

As enacted, the statute incorporated the $350,000- and $1,000,000-dollar-volume threshold for construction and retail-service enterprises, respectively,[145] and

---

[141]S. Rep. No. 145, at 101. Goldwater had noted a year earlier that a "substantial segment of those in the construction industry would satisfy these tests, because many of them have at least one employee who receives some materials from out of the State, and do a gross annual business of at least $350,000." 106 *Cong. Rec.* at 16, 213.

[142]S. Rep. No. 145, at 77.

[143]1 William Cook, *A Treatise on the Laws of Corporations* vi (4th ed. 1898).

[144]106 *Cong. Rec.* at 16,213.

[145]Fair Labor Standards Act Amendments of 1961, Pub. L. No. 87-30, § 2(c), 75 Stat. at 66. The $350,000 exemption level for construction appeared in the same new definitions section as § 3(s)(4). In addition to exempting retail and service enterprises doing less than $1 million of business, the amendments excluded any employee employed

defined an "enterprise engaged in commerce or production of goods for commerce" as meaning "any of the following in the activities of which employees are so engaged, including employees handling, selling, or otherwise working on goods that have been moved in or produced for commerce by any person."[146] Congress estimated that about one million of the 4.1 million newly covered employees—leaving 16 million nonsupervisory private-sector employees still outside the reach of the FLSA—were construction workers.[147]

The crucial point about enterprise coverage was and remains that the law did not treat firms situated on opposite sides of the dollar-volume threshold as mirror images of each other: whereas the test was designed to create expanded, blanket, coverage in the larger firms for all employees, regardless of whether they were individually engaged in commerce or the production of goods for commerce,[148] it did *not* create a corresponding blanket small business exemption for the smaller firms. Small firms remained covered, as they had always been, with respect to

---

in an establishment with sales of less than $250,000 even if it was part of an enterprise with sales of more than $1 million. Fair Labor Standards Act Amendments of 1961, Pub. L. No. 87-30, § 9, 75 Stat. 65, 71.

[146]Fair Labor Standards Act Amendments of 1961, Pub. L. No. 87-30, § 2(c), 75 Stat. 65, 66. Five years later a covered enterprise was definitionally simplified to mean "an enterprise which has employees engaged in commerce or the production of goods for commerce, including employees handling, selling, or otherwise working on goods that have been moved in or produced for commerce by any person...." Fair Labor Standards Amendments of 1966, Pub. L. No. 89-601, § 2(c), 80 Stat. 830, 831. In 1974, Congress amended the last part of the provision again to read, as it still does: "or employees handling, selling, or otherwise working on goods or materials...." Fair Labor Standards Amendments of 1974, Pub. L. No. 93-259, § 6(a)(5), 88 Stat. 55, 59. The point of substituting "or" for "including" was to emphasize that the clause "was intended as an additional basis of coverage." S. Rep. No. 690, 93d Cong., 2d Sess. 17 (1974). Congress added "materials" to "make clear the Congressional intent to include within this additional basis of coverage the handling of goods consumed in the employer's business, as, e.g., the soap used by a laundry." *Id.*

[147]S. Rep. No. 145, 87th Cong., 1st Sess. 1, 31 (1961).

[148]The Supreme Court erred in stating that the effect of the introduction of enterprise coverage "was to extend protection to the fellow employees of any employee who would have been protected by the original Act, but not to enlarge the class of employers subject to the Act." Maryland v. Wirtz, 392 U.S. at 188. Enterprise coverage did significantly enlarge the class of employers subject to the FLSA by encompassing for the first time employers whose employees are engaged in "handling, selling, or otherwise working on goods that have been moved in or produced for commerce by any person." Fair Labor Standards Amendments of 1961, § 2(c), 75 Stat. at 66. For tactful recognition of the Supreme Court's misunderstanding, see Wirtz v. Melos Construction Co., 408 F.2d 626, 628 n.5 (2d Cir. 1969); Dunlop v. Industrial America Corp., 516 F.2d 498, 501 n.6 (5th Cir. 1975).

those employees who were engaged in commerce or the production of goods for commerce. The advent of enterprise coverage did not affect individually based coverage at all in firms below the enterprise-coverage threshold.

A construction employer sought to have enterprise coverage declared unconstitutional on the grounds that Congress lacked the power to regulate firms engaged in handling goods that have left the stream of interstate commerce and come to rest within the state in which they are exclusively used. But the court upheld the innovation to the extent that the employer's activities "exert a substantial impact upon commerce among the several states, which commerce is integrally related to the national economy and the general welfare of the workers therein."[149]

The expanded enterprise coverage of the 1961 amendments did not, however, afford protection to all workers. The $350,000 coverage threshold for construction enterprises still excluded 616,000 nonsupervisory construction employees as of 1964. Of this number, 423,000 or 69 percent were also not covered by state minimum wage laws.[150] The Eighty-Ninth Congress of 1965-66, the executor of President Johnson's Great Society, completed the work of extending coverage to virtually all construction workers by establishing zero-dollar enterprise coverage.[151]

Three identical administration bills were filed on May 18, 1965 by Congressmen Powell (chairman of the House Education and Labor Committee), Roosevelt, and Dent, which would have enlarged coverage by creating an across-the-board threshold of $250,000 in annual sales for enterprise coverage.[152] The hearings that began a few days later provoked hardly any response from construction employers. The only testimony came from the National Electrical Contractors Association, whose public relations director stated that the industry was composed primarily of small businesses employing fewer than 10 workers. He never mentioned the lower coverage threshold at all, instead focusing on the proposed double pay for overtime, which at $9.42 "would seriously be personally attractive enough to me to make me want to enter the industry tomorrow, on the union side."[153] The first appearance of first-dollar coverage for construction employers was H.R. 10518, which Representative Roosevelt introduced on August 17, 1965. The bill established this expanded coverage for enterprises engaged in

---

[149]Wirtz v. Mayer Construction Co., 291 F. Supp. 514, 517 (D.N.J. 1968).

[150]U.S. DOL, Wage and Hour and Public Contracts Divisions, *Minimum Wage and Maximum Hours Standards Under the Fair Labor Standards Act*, tab. 3 at 4 (1966).

[151]Fair Labor Standards Amendments of 1966, Pub. L. No. 89-961, § 102(c), 80 Stat. 830, 832 (1966).

[152]H.R. 8259, 89th Cong., 1st Sess., § 202 (1965). See also H.R. 8260 and 8261.

[153]*Minimum Wage-Hour Amendments, 1965: Hearings Before the General Subcommittee on Labor of the House Committee on Education and Labor*, 89th Cong., 1st Sess. 1662-63 (1965).

laundering, cleaning, and repairing clothing or fabrics as well.[154] The House Committee on Education and Labor reported the bill out a few days later. The report offered no explanation for the change, stating merely that: "There is no dollar volume test for laundries, drycleaning, or construction enterprises."[155]

The minority members of the committee stressed that the new coverage threshold "thrusts deeply into the 'small business' segment of the American economy," which all administrations were "dedicated to protecting against the threat of ultimate obliteration." The minority was too preoccupied with yet another "emasculation of the interstate commerce clause" to focus on the lack of a dollar-volume test for construction. Indeed, it pessimistically viewed the "few meager dollar volume limitations" as having "thinly disguised" the disappearance of that clause. Projecting the trajectory of reduced coverage thresholds, the minority "predict[ed] that eventually, and the time is not far off, even these limitations will be eliminated, and the National Government will become the regulator of all business, private as well as public, local as well as interstate, unless those of us who are concerned to protect the Federal-State character of our Government effectively call a halt."[156] More than two decades would pass before this exhortation would bear fruit.

The process of enacting amendments to the FLSA, which was complicated by the strong resistance mounted against the inclusion for the first time of some farm workers, was prolonged into the next session. In 1966 the main bill was H.R. 13712, introduced on March 16 by Representative Dent, a former union official and long-time vigorous advocate of minimum wage regulation. It too included zero-dollar coverage for construction in his bill.[157]

The sole congressional voice in opposition to the full coverage of construction in 1965-1966 was Representative Dave Martin of Nebraska, a Republican member of the subcommittee of the House Education and Labor Committee that considered the FLSA amendments, who was himself a small business owner. His animus, however, was hardly confined to the construction provision. Rather, he regarded the whole bill as a "continuation of the socialistic trend which started in these United States some 30 years ago."[158] Regardless of his ideologically confused nomenclature, Martin had accurately foreseen in 1961 that the purpose of the new commerce coverage language was "to get the concept accepted that retail businesses should be included, and then, eventually, every single retail store in the

---

[154]H.R. 10518, 89th Cong., 1st Sess., § 102(c) (1965).

[155]H. Rep. No. 871: *Fair Labor Standards Amendments of 1965*, 89th Cong., 1st Sess. 10 (1965).

[156]H. Rep. No. 871, at 76, 77, 79-80.

[157]H.R. 13712, 89th Cong., 2d Sess, § 102(c) (1966); telephone interview with Rudy Oswald, retired chief economist of the AFL-CIO, Potomac, MD (Dec. 4, 1997).

[158]107 *Cong. Rec.* 4646 (1966).

United States...."[159]

At one of the minimum wage hearings Martin referred to the "inequity" that laundries, drycleaners, and construction businesses would "not have any exemption from total sales" and would "automatically come under the provisions of the minimum wage law."[160] That these businesses were "completely covered by the law" would, Martin asserted, "work a severe hardship" on small laundries and drycleaners

> as well as the construction industry and in small towns. I am thoroughly familiar with this because I am in the business. In smaller towns we have these fellows who go out, smaller contractors, carpenters, with one employee. In the summer months when the weather is good and it is proper for construction, they got in and work 10, 12, 14 hours a day and they work on Saturdays. They do not pay any attention to overtime. This is traditional. Yet they are not going to have any exemptions. They are fully covered and are subject to the severe penalties of time and a half and you are going to find...that it is going to raise the cost of housing and remodeling, and so on, in many of your localities throughout the entire country. It is not a fair shake for these people not to give them the same exemptions that you give others.[161]

Dent was eager to respond to this attack. His answer with respect to the laundry industry was straightforward and situated on the national organizational level: for the first time ever, "a complete agreement has been obtained from all" sectors of the industry—commercial, home, and linen. "No one has received a letter from a responsible laundry association against this legislation." Dent's approach to construction was, in contrast, personal and anecdotal: "In the construction field, where I am having construction done right now, I cannot get a big contractor to do a remodeling job. I am paying $4.60 an hour for carpenters and $2.10 for labor. They are not even union; they are not organized. And my town is as small as yours.... You are talking of the past when you refer to wages below $1 an hour. You are not talking about the present day."[162] The absence of any reference to organizational agreement with employers' associations may, possibly,

---

[159]H. Rep. No. 75 at 77.

[160]*Minimum Wage: Hearings Before the House Rules Committee*, 89th Cong., 2d Sess. 83 (1966).

[161]*Minimum Wage: Hearings Before the House Rules Committee* at 11-12.

[162]*Minimum Wage: Hearings Before the House Rules Committee* at 12. Martin was aware of the involvement of employers' organizations. Later in the hearing he explained to another congressman that "the Dent bill, was not written, I must admit, really, by the committee itself. We considered it after it was drawn up, but the subcommittee chairman after consultation with people in various industries and trade associations that are affected wrote up this legislation himself and then the subcommittee was called into session and the bill was presented to us." *Id.* at 83-84.

have been even more significant than its presence in the case of laundries—as suggestive of employers' indifference to the commands of the state at a time when the commands of the labor market made minimum wage and overtime regulation moot. In the mid-1960s, as construction wage rates rose strongly in conjunction with the Vietnam War-driven military industrialization of the economy to the irritation of nonconstruction firms as well, and construction employers offered scheduled overtime hours as a method of recruiting workers in a tight labor market,[163] avoiding the minimal requirements of the FLSA was hardly a high priority for construction employers.[164]

Martin was also alone in seeking to remove the first-dollar coverage provision for laundries and construction from the bill on the House floor. In offering his amendment on May 25, 1966, Martin pointed out that in the original administration bill of the previous May these industries had been included under the general dollar-volume provision: "But somewhere along the line, it was removed." Once again playing his foil, Dent emphasized that all the laundry and cleaning employers' groups had "endorsed this legislation unanimously." If, as Martin asserted, segments of the coin-operated laundry industry opposed the provision, Dent saw all the more reason not to "exempt an industry that automates...." Moreover, Dent found on his own examination that "most of the coin-operated laundries, where they have employees, are owned by persons who play golf regularly, who go to Florida regularly, and have come here to Congress crying about being put out of business, riding here in Cadillacs." Finally, Dent refuted Martin's claim of inequity by replying that "the best measure of fairness has to come from those affected. If those affected are not protesting, then we cannot accept the charge of unfairness." At that point the House rejected Martin's amendments.[165]

Dent's rule-of-thumb is plausible—but only if the affected are aware of what the legislature has in store for them. At the time of the 1989 FLSA amendments, that proviso would be invalidated: it is doubtful whether a single affected worker was aware of the exemption of small businesses from enterprise coverage.

Congress unabashedly boasted of the expanded coverage that the new amendments created. The Senate report declared that its bill would bring under coverage 7.2 million of the 17.7 million uncovered private nonsupervisory

---

[163]"Chicago Employer Groups Impose Overtime Ban in Effort to Restrain 'Pirating' of Workers," *Construction Lab. Rep.*, No. 546, Mar. 9, 1966, at A-3; Don Sider, "The Big Boondoggle at Lordstown," *Fortune*, Sept. 1969, at 106, 109; Business Roundtable, *Coming to Grips with Some Major Problems in the Construction Industry* 1, 7 (1975 [1974]).

[164]See generally, Marc Linder, *Wars of Attrition: Vietnam, The Business Roundtable, and the Decline of Construction Unions* (1999).

[165]112 *Cong. Rec.* 11369-71 (1966).

employees.[166] When the leading construction trade journal reported in September 1966 that the additional coverage of eight million was the greatest extension in the history of the FLSA, and that the added coverage of 583,000 construction workers had been achieved by "dropping all dollar volume restrictions," the *Engineering News-Record* did not even hint that this "legislative plum" to the AFL-CIO would be problematic for employers.[167] Indeed, despite the evidence of any public lobbying in the formal legislative history, one AFL-CIO official recalled that while most construction firms were indifferent to the change, some actually supported it on the grounds that it disposed of a problem that had arisen under the 1961 enterprise coverage dollar-volume threshold: they did not know at the beginning of the year whether they would be covered.[168]

As a result of the first-dollar enterprise coverage, the 1966 amendments "extended coverage to...the entire construction industry,"[169] entitling virtually all construction workers to the minimum wage and premium overtime.[170] For the next two decades, only one-half of one percent of the three to five million construction workers were excluded from the minimum wage. Presumably the only reason that even a minuscule 17,000 to 22,000 workers annually fell into this category[171] was that Congress defined a covered enterprise as having "employees...handling, selling, or otherwise working on goods that have been moved in or produced for

---

[166]S. Rep. No. 1487, reprinted in 1966 U.S. Code Cong. & Adm. News 3002, 3005, 3007.

[167]"Minimum Wage Boosted by Congress," *Engineering News-Record*, Sept. 15, 1966, at 312. See also *Construction Lab. Rep.*, No. 587, Dec. 21, 1966, at A-6; U.S. Dept. of Labor, Wage and Hour and Public Contracts Divisions, *Construction Industry Under the Fair Labor Standards Act as Amended in 1966* (WHPC Pub. 1163, 1966).

[168]Telephone interview with Rudy Oswald, Potomac, MD (Dec. 4, 1997). In 1966 Oswald was an AFL-CIO staff economist; he later became chief economist before retiring recently.

[169]1 *Report of the Minimum Wage Study Commission* 4 (1981).

[170]Arthur B. Smith, Jr., *Construction Labor Relations* 194 (1984) (noting that the 1966 amendments brought all construction firms within the FLSA regardless of dollar-volume and that the coverage tests are "liberal and easy to meet").

[171]U.S. DOL, *Minimum Wage and Maximum Hours Standards Under the Fair Labor Standards Act: 1988 Report to the Congress Required by Section 4(d)(1) of the Fair Labor Standards Act*, tab. A-2 at 58-69 (1989); U.S. DOL, *Minimum Wage and Maximum Hours Standards Under the Fair Labor Standards Act: Reports to the Congress Required by the Fair Labor Standards Act*, tab. 7 at 25 (1991). In September 1989, shortly before Congress curtailed coverage for construction, only 68,000 or 1.3 percent of all nonsupervisory employees in the industry were not subject to the overtime provision. *Id.*, tab. 10 at 31. It is unclear why this figure was three times greater than the number excluded from the minimum wage.

commerce...."[172] Regardless of whether Congress thought about the question and literally meant that enterprise coverage required an employer to employ at least two employees, the DOL and the courts have consistently interpreted it that way.[173]

6. Trial Run for the 1989 Small-Business Exemption: The 1977 Amendments

> Small businesses are the most vibrant segment of our economy. They are responsible for the lion's share of job growth and ingenuity.[174]

In spite of this clear thrust toward universal coverage in the 1960s, the reversal of progressive reductions in the coverage threshold in 1989 was not unprecedented. A Democratic-controlled Congress initiated the process in 1977 when it increased the dollar volume for retail and service enterprises in stages from $250,000 to $362,500 from 1978 to 1981.[175] Neither the House nor Senate bills nor committee reports contained such a provision, which was added as a last-minute floor amendment in both Houses.[176]

The differences among the various amendments revealed congressional ambivalences on the subject of privileging small employers to impose unfair labor standards on their employees that were remarkably absent from the debates in 1989. In the House, congressmen explicitly viewed the three different proposals in 1977 as embodying more and less radical programs. Representative Michael Blouin, a Democrat from Iowa, offered the first amendment, which would have required the Secretary of Labor annually to adjust the dollar-volume threshold for retail and services enterprises by the same percentage by which the price index

---

[172]Fair Labor Standards Amendments of 1966, Pub. L. No. 89-601, § 102(c), 80 Stat. 830, 831.

[173]Employment Standards Administration, WHD, "Fact Sheet No. 14: Coverage Under the Fair Labor Standards Act" (http://www.dol.gov/dol/esa/public/regs/compliance/whd/whdfs14.htm); Rhude v. Jansen Construction Co., 369 F.2d 806 (5th Cir. 1966); Robertson v. Dailey Electric Supply Co., 369 F. Supp. 1069, 1071 (N.D. Tex. 1974).

[174]H. Rep. No. 586: *Small Business Job Protection Act of 1996: Report of the House Committee on Ways and Means*, 104th Cong., 2d Sess. 61 (1996).

[175]Pub. L. No. 95-151, § 9(a), 91 Stat. 1245, 1251 (1977).

[176]Former Representative Michael Blouin, who played a significant part in the 1977 debates, stated that the fact that the amendment was added in the floor debates indicated that the issue was too difficult to resolve in committee even if the floor debate was choreographed. Telephone interview with Michael Blouin, Cedar Rapids, IA (Dec. 12, 1997).

increased. Blouin, who was concerned that inflation had subverted the $250,000 threshold, proposed to confine the increase to a prospective application to businesses that he estimated employed no more than seven employees. His reason for not raising the level immediately to the $475,000 range that inflation-indexing would have suggested was the "real inequity" of "uncover[ing]" four million workers who had become entitled to the minimum wage. Although Blouin believed that Congress could deal with the four million uncovered workers for the future, it is unclear how he envisaged solving the problem caused by every creation of an enlarged sector of lawful unfair labor standards—namely, that "no one wants to force a smaller concern into a negative, competitive situation against a bigger concern that can afford the added impact of higher wages when the smaller company cannot."[177]

Republican Representative John Ashbrook had no patience with Blouin's long-term approach. Instead, he proposed an immediate increase of the threshold to $500,000 and application to all businesses. Ashbrook intended to avoid "wage slicing" by prohibiting employers who had been covered from decreasing the wage of any employee who had received the minimum wage while the employer was so covered[178]—a clause that Congress would thenceforth self-congratulatorily call "preservation of coverage."[179] Democratic Representative Jake Pickle of Texas liked to think of his amendment as a compromise between the other two in that his neither extended beyond retail and service businesses nor applied indexing. Driven by complaints he had received from gas station operators among his constituents whose profits margins had shrunk even without having been covered by the minimum wage, Pickle sought to protect them from business failure as inflated gasoline prices pushed their sales above the threshold, subjecting them to the FLSA. More generally, he argued that the $250,000 threshold was "grossly unfair to small businesses. It must be updated or we will drive out of business thousands of small businesses...." Like other proponents of an increase, he distorted the history of the FLSA by claiming that "[t]here has always been a basic exemption for small business under the minimum wage law."[180] This conflation of a business's intrastate character with small size served to justify Pickle's indifference to the fate of the workers whom he intended to uncover:

> the only real argument that can be made against my amendment is that it might take a lot of people out from under coverage of the Minimum Wage Act. I admit that. ... But it is also a fact that many of these same people were brought under the act simply because of

---

[177] 123 *Cong. Rec.* 29,467-68 (1977).

[178] 123 *Cong. Rec.* at 29,468.

[179] Fair Labor Standards Amendments of 1977, Pub. L. No. 95-151, § 9(a), 91 Stat. 1245, 1251 (1977).

[180] 123 *Cong. Rec.* at 29,469.

inflation. We are not removing new people from coverage, but rather putting them back in the same status they would have been [in] prior to the increase of wages and prices since 1969 or 1973. ...

The committee would want you to believe that we are ruthlessly removing millions from the Wage and Hour Act, that it is a march backward. That is not so. Over 80 percent of the present workers covered are drawing over $3 per hour now—and would not be affected. All we are doing is restoring the equivalent level of 10 years ago.[181]

Pickle's lack of concern as to the future impact was unjustified since employers would have been legally free under his amendment to cease paying the minimum wage even to those previously covered. His position did, however, have the virtue of consistency in one respect: by excluding construction and the other first-dollar-coverage industries from his proposal, he was able to avoid the obvious objection that Congress had not intended to link the proportion of covered workers to some inflation-adjusted sales volume standard. But even with regard to the retail and service industries, the fact that Congress in 1961 and 1966 had planned to drive down the thresholds over time, strongly suggested that its objective was not a stationary proportion of employee coverage, but a progressively rising one as more modern conceptions of interstate commerce permitted the legislature to make plausible the federal regulatory role over labor markets that had once appeared peculiarly committed to local—or, more realistically, no—governmental control at all.

In an instrumental sense, however, Pickle's distorted legislative history was irrelevant: the FLSA, like any other statute, is not a constitution requiring a complicated amendatory process or supermajority favoring change. A majority in each Congress is free to rewrite future history by altering that body's intent. That the new majority found it inadvisable to declare the new pro-employer bias all too bluntly, instead hiding behind an erroneous or perhaps even mendacious rewriting of legislative history, suggests that the residual force of the older impulse toward universal coverage was still potent. The success in 1977 insured that it would no longer be by 1989.

After the House defeated Ashbrook's amendment and passed Pickle's,[182] the Senate took up the same question in debating various amendments to S. 1871. Senator John Tower was the first to take up the cudgels for "'small, small businesses'—those retail and service establishments which range from the traditional 'Mom and Pop' stores to those which may employ...15 or 20 workers."[183] Unable to buttress his claim that "[t]hroughout the history of the minimum wage law, Congress has recognized the need to provide some sort of

---

[181] 123 *Cong. Rec.* at 29,470.

[182] 123 *Cong. Rec.* at 29,471-72.

[183] 123 *Cong Rec.* at 32,893.

relief for these smaller businesses," Tower was constrained to concede that the original exemption for intrastate commerce did not involve a "dollar volume test."[184] Unable to deal with the universalist thrust underlying the creation of first-dollar coverage for construction and laundries in 1966, Tower evaded the issue by claiming: "From what I have been able to determine, there was very little discussion of this action during floor debate."[185] To provide a rationale for his proposed restoration of the $1 million threshold from 1961—which Senator Harrison Williams called "a giant step backward in terms of the whole scope...and coverage" of the FLSA[186]—Tower stood the original purpose of the act on its head. Whereas Congress in 1937-1938 had striven to weaken if not eliminate wage cutting as a competitive tool that kept inefficient firms afloat, Tower argued that the exemption was necessary to "offer some assurance to these very small firms that they will be able to maintain a position of competition; that they will not be swallowed up by huge companies or forced out of business altogether."[187] Tower sought to justify his expulsion of 4.8 million workers from protection—"only 1 million" of whom were below the minimum wage—by asserting that even some small employers earned less than the minimum wage.[188] Tower received his most vigorous support from Senator Goldwater, who, reminiscing about how he had considered $300,000 good sales when he first went into business ("Today we do $31 million"), would have raised the threshold to $2 million.[189]

Senator Leahy then proposed an alternative amendment under which the threshold would have been raised to $500,000; thereafter it would have been raised by the same percentage by which the minimum wage was raised. Leahy, too, was little concerned with the minimum-wage workers whom his proposal would have expelled from the FLSA: after all, "the vast majority are part-time unskilled workers who are in marginal jobs." And in any event, the exemption would be doing them a favor since "[i]t would be tragic if their employment prospects would disappear because the small business employers could no longer afford to keep them hired."[190] Because Tower was convinced that his side had been dealt a "stacked deck"—"organized labor has dictated that there can be no exemption for any small businesses"—he agreed to accept Leahy's lower threshold.[191] In a

---

[184] 123 *Cong. Rec.* at 32,894. Congress in 1938 excluded "any employee engaged in any retail or service establishment the greater part of whose selling or servicing is in intrastate commerce." FLSA, § 13(a)(2), 52 Stat. at 1067.

[185] 123 *Cong. Rec.* at 32, 894.

[186] 123 *Cong. Rec.* at 32,896.

[187] 123 *Cong. Rec.* at 32,894.

[188] 123 *Cong. Rec.* at 32,894.

[189] 123 *Cong. Rec.* at 32,894.

[190] 123 *Cong. Rec.* at 32,895.

[191] 123 *Cong. Rec.* at 32,894, 32,895.

further effort to secure Democratic votes, Tower and Leahy then accepted a grandfather amendment offered by Senator Pell, which prohibited newly uncovered employers from lowering the wage of any employee who had previously received the minimum wage.[192]

At this point Senator Harrison Williams offered what was perhaps the historically and analytically most accurate accounts of the function of the threshold. One of the staunchest congressional advocates of labor standards, in 1971 Williams had introduced a bill in the Senate that would have eliminated the enterprise coverage dollar-volume test, thus including within coverage all enterprises engaged in commerce.[193] Measured against the FLSA's "principal thrust and purpose" to expand coverage, the proposal to increase the dollar-volume test to reflect price increase

> misconceives the history and purpose of the enterprise definition in the act. In 1961, Congress established a $1,000,000 enterprise test of coverage to assure that the act would reach all employees of firms engaged in interstate commerce. However, individual employers [sic] who were, themselves, engaged in interstate commerce were still entitled to the minimum wage, even if their employer did not meet the enterprise test.
>
> At the same time, Congress adopted a separate dollar test for retail and service establishments [which] were given a complete exemption from minimum wage and overtime provisions, even with regard to their employees who were individually engaged in interstate commerce, if the establishment had a gross annual dollar volume of less than $250,000.
>
> Five years later, in 1966, the Congress purposefully reduced the dollar volume test for coverage under the enterprise definition...as a means of expanding the act's coverage. As this was done, it became unnecessary and redundant to maintain the lower dollar volume test of coverage in the retail and service establishment exemption in section 13(a)(2).... Accordingly, in conjunction with the reduction of the enterprise dollar test, the act was amended to delete the dollar test for the retail and service establishment exemption. That exemption, under present law, depends upon the dollar test under the enterprise provision...in section 3(s).
>
> Thus, the proposed amendment would, in effect, not only create an exemption for 400,000 workers employed in enterprises, but it would also reduce coverage to an unprecedented degree, by removing from coverage 3.8 million employees of retail and service establishments.
>
> There is no predicate for this drastic reduction in...coverage.... It is not needed as a means of providing protections for "mom and pop" stores. That is already done explicitly by the act.[194]

---

[192]123 *Cong. Rec.* at 32, 896.

[193]S. 1861, 92d Cong., 1st Sess., § 2(f) (1971); *Fair Labor Standards Amendments of 1971: Hearings Before the Subcommittee on Labor of the Senate Committee on Labor and Public Welfare*, 92d Cong., 1st Sess. 17 (1971).

[194]123 *Cong. Rec.* at 32,896.

Tower evaded a discussion of the history of the relationship between the enterprise coverage thresholds and the exemption thresholds. He charged in rebuttal that instead of denying workers a raise by increasing the threshold, Congress would be denying them a job altogether by failing to exempt small businesses.[195]

An increase in the enterprise threshold was foreordained when Senator Dale Bumpers, a Democrat from Arkansas, proposed a compromise, raising the level in stages to $325,000 by 1980. Bumpers would have accepted a higher level, but recognized the "incalculable damage to millions of employees" that it would do. The fact that the House had already passed a bill with a $500,000 level made it clear to Bumpers that some figure between his and that figure would become law. Yielding to the same realism, Williams immediately expressed his support.[196] Pro-labor supporters were also able to secure a "step-grandfather clause," permitting newly uncovered employers not to pay the higher minimum wage to existing employees, but requiring them to pay those workers no less than the old lower minimum wage and overtime.[197] True to Bumpers' prediction, from the conference between the two Houses emerged a compromise provision under which the exemption level was raised in stages to $362,500 effective 1981.[198]

7. Expanding the Class of Exempt Small Businesses: The 1989 Amendments

I regret that today we give up territory that Congress has fairly claimed, that we take a backward step from the measures Congress designed to protect the lowest paid and weakest group of wage earners in the Nation.[199]

If a Democratic administration and a Democratic Congress found no way to avoid an increase in the enterprise coverage threshold as the price to pay for increasing the minimum wage in the 1970s, it should have been a foregone conclusion that the two would, at the very least, have to be yoked to each other during the Reagan years—if that most anti-labor presidency since the 1920s ever supported an increase in the minimum wage on any terms. Nevertheless, despite these unpropitious circumstances, Senator Edward Kennedy and Representative Augustus Hawkins, the chairmen of the Senate and House labor committees,

---

[195]123 *Cong. Rec.* at 32,897.

[196]123 *Cong. Rec.* at 32,899.

[197]123 *Cong. Rec.* at 32,900. The final vote on the whole bill was 63 to 24. *Id.* at 32,908.

[198]Pub. L. No. 95-151, § 9(a), 91 Stat. 1245, 1251 (1977).

[199]Mitchell v. H. B. Zachry, Co., 362 U.S. at 310 (Douglas, J., dissenting)..

introduced short bills at the beginning of the last Congress of Reagan's presidency in 1987 to raise the minimum wage to restore the purchasing power that had been eroded since the last increase to $3.35 in 1981. In addition to increasing the wage to $4.65 by 1990, they provided for indexation, which had long been sought but never achieved by labor supporters: the minimum wage was to be revised annually so as to equal 50 percent of the average private, nonsupervisory, nonagricultural hourly wage. The bills manifestly embodied maximalist demands since they contained no other provisions.[200]

That a minimum wage increase unaccompanied by an increase in the enterprise coverage dollar-volume threshold was politically unacceptable became clear at a hearing later that year before the House Committee on Small Business. Titled, *Minimum Wage Increase*, the hearing highlighted "horror stories...from small businessmen who are virtually making less than their employees." To mitigate this inversion of the natural class order, congressmen immediately proposed raising the threshold to $500,000 or $600,000.[201] Because 55 to 60 percent of the membership of the National Federation of Independent Business (NFIB), one of the most potent congressional lobbyists, had annual sales of less than this amount, this threshold would have conveniently exempted more than half of that organization's members. Ominously, Sar Levitan, arguably the most vociferous academic proponent of the minimum wage, when asked his opinion about such a step, responded that it "might be worth considering." Unsurprisingly, the committee displayed no interest in his further remark that, because some $500,000-per-year businesses were "prosperous and highly profitable" and thus "not struggling to make a living," he would need more information before judging a universal $500,000 exemption.[202] The next year the House Committee on Small Business issued a report recommending a study of the impact of this exemption since retail and service firms with less than $362,500 in sales employed the largest number of uncovered workers—six million. To be sure, the committee was concerned with the impact on the "many employers whose gross volume of sales...has gone above $362,500" and had thus "'slipped under' minimum wage coverage," rather than with the consequences for their employees.[203]

By March 1988 it became clear that the maximalist demands were unrealizable. At a mark-up session of H.R. 1834, the House Subcommittee on Labor Standards not only voted to drop the indexing feature, but approved an amend-

---

[200]S. 837, 100th Cong., 1st Sess. (1987); H.R. 1834, 100th Cong., 1st Sess. (1987).

[201]*Minimum Wage Increase: Hearing Before the House Committee on Small Business*, 100th Cong., 1st Sess. 29 (1987) (Rep. Bilbray).

[202]*Minimum Wage Increase: Hearing Before the House Committee on Small Business* at 32-33.

[203]*The Minimum Wage and Small Business: A Staff Report of the Committee on Small Business*, 100th Cong., 2d Sess. 28-29 (1988).

ment, submitted by Representative Bob Wise, a Democrat, by 6 to 3, to increase the enterprise coverage threshold to $500,000. The three no votes came from Republicans, who voted for an even more expansive amendment of Representative James Jeffords—who would soon play a key role in the exemption debates—to raise the level to $1 million.[204]

At the mark-up session of the full House Committee on Education and Labor on March 16,[205] Jeffords offered another amendment to H.R. 1834 concerning enterprise coverage. It would have raised the threshold to $500,000 and extended it to all enterprises with the exception of public agencies.[206] Jeffords, who later received the Guardian of Small Business Award from the NFIB,[207] described his goal as "trying to...basically, get us one set of rules to cover small businesses so that they will know as to whether they are or are not exempt, and to reduce the amount of confusion and therefore the amount of potential violations." In contrast, merely raising the threshold, as Wise's amendment did, "did not undo many of the complicated differentiations among different types of businesses"—the "host of special rules that make compliance and enforcement much too difficult." In this context Jeffords mentioned that merely "engaging in laundering or cleaning or repairing of clothing triggers coverage, as does being in the construction business."[208]

Chairman Hawkins opposed the amendment as "highly defective and highly destructive. It turns the clock back, actually, several years." He contended that some industries, such as industrial laundries, did not want to be exempt by a higher

---

[204]"House Panel to Take Up Minimum Wage Legislation," *Daily Lab. Rep.*, Mar. 3, 1988, at A-7 (Lexis); "House Subcommittee Approves Minimum Wage Increase by Vote of 6-3," *id.*, Mar. 4, 1988, at A-14 (Lexis). Jeffords' amendment limited the exemption to companies with 20 or fewer employees.

[205]See generally, "House Labor Panel Reports Out Bill Increasing Minimum Wage," *Daily Lab. Rep.*, Mar. 17, 1988, at A-10 (Lexis).

[206]Amendment to Committee Print of H.R. 1834 Offered by Mr. Jeffords, § 3(a). The amendment, which is marked "JEFFOR378" and dated "3/15," is included in a file, "Full Cmte. Mtg., March 16, 1988, H.R. 1834, Fair Labor Standards Act (continued)," which Silvia Riley, an employee of the House Committee on Education and the Workforce," made available in Room 2181 of the Rayburn House Office Building on Jan. 14, 1998, to Bruce Goldstein, who photocopied it. In 1988 Riley had been the Republican Clerk of the committee.

[207]*Lab. L.J.*, Feb. 1997 (inside front cover) (1994 award).

[208]"Stenographic Transcript of Hearings Before the Committee on Education and Labor, House of Representatives, Markup of H.R. 1834, Minimum Wage Legislation Wednesday March 16, 1988" at 55-56. This transcript, which was also included in the file, "Full Cmte. Mtg., March 16, 1988, H.R. 1834, Fair Labor Standards Act (continued)," apparently, like all mark-up transcripts, may not be duplicated. The quotations in the text are taken from Bruce Goldstein's extensive and verbatim notes.

dollar-volume threshold because they wished to avoid "cutthroat competition." Hawkins also argued that many health care workers would lose minimum wage coverage. Finally, he urged rejection of an across-the-board exemption on the grounds that small businesses received subsidies and other government assistance.[209] Even Representative Wise, who had proposed increasing the enterprise coverage threshold to $500,000, based his opposition to Jeffords' amendment on the "concern...that it would eliminate some of the traditional areas where minimum wage has applied."[210]

Republican Representative Steve Bartlett voiced his support for the expansion of the threshold by embellishing on the reasons advanced by Jeffords. He asserted, without empirical corroboration, that because there were too many different rules, "you won't find a small business that is employing the small business exemption. It is not usable because it is not understandable."[211]

Following the 14-19, virtually straight party-line vote rejecting Jeffords' amendment,[212] the full committee approved the increase in the enterprise test to $500,000 for retail and services businesses alone.[213]

The House Education and Labor Committee in reporting out the bill took numerous liberties with historical truth. The committee declared that by "proposing an adjustment in the definition of an enterprise engaged in commerce," it "continues to support the principle of a true small business exemption." Apart from the fact that Congress lacked a tradition of articulating, let alone enacting, a small business exemption, the committee's account of the "history of periodically adjusting the enterprise threshold test" conveniently omitted Congress's act of "adjusting" it down to $0 for the construction and laundry industries. Instead, it stressed that "[i]n recent years the movement has been upward"—suppressing the fact that the downward and upward "adjustment" embodied radically different

---

[209]"Stenographic Transcript of Hearings Before the Committee on Education and Labor, House of Representatives, Markup of H.R. 1834, Minimum Wage Legislation Wednesday March 16, 1988" at 60-61.

[210]"Stenographic Transcript of Hearings Before the Committee on Education and Labor, House of Representatives, Markup of H.R. 1834, Minimum Wage Legislation Wednesday March 16, 1988" at 62.

[211]"Stenographic Transcript of Hearings Before the Committee on Education and Labor, House of Representatives, Markup of H.R. 1834, Minimum Wage Legislation Wednesday March 16, 1988" at 63.

[212]"Stenographic Transcript of Hearings Before the Committee on Education and Labor, House of Representatives, Markup of H.R. 1834, Minimum Wage Legislation Wednesday March 16, 1988" at 68-71. Rep. Penny, a Democrat from Minnesota, not only voted for the Jeffords amendment, but spoke in favor of it on the grounds that small businesses should be subject to state minimum wage laws. *Id.* at 65-67.

[213]H.R. 1834, 100th Cong., 2d Sess., § 3, printed in, H. Rep. No. 560: *Fair Labor Standards Amendments of 1988*, 100th Cong., 2d Sess. 1, 2 (1988).

labor standards policies. Since the vast majority of U.S. workers were employed in large enterprises, the committee's belief that the $500,000 level "preserv[ed] coverage for the vast majority of workers" was misleading. Then in a tour de force of double talk, the House committee report argued that the "hold harmless" provision prohibiting newly exempt employers from reducing existing employees' wages below the previous minimum wage "will insure that no employee will be adversely affected by the Committee amendment."[214] The committee failed to explain in what sense it had not "adversely affected" workers who, unlike their relatives, friends, neighbors, acquaintances, and most of the working class, would no longer be entitled to the current minimum wage. Moreover, all workers employed in the labor market penumbra of such exempt firms would feel the downward pressure of their lawfully unfair labor standards.

In the following months, members of Congress were "bombarded" with claims that an increased minimum wage would injure small businesses.[215] By June, when the Senate Labor Committee met in executive session, even Kennedy was constrained to offer a substitute bill that not only scaled back the minimum wage increase, but also raised the exemption level to $500,000.[216] Kennedy was presumably retreating in the face of Republican amendments, mobilized by Senator Dan Quayle, to increase the level to $600,000 for all businesses.[217] In the event, Quayle and the other Republicans decided not to press their amendments, which had no chance of passage in committee, waiting instead for the floor debates.[218] Chairman Kennedy, in reporting out a bill with the higher $500,000 enterprise threshold, took a different justificatory tack than his House counterpart. Without explaining why, he declared that the committee took the position that "with the increase in the minimum wage there should be a commensurate increase in the Retail-Service Enterprise Test." The committee boasted of having achieved an almost mathematical equality—35.8 percent and 37.9 percent, respectively. Unlike the House committee, the Senate committee refrained from claiming that the higher exemption had not adversely affected any worker; it even conceded that 1.15 million workers would be added to the group of the exempt.[219]

---

[214]H. Rep. No. 560, at 11.

[215]"Backers of Minimum Wage Increase Seek Support Among House Members," *Daily Lab. Rep.*, May 6, 1988, at A-11 (Lexis).

[216]"Minimum Wage, Plant Closing Bills Are Focus of Attention in Senate," *Daily Lab. Rep.*, June 23, 1988, at A-5 (Lexis).

[217]"Senate Labor Panel to Vote on Minimum Wage, House Republicans Weigh Compromise Offer," *Daily Lab. Rep.*, June 21, 1988, at A-12 (Lexis); "Senate Panel to Vote June 29 on Minimum Wage Compromise," *id.*, June 24, 1988, at A-8 (Lexis).

[218]"Senate Labor Committee Clears Bill to Raise Minimum Wage to $4.55 an Hour," *Daily Lab. Rep.*, June 30, 1988, at A-1 (Lexis).

[219]S. Rep. No. 430: *Minimum Wage Restoration Act of 1988*, 100th Cong., 2d Sess.

Although the stage had been set for floor debates in both Houses over more far-reaching exemptions, they failed to materialize. After Senate Democrats withdrew the bill in September in the face of a successful Republican filibuster, the House never debated the bill at all in 1988.[220]

In the wake of Vice-President Bush's election as president, Hawkins and Kennedy continued to accommodate political realities. H.R. 2 and S. 4, which they introduced on January 3, 1989, both retained their earlier bills' higher $500,000 enterprise coverage threshold for retail and service employers.[221] Following testimony by Secretary of Labor Elizabeth Dole to the labor committees in both Houses of Congress on March 3 and 4 that President Bush would not sign a bill increasing the minimum wage unless the amendments extended what she erroneously called the "small business exemption" (at the $500,000 level) to "all businesses,"[222] the Senate committee on March 13 reported out a bill containing "a revised enterprise test...almost identical to the provision sought by the Administration." Covering up the fact that construction workers, for example, would, for the first time in almost a quarter-century, lose their universal coverage, the committee chose to describe the radical change euphemistically: "the test for small business enterprises is altered to a uniform $500,000 in gross annual sales, eliminating several of the separate tests." The committee stressed that "this more streamlined version of a threshold test...goes a long way toward simplifying this section."[223]

This emphasis on uniformity and streamlining accommodated the concerns of Senator Jeffords, who a year earlier, as a member of the House, had unsuccessfully proposed a similar amendment. Jeffords purportedly articulated the change as a mere "housekeeping" measure designed to "harmonize" coverage.[224] Since

---

24 (1988).

[220]134 *Cong. Rec.* 25,290 (1988). No proposals for a higher or broader exemption were discussed during the Senate debate.

[221]H.R. 2, 101st Cong., 1st Sess., § 3(a) (1989); S. 4, 101st Cong., 1st Sess., § 3(a) (1989).

[222]*Minimum Wage Restoration Act of 1989: Hearing Before the Senate Committee on Labor and Human Resources*, 101st Cong., 1st Sess. 26 (1989).

[223]S. Rep. No. 6: *Minimum Wage Restoration Act of 1989*, 101st Cong., 1st Sess. 28-29 (1989). The reports in the *Daily Labor Report* overlooked this change. "Senate Panel Oks Minimum Wage Hike, Rejects Administration's Proposal," *Daily Lab. Rep.*, Mar. 9, 1989, at A-14 (Lexis); "House Subcommittee Reports Bill Reports Bill to Raise Minimum Wage," *id.*, Mar. 10, 1989, at A-9 (Lexis).

[224]Telephone interview with Mark Powden, Washington, D.C. (Dec. 4, 1997). In 1988-89 Powden had been Jeffords's legislative director; at the time of the interview, he was staff director of the Senate Labor and Human Resources Committee, of which Jeffords is chairman.

Jeffords was not viewed as an enemy of labor,[225] his sponsorship of this change enhanced its appearance as a neutral measure.

The Senate committee also suggested that the higher threshold for enterprise coverage would not lead to a net reduction in the total number of workers covered because the newly excluded employees would be approximately equal to the number of employees "added to the coverage of the Act by the removal of the section 13(a)(2) and 13(a)(4)."[226] Although the report nowhere explained this step, it was referring to the bill's conforming amendment that proposed deletion of sections containing exclusions of employees of certain local retail and service employers.[227] This clear statement of the additional coverage that would result from the deletion, which Jeffords had also proposed in his unsuccessful 1988 amendment,[228] is significant because it refutes the claim made by small employers and Republicans in 1990 and later that a drafting error had produced the deletion as a result of which some workers retained individual coverage.

The one respect in which the Senate provision did not conform to the Bush administration's requirements was the preservation of first-dollar coverage for public hospitals. This exception was the result of expeditious lobbying by the American Federation of State, County and Municipal Employees.[229] That success suggests the possibility that prompt and coordinated lobbying by the construction unions to retain universal coverage might have produced the same result.[230]

The House bill, reported out on March 20, which continued to include the higher $500,000 threshold, lacked the across-the-board extension.[231] The committee's explanation of the increase differed from the one that it had issued a year earlier only in having deleted the misleading claim that "the vast majority of workers" remained covered. Instead, it inserted another misleading claim—that the $500,000 level was less than "the historic $1,000,000 threshold" from 1961.[232] Since that level had already been reduced to $250,000 by 1966, it is unclear in what sense the threshold that had prevailed for only a few years could qualify as

---

[225]Telephone interview with Jim Riley, Washington, D.C. (Dec. 9, 1997). Riley was chief majority counsel to the Labor Standards Subcommittee of the House Education and Labor Committee from the mid-1980s to 1995, and was at the time of the interview a Federal Mine Safety and Health Review Commission commissioner.

[226]S. Rep. No. 6 at 35.

[227]S. 4, 101st Cong., 1st Sess., § 3(c)(1) (Mar. 13, 1989); S. Rep. No. 6, at 7.

[228]Amendment to Committee Print of H.R. 1834 Offered by Mr. Jeffords, § 3(c).

[229]Telephone interview with John Zalusky, Washington, D.C. (Dec. 9, 1997). Zalusky was an AFL-CIO economist at the time and involved in the FLSA negotiations.

[230]Telephone interview with John Zalusky, Washington, D.C. (Jan. 26, 1998).

[231]H. Rep. No. 11: *Fair Labor Standards Amendments of 1989*, 101st Cong., 1st Sess. 3 (1989).

[232]H. Rep. No. 11, at 14.

"historic."

But almost immediately following the issuance of the House report on March 20, a "deal" was struck that the committee would support floor amendments embodying the extension of the $500,000 threshold to industries other retail and service.[233] On March 21, the House Rules Committee recommended passage of a House Resolution, according to which Representatives William Goodling and Austin Murphy, the ranking Republican on the Education and Labor Committee and the chairman of the Labor Standards Subcommittee, respectively, would be permitted to offer for debate an amendment in the nature of a substitute that included the higher across-the-board threshold.[234]

The House debate on March 22-23 took place as choreographed by the deal. Representative Murphy, bowing to the "political reality" of an offer by the Bush administration to do what Reagan had refused for eight years—namely, to sign an increase in the minimum wage—met the other "[c]oncerns of the business community" by agreeing to a $500,000 "exemption ceiling for all businesses" except hospitals.[235] In contrast, Representative Hawkins recorded his surprise—disingenuously, since he had already acquiesced in the higher threshold a year earlier—that his maximalist demand had not sailed through the Reagan administration: "I never dreamed, as the author of this little bill merely calling for some adjustment in the [minimum rate] rate based on the erosion that inflation has caused, that the bill would have picked up such baggage as it has—the tip credit, the small business exemption, the training wage. Unfortunately that is so."[236]

No member of the House spoke against the increase in, or expansion of, the enterprise threshold. Among the very few speakers who even mentioned the issue, two Democrats, including one of the sponsors of the Murphy amendment, misstated the scope of the proposed enterprise coverage provision. Representative Thomas Ridge, the co-sponsor, stated that: "As I interpret the exemption, even agribusiness of $500,000 or less is included in this particular exemption...."[237] And Representative Bill Richardson, who admonished his colleagues not to "break the backs of small business owners who provide employment for many minimum wage workers," opined that "many of the small farm and cattle ranches in my district will be exempted from minimum wage requirements."[238] Although none of their more

---

[233]Telephone interview with Jim Riley, who emphasized that, like many such deals, this one was—and had to be—concluded within a few hours.

[234]H. Rep. No. 13, 101st Cong., 1st Sess. 2, 4-5 (1989). Interestingly, the provision in Goodling's amendment was labeled "Small Business," whereas in Murphy's it was called "Change in Enterprise Test."

[235]135 *Cong. Rec.* 5142-43 (1989).

[236]135 *Cong. Rec.* at 5155.

[237]135 *Cong. Rec.* H860 (Lexis).

[238]135 *Cong. Rec.* at H849 (Lexis).

knowledgeable colleagues corrected them, their understanding was incorrect: since "[v]irtually all" farmworkers are individually engaged in the production of goods for commerce,[239] those working for farmers with annual sales below the enterprise coverage threshold remain subject to individual coverage. Only in the extraordinary case of farms that produced crops to be sold to consumers exclusively within the same state would farmworkers be excluded from coverage.[240] The misinterpretation was, to be sure, largely academic: 62 percent of nonsupervisory agricultural employees were already excluded from the minimum wage and 100 percent from overtime by various other provisions.[241] As expected, the House then voted 248 to 171 for the compromise, the negative votes coming largely from those opposed to an increase in the minimum wage.[242]

The debate in the Senate in April also generated no substantive discussion of the expanded enterprise coverage exemption. Despite the fact that Congress then passed a FLSA bill that embodied many of the preconditions that the Bush administration had laid down—including the almost universal $500,000 threshold for enterprise coverage—the president vetoed it on June 13 on the grounds that the increase in the minimum wage (from $3.35 to $4.55 in three years) was "excessive."[243] Once the House proved incapable of overriding the veto (the 247 to 178 vote being very similar to the original vote),[244] Democratic legislators were forced to accommodate the administration further, but not with respect to the enterprise coverage threshold.[245]

---

[239]WHD, "Fact Sheet No. 012: Agricultural Employers Under the Fair Labor Standards Act (FLSA)" (http://www.dol.gov/dol/esa/public/regs/compliance/whd/whdfs12.htm).

[240]"Goods are produced 'for' such commerce where the employer intends, hopes, expects, or has reason to believe that the goods...will move" in interstate commerce. If such movement "can be reasonably anticipated by the employer" when his employees work on them, "it makes no difference whether he himself or a subsequent owner...of the goods put the goods in interstate...commerce." 29 C.F.R. § 776.21(a).

[241]29 U.S.C. § 213(a)(6); S. Rep. No. 117: *Fair Labor Standards Amendments of 1989*, 101st Cong., 1st Sess. Tab. 2 at 22, tab. 4 at 24 (1989). Agricultural workers are excluded principally by virtue of their employment by employers "who did not, during any calendar quarter during the preceding calendar year, use more than five hundred man-days of agricultural labor." 29 U.S.C. § 213(a)(6) (A).

[242]135 *Cong. Rec.* at 5256-57.

[243]"Message to the House of Representatives Returning Without Approval the Fair Labor Standards Amendments of 1989," in *Papers of the Presidents of the United States: George Bush: 1989*, at 724 (1990).

[244]135 *Cong. Rec.* at 11,776.

[245]S. Rep. No. 117; H. Rep. No. 260, 101st Cong., 2d Sess. (1989).

8. The High Price of a Small Increase in the Minimum Wage

[I]n 1989, the Senate agreed to increase the small business exemption from $362,500 to $500,000. The clear intention was to protect the jobs of those who work in the smallest companies from the backlash of a higher Federal wage.[246]

The changes ultimately embodied in Public Law 101-157 (enacted on Nov. 17, 1989, and made effective April 1, 1990) included the increase of the enterprise coverage threshold to $500,000 and its extension to all businesses except public and private hospitals, schools, and institutions for the aged.[247] Under the heading, "Preservation of Coverage," the amendment also required any enterprise that on March 31, 1990 was subject to the minimum wage provision of the FLSA, but is, as a result of the amendment, no longer subject to it, "to pay its employees not less than the minimum wage in effect...on March 31, 1990" ($3.35), and to pay its employees time and one-half for overtime hours.[248]

This "preservation of coverage" clause, which the committees had falsely characterized as a hold-harmless provision for the benefit of workers, was deeply flawed. To begin with, the requirement that employers continue to pay $3.35 per hour in perpetuity became, as soon as the higher minimum wage went into effect on April 1, 1990, a government-enforced invitation to impose unfair labor standards; with time, as the wage level rose, it could only become even more grotesque. Newly exempt enterprises' ongoing obligation to pay overtime was subject to the same criticism in the sense that to minimum wage workers they were required to pay time and one-half only on that obsolete $3.35 or whatever substandardly depressed wage rates they were paying their workers. In addition, even this diluted duty was undermined by employers' practice of going out of business and reopening as a new entity in order to extricate themselves from even this stepgrandfather clause. Such churning is a particularly prevalent ploy in construction,[249] where large numbers of small firms without any self-detriment seasonally "go in and out of business" anyway.[250] DOL enforcement officials acknowledge that such disappearances and reappearances have made a dead letter

---

[246]137 *Cong. Rec.* S.1584-85 (1991) (Sen. Bumpers).

[247]Fair Labor Standards Amendments of 1989, Pub. L. No. 101-157, § 3(a), 103 Stat. 938, 938.

[248]Fair Labor Standards Amendments of 1989, Pub. L. No. 101-157, § 3(b), 103 Stat. at 939.

[249]Telephone interview with Rudy Oswald, Potomac, MD (Dec. 4, 1997). Oswald, now retired, was for many years the chief economist of the AFL-CIO.

[250]*The Family Friendly Workplace Act: Hearing Before the Subcommittee on Employment and Training of the Senate Committee on Labor and Human Resources*, 105th Cong., 1st Sess. 9 (S. Hrg. 105-12, 1997) (Senator Dodd).

of the provision in construction.[251] Moreover, since the DOL is prohibited from requiring firms to keep records more than three years, it is, in its view, by now no longer able to prove that employers owe any residual obligation dating back to the period before April 1, 1990.[252]

But even apart from such tactics, the robustness of the so-called hold-harmless provision becomes moot over time: given the enormous turnover rate among small construction entities, as pre-1990 small firms go out of business forever and wholly unrelated new small ones are formed, the only ones who will be held harmless, as it were, are these post-March 31, 1990 start-up firms, which are freed from FLSA obligations and free to compete with larger firms on the basis of lawfully lower wages. And even if construction labor market forces compel payment of wages in excess of the minimum wage, the more important issue is nonpayment of overtime, which is "'a very big problem'" even among covered employers.[253] Finally,

---

[251]Telephone interview with Don Chleborad, DOL, Des Moines, IA (Nov. 21, 1997). Strong grounds exist for believing that the DOL has yielded too quickly on this point. Even in the more tenuous case of a bona fide buyer of a corporate employer, courts have held that such a successor may be held liable for the seller's FLSA liabilities where "the new business retains common aspects of the prior business sufficient to allow the legal conclusion of 'successorship'" and the successor knew of the FLSA violations at the time it bought the business. Criteria for testing retention of common aspects of the business include: substantial continuity of the same business operation; use of the same plant; the same or substantially same work force; the same jobs under the same working conditions; the same supervisors; the same machinery, equipment, and methods of production; and the same product manufactured or service offered. Brock v. LaGrange Equipment Co., 107 Lab. Cas. ¶ 34,967 at 45,209 (D. Neb. 1987). *See also* Steinbach v. Hubbard, 51 F.3d 843, 846 (9th Cir. 1995); 29 C.F.R. § 825.107(a) (factors for determining whether an employer is a successor in interest under the Family and Medical Leave Act) . The case of a small construction business owner who merely goes in and out of business would be much easier to resolve. First, it would be unnecessary to prove that he knew of the minimum wage or overtime liability. Second, if he merely closed down one sole proprietorship and opened another, his person would create the identity. Third, even if he closed down a sole proprietorship and incorporated or closed one corporation and reincorporated, if the business were otherwise unchanged, the requisite "degree of business continuity" would be proven. Since Congress's purpose was "Preservation of Coverage," permitting such alter ego transactions to wipe out residual overtime liability would make a mockery of congressional intent. Finally, if small construction companies customarily suspend operations during the winter anyway, it would, likewise, contravene congressional intent to recognize such temporary closures as terminating overtime coverage.

[252]29 C.F.R. § 516.5; telephone interview with Richard Brennan, DOL, Division of Policy and Analysis, Washington, D.C. (Dec. 8, 1997).

[253]Stephanie Armour, "More Workers Putting in Free Overtime Hours," *USA Today*, Jan. 14, 1998, at 5B (quoting John Fraser, Acting Wage and Hour Administrator). Charles Ciccone, "The Small Business Exemption in the Fair Labor Standards Act: Number of

Congress drained whatever residual force remained in the "preservation of coverage" provision by failing to codify it as it had in 1977. Consequently, only the utmost diligence or serendipity would lead even a lawyer to stumble over it in the session law or the notes to the *United States Code*.[254]

Congressional justification in 1988-1989 of the increase in the enterprise coverage dollar-volume threshold as merely adjusting for inflation might have made sense if it historically had been Congress's intent to maintain coverage at some fixed level. But the structure of the 1966 amendments, which lowered the threshold for retail and service enterprises from $1,000,000 to $500,000 and $250,000 in two stages, clearly pointed in the opposite direction. One of the conservative Republican opponents of minimum wage regulation underscored this intent in 1966. Senator Paul Fannin, objecting to the lowering of the enterprise coverage threshold to $250,000, quoted the 1961 Senate report to the effect that the $1 million threshold established in that year for retail and service enterprises was designed to insure that "small local business" would not be affected. He then asked rhetorically: "Is it possible that in the short space of 5 years our opinions on this vital point have changed 75 percent? Is it now felt that a small store with, say, six or eight employees, should be subject to the voluminous provisions of the Fair Labor Standards Act?"[255]

Creation of first-dollar coverage for construction and laundry enterprises was an unambiguous answer: in pushing out to the limits of its interstate commerce powers, Congress made clear not only that it regarded as engaged in activities affecting commerce more and more businesses that it once classified as merely local, but that the "small" in "small local business" would have to dwindle in tandem with the "local." Congress's attempt in 1989 to justify the increase and extended application of the enterprise threshold level on the grounds that "a single small business threshold" was obviously superior to the existence of "several confusing standards to determine applicability of the Act" and "should make it much easier to determine which enterprises are covered and which are not,"[256] overlooked the fact that nothing could be less confusing than the universal first-dollar coverage that had prevailed in construction for a quarter-century[257]—nothing, that is, except the universal exclusion associated with repeal of the

Employees Subject to the 1989 Amendments" at 5-6, in *CRS Report for Congress* (Cong. Res. Serv., 91-307 E, Apr. 2, 1991), totally overlooks the question of overtime in construction.

[254] 29 U.S.C. § 203 at 60 (1994).

[255] S. Rep. No. 1487, in 1966 U.S. Code Cong. & Ad. News 3002, 3043.

[256] H. Rep. No. 260, 101st Cong., 1st Sess. 39, 18 (1989).

[257] Confusion did not, however, disappear entirely. The judge in Donovan v. Doyon Drywall, Inc., 1982 U.S. Dist. Lexis 13705 (M.D. Fla.), proceeded from the misunderstanding that in order to meet the enterprise coverage test, construction employers

FLSA, which was not yet on the practical agenda at that time.[258]

9. Here an Exemption, There an Exemption: Today Enterprise Coverage, Tomorrow Individual Coverage?

There is a certain number of marginal industries which for one reason or another cannot pay a wage which...all of us might believe to be a desirable wage. Society must choose whether it wishes to have those marginal industries continued on a basis of what might be termed marginal wages, or whether it wishes to eliminate them from industry and their production taken off the market, and support them on relief or by other means.[259]

The provision in the 1989 FLSA amendments dealing with enterprise coverage included "conforming amendments," which deleted §§ 213(a)(2) and (4) of the FLSA.[260] Section 213(a)(2) had, beginning in 1961, excluded even from individual coverage under the minimum wage and overtime provisions any employee in any retail and service establishment more than one-half of whose sales were made intrastate if the establishment was either exempt from enterprise coverage or was in a covered enterprise but the establishment's annual sales were less than $250,000.[261] As of the time of the 1989 amendments,[262] section 213(a)(2)

---

had to do at least $250,000 of business. Since the employers did reach that level, the error was harmless.

[258]Despite the expanded small business exemption, Senator Hatch still believed that small businesspeople would suffer as a result of the passage of the amendments. He therefore (unsuccessfully) proposed an amendment prohibiting the 101st Congress from increasing the business costs of any small business (defined as employing 50 or fewer people or having gross receipts of less than $1 million) by enacting legislation requiring additional paperwork, capital expenditures, compliance costs, or taxes. 135 *Cong. Rec.* at 27,855.

[259]*Fair Labor Standards Act of 1937* at 658 (testimony of Noel Sargent, secretary, National Association of Manufacturers).

[260]Fair Labor Standards Amendments of 1989, Pub. L. No. 101-157, § 3(c)(1), 103 Stat. at 939.

[261]Fair Labor Standards Amendments of 1961, Pub. L. No. 87-30, § 9(a)(1), 75 Stat. at 71. From 1938 to 1949, the provision referred simply to retail and services establishments "the greater part" of whose sales was in intrastate commerce. FLSA, § 13(a)(2), 52 Stat. at 1067. The use of 50 percent as a marker of local businesses was inserted in 1949 to "obviate" Supreme Court decisions and rulings by the Wage and Hour Administrator that Congress deemed to "sweeping." Fair Labor Standards Amendments of 1949, ch. 736, § 11, 63 Stat. 910, 917; H. Conf. Rep. No. 1453, 81st Cong., 1st Sess., *reprinted in* 1949 U.S. Code Cong. Serv. 2251, 2263-64.

[262]When the 1966 amendments lowered the retail and service enterprise coverage

stated that the minimum wage and overtime provisions did not apply to "any employee employed by any retail or service establishment...if more than 50 per centum of such establishment's annual dollar volume of sales of goods or services is made within the State in which the establishment is located, and such establishment is not in an enterprise described in section 203(s)...."[263]

This exclusion relieved such locally oriented retail and service establishments of minimum wage and overtime obligations vis-à-vis an estimated 3,415,000 employees as of September 1988.[264] The obvious purpose and effect of the deletion of this exclusion were, as President Bush's Secretary of Labor observed in her statutorily required annual (1990) report to Congress on minimum wage and overtime coverage,[265] to entitle employees of such formerly doubly and wholly exempt enterprises to minimum wage and overtime payments "insofar as they are individually engaged in commerce, in the production of goods for commerce or an activity which is closely related and directly essential to such production, in a workweek."[266] That the intent behind the combined increase in the threshold and deletion of the former exclusions was not to exempt all small firms entirely is clear from the statement in the final House committee report that the amended enterprise test in conjunction with the deletion of §213(a)(2) would "exempt *most* small businesses from the FLSA if their annual volume of sales...is less than $500,000."[267]

About the time the higher minimum wage of $3.80 was to go into effect in April 1990, small business owners and congressional Republicans began claiming

---

dollar-volume threshold to $250,000 as well, the separate but identical dollar-volume for establishment exemption from all coverage became redundant; it was finally deleted as of 1977, from which time forward the enterprise coverage dollar-volume threshold also determined the establishment threshold. 29 U.S.C. § 213(a)(2) (1964, 1970, 1976). For a good overview of the history of the changes in § 13(a)(2), see Conrad Fritsch, "Exemptions from the Fair Labor Standards Act, Retail Trade and Services," in 4 *Report of the Minimum Wage Study Commission* 1, 13-18 (1981). The very complex regulations are found at 29 C.F.R. §§ 779.300-343.

[263]29 U.S.C. § 213(a)(2). The other section that Congress repealed, 29 U.S.C. § 213(a)(4), excluded from minimum wage and overtime coverage employees of an exempt retail establishment (under § 213(a)(2)) if it was recognized as a retail establishment despite making or processing at the retail establishment the goods that it sells "Provided, That more than 85 per centum of such establishment's annual dollar volume of sales of goods so made or processed is made within the State in which the establishment is located."

[264]S. Rep. No. 117, tab. 2 at 23. 29 U.S.C. § 213(a)(4) affected only 8,000 employees.

[265]29 U.S.C. § 4(d)(1).

[266]U.S. DOL, Employment Standards Administration, *Minimum Wage and Maximum Hours Under the Fair Labor Standards Act* 4 (1991).

[267]H. Rep. No. 260, Pt. 1, at 39 (italics added).

that a drafting error had vitiated the increase in and expansion of the enterprise coverage exemption. As an official of the chief lobbyist on this matter, the National Restaurant Association (NRA), declared: "'This was absolutely a mistake....'"[268] They complained that no one had foreseen that the deletion of § 213(a)(2) would mean that individual coverage would be preserved for some workers individually engaged in commerce or production of goods for commerce even in enterprises falling below the enterprise coverage threshold.

The NRA spearheaded claims by small businesses that the deletion of § 213(a)(2) "in effect, repealed the small business exemption" that had been in existence since 1961, making it "virtually useless in most instances." The NRA complained that a restaurant that had, under prior law, been exempt both under enterprise coverage and with regard to individual coverage by virtue of § 213(a)(2), was now for the first time, even if it did less than $500,000 of business, liable for the minimum wage vis-à-vis "employees who handle or process cash, checks, and credit card charge slips, take telephone reservations from customers calling from out-of-state, unload goods shipped from another state, and deliver mail to the post office."[269]

A few months after the 1989 amendments had gone into effect, some legislators began trying to undo the survival of individual coverage in firms exempt from enterprise coverage. On July 20, 1990, Representative Penny and 17 others introduced a bill to amend the FLSA so as to confine coverage only to employees of enterprises engaged in commerce or in the production of goods for commerce.[270] A few days later, Representative Murphy introduced his "Fair Labor Standards Technical Amendments," which would have achieved the same end.[271] No action was taken on these efforts to deprive workers of individual coverage, but on October 17, 1990, Secretary of Labor Dole informed Senate Majority Leader George Mitchell that the so-called conforming amendment had had the "'inadvertent effect' of bringing individual employees of small firms under the law

---

[268]"White House Pushing To Modify Minimum Wage," *Lab. Rel. Rep.*, Dec. 10, 1990, at 463, 464.

[269]"White House Pushing To Modify Minimum Wage" at 464. The DOL does take the position that "a waitress or cashier who handles a credit card transaction would in all probability be subject to the Act." WHD., "Fact Sheet No. 002: Restaurants and Fast Food Establishments Under the Fair Labor Standards Act (FLSA)" (http://www.dol.gov/dol/esa/public/regs/compliance/whd/whdfs2.htm). On the wide-spread violations in restaurants unrelated to the exemption of small businesses from enterprise coverage, see Brian Tumulty, "Work Violations Rob Employees: Unpaid Overtime Is the Worst Problem, Agency Says," *Idaho Statesman*, Dec. 20, 1997, at 1a (Lexis).

[270]H.R. 5340, 101st Cong., 2d Sess. (1990).

[271]H.R. 5382, 101st Cong., 2d Sess. (1990).

for the first time."[272] The next day, the House considered two unrelated issues left over from the 1989 bill. Representative Murphy, the chairman of the Labor Standards subcommittee, sought to "accommodate two separate groups of employers" with regard to matters that the 1989 act had not made "clear" or had "failed to exempt." Representative Bartlett tried to use the occasion to persuade his colleagues that these points were only "two of the four mistakes, drafting mistakes, that were made in the passage of the Minimum Wage Act of 1989."[273] Bartlett considered it "important for Members to understand" that these other two "mistakes...were generally acknowledged to be mistakes." Who had made these "mistakes" and how, Bartlett did not reveal, although he certified they had not been made by Murphy or Goodling, the ranking Republican. Unable to state comprehensibly (or grammatically) what in fact Congress had done, Bartlett, who urged that "the mistakes...be corrected...at some point" that session, asserted that:

> [T]he words of the committee report in section 3, section 3 amends the enterprise test to exempt most small businesses from the FLSA [i]f their annual volume of sales or business done is less than $500,000. Nevertheless, the drafting of the 1989 act, drafted the small business exception which had been in effect since 1961 to totally remove the exemption from small business, not a result that anyone so far as I know had intended, and clearly not the intent of that act.[274]

Although it is admittedly impossible to know what Bartlett meant, others soon made it clear. On the last day of the 101st Congress, Senator Bumpers, on behalf of himself and 16 Democratic and Republican colleagues, introduced the last bill in the Senate, which would have eliminated individual coverage, retaining minimum wage and overtime coverage only for employees employed in an enterprise engaged in commerce or in production of goods for commerce.[275] Bumpers immediately returned to the issue in the next session. Early in 1991, two southern Democrats, Bumpers in the Senate and Mike Espy in the House, introduced bills identical with the earlier proposal. These proposals were disingenuous in the sense that their sponsors falsely advertised them as a mere technical correction designed to restore the status quo ante 1989. In fact, they were a radical break with a half-century of FLSA coverage: they would not merely have reinstated the limited exemptions for local retail and service establishments under §§ 213(a)(2) and (4), but would have eliminated individual-based interstate commerce coverage entirely in all businesses with less than $500,000 of sales in

---

[272]"White House Pushing To Modify Minimum Wage" at 464.

[273]136 *Cong. Rec.* H10,563 (1990).

[274]136 *Cong. Rec.* at H10564.

[275]S. 3271, 101st Cong., 2d Sess. (1990).

all industries.[276]

In explaining the basis of his proposal, Bumpers distorted the history of the FLSA: "Since the enactment in 1938, the Fair Labor Standards Act has provided an exemption for small businesses.... Unfortunately, under current law, that exemption does not exist for all practical purposes."[277] Both of these claims are incorrect. From the outset the FLSA excluded from coverage firms, regardless of size, not engaged in interstate commerce or production of goods for commerce. The exemption from enterprise coverage, which did not begin until 1961 and which Congress increased and expanded in 1989, continues to exist for retail and service firms, but Congress expressly meant to trade it off for inclusion of those employees who are individually engaged in commerce.

The other Democratic senator from Arkansas, David Pryor, supplemented the distortion with respect to its operation. He asserted that "through an unintended deletion of a section of the...FLSA..., all businesses that had employees engaged in interstate commerce would be covered in full...."[278] This claim is false: no employer forfeits its enterprise coverage exemption with respect to employees not engaged in interstate commerce merely because other employees are so engaged. Senator D'Amato offered the most extreme attack by falsely asserting that the "deletion error" not only had left the DOL with "no choice but to determine that all businesses with employees engaged in interstate commerce are not covered under the small business exemption," but that it "will place hardships upon small businesses that have been unheard of in over 50 years of labor law."[279] A determination by the DOL that some employees are individually covered in no way affects a small business's exemption from enterprise coverage vis-à-vis its other employees. Outside of the retail and service sector, newly uncovered construction firms also refute D'Amato's claim since very few if any of their employees are individually engaged in interstate commerce.

Small business lobbyists' success in securing 48 senatorial co-sponsors for Bumpers' bill sufficed to persuade the Democratic leaders of the Labor Committee that they would "have to negotiate some kind of compromise with him to try to limit the damage."[280] In the event, the adamant rejection by Representative William Ford, the new chairman of the House Education and Labor Committee, of a proposal that would expel so many workers from coverage doomed the

[276]S. 349, 102d Cong., 1st Sess. (1991); H.R. 1237, 102d Cong., 1st Sess. (1991).

[277]137 *Cong. Rec.* S1584 (1991) (Lexis).

[278]137 *Cong. Rec.* at S1585 (Lexis).

[279]137 *Cong. Rec.* at S2241 (Lexis).

[280]Sarah Fox, "Background on Bumpers' Minimum Wage Amendment" 6 (July 19, 1991). Fox wrote this internal memo when she was chief majority counsel of the Senate Labor and Public Welfare Committee.

initiative.[281]

The allegation that no one realized the consequences of deleting § 213(a)(2) or that it was a drafting error is directly contradicted by the contemporaneous legislative history. During the debate over H.R. 2 on March 23, 1989, for example, Representative Goodling, a senior Republican member of the Labor Committee, inserted into the record the DOL's estimate of the economic effects of the increase in the small business exemption. This Bush administration DOL document is important because it refutes the claim that no one understood that the deletion of the exemptions in §§ 13(a)(2) and (4) meant that individual coverage would survive the exemption from enterprise coverage. The DOL unambiguously stated that the increase in the enterprise threshold to $500,000 "would exempt additional jobs from the minimum wage, as additional establishments would revert to individual coverage...."[282]

Still more pertinent to understanding the purpose of the deletion is its author. Jeffords, a Republican, as a member of House labor committee in 1988 and the Senate labor committee in 1989, proposed the deletion of § 13(a)(2) in tandem with his plan to raise, universalize, and make uniform the various dollar-volume tests.[283] One purpose of the deletion was to simplify the small business exemption rules and to reduce the number of violations.[284] The other purpose was to accommodate pro-labor members who were concerned about the loss in coverage that would result from the higher and expanded threshold. Jeffords expressly viewed the deletion of § 213(a)(2) and (4) as bringing into coverage about as many workers as the higher threshold would exclude—3 million. He and his staff characterized this trade-off as a "wash."[285] When he explained his proposal to the House Labor Standards subcommittee in 1988, to be sure, the "members' eyes glazed over" in reaction to the complexities, but "what everyone understood was that it was a 'wash.'"[286] Most importantly, at the full committee mark-up hearing

---

[281]Telephone interview with Ross Eisenbrey, Washington, D.C. (Dec. 18, 1997). In 1988-89 Eisenbrey was legislative director to Representative William Ford, the second ranking Democrat on the House Education and Labor Committee and ex-officio member of the Subcommittee on Labor Standards. At the time of the interview, Eisenbrey was Associate Director for Legislative Affairs at the DOL.

[282]135 *Cong. Rec.* 5244 (1989).

[283]James Riley, the chief counsel and staff director of the House Subcommittee on Labor Standards in the late 1980s, speculated that Jeffords used the across-the-board $500,000 threshold as a "cover"—to appear to be "carrying water for the president," and thus not to be "suspect" to the Republicans. Telephone interview with Riley.

[284]"White House Pushing To Modify Minimum Wage" at 465.

[285]Fox, "Background on Bumpers' Minimum Wage Amendment" at 3; telephone interview with Mark Powden.

[286]Telephone interview with Ross Eisenbrey. Independently, John Harvey, the chief

in 1988, although Jeffords conceded that "precise figures were not available" and that minimum wage coverage would decrease in some occupations, he definitively declared that "there is no question...that there will probably be a net increase in coverage."[287]

This clear contemporaneous record that the trade-off was public and known[288] is, curious as it may seem at first blush, not inconsistent with evidence that some heavily involved employers' associations nevertheless did not understand that individual coverage survived.[289] Staunchly pro-labor congressional staffers freely admit that small business representatives were being honest when they protested that they had not understood that the trade-off resulted in the preservation of individual coverage. The majority counsel of the Senate Labor and Public Welfare Committee, for example, wrote that in mid-1990, a few months after the amendments had gone into effect, the NRA "lobbyists realized what they'd agreed to and started screaming bloody murder."[290] A House labor committee staffer and later DOL legislative affairs director explained the ignorance as the result of the

---

labor counsel on the Senate Labor and Public Welfare Committee in 1989, stated that when he and Mark Powden, Jeffords's legislative director, went to the DOL to figure out exactly how many employees would be excluded and included by the amendments, the answer was that it was "a wash." Telephone interview with Harvey.

[287]"Stenographic Transcript of Hearings Before the Committee on Education and Labor, House of Representatives, Markup of H.R. 1834, Minimum Wage Legislation Wednesday March 16, 1988" at 57-58.

[288]Harvey stated that he and Powden realized that small business was still subject to individual coverage. Telephone interview with Harvey. Inconsistent with this account is the version furnished by James Riley, chief counsel and staff director of the House Subcommittee on Labor Standards. He stated that he and the other staffers who drafted the deletion "sort of pulled a fast one." As part of a "word game" in which staffers and opposing lobbyists are continually engaged, they were testing the skills of their opponents' lawyers: "If they're so much smarter, let them figure it out." Stressing that the game was "not deceitful," Riley observed that staffers were "obstinate" and enjoyed showing how "clever" they were. Telephone interview with Riley. Eisenbrey strenuously discounted this version, but agreed that Riley did try to "pull the wool over the eyes" of the other side by writing a committee report that was not truthful. As a result of the incident, Murphy felt constrained to support the "correction" in 1990. Eisenbrey did not find it inconsistent with his account that Riley had related that after the controversy had broken out, Murphy had smiled and said to Riley: "I see you're up to your old tricks again." Telephone interview with Eisenbrey.

[289]Senator Kennedy conceded seven years later: "It is clear that some Members of Congress thought they were voting for a blanket small business exemption when they voted to increase the threshold for the enterprise test to $500,000. But those Members of Congress were ignoring the longstanding principle of individual coverage—which the 1989 act did not abandon, and with good reason." 142 *Cong. Rec.* at S7355.

[290]Fox, "Background on Bumpers' Minimum Wage Amendment" at 4.

fact that some lobbyists are simply "lazy"; and although such "incompetence" is not extraordinary, he conceded that this issue had been a "pretty big one" for them to have missed.[291]

The suspicion that few legislators, lobbyists, or employers understood enterprise coverage and its relationship to individual coverage is confirmed by the fact that even a quasi-official source fell victim to a primitive misunderstanding. A 1991 study of "The Small Business Exemption in the Fair Labor Standards Act: Number of Employees Subject to the 1989 Amendments," published by the Congressional Research Service, a department within the Library of Congress that analyzes the advisability of legislative proposals for congressional committees,[292] cited, without correction, a complaint that a cashier working in a restaurant with less than $500,000 in sales would be covered "because the cashier worked with a cash register that was 'moved in or was produced for commerce'...."[293] In fact, the cashier would be no more covered than the waiter who served food on dishes produced for commerce, or the roofer, employed by a construction business doing less than $500,000 of business, who used nails produced for interstate commerce. They would not be covered because their employers are not subject to enterprise coverage and they are not individually engaged in interstate commerce. If a relatively simple key concept in a statute as brief and straightforward as the FLSA is so mystifying to professional participants in the legislative process, the level of legislators' comprehension of something as impenetrable as the Internal Revenue Code can only be imagined.

Despite the failure of the Bumpers bill in 1991, the NFIB and NRA have continued to lobby Congress to broaden the exemption of small businesses. In 1995 the NFIB urged Congress to eliminate individual coverage "so small businesses can get relief from the mandates of the FLSA and begin to expand their businesses and create more jobs." [294] In 1996 they again prevailed upon legislators to renew the effort to eliminate individual coverage for employees of employers not subject to enterprise coverage. This insistence that small employers should be free to propagate unfair labor standards is remarkable in light of the astounding results that the NFIB has published of polls of its own members on this issue. When the NFIB asked its members—who typically employ five people and gross $350,000 annually[295]—in 1987: "Should the exemption for minimum-wage laws for small

---

[291]Telephone interview with Eisenbrey.

[292]2 U.S.C. § 166(d)(1).

[293]Ciccone, "The Small Business Exemption in the Fair Labor Standards Act: Number of Employees Subject to the 1989 Amendments" at 2.

[294]*Hearings on the Fair Labor Standards Act: Hearings Before the Subcommittee on Workforce Protections of the House Committee on Economic and Educational Opportunities*, 104th Cong., 1st Sess. 236, 238 (1996) (statement of NFIB).

[295]*The Family Friendly Workplace Act* at 65 (prepared statement of Susan Eckerly,

retail and service firms be increased?," 47 percent were opposed and 9 percent undecided. Even in 1995, five years after the $500,000 enterprise coverage threshold had gone into effect, 23 percent were opposed and 10 percent undecided when asked: "Should all small businesses with less than $500,000 in annual gross sales be exempt from FLSA requirements?"[296] Little wonder that in 1996 Representative John La Falce, formerly chairman of the House Committee on Small Business and then its ranking minority member, found that small businesses are not "notably concerned about" an increase in the minimum wage. He related that when the SBA brought to the attention of tens of thousands of small business owners in connection with the 1995 White House Conference on Small Business that bills had been introduced to increase the minimum wage, "the top 403 recommendations coming from the regional conferences to be considered at the National Conference did not include the minimum wage issue. This was not even on the radar screen of the small business community."[297]

Nevertheless, the legislative push to increase the minimum wage in 1996 prompted renewed efforts to eliminate individual coverage. Representative Goodling, the chairman of the former House Labor Committee (renamed Committee on Education and Workforce Development by the new Republican majority), offered a "poison pill amendment"[298] which would, again, have totally eliminated individual coverage with respect to the minimum wage and overtime.[299] Despite the fact that Goodling himself in 1989 had inserted into the *Congressional Record* the DOL report that clearly stated that the small businesses losing their § 213(a)(2) exemption would revert to individual coverage, in 1996 he asserted that the legislation had "inadvertently" produced that result; indeed, he went so far as to claim that such individual coverage was precisely "what they tried to correct in 1989."[300]

The one respect in which Goodling's logic was unassailable was the argument that it was "silly" for the law to treat differently two people working next to each other performing exactly the same duties except that one made interstate telephone calls and the other only in-state calls.[301] The Wage and Hour Administrator had made the same argument after World War II, President Truman repeated it, President Eisenhower's Secretary of Labor echoed it in the 1950s, and the

---

director of Senate federal government relations, NFIB).

[296]NFIB, Mandate (www.nfibonline.com/cgi-bin/search.pl/mandatesearch/).

[297]*Small Business and Entry-Level Employees: How to Increase Take-Home Pay and Keep America Working: Hearing Before the House Committee on Small Business*, 104th Cong., 2d Sess. 5 (1996).

[298]142 *Cong. Rec.* H5506 (1996) (Rep. DeLauro).

[299]142 *Cong. Rec.* at H5534.

[300]142 *Cong. Rec.* at H5534.

[301]142 *Cong. Rec.* at H5540.

legislators who amended the FLSA in 1961 finally crafted a remedy for this anomaly. That remedy for this obsolete residue of federalism was enterprise coverage—precisely the institution that Congress began whittling away in 1977 and that Goodling wished to eliminate for as many firms as possible. The difference between him and the earlier advocates was manifest: whereas they wished to create uniformity by conferring coverage on both intra- and interstate commerce workers,[302] Goodling's goal was coverage for neither.

In an era in which employers and politicians ceaselessly admonish workers that no one, big or small, is immune from the competitive forces of one globally interconnected economy, which imperiously demands dislocations and belt-tightening, it is grotesque to base the national wage and hour law of the world's largest economy on an antiquated distinction between intrastate and interstate commerce "that would serve only an 18th-century economy...."[303] To condition an entitlement to extra payment for overtime work on whether a roofer happens to unload a truck that just crossed a state border with shingles manufactured in another state degrades industrial policy to a childish game.[304] No political-economic or moral reason can justify FLSA protection for the maids who clean houses while denying it to those who repair the roofs on the self-same houses—especially since only the roofers work for profit-making commercial enterprises. Goodling, if he focused on it, would presumably resolve this anomaly by leveling the maids down to the roofers' excluded status, but only universal

---

[302]Goodling's predecessors were, however, not completely consistent: the 1961 amendments, after all, were the origin of §§ 213(a)(2) and (4), which deprived employees of local retail and service establishments, which fell below the enterprise coverage threshold, of minimum wage and overtime protection even if they were individually engaged in interstate commerce.

[303]United States v. Lopez, 514 U.S. at 574 (Kennedy, J., concurring). For well-reasoned arguments that eighteenth-century discourse and early nineteenth-century and some early-twentieth-century Supreme Court decisions embodied much more expansive understandings of the congressional power to regulate commerce, see Robert Stern, "The Commerce Clause and the National Economy, 1933-1946," 59 *Harv. L. Rev.* 645, 647-53 (1946); 1 William Crosskey, *Politics and the Constitution in the History of the United States* 17-292 (1978 [1953]).

[304]The FLSA applies to construction "employees who are regularly engaged in ordering or procuring materials and equipment from outside the State or receiving, unloading, checking, watching or guarding such goods while they are still in transit. For example, laborers on a not covered construction project who regularly unload materials and equipment from vehicles or railroad cars which are transporting such articles from other States are performing covered work." 29 C.F.R. § 776.23(d)(1) (1997). "Similarly, employees who regularly use instrumentalities of commerce, such as the telephone, telegraph and mails for interstate communication" are subject to the FLSA. 29 C.F.R. § 776.23(d)(2).

coverage avoids the distributive injustice of making impoverished workers subsidize wealthier consumers or employers.

The so-called preservation of coverage provision in Goodling's amendment was much narrower than that adopted in 1989: it would have required newly uncovered employers to pay the old lower minimum wage and overtime only to employees who had been, but were no longer, entitled to the minimum wage.[305] Despite this blatant contraction of coverage, Goodling boasted that he had "grandfathered all of these people who are now inadvertently receiving this money." And even if Goodling had not preserved their entitlement to the obsolete minimum wage, the number of affected employees would, he argued, not be significant anyway: "if we look at all the exemptions that are presently in the law, we will find that there are not that many [employees] left...."[306] Goodling seemed oblivious of where the logic of his (empirically unsound) argument led—namely, to the recognition that the problem he was seeking to solve could also not have been significant. What he had not overlooked, however, was the possibilities that the amendment would open up for small employers: "He acknowledged that some employers might use the opportunity to cut the pay of new hires below the minimum wage, 'if they can find people willing to work for it.'"[307]

Even if the Goodling amendment had not been defeated 229 to 196,[308] President Clinton, who pronounced the initiative "a giant fraud on the American people," threatened to veto the minimum wage bill: "Eliminating the minimum wage is no way to increase it. We must not tolerate sweatshops and a repeal of wage protections for millions of Americans as a condition of assuring a living wage for some workers."[309] The sentiment was as economically and morally sound as it was historically disingenuous: Democrats had been agreeing to that compromise since 1977 when they voted to reverse the pattern set in 1961 and increased the enterprise coverage threshold. The same historical caveat is applicable to the impeccable logic behind Clinton's threat to veto the counterpart amendment in the Senate a month later: "It doesn't matter the size of your employer, you can't raise a family on $4.25 an hour."[310]

The Democrats' spirited pro-labor defense of residual individual coverage in small businesses exempt from enterprise coverage should, finally, not deflect

---

[305]142 *Cong. Rec.* at H5534.

[306]142 *Cong. Rec.* at H5535.

[307]David Hess, "GOP Move Could Scuttle Wage Hike, Would Exempt Millions of Jobs," *Bergen Record*, May 23, 1996, at A10 (Lexis).

[308]142 *Cong. Rec.* at H5543.

[309]"Republicans Try to Limit Wage Hike," *St. Louis Post-Dispatch*, May 23, 1996, at 1A (Lexis).

[310]"Minimum Wage Bill Faces Veto over GOP Amendments, Clinton Says," *Daily Lab. Rep.*, July 2, 1996, at D13 (Lexis).

attention from the marginal importance of individual coverage for marginalized workers. The apprehension of retail and service employers exempt from enterprise coverage that DOL enforcement agents, in the course of investigating them, might discover violations with respect to employees individually engaged in interstate commerce may, to be sure, deter such firms from committing minimum wage and overtime violations.[311] But given the meager level of DOL enforcement in general, vindication of rights under the FLSA must rely on workers' self-reliance. And here the preservation of individual coverage in otherwise exempt firms is much too arcane and convoluted to expect many workers to be aware of, let alone understand, what legislators and lobbyists had not.

10. Does the FLSA Now Have Or Has It Ever Had a Small-Business Exemption?

There is an exemption provided in this [FLSA] bill for employers employing less than a specific number of persons.... I think this is not a good idea. These small employers, while frequently very fine men often bring about restricted and inequitable price competition. If they are permitted to cut wages and work hours beyond that of the general producer, they become at once the price competitors of everybody else and tend to work a great hardship upon some larger establishment which must maintain the price and wage level. Moreover...it would encourage the formation of small units...which...in many industries are not the most efficient use of the capital investment.

I think it...also...places at a great disadvantage those workers who are so unfortunate as to find their only livelihood in working for one of these small employers.[312]

Without any doubt, Congress knows how to write a small-business exemption into a labor-protective statute when it so desires. For example, Title VII of the Civil Rights Act of 1964 and the Americans with Disabilities Act define a covered "employer" as employing 15 or more employees.[313] The Age Discrimination in Employment Act sets the threshold at 20 employees.[314] The Worker Adjustment

---

[311]Fox, "Background on Bumpers' Minimum Wage Amendment" at 5, related that the Field Labor Directors Association, which represents managers and supervisors in DOL regional offices, had advised the Senate Labor Committee that the removal of individual coverage would impede enforcement even with respect to workers subject to enterprise coverage because proving individual coverage does not require access to employers' records to determine whether they are doing $500,000 business.

[312]*Fair Labor Standards Act of 1937: Joint Hearings* at 183-84 (statement of Secretary of Labor Frances Perkins).

[313]42 U.S.C. § 2000e(b); 42 U.S.C § 12111(5)(A). Originally Congress set the threshold under Title VII at 25 in 1964.

[314]29 U.S.C. § 630(b).

and Retraining Notification Act does not apply to employers with fewer than 100 employees.[315] Other federal and state statutes also use such employee size-class thresholds to exempt small businesses from regulation and thus to deprive their employees of the relevant protections.[316] Congress chose not to create such an express small-business exemption in the FLSA in 1938 despite the example of the Social Security Act, which in 1935 imposed unemployment taxes only on employers of at least eight employees.[317] Nor did Congress in the intervening years amend the FLSA to add a general employee-size-based exemption, although it has in a very few instances established such a criterion excluding employees of employers in certain industries.[318]

Congress's reasons for creating small-business exemptions vary from statute to statute. The basis for privileging owners of small businesses to discriminate against black (or other nonwhite or female) workers was an analogy between such workplaces and private social settings: the legislature would no more compel him to rub shoulders with a black person in the shop he owned than it would require him to invite that person to dinner at his home. "[W]hen a small businessman who employs 30 or 25 or 26 persons selects an employee," Senator Cotton declared, "he comes very close to selecting a partner; when a businessman selects a partner, he comes dangerously close to the situation he faces when he selects a wife."[319]

In contrast, when legislators, unsuccessfully, sought to insert an employer size-exemption in the Occupational Safety and Health Act (OSHAct), proponents argued that coverage was unnecessary: the close employer-employee relationship means that small employers keep close contact with their workers and have an obvious interest in the safety.[320] Thus whereas at least some legislators were willing to concede that small employers might discriminate against black workers,

---

[315]29 U.S.C. § 2101(a).

[316]For a catalog, see Clark Judge, "Thresholds of Pain," *Wall St. J.*, Aug. 10, 1994, at A8 (Westlaw).

[317]Social Security Act, ch. 531, § 907(a), 49 Stat. 620, 642 (1935).

[318]For example, forestry workers are excluded from overtime if their employer employs fewer than 9 workers. 29 U.S.C. § 213(b)(28) (1994). Agricultural employees are excluded from minimum wage and overtime if their employers did not use more than 500 man-days of agricultural labor in any calendar quarter in the previous calendar year. 29 U.S.C. § 213(a)(6)(A).

[319]110 *Cong. Rec.* 13,085 (1964) (Sen. Cotton).

[320]118 *Cong. Rec.* 31,314 (1972) (Rep. Rousselot). In 1972 the House and Senate both voted in favor of a rider to an appropriations bill that would have created a small-employer exemption, but President Nixon pocket vetoed the bill. 118 *Cong. Rec.* at 31,307-20, 37,203. In order to stave off further congressional action, OSHA in 1977 issued a regulation creating an exemption from paperwork requirements for employers of 10 or fewer employees. 29 C.F.R. § 1904.15.

and openly advocated grandfathering in such prejudice at close quarters, they denied that employees of small employers were exposed to significant safety or health risks. Unlike the situation with regard to discrimination, small-business advocates were constrained to deny their opponents' empirical premise that an exemption from the OSHAct "would almost give a license to kill."[321] In the event, as the regulations emphatically observe:

> The legislative history [of OSHAct]...clearly shows that every amendment or other proposal which would have resulted in any employee's being left outside the protections afforded by the Act was rejected. The reason for excluding no employee, either by exemption or limitation on coverage, lies in the most fundamental of social purposes of this legislation which is to protect the lives and health of human beings in the context of their employment.[322]

Neither of the justifications advanced for small-business exemptions under Title VII or the OSHAct, however, applies to the FLSA. No legislator has argued that small employers should be privileged to exploit their workers because it would be socio-psychologically presumptuous of Congress to prohibit employers from taking advantage of workers with whom they rub shoulders every day. By the same token, no legislator has asserted that FLSA coverage is superfluous because small employers have an obvious interest in paying their workers well: the whole point of the exemption is to enable them to accumulate and reinvest the difference between the minimum wage and overtime premium that they are not required to pay and the lower wage that the unfettered labor market permits. One important reason that even Democrats and liberals have accepted a small-business exemption from the FLSA must be that they reject the analogy to the OSHAct—they must deny that the exemption 'would almost give a license to starve.'

Despite this aberrant statutory history, pro-employer partisans have taken absolutist positions on the question of whether the FLSA provides a small-business exemption. Senator Dole belonged to the fringe of the pro-employer extreme by virtue of adding a chronological component: "There has always been a basic exemption for small business under the Minimum Wage law."[323] In fact, however, it is more accurate to state that the dollar-volume thresholds for enterprise coverage, which were not introduced until 1961, did "not establish, and w[ere] not intended to establish, a 'small business exemption,'" and that the (erroneously labelled) "Exemptions" section of the FLSA, "does not include—and has never included—any general exemption for small businesses."[324]

---

[321]118 *Cong. Rec.* at 21,103 (Rep. Flood).

[322]29 C.F.R. § 1975.3(b).

[323]123 *Cong. Rec.* at 32,907.

[324]Fox, "Background on Bumpers' Minimum Wage Amendment" at 1, 2. On how

Representative Goodling, in pleading for adoption of his amendment to eliminate individual coverage under the FLSA, cited the aforementioned statutes as proof that "the small-business exemption...is what we do in every piece of legislation."[325] If Congress were to insert a general small-business exemption into the FLSA, there is no doubt that the Supreme Court would hold that Congress faces no insuperable constitutional due process or equal protection obstacles in choosing to permit small employers to subject their workers to the kinds of exploitation and discrimination that it has otherwise outlawed. Indeed, on the very day that the original FLSA bill was introduced in 1937, the Supreme Court rejected such a challenge to the Unemployment Compensation Act of Alabama, which in conformity with the unemployment tax provisions of the Social Security Act, did not tax employers of fewer than eight employees:

> [T]his is the type of distinction which the law is often called upon to make. It is only a difference in numbers which marks the moment when day ends and night begins, when the disabilities of infancy terminate and the status of legal competency is assumed. It separates large incomes which are taxed from small ones which are exempt, as it marks here the difference between the proprietors of larger businesses who are taxed and the proprietors of smaller businesses who are not.
>
> [I]t cannot be assumed that the legislature could not rightly have concluded that generally the number of employees bears a relationship to the size of the payroll and therefore to the amount of the tax, and that the large number of small employers and the paucity of their records of employment would entail greater inconvenience in the collection and verification of the tax than in the case of larger employers.[326]

The Supreme Court's deference to legislative economic policy decisions of this type long antedated the New Deal and remains robust.[327]

To be sure, the original FLSA bill required the Labor Standards Board (which was ultimately never established) to provide by regulation that payment of substandard wages or maintenance of substandard hours by "any employer employing less than [blank] employees shall not be deemed to constitute a substandard labor condition...." Yet even this concession to small employers was to be withdrawn when the board found that "the maintenance of the appropriate labor standard by such class of employers is necessary or appropriate in order to

---

exclusions of employees in § 13 came to be misleadingly labelled exemptions, see above chapter 2.

[325]142 *Cong. Rec.* at H5535.

[326]Carmichael v. Southern Coal and Coke Co., 301 U.S. 495, 510-11 (1937).

[327]E.g., Middleton v. Texas Power & Light Co., 249 U.S. 152, 159 (1919) (upholding state workers compensation statute that did not apply to employees of employers of five or fewer employees).

carry out the purposes, or prevent the circumvention" of the FLSA.[328] Congress, however, decided not to proceed with even such a conditional across-the-board exemption for small employers as defined by the number of employees or any other size criterion. The floor debate in the Senate two months later revealed the political-economic and moral reasons for eschewing a general small-business exemption.

After an amendment was proposed exempting any firm employing 10 or fewer persons, Senator Hugo Black explained that the original bill had left the employee-threshold blank both because he was unsure as to whether there should be such an exemption and because he believed that the Education and Labor Committee and the whole Senate should debate the issue.[329] Black then noted that numerous statutes (such as the unemployment tax provision of the Social Security Act enacted by Congress just two years earlier) exempted employers with fewer than eight workers, while some state compensation laws set the threshold at three or five workers. Some people had taken the position that enforcement problems suggested the wisdom of exempting very small employers, while others—in particular, large employers—believed that "the law should apply to all employers, whether they employ 1 or 20 or 5,000 persons." Ultimately the committee decided that "the law should apply to all alike."[330]

The discussion leading up to the vote on the exemption amendment was dominated by the following dialogue between Senator Robert Wagner and Senator David Walsh:

> Mr. WAGNER. Would not the effect of the amendment be that the character of competition which we are seeking to prevent, namely, exploitation as against efficiency, would continue, because the small sweatshop, employing just a few persons, would continue to pay low wages in competition with the employer who pays reasonable wages?
>
> Mr. WALSH. The Senator from New York is absolutely correct. If this bill...has any merit at all...it is that it is designed to protect and prevent the exploitation of men and women wage earners in small establishments. Those working in establishments having less than 10 employees number approximately 200,000. The bill is on the theory that such workers cannot organize, cannot enjoy collective bargaining, cannot have the benefit of

---

[328]S. 2475, § 6(a).

[329]Black did not draft the bill, which was drafted by two New Deal insiders, Thomas Corcoran and Benjamin Cohen. Their April 30, 1937 draft left the number of employees blank. "Confidential Revised Draft April 30, 1937," § 5(a), National Archives, Labor Dept. Records, Labor Standards—1937 File, Fair Labor Standards Bill File. In their May 20, 1937 draft, which is otherwise identical with the actual bill, the number "15" is written in the blank, but it is unclear by whom. "Confidential Revised Draft May 20, 1937," § 6(a), National Archives, Labor Dept. Records, Labor Standards—1937 File, Fair Labor Standards Bill File.

[330]81 *Cong. Rec.* at 7863-64.

> the large units of employees who can organize and bring the pressure of a great labor organization to bear against the employer in order to obtain decent wages and reasonable hours of employment. ...
>
> The theory upon which the bill has merit...is that small-wage earners in small industries scattered all over the country in competition with large industries, because of their locality, because of the fact that they cannot organize, because of the objections of their employers to organized labor unions, have no power of asserting their human right to social justice.
>
> What is social justice? Social justice means that we as legislators should extend to the unfortunate human beings those social rights which they could demand if they had the power of unity of action. Social justice means that government will take a hand in helping to uphold and support individuals and small groups of individuals who have not the power of pressure possessed by labor organizations. ...
>
> ... Senators can visualize the kind of men who operate sweatshops in the great cities of the country suddenly dividing their 60 or 70 or 80 employees into units of 8 or 9, with a brother-in-law or cousin or aunt or uncle in alleged ownership of the establishment, and thus evading...the application of the law; then sending their goods into the central markets in competition with large employers who obey and respect the law.[331]

Fully aware that the exemption for firms with fewer than 10 or fewer employees would have exempted a large proportion (more than one-half) of the estimated universe of covered employers, employing only about one-twentieth of all covered employees,[332] the Senate, scarcely two months after the original bill had been introduced, rejected the amendment by a vote of 52 to 31.[333] This fleeting and unenacted existence of a real small-business exemption, taken together with intense congressional concern over the possibility that the Supreme Court would invalidate any statute that sought to regulate non-interstate commerce, strongly suggests that any exemptions of local and small businesses were not grounded in the firms' size per se, but merely used size as an indicator that they were not "seriously competing with and having a substantial effect upon the flow of interstate commerce."[334] Consequently, by the mid-1940s, once the Supreme Court had made it clear that it would uphold a much broader exercise of the commerce power, it was foreseeable that Congress would eventually provide wage and hour protection to ever larger numbers of workers employed in firms formerly deemed "local and small."

---

[331]81 *Cong. Rec.* at 7885-86.

[332]81 *Cong. Rec.* at 7800-7801. The proportions are not precise because the data referred to employers with 1-5 and 6-20 employees.

[333]81 *Cong. Rec.* at 7887-88.

[334]81 *Cong. Rec.* at 7648 (Sen. Black).

11. The Economic Basis of the Small-Business Exemption

Congress made it clear that by fixing a dollar volume test it was not concerned with profit, but with impact on commerce measured by inflow of money.[335]

Even if the boosterist claim that small firms are a job growth machine were valid, the mere creation of jobs in firms that on average offer lower wages, fewer and inferior nonwage financial benefits, worse working conditions, fewer opportunities for acquiring greater skills, and less job security is no reason to require their employees to subsidize them to the detriment of larger firms. A recent study of wage levels by size of employer revealed that the average hourly wage earnings of full-time workers in firms with 500 or more workers were 43 percent to 28 percent higher than those in firms with fewer than 100 employees between 1983 and 1993. This gap is an understatement because it excludes probably lower-paid part-time workers, who are more prevalent in small firms. If wage date were available for firms with fewer than 10 workers, the wage gap would presumably be even wider.[336] The fact that wage levels rise directly with firm size is closely linked to the fact that unionization rates are similarly differentiated.[337]

Promoting small construction businesses by exempting them from labor standards laws not only deprives workers of the protections of those mandates, but also subjects them to other substandard conditions that are, to be sure, not unlawful, but are manifestly consequences of this sector's small and stagnant character. Health insurance is a prime example. As the Small Business Administration concedes: "Most companies without coverage are in the retail trade and construction industries. ... More than 50 percent of all small construction companies with fewer than 10 employees...are without insurance plans."[338] In 1993, only 22 percent of employees of construction firms with fewer than 10 employees were covered compared with 61 percent in firms with more than 500 employees.[339] In general, small firms offer markedly fewer benefits than their larger competitors. Only one-fifth of workers in firms with 1-24 employees had pension plans compared to almost nine-tenths of those in firms with 500 or more workers.[340]

---

[335]Mack Player, "Enterprise Coverage Under the Fair Labor Standards Act: An Assessment of the First Generation," 28 *Vand. L. Rev.* 283, 331 (1975).

[336]Richard Boden, "Changes in Wages and Worker Attributes by Firm Size, 1983-1993," *Bus. Economics*, July 1997, at 37.

[337]*The State of Small Business: A Report of the President,* tab. 4.15 at 262 and tab. 4.19 at 271 (1984) (data for 1978 and 1979).

[338]*The State of Small Business: A Report of the President: 1994*, at 68 (1995).

[339]*The State of Small Business: A Report of the President: 1994*, tab. 2.15 at 92.

[340]*The State of Small Business: A Report of the President* tab. 4.16 at 266 (1984) (data

Moreover, empirical confirmation of disproportionate job creation in small firms would not in itself be grounds for according them preferential legal treatment: "The relevant question is what market failure the preferential policies are expected to address. The small business sector is not obviously undersized because of product or labor market imperfections...."[341]

In raising the dollar-volume threshold of and incorporating construction employers into the exemption, Congress ignored and contradicted the recommendation of its own Minimum Wage Study Commission (MWSC), which it established in 1977 to report on the social, political, and economic ramifications of the FLSA with particular reference to exemptions.[342] The commission in 1981 urged the complete elimination of the exemption for retail and service enterprises because such a move was consistent with the FLSA's major objective of placing a floor under all workers' wages. The change would not only have brought under the act the largest group of excluded nonsupervisory workers, but would have imposed only a "minimal" cost on employers since three-fourths of the workers were already receiving the minimum wage and one-half of the exempt firms would not experience higher wage costs.[343]

It is by no means unimaginable that a majority of the Congress will one day decide to impose the same type of discriminatory yet constitutional universal small-employer exemption on the FLSA that it has incorporated into more recently enacted labor-protective statutes. But if and when the national legislature decides that the same small employers whom it has privileged, for example, to withhold a livelihood from workers against whose race, ethnicity, or gender they are prejudiced, must also be permitted to operate otherwise unlawful sweatshops, this ill-advised step should be done openly and not in some convoluted fashion through the use of exemptions from exemptions, which even many legislators and lobbyists are intellectually incapable of grasping. Congress should be required to state directly to the affected workers that it has chosen to sacrifice them on the altar of an unproven, ideologically driven speculation—that the smallest firms grow into large ones and provide the bulk of new employment in the United States—and to confine minimum wage and premium overtime coverage and the ban on oppressive child labor to those firms that, as a result of the operation of market forces, are more likely to comply with fair labor standards anyway.

A direct criterion of labor-use intensity (such as the number of workers) may,

---

for 1979).

[341]Steven Davis, John Haltiwanger, and Scott Schuh, *Job Creation and Destruction* 171 (1996).

[342]Fair Labor Standards Amendments of 1977, Pub. L. No. 95-151, § 2(e)(1)(H), 91 Stat. 1245, 1247.

[343]1 *Report of the Minimum Wage Study Commission* 121 (1981).

as the MWSC noted in 1981,[344] be more rationally related than annual sales to the purported objective of the exemption. Its straightforwardness would, in any event, subject legislators to more focused scrutiny of the impact. Neither criterion, however, can claim to be optimally suited to the purpose of the small-business exemption, which is to relieve small firms that are not profitable enough both to accumulate capital for expansion and to offer standard working conditions of the obligation to pay fair wages. Both sales and number of employees suffer from overbreadth: neither size criterion is unambiguously positively correlated with profitability. As the MWSC noted: "The most common rationale...to justify the existing minimum wage exemptions...is the perceived relationship between small size and low profit rates."[345]

If profitability is the criterion that Congress is targeting, why should small but profitable firms not be required to pay the minimum wage? Why should small firms that have remained small for many years not forfeit the presumption of being rising stars of job creation? Why should larger firms that by virtue of contraction have fallen into the status of small businesses be entitled to impose unfair labor standards on their workers? Even advocates of a small-business exemption acknowledge the need to differentiate. In the words of a Republican congressman: "If we are going to grant a small-business exemption under the Federal minimum-wage requirement, it ought to apply only to businesses that are in a startup mode during that first year or two of operation when the survival of the small business is so tenuous."[346] Such an apprentice-entrepreneur approach would be a quasi-counterpart to the so-called training or opportunity wage that Congress enacted in 1989 and 1996, permitting employers to pay newly hired teenage workers the out-of-date lower minimum wage for the first 90 days.[347]

If, as advocates of small business assert, "[s]mall size, in and of itself, does not dictate low profitability,"[348] why do such firms require any government-enforced subsidies from their employees? This question is so much the more appropriate since boosters suggest that many workers of "start-up firms" are themselves so entrepreneurial that they willingly accept "as little cash wages as the workers need to survive. All workers are [independent] contractors so as to reduce cash flow during the critical early start-up period. It is difficult to criticize these firms for abusing the law, for, if they had to pay cash wages, unemployment insurance, and

---

[344]1 *Report of the Minimum Wage Study Commission* at 112-13.

[345]1 *Report of the Minimum Wage Study Commission* at 112.

[346]142 *Cong. Rec.* at H5539 (Rep. Frank Riggs, Cal.).

[347]29 U.S.C. § 206(g). The training or opportunity small business exemption would still be more capacious because it does not require employers to pay even the lower minimum wage to new employees.

[348]Bruce Kirchhoff, *Entrepreneurship and Dynamic Capitalism: The Economics of Business Firm Formation and Growth* 30 (1994).

Social Security, they probably would soon exhaust their cash resources and go out of business."[349] By freeing small employers from the mandates of fair labor standards,[350] Congress has privileged them to impose such entrepreneurialism on workers too risk-averse to forgo wages in order to catapult themselves to millionaire-status in the service of the next Bill Gates.

Bruce Kirchhoff, a former chief economist of the SBA and one of the foremost academic boosters of small business, concedes that in addition to "potential creative destroyers that need encouragement" and "eventually come into the tax system," "some small-firm owners are dishonest and have no intention of ever entering the tax system. They and their firms remain in the underground economy for their entire existence." Nevertheless, Kirchhoff not only offers no method of distinguishing between the two for enforcement purposes, he fears that "efforts to force compliance could easily create additional barriers to entry of new firms." Consequently, with regard to the 2 million firms that purport to have no employees at all, he holds that "the problem of firms failing to comply with the intent of the unemployment insurance and Social Security laws is a trade-off between allowing for 4 percent noncompliance or instituting more enforcement, thereby discouraging potential growth firms from starting. The present system seems acceptable when analyzed this way."[351] To make it even more acceptable, Kirchhoff transmogrifies criminal violations of the Internal Revenue Code into a neutral "opt[ing] out of the formal employer role."[352] If boosters are not too embarrassed to condone outright illegalities for the greater good of small businesses, no wonder they fervently support lawful exemptions from minimum wage and overtime obligations.

Kirchhoff's framework demonstrates that the FLSA exemption for small construction employers is not an isolated or idiosyncratic development in public policy. It fits in snugly with the self-help measures that employers, especially in construction, have increasingly adopted over the last 20 years to rid themselves of the costs of what they view as financially obnoxious government-mandated social and labor protections. In order to evade employment taxes, for example, construction employers have been pioneers in—as a congressional committee entitled a hearing on the subject in 1991—*Exploiting Workers by Misclassifying Them as Independent Contractors*.[353] As the president of the AFL-CIO Building

---

[349]Kirchhoff, *Entrepreneurship and Dynamic Capitalism* at 112.

[350]David Birch, *Job Creation in America: How Our Smallest Companies Put the Most People to Work* 17 (1987), also praises the "aggressive, ambitious people who are in the shop weekends and labor at low wages for a chance at a piece of the action."

[351]Kirchhoff, *Entrepreneurship and Dynamic Capitalism* at 112-14. The 4 percent figure refers to national noncompliance with respect to 4 percent of all employees.

[352]Kirchhoff, *Entrepreneurship and Dynamic Capitalism* at 107.

[353]*Exploiting Workers by Misclassifying Them as Independent Contractors: Hearing before the Employment and Housing Subcommittee of the House Committee on*

and Construction Trades Department recently testified to Congress: "Every day, we see construction sites where there are scores, or even hundreds of workers, and yet every single worker is being treated as an independent contractor."[354] The WHD reports that construction contractors are national leaders in misclassifying employees as independent contractors for FLSA purposes.[355] That larger firms resort to illegalities in order to be able to impose the same unfair labor standards that their smaller rivals are lawfully privileged to offer is hardly surprising in a competitive industry.[356] Indeed, labor market standards appear to be so debased in residential construction that only a "severe shortage" can force builders to "adopt[] all manner of tactics" including even "paying overtime."[357]

Small firms, however, generally make more intensive use of so-called independent contractors than large firms. A survey commissioned by the SBA found that in 1989 the number of days worked by independent contractors as a proportion of all days worked by "regular employees" were 84 times greater in firms with fewer than 25 employees than in firms with 500 or more.[358]

Since the Census Bureau derives its sample of construction employers with payroll from the "list of all construction companies in the active records of the Internal Revenue Service...which were subject to payment of Federal Insurance Contributions Act (FICA) taxes,"[359] a rise in the number of construction establishments without payroll as a share of all establishments serves as an indicator of the spread of the independent contractor scam. Indeed, this proportion has steadily increased in the construction censuses from 52.5 percent in 1972 to

---

Government Operations, 102d Cong., 1st Sess. (1991).

[354]*Employment Classification Issues: Hearings Before the Subcommittee on Oversight of the House Committee on Ways and Means*, 104th Cong., 2d Sess. 311 (1996) (statement of Robert Georgine).

[355]U.S. Wage and Hour Div., "Fact Sheet No. 013: Employment Relationship Under the Fair Labor Standards Act (FLSA)" (http://www.dol.gov/dol/esa/public/regs/compliance/whd/whdfs13.htm).

[356]"Roofing Company Pays $857,000 in Back Wages," *Las Vegas Review-Journal*, Nov. 5, 1997, at 2D (Lexis) (residential roofer failed to pay overtime); "Drywall Settlement May Spur Other Workers," 141 *Lab. Rel. Rep.* 400, 403 (Nov. 30, 1992) (dozens of suits filed against most of the major drywall contractors in southern California for violating the overtime provision of the FLSA).

[357]Lew Sichelman, "Labor Shortage: Nationwide Problem Impacts New-Home Quality and Completion," *San Diego Union-Tribune*, Oct. 19, 1997, at H-1 (Lexis).

[358]U.S. Small Business Administration, *The State of Small Business: A Report of the President* 63 (1991). The figures were 2.52 percent and 0.03 percent respectively.

[359]U.S. Bureau of the Census, *1992 Census of Construction Industries: Subject Series: Legal Form of Organization and Type of Operation* at vi.

70.2 percent in 1992.[360] Among special trade contractors, establishments without payroll accounted for 75.6 percent of all (1.5 million) establishments in 1992. Since it is implausible that, for example, in 67.9 percent of roofing establishments only the owner works,[361] presumably hundreds of thousands of special trade contractors are classifying their workers as nonemployees. The explosion of firms that report having no employees and the concomitant phenomenon of "[e]very independent contractor becom[ing] a zero-employee firm"—both of whom "choose to avoid government payments for benefits they think they do not need"—are, for Kirchhoff, positive manifestations of a "changing society.... And change is the stuff of dynamic capitalism."[362]

Relegating workers to employment in the subminimum-wage sector thus reveals itself to be part and parcel of the same approach that encourages self-employment for the unemployed.[363] Those who see small firms as Schumpeterian creatively destructive engines of job growth praise them as peculiarly suited to the U.S. economy, which "is a seething mass of pushing, shoving, and manipulating firms that are attempting to acquire market share and win profits." In such an economy workers figure as "probably the most flexible resource.... They can be hired, fired, transferred, trained, and retrained."[364] Excluding more and more workers from mandatory labor standards regimes serves as a kind of proto-deregulatory experiment; and if the new devotees of entrepreneurialism favor

---

[360]Why it declined slightly from a high of 71.8 percent in 1987 is unclear. The figures in 1967, 1977, and 1982 were 53.6, 59.9, and 66.9 percent respectively. Calculated according to U.S. Bureau of the Census, *Census of Construction Industries, 1967: Type of Operation and Legal Form of Organization*, tab. 1 at 1-3 (1970); U.S. Bureau of the Census, *1972 Census of Construction Industries: Industry Series: United States Summary—Statistics for Construction Establishments with and Without Payroll*, tab. A1 at 1-2 (1975); U.S. Bureau of the Census, *1982 Census of Construction Industries: Industry Series: U.S. Summary: Establishments with and Without Payroll*, tab. 1 at 3 (1984); U.S. Bureau of the Census, *1987 Census of Construction Industries: Industry Series: U.S. Summary: Establishments with and Without Payroll*, tab. 1 at 7 (1990); U.S. Bureau of the Census, *1982 Census of Construction Industries: Industry Series: U.S. Summary: Establishments with and Without Payroll*, tab. 1 at 3 (1984); U.S. Bureau of the Census, *1992 Census of Construction Industries: Industry Series: U.S. Summary: Establishments with and Without Payroll*, tab. 1 at 27-5 (1996).

[361]Calculated according to U.S. Bureau of the Census, *1992 Census of Construction Industries: Industry Series: U.S. Summary: Establishments with and Without Payroll*, tab. 1 at 27-5.

[362]Kirchhoff, *Entrepreneurship and Dynamic Capitalism* at 111.

[363]Marc Linder, *Farewell to the Self-Employed: Deconstructing a Socioeconomic and Legal Solipsism* 94-96 (1992); U.S. DOL, Unemployment Insurance Service, *Self Employment Programs for Unemployed Workers* (1992).

[364]Kirchhoff, *Entrepreneurship and Dynamic Capitalism* at 144.

macroeconomic "turbulence, not equilibrium,"[365] depriving workers of protections such as the minimum wage and premium overtime appears optimally suited to the intensification and acceleration of their degradation into mere "flexible resources."

Exempting small employers from compulsory fair labor standards as a means of promoting capital accumulation[366] and their expansion into larger enterprises would make sense from this neo-entrepreneurial perspective only if experience demonstrated that small firms typically grow into large ones. In fact, however, the typical pattern is that only a tiny minority of firms doing less than $500,000 of business annually develop into larger businesses even when they are legally privileged to impose unfair labor standards on their workers. Even Bruce Phillips, the director of the Office of Economic Research of the SBA, a federal agency whose mission is advocacy, concedes that perhaps 5 percent of firms of such size grow, whereas "most vegetate" or go out of business.[367] And in a study that Phillips published using the SBA's establishment longitudinal microdata based on Dun and Bradstreet files, he found that: "New construction firms face a lower chance of survival than firms in any other industry."[368]

But even if very small firms generated a disproportionately large volume of employment, two questions would have to be posed concerning this development. If, on the one hand, this growth takes place by means of displacement of the production, market share, or employment accounted for by higher-wage larger firms, why should the state intervene to achieve or reinforce such a debasement of labor standards? On the other hand, if small firms can generate large numbers of jobs without having to rely on a statutory exemption from fair labor standards, why is the state imposing a superfluous detriment on their employees?

Close observers of the roofing business confirm the inapplicability of neo-entrepreneurial theory to the industry. A roofing contractor in the Iowa City area—whom both the Roofers Union and the National Roofing Contractors

---

[365]Kirchhoff, *Entrepreneurship and Dynamic Capitalism* at 144.

[366]Marx noted that the subversion of the customary standard of living played an important role in the real world: "The forcible reduction of the wage below this value [of labor power]...transforms, in fact, within certain limits, the worker's necessary consumption fund into an accumulation fund of capital." 1 Marx, *Das Kapital* at 626.

[367]Telephone interview with Bruce Phillips, Washington, D.C. (Dec. 2, 1997). These 5 percent ("gazelles") account for three-fourths of new jobs created by small businesses. William Dennis, Jr., Bruce Phillips, & Edward Starr, "Small Business Job Creation: The Findings and Their Critics," *Bus. Economics*, July 1994, at 23, 25. The SBA formerly leased Dun & Bradstreet data files covering the years 1979 to 1990 that would have made it possible to do longitudinal cohort studies answering the question as to what happens to such firms. When the Congress cut off the funding for the data program, the SBA had to return to the data files.

[368]Bruce Phillips & Bruce Kirchhoff, "Formation, Growth and Survival: Small Firm Dynamics in the U.S. Economy," 1 *Small Business Economics* 65, 70 (1989).

Association characterize as a good employer—states that only one small roofing contractor among the scores that have come and gone during the previous 15 years became a larger and reputable employer. A combination of their exemption from the FLSA and their violation of the social security, unemployment and workers compensation laws, and OSHA regulations enables small contractors to submit bids 30 percent lower than larger reputable firms can and to monopolize the residential roofing sector. Since the small contractors' unlawfully lower labor costs are proportionally even lower than their bids, such contractors, who on average employ five to seven workers, can secure annual profits in the $30,000-$50,000 range on $250,000 of business.[369]

Calculating the profitability of small firms on a national level was made impossible, ironically, by the Reagan administration, which terminated publication of Internal Revenue Service (IRS) data broken out for size-classes and sub-industries.[370] In the last year (1980) for which the IRS published such data for sole proprietorships, which constitute 81 percent of all special trade contractors,[371] net income as a percentage of business receipts declined almost monotonically—from 44 percent in firms with receipts between $5,000 and $10,000 to 4 percent in those with receipts between $5 million and $10 million. Firms with receipts between $100,000 and $250,000 and between $250,000 and $500,000 achieved quite solid profit margins of 14 percent and 11 percent, respectively.[372] This monotonic ordering could indicate that the smaller the firm the more the owner generated profits by scrimping on personal consumption,[373] but given small special trade

---

[369]Telephone interview with Kurt Tjemeland, T & K Roofing, Ely, IA (Dec. 2, 1997).

[370]1980 was the last year for which such data were published for sole proprietorships, and 1981 was the last year for which the IRS issued sole proprietorship income statistics in a separate publication as it had for many years. Thereafter the IRS published data only in very abbreviated form in an annual article in *SOI Bulletin*. IRS, *Statistics of Income—1981: Sole Proprietorship Returns* iii (1982); Raymond Wolfe, "Sole Proprietorship Returns, 1982," *SOI Bulletin*, Summer 1984, at 17. The IRS refuses to run the data even for researchers who offer to pay for them. Telephone interview with John Comisky, IRS, Statistical Information, Washington, D.C. (Jan. 2, 1998).

[371]Calculated according to U.S. Bureau of the Census, *1992 Census of Construction Industries: Subject Series: Legal Form of Organization and Type of Operation*, tab. 1 at 6 (1995).

[372]Calculated according to IRS, *Statistics of Income 1979-1980: Sole Proprietorship Returns*, tab. 11 at 169 (1982). The category "net income" is net of deficits. This perfect monotonicity was not a quirk of 1980. In 1972, for example, special trade contractors' net profit as a proportion of business receipts declined from 49.9 percent in the $2,500-$5,000 receipts class to 4.0 percent in the $1 million-and-over class. Calculated according to IRS, *Statistics of Income 1972: Business Income Tax Returns*, tab. 2.3 at 20 (1976).

[373]Bruce Phillips, Director of Economic Research, Office of Advocacy, U.S. Small Business Administration, suggested this interpretation. Telephone interview (Jan. 5,

contractors' relatively meager capital investment expenditures, it is also possible that the profits are consumed instead of reinvested. This latter scenario of prodigality would indisputably contradict the purpose behind the FLSA exemption for small employers. But even the former scenario of prudent thrift would not support the exemption: for if small entrepreneurs can achieve the requisite level of profitability by temporarily cutting back on their own consumption, why should the state exempt them from this Faustian conflict between accumulation and consumption by imposing this "self-denial"[374] on their employees? After all, it is entrepreneurs' very "abstinence," according to one strand of economic theory, that entitles them to part of their profit.[375]

The data that the IRS still publishes for corporations reveal a somewhat different pattern. But here, too, construction firms with business receipts between $250,000 and $500,000 are shown to be more profitable than most firms in larger size-classes.[376]

A unique study carried out by the Bureau of the Census in connection with the 1987 and 1992 Economic Census revealed how profitable many small businesses are. Based on a sample of the universe of more than 17 million firms in 1992, the Bureau determined that of firms with receipts between $100,000 and $199,999, 4.8 percent recorded net profit of $100,000 or more, while 32.4 percent achieved net profit of $25,000 to $99,999. The corresponding proportions for firms with receipts between $200,000 and $249,999 were 9.3 percent and 27.4 percent, respectively; for those with receipts between $250,000 and $499,999, the proportions were 13.7 percent and 28.7 percent. If the universe is restricted to the 10 million "Nonminority male-owned businesses"—special trade contractors are

---

1998).

[374]John Stuart Mill, *Principles of Political Economy* 729 (new. ed., W. Ashley ed., 1926 [1848]).

[375]Eugen von Böhm-Bawerk, *Geschichte und Kritik der Kapitalzins-Theorien* 241-61 (4th ed. 1921 [1884]).

[376]The IRS does not publish data, broken out for size-classes, on corporate special trade contractors; these data refer to all construction corporations. Net income (less deficits) as a proportion of total receipts amounted to 1.2 percent in corporations with $250,000 to $500,000 of business receipts. The highest proportion, in corporations with business receipts between $5 million and $50 million, was 1.6 percent. Calculated according to IRS, *Statistics of Income—1992: Corporation Income Tax Returns*, tab. 5 at 49-50 (1995). The only data that the IRS currently publishes on special trade contractors broken out for size classes refer to assets size-classes. Net income as a proportion of total receipts in the smallest class (having less than $100,000 in assets) amounted to 1.6 percent. This level exceeded that in the classes with $100,000 to $5 million in assets; the highest proportion, 3.3 percent, was found in corporations with $100 million to $250 million in assets. Calculated according to IRS, *Source Book: Statistics of Income: Active Corporation Income Tax Returns, July 1991-June 1992*, at 28 (n.d.).

overwhelmingly white men—these proportions ran even higher. In the $250,000-$499,999 size-class, for example, 15.7 percent of the firms recorded net profit of $100,000 or more, while 30.3 percent reported $25,000 to $99,999. (The corresponding proportions in 1987 had been very similar: 13.5 percent and 31.5 percent.) The total of 46 percent was only marginally lower than the 47.8 percent in the $500,000-$999,999 size-class.[377] Why firms this profitable require state-enforced subsidies from their employees is a mystery.[378]

Despite such profits, the representative small construction employer has not used its exemption from mandatory fair labor standards to invest in additional capital equipment or to hire additional workers. The quinquennial Census of Construction Industries reveals that from 1987 to 1992, while the overall value of business done by special trade contractors rose by 8 percent, average annual capital expenditures in establishments doing less than $500,000 of business declined 17 percent, from $3,884 to $3,239. The average number of employees employed by such establishments also declined—from 3.4 to 2.9.[379] Admittedly, these census

---

[377] Calculated according to U..S. Bureau of the Census, *1992 Economic Census: Characteristics of Business Owners*, tab. 27b at 224; U.S. Bureau of the Census, *1987 Economic Censuses: Characteristics of Business Owners,* tab. 21b at 156-57. These proportions are understated because the denominator includes owners who did not respond to the question.

[378] To be sure, not all of these firms had employees. The Census of Construction Industries cannot be used to calculate profit rates because it does not collect comprehensive data on costs, but it does permit comparisons among size-classes of employers with respect to a kind of profits category—value added minus payroll, rental cost for machinery, equipment, and buildings, and capital expenditures. A crude surrogate for the rate of profit results from dividing this figure by value added. In 1992, this 'rate of profit' was 40.8 percent among special trade contractors doing $250,000-$499,999 of business and 40.4 percent among those doing more than $10 million of business. Calculated according to U.S. Bureau of the Census, *1992 Census of Construction Industries: Industry Series: United States Summary: Establishments with and Without Payroll*, tab. 9 at 27-15 (1996). The corresponding figures for 1987 were 41.5 percent and 42.8 percent, respectively. U.S. Bureau of the Census, *1987 Census of Construction Industries: Industry Series: United States Summary: Establishments with and Without Payroll*, tab. 10 at 19 (1990). The minuscule difference between small and large firms suggests that the former require no state-enforced subsidies from their employees to become profitable enough to accumulate competitively.

[379] Calculated according to U.S. Bureau of the Census, *1987 Census of Construction Industries: Industry Series: United States Summary: Establishments with and Without Payroll*, tab. 10 at 19; U.S. Bureau of the Census, *1992 Census of Construction Industries: Industry Series: United States Summary: Establishments with and Without Payroll*, tab. 9 at 27-15. Total capital expenditures among all special trade contractors declined 3 percent from 1987 to 1992; they increased in the largest entities. The monetary amounts are not adjusted for inflation.

data cannot reveal whether individual employers doing less than $500,000 of business expanded into larger size-classes. Nevertheless, the impact of the FLSA exemption should also be observable within the small business sector: new (or already existing) small businesses should be using the additional profit that the payment of lawfully substandard wages makes possible to hire more workers and invest in more capital equipment.

Why profitability on this scale fails to lead to capital investment and expansion is a question for small-business boosters to explore. Why employers appropriating such profits should be entitled to government-enforced subsidies from their workers in the form of substandard wages is a troubling labor policy question that Congress has not troubled to answer. The burden rests with the national legislature to explain why condemning the vast majority of employees of such firms to vegetate in perpetuity in the backwaters of substandard labor conditions in order that a tiny minority of firms might advance is not an irrational industrial policy—especially since some of those few dynamic firms would have expanded even if they had been subject to the FLSA.

Moreover, contrary to small business boosters, who assert that small business has become the job growth engine of the U.S. economy,[380] the kinds of small firms that benefit from the FLSA small-business exemption have not produced any increase in their share of total jobs. Table 4-1 shows that the share of the total number of employees accounted for by the smallest establishments and enterprises[381] in recent decades has actually declined marginally.[382]

---

[380]Birch, *Job Creation in America.* For a critique, see Davis, Haltiwanger, and Schuh, *Job Creation and Destruction* at 57-81. Charles Brown, James Hamilton, and James Medoff, *Employers Large and Small* 24 (1990), argue that small firms' disproportionate share of new employment "is an accident of birth—new firms happen to be born small. Since new businesses account for more than 100 percent of the net increase in employment, and new businesses rarely start out with 100 or more employees, it is almost inevitable that small firms will account for a disproportionate share of new employment. Once established, however, small firms are not on average very hardy."

[381]Data for establishments are available for years prior to 1974, but not for the size-classes used here.

[382]The stagnant or declining share of the smallest establishments/enterprises could be masking the growth of such entities into larger ones; the stagnant or declining share could, however, also mask an even stronger decline caused by the reverse process of the shrinkage of larger entities into smaller ones. Only longitudinal studies of identified individual businesses could settle this question. If the long-term stagnant share of total employment accounted for by the smallest entities means that the number of jobs annually created and disappearing are in equilibrium, this sector cannot qualify as the especially dynamic growth machine that boosters have vindicated for it. Zoltan Acs & Bruce Phillips, "Why Does the Relative Share of Employment Stay Constant?" (Ms., Babson Entrepreneurship Conference, Apr. 16-20, 1997), concede the stagnant share of

Table 4-2, which displays the same data for the construction industry, reveals a different pattern. The increase in the share of employment accounted for by the smallest construction establishments during the years following the creation of the $500,000 enterprise coverage threshold in 1990 is—despite some fluctuations over time—consistent with the hypothesis that the lawful privilege to impose unfair labor standards has promoted the competitiveness of such firms.

Aggregate data for the construction industry, however, are misleading since small entities are much less prominent in certain sectors than in others. Examining the special trades contractors, the stronghold of small businesses, sharpens the focus. In the years immediately following the increase in the enterprise coverage threshold from 0 to $500,000, special trades contractor establishments with fewer than 10 employees raised their share of total employment every single year; the increase, from 27.0 percent in 1989 to 31.2 percent in 1993, amounted to 15.6 percent overall. In roofing, the monotonic increase from 24.3 percent to 28.8 percent in 1994 amounted to 18.5 percent.[383]

---

employment in small firms generally over time, but contend that it is the result of many of the highest growth small firms' becoming or being acquired by large firms. Even using longitudinal data, however, Kirchhoff found that firms with 1 to 19 employees accounted for only 26 percent of the net employment increase between 1976 and 1986. Part (perhaps half) of this increase was accounted for by the growth in small firms that became large. Krichhoff, *Entrepreneurship and Dynamic Capitalism* at 125-28.

[383]Calculated according to U.S. Bureau of the Census, *County Business Patterns 1989: United States*, tab. 1b at 7; U.S. Bureau of the Census, *County Business Patterns 1993: United States*, tab. 1b at 7 (1995); U.S. Bureau of the Census, *County Business Patterns 1994: United States*, tab. 1b at 7. The proportions accounted for by small specialty contractor and roofing firms declined again through 1997. U.S. Bureau of the Census, *County Business Patterns 1997*, tab. 1b at 7. Roofing includes siding and sheet metal work. Data on the number of employees in each size class are not published for Iowa, but roofing establishments with 1 to 4 employees as a proportion of all such establishments rose from 56 percent to 63 percent from 1989 to 1995. U.S. Bureau of the Census, *County Business Patterns 1989: Iowa*, tab. 1b at 3 (1991); U.S. Bureau of the Census, *County Business Patterns 1995: Iowa*, tab. 1b at 3 (1997).

Table 4-1: % of Employees in Small and Large Establishments/Enterprises, 1963-97

Year	Establishments with...employees			Enterprises with...employees		
	1-4	**5-9**	**500+**	**1-4**	**5-9**	**500+**
1963				7.7	6.9	47.1
1967				6.8	6.7	46.8
1972				6.4	7.0	46.5
1974	7.2	8.2	24.3			
1977	7.4	8.8	22.5	6.2	7.0	47.5
1982	6.9	8.9	21.3	8.0	8.4	41.3
1987	6.7	9.1	19.4	6.0	7.5	43.3
1989	6.3	8.8	20.1			
1992	6.5	9.1	20.0	5.7	6.7	47.3
1994	6.3	8.8	19.8			
1995	6.2	8.6	19.9			
1996	6.2	8.5	19.9			
1997	6.1	8.5	19.7			

Sources: See table 4-2

Table 4-2:% of Employees in Small and Large Construction Establishments/Enterprises, 1963-97

Year	Establishments with...employees			Enterprises with...employees		
	1-4	5-9	500+	1-4	5-9	500+
1963				n.a.	n.a.	n.a.
1967				12.7	12.3	13.5
1972				12.1	12.3	14.3
1974	10.9	12.2	10.0			
1977	13.8	14.6	11.4	13.8	14.3	17.9
1982	12.0	13.0	12.7	13.0	12.7	18.8
1987	11.5	14.1	6.7	12.5	14.5	11.7
1989	11.0	13.7	6.6			
1992	13.5	15.3	6.0	14.9	15.0	9.9
1994	13.3	15.1	5.7			
1995	12.8	14.6	5.6			
1996	12.8	14.4	5.6			
1997	12.3	14.0	5.7			

Sources: **Establishments:** U.S. Bureau of the Census, *County Business Patterns 1974: U.S. Summary*, tab. 1B at 3 , 8 (1977); idem, *County Business Patterns 1977: United States*, tab. 1B at 3, 8 (1979); idem, *County Business Patterns 1982: United States*, tab. 1B at 3, 8 (1984); idem, *County Business Patterns 1987: United States*, tab. 1b at 3, 7 (1990); idem, *County Business Patterns 1989: United States*, tab. 1b at 3 (1991); idem, *County Business Patterns 1992: United States*, tab. 1b at 3, 6 (1994); idem, *County Business Patterns 1994: United States*, tab. 1b at 3, 6 (1996); idem, *County Business Patterns 1995: United States*, tab. 1b at 3, 6 (1997); idem, *County Business Patterns 1996*, tab. 1b at 3, 6 (1998); idem, *County Business Patterns 1997*, tab. 1b at 3, 6 (1999). **Enterprises**: U.S. Bureau of the Census, *1967 Enterprise Statistics*, Part 1: *General Report on Industrial Organization*, tab. 3-1 at 164-67 (1972); idem, *1972 Enterprise Statistics*, Part 1: *General Report on Industrial Organization*, tab. 1 at 142, 144 (1977); idem, *1977 Enterprise Statistics: General Report on Industrial Organization*, tab. 3 at 146, 148 (1981); idem, *1982 Enterprise Statistics: General Report on Industrial Organization*, tab. 3 at 93, 96 (1986); idem, *1987 Enterprise Statistics: Company Summary*, tab. 3 at 17, tab. 2 at 13 (1991); idem, *1992 Economic Census—Enterprise Statistics* (http://www.census.gov/agfs/ent/view/us_emp.txt).

These increases more robustly confirm the prediction that small firms legally privileged to superexploit their workers will secure a competitive advantage. These proportions and increases are, moreover, underestimates because the annual *County Business Patterns* data for single-establishment firms derive from employment tax filings with the IRS and thus exclude workers whom small employers disproportionately and increasingly treat as nonemployees.[384] The quinquennially collected firm-level data reveal a similar pattern: the proportion of all employees accounted for by firms employing fewer than 10 employees rose from 30.9 percent in 1987 to 33.1 percent in 1992.[385]

Finally, the congressional policy exempting small employers from the general obligation to comply with fair labor standards is not entirely consistent with the overall federal policy promoting small business, which dates back to the beginning of the first Eisenhower administration:

> The essence of the American economic system of private enterprise is free competition. Only through full and free competition can free markets, free entry into business, and opportunities for the expression and growth of personal initiative and individual judgment be assured. The preservation and expansion of such competition is basic not only to the economic well-being but to the security of this Nation. Such security and well-being cannot be realized unless the actual and potential capacity of small business is encouraged and developed. It is the declared policy of the Congress that the Government should aid, counsel, assist, and protect, insofar as is possible, the interests of small-business concerns in order to preserve free competitive enterprise, to insure that a fair proportion of the total purchases and contracts or subcontracts for property and services for the Government (including but not limited to contracts or subcontracts for maintenance, repair, and construction) be placed with small-business enterprises, to insure that a fair proportion of the total sales of Government property be made to such enterprises, and to maintain and strengthen the overall economy of the Nation.[386]

Revealingly, for purposes of implementing this congressional policy and determining whether a business is small enough to be eligible for government programs and preferences,[387] the SBA has established size standards for a large number of industries. For general building contractors and heavy construction a small business is defined as having annual receipts of less than $17 million, while special trade contractors must fall below $7 million.[388] This standard-setting is

---

[384]On the data source, see U.S. Bureau of the Census, *County Business Patterns 1992: United States* v (1994).

[385]Calculated according to U.S. Bureau of the Census, *1987 Enterprise Statistics: Company Summary*, tab. 3 at 19; U.S. Bureau of Statistics, *1992 Enterprise Statistics*.

[386]15 U.S.C. § 631(a) (1994) (enacted 1953).

[387]13 C.F. R. § 121.101 (1997).

[388]13 C.F.R. § 121.201.

particularly significant since at the time the SBA knew that the average size of construction firms was three employees and $300,000 in annual sales.[389] If Congress had adopted such a small-business standard for the FLSA, fewer than 5,000 (or 1 percent of all) construction companies would be covered and 75 percent of all construction employees would be excluded from the statute.[390] Such an enormous breach in labor standards was apparently too much even for the Bush administration.

12. The Quantitative Impact of the Exemption of Small Businesses

> The Committee bill also updates the provision in Section 3(s) of the Act that prevents newly exempt employers from lowering their employees' wages below the previous minimum wage rate under which they had been covered.... This hold harmless provision will insure that not [sic] employee will be adversely affected by the Committee amendment.[391]

The typographic carelessness of the House Committee on Education and Labor in assuring workers that they would not suffer any disadvantage as a result of the higher $500,000 exemption level for their employers was a bad omen for the assertion's truthfulness. But before its validity can be probed, its existence and meaning must be known. Yet, even today many close observers of labor standards legislation are surprised to learn that a significant proportion of construction workers work in firms doing less than $500,000 of business.[392]

Two years before Congress exempted small construction firms, the Bureau of the Census's *1987 Census of Construction Industries* ascertained that 1,256,597 employees were employed in establishments doing less than $500,000 worth of business. They accounted for 25 percent of the slightly more than 5 million construction employees, while the 388,687 establishments falling below the $500,000 threshold represented 71 percent of all construction establishments with payroll.[393] The next economic census, carried out in 1992, two years after the

---

[389]49 Fed. Reg. 5024 (1984) (Lexis).

[390]Estimated according to data in U.S. Bureau of the Census, *1992 Economic Census—Enterprise Statistics* (pre-publication data emailed by U.S. Bureau of the Census, Dec. 1, 1997). Since the SBA threshold size class fell in the middle of one used by the Census Bureau, an estimate had to be made.

[391]H. R. Rep. No. 260 Pt 1: Fair Labor Standards Amendments of 1989, 101st Cong., 1st Sess. 18 (1989).

[392]E.g., telephone interview with Sarah M. Fox (Dec. 4, 1997).

[393]U.S. Bureau of the Census, *1987 Census of Construction Industries: Industry Series: United States Summary: Establishments with and Without Payroll*, tab. 2 at 8 (1990).

small-business construction exemption had gone into effect, revealed that the 1,157,141 employees in such establishment still accounted for 25 percent of thc estimated 4,668,280 construction employees, while the 413,435 establishments doing less than $500,000 of business represented 72 percent of all establishments with payroll.[394] In Iowa, a state with no overtime statute and a very weak minimum wage statute (which was, coincidentally, not enacted until 1989),[395] fully 30 percent of all construction employees are excluded from the FLSA.[396]

In order to put the census data on the same enterprise basis as the FLSA coverage definition, the data from the only Bureau of the Census program that consolidates establishment data within enterprises can also be used.[397] They reveal

---

[394]U.S. Bureau of the Census, *1992 Census of Construction Industries: Industry Series: United States Summary: Establishments with and Without Payroll*, tab. 9 at 27-14 (1996).

[395]Iowa Code § 91.D (1997). Because the statute was enacted shortly before the 1989 amendments to the FLSA and has never been amended, it seems to apply only to retail and service employees of employers doing an annual business of between $300,000 to $500,000. But see Iowa Op. Att'y Gen. 1989-90, at 94 (Nov. 1, 1990). The regulations, which are largely taken verbatim from the FLSA regulations, suggest that coverage is greater and includes all construction firms falling below the FLSA threshold.

[396]U.S. Bureau of the Census, *1992 Census of Construction Industries: Geographic Area Series: West North Central States*, tab. 7 at IA-10 (1996).

[397]Since the economic censuses conducted by the Bureau of the Census are based on establishments, whereas coverage under the FLSA is keyed to enterprises, it might seem that the establishment data in the text vastly overstate the effect of the small business exemption. Despite the definitional differences, however, the construction establishment-based employment data are very close approximations of enterprise-based coverage. The FLSA defines an enterprise as "the related activities performed (either through unified operation or common control) by any person or persons for a common business purpose, and includes all such activities whether performed in one or more establishments or by one or more corporate or other organizational units...." 29 U.S.C. § 203(r)(1). The Bureau of the Census defines a construction establishment "as a relatively permanent office or other place of business where the usual business activities related to construction are conducted." U.S. Bureau of the Census, *1992 Census of Construction Industries: Subject Series: Legal Form of Organization and Type of Operation* v (1995). But these potentially significant differences are neutralized by the fact that the establishments of multi-establishment companies, which accounted for fewer than 2 percent of all establishments with payroll and fewer than 1 percent of all establishments, are, on average, so much larger than single-establishment firms and so far exceed the $500,000 exemption level that no appreciable number of them could have fallen below that threshold. In 1992, the average value of construction work performed by establishments (with payroll) of single-unit companies was $741,000 compared with $10.5 million for establishments of multi-unit companies. *Id.*, tab. 2 at 8. This disparity also applies to the generally small special trade contractors. In roofing, siding, and sheet metal work, for example, the average value of construction

that in 1992 1,194,856 employees or 26 percent of all construction industry employees were employed in the 73 percent of all companies in the receipt size classes below $500,000.[398] Both of these proportions were one percentage point higher than in 1987.[399]

Since the most concentrated impact of the small-business exemption is on the so-called special trades contractors, which are on average smaller than other building companies, the corresponding data for this sector are presented here. In 1992, the average construction industry establishment with payroll did $941,000 of business and employed eight employees; among special trades contractors the corresponding figures were $600,000 and eight employees. The special trades are, in other words, both smaller and more labor intensive. Whereas in the construction industry as a whole, establishments with payroll employing one to four workers did $198,000 of business, similarly situated special trade contractors did only $140,000 of business; the corresponding figures for establishments employing five to nine employees were $591,000 and $436,000 respectively. Consequently, a larger

---

work done was $567,000 and $3.6 million, respectively. *Id.*, tab. 2 at 11. The disparity is also found regardless of how many establishments the company owns. For example, in 1982, the average receipts of construction establishments of companies owning or operating only two establishments were more than seven times greater than those of single-establishment entities. U.S. Bureau of the Census, *1982 Enterprise Statistics: General Report on Industrial Organization*, tab. 5 at 214 (1986). Since, therefore, virtually all establishments doing less than $500,000 of business are single-establishment firms, employment data for such establishments are in effect enterprise-level data. The Census Bureau's definition of a "company" is similar to the FLSA definition of "enterprise": it includes all establishments under its ownership or control and, if a parent company, all establishments of its subsidiaries. U.S. Bureau of the Census, *1992 Census of Construction Industries: Subject Series: Legal Form of Organization and Type of Operation* at 4.

[398]U.S. Bureau of the Census, *1992 Enterprise Statistics: Company Summary*, tab. 4 at 15 (1997).

[399]U.S. Bureau of the Census, *1987 Enterprise Statistics: Company Summary*, tab. 5 at 60. The annual Bureau of the Census data series, *County Business Patterns*, yields similar results. According to the 1992 Census of Construction Industries, 5.0 employees worked on average in establishments doing $250,000 to $500,000 of business; conversely, establishments with 5 to 9 employees, did on average $591,000 of business. Thus a close correlation obtains between doing $500,000 of business and employing six to seven employees. Since *County Business Patterns* uses size classes of 1-4 and 5-9, in 1994 approximately 900,000 employees were employed in construction firms with fewer than seven employees; they represented about 19 percent of all construction employees U.S. Bureau of the Census, *County Business Patterns 1994: United States*, tab. 1b at 6. Similar proportions can be calculated from special tabulations for the Small Business Administration. *The State of Small Business: A Report of the President: 1994*, tab. A7 at 182-83, tab. A8 at 206-207 (data for 1990 and 1991).

proportion of special trades contractors are exempt and a larger proportion of their employees are excluded from the FLSA than for thc industry overall: 76 percent of establishments and 825,790 employees or 30 percent of all employees.[400] On an enterprise basis, 31 percent of employees in 1992 were employed by the 77 percent of special trade contractor companies with less than $500,000 in receipts.[401]

These figures represent the upper limit of the number of construction workers lawfully excluded from mandatory minimum wage and overtime compensation.[402] Some employees of small construction firms may work under collective bargaining agreements that provide for such payments. Employers of others may make such payments voluntarily. A few may be covered because they are individually engaged in commerce by virtue of unloading trucks that crossed a state line to delivery materials.[403] Still others may be covered by state laws.

---

[400]U.S. Bureau of the Census, *1992 Census of Construction Industries: Industry Series: United States Summary: Establishments with and Without Payroll*, tab. 8-9 at 27-12-27-15.

[401]U.S. Bureau of the Census, *1992 Economic Census—Enterprise Statistics*. Both proportions were the same in 1987. U.S. Bureau of the Census, *1987 Enterprise Statistics: Company Summary*, tab. 5 at 61.

[402]The last set of coverage estimates that the DOL published, six months after the 1989 amendments had gone into effect, were implausible: the 75,000 construction employees excluded from the minimum wage and the 120,000 excluded from overtime in September 1990 represented only 1.4 percent and 2.5 percent, respectively, of the total number of nonsupervisory employees in the industry. U.S. DOL, Employment Standards Administration, *Minimum Wage and Maximum Hours Standards under the Fair Labor Standards Act*, tab. 7 at 27, tab. 10 at 33 (1993). Bizarrely, when the DOL published new estimates in 1998, the number of construction employees excluded from the minimum wage and overtime for 1990 had been revised down to 50,000 for both despite the fact that the revisors' methodology was based on the old data. U.S. DOL, Employment Standards Administration, *Minimum Wage and Maximum Hours Standards under the Fair Labor Standards Act*, tab. C1a90 at 116, tab. C1d90 at 122, 129 (1998). One of the two revisors conceded that the DOL's data for 1990 were a "black box," which they had not been able to inspect and analyze. He also conceded that he could not vouch for the accuracy of the data for construction, and that someone who was intimately familiar with the 1989 amendments and their effects on coverage construction workers would be in a position to make more informed estimates. Telephone interview with Daniel Hodge, Employment Research Corporation, Ann Arbor, MI (Nov. 12, 1999).

[403]"Workers employed on new construction not yet dedicated to interstate commerce are not covered unless they are engaged in ordering and purchasing, receiving and unloading materials from outside the state so as to make these activities a part of interstate commerce." Statement of the Director, Wage and Hour and Public Contracts Div. (Dec. 3, 1948), reprinted in 1 *Lab. L. Rep.* ¶25,150C.10 at 37,366 (CCH, 1997). More recently the WHD stated that: "Of course, employees engaged at the construction site in receiving materials which are still moving [in] interstate commerce would be individually

The fact that many states lack a statutory minimum wage or, more importantly, a premium overtime law undercuts an argument put forward by liberal supporters' of compromise with the Bush administration that most of the workers excluded by the higher exemption level would be held harmless by their coverage under the state laws.[404] The Bush administration itself used this argument. As former Secretary of Labor Dole claimed: "Most states have their own minimum wage laws (and some had higher minimum wage levels than that provided under Federal law) that would reach these small employers."[405]

In fact, as of September 15, 1999, seven states (Alabama, Arizona, Florida, Louisiana, Mississippi, South Carolina, and Tennessee) had no minimum wage statutes at all. In addition, ten other state minimum wage laws prescribe a minimum wage rate far below the federal rate of $5.15: Georgia ($3.25), Kansas ($2.65), Minnesota ($4.90 for enterprises with annual receipts of under $500,000), Montana ($4.00 for business with gross annual sales of $110,000 or less), New Mexico ($4.25), New York ($4.25), Ohio ($2.80 to $4.25 depending on employer's annual sales volume), Oklahoma ($2.00 for employers with less than $100,000 in annual gross sales or fewer than ten employees at any one location), Texas ($3.35), and Wyoming ($1.60). Numerous states create coverage thresholds in the form of a minimum number of employees that exclude large numbers of employees: Arkansas (4), Georgia (6), Illinois (4), Indiana (2), Michigan (2), Nebraska (4), Vermont (2), Virginia (4), and West Virginia (6).[406] Eighteen states have no overtime law at all. In the states that do have overtime statutes, the aforementioned coverage-restricting conditions also apply; in addition, Alaska excludes from the overtime entitlement employees of employers with fewer than four employees. Moreover, additional overtime coverage restrictions and exemptions further limit their applicability. For example, the overtime premium does not apply to employees in retail or service businesses with annual sales of less than $500,000 in Missouri, or retail or service establishments in Vermont;

---

covered...." 2 WHD, *Wage and Hour Division Field Operations Manual* ch. 11c10 (Apr. 24, 1994).

[404]When John V. Harvey, Jr., the chief majority counsel for Senate Labor and Public Welfare Committee in 1989, made this argument during an interview in 1997 and was informed that many states lack minimum wage and especially overtime laws, he admitted that he had also been unaware of that fact in 1989. Telephone interview with John V. Harvey, Jr., vice-president, employee relations, Owens-Corning, Ohio (Dec. 9, 1997).

[405]Letter from Elizabeth Hanford Dole to Marc Linder (Jan. 14, 1998).

[406]A Georgia state senator with plans to introduce legislation increasing the state minimum wage observed that: "'Many Georgians will be shocked to learn that there are people around our state who are working for below the minimum wage because...the company they work for is not subject to the federal minimum wage law.'" "Senator Keys on Minimum Wage," *Augusta Chronicle*, Jan. 10, 1998, at C3 (Lexis).

employees are also excluded in enterprises with annual sales below $250,000 in Nevada.[407]

Overall, then, the states have always offered and continue to offer only spotty back-up protection to workers excluded from the FLSA. Consequently, a large number of construction workers, especially those in the nonmechanical trades such as roofing, carpentry, and painting, and in (single-family) residential building in general,[408] are no longer entitled to and do not receive premium wages for overtime.

13. Why Was and Is the Exclusion of Construction Workers in Small Firms Almost Unknown?

The Committee is aware that the low-wage worker, whose economic status is in large part determined by the FLSA, does not typically communicate with the Congress either by testifying on bills or by writing letters outlining his position on the legislation. [T]he Congress must represent the public conscience in the matter of low-wage workers and minimum wage legislation.[409]

Ignorance of the existence of the small construction firm exemption, at the time of its enactment and even today, is extraordinarily widespread. Although even many legislative leaders and their staffs were ignorant of the impact that the $500,000 threshold would have on construction workers, Congress was not unaware of the general wage-cutting consequences that restricted coverage would bring in its wake. During the debate over H.R. 2 in 1989, Representative Goodling inserted into the record the DOL's estimate of the economic effects of the increase in the small business exemption. The analysis presented by the Bush administration's DOL was subordinated to its speculation that increasing the minimum wage to $4.25 would destroy 450,000 jobs. The higher exemption threshold figured, together with the increased tip credit and introduction of a so-called training wage, merely as "job loss offsets." In other words, the DOL viewed the disentitlement to the minimum wage solely as a positive development—as

---

[407]U.S. DOL, "Minimum Wage Laws in the States," (Sept. 15, 1999) (http://www.dol.gov/dol/esa/public/minwage/america.htm). It was not until December 1997 that the construction industry was added to the list of industries covered by Colorado's minimum wage and overtime regulation. Monique Tuttle, "New Colorado Minimum Wage Order Includes Construction Industry," *Colorado Employment Law Letter*, Dec. 1997 (Lexis).

[408]Not surprisingly, homebuilding was, not so long ago, called "The Industry Capitalism Forgot," *Fortune*, Aug. 1947, at 61.

[409]S. Rep. No. 690: *Fair Labor Standards Amendments of 1974*, at 34.

"sav[ing]" jobs. The higher dollar volume was estimated to exempt 1.1 million retail and service jobs from the minimum wage and two million jobs in the other affected industries, for a total of about three million lost jobs. The DOL viewed the new $500,000 threshold as reducing job opportunity losses by a net of 4 percent or 18,000 jobs. This job-saving effect would, according to the DOL, have been greater if state minimum wage laws had not intervened: they "effectively nullify" the increase in the coverage threshold by preserving minimum wage protection for about half the affected workers.[410] Thus instead of regarding the state laws as a safety net for workers expelled from the FLSA, the DOL perversely deemed them to be thwarting the effect that Congress had intended for the higher threshold as a compensation for the higher minimum wage.

Interviews with key congressional committee staff members and employer and union lobbyists reveal how widespread the ignorance of the exemption and its impact on construction workers was. The chief counsel and staff director of the Subcommittee on Labor Standards of the House Committee on Education and Labor in the late 1980s and early 1990s, James Riley, was crucially involved in drafting the amendments and writing the committee reports. Although he knew that the bill extended the $500,000 coverage threshold to the construction industry, not even he realized at the time that the bill was taking away universal coverage from construction workers. Indeed, the only interest that the $500,000 threshold sparked in the House committee was a speculative one: staffers worried that it might have been a "stalking horse" or trial balloon for Republican efforts to increase the coverage threshold under the Davis-Bacon Act. That law requires the payment of locally "prevailing" wages, as determined by the Secretary of Labor, under all federal building contracts over the virtually nominal level of $2,000.[411] Although Republicans continued to seek an increase in the coverage threshold (in addition to repeal of the statute altogether), they in fact never used the higher FLSA threshold as a precedent. In retrospect, Riley conceded that "we probably shot ourselves in the foot" with the $500,000 exemption, which "you've now discovered is hurting construction workers."[412]

Experienced DOL enforcement and compliance officers are well aware of the changes that the 1989 amendments wrought with respect to the construction industry, but the current acting Wage and Hour Administrator, a long-serving career civil servant, had not realized that construction had not been in the group of

---

[410]135 *Cong. Rec.* 5243-44 (1989).

[411]29 U.S.C. § 276a.

[412]Telephone interview with Riley. John V. Harvey, Jr., the chief labor counsel on the Senate Labor and Public Welfare Committee, disagreed. With the hindsight knowledge of how many construction workers have been excluded from the FLSA, he still felt that everyone in 1989 recognized that the expanded exemption would bring about some such consequences if not precisely these. Telephone interview with Harvey.

industries subject to the $362,500 threshold in the years before 1989.[413]

Few people were closer to FLSA lobbying in 1989 than Robert McGlotten, the legislative director of the AFL-CIO. For example, the AFL-CIO put out a news advisory on March 22, 1989, that McGlotten would be available to the media immediately after the House vote on the minimum wage in front of the House press gallery.[414] Yet in an interview eight years later, when asked about the inclusion of construction in the $500,000 small business exemption, McGlotten said: "No one caught it. I'm hearing about it for the first time from you."[415] Other insiders contradict this claim. John Zalusky, an economist with the AFL-CIO in 1989, called it "bullshit." Zalusky stated that he foresaw and raised "bloody murder" about the consequences of the exemption, but was, despite his prediction that it would later "bite them in the rear," unable to persuade officials of the Building and Construction Trades Department of the AFL-CIO to focus on the issue.[416] John Harvey, who was the chief labor counsel of the Senate Labor and Public Welfare Committee in the late 1980s, also characterized McGlotten's claim as "baloney."[417]

Jay Power, who was the AFL-CIO's chief lobbyist on the FLSA in 1989, stated that since the building trades unions did not express any interest in the issue, the inclusion of construction in the enterprise coverage exemption was "not that big a deal" for the AFL-CIO.[418] Donald Elisburg, who had been the Assistant Secretary of Labor for Employment Standards in the Carter administration and has

---

[413]Telephone interview with John Fraser, DOL, Washington, D.C. (Dec. 8, 1997).

[414]"News Advisory," PR Newswire, Mar. 22, 1989 (Lexis). On Nov. 1, 1989, McGlotten, on behalf of the AFL-CIO, wrote Representative Austin Murphy supporting the compromise with the Bush administration on amending the FLSA. 135 *Cong. Rec.* H7868 (1989) (Lexis).

[415]Telephone interview with Robert McGlotten, Washington, D.C. (Nov. 25, 1997). "After nearly three decades at the AFL-CIO, the labor movement's top lobbyist" retired in 1995 to become a lobbyist for Philip Morris and other clients. "Labor's Private Weapon," *Legal Times*, Apr. 24, 1995, at 5 (Lexis) (quote); "Highlights of Recent Lobby Registration," *Legal Times*, Mar 24, 1997, at 42 (Lexis).

[416]Telephone interview with John Zalusky, Washington, D.C. (Dec. 9, 1997). Zalusky recently retired from the AFL-CIO. Zalusky added that his own union, the International Brotherhood of Electrical Workers, had complained but to no avail.

[417]Telephone interview with John V. Harvey, Jr., Ohio (Dec. 9, 1997). After working for General Electric, Harvey became the vice president for employee relations at Owens-Corning Glass. With respect to assessing plausibility and credibility, it is unclear why McGlotten would untruthfully characterize himself as having been an incompetent lobbyist in preference to stating that his immediate constituents, the building trades, were indifferent, or that the exemption was a necessary trade-off for an increase in the minimum wage.

[418]Telephone interview with Jay Power, AFL-CIO, Washington, D.C. (Dec. 17, 1997). Power himself came to the AFL-CIO from the Carpenters Union.

remained close to the AFL-CIO, emphasized that the building trades unions have always been so exclusively focused on the Davis-Bacon Act that they deferred to the AFL-CIO in all matters relating to the FLSA.[419] Construction unions' neglect of the FLSA has in large part been a function of their historical successes in securing far superior wage and hour provisions in their collective bargaining agreements than the FLSA offers. In that sense, the lack of coverage under FLSA could be regarded as a desirable organizing tool rather than a deficiency to be remedied by lobbying.[420]

Against this background, it is hardly astonishing that in 1991, when Zalusky was seeking to mobilize opposition to the Bumpers bill (which would have eliminated individual coverage in retail and service firms already exempted from enterprise coverage), his effort to explain why the exemption from enterprise coverage for small construction employers should be repealed "didn't really register" with Robert Georgine, the president of the Building and Construction Trades Department.[421] The peripheral importance of the FLSA is underscored by the fact that the director of research of the Building and Construction Trades Department of the AFL-CIO not only had never heard of the small construction firm exemption, but expressed strong doubt that it even existed.[422] The vice

---

[419]Telephone interviews with Donald Elisburg, Washington, D.C. and Chicago, IL (Nov. 1997). The building trades unions' lack of familiarity with the FLSA and exclusive focus on Davis-Bacon are corroborated by Zalusky and Terry Yellig, an attorney who represents the construction unions. Telephone interview with Terry Yellig, Washington, D.C. (Jan. 26, 1998). Support for this view is also found in *1976 National Jobs Conference of the Building and Construction Trades Department AFL-CIO* 93-95 (1976), which devotes the chapter, "Labor Standards—Protect the Tradesman," to Davis-Bacon, without ever mentioning the FLSA

[420]This logic is, to be sure, contradicted by construction unions' traditional practice of organizing construction companies rather than workers. Until the extraordinary successes of the antiunion open-shop movement in the 1970s, "the building trades have organized relatively few workers, relying instead on the fact that the construction market has been dominated by union contractors who get their labor through union hiring halls." "Open-Shop Construction Picks Up Momentum," *Bus. Wk.*, Dec. 12, 1977, at 108. See also Jerry Flint, "Building Unions Plan Organizing Campaign," *N.Y. Times*, Dec. 1, 1977, at A18, col. 1.

[421]Telephone interview with Zalusky (Jan. 26, 1998). Georgine, who remained president of the Building and Construction Trades Department until 2000, had no independent recollection of the debates over the 1989 FLSA amendments according to his attorney. Telephone interview with Yellig.

[422]Telephone interview with Adam Pagnucco, Washington, D.C. (Nov. 24, 1997). Despite this obvious ignorance, the president of the Building and Construction Trades Department asserted in 1998: "Since the early 90s, we have been working on corrective strategies...." Letter from Robert Georgine to Marc Linder (Feb. 10, 1998). Georgine did

president in charge of organizing at the Roofers Union stated that he had never heard of the de facto exemption of small contractors from the FLSA. He suggested as the reason for his lack of familiarity with the exclusion the fact that the union did not organize residential roofing or small roofing contractors in general. He strongly suspected that the kinds of employers with which the union dealt had also never heard of the law.[423] In the field, the answer the was the same. For example, the Roofers Union regional organizer in the Midwest (including Iowa) had never heard of the amendment.[424]

Other unions of nonmechanical construction trades were similarly in the dark about the small-business exemption. The director of the legislative affairs for the United Carpenters and Joiners Union stated that he knew of the $500,000 threshold, but did not realize that it applied to construction.[425] The general counsel of the Painters Union, though unfamiliar with the exemption, suggested that educating employees of small construction contractors as to their lack of an entitlement to overtime would be a good organizing tool.[426]

Construction employers' associations were equally ignorant of the exemption. Neither the executive director for congressional affairs of the AGC, an organization of larger general contractors, nor the legislative affairs official at the antiunion Associated Builders and Contractors had ever heard of it.[427] The director of government relations at the National Roofing Contractors Association explained his ignorance of the threshold by reference to the composition of the organization's membership: because the 3,500 members averaged $3.5 million in annual business, the issue was, as so many other lobbyists and congressional staffers also put it, "below the radar" of larger contractors.[428]

---

not identify these "strategies." According to an attorney for the Building and Construction Trades Department, no such strategies existed precisely because the unions were unaware of the small-business exemption. Telephone interview with Terry Yellig, Washington, D.C. (Feb. 20, 1998).

[423]Telephone interview with John Martini, United Union of Roofers, Waterproofers, and Allied Workers, Washington, D.C. (Nov. 21, 1997). On the relatively low degree of unionization in single-family residential construction, see Herbert Northrup and Howard Foster, *Open Shop Construction* 49-71 (1975).

[424]Telephone interview with Carl Keeton, Kansas City, MO (Nov. 26, 1997).

[425]Telephone interview with Jim Kolb, Washington, D.C. (Dec. 17, 1997).

[426]Telephone interview with Dick Sigmond, Philadelphia (Jan. 26, 1998).

[427]Telephone interview with Jeff Shoaf, Washington, D.C. (Nov. 24, 1997); telephone interview with Austin Fulk, Virginia (Nov. 24, 1997).

[428]Telephone interview with Craig Brightup, Washington, D.C. (Nov. 26, 1997). The largest roofing contractor in the United States, Centimark Corp., had revenues of $175 million in 1996—three times greater than the second largest. Gary Tulacz, "The Top 600 Specialty Contractors," *ENR*, Oct. 6, 1997, at 52 (Lexis).

Ignorance of the small-business exemption from enterprise coverage is by no means restricted to employers and workers organizations. Seven years after the amendments were enacted, even the highly respected *Congressional Quarterly* disseminated false information about it. In reporting on the aforementioned unsuccessful efforts in 1996 to eliminate individual employee coverage in enterprises doing less than $500,000 of business, the weekly magazine asserted that the 1989 amendment

> ultimately ended up contracting the small-business exemption, not expanding it. ... Since then, the Labor Department has interpreted the law to mean that any small-business employee engaged in interstate commerce in any way—including using materials produced in another state or answering out-of-state phone calls—had to pay the minimum wage and overtime. Wage and hour laws now apply to virtually all U.S. workers.[429]

Every single statement in this quotation is false.[430] Before 1990, virtually all construction firms, for example, were covered by the FLSA. From 1990 on, no construction firm doing less than $500,000 in business has been subject to enterprise coverage. Only construction workers individually engaged in commerce or production of good for commerce would be covered. The DOL has not interpreted the FLSA to mean that any small-construction (or retail or service) business employee merely using materials produced in another state is entitled to the minimum wage or overtime: such an expansive interpretation is permissible only under the inapplicable enterprise coverage standard. In fact, DOL enforcement officers, all-too-well informed of the restrictiveness of the 1989 amendment, bemoan the fact that precious few small-business construction workers are still covered.[431] Finally, contrary to the magazine's assertion, millions of employees of small businesses are now uncovered in addition to the millions who had been previously uncovered.

The same article in *Congressional Quarterly* goes on to quote David Card, a labor economist who gained name recognition and helped shape national minimum wage policy in recent years with much criticized studies showing that an increase in the minimum wage can lead to increased rather than diminished employment.[432]

---

[429]Jonathan Weisman, "Exemption for Small Business......Isolated, Attacked and Defeated," *Cong. Q.*, May 25, 1996, at 1462.

[430]Two weeks later the magazine repeated the false statement. Jonathan Weisman, "Senate May Reprise 1989 Fight Over 'Training Wage,'" *Cong. Q.*, June 8, 1996, at 1600, 1601.

[431]Telephone interview with Don Chleborad, DOL, Des Moines, IA (Nov. 21, 1997). See also telephone interviews with Gail Coleman, Solicitor's Office, DOL, Washington, D.C. (Nov. 25, 1997); Leif Jorgenson, FLSA attorney, DOL, Washington, D.C. (Nov. 1997); Frank Laruffa, WHD, DOL, Washington, D.C. (Nov. 1997).

[432]David Card and Alan Krueger, *Myth and Measurement: The New Economics of the*

The magazine quoted Card as saying that "a company that grosses $500,000 a year is very small, perhaps a two-man exterminator firm or a carburetor cleaner." This cavalier comment, based on empirical ignorance of how widespread and large such firms are, trivializes an important problem. Although he might be right that a McDonald's, if it were small enough to qualify for exemption from enterprise coverage, would suffer from publicity over lawfully paying subminimum wages, such exposure does not faze local roofers.[433]

So thick is the confusion as to what the 1989 amendments did—or perhaps, even more troublingly, what FLSA coverage and exemptions are all about—that in a letter that took many weeks to draft, former Secretary of Labor Dole explained the purpose behind the single-level small-business enterprise coverage threshold as eliminating "the crazy quilt of exemptions, such as complete exemption for laundry firms."[434] Apparently, the Secretary of Labor believed either that coverage of laundries was actually expanded by the 1989 amendments or that first-dollar coverage constituted a kind of exemption from exempt status.

At the other end of the disinformation spectrum, in 1996 Secretary of Labor Robert Reich disingenuously declared in a letter to the Speaker of the House, Newt Gingrich, that the proposal to eliminate individual coverage in firms exempt from enterprise coverage "'invites a return to the sweatshop conditions that Americans abhor.'" Magnifying his hyperbole in an interview with *The New York Times*, Reich asserted that the exemption "would create an incentive to a lot of businesses to subcontract their work to new, tiny subcontractors paying 50 cents to a dollar an hour.' That, he said, would provide 'another incentive for illegal immigration.'"[435] If any of these tactically opportunistic partisan assertions were accurate,[436] they

---

Minimum Wage (1995).

[433]Weisman, "Exemption for Small Businesses" at 1463. Card's claim that the exemption is irrelevant in the sense that any employer that "does not want to pay the minimum wage simply will not" regardless of whether it is exempt sounds plausible, but when he adds that the only penalty for failure to pay is merely paying the back wages due, he overlooks that in private suits brought by workers employers in the vast majority of cases will have to pay double the wages owed as well as the workers' attorney's fees. FLSA, § 216.

[434]Letter from Elizabeth Hanford Dole to Marc Linder (Jan. 14, 1998).

[435]Adam Clymer, "Clinton Says He Will Veto Republican Plan in Wage Bill," *N.Y. Times*, May 23, 1996, at B10, col. 1 (Lexis).

[436]If Reich was referring to manufacturing sweatshops, even if their owners were lawfully able to take advantage of the exemption from enterprise coverage, individual workers would still be covered because they produce for interstate commerce. As his own agency notes: "It has been the experience of the Wage and Hour Division that virtually all employees of manufacturers are covered by the Act's provisions." Wage and Hour Div., Fact Sheet No. 9: Manufacturing Establishments Under the Fair Labor Standards Act (FLSA)" (http://www.dol.gov/dol/esa/public/regs/compliance/whd/whdfs9.htm).

applied with much greater force to the original $500,000 exemption in 1989, which the Democratic majority not only supported, but also described as a "true small business exemption."[437] In this context, Senator Bond was generous in 1996 in characterizing as "odd" Democrats' complaints about the effort to exclude small-business employees from the minimum wage increase: "Many of them happily voted for similar poison" in 1989 when they agreed to exempt small businesses from enterprise coverage.[438]

If, in one disparaging view of the unscientific character of congressional policymaking, Congress engages in "legislation by anecdote,"[439] not only was the process culminating in the exclusion of small construction firms from enterprise coverage in 1989 not guided by anecdotes, but those who should have purveyed the anecdotes or antidotes to them were nowhere to be seen. Small contractors became, according to virtually all the participants, the inadvertent beneficiaries of Senator Jeffords' drive to create a uniform dollar-volume threshold.[440] Although Jeffords did not have the construction industry specifically in mind, his goal of simplifying enforcement by means of uniformity could, in the abstract—that is, abstracting from the link to unemployment—have been achieved even more readily by bringing the other industries down to construction's zero-dollar threshold. However, since wealth redistribution from workers to their small-business employers was one of the priorities of the general small business lobby, to which many legislators were committed, universal application of enterprise coverage would have been politically impossible. Uniformity had to be joined to an increase in the dollar volume. Because the outcome of a compromise was, in this sense, preordained, no one in construction had to spend political capital on this issue.

Contractors small enough to be eligible for the exemption did not lobby for it—former Secretary of Labor Dole, for example, does "not recall...any meetings with construction industry representatives to discuss the issue"[441]—nor did their

---

[437]H. Rep. No. 260, Part 1: *Fair Labor Standards Amendments of 1989*, 101st Cong., 1st Sess. 18 (1989).

[438]142 *Cong. Rec.* S7411 (1996).

[439]Telephone interview with Richard Brennan.

[440]Former Secretary of Labor Dole asserted that "while there was no particular focus on small construction firms, the changes affecting them were not inadvertent." Her reasoning, however, is a non sequitur. While conceding that she does "not recall any focus on small construction firms," she derives the intentionality merely from the perceived benefits: "By eliminating coverage for t he smallest of businesses, we both eliminated the burden of a higher minimum wage on these businesses and reduced the Federal government's own regulatory burden in dealing with a large number of businesses that do not have a significant impact on interstate commerce." Letter from Elizabeth Hanford Dole to Marc Linder (Jan. 14, 1998).

[441]Letter from Elizabeth Hanford Dole to Marc Linder (Jan. 14, 1998).

larger competitors or construction unions oppose it. Since contractors of this size were, by and large, not members of any construction employers association, they lacked the organizational wherewithal to apply pressure in any event. (To the extent that small contractors were violating various other labor-protective laws by unlawfully classifying their workers as nonemployees, they would, in any event, have had no incentive to call attention to themselves.) Since associations of larger contractors believed that their members were insulated from bid competition with such firms, and unions believed that their members were insulated from labor market competition radiating from such firms, the sudden withdrawal of the entire under-$500,000-per-year sector from wage-and-hour enforcement was, in the almost universally used locution, "underneath the radar" of their lobbyists. As a result, Congress was deprived of even the pseudo-information generated by the carefully choreographed personal presentation of point-counterpoint anecdotes characteristic of hearings. Since virtually no one in or around Congress realized that after a quarter-century of universal coverage, more than 70 percent of all construction firms would be reassigned to the unfair labor standards regime,[442] Congress could not even pretend that it had weighed the consequences of such unmediated and massive labor market deregulation. Whether such ignorance-based legislation generates a political-economical and moral environment superior to that associated with the same exclusionary outcome arrived at by an avowedly anti-labor process is a nice question.

A radically different interpretation of these attitudes and legislative policies, at least on the part of the unions, is, to be sure, possible. To the extent that the AFL-CIO was aware of the expansion of the small-business exemption in 1989, the labor movement's acquiescence in, and the decision to subordinate any opposition to, the amendment to the overriding need for an increase in the minimum wage could be viewed as noble if not entirely altruistic. After all, the vast majority of workers—such as migrant farm laborers—who are actually paid the minimum wage and whose weak labor market position would generate subminimum wages in the absence of a compulsory statutory norm,[443] are not union members. Increases in the minimum wage may help ratchet up the whole wage structure for unionists. Nevertheless, the AFL-CIO's or the building trades unions' willingness to sacrifice the immediate interests of hundreds of thousands of construction workers in coverage under the FLSA for the sake of a more livable wage for millions of even more impoverished workers should be acknowledged as an act of solidarity.

---

[442]According to Gail Coleman, "no one focused on" the exclusion of the construction industry. Telephone interview with Coleman.

[443]Marc Linder, *Migrant Workers and Minimum Wages: Regulating the Exploitation of Agricultural Labor in the United States* (1992).

14. Conclusion

> [E]very time we have had a minimum wage increase, we have always...made the exceptions and the exemptions, so that small businesses could provide those jobs for those most in need, and so small businesses could create those jobs that small businesses must create if as a matter of fact we are going to have a growing economy.[444]

Focusing on the construction industry underscores one crucial way in which the pernicious impact of unfair labor standards on the rest of the economy may be different today than it was in the early years of the FLSA. In 1949, the Truman administration, viewing the president's election in 1948 as a repudiation of the antilabor policies of the Republican-dominated Eightieth Congress, proposed amendments to the FLSA that would have significantly expanded the universe of covered workers by pushing "the commerce power of Congress exercised to its fullest constitutional extent...."[445] In explaining the planned expansion to the House Committee on Education and Labor, the Secretary of Labor, Maurice Tobin, noted that one of the FLSA's original objectives was to guard fair employers "from unfair wage chiseling by the few." Within the "part of our industrial community" operating under the act's "minimum ground rules" unfair competition had largely been "wiped out." However:

> there is another large part of the same general community for whom the labor costs, the wage rates, the hours of work, and the rules on child labor are whatever is required by the forces of competition. In this group are the workers who are not favored by State laws or self-organization. Yet their employers are frequently in the same competitive markets with those who must comply with the Fair Labor Standards Act.
>
> I cannot escape the conclusion that what is good for one group of employers is equally good for those who compete with them. I am impressed with the fact that it is pretty hard for a fair employer to live by the rules and stay in business in bad times when his competitor is free to cut labor costs and undersell him. Moreover, the employers and employees who are not subject to the act are left to be the victims of the same type of vicious competition among themselves which helped to create the greatest depression in our history.[446]

There is little doubt that Tobin correctly assessed the depressed conditions in the exempt sector both then and now. Less certain is the continuing validity of his

---

[444] 142 *Cong. Rec.* at H5534 (Rep. Goodling).

[445] William S. Tyson, "Memorandum: Scope of section 3(n)," in *Amendments to the Fair Labor Standards Act of 1938: Hearings Before the House Committee on Education & Labor*, 81st Cong., 1st Sess. 121 (1949).

[446] *Amendments to the Fair Labor Standards Act of 1938: Hearings Before the House Committee on Education & Labor* at 15 (testimony of Maurice Tobin).

conceptualization of the competitively ramifying effects of the substandard sector on the covered sector. As recently as the 1960s, the relationship between the two sectors assumed a different character than today. At that time, too, some craft unions often refrained from organizing residential building, but the strategic objective was accommodation. Unions "prefer that small home builders find in the nonunion market the lower wages and flexibility that craft lines deny. For the union man, the nonunion sector serves as a buffer. When union-scale heavy construction jobs are unavailable, craft union members can temporarily move into the home-construction field. Such buffer arrangements also provide flexibility in bargaining with management, for the craft world provides a variety of escape hatches. A craftsman can strike in the unionized sector while working in the nonunionized."[447] The "flexibility" characteristic of that period would not have embraced today's prospect of temporarily working, not merely below the high standards of union contracts, but in derogation of statutory norms. Substandard conditions in residential building may have rendered that sector almost as inaccessible to union workers as it is to law-abiding employers.[448]

If, as the case of the construction industry today appears to show, employers in the two sectors operate in noncompeting product markets and do not compete for the same groups of workers, it is possible that labor standards in the covered sector are largely impervious to the corrosive impact of wage chiseling. Whether this hypothesis is objectively true or not—and surely the exemption from the FLSA of contractors doing less than $500,000 of business must exert a wage-depressing competitive impact on covered employers doing somewhat more than $500,000 of business—construction employers associations and unions, as the aforementioned interviews reveal, seem to act on the assumption that it is. For not only did construction employers not lobby for and unions against the small-business exemption in 1989, their lobbyists and legislative directors were unaware of its inclusion in the amendments. More astounding yet, eight years later, when interviewed about their positions on the exemption, most of them were flabbergasted to hear that it even existed. In self-exculpation, union officials explained that they do not organize such small firms, while employers' representatives stated that their members' businesses were far larger than the

---

[447]Margaret Chandler, "Craft Bargaining," in *Frontiers of Collective Bargaining* 50, 58 (John Dunlop & Neil Chamberlain eds., 1967). For evidence that unionized workers sometimes forgo overtime as an accommodation to employers, see Barry Whelchel, "Informal Bargaining in Construction, 10 *Ind. Rel.* 105, 107-109 (1971).

[448]The greater price sensitivity among house buyers and the associated reduced ability of residential builders to pass their increased costs on have long intensified competitive pressures and demands for downward wage flexibility in residential construction. John Dunlop, "Labor-Management Relations," in *Design and Production of Houses* 270 (Burnham Kelly ed., 1959).

exemption threshold and did not engage in the kind of building operations typically performed by small contractors.

In fact, however, the groups do compete. Traditionally, during cyclical downswings, large firms, "in order to maintain their level of output, will not hesitate to bid on construction projects which are normally left to the smaller firms."[449] For example, a reputable roofing contractor in the Iowa City area observes that larger roofing contractors could traditionally make a living from commercial projects in upswings, but needed residential work to sustain themselves during recessions. The domination of the residential sector by unfair labor standards has deprived some larger and law-abiding firms of that safety valve, undermining their long-term viability.[450] And labor union economists agree that, regardless of the sectoral organizing strategy of building trades unions, there is a standards-depressing spill-over effect from the residential to the commercial construction labor market.[451]

Ominously, the single-family housing sector of roofing, in which lawless microfirms are the norm, has been expanding its share of the roofing business. In 1997, the average (mean) establishment among the 17,861 establishments (with payroll) in this subsector employed only 4.9 employees and did construction work valued at only $429,000; among firms that were 100 percent specialized in single-family houses, the corresponding averages were even lower: 3.8 employees and $347,000.[452] The expansion of this subsector at the expense of others between 1982 and 1997 is documented in Table 4-3:

Whereas in 1982 roofing establishments in single-family housing had accounted for 37.8 percent of all 21,152 roofing establishments and 19.2 percent of all 191,489 roofing employees, by 1997 these shares rose to 58.5 percent of 30,557 establishments and 34.5 percent of 253,315 employees. Among the establishments 100 percent specialized in single-family housing, the shares rose from 16.9 percent and 6.8 percent in 1982 to 28.0 percent and 12.7 percent in 1997, respectively.

---

[449]Peter J. Cassimatis, "The Performance of the Construction Industry, 1946-1965" at 295-96 (Ph.D. diss., New School for Social Research, 1967).

[450]Telephone interview with Kurt Tjemeland, T & K Roofing, Ely, IA (Dec. 2, 1997).

[451]Telephone interview with John Zalusky, Washington, D.C. (Dec. 9, 1997). Zalusky was an AFL-CIO economist until his retirement and was involved in the 1989 FLSA negotiations.

[452]U.S. Census Bureau, *1997 Economic Census: Construction: Industry Series: Roofing, Siding, and Sheet Metal Contractors* tab. 8 at 12 (Oct. 1999).

Table 4-3: Expansion of Single-Family-Housing Roofing Sector, 1982-97				
	1982	1987	1992	1997
SFHR establishments as % of all roofing establishments	37.8	44.0	48.9	58.5
Employees in SFHR establishments as % of all roofing employees	19.2	24.9	31.7	34.5
100%-specialized SFHR establishments as % of all roofing establishments	16.9	17.4	20.3	28.0
Employees of 100%-specialized SFHR establishments as % of all roofing employees	6.8	7.1	10.1	12.7

Sources: U.S. Bureau of the Census, *1982 Census of Construction Industries: Industry Series: Roofing and Sheet Metal Work Special Trade Contractors* tab. 8 at 18-10 (1984); U.S. Bureau of the Census, *1987 Census of Construction Industries: Industry Series: Roofing, Siding, and Sheet Metal Work Special Trade Contractors* tab. 8 at 18-10 (1990); U.S. Bureau of the Census, *1992 Census of Construction Industries: Industry Series: Roofing, Siding, and Sheet Metal Work Special Trade Contractors* tab. 8 at 18-10 (1995); U.S. Census Bureau, *1997 Economic Census: Construction: Industry Series: Roofing, Siding, and Sheet Metal Contractors* tab. 8 at 12 (Oct. 1999).

Employers' and unions' subjective belief in the thesis of noncompeting groups would bode well for the further evisceration of the FLSA. Advocates of governmental deregulation would face fewer obstacles to achieving their goals if organized capital and labor were to remain indifferent to efforts to cut back coverage incrementally. Such a scenario was conjured up a half-century ago, when Ralph Gwinn, a Congressman from New York who detected socialism in the most unlikely places,[453] engaged William McComb, the Wage and Hour Administrator, in the following colloquy:

Mr. GWINN. It is because people chisel that you think the Government must manage the economy to the extent that you propose?
Mr. MCCOMB. It is because some employers will pay as little as they can for their employee's work.
Mr. GWINN. How many?
Mr. MCCOMB. Well, it would just take a very small percentage. You have spoken of free competition. ...
Mr. GWINN. How many of the employers, do you say, are chiselers?

---

[453]Gwinn spoke of "socialist Federal regulation of prices and wages...." *Amendments to the Fair Labor Standards Act of 1938: Hearings Before the House Committee on Education & Labor* at 98.

Mr. McCOMB. A very small percentage of them.
Mr. GWINN. How small?
Mr. McCOMB. Oh, less than 5 percent....
Mr. GWINN. All right; then you would subject our whole economy in this area to management from Washington, and all of your inspectors and all of the expenses of the taxpayers that are involved, and all the bookkeeping that is involved, and the uncertainties, and the ill will because 5 percent of our employers, you say, are chiselers?
Mr. McCOMB. ...I will have to disagree with you, that there would be a great deal of ill will. I know of many, many employers who want to pay a decent wage, but if they must compete with the man who is paying a very low wage and has no regard for the living conditions under which his workers must live, those employers must pay low if they are going to compete with the others. ...
Mr. GWINN. You have great faith in our free economy and in the honesty of 95 percent of our employers?
Mr. McCOMB. Yes, I do.
Mr. GWINN. If a majority of them come forward in these hearings and say they will take their chance on competition with the 5 percent of the chiselers, are you willing to leave this law to their judgment in that regard?
Mr. McCOMB. I do not think you could.[454]

The Wage and Hour Administrator may not have thought it possible 50 years ago,[455] but if unions and covered employers no longer believe that they compete with and if they thus no longer need to be "protected against the unfair methods of competition of those who utilize sweatshop methods to gain a competitive advantage,"[456] their indifference to the exemption of small firms may help vindicate Gwinn's deregulatory program yet. If unions are in fact operating under that belief, then they have turned their backs on the key insight that they themselves successfully imparted to Congress in 1966. As the Building and Construction Trades Department president explained to the Senate Subcommittee on Labor:

because of problems peculiar to this industry, we believe that Congress should eliminate the requirement...under which an enterprise...must have an annual gross of business done exceeding $250,000 before the provisions of the amended act will become applicable to it.

---

[454]*Amendments to the Fair Labor Standards Act of 1938: Hearings Before the House Committee on Education & Labor* at 103-104.

[455]At that time it was still de rigueur in the construction industry to find that: "For the well-established employers, it is...important to have a floor under competitive labor costs. Otherwise, the threat is always present of a competitor securing cost advantages through undercutting labor standards." Frank Pierson, "Building-Trades Bargaining Plan in Southern California," 70 *Monthly Lab. Rev.* 14, 14 (1950).

[456]*Fair Labor Standards Act of 1937*, at 3 (statement of Asst. Atty. Gen. Robert Jackson).

> The use of a volume-of-business test presupposes that there is some difference in the nature of operations between small and large enterprises...in an industry. In other words, Congress may consider itself justified in imposing different requirements on larger business units within an industry tha[n] it imposes on smaller ones if it can be assumed that different sized business units do not directly compete with each other. This assumption does not hold true in the construction industry.[457]

If a rational industrial policy of any kind underlies the expanded small-business exemption, it must be based on the conclusion that such a rigid "dual economy" has emerged that larger firms and primary-sector unions can ignore wage-chiselers with impunity, many of whose employees will increasingly become those whom Congress has expelled from the welfare rolls.[458] Alternatively, the policy of exempting small firms from the FLSA must also assume that all small employers are willing to become wage-chiselers: Congress's decision to subject all employers below the $500,000—and, in the future, perhaps an even higher[459]—threshold to the withering competition of unfair labor standards tendentially compels even well-intentioned employers to reproduce the conditions prevailing among their most rapacious rivals.

Above all, however, a rational industrial policy informing revision of the FLSA presupposes, at the very least, an explicit economic theory and unbiased empirical studies, which have been conspicuously absent.[460] A democratically organized discussion comparing the class-based distribution of the benefits and deprivations of universal coverage and selected exemptions would require a measure of honesty and comprehension on the part of legislators and interest and intelligence on the part of intervening participants that had never been prominent in earlier FLSA debates, and has virtually disappeared since the 1980s.

---

[457]*Amendments to the Fair Labor Standards Act: Hearings before the Subcommittee on Labor of the Senate Committee on Labor and Public Welfare*, Pt. 2, 89th Cong., 1st Sess. 1068 (1965) (letter from C. Haggerty to Sen. Pat McNamara, July 19, 1965).

[458]*E.g.*, Tony Horwitz, "Poor Prospects: Paring Welfare Rolls Proves a Huge Grind for Everyone Involved," *Wall St. J.*, Nov. 4, 1997, at A1 (Westlaw).

[459]Passage of future bills introduced by Democrats to increase the minimum wage may, once again, be conditioned on an increase in the small-business exemption threshold. Although an attorney to the Building and Construction Trades Department recommended to the organization that it seek to repeal the exemption, it did not follow that advice. Telephone interview with Yellig (Feb. 20, 1998).

[460]The one chief exception was the seven volumes of the *Report of the Minimum Wage Study Commission* (1981).

Index